Second Edition
Canadian Criminology

John A. Winterdyk

Mount Royal College

PEARSON

Prentice
Hall

Toronto

National Library of Canada Cataloguing in Publication

Winterdyk, John
    Canadian criminology / John A. Winterdyk.—2nd ed.

Includes bibliographical references and index.
ISBN 0-13-123425-0

1. Criminology—Textbooks. 2. Crime—Canada—Textbooks.
I. Title.

HV6025.W56 2005   364   C2005-901441-5

ISBN 0-13-123425-0

Vice President, Editorial Director: Michael J. Young
Acquisitions Editor: Ky Pruesse
Executive Marketing Manager: Judith Allen
Developmental Editor: Patti Altridge
Production Editor: Richard di Santo
Copy Editor: Eliza Marciniak
Proofreader: Trish O'Reilly
Production Coordinator: Janis Raisen
Permissions Manager: Susan Wallace-Cox
Page Layout: Laserwords
Art Director: Julia Hall
Cover and Interior Design: Anthony Leung
Cover Image: GettyImages

2 3 4 5 6 7 8 DPC 09 08 07 06
Printed and bound in Canada.

Statistics Canada information is used with the permission of the Minister of Industry, as Minister responsible for Statistics Canada. Information on the availability of the wide range of data from Statistics Canada can be obtained from Statistics Canada's Regional Offices, its World Wide Web site at http://www.statcan.ca, and its toll-free access number 1-800-263-1136.

Table of Contents

Introduction

Criminology and crime remain hot topics these days. One cannot read the paper or watch the news without being bombarded with local crime stories, let alone accounts of national-level or international crimes. Many criminology and criminal justice programs have to turn students away because there are not enough seats available in their programs to accommodate them all. The general interest in criminology, and more particularly in Canadian criminology, is also being reflected in the growing number of crime fiction books and academic books.

Almost as quickly as the interest in criminology has grown so has the understanding of crime and criminality. Criminology is a dynamic area of study that is continually evolving in its aim to better understand and control crime and criminal behaviour and ultimately remove social inequalities.

The new edition of this book continues to reflect the growing acceptance of an integrative and interdisciplinary approach to the study of crime and criminality. The content in the existing chapters has been updated, and the discussion of theory has been streamlined into three chapters in order to allow a new chapter on victimology—again a reflection of the evolving nature of the discipline. Furthermore, in an effort to make the text more student-friendly, most chapters have been shortened by reducing secondary material while retaining key information. Changes to pedagogical features include streamlining the Learning Objectives, presenting the Summary in point form, and limiting the Discussion Questions to five per chapter (see below for further details).

As in the first edition, the traditional subject areas found in more conventional criminology textbooks are still covered. Opening **Section I**, **Chapter 1** introduces the reader to the meaning of crime, deviance, and criminology. It also traces the evolving history of criminology and provides the basis for understanding why an interdisciplinary and integrated approach is necessary for criminology. **Chapter 2** examines the role of the public and the media. Both play an integral role in forging the identity and the issues examined by criminology, as well as directing criminal justice policy. The chapter offers an overview of why criminology needs to understand the importance of the role of the public and the media when studying crime.

Criminological theory and criminal justice policy are influenced by cultural values and politics. These elements can be tempered by examining objective criminological data. In **Chapter 3**, the general aims of criminological research are explored. Then the various methods of collecting and analyzing information about crime and criminals are reviewed. Such data can be used to support policies and educate the public. **Chapter 4** continues to remain a unique feature of this book, not found in other introductory criminology textbooks. While many such books include some coverage of the history and the evolving nature of the discipline, this chapter explores in more detail the major schools of criminological thought and presents profiles of important pioneers (including Canadian pioneers) of criminology. The underlying assumption is that an appreciation of our heritage is an essential ingredient in preparing for the future. It is hoped that this historical discussion will help students appreciate the heritage of and the need for Canadian criminology and will prompt other authors to expand their historical coverage.

In **Section II**, attention shifts toward criminological theories. Criminological theories represent the various epistemological perspectives used to engage in criminological inquiry. Textbooks vary in their orientation and method of coverage, but they generally reflect competing disciplinary approaches rather than offering an interdisciplinary, integrated approach. In this book, in keeping with the interdisciplinary approach, the major criminological theories are divided into the three primary disciplinary areas: biology (**Chapter 5**), psychology (**Chapter 6**), and sociology (**Chapter 7**). Each chapter in this section covers the primary theories stemming from the given discipline, as well as examines some newer integrated and interdisciplinary approaches that include aspects of the discipline. Recognizing that many criminology and criminal justice programs include a course on criminological theory, the intention here is to provide an overview and not a comprehensive summary of all the theories.

Section III is divided into seven chapters. **Chapter 8** includes an overview of the violent crimes that are most recorded by the police and the trends that draw the most attention from the media and the public. In addition, there is a brief overview of some of the emerging forms of violence, such as hate crime, stalking, and terrorism. **Chapter 9** includes an overview of crimes against property. In particular, the chapter focuses on conventional property-related crimes such as fraud, theft, arson, and motor-vehicle crimes. In **Chapter 10**, the focus shifts to organized and corporate crime, sometimes referred to as non-conventional crime. In addition to reviewing current trends, the chapter addresses some of the explanations of these types of crime. **Chapter 11** addresses what are often referred to as public order offences, such as gambling, prostitution, and substance abuse. Although these crimes often involve organized crime groups, they have been placed in a separate chapter because of their general nature. They are sometimes also referred to as victimless crimes, since those involved are often willing participants. These are crimes concerned with issues of morality, which some argue do not belong in the domain of state control. However, regardless of moral issues, these behaviours involve acts that have a direct impact on public safety and well-being.

Chapter 12, which is new to this edition, deals with the subject of victims and victimology. Victimology has recently become more mainstream in Canadian criminology and therefore rightfully deserves a whole separate chapter. Another important topic that has recently gained attention—women and crime—is dealt with in **Chapter 13**. There was considerable outside support for this chapter, yet divergent opinion about its format. Although criminologists have been paying increasing attention to female crimes, this is an area that can be characterized as being still in its infancy. In the chapter, an overview of the history and current status of a criminological understanding of female crime is provided.

Finally, in **Chapter 14**, the focus shifts to future criminological issues. Issues such as the future of crime, the need for comparative research, the knowledge explosion in criminology, and crime prevention are examined. The chapter concludes with an overview of restorative justice—one of the dominant emerging trends in criminology that reflects an integrated and interdisciplinary approach to social order.

Where appropriate, the text includes overviews of some of the major historical antecedents, key concepts, and important findings that highlight the relevance of topics under consideration to the study of crime and criminality. In this way, the reader can acquire an appreciation of how the discipline has evolved as well as how current theories have come into the fold.

In order to facilitate better understanding of the content, each chapter begins with a set of five important **Learning Outcomes**. The outcomes are intended to help the reader focus on important conceptual aspects of the text. At the end of each chapter is a set of **Discussion Questions** that are intended to help integrate the material, as well as a list of **Key Concepts** and **Key Names** (where appropriate). Each chapter concludes with a list of helpful **Weblinks** that contain further information on the topics discussed.

At the end of the book is a **Glossary** of the concepts highlighted in bold throughout the chapters. Although such a list may appear redundant, standardization is becoming increasingly important as criminology continues to evolve and become increasingly international in scope. Readers are likely to find some discrepancies because of different theoretical perspectives used by different researchers and authors, but overall the definitions found in the Glossary should help develop a better understanding of criminology.

Supplements

To help students and instructors get the most out of this textbook, I have prepared, with the assistance of Kiara Okita, an **Instructor's Manual** and a **Test Item File** that can be downloaded by instructors from a password-protected location on Pearson Education Canada's website. To get to these files, simply search for this textbook in the online catalogue at **vig.pearsoned.ca**, then click on "Instructor" under "Resources" in the left-hand menu. Contact your local sales representative to obtain further information or a password.

The website dedicated specifically to this book—**www.pearsoned.ca/winterdyk**—offers additional resources. On this site, instructors and students are able to access **PowerPoint slides** that summarize each of the chapters. An **updated chapter on crime and criminal law** is also available, along with several supporting **appendices**.

Although I continue to try to do justice to the evolving nature of criminology by adopting an interdisciplinary and integrated approach, I must call on students and instructors to fill some voids from time to time. I see this edition—like criminology itself—as a work in progress. Should you find this book interesting and intellectually stimulating, then my efforts have not been in vain. Nevertheless, rest assured the journey is not complete and that constructive feedback is always welcome. Finally, please feel free to visit the website of the Department of Justice Studies at Mount Royal College, at **www.mtroyal.ab.ca/healthcomm/justice.shtml**, where I and my colleagues have compiled a list of helpful criminology websites and related internet links.

John Winterdyk
Department of Justice Studies
Mount Royal College
Calgary, Alberta T3E 6K6
e-mail: **jwinterdyk@mtroyal.ab.ca**
fax: 403-240-6201

Acknowledgments

Although I am solely responsible for the content of this textbook, it reflects the input and support of numerous people. While some of these persons are aware of their impact and/or contributions, many are not. I am indebted to all of them. And while not everyone's name may appear below, my heartfelt thanks goes out to them all.

Whenever I undertake an effort such as this book, I realize not only how important friendships and loved ones are but how important it is for us to recognize and appreciate that we are all one.

My grandfather, Dirk Winterdyk, has been the most influential academic force in my life. In addition to embodying all the quintessential traits of a wonderful grandfather, he was an educator extraordinaire, and his ideas and enthusiasm have remained a powerful influence on me. Throughout my school years, I have been touched in various ways by the ideas and works of Vern Schafer, Ronald Roesch, Ray Corrado, Vince Sacco, Paul Maxim, Paul and Patricia Brantingham, Elizabeth Loftus, Hans Eysenck, and C.R. Jeffery. I would also like to acknowledge several of my fellow graduate students who in their own way helped me to survive the demands of graduate school so that I can enjoy what I do today. Those were truly memorable times. Thanks in particular to Dan Beavon, Jane Debbo, Linda Fischer, David Horne, Klaus Kohlmyer, and my academic partner in "crime" Darryl Plecas.

Of my colleagues at Mount Royal College, I would like to recognize Sandie McBrien, who provided invaluable feedback on the first edition, and more recently Doug King, who allowed me to spend the time I needed to get the revisions completed on time for this edition. Kiara Okita, who has become an invaluable research assistant and friend, gave an unbelievable amount of her time and energy in assisting me in completing this project. I look forward to her success as she moves on with her academic interests and hope to return the generosity and kindness. Rosalynn Hupkes helped track down a number of references and permissions and proofed several chapters during the crunch period. Michael O'Connell with the A-G Department and Victim Services in Adelaide, Australia, and Leslie-Anne Keown at the University of Calgary provided invaluable reviews of the victimology chapter.

I would like to acknowledge the enduring support, patience, and tolerance of my life partner, Rosemary. And while neither of us is perfect, she is the true pillar of strength in our relationship and throughout this project! I would also be remiss if I neglected to recognize our two boys—Michael and Alex. Wrestling, playing chess, cycling, and playing board games keep reminding me that there is more to life than work.

Last but not least, I would like to thank Pearson and my sponsoring editor, Carolin Sweig, who provided the encouragement and support to embark on updating the text. I would also like to thank Patti Altridge, developmental editor, who diligently helped nurse and nudge this edition into completion. Her sense of humour also helped make the tough days a lot easier to deal with. And I want to thank Eliza Marciniak, my copy editor, whose editing skills rival anything I've ever had the pleasure to experience. Again, I would like to thank all the anonymous reviewers who spent many hours offering constructive criticisms and insightful suggestions for this edition.

CHAPTER 1

Criminology: Its Nature and Structure

"When there is crime in society there is no justice."

Plato

"Crime, for its part, must no longer be conceived as an evil that can not be too much suppressed...crime is not pathological at all... and its true function must be sought elsewhere."

Émile Durkheim (1858–1917)

Learning Outcomes

After you have completed this chapter, you should be able to:

- Understand the complexity of both criminology and crime, particularly within a Canadian context.
- Differentiate between crime and deviance and identify other misconceptions about criminology.
- Understand the role of criminologists, their various methods of inquiry, and the elements that make up the discipline of criminology.
- Recognize the many ways we gain knowledge regarding crime.
- Appreciate the impact of the social sciences on the development of criminology and recognize the necessity for an integrated and interdisciplinary approach.

Introduction

Although the chapter's opening quotations are both about crime, they reflect diametrically opposing views. Welcome to the controversial subject of crime and, more generally, the discipline of criminology.

Before we begin, take a few minutes to answer a few questions that I like to ask my students at the start of my introductory criminology classes. You might want to do this exercise in a group setting and jot down your responses.

- What does criminology mean to you?
- What does the word "crime" mean?
- Is there a difference between crime and deviance?
- Who is a criminal?
- What do criminologists do?

While these are specific questions, you will likely get a wide range of responses. Explore possible reasons for this with your classmates.

The questions below are a little more abstract but are ones that we have probably all thought about at some point. Follow the same procedure as you did with the previous questions.

- Has crime increased?
- What are the most serious crimes and why?
- Who is committing the most crimes and why?
- Do you feel that capital punishment (the death penalty) should be reinstated and why?
- Why does the crime rate vary within Canada and internationally?
- Why are certain types of crimes committed by certain individuals and not others?
- Why do different people respond differently to alleged criminality?
- What can we do to control crime?

These questions are intended to get you thinking about the sources of information about crime and our perceptions of crime and criminality. They also serve to establish a foundation on which we can begin to examine some misconceptions about crime and criminality, as well as develop a framework in which to study criminology.

When I teach, I like to end the introductory portion of the first class by asking students why they are taking the course and/or are enrolled in criminology. Again, take a few minutes to share your impressions. Do some of you want to work with young offenders, to be police officers, to practise criminal law, to study forensics, or are you just taking the course as one of your electives? If the responses are varied, what conclusion might you be able to draw about criminology as a discipline and about what it has to offer interested students?

The answers to the two sets of questions above are the cornerstones and building blocks of this course. In this chapter, we will begin by examining the fundamental principles of crime, criminality, and deviance. We will then look at the historical roots of criminology. This historical overview will provide the backdrop that will allow us to understand and appreciate how and why criminology has evolved into an enterprise that has become increasingly integrated and interdisciplinary in nature. The chapter will conclude with some practical issues that criminologists must consider. Before we begin, however, let's examine why this textbook has adopted a Canadian slant.

A Canadian Flavour, Eh!

As reflected in the title, this book is not only an introduction to criminology, but also an introduction to Canadian criminology. Is there a difference? Is there any constructive purpose in trying to separate Canadian criminology from criminology in general? Some Canadian criminologists have noted that we are modest players on the international scene. For example, a review of articles in such journals as the *Canadian Journal of Criminology and Criminal Justice* will reveal how we regularly give credit to the same scholars, most of whom are American. And we are not the only ones who regularly turn to American sources for our theoretical perspectives and notions of what is important in criminology. In his book on comparative juvenile justice, Winterdyk (2002) presents 18 different countries and shows that most of them trace the inception of their respective juvenile justice systems to the influence of the American model used at the turn of the 1900s. Although youth crime has remained a universal issue, six different juvenile justice models have emerged over the years as a result of different cultural, geographical, political, and social attributes unique to each country. Canada and the United States do differ in significant ways as far as crime is concerned (see Box 1.1).

REALITY CHECK BOX 1.1

CANADA AND THE UNITED STATES: DIFFERENCES THAT COUNT

Even though Canada and the United States share a common heritage, there are a number of unique social, cultural, and political differences that make our differences count.

	CANADA	UNITED STATES
Population (2001)	30.0 million (approx. 3 per km^2)	281.4 million (approx. 28 per km^2)
Languages	English/French	English
Visible minorities	East Indians/other Asians/ Caribbean	African-American/ Hispanic
Indigenous peoples	First Nations People/ Métis/Inuit	Native Americans/ Alaska Native Americans/Asian/ Pacific Islanders
Government	parliamentary/ constitutional monarch	Federalism executive/bicameral
Basis of government	*Constitution Act*/Charter of Rights and Freedoms	US Constitution/ Bill of Rights

	CANADA	UNITED STATES
Criminal law	national *Criminal Code*	state criminal statutes/ federal statutes
	Youth Criminal Justice Act (federal)	state juvenile acts
	• age limits 12–17	• age variable
	• modified justice model	• crime control model
	no capital punishment	capital punishment
	indictable/summary offences	felonies/misdemeanours
Justice officials	appointed by government	county sheriffs/city and county prosecutors/ state judges—all elected
Policing	municipal/provincial/federal	municipal/county/state/ federal
Sentencing	indefinite	indeterminate/ determinate, varies from state to state
Corrections	federal/provincial	federal/state
	• jurisdiction determined by length of sentence	• jurisdiction determined by code violation
Crime rates (2002)	4944 per 100 000*	4118.7 per 100 000**
Violent crime	969	494.6
Property crime	3975	3624.1

* CCJS, 2004, 24(6):17.

** Based on FBI Uniform Crime Reports, 2002, Table 2.

Note: Statistics Canada and the FBI use different recording practices, which makes direct comparison difficult.

These differences do not mean that one country's system or criminological approach is better than the other's. The two are simply different and, if for no other reason, deserve to be treated as such. Since the late 1970s, Canadian criminology has been forging its own identity, as evidenced by the growing number of criminology programs, criminology books with a Canadian focus, and Canadian-based criminologists who have made significant theoretical and practical contributions to criminology. This textbook provides students with an introduction to criminology that, where appropriate, places the content within a Canadian context.

This textbook is also biased toward the work of Canadian criminologists. The premise for this orientation and emphasis is based on feedback from my students over the years. They want Canadian content. However, they also want Canadian material put into a realistic perspective. Therefore, where appropriate, international material has been used in an effort to provide a balanced overview and one that will enable practical and, I hope, insightful conclusions and comparisons.

Criminology, Crime, and Deviance

"The objective of criminology is the development of a body of general and verified principles and of other types of knowledge regarding this process of law, crime, and treatment." Sutherland & Cressey, 1960:3

What Is Criminology?

Many introductory textbooks define criminology as the scientific study of crime, criminals, and criminal behaviour. This general sociological definition was first introduced by Edwin Sutherland in one of the first criminology textbooks in North America, during the 1920s (see Chapter 7). While the definition tells us that criminology is a scientific discipline, it says nothing about the meaning of the terms "crime," "criminals," and "criminal behaviour." A more precise description of what criminology means is dependent on the disciplinary orientation used to define the nature of crime and criminals (see Box 1.2). Thus, **criminology** can be defined as *the scientific study of human behaviour, crime causation, crime prevention, and the punishment and rehabilitation of offenders*.

The study of crime emphasizes the scientific study of human behaviour. Criminology attempts to explain how and why crime occurs. Therefore, a **criminologist** is *a behavioural scientist who is interested in the identification, classification, and description of types of criminal behaviour*. Since a criminologist is concerned with the study of human behaviour, he or she draws on the behavioural sciences rather than the elements of the **criminal justice** system (e.g., law enforcement, courts, and corrections) to explain criminal behaviour. The behavioural sciences can include a wide range of subject areas, such as biology, anthropology, economics, political science, psychology, and sociology, as well as policy sciences, such as criminal law, policy, administration, and ethics. Therefore, criminology is an **interdisciplinary** and **integrated** science.

Until recently, most criminologists tended to be trained in a particular discipline (e.g., biology, political science, sociology, psychology, or law). As a result, they tended to be specialists who, while acknowledging other disciplinary perspectives, studied crime and justice in accordance with their particular disciplinary training. However,

TWO MISCONCEPTIONS ABOUT CRIMINOLOGY

While criminology is the disciplined study of crime and crime control, it has had to contend with a number of misconceptions that arise from its efforts to apply its findings to practical policy. For example:

1. Criminologists have been crusaders for fair laws, fair punishment, more reliable treatments, removal of the death penalty, and a better sense of social justice. For this reason, criminology has often been viewed as a *humanitarian* movement (see Chapter 4). However, it is also a *scientific discipline* that relies on empirical evidence to support humanitarian reforms.
2. The norms, beliefs, and values of society often dictate the formalization of laws. Consequently, some mistakenly think that criminology is a *normative* discipline concerned only with understanding the values and norms of society. While criminologists do study the relationships between norms and their entrenchment into the values and practices of society, the method adopted is non-normative. Rather, criminology is scientific and interdisciplinary in its approach to the study of criminological issues.

How might humanitarian and normative issues either assist or hinder our understanding of crime and its control?

---

as the discipline has evolved, an increasing number of scholars are being educated in an integrated and interdisciplinary environment. These criminologists believe that the various disciplinary perspectives are interrelated and provide a richer approach to methodological, practical issues, and theoretical debates than that of a single discipline or body of knowledge.

The plea for an interdisciplinary approach can be traced back to at least 1933, when Jerome Michael and Mortimer J. Adler, in their book entitled *Crime, Law and Social Science,* called for the establishment of a separate criminology program in which criminal law and the behavioural sciences would be taught in an integrated and interdisciplinary manner. However, during its gestation period in North America, sociologists (in particular those following the Chicago School, as explained in Chapter 7) quickly came to dominate criminological thought and research. It wasn't until the 1960s, with the flourishing of criminology, that the schools provided criminology with an opportunity to evolve an interdisciplinary approach and to bridge paradigmatic differences. Noted scholars such as C.R. Jeffery (1978, 1990) in North America and Sir Leon Radzinowicz (1965) in Europe have championed the cause. In Canada today, the integrated and interdisciplinary approach to the study of crime is attracting a growing number of followers.

What Is Crime?

"Everyone knows what crime is, or so it seems." Silverman, Teevan, & Sacco, 1991:1

Crime (from the Latin word *crimen*, meaning "accusation") is a generic term that people use to refer to a wide range of acts that have been socially, culturally, and/or legally defined as being "wrong" or "anti-social" (Siegel, 1995). Crime is a social phenomenon that commands considerable attention from the (Canadian) public. Canadian criminologist John Hagan (1987), while commenting on crime, simply described it as a "hot" topic.

The meaning of crime has changed over time. Originally, crimes were private wrongs. Individuals who were wronged would seek "self-help" retribution, or revenge, against the wrongdoer or the wrongdoer's family. In time, this practice of personal justice broke down as the family structure changed and private vengeance became difficult to enforce. This gave way to the emergence of the legal concept of crime that today is commonly used within the criminal justice system. A legal definition of crime simply states that a crime is *what the law proclaims it to be*, and it is *an act punishable by law*.

Crime vs. Offence

In the media, the terms "crime" and "offence" are sometimes used interchangeably. Is there a difference? British criminologist Nigel Walker (1987) has observed that the concept of crime used to mean a serious breach of criminal law. The Scots and French still distinguish between "crimes" (breach of the law) and "offences" (violation of morality), while in the United States, crimes are distinguished based on a perceived serious breach of law. Less serious crimes or breaches (e.g., public drunkenness) are called "misdemeanours," while the more serious offences (e.g., murder or rape) are called "felonies." Until 1967, England made the same distinction. However, that country now simply classifies crimes as "arrestable" and "non-arrestable" offences. Arrestable offences are crimes for which a person can be arrested without a warrant, while non-arrestable offences require a warrant (see Box 1.3).

A CLOSER LOOK BOX 1.3

BE CAREFUL WHAT YOU DO!

According to the Law Commission of Canada, there are more than 40 000 crimes and offences that appear in federal and provincial laws and regulations as well as in local government statutes and bylaws.

In Canada, we use the term "indictable" to refer to more serious crimes (e.g., homicide, assault, and robbery). The penalty for **indictable offences** varies depending on the seriousness of the crime. The other term used is **summary offences**. Summary offences denote less serious crimes (e.g., certain types of property offences and theft or fraud under $5000). Summary convictions carry a general punishment "of a fine of not more than $2000 or imprisonment for six months or both." *Therefore, crime refers to the general infraction, while offence refers to the specific crime, such as homicide, theft, and robbery.*

While the term "crime" is central to criminology, there is not a universal definition! We can note, however, that all definitions are based on legal constructs that define crime as the violation of a criminal law. In other words, *without law there is no crime— nulla crim sin lege.* Furthermore, we can note that the meaning of crime can vary with time and place, since those who make the law also change over time. What is fundamentally important to recognize is that how we define a crime will influence how we view and study it. In Section II of this book, we will examine the theories criminologists use to study crime and criminals.

Although there is no universal definition of crime, we can note that the term is a normative one (i.e., based on norms and values) that carries a negative connotation. Any definition is influenced by our *frame of reference*, that is, the product of our economic, ideological, political, social, and disciplinary training. For the purpose of this book, **crime** is defined as a socially constructed concept used to categorize certain behaviours as requiring formal control and warranting some form of social intervention.

The list of what constitutes a crime is long and varied. One method that has been used to organize the various types of crimes is to divide them into conventional and non-conventional categories (although other classifications exist). **Conventional crimes** have been characterized as those crimes committed by individuals or small groups in which some degree of direct (e.g., personal) or indirect (e.g., property) contact occurs. These crimes can include street crimes such as robbery, assault, motor-vehicle theft, and break and enter. They are also the kinds of offences that most frequently come to the attention of the criminal justice system as well as the media. As Canadian sociologist Daniel Koenig (1992) observed, conventional crime represents a subset of crime and may or may not include offences that cause great financial loss, physical harm, or death. In Chapters 8 and 9, we will focus on the most common of the conventional crimes and take a look at some of the emerging variations of these crimes (e.g., stalking, home invasion, and hate crime).

Non-conventional crimes are those offences not usually pursued by the criminal justice system. Yet their social, financial, and personal impact may be far more serious than that of conventional crimes. For example, computer crimes have been described as a type of theft, but the impact of these crimes can have a devastating and more far-reaching impact than "simple" theft. Other examples of non-conventional crime include organized crime, various public order crimes, various forms of terrorism, transnational crime, and white-collar crime (see Box 1.4). In addition, as with conventional crimes, there are emerging forms of non-conventional crimes that the criminal justice system is only now realizing or that have appeared in response to some social, economic, or political situation (e.g., Russian Mafia, trade in human organs, or child pornography on the Internet). We will examine some of these crimes in Chapters 10 and 11.

Regardless of whether we are dealing with conventional or non-conventional crimes, all crimes are defined by laws.

Deviance

Deviance is another concept that is sometimes misunderstood and deserves clarification. While the term is occasionally used interchangeably with the word "crime," there are subtle differences in meaning.

Deviant behaviour encompasses a wide spectrum of conduct that, to varying degrees, may be considered offensive. **Deviance** *involves actions that depart from social norms. These actions may or may not be against the law.* For example, is the use of a "soft drug," such as marijuana, illegal? Is its use considered deviant? Boyd (1993) cites studies that found the use of marijuana to be quite common. For example, the Canadian Medical Association estimates that 1.5 million Canadians smoked marijuana recreationally in 2003. Using Canadian data, Boyd also observes that "[m]ore than 90 per cent of those jailed for cannabis possession receive sentences of less than six months in prison" (1993:79), and in 2003 an estimated 600 000 Canadians had criminal records for marijuana possession (Up in smoke? 2004). Since so many people experiment with marijuana and the court imposes relatively light sentences, should we continue to view the use of marijuana as deviant or simply as a social deviation? Is marijuana any more socially harmful than alcohol or cigarette smoking? A 2002 report by the Senate Committee on Illegal Drugs concluded that marijuana "is less harmful than alcohol" (Up in smoke? 2004).

For obvious reasons, society cannot and would not sanction all undesirable behaviour, but where do we draw the line? The line between crimes and non-crimes or deviance or even normal behaviour is often a fine one. Hence, Boyd's discussion of illicit drugs serves to illustrate the point that the concept of crime is relative (to time and place) and evolutive (a term coined by Maurice Parmalee in 1918, meaning changing)?

The relativity of crime is an important concept because it reflects the attention that should be placed on how we respond to criminal acts as well as the extent to which we want to control social behaviour. The concept of crime as a **relative** construct is also important because by definition it is fundamentally incompatible with the notion that criminals are born to crime or predisposed to crime through heredity. This idea has major theoretical implications, some of which we will explore in Section II.

The notion of crime as **evolutive** refers to the historical pattern: there are ample indicators that acts deemed criminal at a given time, in a given community, often turn out to have a different or more positive value at another point or in another community. Examples in Canadian history include prohibition, abortion, and the use of morphine and marijuana. At one time or another, all these behaviours were illegal before being legislated legal, or at least socially tolerated.

But what, if any, boundaries of criminalization should be set? Is criminal behaviour qualitatively different from non-criminal behaviour? Answers to such questions can also have social policy implications and represent major challenges to criminologists.

The Crime and Deviance Hierarchy

University of Toronto criminology professor John Hagan (1985) developed a schematic diagram to illustrate the difference between crime and deviance. As illustrated in Figure 1–1, the difference between what is a crime and what is simply deviant is sometimes subtle. At the bottom of the pyramid there are *social diversions*, which are minor forms of deviance that are considered relatively harmless. Examples include non-criminal violations of public and financial trust. Meanwhile, *social deviations* include those behaviours that are not criminal but are considered disreputable. Such behaviour could include an individual's preference in dress, language, and lifestyle. In certain social settings, however, a social deviation may be regulated, such as a school dress code or the use of offensive language directed toward a police officer or the court.

At the top of the pyramid are those behaviours that are generally considered very harmful; there is also strong support to sanction and control such behaviour. These are referred to as **consensus crimes**. Examples of consensus crimes in Canada include homicide, sexual assault, and treason. However, not everyone necessarily agrees that these crimes are wrong or that they should be considered crimes at all.

The **conflict crimes** and social deviation crimes represent actions for which there is mixed support as to whether they should be considered crimes, even though they are

F I G U R E | 1—1

HAGAN'S PYRAMID: CONSENSUS VS. CONFLICT

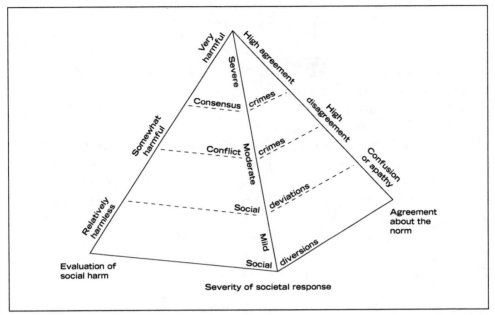

Source: J. Hagan, "The Disreputable Pleasures," Toronto: McGraw-Hill Ryerson Ltd., 1991. Reprinted with permission.

legally defined as such. Currently in Canada, these include using marijuana for medicinal purposes, procuring the services of a prostitute, appearing topless in public in some provinces, driving without your seat belt fastened, or smoking in a public place.

In essence, we can say that our perceptions of behaviours are not constant. Our attitudes about them can vary over time and from one place to another. This shifting of our definitions of deviant behaviour closely parallels our concepts of crime.

Sacco and Kennedy (1988:7) perhaps best encapsulated the meaning of deviance when they wrote, "the essence of deviance is to be found not in the behaviour defined as deviance, but in the social processes that define deviance." That is, deviance is defined by the norms and values within society. While these are usually defined by the majority, they can also be defined by a minority group that sees certain societal practices as deviant.

What is key is not just why an act becomes deviant but why people behave in ways unacceptable to most of us. Furthermore, as criminologists, we are interested in the concept of deviance and its relationship to criminality.

So far, we have defined the major concepts and terms that make up the terminology of criminology. We have seen that their meanings are specific and perhaps somewhat complex. Next, we will look at how criminology and its terms originated.

The Origins of Criminology

As early as 2000 BC, the subject of crime was a point of debate among philosophers, legal scholars, medical doctors, and even theologians. Socrates, for example, was known to have commented on the plight of young people; he argued that they were disrespectful and in need of punishment. During your higher education, you might study crime as part of the curriculum in any number of fields. Naturally, as noted earlier, your approach and understanding would be greatly influenced by the particular disciplinary orientation—i.e., its *frame of reference*. For example, how might a lawyer, as opposed to a theologian, approach the causes of crime? What line of reasoning would each be likely to adopt when considering an appropriate response to a criminal offender?

For centuries, the fields of inquiry mentioned above (that is, philosophy, law, medicine, and theology) constituted the core means by which to study crime—by studying human behaviour. However, it was not until the works of several social philosophers in the 18th and 19th centuries that the natural and social sciences became recognized as disciplines. This era is often referred to as the Enlightenment because of the marked proliferation of non-secular intellectual thought (see Chapter 4).

The Emergence of Criminology

In 1885, Raffaele Garofalo, an Italian law professor and former student of Cesare Lombroso, coined the term "criminologia," and the French anthropologist **Paul Topinard** (1830–1911) used it for the first time in 1879, as "criminologie." Both Garofalo and Topinard used their terms in reference to the study of punishment and treatment of criminals rather than the scientific analysis or observation of crime and criminals. Not only did this reflect their respective disciplinary training, but it also had a significant impact on the meaning of criminology for nearly a century thereafter. Writers and thinkers of the time were more interested in reforming criminal law than in attempting to understand the etiology (i.e., origin) of criminal behaviour. This orientation is referred to as the classical school of criminological thought.

At the turn of the 20th century, one of the leading European criminologists, Bernaldo de Quirós (1873–1969), noted that the science of criminology was a secondary evolutional consequence of the study of penology (i.e., the study of punishment) (Quirós, 1969 [1911]). In fact, two of the major reformers of the time, Cesare Beccaria (1738–1794) from Italy and Jeremy Bentham (1748–1832) from England, wrote about penal reforms based on humanitarian grounds and classical principles rather than scientific ones.

Gaining Stature

The late 1800s were a period of considerable change for criminology. As it gained acceptance around the world, universities began to offer courses in programs that specialized in criminology. Today, in Canada, we have three different, although not necessarily independent, criminology-oriented programs. They include:

1. Criminology—focusing on the etiology of crime,
2. Criminal justice—focusing on the agencies of social control, and
3. A "human justice" program at the University of Regina focusing on preparing undergraduate students for employment in the criminal justice field, as well as conducting research within the province.

The growing acceptance of criminology as a subject of study coincided with a shift from legal reforms to a more scientifically oriented approach. In North America, the first real breakthrough for criminology as a discipline occurred in 1918 when **Maurice Parmalee** (1882–1969), a sociologist, wrote the first textbook on criminology, albeit with a sociological orientation. It was simply titled *Criminology*. Even though Parmalee drifted into criminological obscurity, Edwin H. Sutherland's *Principles of Criminology*, which appeared six years later, in 1924, became a major force in furthering the influence of sociological positivism (Gibbons, 1979). His textbook, with updates and later revisions with his former student Donald R. Cressey, had been reprinted more than a dozen times by the early 1980s, a testament to its content, ideas, and enduring impact on criminological thought. While Sutherland is generally regarded as the most influential North American criminologist, John Henry Wigmore, former dean of the law faculty of Northwestern University in Chicago, is recognized as the first to give criminology a credible platform in North America. Wigmore arranged for the first conference on the subject in 1909. Out of the conference proceedings emerged the prestigious publication for scholars in which to publish their related works, the *Journal of Criminal Law and Criminology*.[1]

Sutherland's work spawned a plethora of sociologically based textbooks dealing with the subject of criminology. Furthermore, between 1930 and 1950 in North America, that orientation helped forge an alliance between criminology and sociology departments (see Reckless, 1970). Many of the more prominent sociological theories of crime emerged during this era (see Chapter 7).

In summary, we can see that the discipline of criminology has not only evolved in its meaning and scope but continues to be a fluid and evolving area of study. Criminologists are no longer concerned with just penology or the sociology of law. Rather, criminology can be, and has been referred to as, a criminological enterprise. Let's explore what is meant by this phrase.

The Criminological Enterprise: What Criminologists Do

Today, criminology is increasingly recognized and accepted as an interdisciplinary and multifaceted enterprise. The notion of **criminological enterprise** can be attributed to the writings of Marvin Wolfgang and Franco Ferracuti (1967), who recognized that the study of criminology involves several sub-areas, such as biology, law, psychology, psychiatry, and sociology. We can say it is multifaceted because it encompasses the study of several major areas, where they pertain to the subject of crime and criminality. In such an enterprising discipline, a criminologist is likely to specialize in one or more of these sub-areas.

Students studying criminology are usually required to take at least one course in each of several primary sub-areas. So let us take a brief look at the core sub-areas (Figure 1–2) that make up the criminological enterprise.

1. *Criminal statistics*: In an effort to understand, describe, predict, and access the impact of crime prevention or intervention programs, researchers often rely on crime data. For example, how serious is the incidence of youth crime in Canada? When and where does it usually occur? Will the replacement of the *Young Offenders Act* with the *Youth Criminal Justice Act* help control the problem? How do youth crime rates in Canada compare to those in other nations? Answering these types of questions involves gathering scientific data from a variety of sources and using appropriate research methods and statistical tools.

By "scientific," I mean data that can be observed and (repeatedly) measured to test theories and ideas for their validity and reliability. Otherwise, if we obtain information based on erroneous sources, we might make a decision that could be counterproductive. For example, should we reinstate capital punishment? Would that behaviour act as an effective deterrent? Will requiring Canadians to register their firearms reduce the incidence of offences resulting from the use of firearms?

FIGURE 1–2

THE CRIMINOLOGICAL ENTERPRISE

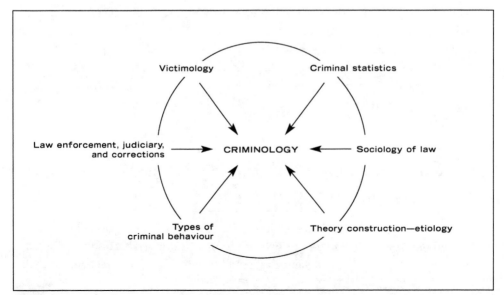

Obtaining dependable answers to these and many other criminological questions is critical if the criminal justice system is going to maintain social control and command the support of the populace (see Box 1.5). Hence, criminal statistics is one of the most crucial aspects of the criminological enterprise. In Chapter 3, we will review some of the data-gathering techniques commonly used in the study of issues related to criminology. In Chapters 8–13, we will examine how data can be used to describe the patterns and characteristics of crime.

A CLOSER LOOK BOX 1.5

THE COST OF CRIME

If crime were still at 1962 levels, Nova Scotians would be saving about $750 million a year or $2200 per household, money that would be available for investment in more productive and welfare-enhancing activities (GPI Atlantic, 1999).

2. *Sociology of law*: In Canada, as elsewhere around the world, the provinces and federal government are constantly concerned about maintaining social order. Criminal law, as prescribed in the Canadian *Criminal Code*, is the backbone of the formal description of non-acceptable behaviour. The *Criminal Code* also describes the range of punishment, rules of law, and the limits of law. For example, in Canada, there can be no crime without a law, and those under the age of 12 are considered mentally incapable of committing a crime.

These formal definitions are all very well, but they leave many questions unanswered. For example, how do laws come into effect? Do they help ensure a better quality of life and safer communities? Do they give rise to a feeling that justice has been exacted for those who have violated the law? Was Paul Bernardo punished fairly for the killing of two girls in Ontario? Was it fair, or right, that in December 1997 he was granted the right to have a public defender plead his appeal? Was it fair that his wife and partner in crime, Karla Homolka, had further charges dropped because of her plea bargain arrangement prior to the full disclosure of her involvement?

The sociology of law is concerned with determining the origin of law and legal thought. By examining the past, criminologists try to gain a better understanding of how various economic, political, and social forces work to influence the formalization of social control and social order. Noted American criminologist Richard Quinney (1977) argued that the definition of law is created by authorized agents who have vested interests. Is this true? Who decides whether soliciting should be legal? To what extent is law an effective instrument for curbing the downloading of illegal material off the internet or cigarette smuggling? Should the law be used to regulate issues of morality (e.g., how old you have to be to buy alcohol, purchase pornographic literature, etc.)? The sociology of law is also concerned with the study of how and why changes in the law occur. Crime being a relative and evolving concept, the law must be sensitive to changing conditions within society. It is interesting to note that Edwin Sutherland (1947) observed that the sociology of law received little attention during the early years when sociology dominated criminological thought. It was accepted as a given. However, as the discipline of criminology evolved, so did its focus.

3. *Theory construction—etiology*: This area of study has grown considerably throughout the 20th century. It is concerned with understanding **etiology**—the causes of crime and its rates and trends—as well as predicting individual or group behaviour. For example, why and how could Robert Picton kill over 30 women and bury them on his farm within an urban setting? How is it that two middle-aged brothers could return years later to the home of their teacher in Cardstairs, Alberta, and turn the elderly woman upside down and then drop her to the floor? How is it that several teenagers could gang up on another teenager, Reena Virk, and kill her? How could otherwise well-trained and disciplined Canadian soldiers, while serving in Somalia in the mid-1990s, kill innocent local residents? Were the offenders suffering from some biological or neuropsychological problem? Was their behaviour somehow learned? Were there other social, economic, or mitigating causal factors?

In order to answer these kinds of questions in an objective and "value-free" manner, criminologists rely on criminological theories to help describe, explain, and predict criminal behaviour. This approach is also known as a scientific approach—using facts to speak for themselves.

All theories, however, reflect the ideological or political sentiments of the day. In the 1960s, Cloward and Ohlin's theory of differential opportunity arose in part because of the political belief that lack of opportunity was the root of most crime. In fact, in the United States, the Kennedy and Johnson administrations launched all-out campaigns against what was believed to be the root of crime—the slums. The $12 million initiative referred to as the War on Poverty involved a program called Mobilization for Youth, based in the slum areas of New York City. Unfortunately, as a result of poor management and practical and conceptual limitations, the program was unable to bring about structural social changes to the slums. The initiative was, however, instrumental in establishing such well-known programs as Job Corps, VISTA, neighbourhood legal services, community action programs, and one of the most successful programs—Head Start (see Krisberg & Austin, 1978).[2]

Because the study of criminology is interdisciplinary in nature, there are a variety of criminological theories and theoretical orientations. Researchers have developed several methods for classifying these variations, but almost every criminology textbook offers a somewhat different twist on these classifications. Unfortunately, this practice has done little to facilitate students' understanding of theories—and it also reflects the ideological biases and conflicts that permeate the study of crime and criminality. For the purposes of this book, we will group theories according to their disciplinary orientations (Chapters 5–7) in an effort to demonstrate the need for an integrated and interdisciplinary or "bridging theories" orientation.

4. *Types of criminal behaviour*: The use of criminal typologies is a way of trying to understand and organize behaviour. In official police data (known as the Uniform Crime Reports), crimes are recorded according to specific types as defined by law. Many criminologists believe that different crimes have different explanations and causal factors. For example, Fredrick Desroches's *Forces and Fear: Robbery in Canada* (1995) is a fine analysis of robbery including a discussion about how we might consider preventing robberies. Silverman and Kennedy (1993) offer a similar study of murder in Canada.

Criminologists interested in this sub-area of study often attempt to link crime types with criminal behaviours, that is, explain how different types of criminals commit different types of crimes. This is known as crime typology. This area of inquiry is concerned with understanding the causes and motivation underlying, for example, violent crime, corporate crime, serial murder, property offences, or soccer hooliganism. In Section III of this book, we will address some of these areas.

5. *Law enforcement, judiciary, and corrections*: The criminal justice system (CJS for short) consists of three formal elements: detecting crime, processing criminals, and protecting society (see Box 1.6). How these elements, individually and collectively as a system, fulfill these tasks is subject to much debate and research (see, for example, Schmalleger et al., 2004). For this reason, many criminology programs offer several courses that allow the student to examine each element in detail. Therefore, we will not be examining these elements in any specific chapter. Only those issues pertinent to the study and etiology of crime and criminals will be covered.

A CLOSER LOOK BOX 1.6

THE COST OF OPERATING THE CRIMINAL JUSTICE SYSTEM

After adjusting for inflation, the per capita cost of crime has risen dramatically from $4.38 per Canadian in 1961 to $16.85 per Canadian in 1980 (Griffiths & Verdun-Jones, 1989) to $340 for every person in 1994/95 (CCJS, 1997, 17(3)). Total government spending on police, courts, legal aid, and corrections increased 13 percent (after inflation) between 1988/89 and 1992/93 to $9.57 billion (Easton & Brantingham, 1998) and over $17 billion for 2002/2003.[3]

---

6. *Victimology*: In recent years, the growing awareness of criminal–victim relationships has prompted both public and academic interest. The origins of this sub-area of study go back to some of the early positivists (Lombroso, Garofalo, Ferri, and Tarde, among others) who recognized the importance of the victim's relationship to the crime he or she suffered and to the offending individual. As Ellis (1986) has noted, the relationship is not always clear. One of the pioneers of victimology, Hans von Hentig (1948:383), posited that many victims precipitate their own victimization through their lifestyle,

mannerisms, or other forms of behaviour and expression—"the relationships... are much more intricate than the rough distinction of criminal law." A classic analogy, taken from von Hentig's early work, might be that someone who goes to seedy bars alone and is not dressed to fit in may be inviting trouble. Based on Fattah's (1991:101) typologies, such a potential victim could be described as a *deserving victim* because his or her "reckless behaviour (is) seen as deserving their victimization."

Victimology can also include the scientific study of the relationship between the victim and the criminal justice system (see Box 1.7). Ellis has pointed out how victims can be further victimized by the system. This can involve insensitive questioning by police, harsh cross-examination in the courts, or withholding of evidence until a case is resolved.

Alternatively, the state can be viewed as an offender: it could neither provide sufficient protection for the victim, nor could it restrain or deter the criminal, because of some fault in the social control network. As well, there could be connections between victims and other societal groups and institutions, such as businesses, the media, and social movements. We will further explore the topic of victimology in Chapter 12.

REALITY CHECK BOX 1.7

FROM VICTIM TO VINDICATED

One of the controversial issues that has plagued the criminal justice system has been its inability to ensure due process and reach a just decision as to the guilt or innocence of an accused based on legal protocols. John Monahan (1981) wrote about the issue of *false positives* (incorrect predictions of behaviour) among psychiatric predictions of the future dangerousness of offenders. If psychiatrists can be wrong 56 to 80 percent of the time, how often are innocent people falsely convicted when lawyers and judges regularly make decisions on interpretation of the law? What price is society willing to pay for a sense of security? What are the moral and ethical limits to justice being exacted? Does society have the right to make examples of innocent people? How can criminology help to reduce these problems?

Science can, and has, played a critical role in protecting the rights of the innocent and ensuring the conviction of the guilty. One of the more powerful scientific tools, in recent years, has been the development of the DNA test in 1988. DNA testing was introduced into Canada in 1989, and the first case in which it was successfully used to free a wrongfully convicted individual occurred in January of 1995. Guy Paul Morin, who had been charged with the brutal sex slaying of a young girl in 1984, was finally proven innocent. Another case of note is that of David Milgaard, who spent 23 years behind bars for a murder he didn't commit. He was finally released from prison in 1992 and his name was cleared in 1997, when the Supreme Court of Canada admitted that, based on the DNA evidence, there had been a miscarriage of justice. Conversely, in October of 1995, Jason Scott Good of British Columbia was finally convicted of slaying Denny MacDonald, using DNA testing results.

THE DARK FIGURE OF CRIME

The 1993 victimization survey, the General Social Survey (GSS) of Canadians, revealed that 90 percent of sexual assaults went unreported to police, along with 53 percent of robberies. The same survey reported that more than 70 percent of perceived violent criminal incidents were not reported to the police (Johnson, 1996a).

In summary, as an enterprising and interdisciplinary area of study, criminology has evolved to become a multifaceted discipline. Its sub-areas often pursue the same issues (such as the possible means of controlling criminality), but generally come out with different solutions or interpretations. This often presents major hurdles when trying to make sound policy. As the great Greek philosopher Plato observed over 2000 years ago, "existing conditions are imperfect reflections of operating principles" (cited in Wright & Fox, 1978:317). Furthermore, this lack of consensus can lead to confusion. So how does criminology attempt to make sense of crime, and how can it put that knowledge into effect?

In the next two sections, we will review the primary disciplinary perspectives that make up the study of crime and criminality. Then we will look at the importance of linking criminological findings with policy.

Viewing Crime Through the Eyes of a Criminologist

"Crime is present not only in the majority of societies of one particular species but in all societies of all types." Émile Durkheim (1858–1917)

We have just identified the main sub-areas of study within criminology. What we did not clarify is how criminologists view crime. Because of the complexity of crime and its pervasive influence on all levels of society (e.g., economically, politically, environmentally, and even spiritually), virtually every major discipline has contributed something to the study of crime. Criminologists, regardless of their disciplinary bias or theoretical orientation, however, are all primarily interested in the study of human behaviour or, more specifically, crime and criminality (i.e., Why are crimes committed by certain individuals and not others?).

We will summarize six of the more important criminological specialties that you are likely to be exposed to as a student of criminology.

1. *Sociology*: Sociology is the science of interaction among people, the effects of the interaction on human behaviour, and the study of the forces (such as values, norms,

mores, and laws) that underlie regularities in human behaviour. In essence, sociologists are interested in the study of culture and social structure. The French sociologist Émile Durkheim (1895) defined crime in this way: "An act is criminal when it offends the vigorous and well-defined states of the collective conscience."

Sociology, like all other major disciplines, views crime and criminal behaviour from a variety of perspectives. These range from *social structure* to *social process* to *social organization* orientations, as discussed in Chapter 7. The sociological perspective is the most dominant criminological perspective in North America.

2. *Psychology*: Psychology is the science of individual behaviour. More than 2000 years ago, Plato, in *The Republic*, not only spoke about assigning citizens to different roles based on their aptitudes, but also advocated that measurements of peoples' aptitudes be developed. Psychologist Olaf Kinberg (1960) defined crime as "a form of social maladjustment which can be designated as a more or less pronounced difficulty that the individual has in reacting to the stimuli of his environment in such a way as to remain in harmony with that environment."

WHAT DO YOU THINK? BOX 1.9

ARE CRIMINALS INTELLIGENT AND/OR CREATIVE?

Noted Harvard University psychologist Howard Gardner published his controversial book *Frames of Mind: The Theory of Multiple Intelligence* in 1983, refining his theory that intelligence cannot be measured through intelligence quotient tests. Gardner believes we have multiple intelligences: linguistic, logical/mathematical, musical, spatial, bodily kinesthetic (e.g., skills possessed by athletes, actors, and dancers), interpersonal, intrapersonal, and even naturalistic (e.g., a good understanding of flora and fauna). For example, have you ever felt you were better suited to, or felt more comfortable with, one of these areas than others? To support his general premise, Gardner cites an example of the frontal lobes of an individual being removed so that he is never able to move again, yet can still score 130 on an IQ test. Rather than believing that IQ alone is indicative of what we are capable of, Gardner suggests we need to broaden our understanding of intelligence (Jahrig, 1996). Platt (1969) suggests that *creativity* may be a better indicator of intelligence. In order for a crime to be successful, a criminal must not only be intelligent enough to form the intent but also display a degree of creativity that enables him or her to evade apprehension. Guilford (1954) has defined creativity as behaviour characterized by fluency, flexibility, and originality.

What kind of implications might this have for our attempts to understand criminal behaviour and our response to it? Do you think that social forces in life are more important than individual factors in determining criminal behaviour?

As with most other social sciences, the manner in which individual behaviour can be tested and quantified varies depending on one's orientation. For example, one can focus on mental abilities such as IQ (see Box 1.9) as a gauge of normality, or on differences in physical characteristics (see Chapter 5). In addition, psychologists focus on differences in personality and mental characteristics of criminals. Even as early as the fourth century BC, the father of modern medicine, Hippocrates, associated physical characteristics with behaviour.

Although psychology is a popular area of study, it is less well-established in criminological literature than the sociological perspective. One of the more notable Canadian contributions include Donald A. Andrews and James Bonta (both at Carleton University), who collaborated to produce *The Psychology of Criminal Conduct*. In their 1998 preface, Andrews and Bonta offer a strong argument on the need for a psychological examination of criminal conduct, commenting that sociologists have tended to discredit and often ignore individual elements in explaining criminal behaviour. We will examine some of the different psychological interpretations of crime in Chapter 6.

3. *Biology*: Bears know when to hibernate, salmon always return to the river they were spawned in, and vultures seem to know when death is close at hand. These are instinctual and biologically triggered mechanisms. Why could it not be possible that certain human traits are biological, or "hard-wired"? Or that certain crimes are a function of chemical, genetic, and/or neurological influences? In Chapter 5, we will examine some of the traditional and more recent biological interpretations of criminal behaviour.

Until recently, the biological perspective was met with a fair degree of skepticism. However, the book that had perhaps the greatest impact on the re-emergence of biological explanations of crime is the acclaimed 1985 work of J.Q. Wilson and R. Herrnstein, *Crime and Human Nature*. The biological perspective has evolved into an interdisciplinary perspective and appears to be gathering a strong following.

4. *Economics*: To paraphrase a famous dictum from the works of Karl Marx (1818–1883), "money is the root of all evil." Over the years, many studies have been done, demonstrating a link between unemployment, economic recession, and capitalism that forms the basis of all crime. Is it possible that crime is a function of competition for limited resources and/or social status/power? Do people who have "everything" commit as many crimes as those who do not?

Karl Marx is the one most often associated with this notion of economic determinism and its relationship to crime. However, other than using economics as an explanatory variable (or as part of a grander theoretical model), few researchers since the classic work *Criminality and Economic Conditions* in 1905, by the Dutch criminologist Willem Adriaan Bonger (1876–1940), have produced a book using economics as the primary predictor (dependent variable) of crime.

Although the economic perspective of crime has never been as widely embraced as some of the other perspectives by Canadian criminologists, there have been a number of interesting works that can (however loosely) be aligned with that view.

5. *Geography/environment*: Crime cannot occur in a vacuum. Take a minute to reflect on some of your favourite crime or horror movies. Are there "typical" scenes that tend to show up often? How about a foggy night down by the waterfront, or an unlit alleyway in a rundown area of town, or even a clear night with a bright full moon? Criminologists have developed sophisticated models and theories based on a wide range of environmental factors such as phases of the moon, barometric pressure, and even the physical appearance and layout of a business, residence, social area, or community. Is it possible that crime rates are a by-product of physical and environmental forces?

What is unique about this theoretical orientation is that the results from this line of inquiry can often be used in a proactive and preventive manner. For example, adding an alarm system to your new home or making sure that your lawn is cut and mail picked up while you are away are simple crime prevention designs using elementary environmental modifications.

6. *Political science*: How is it that a small but empowered group of officials can produce laws or ignore the will of the public they serve? How criminal justice officials make decisions has a direct impact on the community at large. In addition, since criminal justice, like most social service systems, is not perfect, it presents many interesting issues for study.

All societies require some coordination among people. The more complex and heterogeneous societies are, the greater the need for a formal infrastructure that tries to coordinate all the activities that might affect its citizens. This can range from identifying privileges, rights, and obligations to defining the administration of justice. The organizing principles of a country, province, or municipality "indicate how conditions and concepts such as life, liberty, property, civil rights, prestige, status, jobs, and information should be distributed among members of society" (Wright & Fox, 1978:314).

As a student of criminology, you might be interested in trying to understand why it took more than 20 years of debate before the *Young Offenders Act* was passed in 1984 (see Fetherston, 2004). You might also ask what the politicians were trying to accomplish, and whose interests were being served—especially given the act's public reception. Alternatively, you might ask why political decisions do not always appear to reflect the interests of society. For example, why is it that capital punishment has not been reinstated when, in a 1995 Ipsos-Reid survey, 69 percent of Canadians supported its reintroduction for heinous capital crimes. By 2001, the support dropped to 52 percent. Why the decline? It has been suggested increased publicity and wrongful convictions, controversy in the United States, and easier access to DNA testing may account for it.

Throughout this textbook, and in particular in Chapter 14, we will see how political science as well as the other disciplines have contributed to the study of criminality and social policy.

Finally, it is interesting to observe that while North American criminologists tend to align themselves with one of the above social science perspectives when studying crime, Europeans have approached crime from a legalistic standpoint.[4] For example, most European criminologists are predominantly lawyers by training who have taken an interest in social science (see Winterdyk & Cao, 2004). Yet neither approach seems to be very successful at solving the crime problem.

Criminology—An Integrated and Interdisciplinary Approach

Until recently, few Canadian criminologists had been trained within a criminology program. This is primarily because criminology programs in Canada did not exist until 1960 and graduate-related programs until some years after. Furthermore, in the past criminologists have usually come from diverse fields, with sociology and psychology representing their primary orientation. However, since Denis Szabo's pioneering efforts, a growing number of criminology, criminal justice, and human justice programs have sprung up across the country. Chunn and Menzies (1997:18) estimate that over the years, "nearly 1,000 students have graduated from Montreal, Toronto, Ottawa, and Simon Fraser Universities with MA, MSc, MCA, or PhD degrees in criminology. Today five schools offer graduate-level programs in criminology"[5] and have become increasingly interdisciplinary in their approach to the study of crime and criminality (see Figure 1–3 and Box 1.10). The new undergraduates and graduate students will further help shape the interdisciplinary and integrated identity of the discipline.

FIGURE 1–3

INTERDISCIPLINARY CRIMINOLOGY

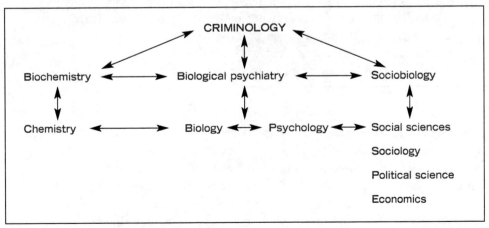

Source: Adapted from C.R. Jeffery, *Criminology: An Interdisciplinary Approach* (Englewood Cliffs, NJ: Prentice-Hall, 1990).

SO MANY QUESTIONS AND SO FEW ANSWERS!

A critical review of the literature reveals that there are both disciplinary and ideological arguments for trying to address only certain questions and issues as they pertain to criminology (see, for example, Shearing, 1989; Miller, 1973). However, it is the intent of this book to argue that an interdisciplinary, holistic, and flexible approach may be more realistic and practical. The following lists offers a cross-section of questions you can explore individually or with your classmates. There are no right or wrong answers. Rather, the exercise serves as an introduction to the complexity of crime and demonstrates how difficult it is to solve criminological issues.

How might one best begin to answer each of the questions?

1. Is crime (really) increasing in Canada? If so, why is it increasing? What factors play a major role in understanding crime patterns (e.g., age, gender, region, climatic conditions)?
2. Are certain groups in Canadian society overrepresented in the Canadian justice system? If so, why? Is the CJS racist? If so, is anything being done to correct the situation?
3. Should pornography be censored? Should lap dancing be banned? Should prostitution be legalized? Why were/are certain books (such as Canadian author Margaret Laurence's *The Stone Angel* and *The Diviners,* and J. D. Salinger's *Catcher in the Rye*) banned from public schools?
4. Should soft drugs such as marijuana be legalized? Why do we allow people to drink alcoholic spirits and smoke cigarettes when we know these substances can lead to premature death? Would legalizing drugs help the CJS?
5. Should the insanity defence be abolished?
6. Should terminally ill patients be allowed to have assisted suicide?
7. Do we need more prisons? Is punishment the best way of dealing with criminal offenders? Should men and women in prison be allowed conjugal visits?
8. Are victims' rights and assistance programs succeeding?
9. Should we focus on general theories of crime as opposed to specific ones?
10. Should criminology be recognized as a separate discipline?

An integrated and interdisciplinary approach attempts to treat all disciplinary perspectives equally, as well as integrating the competing notion that crime is a product of choice or free will as opposed to being a product of fixed external and internal factors.

For example, why did former NHL hockey czar, Alan Eagleson, commit fraud in 1996 against the players who had entrusted him with the management of their pension funds? Those who support the free will model might say he knowingly calculated the risk based on his influential position, limited knowledge, and/or concern of his agents. He responded to an "opportunity" that seemed too good to ignore. By contrast, it may also have been true that pressure from his legal firm to generate revenue, family stress, and/or a troubled childhood predisposed him to commit the offence.

An integrated and interdisciplinary approach would say that Eagleson committed the crime based on a combination of rational and irrational factors. Once tempted, he may have become consumed by greed and lost sight of his ability to maintain any perspective (see Box 1.11).

Hence, an integrated and interdisciplinary approach may be general (e.g., all crimes) or specific (e.g., a particular crime) and may rely on some perspectives more than others to understand a situation.

FYI BOX 1.11

WHAT ARE YOUR CHANCES—CAN YOU BELIEVE WHAT YOU READ?

In 2002, there were 2.6 million *Criminal Code* incidents (excluding traffic incidents), and there were nearly 30 million Canadians of which approximately 21 million were of legal age. Therefore nearly 1 in 10 Canadians could have committed a crime. The official crime rate is about the same as it was in 1979! (CCJS, 2003, 23(5)).

Can different theoretical perspectives offer politicians informed responses to the criminological issues confronting society?

Can These Ideas Work? Bridging Theory and Policy

"Every man is guilty of all the good he didn't do." Voltaire (1694–1778)

The subject of crime, as John Hagan (then president of the American Society of Criminology) said in 1987, is "hot." It receives considerable media coverage, and levels of public fear are higher than ever before. Annual surveys conducted across Canada for *Maclean's* magazine all report that Canadians rank crime as an important issue.

Politicians often run their campaigns around crime issues—especially Stephen Harper's Conservative Party of Canada (see **www.conservative.ca**). Allan Rock (minister of justice in 1996) was applauded for taking a hard stand against crime when he toughened the *Young Offenders Act* and repealed Bill 745 (the "faint hope" clause, as it was referred to in the press). The bill had opened a loophole for serious offenders to get out on early release. In 1998, following Ontario's example, Alberta began to seek public input on revamping the justice system. Alberta's minister of justice, John Havelock, explained that Albertans were disgusted with the government's apparently lax attitude toward justice. Is this an astute observation or simply a means by which the government can absolve itself from responsibility if the public's ideas do not work?

As has been noted already, criminology is an "applied" social science. Criminologists use their theoretical perspectives to study crime and formulate workable solutions to the problem. This book deals with the challenge of bridging theory and policy in criminology. It is a challenge because despite numerous studies and policy recommendations, the successes in this area have been few. Furthermore, there are often competing approaches to addressing the same issue. For example, what is the best method of dealing with sex offenders? Different explanations and different solutions have been put forth, yet according to official statistics the rate of incidence of sexual assaults has not declined significantly.

While criminologists may not boast a perfect track record, making policy decisions without theoretical guidance would be like playing Russian roulette. There would be no basis on which to decide how to respond to sex offenders or how to address any other issue confronting criminologists and the criminal justice system. Hackler (1994:62–63) offers an interesting explanation for the dilemma:

> If criminologists would be *inconsistent* in their ideology and more *consistent* in their use of science, we would probably create a more reliable knowledge base. In the end, this could contribute to a better society.... Criminologists in Canada would probably be more productive if they understood and utilized scientific procedures more than they do at present.

Despite the difficulties confronting criminologists in conducting sound research and being able to make sound policy recommendations, criminology has much to offer in the study of crime. For example, without scientific proof, capital punishment would likely be reinstated, we would likely still be torturing wrongdoers, and we might never have introduced such programs as victim–offender reconciliation and community service order or used DNA technology in investigative work.

Throughout this textbook, there are examples of how theory, coupled with research, has been used to lead to social policy (see Chapters 8–13).

A final point about integrating theory and policy that deserves mention is the ethical issues criminologists must face when espousing a theoretical perspective or offering policy recommendation. There are potential social and political consequences to doing applied research. As Barak (1997:10) cautions, however, "criminological knowledge is also a product of ethics and notions of justice." In other words, policy recommendations are driven by the dominant and prevailing values and disciplinary structures of the time.

When Do They Go Public? Ethical Issues

The study of any social issue with the intent of proposing solutions raises ethical dilemmas. Ekstedt and Jackson (1997:242) define ethics as "the application of moral values or principles to decisions in public or private life."

Researching a social issue such as child abuse or prostitution, or deciding whether to subject inmates to "experimental" treatment programs, can involve profound ethical issues. For example, many people's lives may be affected by these findings—be it regarding chemical castration (see Is chemical castration..., 1996); legalizing prostitution (see Liberator, 2003); random drug testing of police officers in England (Random drug..., 1996); or managing sex offenders (Sex offender recidivism predictor, 2004). In October 1970, the federal government enacted the *War Measures Act* in response to the controversial activities of the FLQ (Front de libération du Québec). Before that, the FLQ had plotted to kidnap the United States' and Israel's consul-generals in Montreal. They had planted a bomb in the Montreal Stock Exchange, which injured 27 persons, and had been involved in the murder of a member of the Quebec cabinet, Pierre Laporte.

When might any of the above examples represent an infringement of our basic civil liberties and a violation of our moral standards? How should criminologists interpret such issues? How do we separate prevailing competing disciplinary biases and values to address criminological concerns?

Given the dynamic nature of crime, some criminologists try to understand the extent to which society attempts to maintain social order and the extent to which the public is prepared to acquiesce in that attempt. In addition to dealing with these practical and ethical issues, we need to consider how the findings can, or should, be used: toward social control or (one of the central themes of this book) crime prevention? There is also the issue of which criminological perspective to study. Answers to these questions can, in part, be found within whatever disciplinary perspective is being used.

In summary, criminologists need to exercise caution when interpreting their findings. They should ground their research in sound theories and sound methodologies. However, they also need to move beyond conventional ideas and strive to create new images and new meanings for concepts that do not work. This postmodernist conceptualization embraces an integrated and interdisciplinary approach. Then these findings should be replicated over time and in different settings before they are applied. This is why many criminologists are reluctant to state anything conclusively. As you read the conclusions to research reports or journal articles, you will inevitably notice this fact.

Summary

- Canadian criminology can justifiably be examined from a *Canadian perspective*, as evidenced by the number of emerging diploma and degree programs across the country and the studies and scholars that have already made their mark on the international scene.

- While criminology is a comparatively young area of inquiry, it has and continues to evolve into an *integrated* and *interdisciplinary* science that involves the study of human behaviour in a systematic and objective manner.

- Although sociological thought has played a major role in North American criminological thought, no single theory can provide all explanations regarding the crime problem. Yet, as the noted American sociologist Thomas Kuhn (1970), among others, noted, the paradigm criminologists use will naturally influence the type of information sought, strategies employed, and interpretations made.

- As an applied science, criminology uses *theory* and *research* methods to explain the causes of criminal behaviour, often to help guide *policy-making* throughout the criminal justice system. Consequently, criminologists often face *ethical issues* when conducting research.

- Criminology is akin to a living organism, dynamic, evolving, and challenging. Embracing an integrated and interdisciplinary approach to the study of behaviour offers opportunities within a large number of professions and related areas of employment and study.

Discussion Questions

1. What is the importance of:

   a. studying criminology within a Canadian context?

   b. understanding criminology's historical roots?

2. Provide examples of ethical issues faced by criminologists and how they can be resolved.

3. The use of medicinal marijuana is one example of the relative and evolutive nature of a criminal/deviant behaviour. Provide other examples. Explain how these behaviours have or are changing and speculate as to why.

4. What are the major elements of the criminological enterprise?

Key Concepts

conflict crimes	consensus crimes	conventional crimes
crime	criminal justice	criminological enterprise
criminologist	criminology	deviance
etiology	evolutive	indictable offences
integrated	interdisciplinary	non-conventional crimes
relative	summary offences	

Key Names

Maurice Parmalee
Paul Topinard

Weblinks

www.stmarys.ca/administration/library/subjects/criminology.htm St. Mary's University has one of the fastest growing criminology programs in the Maritimes; its library's website contains good links.

www.ualr.edu/~alpatenaude/page4.htm Prof. Patenaude has put together a website with numerous criminology and criminal justice links focusing on topics relevant to the study of Northern justice.

www.socialsciences.uottawa.ca/crm/eng/links.asp This website from the University of Ottawa's Department of Criminology offers useful links.

Endnotes

1. Other major contributions of historical note include John L. Gillin's 1926 textbook *Criminology and Penology* and Philip A. Parsons's textbook *Crime and the Criminal*, also published in 1926 (see Gibbons, 1979:34). Gillin's textbook included 36 chapters that were divided into two main sections—theoretical explanations of crime and punishment and control of crime. His etiological approach paralleled that of Parmalee. Parsons's book, while having drawn fewer accolades than Gillin's or Sutherland's, was intended for the general public and college students (Gibbons, 1979).

2. These views were also clearly reflected in Michael Harrington's 1962 book *The Other America: Poverty in the US* (NY: Penguin). The book has been credited with sparking the War on Poverty.

3. *Juristat* reports note that these figures do not reflect all government spending! They neglect to explain which elements of government spending are not included in the estimates.

4. Among some key names one is likely to come across are: David Farrington and Barbara Wooten from England; Nils Christie from Norway; Josine Junger-Tas and Gert-Jan Terlouw from the Netherlands; David Garland from Scotland; and Hans-Jörg Albrecht, Hans Juergen, and Hans-Jörg Kerner from Germany.

5. The University of Montreal was the first to grant a doctoral degree in criminology in 1968. Simon Fraser began its doctoral program in 1985; the University of Toronto, in 1990–91; and the University of Ottawa, around 2002.

CHAPTER 2

Images of Crime and Its Control

"Accounts of life in the urban centres of the late 1800s and early 1900s are hair-raising. Crime was a real threat, but then as now the picture of the crime problem painted by official statistics was seriously distorted..."

H. Pepinsky & P. Jesilow, 1984:22

Learning Outcomes

After you have completed this chapter, you should be able to:

- Recognize the various methods of forming images of our reality.

- Know what influences our frame of reference.

- Identify the five basic ways in which we acquire knowledge and understanding.

- Understand the difference between rationalism and empiricism and how they affect our conception of crime and criminality.

- Discuss and appreciate the importance of ethics in disclosure and have an appreciation of the social responsibility inherent in social science discovery and disclosure.

Assuming you have read Chapter 1, you now know that the complex subject of crime has been influenced by different ideologies and disciplinary perspectives. In fact, even among those who consider themselves criminologists, there is some disagreement over what criminologists should be studying, how they should study it, and what they should call their studies. In Section II of this book, we will examine some of these diverging views. However, before we do, let us look at some of the images the public has of crime, as well as the role of mass media in shaping our images of crime.

Up until the early 1970s, researchers tended to examine only people's perceptions of crime. They felt that the public was greatly concerned about crime and that the mass media played a significant role in the creation and dissemination of perceptions of crime. Roberts et al. (2003), among others, point out that most people are quite naive when it comes to knowing the "truth" about the extent of crime and/or how the criminal justice system works in general. Yet, as Ballard (1998) noted, media coverage of crimes can play a major role in the legislative processes that may not always be warranted.

While the average person has a general knowledge on the topic of crime, this awareness, as some researchers have observed, tends to be based on an information-rich and knowledge-poor foundation. How do we form opinions about the world of crime around us? To what extent is our fear of crime justified? Do the media distort crime news? Are official sources of crime data reliable?

The objective of this chapter is to examine how people come to know about and form perceptions of crime and criminality. After some initial discussion, the chapter will focus on the four main methods of how people come to perceive their reality.

Public Perceptions of Crime

"Ignorance is preferable to error; and he is less remote from the truth who believes nothing, than he who believes what is wrong." Thomas Jefferson (third president of the USA, 1801–1809)

Before delving into methods of knowing, it is helpful to clarify a few terms of reference about the concept of image formation. How we form images of our reality has been the subject of numerous philosophical debates and social science studies. Kerlinger (1979), for example, notes that *knowledge* can be viewed as either being *dynamic* or *static*. "The static view holds that science is an activity that contributes systematized information to the world" (ibid.:7). It views knowledge as cumulative to the extent that we keep inquiring.

The dynamic view, by contrast, regards knowledge as a process of self-discovery. Knowledge is seen to be important in and of itself, but it serves only as "a base for further scientific theory and research" (ibid.:7). The view, or *frame of reference*, we choose is influenced by our socialization process, psychological character, and various biological factors. Nettler (1984), among others, has observed that how we view something is not necessarily the same as our knowledge about something. You might believe that capital punishment is an effective deterrent, but over the years, research (i.e., knowledge) has continually been unable to support your view. Furthermore, the type and amount of reading or viewing you engage in will determine how much knowledge you have to make an informed decision about a particular issue. For example, because the media have a code of conduct that requires them to report the news accurately, we may feel that they are reliable sources of crime information. However, knowing that they also "focus upon what is out of place: deviant, equivocal, and unpredictable"

(Ericson, Baranek, & Chan, 1991:4) provides additional insight into the role of the media that may help us view such news more cautiously. Yet the public may not always be aware that this is the case. A number of studies have shown that as many as three-quarters of people polled overestimate the amount of crime involving violence (see Ekstedt & Jackson, 1997; Roberts et al., 2003). Therefore, there are many avenues by which to gain knowledge, and they do not always result in the same outcome! How then does the public acquire its knowledge about crime?

General Methods of Knowing

What is the difference between knowledge, belief, and truth? Based on information (such as crime statistics) available to you, you might *know* that the crime rate declined throughout 1990s and into the new millennium. However, based on personal experience and/or other methods of knowing, you might not *believe* everything you read (see Box 2.1). So what is the *true* (real) scenario?

The great French philosopher René Descartes (1596–1650) introduced us to the *method of doubt*. Unless every belief can be demonstrated with absolute certainty, then we must doubt its existence. He introduced the concept of **rationalism**, which means that knowledge is based on reasoning. It is from Descartes's work we have the famous saying "I think, therefore I am." Another way of understanding knowledge comes from the **empiricist** perspective. Such great scholars as John Locke (1632–1704) and David Hume (1711–1776) argued that knowledge comes though experience. Locke used the analogy of *tabula rasa*: our minds begin as a blank slate on which life experiences form our reality (Wolff, 1971).

If one considers the work of Immanuel Kant (1724–1804), perhaps one of the greatest thinkers since Aristotle and Plato, then the line between fact and fiction becomes even more nebulous. In his work titled *Critique of Pure Reason*, published in 1781, Kant argues that we never have knowledge of reality. Instead, our mind forms our appearances of reality. Hence, *our ways of acquiring knowledge simply represent the mental window through which we view and construct our reality*. Therefore, it is possible for two researchers (or other people) to describe the same thing from two different paradigms and produce considerably different accounts. It is not unlike the Crown and defence bringing in their own experts to counter each other's sworn impressions. Each believes their experts' knowledge to be superior to and therefore more believable than those of the other's experts. Yet all the experts are speaking on the same subject. Who is telling the "truth"? We must assume they all are, since their testimony is provided under oath!

While it is beyond the scope of this chapter to debate the strengths and weaknesses of the above views, they serve as reminders that what we believe to be facts may be only illusions compared to a greater reality that we have not yet seen. Change in our knowledge can occur through what Thomas Kuhn (1970) called a **paradigm shift**. This concept encapsulates the premise that there can be no one objective truth but rather multiple theories that arise from the different beliefs and values that researchers and scientists have. Hence, reality can be described as consisting of multiple paradigms (beliefs) or theories. However, research paradigms come under scrutiny; when new findings overwhelm previous knowledge, researchers experience a paradigm shift. For example, criminology was once dominated by law and the sociological perspective. However, as we have gained more empirical knowledge about crime and criminality, we have seen a shift toward embracing other perspectives, such as psychology, political science, and an interdisciplinary approach (Cao, 2004).

So again we come back to the importance of knowing. It can perhaps be generally said that whether we choose to view crime as either "bad" or "good," functional or dysfunctional, it is a phenomenon that draws considerable attention. What does crime mean? What does it really represent? What can or should we do about crime? And why do some people tend to commit more of certain crimes than others?

Criminology, like any area of study, is a collection of information about issues and concerns that forms a knowledge base. This knowledge base becomes the foundation for theory, policy, and social and political responses.

In more concrete terms, criminologists have synthesized the above issues into two principles of crime. The concept of crime is both *relative* and *evolutive*.

Consider the following example. On Sundays in Indonesia, it is illegal to express affection in public; doing so can result in a prison sentence. But if you were to visit the beautiful open squares in Rome on a warm Sunday, you would likely find the steps covered with lovers showing their affection. Similarly, in Canada, such expressions are not sanctionable unless they violate public conduct orders. The above example illustrates two points. First, our knowledge of crime is limited by our knowledge of social and cultural values around the world. Second, the concept of crime is relative to time, place, culture, and values. Therefore, we can further note that there are no absolutes about our knowledge of what constitutes a crime.

Consumption of certain substances constitutes a good example of crime as evolutive. Today, we view alcoholism as a disease (a position endorsed by Alcoholics Anonymous), but at the turn of the century it was seen as a moral failing (Schlaadt, 1992). In Canada, the 1878 *Dominion Temperance Act* gave local jurisdictions the right to vote "dry" (Hatch, 1995). Both the *Dominion Temperance Act* and World War I brought about the prohibition era in Canada. By the 1960s, however, ads associating alcohol consumption with good times were readily displayed on television and in print! While alcohol consumption was frequently forbidden in the late 1800s and early 1900s, it was legal to consume cola nuts and marijuana. In fact, Coca-Cola used to have a cola nut base—hence the word "cola" to mean this kind of soft drink. Today, cola nuts are on the Olympic list of banned substances because they have a stimulant effect on the body. Since the banning of cola nuts, Coca-Cola has substituted sugar and caffeine. When consumed in excessive amounts, both also have addictive properties, but they are legal (Fishbein & Pease, 1996).

What constitutes a crime can change over time. The definition and meaning of crime is influenced by changing values and beliefs. For example, homosexuality is no longer a crime; in many jurisdictions, smoking in public places is a violation; and not wearing your seat belt, or bicycle helmet in some parts of Canada, is now a crime.

What is the purpose of making laws that have no permanence? Why do we create laws that in a few years may be considered either too liberal or conservative? Do such laws have a place in our complex society? How do we *know* when to legislate laws or to repeal them? What constitutes a majority of opinion?

In summary, our images of crime involve a complex interplay of the knowledge (i.e., information) we have available and the choice we make as to how strongly to believe such information (i.e., based on experience, values, and norms). We have also seen that what may appear factually accurate at one point in time and place may later take on a different meaning. Collectively, the ethical implications of these elements play an important role in how, when, and why we control crime.

Acquiring Knowledge on Crime

In the previous section, we noted that the line between fact and fiction is often obscure and subject to change. The problem is further complicated by the fact that our world has become so highly specialized. It is no longer possible for the average person to be a "jack of all trades." Instead, we tend to acquire varying degrees of expertise in one or two areas. We tend to develop and master specialized skills that enable us to obtain employment that often requires them. For example, police officers must go through rigorous physical and personality screening procedures before they are accepted into the police training academy. Then they must successfully complete the training, in many cases at their own expense, before they become police officers. The days of going straight from high school into a police force are becoming increasingly rare.[1]

In 1984, Canadian sociologist Gordon West identified four major influences that shape our images of juvenile delinquency that can also be generalized to crime. They include: (1) personal knowledge, (2) the mass media, (3) official state knowledge, and (4) sociological knowledge. We will examine the first three influences and, based on the assertions made about criminology being interdisciplinary and integrated, we will expand on the fourth point to include theoretical knowledge.

Because crime is so pervasive today, the public relies on a variety of sources to obtain some understanding of a subject that, according to various polls over the years, ranks consistently at or near the top of social concerns (Gallup Polls, 2004). Based on the work of Kidder and Judd (1986), we will review five basic means by which we acquire information and understanding about crime and criminological issues. They include:

1. *Speculation and logical analysis.* We often form conclusions based on what appear to be logical speculations. For example, being idle provides free time and boredom, which in turn can lead to committing deviant acts to alleviate that boredom. However, our deductive process may be influenced by our limited knowledge and our wishes and desires, as well as our capacity to ignore contradictions in our thinking.

2. *Authority*. An authority (such as the Bible, a parent, a teacher, or an "expert") says that something is so, and we accept it as fact. Using an expert to affirm our belief lends credibility to it. In fact, research shows we are likely to seek out experts with whom we can identify, just as we tend to seek out friends and partners with whom we feel a "connection."

3. *Consensus*. Rather than appeal to wisdom, we appeal to the wisdom of our peers. Our peers, however, are likely to share the same views as those inquiring. Kidder and Judd (1986:15) note that "groups of people can be notoriously poor as independent judges."

4. *Observation*. You might have heard that a certain instructor is very demanding. To decide whether you should avoid taking a course taught by this instructor, you decide to sit in on a class and observe for yourself. Since you are limiting your impressions to one or two classes and the opinions of others, you might not be objective in your assessment.

5. *Past experience*. Kidder and Judd suggest that this is the most common means of generating support for our hypotheses. We draw on prior instances or events that confirm our assumptions and then attempt to modify incongruent elements.

BY THE NUMBERS BOX 2.1

PUBLIC PERCEPTIONS: FACT VERSUS FICTION

- A special report feature in the *Calgary Herald* (Public perception of crime, 1996) noted that people's concern for personal safety increased from 56 percent in 1991 to 62 percent in 1996. In fact, however, the number of criminal incidents (and their rates) has been declining in recent years, both nationally and regionally. For example, in spite of Calgary's continual growth, the city experienced a drop in its official crime rate but a slight increase in perceived levels of fear.

- In 1998, 77 percent of Canadians believed that sentencing of young offenders was too lenient (CCJS, 2003, 23(3)). Yet we have one of the highest incarceration rates of young offenders in the Western world (Winterdyk, 2002).

- A federal report in 2001 by Karin Stein found that "overall, Canadians do not consider crime to be a 'top-of-mind' concern. Public concern has fluctuated little over the years, and been decreasing of late."

Why do people seem to have the wrong impression about crime? There are a number of possible explanations. With fiscal cutbacks, police are prioritizing responses, the public may be reporting less as their faith in the system wanes, and the increase in youth crime may be distorting the overall perception and trend. Nevertheless, your odds of being a victim of a violent crime are 1 in 119; of a property crime, 1 in 14; of death from a heart attack, 1 in 538; of dying from smoking, 1 in 606; of dying in a fatal car accident, 1 in 10 526. Therefore, perhaps our fears are not illogical. What do you think? (See Chapter 3 for further discussion.)

Studies have shown that information that is consistent with our expectations is more easily remembered than information that is not. Therefore, it is generally "unlikely that hypotheses will be disconfirmed by recollected observations" (Kidder & Judd, 1986:17).

Although the above methods of knowing are readily available to most people, certain critical elements are often absent. Most importantly, many people are not systematic or objective in their approach. They do not use a representative sample; typically, they instead use small samples based on a limited number of questions. These approaches are "naive" in nature (see Box 2.1). By contrast, scientific inquiry relies on the collection of observable and measurable data in which ideas are tested following prescribed methodological techniques (see Chapter 3). These techniques are the subject of research methods courses that most criminology programs require their students to take.

What is needed to help separate facts from public misconceptions is the use of the scientific method of inquiry. The primary building blocks involve four steps. The process is illustrated in Figure 2–1. The fact that the model is circular indicates that knowledge

FIGURE 2–1

THE WHEEL OF RESEARCH

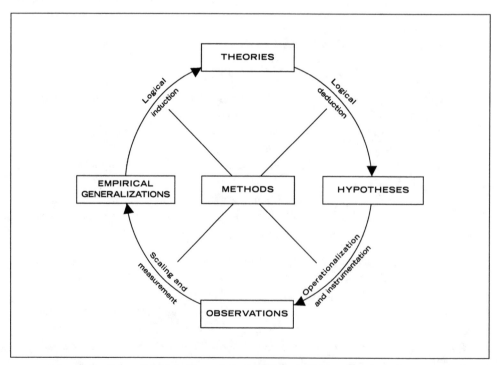

Section I: Foundations of Criminology

is a process of retesting and refining our understanding of a phenomenon, program, or event. Theories, for example, are constantly being tested under different conditions to see whether they can stand up to the rigours of objective evaluation and the passage of time. Theories that do so tend to become the dominant perspectives embraced by researchers. (We will examine some of these perspectives in Chapters 5–7.) These naive methods of gathering information can sometimes result in misconceptions of crime because our perceptions are often coloured by one or more of the above factors.

Personal Knowledge and Crime

The viewpoints formed by the public can have a dramatic impact on the criminal justice system and on criminology in general. Public pressure has been successful in bringing about judicial reform. The public has been described as the *hidden element* of the criminal justice system (Griffths & Verdun-Jones, 1994). In many cases, it is the public that dictates how money is spent in addressing crime and criminality, including the administration of criminal justice.

One of the more dramatic examples in recent years has been the growing dissatisfaction the public has had with young offenders, fuelled by stories such as the 1992 case of Ryan Garrioch, who was murdered in his school yard as a result of a dispute with another youth; the 1995 incident in Montreal that involved the senseless killing of Reverend Frank Toope and his wife for a paltry $100 and some jewellery; or the 2002 case of a Nova Scotia youth who committed suicide after being involved in extortions by a local youth gang. These and other cases have contributed to public criticism of the juvenile justice system, in particular the *Young Offenders Act*. Public outcry at these incidents eventually led to an increase in the penalty for murder, from seven to ten years. However, in 1999, a bill was tabled to replace the former *Young Offenders Act* with the *Youth Criminal Justice Act*; the new legislation came into force on April 1, 2003. The act promotes various current social values that have the potential to gain public confidence and curb the tide of public criticism.

Similarly, a growing decline in public confidence in the criminal justice system, in particular because of certain sentencing and correctional practices, prompted the so-called *Daubney Report* (titled *Taking Responsibility*) to verify the impressions expressed by the public in the media. Subsequent studies by Doob and Roberts (1982) and, more recently, Roberts and Sanders (2004) indicated, however, that most Canadians appear to have limited knowledge about the actual crime rate and tend to overestimate the amount of violent crime, along with being ill-informed about other key aspects of criminal justice functions. Similar observations have also been reported in the United States (see Barkan & Cohn, 1994) and in Germany (see Boers & Sessar, 1991).

Public images of crime and criminality can have a direct impact on how people conduct themselves. According to Sacco and Kennedy (1998), women tend to feel less safe alone at night, and seniors are more fearful of being victimized than are other age groups. Because of their fear, some people go to great lengths to secure their property, from using sophisticated car and house alarms to carrying protective devices such as pepper spray and personal alarms. Based on 1996 figures, Canadians spend approximately $195 million—that is, between 2.3 and 5.3 percent of the nation's gross domestic product (GDP)[2]—on personalized security systems (Easton & Brantingham, 1998). Do these devices work? Are they necessary? Has their presence created other problems? In 2001, the Pembina Institute in Alberta reported that crime had increased 264 percent in the province since 1961, even though Albertans were spending more on alarms, home security, locks, etc. (Taylor & Anielski, 2001). Consider the following news items:

- "Lorrie McClinton has a big dog, bolts her doors and keeps a knife and a baseball bat nearby." This was the photo caption to an article on peoples' increasing fear levels of being victimized (*Maclean's*, 1991:30).
- Sales of The Club, a steering-wheel lock to discourage auto theft, increased from $22 million in 1990 to $107.3 million (US) in 1992 (*Business Week*, 1993). Yet, according to Statistics Canada, the rate of auto theft increased from 184 per 100 000 in 1983 to 355 by 1993 and 514 by 2002 (CCJS, 2003, 23(5)). Based on his review of Canadian motor vehicle theft, Morrison (1996) observed that, contrary to advertisement claims for automobile security devices, "little is known on the deterrent effect of anti-theft devices."

Public perception of the risk of being victimized by crime versus the actual risk varies according to factors related to lifestyle, age, gender, occupation, and a variety of personal attributes (see Karman, 1990; Stein, 2001).

Beginning in the 1980s, Canadian researchers have conducted major victimization studies. Brillon (1987) and, more recently, Fattah and Sacco (1989) examined victimization among seniors. They observed that actual victimization of seniors (i.e., 65 years of age or over) was low, but that fear levels increased due to feelings of fragility and defencelessness. Vulnerability factors included:

1. *State of health*: 28 percent of seniors versus 19 percent of those in the 18–24 age bracket required hospitalization after being victimized.
2. *Financial situation*: 65 percent of those surveyed experienced a drop in income. Two-thirds of those people experienced a 25 percent drop in income levels.
3. *Social milieu*: Due to their lifestyle, seniors are generally less informed about their risks than younger generations.

Until Brillon's study, very little research had been conducted on the victimization of seniors, but more recently studies of elder abuse and other forms of elder victimization have been growing. We now know, for example, that seniors are more likely to be victimized at, or near, their homes than are other age groups. Although many older people believe they are likely to become victims of crime, the rates of both theft and violent crime against seniors dropped between 1973 and 1993. A 2002 report by Health Canada stated that seniors are significantly less likely to encounter violent crimes than are younger age groups. While in 2001 those over 65 constituted about 16 percent of the Canadian population, violent crimes against them accounted for only 3 percent of the total. About half of these involved minor assaults, as compared to 68 percent for younger victims.

While we should not view the problem lightly, Canadian criminologist Brian Maclean (1986) argues that the growing awareness of victimization may well represent an excuse for widening the net of social control. He notes, for example, that the rate of criminal justice spending increases faster than the rate of growth for overall state expenditures. Yet crime rates remain comparatively stable. In fact, during the mid-1990s and into the new millennium, there was a decrease in crime rates. Maclean also points out that conviction rates have remained relatively stable over the years.

As noted in the biographical sketch of Denis Szabo in Chapter 4, there are two sides to social reality. There is the social reality as perceived by the public and that perceived by researchers and criminology/criminal justice officials. The challenge for criminologists is to try to discern which reality is more plausible and how to balance the two perspectives. This is why most criminologists ground their research in theoretical principles and empirical data. However, it is clear how the public can become confused or misled when trying to learn about the realities of crime.

Mass Media Knowledge and Crime

"It is likely that in one week of prime-time television drama one will see more homicides than will occur in Canada in the course of a year." Silverman, 1988:209

Much of what people know about the issues in the world come not from direct experiences but from media portrayals. And there is plenty to choose from. Most radio stations, including CBC radio, provide news on an hourly basis. On television, there are several all-news stations, such as CNN and CBC Newsworld, plus scores of crime-based dramas, movies, and documentaries that are aired regularly. These media, in many respects, represent our conventional methods of knowing. They represent authority (the trusted news anchor), consensus (all the channels tend to cover the same stories), and observation (we see pictures of the crime around us); as well, the news is often just "more of the same." In fact, one of the experiences that can account for an increase in crime is that media-sensitive crimes can promote a feedback loop that can impact people's willingness to report crimes, as well as their perception of crime seriousness. In addition, television, radio, and newspapers are entertainment media that must sell themselves to the public.

Dr. Leonard Eron, from Yale University, was the first to study the relationship between TV watching and subsequent aggressive behaviour. He argued that the best predictor of violence among young males was the amount of television watching they did (Stutman, 1995). Using Canadian data, Smith (1983) found that the public and policy-makers are generally concerned about the effects of television and movies on violent behaviour. Ericson, Baranek, and Chan (1987, 1991), and others, have found that the presentation of news content varies between TV broadcasting and print because of the distinct format differences; however, the research has been unable to find consistent patterns. For example, Gollin (1988), vice-president of a national advertising agency, argues that the impact of the mass media is far less than critics fear and that the media simply reinforce prevailing attitudes and beliefs. At the other end of the spectrum, the group Christianity Today (2000) argues that the media, by displaying violence, sex, and crime, undermine morality in society. Yet Laval University researchers found that violence content of television programming in Canada is about 23 percent less than that violence content on American television (Alter, 1997).

The lack of congruence in the literature reflects not only the different intellectual heritage of the authors but also methodological limitations. Such limitations include being able to control for the characteristics of the source or controlling less tangible elements, such as public interest and the characteristics of viewers/readers.

Representative crime coverage falls into a catch-22 territory because people are inclined to pay to see only what fits their frame of reference. Therefore, the media have a stake in reinforcing certain images. Moreover, since most people have limited access to or experience with crime, their misconceptions are perpetuated in the media (Silverman, 1988). The formations of such misconceptions have been well documented in the literature. Among the first to point them out was the noted social psychologist Albert Bandura, originally from Mundare, Alberta.

The Mitigating Role of the Media

Bandura (1979), in a series of experiments, found that one way in which behaviour is learned is through *symbolic modelling*. Drawing on the principles of the *social learning theory* (see Chapter 6), Bandura observed that children readily imitated behaviour they observed on television and controlled video presentations. This process is referred to as *vicarious reinforcement*. The theory asserts that our social environment contributes to the learning process. Given this line of reasoning, it is possible to learn not only from those around us, but also from what we see, hear, and read, as well as from those with whom we associate.

How, or why, people imitate what they see, read, or hear is not clear, but there is sufficient scientific evidence to indicate that imitative and vicarious learning does occur at some level. For example, if violence and punishment are used in the home to settle disputes, children are likely to model that behaviour when they find themselves in a similar situation. The role of vicarious modelling has been extensively documented in child abuse literature (see Trocme et al., 2001).

Using several figures from the National Centre of Health Statistics, sociologist David Phillips found that suicides increased significantly just after the appearance of a non-fictional suicide story on television. In conjunction with related studies, Phillips concluded, "all these findings support the hypothesis that publicized suicides trigger imitative behaviour," sometimes in overt ways (an explicit suicide) or covertly (in the form of automobile or aircraft accidents) (cited in LaHaye, 1988:114). In addition, while an association between what we are exposed to and what we do does not imply a causal relationship, the media do appear to play a role in influencing human behaviour. However, since we do not have a clear picture as to the strength of the relationship, nor fully understand why some people are more susceptible to media images than others, the role of the media and crime will continue to intrigue behavioural scientists.

In Chapter 6, we will explore other elements of the social learning and cognitive theory, which, according to Stitt and Giacopassi's (1992) research on theories, are among the most frequently tested theories in criminology.

A Growing Concern

Since the 1960s, there has been a dramatic growth in news media coverage of crime (Wilson, 1994) (see Box 2.2). Is this due to an increase in crime or is it a response to the media's realization that sensational news sells? What type of crime stories do you typically hear, see, or read about? Is the coverage representative of the "true" crime picture offered by official sources? Does the coverage provide a fair balance of local, national, and international crime experiences? If you answer no to any of these questions, what concerns or issues might that raise regarding our understanding of crime?

A report from a conservative think tank (*Fraser Forum*, 1996) pointed out that while the murder rate declined each year between 1991 and 1995, media coverage increased significantly. It also noted that even though in 1995 just 16 percent of the murders were committed by someone unknown to the victim, these types of cases were overrepresented in the media (e.g., 54 percent of CBC and 66 percent of CTV coverage). In fact, only "18 per cent of CBC and 11 per cent of CTV news stories on Canadian murder focused on those committed by someone known to the victim."

FYI BOX 2.2

MEDIA VIOLENCE

- Children's programs were 68 percent more violent than programs for adults.
- Though the murder rate has dropped since 1994, media reports of murder were 33 percent more frequent in 1998 than in 1997 (Quick facts, 1998).
- A 2001 report by the Quebec Superior Council of Education noted that "repeated exposure of media violence is among the 3 major factors responsible for causing a 300% increase in youth violence over the last 15 years of kids with troubled behaviour" (Brodeur, 2002).
- Overall, 61 percent of American programming had violent content (*CNN interactive*, 1998). In a 2002 American research study, Blakey reports that the average child has seen 100 000 acts of violence and 8000 murders on television by the time he or she leaves elementary school.

In a study by West (1984), a survey revealed that stories about delinquency and crime tended to feed on **moral panic** rather than being based on actual behaviour. For example, in 1992, stories surrounding the Ryan Garrioch case tended to focus on the growing problem of violent youth crime and the need for amendments to the *YOA* (Seskus, 2004).

The type of coverage by the various media was similar to the infamous and sensationalized killing of a 12-year-old Toronto youth in July 1977. The youth was "homosexually assaulted and raped, forced to take illicit drugs, then murdered" (West, 1984:5). The story received considerable coverage, but no mention was made of the rarity of such crimes, the risk of victimization, or the fact that physical coercion for this type of crime was also very uncommon. Instead, the media focused on stories such as campaigns to clean up Yonge Street and to combat homosexuality.

As Ericson et al. (1991) found in their extensive study on the role of the media in Canada, the media are powerful and persuasive. But the public's fascination with crime often has little to do with the reality of crime. For example, Chermak (1995) suggests that our reading of crime news is a "ritual move exercise" that is not dissimilar to other routines we engage in, such as exercising, having our morning coffee, or late night snacks. Similarly, David Grossman (2002), acknowledged expert on violence, argues that as a society we have become desensitized to violence through what is displayed through the mass media.

From a criminological standpoint, it may be interesting to explore the relationship between the frequency with which people attend to the news media and their perceptions of crime. What kind of impact does TV and/or violent video games have on people's perception of the seriousness of crime?

Several years ago, an Ontario-based study reported that there was a significant relationship "between media use and perceptions of crime seriousness" (Geboyts, Roberts, & DasGupta, 1988:3). The more people watched television news, the higher their ratings of crime seriousness became. The researchers also found that women and those respondents who had not been victimized within the past year expressed greater fear than did males and recent victims. Geboyts et al.'s work reaffirmed the findings of earlier Canadian studies by Akman and Normandeau (1967), Sacco (1982), and, more generally, the views expressed by the Canadian Coalition Against Violent Entertainment and the Coalition for Responsible Television. What was not taken into account were any possible social, economic, and/or demographic variables.

Since the 1970s and the video game Pong, electronic interactive games have become one of the most popular forms of entertainment—particularly among young people. David Walsh of the National Institute on Media and the Family reports that youth between the ages of 7 and 17 play for an average of eight hours per week. And while many games offer practical problem-solving skills, a growing number of games have less social merit but appeal to young minds that are looking for active stimulation (see Anderson & Dill, 2002).

In 1991, Martinez (cited in Barbara, 1995) presented a report to the CRTC in which he provided a detailed analysis involving hundreds of studies that link radio and television violence to individual aggression and violent crime. In particular, the report noted that children are particularly affected by media violence. In a follow-up study done 30 years after the initial study, Leonard Eron found that viewers become less sensitive to the pain and suffering of others, more fearful of the world around them, and likely to behave in aggressive or harmful ways toward others. Anderson and Bashman (2001) came to a similar conclusion. However, their report points out that adults can also be affected by media violence because it tends to erode their ability to socialize and their moral development. Members of the Canadian Coalition Against Violent Entertainment and the Coalition for Responsible Television report that violent content on television increased over 30 percent during the late 1970s and early 1980s.

Statistics Canada data indicate that in 2001 Canadians viewed nearly 23 hours of television per week. Children (2–11 years) viewed nearly 15.5 hours, with 79 percent of youth ages 9–17 watching 1 or more hours per day (Media Awareness Network, 2002). An American study by Burns (1989:35) reports that the average 18-year-old has spent about 12 000 hours in the classroom, approximately 22 000 hours watching television, and 3600 hours in direct contact with parents; in the meantime, he or she has watched close to 100 000 beer commercials. The authors conclude, "it is clear that electronic input into the minds and brains of our young is an overwhelming fact in our society."

Some argue, of course, that viewers dictate programming by making television stations aware of their interests and concerns. The manager of a television station in Ontario has been quoted as saying, "The fastest way I can go bankrupt is to program shows that you will not watch" (Marron, 1983).

Linking Anti-Social Behaviour to Television Viewing

It cannot be denied that many television programs and interactive video games contain violence in one form or another, be it physical, verbal, or (occasionally) symbolic. Moreover, even though there have been "more than 1,000 studies published worldwide on violent entertainment" (Brady, 1992, cited in Murphy, 1995:109), the evidence has not always been conclusive. As early as the late 1950s, researchers began to examine the relationship between television viewing and maladaptive behaviour. Most studies failed, at that time, to find any significant relationship between the viewing of violence on television by children and subsequent maladaptive behaviour. Most other studies since, especially those done by Bandura and his colleagues in the 1960s, have consistently shown an increase in anti-social and aggressive behaviour because of exposure to aggressive models. In addition, as former CRTC chairman Keith Spicer noted, "common sense tells us that this must be true ... why else do advertisers spend millions on television commercials if there is no impact on our behaviour?" (Murphy, 1995:109). An informal survey by an Ottawa newspaper in July 2000 found that two 14-year-old boys were able to rent games intended for persons 17 or older from every video store they visited.

The evidence points to a relationship between the viewing of violence and subsequent maladaptive behaviour. Moreover, while there might not be a direct link, some experts suggest that the cumulative effect of such exposure can be harmful to future behaviour. Television viewing has steadily declined since 1995 (Television viewing, 2001); for example, in 2001, children aged 2–11 averaged 2.2 hours of viewing per day, down from a peak of 3.4 hours in 1987, while youth aged 12–17 averaged 2.6 hours. Interestingly, in 2001, adults averaged almost 3.1 hours per day (Television viewing, 2001). (For more details, see Media Awareness Network's website at **www.media-awareness.ca**).

Understanding how the public forms its opinions and its understanding of criminological issues is important as these opinions can, and have, impacted criminal justice policy and practices. A few years ago, for example, the Calgary Police Association placed an ad in one of the local papers with the caption, "We have just one police officer for every 674 Calgarians." It seems clear the police were using the media venue to gain public support in their fight to have the city allocate more funding for law enforcement. The ad began by citing police ratios of between 439 and 571 to one in most other major Canadian cities. And while it acknowledged the level of satisfaction Calgarians expressed toward the police, it stated that unless things change, "sooner or later, something's got to give." Interestingly, the ad neglected to mention that there is no research supporting the premise that increases in the number of police officers reduce crime, improve response time, or improve overall service. Conversely, the police have also used the media through cooperative initiatives to combat crime, such as Crime Stoppers. However, while most Crime Stoppers programs can point to their success (see Box 2.3), it is not clear to what extent programs such as *America's Most Wanted* and *American Justice* create an unreal perception of crime seriousness, increase public fear levels, and generate the sale of unnecessary security devices. For criminologists, these types of questions have both theoretical and ethical implications and raise further questions as to the role of the media as a social and political instrument in the fight against crime.

Theoretical Explanations

Basing his argument on the principles of the *conflict theory* (see Chapter 7), Richard Quinney (1970) argued that various media are among the vehicles within a capitalistic society that are used to interpret social reality in terms of interpersonal violence and property crimes. He further argued that the media tend to convey an image of rapidly increasing crime rates. These views have been more recently supported by the *left realist* perspective in the writings of Jock Young (1986) and others. It can be said that collectively, the media play a significant role in society "because they have the power to decide what issues are worthy of public consumption and crime is an important topic in society" (Chermak, 1995:167). Is this interpretation of the role of the media "real" or simply the product of *social constructionism*—i.e., if we pay it enough attention, it suddenly becomes a social issue? Lippert (1990), in his study of Satanism in Canada, suggests that the perceived problem of Satanism may be nothing more than a perceptual image fed by the media. However, if the media are so influential, why then do not

CRIME STOPPERS—A COMMUNITY EFFORT

In July 1976, in Albuquerque, New Mexico, a university student was killed during a gas station robbery. After nearly two months of investigation, police were unable to come up with any leads. Then police detective Greg MacAleese obtained permission to re-enact the crime on a local station. A reward was offered to anyone who could provide information leading to an arrest. Within 72 hours of the re-enactment being aired, the police had enough leads to arrest the two men responsible for the killing. This was the beginning of Crime Stoppers.

Today, there are more than 950 Crime Stoppers programs worldwide. Most major cities across Canada have a Crime Stoppers tip line and use television and/or radio to seek public support for difficult-to-solve cases and/or wanted persons. Rewards of up to $2000 are offered to anyone providing information leading to an arrest. All information can remain anonymous if the caller so wishes. Funds for the project are supported by donations of money, goods, or services from the community.

Crime Stoppers International statistics indicate a noticeable growth in the effectiveness of the program:

- 577 688 cases cleared in 1997 vs. 1 128 075 cases cleared by March 2004.
- $40 004 333.00* in 1997 vs. $68 387 636 in 2004 paid out in rewards.
- $1 017 169 438 in 1997 vs. $1 646 079 389 in 2004 in recovered property.
- $3.6 billion in 1997 vs. $4.6 billion in 2004 total money recovered.
- 112 595 in 1997 vs. 528 551 in 2004 total convictions made (CSI Statistics, 1997 and March 2004).

In Canada, provinces such as British Columbia also have successful Crime Stoppers programs. Their very first program started in 1982, and by 2003, there were 42 Crime Stoppers programs throughout the province. The province's tip line has produced the following data:

- 22 551 cases cleared in 2003.
- 16 412 arrests.
- $54 612 062 in property recovered in 1982–2003.
- $35 307 650 seized in illegal drugs in 1982–2003.
- $1 832 210 paid out in 2003 in rewards (BC Crime Stoppers, 2003).

In 1997, the Canadian Supreme Court ruled that police do not have to disclose any information they received through Crime Stopper tips.

---

* All cash amounts in this list are given in Canadian dollars.

even more viewers, both young and old, commit crime? If the media are such powerful communicators, when should censorship be enforced? Should the networks adopt a voluntary rating system as opposed to government interference? Where do we draw the boundaries of freedom of speech and expression? Where does the role of parental responsibility come into play?

One recent example, from the United States, involved a debate over whether executions should be permitted on television. The notion of public executions serving as a deterrent is not new. Executions were carried out during the Roman Empire and again with great regularity during the Inquisition and the French Revolution, and did little to deter people from committing more crimes (Johnson, 1988). Meanwhile, in Canada, there has been controversy about the use of the V-chip in lieu of the media monitoring themselves. Invented by Vancouver engineer Tim Collins, the chip is designed to help parents screen out sex and violence on television. Collins notes that in spite of growing public concern, the public is "not winning the battle in the United States." Former president Bill Clinton signed a law requiring all new television sets to have a V-chip by 1998. The Canadian Radio-television and Telecommunications Commission began to support the use of V-chip technology in 2000; by 2003, more than 200 000 Canadian homes had V-chip–equipped television sets, and broadcasters had begun to encode their programs, enabling the use of V-chip technology.

In summary, while social scientists may not fully understand how media coverage of crime or the availability of interactive videos affect public perceptions of crime or behaviour, we do know that the media provide information, and some more than others. But, in defence of the electronic media, no or few studies have ever proven that reading, viewing, or hearing about violence leads to violent behaviour.

The difficulties in studying the impact of the media include understanding how people respond to different channels of information (radio vs. newsprint vs. television vs. the internet), which ones they prefer to rely on, how their personal experiences preceding participation in the survey have influenced them, and what their state of emotional and physiological arousal is at the time. The problem in discussing the impact of media on crime is analogous to selecting jury members for a case that has received considerable media attention. Almost everyone will have heard something about it, so it is impossible to determine anyone's objectivity.

Official Knowledge and Crime

Within the criminal justice system, there are three primary sources of official knowledge: the police, the judicial system, and the corrections system. As we will see in Chapter 3, these sources are required by law to produce information, primarily in the form of statistics, that are intended to reflect their performance. The collection and dissemination of these data can be viewed as a form of public accountability. Many of the statistics and general information used by the media and criminologists come from these primary sources. For example, the federal justice department regularly provides press releases to the media covering a wide range of issues and information requests. In addition, the Canadian Centre for Justice Statistics annually publishes information service bulletins titled *Juristat*. These publications summarize criminal justice information on a variety of topics, ranging from criminal justice expenditures to violent offences among young offenders to issues related to sentencing and correctional and law enforcement practices.

Unfortunately, these statistical data have inherent limitations, since the information collected is dependent on being reported or processed by the criminal justice system. Let us take a brief look at some of these limitations before offering a rationale for their use.

Limitations of Official Data

In Canada, the system for collecting and disseminating criminological data has evolved with the growing demands for that knowledge, both in the professional and public sectors. It is important to identify common errors that plague those who use criminological data. The use of such data is based on sampling, an important factor for virtually any survey project. Counting anything is always subject to limitations. These limitations affect the **reliability** (i.e., does the instrument measure the event consistently each time?) and **validity** (i.e., does the instrument measure what and only what it is supposed to measure?).

Random error refers to the unintentional mistakes made during the data collection process. For example, all municipalities are required to report counts of the same criminal offences to Statistics Canada. However, due to variances in administrative differences, enforcement practices, or even public attitudes, there may be unknown errors in their counting procedures. One way to minimize the amount of random error is to have a large enough sample.

Systematic error refers to a predictable error during the data collection process. When recording crime data, municipalities need to be sensitive to such details as the difference in the reporting rates between certain property-related offences and most serious violent crimes. For example, it is a well-established fact that property crimes are more likely to go unreported than are most serious violent crimes. Therefore, researchers know that the margin of error for officially recorded property crimes is greater than that for serious violent offences. It is necessary to know the differences regarding the dependent variables (i.e., types of crime) to properly control for systematic error.

Measuring crime data at different stages can lead to potential interpretative errors. For example, consider the history of marijuana legislation. During the 17th and 18th centuries, the French Royal Warehouses promised to buy all the hemp that Canadian farmers could grow. Then in the 1920s, Emily Murphy wrote articles that talked about the evils of smoking narcotics. The articles provided the RCMP and the government with the leverage needed to make hemp illegal, under the name of "marijuana," in the *Opium and Narcotic Drug Act* of 1923. In 1971 and again in 1993, "smoke-ins" were held in Vancouver, which in turn spawned a number of grassroots organizations that demanded the law be changed. In 1996, the Liberals attempted to pass a bill that would make the penalties for marijuana offences, covered by the *Controlled Drugs and Substances Act*, even harsher. Bill C-38, also introduced by the Liberals in 2003, proposed to relax the penalties for minor possession and consider legalizing its use for medical purposes. In fact, in January 2003, an Ontario judge ruled that Canada's law for minor possession (less than 30 grams) was no longer valid (Up in smoke? 2004). On November 1, 2004, the federal Liberal Party reintroduced a bill decriminalizing possession of small amounts of marijuana and hashish, in sharp contrast to harsher US penalties. As this example illustrates, social climate and legislation can change significantly over the years, so it is important to understand the context surrounding the collection of certain information.

Similar examples can be found for prostitution (Lowman, 1995; Sansfacon, 1985), murder (Boyd, 1991), crimes against women in Canada (Boritch, 1997), and, more generally, official crime data. Before 1962, when the Uniform Crime Reporting process was introduced, Canada did not have a standardized crime recording procedure for the provinces. These and other studies illustrate that even if organizations such as the police are not making recording "errors," crime recording variations between and within systems are inevitable.

Interpreting data at different stages of the system represents another potential pitfall when using official data sources. When you examine Canadian crime statistics (or crime data from any other country) that span a significant period of time, you will most likely observe that data are not always reported and recorded in the same manner from year to year (see above). This variation may be the result of administrative changes, changes in the law, or some other intervening variable that is not always readily observable. Overlooking such differences in the data can lead to serious errors in the interpretation.

Another factor that can affect the interpretation of crime data is what is referred to as the **crime funnel**. This concept is based on the knowledge that the numbers of cases at each level get smaller as a result of information processing. For most offenders, the police are the point of contact with the criminal justice system. Whether the police lay a charge or not determines whether the offence proceeds to the next stage of the system. Then, depending on the decision of the courts, the case may or may not proceed beyond the court level.

Similarly, depending on what type of crime data municipalities are collecting, its relevance can be affected by the social, cultural, and/or political climate at the time. Hence, certain assumptions about the reliability of the source may warrant scrutiny.

We can see, then, that these "information contaminants" carry potential risks for interpreting data at different stages of the system. Fortunately, steps can be taken to identify potential pitfalls. Researchers need to be familiar with the characteristics of their crime statistics in order to be able to draw valid conclusions. Understanding the various types of systematic and/or random errors can enable researchers to make sound comparisons and analysis. It is important to be aware, however, that no matter how diligently data are collected, or at what level they are accessed, all crime statistics are, at best, only suggestive in what they reveal about the true nature of crime.

Why Use Official Data?

Criminologists have long debated the merits and the intent behind official data sources. Those with a more *critical*, or *radical theoretical*, orientation suggest that official sources are controlled by the ruling classes. To them, information reflects the interests of the state in such a way that it allows it to continue to exert control or engage in **net widening** activities. For example, are there more laws today than there were 50 years ago? Are there more police officers per capita than there were 50 to 100 years ago? Who is primarily responsible for legislating new criminal laws? Why are there so few statistics on white-collar crime, political crime, and environmental crime? Some of these issues will be explored in subsequent chapters. At this point, however, it can be noted that official data, according to the conflict perspective, serve only the interests and needs of those recording it. They are simply doing what they need to do in order to meet their own goals and objectives.

The *consensus model*, or the *moderate/conservative view*, offers a different picture. Synnott (1996:11) suggests that "indeed the 'small c' conservative perspective paradigm is the dominant paradigm in Canada." This view asserts that official sources provide the information that the public appears to want. As Émile Durkheim, the prime consensus theorist, once noted, all events serve a purpose. The media are simply part of a unity of interdependent institutions that serve to maintain the social structure. So are we more interested in general information than in understanding the causes of the acts? Again, there is no clear answer to such a question. Rather, it depends on one's frame of reference and knowledge base.

Theoretical Knowledge and Crime

While theoretical concepts are supposedly based on scientifically verifiable and reliable observations, the **operationalization** of variables is often subject to criticism. The criticism is premised on concerns about how a construct is defined in terms of specific operations, measurement instruments, or procedures. An operational definition is sometimes referred to as the indicator or measure of a construct. For example, are official crime data reliable indicators of youth crime? Numerous self-report studies have shown official data to be limited for most property-related offences. Theoretical knowledge, on the other hand, often has a direct impact on public opinion and social policy (DeKeseredy & Schwartz, 1996). By way of example, beginning in 1965, a growing volume of literature in the area of developmental psychology provided some of the critical information for the eventual replacement of the 1908 *Juvenile Delinquency Act* with the 1984 *Young Offenders Act* and later the 2003 *Youth Criminal Justice Act* (Fetherston, 2004). Similarly, after Robert Martinson published his controversial, yet widely read, work on how "nothing works" in 1974, there was a dramatic shift away from the rehabilitative models to a more conservative approach to justice administration. The growth of rehabilitation programs had corresponded to the emergence of positivism and psychology in the 1960s and early 1970s (Williams & McShane, 2002).

Theoretical perspectives in other areas of inquiry, besides those specifically applicable to the study of crime and criminality, also have much to contribute to criminology. Theories of knowledge are one example. In order to understand crime and criminality, it is important to realize that how we form our sense of reality is fundamental to how we think about problem solving. In recognizing the complexity of human behaviour, criminological knowledge needs to be interdisciplinary in nature and embrace theories that bridge the social and physical sciences. Without this integration of theory, criminology's ability to move forward as a science will be greatly hampered.

The Ethical Dilemmas in Conducting Criminological Research

This chapter has addressed different aspects of how we come to form perceptions of reality and acquire knowledge. By now, you have probably deduced that the understanding of how we acquire knowledge, what it means, and what it represents is filled with controversy. Yet, notwithstanding some of the issues discussed, it can be noted that whether knowledge comes through personal experience, via the media, through official accounts, or based on theoretical knowledge, it should pass the same "test of meaningfulness, verifiability, and reasonableness before it can be accepted" (Wolff, 1971:257). This is especially pertinent when one recognizes criminology's potential political and social implications. The lives of numerous people can be directly or indirectly influenced by criminological findings.

Since knowledge can be said to be *relative* and *evolutive*, how then do the media and/or criminologists rationalize the disclosure of what they believe to be meaningful, verifiable, and reasonable? For example, public opinion surveys show that most Canadians are in favour of:

- Reinstating capital punishment.
- Increasing penalties for young offenders.
- Lowering the age of responsibility.
- Using fixed sentences for serious crimes.

Although criminologists strive to remain objective in their research, funding for research endeavours has increasingly come from various government sources and the private sector (see Murphy & Stenning, 1999). This has not only influenced the direction of criminological inquiry but also dictated what can be studied—for example, crime in the aftermath of the 2001 terrorist attacks, the human sex trade, or computer crime (Clairmont, 1999). Criminologists who study these and other controversial topics have found themselves divided on even the most basic criminological issues, such as:

- What should criminologists study?
- What is crime?

- Is criminal behaviour predetermined?
- Should we have gun control?
- Is punishment good crime control?
- Are prisons a good idea?

It is important to recognize the power of an applied discipline. As we have seen, crime affects us all, either directly or indirectly. Therefore, criminologists must not only be aware of the ethics of their profession, but they must also be prepared to defend their work in the light of public scrutiny. They also need to feel self-conscious about what they say, how they gather data, how they disseminate the findings, and what the short- and long-term implications might be. Scientists have a moral, ethical, and social responsibility to examine their goals and the implications of their findings.

Finally, perhaps all researchers could adopt the oath traditionally sworn by physicians, "Above all do no harm."

Summary

- While the public's knowledge of crime is often naive and limited, public perceptions of crime can have a direct influence on criminal justice policy.
- The general public gains its knowledge of crime from four primary sources: personal experience, mass media, official crime data, and theoretical evidence. Each of these has both strengths and weaknesses.
- Concepts of crime have historically been subject to paradigm shifts, which shows that crime is a *relative* and *evolutive* construct.
- While the mass media undoubtedly affect our knowledge of crime, conventional perspectives of crime and criminality (such as sociology and psychology) have never adequately explained how media influence behaviour. The need for researchers to adopt an interdisciplinary approach is paramount to address these and other issues in order to formulate policies that will balance individual freedoms with the protection of society.
- Ethical dilemmas surrounding when and how information about crime should be shared and used represent a growing area of concern and interest among criminologists, which has resulted in the establishment of ethics review committees in every major educational institution. In order to mitigate the often subjective nature of ethical issues, formal laws have been used in an attempt to ensure a sense of continuity and fairness in our interpretation and handling of crime.

Discussion Questions

1. Where does your knowledge of crime come from, and how accurate do you feel this knowledge is? Does your fear of crime (or lack thereof) relate to this knowledge, and how does it relate to your perceptions of crime?

2. What kinds of challenges do public perceptions of crime pose for criminologists and policy-makers, and how could these challenges be rectified?

3. Which of the four basic kinds of data do you consider superior? Why?

4. Do you have a Crime Stoppers program in your area? If you had information that could assist the police, would you come forward? How would your answer be affected by the reward offered? Do you agree with the concept of Crime Stoppers? Why or why not?

5. How can the public and the media benefit from an integrated approach in criminology?

Key Concepts

crime funnel	empiricist	Juristat
moral panic	net widening	operationalization
paradigm shift	random error	rationalism
reliability	systematic error	validity

Weblinks

www.onlinenewspapers.com This site offers links to a wide range of Canadian newspapers.

www.ipsos.ca Ipsos Canada conducts surveys on a wide range of social, economic, and political issues.

Endnotes

1. Normandeau and Leighton (1990) offer a comprehensive review on the future of policing in Canada. A number of Ontario-based colleges offer police foundation programs designed to assist students in preparing for becoming police officers in Ontario. Similar programs are emerging elsewhere in Canada as well.

2. The GDP calculation varies depending on the method used to perform it.

CHAPTER 3

Gathering and Interpreting Crime Data

"It ain't so much the things we don't know that get us in trouble. It's the things we know that ain't so."

Artemus Ward, cited in Huff, 1954

Learning Outcomes

After you have completed this chapter, you should be able to:

*   Understand the aims of research.

*   Understand and appreciate the purposes of crime data.

*   Identify the main methods of counting crime.

*   Recognize and have knowledge of the official and unofficial crime collection methods and their limitations.

*   Realize the importance of an interdisciplinary, multi-method approach when collecting crime and criminal justice information.

Crime... "It Is Everywhere"

In Chapter 2, it was observed that the public tends to believe that crime is everywhere. As early as 1975, Daniel Koenig, from the University of Victoria, reported that crime was seen to represent a serious concern among Canadians (Linden, 2004). In 1991, a poll conducted by *Maclean's* magazine found that 62 percent of respondents said they are taking more precautions to ensure their personal safety than they used to (Underwood, 1991). The poll also "revealed signs of an increasing interest in handgun ownership" (1991:30). Much of their social reality of crime, however, is based on statistics that, when

reported by the media, are distorted, biased, and otherwise incomplete, or include exaggerated information about ordinary events. Furthermore, if the growth of Canadian criminology programs since the mid-1970s is any kind of indicator, then academics also seem to think that crime and criminality deserve closer attention. A review of international news indicates that crime appears to be omnipresent (see Brady, 1996; also, see the publication titled *Crime and Justice International*).

An additional indicator that might be used as a benchmark of the crime picture is the increase in financial expenditures to support the various elements within the criminal justice system. Griffiths and Verdun-Jones (1989:34) note that "during the twenty-year period 1961–1980, expenditures for criminal justice services in Canada rose dramatically. Total federal spending on police, courts, and corrections in 1961 was $4.38 per Canadian; in 1980, it was $16.85 per Canadian (adjusted to Implicit Price Index)." In 1980, annual expenditures were nearly $4 billion; in 1989–90, expenditures had risen to $7.7 billion (Griffiths & Verdun-Jones, 1994) and by 2001–2002, the budget totalled more than $11 billion or $362 per Canadian (CCJS, 2002, 22(11)).

BY THE NUMBERS BOX 3.1

WHERE DOES THE MONEY GO?
JUSTICE SPENDING IN CANADA, 2000–2001

Area	Percentage of Total Criminal Justice Budget
Policing	61
Adult corrections	22
Courts	9
Legal aid	5
Prosecution	3

Source: CCJS, 2002, 22(11):1.

While Chapter 2 focused on the *qualitative*, *subjective*, and *ideological* reconstruction of criminological phenomena, this chapter will focus more on the *quantitative*, *objective*, and *empirical* statistical reconstruction of crime.[1] We will first discuss the purpose of studying criminological relations and gathering crime data. The main methods of obtaining crime data will then be examined in terms of their strengths and weaknesses. We will conclude with a discussion on research methods and the importance of a multi-method approach to crime data.

Before we proceed, it should be pointed out that this chapter focuses only on the primary sources of collecting crime data. Depending on the issue being studied, other valuable sources range from data from hospitals, insurance companies, banks, and high school and university surveys to archival data and academic literature. Most criminology programs offer qualitative and quantitative research methods courses in which students learn to use a variety of information sources to answer criminological issues from a rich interdisciplinary perspective.

The Purpose of Studying Criminological Relations

Correlation and Crime

One of the oldest formal techniques for trying to understand crime is to examine those factors that are associated with the phenomenon being studied. Nothing happens in a vacuum. For a ball to move, there has to be some type of energy directed at the ball. For a crime to occur, there has to be a target, and the offender must be motivated and must have the skills to commit the crime.

Hartnagel (1995:95) notes that discovering correlates or relationships is "an important first step for any scientific discipline such as criminology." While correlations do not imply *cause*, they are often seen as somehow being related to each other in contributing to a crime. They prompt researchers to examine why and how two (or more) variables correlate. A **correlation** thus refers to an association between two or more phenomena that, based on specified criteria, are related or vary together—as one changes, so does the other. For example, some criminologists have claimed that crime is related to phases of the moon, to economic conditions in society, to the amount of violence on television, and even to different body types. Once correlates have been established, criminologists attempt to discern whether the association somehow contributes or causes a change to the phenomenon in question.

Cause vs. Probability

Cause implies that the occurrence of one event is directly affected by the presence of one or more variables or factors. For example, most people believe that human responses have certain reliable causes. If you stab someone, he or she will probably bleed. If you tell a good joke, people are likely to laugh. However, if you are a trained yogi or Sufi master, you might not bleed if stabbed. In the second example, people might not understand your joke. So believing in a cause does not necessarily imply that an event is must take place. Nothing is ever perfectly predictable. As the social anarchist Paul Feyerabend (1986:55) writes, "no theory ever agrees with all the *facts* in its domain, yet it is not always the theory that is to blame." Many researchers, therefore, prefer to use the term *probability* to express the likelihood that two or more events are related. The process of measuring the probability that certain effects will occur when certain causes are present involves the use of statistical techniques (e.g., chi-square, t-test, analysis of variance, regression, etc.).

The stronger the degree of association between the variables measured, the greater the likelihood that it will be accepted as being true or valid. When researchers test the likelihood of two or more variables, they formulate a *hypothesis* that is usually a declarative statement about the relationship. For example, if you had been abused as a young person (cause), then your chances of becoming an abuser yourself are greater (effect) than if you had not been abused. Theory contains the constructs that are of theoretical interest and that attempt to explicate, or account for, a set of propositions or statements.

The General Aims of Research

As we already discussed, criminologists attempt to follow the scientific method when doing research and interpreting their findings. But, beyond specific aims of a given study, what are the general aims of research? No matter which data-gathering and analytical techniques they use, researchers strive to accomplish any of these four basic aims:

1. *Discovery*: Research can never prove a hypothesis; it can only provide supporting evidence. To the uninitiated, research findings sometimes seem to state the obvious. One of the first observations of this kind I remember reading as a criminology student was the conclusion that if you associated with a "negative element," it would increase your chances of becoming delinquent. I thought, how original, go figure! However, in addition to verifying the "obvious," researchers often also attempt to understand or clarify occurrences that are less straightforward. For example, why doesn't everyone who associates with a "negative element" turn to crime? Similarly, while the practice of punishment and corporal punishment has been around since the dawn of time, it was not until the 1990s that a growing volume of literature suggesting a proactive and restorative stance toward justice started gaining momentum. By examining data through different lenses, researchers are discovering alternatives to punishment. Discovery is thus one of the main aims of criminological research.

2. *Demonstration*: It has often been said that there are very few original ideas, only variations on a few themes. One way to illuminate such assertions is to put an idea or observation to the test—to prove a point, so to speak. This process can offer insight into the relationship between crime and a given idea, such as whether the restorative justice concept works as well in small communities as in major urban settings.

    Not all variations are better than the original version. For example, are new drugs better than the herbs used thousands of years ago by our "primitive" ancestors? Until recently, the Amazon was thought to be little more than a wild jungle where primitive people dwelled. Then the rainforest began to be appreciated for its essential contribution to the world's ecosystem and for its medicinal plants. One such plant that caught North American attention only in the 1990s is gurana. Its natural properties help sustain energy and combat a variety of ailments (see Straten, 1994). Only after scientists have been able to document (i.e., empirically demonstrate) the evidence of the benefits of numerous primitive cures has there been a renewed interest in these old remedies. Closer to home, social control agents have tried to use (demonstrate) punishment as a deterrent. In spite of evidence to the contrary, they have tried to improve (a variation in the demonstration) on their methods of punishment. Yet the results are still the same. Most criminals are seldom deterred by the threat or nature of the punishment.

It is important to realize that research can only be consistent with or demonstrate a hypothesis. No demonstration can ever prove the hypothesis. Just because we might be able to demonstrate that fear of crime is related to safety precautions a person takes does not mean that there are not alternative explanations that are equally consistent with the research results.

3. *Refutation*: Pioneering research by Fattah and others suggested that capital punishment was not an effective deterrent. These studies challenged a long-standing belief and practice and were instrumental in abolishing capital punishment in Canada in the late 1970s. Similarly, in the 1990s, studies on boot camps refuted the notion that hard work, harsh discipline, and a regimented lifestyle deter young offenders from reoffending (Cowles & Castellano, 1995). The highly publicized "Scared Straight" program from the 1970s was also refuted (Lundman, 2001). Yet shortly after its introduction, some Canadians who had only a limited amount of information on which to base their observations noted, "shock treatment, if run properly could be most effective as is proven by ... 'Scared Straight'" (Leard, 1980).

Science provides an opportunity for "checks and balances" of all ideas. Sometimes notions construed with the best of intentions are later refuted as not being sound. After all, we once believed that the world was flat, just as we once believed that the sun circled the earth. While the power of science can provide the objective tools to test (i.e., discover) ideas and gradually move closer to the truth, it can also be used to refute existing beliefs. Canadian criminology pioneers and scholars Ezzat Fattah and Tadeusz Grygier have been strong crusaders against the use of punishment as a means of social control. For example, Fattah (1995) lists nine reasons why punishment does not have justifiable merit as a means of social control (see Box 3.2). Unfortunately, while they have lauded criminologists for their research, Canadian criminal justice policy-makers have done little to embrace their ideas.

4. *Replication*: The more times you can confirm an observation, the greater its predictability and consistency. Academic journals are full of studies that replicate previous studies but using different participants, different settings, and/or additional measures. For example, Sutherland's differential association theory (see Chapter 7) has been the subject of hundreds of articles and earned the respect of most critics (see, generally, Williams & McShane, 1999).

Because social scientists are trained to be inquisitive, critical thinkers and because nothing is absolute, they strive to contribute to the existing state of knowledge. Therefore, theories are constantly evolving and changing. Ecological theories received widespread support between the beginning of the

REFUTING THE "MERITS" OF PUNISHMENT

Consider the following points:

1. Punishment is ineffective: The United States and China, with their high incarceration and execution rates, are prime examples.
2. Punishment achieves nothing: Punishment does little more than breed anger, hostility, resentment, and antagonism; violence breeds violence.
3. Punishment is costly: The financial costs have been escalating year after year (see Crime and punishment ..., 1996).
4. Punishment is degrading, humiliating, and stigmatizing: Any form of deprivation of liberty is degrading and humiliating.
5. Punishment is never personal or individual: Although we might be imprisoning the offender, we are also having an impact on his or her family, friends, and social network. Punishment extends beyond one's immediate circle.
6. Punishment treats human beings as a means to an end: While punishment may have some cathartic effects on the public, it does little for the person being punished. The person is sacrificed to achieve some other goal.
7. Punishment looks at the past: Punishment is retributive in nature. It is retrograde in its approach and does little for the offender's future well-being.
8. Punishment perpetuates rather than settles conflicts: Punishment serves to generate further animosity and antagonism among the parties involved instead of settling conflicts.
9. Punitive penal sanctions amount to punishment of the victim: By its very practice, punishment serves to victimize the victim further. Society also loses, since it refuses to accept failure.

Fattah uses these points to argue in favour of a restorative model of justice, a model that started to receive considerable interest from government and non-government agencies concerned with the growing problems of our current criminal justice system in the mid-1990s. Do these arguments make sense? Do you think the abolition of punishment, or retributive justice in general, could work in our society? What roadblocks might exist?

20th century and the 1940s, when a variety of sociological perspectives gained prominence. Starting in the 1970s, with growing social and political unrest, more conservative interpretations of crime became popular, and conservative strategies to control crime (such as incarceration) were used. When crime increased dramatically and steps had to be taken to understand it, a shift took place from theoretical issues to practical concerns, and a new discipline—criminal justice—emerged (Williams & McShane, 1999). Therefore, while replication can serve a vital function against overgeneralization, researchers need to find a balance so as not to hamper the development of new theories, new approaches, and new (social) policies.

The Purpose of Crime Data

An important sub-area of the criminological enterprise is crime statistics. Criminologists who use **crime data** try to generate *reliable* (i.e., consistent) and *valid* (i.e., accurate) measures of criminal behaviour and criminal trends and patterns. Crime data can also be used to conduct research on crime. Without such data, it would be difficult to construct criminological theories and answer such pressing questions as, "Do the expenditures necessarily reflect an increase in crime?" and "What is the social and financial impact of crime on society and its citizens?"

Since criminologists are interested in crime control, it is important that the measurement strategies used to gather crime data be accurate reflections of what is happening in society. In fact, British criminologist Jason Ditton (1979) suggests that the term "criminology" should be replaced with "controlology" to more accurately reflect what criminologists are concerned with. As Nettler (1987:36) notes, criminological data serve five key purposes:

1. *Description*: Being able to describe the nature and extent of crime is necessary if good crime control policies are to be formed. A description of crime also serves as a barometer of community well-being. As discussed in Chapter 2, the public plays a major role in reporting crime incidents to the authorities. What people choose to report provides a descriptive profile of what they consider worthy of attention. The first step toward being able to understand, explain, and ultimately predict and control crime and criminality is the ability to accurately provide descriptive information about criminal phenomena.

2. *Explanation*: Most criminologists rely on criminological theories to explain crime patterns and trends. Theories enable researchers to extract testable hypotheses that have empirical references. Most research observations rely on quantifiable (measurable) data in order to verify their theoretical statements. Then, based on the empirical findings, researchers are able to either support, or not support, the theoretical assertions tested.

3. *Program evaluation*: As noted above, it is expensive to operate the criminal justice system. Accountability has become a major issue among policy-makers and their constituents. What are we getting for our money?

   An effort to control and/or prevent crime, as well as to determine which control strategy should be used requires the ability to enumerate criminal incidents. In the late 1970s, a pilot program for serious young offenders was established in Ontario. Based on the therapeutic wilderness models popularized by the Outward Bound movement and introduced to North America in the 1960s, the program was carefully monitored financially, and its success was measured against the cost of running the more traditional programs such as probation and community service. After two years, the wilderness program was found to be more expensive to operate than its conventional counterparts. As a result, the project was shut down. What the politicians choose to overlook, however, was the cost-benefit of the program. With a less than 20 percent recidivism rate, the program was considerably more effective than the programs against which it was compared (Winterdyk & Roesch, 1982). However, even data obtained objectively can be subject to different interpretations, depending on whom, and for what, the information is being used.

Program evaluation is easy to conduct, but designing an evaluation and interpreting the data obtained is often challenging. This is one reason why many criminologists suggest that research should be grounded in scientific rigour.

4. *Risk assessment*: While crime may appear to be everywhere, on closer reflection we know that this is not true. By measuring criminal activity in accordance with time, setting, location, and other social and environmental characteristics, criminologists are able to calculate the *relative risk* of being victimized or of becoming an offender (see Box 3.3). In Canada, if you are male, you are more likely to be the victim of homicide, serious assault, and robbery; if you are female, you are more likely to be the victim of sexual assault (Sacco & Kennedy, 1998). Risk assessment for the elderly has become an important area of study in recent years as their numbers continue to increase.

WHAT DO YOU THINK? BOX 3.3

DOES LOCKING UP OFFENDERS HELP?

Based on a survey of 37 000 provincial inmates across seven provinces in the late 1990s, a federal study revealed that about 49 percent of prisoners would likely reoffend. The conclusion was based on a history of prior convictions, behaviour while on supervision, employment history, and substance abuse (Reoffence risk high..., 1998).

5. *Prediction*: From a humanitarian and utilitarian perspective, it would be better to prevent crimes than to react too strongly and punish individuals for their transgressions. Historically, social scientists have been intrigued with the possibility of predicting human behaviour. Many criminologists specialize

in trying to predict who is likely to commit particular types of crimes. Others are interested in trying to articulate what the criminal justice system will be like in the coming decades. For example, what will the law of the future look like? Will we move toward community policing? What will be the impact of future technological developments on the use of DNA? What theories will dominate?

To be prediction-oriented is to be future-oriented, *proactive*, and prevention-oriented. In contract, the punishment model and crime control model are past-oriented and *reactive* to crime. Most of the research conducted by environmental criminologists is prevention-oriented. Various researchers have found, for example, that altering certain environmental factors (street lighting, storefront visibility, street location of businesses, etc.) has a direct impact on crime. Criminals are not interested in being seen, since it increases their risk of being caught. Just as medical and alternative practitioners use the tools of their trade to diagnose potential future risk of heart disease, tooth decay, premature bone deterioration, or aging, criminologists can apply an interdisciplinary approach to predicting who has the potential to become a dangerous offender. Kim Rossmo, a former graduate student at Simon Fraser University, developed a computer-mapping technique referred to as geographic profiling, which can be used to predict where various types of offenders live or work, based on crime site information. This technique relies on innovative research on the spatial behaviour of criminals (see Grescoe, 1996). Unlike the more conventional approaches to studying the "why" of crime, it focuses on the "where" (see Box 3.4).

FYI BOX 3.4

GEOGRAPHIC PROFILING: PINPOINTING CRIME

In a relatively short period of time, geographic profiling has become a new tool in the fight against crime. A growing number of major police forces across Canada—such as the RCMP, the Vancouver City Police, and the Ontario Provincial Police (OPP)—use this computer-based technique to effectively target criminals who commit a series of crimes.

In early 1998, the OPP announced that it would be using Rigel, a computer program developed by Kim Rossomo that can help track down serial killers, repeat rapists, bombers, bank robbers, and arsonists, among other repeat offenders. The Rigel system was able to locate the four-block area where serial killer Clifford Olson had lived. It was also able to identify the St. Catharines area where Paul Bernardo and his wife Karla Homolka lived when they killed two teens in the 1990s. As well, it worked in the case of the Abbotsford killer in the mid-1990s. For addition information of geographic profiling, see **www.comnet.ca/~fbamackay/geo.htm**.

Geographic profiling is based on the premise that we are creatures of habit. It involves collecting as much data as possible about the crime and comparing it to behaviour patterns of persons caught committing such criminal acts. The more data available on a particular type of crime, the greater the likelihood of being able to predict the type of person who commits the crime and their place of residence. For example, do you usually take the same route to and from school every day? Do you usually shop at the same store for your groceries? If you have not already noticed, watch how your fellow classmates come to and leave class. Also note their mannerisms. See if you can differentiate your classmates' movements based on specific characteristics.

Criminology is still a young discipline that is, in many cases, limited in its approach. Developing reliable and valid prediction models is as much an art as a science. Monahan (1981) was among the first to point out the risks in making predictions, especially in the social sciences. One of the most serious risks in trying to predict human behaviour is the high proportion of **false positives**—that is, "misses" or inaccurate predictions. Based on his review of psychiatric predictions of dangerous behaviour, Monahan concluded they were wrong two out of three times. Often, prediction appears to be little more than chance; as Ennis and Litwick (1974) wrote, prediction in the criminal justice system is about as accurate as flipping a coin.

In this section, we have seen that although the purposes of gathering crime data are diverse, such data are essential to the reliability and validity of the study of criminal phenomena. However, in Chapter 2 we learned that some of the purposes have their ethical, practical, and theoretical limitations, so that any crime data—and conclusions drawn from such data—should be viewed with caution, as there will always be some unpredictable influences that may have unwarranted practical consequences.

In the next sections, we will look at the sources of crime data. Before we begin, however, it might be helpful to identify three important terms of reference when talking about crime data. *Actual crime* refers to all crimes that occur but are not necessarily detected, reported, or processed by official criminal justice agencies. *Official crime* refers to those criminal events that have been detected, reported, and recorded in some official fashion (e.g., police data and self-report data). Finally, the *dark figure* of crime refers to those criminal events that go undetected and/or unreported by official criminal justice agencies.

Official Sources of Crime Data

"There are three kinds of lies: lies, damned lies, and statistics." Benjamin Disraeli (1804–1881)

The above quotation reflects the attitude many people have about official crime statistics. As Darrell Huff (1954:8) cautions, "the secret language of statistics, so appealing in a fact-minded culture, is employed to sensationalize, inflate, confuse, and oversimplify." The fact is, however, that statistics are an essential source of information for social scientists and policy-makers.

Section I: Foundations of Criminology

By far the most common measures of crime are official statistics. These types of data are primarily collected by the various elements of the criminal justice system—the police, courts, and corrections. Other public control agencies, such as mental health and social service agencies that deal with alcohol and drug abuse, as well as academics, have come to rely on official data to conduct research and make informed policy decisions.

Police Data

> "The government are very keen on amassing statistics. They collect them, raise them to the nth power, take the cube root and prepare wonderful diagrams. But you must never forget that every one of these figures comes in the first instance from the village watchman, who just puts down what he damn pleases." Sir Josiah Stamp (1880–1941), cited in Nettler, 1987:39.

Historically, the first type of official data to be collected was corrections-based data. Today, however, police reports are the most frequently used form of official crime data (see Box 3.5). This makes sense if we realize that the police are usually the first point of official contact for reported and detected crime.[2]

BY THE NUMBERS BOX 3.5

CRIME RATE DROPS—WE'RE JUST TOO OLD!

Looking through crime data to filter demonstrable, plausible, and irrefutable facts requires some creativity. And sometimes the line between coincidence and fact is little more than a difference in opinion. While some experts were scratching their heads over a decrease in official crime rates between 1991 and 1994, sociologist Rick Linden, from the University of Manitoba, suggested that "we're getting too old to be criminals." Drawing on official crime data as well as demographic data, he noted that most crimes are committed by people between the ages of 15 and 29. The baby boomers were now between the ages of 30 and 50. Linden further observed that similar trends have been observed in many American cities (Crime rate…, 1995).

In Canada, *police data* are based on criminal events that are known to the police. Therefore, unless a crime is reported or detected, it will go unreported, or in some cases unrecorded even if reported. For criminologists, this unknown but assumed quantity of criminal activity is called the **dark figure of crime**. The term was first coined by the British criminologists Richard Hood and Richard Sparks in 1970. The concept of a dark figure of crime has, for some criminologists, become a major area of study in itself. Why do crimes go undetected and unreported? What can be done to improve the detection and reporting of crime? In 1978, University of Ottawa criminologists Waller and Okitiro reported that the dark figure of crime in Canada might have been much greater than was believed. Since then, through public education, changes in demographic characteristics, and increased media attention, reporting rates have gone up.

The collection of police data began in 1920, when the Dominion Bureau of Statistics voluntarily tabulated the crimes known to police forces servicing communities with populations of 4000 or more. As **crime rates** increased, there was a desire to standardize police data and include more detailed information. In 1962, the **Uniform Crime Reporting (UCR)** system was introduced (see Box 3.6). The collection model was borrowed from one already being used in the United States. The results were collated and published by Statistics Canada in the annual Crime and Traffic Enforcement Statistics and can be found today in Statistics Canada *Juristat* publications. Today, police-reported crime statistics are published in a variety of issues under catalogue number 85-002.

The UCR is a standardized survey used by all police departments across the country that collects and collates crime data and makes them available to interested users, government departments, scholars, media sources, special interest groups, and students.

BY THE NUMBERS BOX 3.6

UNIFORM CRIME REPORTS (UCR)

The original UCR survey included the "aggregate" (i.e., total) counts of crime provided by police departments on a monthly basis. These counts, however, were prone to various interpretative problems. For example, aggregate counts did not distinguish between crimes completed versus crimes attempted. In addition, the survey required that only the most serious act be counted if a crime included several offences. This process resulted in a natural attrition of actual offences known to the police.

To correct many of the data deficiencies in the original survey, a revised UCR survey was introduced in 1988. The new UCR shifted from relying on aggregate counts to an incident-based reporting system. Now, rather than providing summaries of criminal events, data are collected on the criminal event, the offender, and the victim on an incident-by-incident basis. Consequently, the UCR data contain more and richer information than in the past. To gain more insight into this issue, look up some crime statistics from the 1960s and/or 1970s. Select a crime, such as homicide, robbery, or motor-vehicle theft. Compare the nature of the statistics with the nature of a current *Juristat* report on the same crime.

The UCR data has generally served to satisfy people's fascination with the question of who was committing crimes, what was happening to offenders, and just how much crime there was. Scholars, criminology students, politicians, government departments, the media, and even the curious public rely on this source when examining the efficiency, effectiveness, and enumeration of criminal justice and crime-related matters.

Since 1981, the **Canadian Centre for Justice Statistics (CCJS)** (see page 72), a division of Statistics Canada, has been responsible for gathering information from 140 police agencies in six provinces, as well as data from the courts and legal aid, corrections, and youth justice agencies. The collective police data account for approximately 46 percent of the national volume of *Criminal Code* violations and make up the data for the Uniform Crime Reports (Hendrick, 1996).

Police crime statistics are divided into two categories, based on the classification of crimes in the *Criminal Code*: summary offences that involve a maximum penalty of six months in jail and/or a fine not exceeding $2000 (unless a different penalty is specified) and indictable offences that involve a maximum penalty of life imprisonment but no maximum fine.[3]

Judicial Statistics

Historically, court records were the first type of official crime statistics to be collected. The French courts began collecting such data in 1825 and published them in *Compte Generale*. Information was gathered on the number of charges and convictions that appeared before the courts (Brantingham, Mu, & Verma, 1995). In addition, information about the offender's gender, income, education, and occupation was collected. The English started collecting court information around 1805, but it wasn't until 1857 that they developed the system in use today.

Not long after the introduction of *judicial statistics*, researchers began to use the data to describe crime trends and patterns. Brantingham and Brantingham (1984) note that André-Michel Guerry and Adolphe Quetelet, from Belgium and France respectively, were among the first to use such data to examine the spatial and temporal distribution of crime, i.e., where and when crime happens. Having information available on age, education, gender, income, and occupation enabled them to conduct studies on suicides (see Durkheim, 1951) and to determine the distribution of the 17 most common crimes by age and gender, as well as in terms of geography (see Elmer, 1982).

Canada started to collect judicial statistics in 1876. Until the late 1960s, judicial statistics were the primary source of national crime statistics. In 1973, due to federal and provincial disputes over jurisdiction and cost, the collection was stopped. National judicial data were not collected again until the CCJS attempted to resurrect the process. In 1991, two publications, with limited data, were published. By 1997, there were approximately a dozen publications. The CCJS also regularly publishes data on youth court statistics through the *Juristat*.

Statistics Canada generally cautions against comparing the cost of court services (see Locke, 1993). This caution aside, it is worth noting that court costs increased from $0.6 billion in 1988–1989 to $1.0 billion in 2000–2001. Expenditures on policing were the fastest-growing component of the justice system. In 2000–2001, policing expenditures were $6.8 billion—up 4 percent from 1999–2000 (CCJS, 2002, 22(11)). Even if the numbers are somewhat suspect, the trend does not bode well for criminal justice administrators, since the increase in expenditures has had no appreciable impact on the crime rate.

To get a more accurate picture of court costs, it would be helpful to know to what extent any variations in the data can be explained by other factors—political (e.g., who is in power), racial/class-based (e.g., what is the proportion of Native and/or marginal groups), or demographic (e.g., what is the proportion of youth). For example, Hackler (1994) offers a comparable argument using the number of Native peoples as a possible means of explaining the higher court costs in the Western provinces.

One way to utilize judicial data is to look at sentencing patterns. These patterns reflect the prevailing judicial practices and trends. For example, Table 3–1 shows that in 2000–2001, the majority of all adult provincial offenders received prison sentences of less than one month. (Though it is worth noting that the data represent only about 30 percent of nationwide coverage). Based on this snapshot of sentencing dispositions, one might want to ask whether we are too "soft" on adult offenders. Or does this sentencing pattern reflect the fact that, contrary to public opinion, most of the crimes committed by offenders are minor in nature?

TABLE 3–1

LENGTH OF PRISON SENTENCES FOR ADULT OFFENDERS, 2001–2002

SENTENCE LENGTH	PERCENTAGE OF ADULTS SENTENCED
1 month or less	54
1–3 months	23
3–6 months	11
6 months–1 year	6
1–2 years	3
2+ years	4

Source: CCJS, 2003, 23(2).

Correctional Statistics

Although English prison statistics date back to 1836, the data appeared only in appendices to special reports. It was not until 1856 that **correctional statistics** became part of a regular composite of criminal statistics. The types of information included in these records included age, gender, education, number of prior convictions, occupation, and birthplace. These procedures remained in place until 1963, when the data were published separately as *Prison Statistics* (Brantingham & Brantingham 1984). With the establishment of the CCJS, statistics on adult correction services have been published annually in the *Juristat* bulletins. The bulletins provide information on the number of persons being held in federal and provincial custody facilities, as well as data on the number of those charged awaiting trial and the number placed under supervision. Limited data are provided on demographic information of offenders (e.g., age, gender, and ethnic background). Data on federal and provincial expenditures are also published.

In 1993–1994, adult corrections cost each Canadian $65 per year, while provincial per capita costs were slightly higher than those for federal institutions ($34 vs. $31 per capita per year) (Trends ..., 1994). Total federal expenditures in 2000–2001 reached $2.6 billion, as compared to $2.2 billions in 1992–1993 (based on constant dollar value) (CCJS, 2003, 23(11)).

For 2001–2002, the Canadian incarceration rate was 133 per 100 000 (down from 155 in 1995–1996), which is significantly lower than in the United States (619) and Russia (694) but significantly higher than in most European countries (CCJS, 2003, 23(11)). On any given day in 2001–2002, there were 155 000 adults in Canadian prisons. The cost of incarcerating offenders is not low. In 2001–2002, it cost an average of $199.57 per day to incarcerate an offender in a federal institution, as compared to $113.14 to supervise an inmate on parole (ibid.). Even so, we continue to rely heavily on incarceration as a means of protecting society. While public protection is the most important part of the mandate of the correctional system, "building more prison cells to lock up more people for longer periods is not an effective response or a greater guarantee for safer communities" (Solicitor General of Canada, 1998). Examining statistics on incarceration enables criminologists and criminal justice agencies to better respond to related issues and endeavour to implement alternatives.

In addition to the data contained in *Juristat*, statistical information on the adult correctional system can be found under government catalogue number 85–211. Correctional Service of Canada also offers some statistical data, in its handy annual booklet that is filled with interesting facts on federal inmate populations. A review of this publication shows that our incarceration rates are increasing and that we are moving toward a more punitive and more expensive correctional system. These official data sources reveal a great deal about the correctional system and raise serious questions about what can be done to address the increasing costs of the current retributive approach to corrections.

What Do Official Data Measure?

The esteemed British criminologist Leslie Wilkins (1915–2000) once noted that official crime data are not, strictly speaking, statistics of criminal events per se. Rather, they reflect police, court, and correctional responses to social behaviour with respect to a particular set of offence categories as defined by the *Criminal Code*. Along this line of reasoning, *symbolic interactionism* (a term coined by Herbert Blumer in 1937) can be used to clarify Wilkins's observation. Blumer (1969:2) identified three premises of the perspective:

1. "Human beings act toward things on the basis of the meanings that the things have for them."

2. "The meaning of such things is derived from, or arises out of, the social interaction that one has with one's fellows."
3. "These meanings are handled in, and modified through, an interpretative process used by the person in dealing with the things he encounters."

Given Blumer's points, it can be said that official statistics are collected and used to meet the collectors' particular needs, since collectors are inclined to collect only data that has meaning to them and that they can use for their own needs. In fact, all organizations have roles and interests that serve to create particular mindsets as to what is important.

At the other extreme of the spectrum, *radical criminologists* see official sources of crime data as nothing more than a measure of political success in that the data "mystify and cloud the fact that the major 'crimes' against society are committed by the state" (American Friends Service Committee, 1971:10–11).

The impetus for such views stems in part from the fact that the volume of recorded criminality is smaller than that of actual criminality. In the first edition of his book *The Disreputable Pleasures*, Canadian sociologist and criminologist John Hagan (1977) discussed the concept of a *crime funnel*, already mentioned in Chapter 2 (see Table 3–2). The extent to which the funnelling effect takes place is subject to considerable debate. At one end of the debate, researchers such as Chambliss (1988), adopting a *conflict/radical* perspective, argue that official statistics are highly unreliable because of competing social factors and political interests. Evans and Himelfarb, on the other hand, are less pessimistic. They conclude their review of UCR data by stating, "we can probably learn something about crime from these data, but we are not sure how much" (1992:78). Nettler (1987:49) concludes that when the various modes of counting yield similar results, confidence in public records increases. However, "judgment is required" when using or interpreting such data.

TABLE 3–2

THE CRIME FUNNEL—CRIME NET

- Total incidents reported to police in 1996 = 2 832 800 (100 percent)
- Offences recorded as actual (determined
  to have occurred) = 96 percent
- Offences cleared = 34 percent
- Offences cleared by charge = 22 percent
- Convictions = 15 percent
- Sentence of custody = 4 percent

Note: Statistics Canada has not produced a crime funnel analysis for some years.

Source: CCJS, 1997, 17(13):1.

Based on absolute numbers (which are what is often reported in the media) in Table 3–3, we might deduce that violent assaults have increased steadily between 1998 and 2002. However, when one takes into account the fact that the population has also increased, the actual rate (number per 100 000) has changed very slightly over the stated period. So, is Canada becoming safer? Are our crime prevention and crime-fighting initiatives working? Or is the decline due to changes in demographic or social structure, or some other social indicator? While crime data offer interesting descriptive information, they do not provide the answers or explanations as to why changes occur. This is where scientific inquiry and knowledge of theoretical explanation come into play.

TABLE 3–3

LEVEL 1 SEXUAL ASSAULTS, 1998–2002

	1998	1999	2000	2001	2002
Absolute number of assaults	183 999	181 330	190 467	191 147	189 158
Number per 100 000	608	594	619	614	602

Source: CCJS, 2003, 23(11):16.

Despite their limitations, official data can serve as useful indicators; it is all a matter of how and for what purpose they are being used. Since crime data do not explain themselves, adopting an interdisciplinary and theoretical approach to using and interpreting official counts of crime is often helpful. While theories are not immune to shortcomings, they offer reasonably objective means to study crime and its control if they are used as part of a structured approach that employs observable and measurable concepts and constructs that can be tested.

One thing is certain: currently there is no sure way of assessing the gap between official and unofficial crime data. Jeffery has offered a scathing yet insightful assessment of how we measure crime. He suggests that "if we had a radar system or an emergency medical system that operated at the level found in the criminal justice system, we would not be alive for very long" (1990:125). Part of the dilemma lies in the relative and changing meaning of crime and the fact that our criminal justice system is reactive in its handling of crime. Therefore, while measuring crime may be of some value when developing theories of crime and criminal law, it serves us less well when developing theories of human behaviour. However, since laws are constantly changing, along with social points of view, such theories will always be limited in their ability to explain and predict.

Factors Affecting Crime Data

Official crime counts are subject to artificial fluctuations. The fluctuation, or distortion, of actual crime can be attributed to a variety of factors that influence the collecting and processing of crime data. They include the following:

1. According to research by Conklin (1975), among others, *media coverage* of crime can influence crime counts. Focusing on certain crimes or crises draws public attention and affects the reporting rates. As noted in Chapter 2, the media can serve as a barometer of public interest.

2. The *dark figure of crime* may be subject to fluctuation over time and even within settings. Fattah (1997), among others, notes that fluctuations in the dark figure can be attributed to variables pertaining to police enforcement practices, victims' willingness to report their victimization, and the public's attitude toward the criminal justice system.

3. *Changes in recording procedures* affect crime data that are collected by the various law enforcement forces throughout Canada and reported to Statistics Canada. From time to time, certain police forces or courts may not be able to provide complete information. For example, a review of annual statistics at different times shows that certain jurisdictions did not provide crime data to Statistics Canada. While Statistics Canada notes these differences, they are seldom discussed by the media, or even, in some cases, in academic accounts of crime. Some of the reasons for non- or overreporting may be:

   a) *Changes in the number of police forces/officers.*
   b) *Changes in police/court administration.* Mandates for policies at the municipal, provincial, or federal level may change (e.g., shift from a crime control model to a community-based prevention model).
   c) *Changes in the legal definition of crime.* On the recommendations of the Wolfenden report in the 1970s, attempted suicide and consensual homosexuality were no longer subject to criminal prosecution. These changes reflected the government's disinclination to interfere with moral issues. In 1985, three major crimes were redefined or amended in the *Criminal Code*: rape (sections 270–273), hate crime (sections 318–320), and prostitution (section 213). In general, these changes reflect the evolving attitudes in public opinion toward accountability and clearer definitions of certain crimes.
   d) *Changes in the population base.* Both the media and the police are notorious for using absolute numbers of crime when trying to create an impact. However, these crime figures are meaningless unless they are linked to population size, political and social changes, or some combination of those factors. Ideally, only crime rates should be used when drawing comparisons.

   Using base rates to convert crime counts to rates that are expressed as the number of crime cases, charges, or complaints per unit volume of the population has become the norm. In Canada, as in many other Western countries, crime reports use units of 100 000 for all crime statistics. For certain crime categories for which the population base is smaller, crime reporting units of 1000 and 10 000 may be used. To calculate the crime rate, the following formula is used:

$$\text{Rate per 100 000} = \frac{\text{\# of reported crimes}}{\text{Total population}} \times 100\ 000$$

Yet in spite of using a common denominator to equalize the counting process, the base rates are prone to several technical problems. First, in Canada, a major census is undertaken only once every 10 years, with a smaller census at the midpoint between each major census. Over that 10-year span, fertility, emigration, and immigration rates can fluctuate significantly (see McKie, 2004), enough to distort the actual crime rates. Even using the midpoint to adjust the base rate is not fail-safe, since the counts are not as comprehensive as those at the 10-year mark.

Other strategies have been suggested as a means of calculating base rates: using counts of the population at risk rather than of the total population (Boggs, 1966); calculating break-and-enter rates in terms of the number of dwellings; basing motor-vehicle thefts on the number of vehicles; and basing sexual assaults on the population of females. However, since circumstances surrounding victims of crime are not consistent, these strategies also have their limitations.

The final technical problem Brantingham and Brantingham (1984:55) identify "involves a change in the *format* used to collect police data." As noted above, redefining certain crimes can cause significant problems for researchers wishing to compare crime data from year to year. The most obvious of these changes occurred in 1962, when Canadian police statistics were completely reorganized. Changes were made again in 1980, with the establishment of the Canadian Centre for Justice Statistics, and collection and recording practices continue to evolve (Ross, 1993).

e) *Changes in public attitudes toward crime and the police.* The Canadian Urban Victimization Survey (CUVS) found that only 42 percent of all recorded crimes are reported by the victim or another member of the public. Depending on the type of offence, only around 30 percent of recorded crimes are the result of police observation or intervention. Therefore, public reporting patterns can have a dramatic impact on crime counts.

As crime rates rose throughout the 20th century, it became increasingly important to establish a comprehensive system that would coordinate criminal justice data and address community justice needs. The Canadian Centre for Justice Statistics was the national response.

Canadian Centre for Justice Statistics

"...no formal system has the ability to count crime with one hundred percent accuracy." Winterdyk, 1996:16

When Uniform Crime Reporting (UCR) was introduced in 1962, official crime counts were considered to be more uniform and reliable than those yielded by previous methods for recording crime data. However, as crime rates increased (from 2771.2 per 100 000 in 1962 to 9233 per 100 000 in 1988) and then dropped (to 8387 per 100 000 in 2002), and as public awareness grew as a result of the spread of mass media, public appetite for the *facts* of crime also grew. As self-report and victimization surveys were introduced during the late 1960s and early 1970s, it became evident that official data were limited. The concept of the dark figure of crime began to draw increasing attention.

Between 1974 and 1981, several task forces and advisory boards attempted to reorganize the national data collection methods in an effort to meet both federal and provincial needs. This seven-year process culminated with the opening of the Canadian Centre for Justice Statistics (CCJS) as a satellite of Statistics Canada, in 1981. For the next six years, the centre continued to be plagued by operational and directional difficulties. A 1984 evaluation gave it a modest passing grade, and its funding was extended for another three years.

In spite of its difficulties, the centre grew. In 1981, it produced only two reports; in 1992, 25. It released 17 publications in 1994, 13 in 1997, and 11 in 2003. Today, the benchmarks of the centre for crime and criminal justice data gathering and publication are the *Juristat* bulletins. These special topical publications not only inform administrators within the criminal justice system about relevant issues, but also fulfill one of the centre's mandates, which is to satisfy the "public's right to know." In addition, the centre undertakes specific studies in such areas as hate crime, impaired driving, and Canada's shelters for abused women(see Box 3.7). However, as several researchers have noted, the CCJS continues to experience difficulties in trying to meet the needs of different sources. Some key limitations include:

- There is no national information on court decisions.
- There are inconsistencies in the way provinces report, as well as count, their crime incidents.
- Data on crime incidents, arrests, charges, convictions, and dispositions lack depth.
- Reports provide little insight into crime and criminal behaviour.
- There are no reports on white-collar crime, organized crime, victimless crime, or other types of non-conventional crime.

In fairness, however, the centre tries to provide information that is of value to policy-makers, criminal justice administrators and planners, academic researchers, the media, as well as the public. And since its inception, it has had a major impact on the study of crime and criminal justice in Canada.

In summary, the official data-gathering techniques in Canada have evolved over the years. Today, the CCJS is the primary source for criminological data. The quality and variety of data have improved considerably since the formation of the service in 1981. In the future, technological changes such as the development of sophisticated internet search engines are likely to contribute to further improvement. However, it is important to remember that criminological data are useful only to the extent to they can be applied or used within a theoretical context. While CCJS provides data on a wide range of topics, not all the data necessarily serve a theoretical function and hence are little more than descriptive information. Therefore, students and scholars are encouraged to familiarize themselves with other significant sources of data. Among the more conventional unofficial sources that criminologists have come to rely upon are victimization surveys, self-report data, and observation data.

Unofficial Sources of Crime Data

Since crime involves both an offender and a recipient of the offence, in certain situations crime data can be obtained from the victim and/or the offender. Data that are obtained directly from the recipient of the offence are called self-report data. Another type of data, obtained either from victims or from others who know victims, is victimization data. A third source is observational or personal data. When collected in a systematic manner, observational data can provide both qualitatively and quantitatively rich detail about the crime and events being observed, but its major drawback is the necessity of being in the right place at the right time to observe. Hence, the first two sources tend to be more accessible and reliable. Without these sources of **unofficial data**, the crime picture would be incomplete, since unrecorded crimes are not reflected in official statistics.

Victimization Data

As will be discussed in greater detail in Chapter 12, the study of victimology is an immensely interesting area of investigation within criminology. In Canada, unlike in many European countries, it is still in its infancy. Even as recently as 2004, courses on victimology were available only in the larger criminology programs and schools in Canada.

As early as 1947, Edwin Sutherland pointed out the public is always the victim of a crime. Sacco and Kennedy (1998) identified three elements that are essential to describing a criminal event; these elements complement Sutherland's observation. The first element is the *precursor* of the event, which refers to the "situational factors that bring people together in time and space." The second element pertains to how *"interactions among participants* define the outcomes of their actions" (e.g., victim–offender relationship). The third element is the *aftermath* of the event. This approach not only offers a convenient mode for studying crime but also illustrates that there is a relationship between the victim and the offender.

Victimization Surveys in Canada and Elsewhere

Victimization surveys (VS) are designed to provide estimates on the nature, frequency, and consequence of crimes that occur by asking people to disclose whether they have been victims of certain crimes over a fixed period of time (usually the past 12 months). Victimization surveys have the potential to also tap into the feelings and attitudes of victims to the criminological and criminal justice's response to their victimization—information not available through official sources. Hence, when conducted properly, victim surveys can serve as an invaluable source of criminological information. We will explore the subject in greater detail in Chapter 12.

In spite of its limited role in Canadian criminology, the use of victimization surveys is more solidly established in Canada than elsewhere. The roots of victimization surveys in North America can be traced back to the efforts of the now defunct Law Enforcement Assistance Administration (LEAA), which funded the first national victimization survey in the United States conducted by Biderman, Johnson, McIntyre, and Weir in 1967 (DeKeseredy & Schwartz, 1996).

In the United States, beginning in 1973 and every year since, the National Crime Survey (NCS)—recently renamed National Crime Victimization Survey (NCVS)—has conducted annual victimization surveys that involve more than 100 000 people who are interviewed several times a year. In their 20th annual report, the NCS included over 120 numerical tables describing criminal victimization (see Greenfeld, 1994). General areas of coverage included costs of crime to victims, the nature and extent of criminal behaviour, probabilities of victimization risks, and victim precipitation of crime and culpability.

Limitations of Victimization Surveys

As much as victimization surveys are used to tap into the dark figure of crime and provide insights into the impact of a crime on the victim, these surveys are not without their limitations. For example:

- Respondents may forget about crimes—especially less serious ones.
- Respondents may be mistaken as to when the incident occurred.
- Respondents may simply not feel comfortable disclosing certain facts and/or details.
- Respondents may fail to clearly understand the questions.
- There may be differences between different social groups of respondents; for example, studies indicate that those better educated have better recall.
- Conducting such surveys tends to be both time-consuming and costly.
- Acquiring stable estimates of less common crimes requires even larger samples that adds to the high cost.

Fortunately, in recent years, there have been many articles written on the subject of victimization surveys, and suggestions for improving the reliability and validity have been put forth. In Chapter 12, we will review and summarize the findings from several major international and national crime victimization surveys.

As researchers increasingly recognize the need for a multi-method approach to collecting data on crime, many of the existing limitations are likely to be addressed. Also, as we move away from what Andrew Karman (1996) terms "offenderology" to being more victim-conscious and integrating victimization into theoretical perspectives, the refinement of victimization surveys is likely to continue. Sociologist Jack Katz (1988), for example, expresses the view that criminologists need to broaden their objective and deterministic perspectives of deviance. He suggests that criminologists need to embrace a spiritual approach. In so doing, criminologists will be able to use victimization data to better understand the role of the victim and offender. Meanwhile, the critical theoretical perspective *left-realism* makes extensive use of victimization data when testing its principles (see, for example, Lowman & MacLean, 1992). Similarly, feminist researchers have not only used victimization data but have developed means of looking into behaviours not covered in traditional victimization surveys. And finally, the University of Leiden in the Netherlands, with support from the Dutch Ministry of Justice and countries participating in the International Crime Victimization Survey (ICVS), is currently coordinating an international survey of victimization suffered by businesses, which will have both theoretical and policy implications. The existence of a variety of victim assistance programs in Canada will undoubtedly help ensure that victimization surveys and the study of victimology in general will become a major force in criminological study.

Self-Report Data

Thorsten Sellin (1931) was one of the first North American criminologists to argue that in order to understand crime, it is important to start by asking about the offender's behaviour and motivation. Since Sellin's article, **self-report studies** have been conducted with young offenders, judges, lawyers, law enforcement officers, inmates, senior citizens, business people, and virtually any sub-population that might be thought to engage in criminal acts.

Self-report studies take a pragmatic approach to the enumeration of criminal behaviour—was a crime committed or not? Based on the responses, the scores are cross-analyzed against the fundamental demographic and socio-economic characteristics of the respondents, such as age, gender, known criminal record, and social class. These data are then used to assess both the validity of criminal justice statistics as a pattern index of crime and the validity of criminological theories based on inferences drawn from the patterns found in criminal justice statistics.

Findings of Self-Report Studies

The flavour of self-report studies has changed over the years. One of the earlier self-report studies was conducted by Austin Porterfield (1943) at Christian University in Texas. Porterfield asked students to respond to a survey on deviant behaviour. While most of his findings might appear trivial by today's standards, he observed that there was a strong gender bias in favour of males—they committed more delinquent acts than females. His more amusing findings showed 79 percent of males admit to using abusive language, and 77 percent admit to throwing spitballs. Only 8 percent admitted to committing break and enter.

The early self-report studies offered criminologists some fruitful insights into their understanding of crime. The studies revealed that the gap between official and self-report data varied by age, gender, offender type, and race. Offenders who are not part of the official data base (i.e., haven't been caught) tend to commit a wide variety of offences, rather than specializing in one type of offending behaviour. Only about one-quarter of all serious, chronic young offenders are officially apprehended.

In Canada, self-report surveys have been limited; those conducted tend to focus on youths and adolescents. For example, during the 1970s and 1980s, two University of Montreal researchers conducted repeated self-report surveys on a large group of high-risk and known delinquent French-speaking boys. The survey included 39 questions asked of the youths about their delinquent behaviour over the past 12 months. The questions covered a broad range of offences, ranging from property-related offences to violence, sexual habits, and crimes against their families. LeBlanc and Frechette (1989) attempted to describe delinquent patterns for all high-risk Canadian boys and men. While their study included some strong elements, they neglected female delinquency and ignored cultural and social differences between English- and French-speaking Canadians. Also, given that they surveyed only urban males in one major city, their generalization to all Canadian youth is highly suspect in terms of reliability and validity.

Limitations of Self-Report Studies

Despite a comparatively long history, self-report studies have been fraught with methodological problems. Until recently, few studies were standardized, as they were often done at different times by researchers with different interests. One exception was the study done by West and Farrington (1977) in England that investigated the development of young offenders in a sample of delinquent and non-delinquent boys over a 10-year period. The authors found that differences did exist between delinquents and non-delinquents on factors relating to family background and several personal characteristics. Similar results have been reported more recently in a study of Chinese delinquents by Wolfgang (1996).

Another limitation of self-report studies has been that they seldom use comparable questions, areas, or time frames. These drawbacks render the studies almost useless for any assessment of the efficiency of criminal justice statistics. Walker (1987) has identified several other factors that bring into question the reliability of self-report surveys. They include the following:

1. Respondent may mistrust the interviewers.
2. Respondents may not answer truthfully because of embarrassment.
3. Respondents may feel a deep sense of guilt and not disclose their behaviour.
4. Respondents may exaggerate the truth, especially if they are young.
5. Respondents may simply forget.

As a result of their numerous methodological limitations, self-report studies are plagued by reliability problems, are of doubtful validity, and have led researchers to draw unfair and incorrect inferences. However, it is possible to minimize the problems by being sensitive to possible limitations and thinking creatively. For example, Dentler and Monroe (1961) found a 92 percent concurrence rate in their two-week follow-up, while Clark and Tifft (1966), who used the threat of using a polygraph test (i.e., a lie detector) on a sample of youths, found the variation between different testing periods to be statistically negligible. In other words, the respondents generally told the truth.

More recently, Junger-Tas, Terlouw, and Klein (1996) have compiled a collection of articles dealing with an international self-report survey of juvenile delinquents. The study was conducted between 1991 and 1993, and the participating countries (most of them European, plus New Zealand and the United States) used a variety of sampling techniques, which made direct comparisons between the countries difficult. Nevertheless, the general findings are consistent with other self-report literature, showing that the ages from 16 to 17 years are the peak ages for offending, that violence is strongly related to lower educational levels, and that school failure is related to violent offences.

In summary, self-report studies have undergone steady improvement over the years, but as DeKeseredy and Schwartz (1996:138) write, "we still have a ways to go to make them completely useful." In the meantime, we should treat these types of studies as reasonably reliable but subject to qualification—that is, less reliable for trivial questions (e.g., theft under $20), for personally embarrassing questions, and for very serious crimes. In addition, researchers need to expand their topic base. For example, our knowledge base about self-report adult crime is very small. Furthermore, the majority of self-report studies have been conducted with male young offenders. This is probably due to the ease of access to this group and the relatively low cost of administering such surveys. However, in spite of the number of self-report studies conducted on young people, the findings have not shed a great deal of light on our understanding of youth crime. For example, Vold and Bernard's (1979:226) observation that "the basic motivations for crime are common in all social classes, not just to the lower class" is not very enlightening.

The limited advances in understanding crime through self-report studies is due in part to the limited methodological limitations discussed above, as well as the lack of an interdisciplinary approach to surveying those who have already committed offences. For example, rather than simply enumerating trends and patterns of offences committed by various groups, self-report surveys could embrace an integrated interdisciplinary approach that includes questions regarding biological and environmental factors that are more in keeping with our understanding of crime and criminality today. Nevertheless, an American study conducted by Michael Hindelang, Travis Hirschi, and Joseph Weis (1981) suggests that official and unofficial data collection techniques have improved over the years and that the problems of accuracy and reliability in self-reports fall well within the range of acceptability. The authors argue that in spite of the skepticism among some criminologists, self-report studies serve an informative function, as long as researchers conduct their research within the methodological parameters identified.

Observational Data

The final source that is regularly used to obtain accurate data on crime is observation or *field research*. As Jackson (1995), among others, has commented, you cannot gain insight into people's motives for committing crimes if you are sitting at your desk analyzing data or reading crime surveys. Would it not be more informative to actually be able to follow and watch a prison riot rather than hand out surveys after the fact? Would it not be more informative to sit in a court and watch a trial unfold or to go on police ride-alongs than administer a survey?

The German sociologist Max Weber (1864–1920) was instrumental in developing methodological approaches that emphasized the importance of how individuals interpret their actions as well as how they interpret the actions and reactions of others.

Weber used the term **Verstehen** to refer to this *qualitative* approach to understanding. The concept is defined as the process of trying to understand an event by placing oneself in the situation and trying to see it through the participant's eyes—aligning oneself with another's social viewpoint. Since Weber's time, some theoretical perspectives have emerged, such as the *symbolic interactionism* perspective (see Ritzer, 1992), the *ground theory* (see Glaser & Strauss, 1973), and the *ethnomethodological* perspective (see Garfinkel, 1967). From this general *social-constructionist* perspective, crime statistics tell us more about the agencies and individuals (e.g., police, courts, and corrections) who are responsible for constructing them than about the crimes and criminals they are reporting.

Over the years, a number of classic studies have employed one of the above perspectives to study crime and criminals. Among these are Sutherland's *The Professional Thief* (1937); Chambliss's *The Box Man* (1975); Snodgrass's *The Jack-Roller at Seventy* (1982); Cromwell et al.'s *Who Buys Stolen Property?* (1993); Skolnick's *Justice Without Trial* (1994); and in Canada, Letkemann's *Crime as Work* (1973). For his book, Letkemann interviewed 45 bank robbers and burglars in an effort to describe and explain the lifestyle of a safe-cracker.

Advantages and Disadvantages of Observational Techniques

All field observation techniques are comprehensive data collection methods. They are excellent techniques for gathering information when going directly to the event is essential or helpful. When events are better observed in their natural setting, observational procedures can be information rich. As Mark Hamm (1998) notes, criminological field research enables the researcher to transcend abstract theoretical analysis by immersing him- or herself in the situated meanings and emotions of the criminal event. These techniques are also useful for gathering data on social processes over time. Collectively, these procedures have a strong appeal to the reader because they have good *face validity*. You report only what you see!

When collecting data in social settings (e.g., inmate vs. guard interactions), observation enables data collection on at least three levels:

1. The act itself, the activities surrounding the act, and the meaning of the activities;
2. The dynamics of the participants and their interrelationships; and
3. The setting in general (Lofland, 1984).

Limitations of Observational Techniques

Observational techniques entail varying degrees of involvement in and observation of the events, which raise certain methodological and ethical considerations. The "tearoom trade" study of homosexual activities by Laud Humphrey (1970) has become a classic case in field research ethics. Humphrey's doctoral dissertation involved observing male homosexuals meeting in public washrooms without getting their consent. Was this a violation of their privacy and personal liberty? Could Humphrey be considered no better than a voyeur? Humphrey admitted to being less than candid with his respondents. Is this practice of deception acceptable? In a report on some of the criticisms, Horowitz and Rainwater (1970) argued that the study was conducted within ethical boundaries. Either way, the point is that collecting data through observational methods can be subject to controversy. As an interesting footnote to this study, Canadian sociologist Fredrick Desroches (1991) attempted to replicate the results of Humphrey's study by means other than personal observations. While his methodology was much different (he used observations made by police), he found the behaviour of male homosexuals to be remarkably consistent over time, from community to community, and across national boundaries.

Another drawback of observational procedures is that they tend to be much more labour-intensive than victimization or self-report surveys. The data obtained are also more subjective, since the type of information gathered is dependent on the recorder's biases and mental and physical limitations. Sample sizes tend to be considerably smaller than in the other unofficial and official means of data collecting. As a result, there is no allowance for causal assertions or generalizations beyond the study group. Nevertheless, as noted above, there have been a number of major studies conducted using field research methodologies. Sometimes field interviews, life history, or biographical interviews are considered more valid and informative than the more standard passive modes of data collection. In response to a growing recognition of the complexity of human nature, field research is being more widely used as either a free-standing method or in conjunction with other methodologies.

Types of Observational Techniques

Two of the more common observational procedures are:

1. *Field observation*: The intent of covert, or *non-participant*, observations is to observe and collect data in its natural setting without altering the setting in any way. While the methodology can be somewhat haphazard, the information obtained can be most enlightening (Jackson, 1999).

   Field observation techniques are the least obtrusive method of the observational techniques. We have probably all engaged in this procedure at some time or other. Going to a hockey or baseball game, sitting at your favorite coffee shop and watching life pass by, or simply hanging around a crime or accident scene and observing the sequence of events all constitute field observation. Field research can provide rich and detailed information. Observing verbal and non-verbal interactions, as well as elements of some theoretical paradigm that you might be testing, can prove very insightful.

2. *Participant observation*: This is a method more commonly used by anthropologists, although the Chicago School used it to produce some classic sociological studies (see Theodorson, 1982). The method involves "going natural" or engaging in *field research*. Humphrey (1970), for example, was a *participant observer* or a "watchqueen," as he termed it. In return for being able to watch, he acted as his study group's watch guard to warn of any unwanted visitors.

The researcher can vary his or her degree of involvement as a participant observer. Some become totally involved in what they are observing. In a classic illustration of this approach, John Howard Griffin had his skin impregnated with a black dye so that he could blend in with the blacks he wanted to observe and live with; he felt that by doing do he could provide a more realistic description of what life was like for blacks in America. For a full account, see his book *Black Like Me* (1961). Although it makes for a compelling story, this type of research is considered to be primarily qualitative. Griffin had become a *complete observer-participant*, whereas the *complete observer* does not participate in anything but only observes, as if sitting behind a one-way mirror.

Engaging in this type of research often places great demands on observers' time. In addition, observers must be able to operate on two levels. First, they must immerse themselves in what they are observing. Second, they must remain detached from what they are observing. Imagine going to your favourite sporting event and being asked to observe but not get personally involved—like a broadcaster or sports reporter. Police officers are also often required to play a passive observational role when conducting an investigation. Ethical dilemmas can arise if they find themselves in a position where an event of which they strongly disapprove might occur. Longmire (1983) found that such dilemmas are common among those who engage in research questions in criminology and criminal justice. Surveying a sample of members of the American Society of Criminology, Longmire found that 63 percent indicated experiencing some ethical dilemmas when conducting research. The most common (9 percent) ethical dilemma pertained to issues surrounding confidentiality. What can observers do to minimize the potential negative effects of research on their subjects? They can follow some of these basic guidelines: don't harm participants, ensure voluntary participation, maintain the anonymity and confidentiality of participants, and be honest at all stages of the study (Jackson, 1999). (If you are interested in substantive issues regarding ethics in criminology and criminal justice policy, consult the journal *Criminal Justice Ethics* for a broad selection of articles and seek out related textbooks.)

Triangulation and Decision-Making

To this point, we have observed that no one data source can measure any crime and criminal justice concerns with complete validity and reliability. Official and unofficial data sources each have their strengths and weaknesses. As criminology moves closer to being more interdisciplinary and integrated, it has increasingly begun to combine qualitative and quantitative methods of data-gathering in order to facilitate more informed decisions. The process of combining multiple sources to better understand criminological phenomena is referred to as **triangulation**. Paul Lazerfeld (1959) and Donald Campbell and Donald Fiske (1959) were among the first to suggest that multiple measurements or *data triangulation* can be used to better illuminate a particular issue. For example, criminologists can recreate a great deal of a past incident by using indirect observations (e.g., examining physical evidence) and combining them with current statistical trends and patterns to better explain and predict the phenomena.

Using triangulation increases *convergent-discriminant* validity. According to Campbell and Fiske (1959:81), by using different data sources "of measuring a construct, the results should be similar, whereas the same method measuring different things should yield dissimilar results." Police data and victimization data provide an official indicator of crime (*convergence*), but the results are seldom identical (*discrimination*), since they measure the same phenomena from different perspectives. Triangulation has enabled criminologists to illuminate the dark figure of crime. In his study of Canadian cheque forgers, Letkemann (1973) included three different sources of information in order to develop his cheque forger typology. A similar method was employed by Boyd (1988), who used at least three sources of information to develop his typology of murderers in Canada.

Research methods textbooks almost unanimously take time to point out that while the validity of information sources is critical, no single method or multi-method strategy can demonstrate or prove any phenomena with one hundred percent accuracy. Rather, the "invalidity is lessened, or researchers are able to express greater degrees of confidence in their data" (Hagan, 1989:247). This is why statistical techniques are used in academic articles to objectively state the degree of confidence found in the data and thereby lend objective support to any policy decisions that might be made based on them.

It is important to remember that as much as solid science relies on reliable and valid data, it is also grounded on sound theoretical underpinnings. Any researcher who does not base his or her research on strong theoretical underpinnings is like a hockey coach coaching without a game plan: bound to make poor decisions and bound to lose in spite of any information. Theory and methodology go hand in hand, and criminological research involves both theory and rigorous *research methodology*. Research methodology is the scientific process whereby criminologists strive to understand and explain criminological issues through a variety of social science methods. Methodology is a sub-area of *epistemology* (the science of knowing) and has also been called "the science of finding out" (Maxfield & Babbie, 1995:5).

It should be pointed out that as sophisticated and structured as research methods may appear to be, they have also been described as an art (Palys, 1997). Even though there are certain fundamental guidelines that researchers attempt to follow when conducting research, the flexibility and quality of their research design is limited by such factors as cost, time, and practicality. Nevertheless, while scientific inquiry may not provide the definitive answers we seek to complex criminological questions, scientific theories offer at least an objective approximation of reality, as they are premised on observable, measurable, and usually empirically testable hypotheses or assertions.

One of the reasons for criminology's lack of "success" in explaining and predicting crime is that most criminologists have viewed and continue to view crime and its causes (as well as its control) from classic one-way cause-and-effect perspective (Normandeau & Hasenpush, 1980). Instead, successful research must recognize the interdisciplinary nature of crime. Crime is influenced by a complex interaction of biological, environmental, political, psychological, sociological, and other factors that are generally beyond the scope of legal mechanisms and decision-makers.

Summary

- Crime data are essential to explaining and describing crime trends and patterns, as well as to developing criminological theory and formulating social policy. Criminal statistics are part of the criminological enterprise.

- Each of the various crime data sources has its strengths and weaknesses, and the choice of which to employ is typically dependent upon the resources available to the researcher and the researcher's training and theoretical bias, combined with the parameters of the phenomena being studied.

- Triangulation is a practical and effective method that can increase the validity of research findings. As Simon (cited in DeKeseredy & Schwartz, 1996:148) observed, "a research method for a given problem is not like the solution to a problem in Algebra. It is more like a recipe for beef stroganoff; there is no one best recipe."

- An interdisciplinary and multi-method approach is recommended when collecting and interpreting criminological information.

Discussion Questions

1. Why is crime data essential to the study of crime, and what are some of the major problems associated with the different sources of crime data?

2. How can the various sources of information on criminal events be used to support or distort actual crime rates?

3. Identify several cases where criminological or criminal justice policies have been, or appear to have been, based on ill-informed decisions. How might such outcomes be avoided?

4. Compare and contrast two or three crimes currently in the news with the official data surrounding the crimes found in a current *Juristat* bulletin. Is the media coverage consistent with the official data? What might account for the differences? What implications might this have for criminal policy?

5. Which form of data do you consider superior: UCR data or self-report data? Why? Which do you think is more predictive of high-risk and/or reoffending behaviours? Based on your answers, how might we determine the best intervention strategies?

Key Concepts

Canadian Centre for Justice Statistics (CCJS)	cause	correlation
	correctional statistics	crime data
crime rate	dark figure of crime	false positive
self-report studies	triangulation	Uniform Crime Reporting (UCR)
unofficial data	Verstehen	victimization surveys

Weblinks

www.statcan/english/sdds/3302.htm This site, hosted by Statistics Canada, provides a detailed overview on the Uniform Crime Report Survey.

www.statcan.ca/english/Pgdb/justic.htm This page provides links to recent justice and crime statistics from Statistics Canada.

www.geographicprofiling.com/geopro/ref-request.htm This site is an excellent Canadian source for those interested in geographic profiling of crime.

www.homeoffice.gov.uk The site of the UK Home Office offers a wealth of data on crime in Britain.

Endnotes

1. The term "objective" refers to the process of using numerical crime data to describe, explain, and predict criminological issues.

2. As early as 1778, Jeremy Bentham recommended that police and court data should be centrally collected and used to measure the moral health of the country.

3. If there have been a number of incidents, the Crown can elect to prosecute them as summary or indictable. This is known as a *hybrid* offence. Examples include impaired driving and theft under $5000.

CHAPTER 4

The History and Pioneers of Criminology

"While we read history we make history."

George William Curtis (1824–1892)

Learning Outcomes

After you have completed this chapter, you should be able to:

- Discuss the three major schools of criminological thought.

- Recognize the impact these schools have had on our current view of crime, criminals, and justice.

- Be cognizant of the pioneers who have contributed to criminological reform in Canada and internationally.

- Appreciate the necessity of an interdisciplinary approach to the study of crime, criminals, and the justice system.

- Recognize the need to include crime prevention in an integrated and interdisciplinary model.

What Is the Point of History?

How often have you heard phrases such as "history just repeats itself," "we've heard it all before," or "we never seem to learn from our past"? In Chapter 1, we saw that people's interest in crime has existed as long as recorded history. Throughout the centuries, scholars have offered various opinions regarding the causes of and "cures" for the problem. Some of these ideas have had an enduring influence on how we view crime and study criminality. However, the scientific study of crime and criminality is a relatively recent development.

In this chapter, we will go into greater depth and examine both the history of criminological thought and some of its major contributors. Throughout this and other chapters, you will find biographical profiles of some of the prominent pioneers of criminology, including Canadian researchers and scholars who have made significant contributions to the discipline.[1] By familiarizing yourself with some of the fundamental ideas and principles of each school of criminological thought and its major contributors, you will gain a better appreciation of how criminology and its sub-areas have evolved into an interdisciplinary area of study.

We will address three major schools of thought: the classical, the neoclassical, and the positivist. In addition, crime prevention, while not generally considered to be a school of criminological thought, will also be discussed, as it is a perspective that is being embraced by a growing number of scholars and by the criminal justice system.

Classical Criminology
The Roots of Social Reform

Classical school of criminology emerged in response to the harsh, retributive punishments that existed throughout the Dark Ages (450–1100 AD), Middle Ages (1100–1300 AD), and the Renaissance (1300–1600 AD). After the fall of the Roman Empire in 476 AD, most of the progressive legal reforms in Europe disappeared and were replaced with superstitions and fear of magic. People who violated social norms were thought to be witches or to be possessed by evil spirits. The Dark Ages were marked by ritualistic torture methods such as burning at the stake and the use of branding, pillory, and the stocks; other variations of humbling corporal punishment survived up to the 17th century. During the 16th and 17th centuries in Europe, justice was extreme in its measures and often involved taking private vengeance for wrongdoings (Johnson, 1988). Some of the more "civil" practices of resolving disputes involved monetary payments.

One of the first attempts to reform and regulate punishment of crime was the introduction of the *Criminal Ordinance* in France in 1670. Its purpose was to codify legal sanctions, with a greater emphasis on severe punishment. However, it was not specific enough with regard to certain types of cases, and it gave judges discretion to diminish or increase punishment (Siegel, 1995).

During this time in Europe's history, punishment was often inconsistent and chaotic. In fact, Martin Luther called for rulers to pursue, beat, strangle, and torture offenders, since rulers were the representatives of divine retribution (Johnson, 1988). Crime was viewed as a rebellious act committed by the poor against the rich and the political structure. Punishment was justified as a means to establish order. Martin et al. (1990) note that peasants, wanderers, and vagabonds were especially disadvantaged under this system. Many were punished for theft that they committed in order to survive. The general acceptance of these views, when combined with famines, wars, excessive taxes, and plagues that characterized this period, meant that social reform was slow in coming.

Toward Enlightenment
in the Renaissance and After

During the Renaissance, Europe started undergoing massive changes. After Polish astronomer Nicholas Copernicus (1473–1543) proved that the earth revolves around the sun, the whole outlook of Western society was forced to change. A more rational, scientific approach to knowing the world slowly emerged. **Jan Weir** (1516–1588), for example, wrote the first refutation of the existence of demons and incantations. He also argued that those thought to be possessed were merely mentally ill—*sans deleria*.

During the Enlightenment era—that is, the period of rapid scientific and intellectual changes in the 17th and 18th centuries—humanism became a significant force that challenged the existing concept of punishment. The prevailing ideology of the time was called utilitarianism. One of its fundamental principles was the notion that punishment should be fair, not cruel, excessive, or capricious. The turning point came on March 2, 1757, after a mentally challenged man, Robert-François Damien, stabbed but did not kill King Louis XV of France (for further details, see Foucault, 1977).

Among the most notable scholars of the Enlightenment was the English philosopher John Locke (1632–1704), who founded the school of empiricism and had a profound impact on political ideology.[2] In France, philosopher and social and political theorist Jean Jacques Rousseau's (1712–1778) ideas also contributed greatly to the emancipation of people from the absolutism of church and state oppression. These ideas appear in his famous political treatise *The Social Contract*, published in 1762. René Descartes (1596–1650), also from France, helped bring mathematics, philosophy, and social science together into a unified scientific method. Other writings spoke to the need for more humane and psychologically oriented methods of child rearing (see DeMause, 1988). Reactions to unfair punishment, abuse of power, and corrupt economic systems that taxed the poor to support the rich and powerful contributed to social revolutions in the American colonies (in 1774) and in France (in 1789).

As the Enlightenment produced many secular ideas, the traditional religious doctrine of divine rule and absolute devotion to the church began to wane and the old aristocracy was called into question. As already mentioned, the prevailing concept of justice was also challenged. One of the leading proponents responsible for spearheading the ideological shift in the way people thought about justice was Cesare Bonesara, Marquis of Beccaria, more commonly referred to as **Cesare Beccaria** (see Box 4.1).

Beccaria's Key Ideas

In their summary of his work, Martin et al. (1990:8) point out that Beccaria "did not specifically set out to develop a theory pertaining to crime and justice, but rather simply wanted to delineate the parameters of a just system with criminals. Whether he intended to or not, Beccaria developed an outline for a theory of justice."

CESARE BECCARIA

Beccaria was born on March 15, 1738, into an aristocratic family in Milan, Italy. In 1758, he graduated from the University of Pavia, where he obtained a law degree (Monachesi, 1973).

Upon graduating, he returned to Milan, where he joined the Accademia dei Transformati, a group interested in literary and social issues. It was through this society that he read some of the great philosophical writings of the day, such as those by Francis Bacon, David Hume, and Jean Jacques Rousseau. He also met and formed a new and stronger political group with Pietro Verri, a noted economist. The new society called itself the Accademia dei Pugni (Academy of Fists).

With much encouragement from Verri, Beccaria wrote about legal and prison reform. Pietro's brother Alessandro took Beccaria into the prisons so that he could see for himself the need to write about penal issues. Beccaria anonymously published his essay *Dei delitti e delle pene* (*On Crimes and Punishments*) in 1764. He was only 26 years of age. This small monograph of approximately 100 pages has been heralded as a masterpiece and the foundation of the classical school of criminological thought.

History is somewhat vague as to whether Beccaria actually wrote the essay himself. In fact, Graeme Newman and Pietro Marongiu (1990) suggest that he may have plagiarized the work. Based on known facts, various scholars feel that Pietro and/or his colleagues may have somehow contributed to the final manuscript (Monachesi, 1973). Either way, beginning with the second edition, Beccaria was listed as the author.

Initially, his treatise was not widely embraced. In 1765, the pope placed Beccaria's work on a list of banned books for its "extreme rationalism" (Beirne, 1991). In time, however, Beccaria's plea for the ending of torture drew increasing international acclaim. The great French philosopher Voltaire (1694–1778) invited him to Paris to meet with his group. Beccaria also received requests from foreign governments to assist with the revision of their criminal codes; Russian Empress Catherine II was among the rulers requesting his help. However, Beccaria did not accept many of the invitations.

Beccaria never produced anything else of note. He eventually took a position as a professor of political economy in the Palatine School, but after two years left to become a magistrate and returned to a relatively quiet life. He died on November 11, 1794, at the age of 56.

In his 1764 essay, *On Crimes and Punishments*, Beccaria argued for a minimal punishment as being necessary for social defence and the protection of society. He emphasized fair and proportionate punishment for the harm done to society, and he embraced the concept of free will, arguing that if three basic conditions could be met, most potential offenders would be deterred. The conditions are *certainty* of punishment, *swiftness* of justice, and measured *severity* of punishment. To this day, many legal systems struggle to maintain these essential elements as part of their criminal justice systems.

In Beccaria's essay (1963 [1764]), it is possible to identify four general and grand principles that epitomize the classical doctrine.

1. *Equality*: All will be treated equally if law is strictly and objectively interpreted. In the classical sense, there can be no consideration of personal character, no entertainment of motive, and no justification for individualized punishment when trying a criminal case. As Beccaria notes, "the measure of punishment is not the sensibility of the crime, but the public injury" (ibid.:70).

2. *Liberty*: We have the inalienable right to be protected from the potential abuses of power by the state. Beccaria states, "only the law can decree punishment for crime" (ibid.:13). As well, the law cannot be applied retroactively, and there can be no punishment without law—"nor can society deprive him of public protection before it has been decided that he has in fact violated the conditions" (ibid.:30).

3. *Utilitarianism*: The major goal of the sovereign is the greatest happiness for the greatest number. Hence, justice should entail utility rather than retaliation and retribution; punishment is to be useful "to instil fear in other men" (ibid.). Therefore, as noted above, punishment should be viewed as a deterrent. Only by ensuring the conditions of certainty, swiftness, and severity is it possible to achieve the maximum deterrent efficiency. "The severity of the punishment of itself emboldens men to commit the very wrong it is supposed to prevent" (ibid.:43); therefore, "it is better to prevent crimes than to punish them. This is the ultimate end of every good legislation" (ibid.:93).

4. *Humanitarianism*: Punishment should be not only fair but humane. Beccaria was opposed to torture and cruel punishment (see ibid.:30–36), and he was against the death penalty (see ibid.:45–52): "This useless prodigality of torments" (ibid.:45) for "[i]t is not the intensity of punishment that has the greatest effect . . . but its duration" (ibid.:46–47).

An Enduring Influence

It has been over 200 years since Beccaria's classic work was first published, and yet it continues to command several pages in virtually every introductory criminology textbook. His fundamental principles still represent the foundation on which social policy in Canada, and in many other countries, is based.

His work, however, has not gone unchallenged (see, for example, Newman & Marongiu, 1990). Criticism should take into account, though, that Beccaria wrote his essay in a time of considerable turmoil, when the scientific technique of gathering objective data to support one's views was not yet in vogue. Furthermore, it was not, apparently, his intention to produce a theory on penal justice (Maconochesi, 1973).

In summary, Beccaria's enduring influence on justice policy and the foundation his work gave to social control theories, social learning theories, and rational choice theories should not be overlooked. His enduring influence on criminology arguably places him in a league by himself and renders him worthy of respect and careful reading to this day.

Many others have carried forward Beccaria's ideas, among them **Jeremy Bentham** (1748–1832) (see Box 4.2). In his *Introduction to the Principles of Morals and Legislation*,

---

DETERRENCE CONCEPTS AND THEORY

Deterrence theory, a fundamental dictum of the classical school, is based on the premise that individuals have free will and that they are rational in their thinking. Proponents of the deterrence theory also base their ideas on learning theory principles.

Zimring and Hawkins (1975) identified two distinct levels of deterrence: The first is *specific*—it focuses on the individual offender by punishing the offender. Offenders learn from their exposure, referred to as *associational learning*: one learns to associate a specific painful stimulus with a specific behaviour pattern. The second level of deterrence is *general*, which refers to the deterrence of non-criminals from any possible future criminal activity. This is *imitative learning*. Through the principles of certainty, swiftness, and severity of punishment, people in general will be deterred from wanting to commit crime. There may, however, be "conditional" circumstances in which legal threats affect only those who are interested in conforming to the norms of society (see Sherman et al., 1992).

published in 1789, Bentham developed the foundation of **utilitarianism**—"the greatest happiness of the greatest number." Like Beccaria, he subscribed to the concept of free will. He argued that people weigh the probabilities of pleasure against the risk of present and future pain. In recognizing the complexity of the process involved in decision-making, Bentham developed a quasi-mathematical formula for calculating how much pain was needed to deter someone from committing an offence. He referred to his formula as *felicitous calculus* (moral calculus) (Geis, 1973). But, as DeKeseredy and Schwartz (1996:164) observed, it might more appropriately be termed "interesting guesswork."

Evaluation of the Classical School

It all sounds good, you may say, but does the fear of punishment really prevent crime? Can criminals be rehabilitated? Attempts to answer these questions have produced many publications, textbooks, and "new and better" programs. This is not the place to try to do justice to such a loaded issue, but a brief observation is warranted at this point.

Overall, the research on deterrence is inconclusive (Paternoster, Saltzman, Waldo, & Chiricos, 1983; Winterdyk, 2000). Some of the earlier studies reported that under certain circumstances, it does appear to work (see Gibbs, 1975). Williams and Hawkins

(1986) found that the fear of arrest could act as a deterrent, especially when linked to the indirect social penalties of arrest. They identified three types of social costs:

1. *Commitment costs*: Arrests may have an adverse effect on future opportunities such as employment.
2. *Attachment costs*: Arrests can result in harm to, or loss of, personal circumstances.
3. *Stigma*: Arrests can negatively affect one's personal and/or public image.

Overall, however, based on his review of the deterrence literature, Akers (1994:55) concludes that the correlations found "between the perceptions of risk and subsequent offenses are too weak to validate deterrence theory." Even when a modified version of the deterrence theory (e.g., Ronald Clarke's rational choice theory) came into vogue, the empirical evidence was limited by the inability of the theory's supporters to clearly define the concepts of "reasoning criminal" or the "rational component" in crime (ibid.).

Although the Canadian public feels generally that the law reflects its values, we tend to be less optimistic about whether the laws are enforced equally (Brillon, 1987). In fact, when there is a high risk of apprehension, the administration of punishment deterrence is likely to have some impact. However, when the risk of sanction is low, deterrence has a limited impact.

As for reforming and rehabilitating criminals, the classical doctrine has met with yet another nemesis. "Success" of punishment or correctional practices is often measured by recidivism, or relapse into crime. Aside from methodological and definitional issues, recidivism rates among both adults and young offenders across Canada are not promising.

Perhaps the most influential modern-day revisionist of the role of punishment has been **Michel Foucault** (1926–1984). Many of his ideas about the role of punishment can be found in his 1977 book *Discipline and Punish*. The essence of his argument is that punishment should not be seen simply as "the independent development of legal or economic institutions" (Barak, 1998:87). Rather, punishment, he argues, is an interrelationship between power, knowledge, and the body that is affected by such factors as economics, social development, political ideologies, and changing mass communication (ibid.).

In spite of its various useful attributes, the classical perspective failed to acknowledge individual differences, motivation, and situational circumstances (Geis, 1973). For example, if you are caught speeding because you are rushing a dying or injured person to the hospital, should you incur the same penalty as when you are speeding simply for pleasure? Similarly, should a woman who kills her partner after years of being physically abused receive the same punishment as someone who kills for greed? Some might argue that "the law is the law" (remember Beccaria's principle of equality), while others might beg for some compassion and discretion when examining certain incident. Mannheim perhaps best summarized the problem with the classical perspective when he said that it is "too static and sterile to guide further progress" (1973:35). These types of issues gave rise to the neoclassical perspective. Before moving on, however, let us take a brief look at the influence that the classical perspective has had on Canadian criminal justice policies.

The Influence of Classical School on Canadian Criminal Justice Policies

Attempts to control crime through the classical doctrines fell short of their good intentions and sound rationales. Nevertheless, some of the major concepts derived from the school are entrenched in the *Canadian Constitution*, the *Criminal Code*, and the *Youth Criminal Justice Act*. These include:

- The idea that humans have free will;
- The concept of utilitarianism;
- The existence of civil rights and due process of law;
- Rules of evidence and testimony;
- Being held accountable for one's misdeeds;
- Determinant sentences;
- The swiftness and certainty of punishment;
- The threat of punishment serving as a deterrent; and
- No justification for capital punishment.

These elements reflect the emphasis on fair and proportionate punishment and have been embraced by the legal system in the ideas of due process and just deserts.

Neoclassical Criminology

The concepts of the **neoclassical school** of thought were first incorporated in the French Penal Code of 1791. Although its assumptions have remained the cornerstone of criminal justice policy, from a criminological perspective the neoclassical school did not receive much attention until the 1980s and 1990s. This revival occurred in response to the failure of rehabilitation and a public outcry for a return to harsher punishments (DeKeseredy & Schwartz, 1996). The public began to demand lengthier prison terms, a return to corporal punishment, and even a reinstatement of capital punishment—a **just deserts** model—and favoured rational choice explanations (see Box 4.4). It generally felt that punishment should fit the crime—a concept in keeping with the classical school.

Spawned by the limitations and criticisms levied at the classical school, the ideas of the neoclassical school were pioneered by Luigi Rossi in Italy and Philip Garraud and Henri Joly in France. While endorsing the major principles of the classical school, this new perspective entailed two fundamental exceptions:

1. Rejection of the rigidity of the classical system of punishment; and
2. A degree of subjectivity when assessing criminal responsibility—that is, **discretion**.

THE SINGAPORE EXPERIMENT

Singapore has one of the most punitive penal codes in the world. In 1994, Singapore drew considerable media attention when Michael Fay, a native of Ohio (then 18 years of age), was detained for defacing automobiles with spray paint. Fay received four lashes after a four-month prison sentence. While the media debated the severity and rationale of corporal punishment, the decline in the crime rates suggests that—it works! The overall crime rates of the United States run between 200 percent and 380 percent higher than those in Singapore (Weichman, 1994). However, while the overall crime rate in the United States decreased from 1988 through 1993, the number of youth crimes increased by almost 30 percent. More than a third of young offenders were caught shoplifting, and about 1 in 10 youths were arrested for stealing. According to official sources, in 2001–2002, Singapore reported a decline in its crime rate for the 11th year in a row—down to 693 per 100 000. Is there merit in the classical approach?

The French Penal Code of 1804–1811 was the first legal code to incorporate these ideas. The Canadian *Criminal Code* has also been written following neoclassical principles.

The neoclassical perspective assumes that individuals choose to commit a crime after calculating whether the crime's potential rewards outweigh its potential risks (Cornish & Clarke, 1986). Today, the neoclassical perspective is generally grouped under the rubric of rational choice theory. The neoclassical perspective assumes that criminals base their decisions on the perceived attractiveness of a target, the absence of guardianship, and level of motivation (Clarke & Felson, 1993).

James Q. Wilson, David Fogel, and Ernest van den Haag have been instrumental in the revival of neoclassical thinking. For example, many of Wilson's ideas and arguments can be found in his frequently cited book *Thinking About Crime* (1975). Wilson argues that since we cannot seem to identify the root causes of crime, policy-makers should direct their attention to better deterring people from committing crimes. This is very much in line with the writings of Beccaria and Bentham. For example, Wilson agrees that punishment should be both swift and certain and that it should be proportionate to the severity of the crime.

However, none of the classical or neoclassical scholars have defined how one measures the degree of seriousness of a crime. Is this a moral issue that implies that crimes are not constant but relative to time and place? Could the seriousness of a crime change with circumstances? For example, during times of war, killing is considered acceptable.

Wilson is less concerned with severity than with certainty and swiftness, because the more Draconian (see Box 4.5) the sentence, the greater the chances for a plea bargain

(Wilson, 1995). A plea bargain is characteristic of the neoclassical approach; it provides an opportunity for the defence and Crown to reach an arrangement in which the accused agrees to plead guilty for certain considerations (Cousineau & Verdun-Jones, 1979).

DRACONIAN LAW AND CAPITAL PUNISHMENT

In 621 BC, Athenian law was codified by the Greek statesman Draco. The codification brought greater equality to all Greeks as the lower class was given the right to vote. Considering this, one may wonder why the term "Draconian law" carries such pejorative connotations. This is easily explained: Draco's codification prescribed death for most criminal offences (Bedau, 1996).

Reference to capital punishment can be found in the Code of Hammurabi, Mosaic Law, and even the Bible, which prescribes death for more than 30 different crimes ranging from murder (see Exodus 21:12) to fornication (see Deuteronomy 22:13) (Bedau, 1996). Canada practised capital punishment until 1976; the last execution took place in 1962 at the Don Jail in Toronto. And although the murder rate increased by nearly 70 percent between 1962 and 1975, the rate had decreased some 30 percent as we entered the new millenium. In 1999, MP John Reynolds of the Reform Party introduced a private member's bill in an effort to bring back capital punishment. In 2001, the Supreme Court of Canada rejected the death penalty as an acceptable element of criminal justice. Even though well-known Canadian criminal lawyer Clayton Ruby notes the reinstatement of capital punishment would be a violation of section 7 of the Charter of Rights and Freedoms, various conservative groups, including the Canadian Association of Chiefs of Police, would still welcome its reinstatement (Canada and the death penalty, 2004).

The death penalty is still in effect in 38 US states—in 2002, there were 3557 inmates on death row. Since January 1, 1973, only 227 people have been granted clemency on humanitarian grounds. And while over 70 percent of Americans continue to support capital punishment (in 2003, Texas executed 33 people), one of the most dramatic shifts in the political landscape came in January 2003, when Illinois governor George Ryan began to empty the state's death row cells.

Whether capital punishment is a Draconian or "cruel and unusual" form of punishment or whether it is a "punishment fitting of the crime" has been subject to numerous philosophical and moral arguments. An Ipsos opinion poll in 2001 revealed that only 52 percent of Canadians support the reinstatement of capital punishment—down from 69 percent in 1995. Residents of Alberta expressed the strongest support (64 percent), while residents of Quebec expressed the weakest support (42 percent). In Ontario and Atlantic Canada, support hovered around 52 percent (Support..., 2001).

How do you feel about the use of capital punishment? Can, or should, it be justified under certain circumstances?

Today, those interested in the neoclassical perspective are mainly economists (DeKeseredy & Schwartz, 1996). Assuming people are rational and calculating, all that differentiates a criminal from a non-criminal is the degree to which an individual feels that the benefits of a criminal act outweigh its cost. An economist might suggest, for example, that the reason property crime is more prevalent than violent crime is that the chances of being caught are considerably less. In addition, the neoclassical perspective is closely aligned with deterrence theory, which assumes that "good" laws (i.e., those involving punishment) can deter criminals. Therefore, the current orientation of the neoclassical perspective is to stress the deterrent effect of punishment. Imprisonment can be justified on the grounds that removal of liberty and social comforts can and should be severe enough to deter not only the specific offender but anyone who might even remotely think about committing a crime.

As mentioned earlier, the literature on deterrence, both specific and general, has not confirmed its effectiveness. Various government studies have shown that approximately 40 percent of prisoners return to their former life of crime on release. In the United States, despite the existence of capital punishment for certain serious offences, these offences are still being committed. In 1995–1996, Ontario and British Columbia introduced zero tolerance for speeding—but people still speed. Cigarette packages clearly advertise the negative consequences of smoking—but statistics show that smoking has increased among young people (McKie & Thompson, 1989). Is there an alternative?

The Italian Positivist School of Criminology

The Roots of Positivism: The Statistical School

Before the emergence of the Italian positivist school, research on crime oriented in that theoretical direction had already been conducted by Adolphe Quetelet (1796–1874) of Belgium and André-Michel Guerry (1802–1866) of France. Both of them were statisticians, and they examined the *social statistics* on information that was available. Their line of inquiry was the forerunner of the *ecological school*. They observed "variations in crime rates by climate and season and...the same age and sex differences we find among criminals today" (Williams & McShane, 1994:3).

Other pre–Italian positivistic research included scientifically oriented studies such as those of Jean Baptiste della Porte (1535–1615), who examined the relationship between body characteristics and crime. He is generally considered to be the founder of human physiognomy (the art of judging character from features of face and form of body). Francis Gall (1758–1828) studied the relationship between the external conformation of the brain and behaviour. This "science" is referred to as *phrenology*. Gall and

Johann Spurzheim (1776–1832) collaborated to map the relationship of bumps on the head to behaviour, especially abnormal behaviour. Spurzheim later acknowledged that the bumps were predisposing factors and that free will could be a mediating factor.[3]

Toward the latter half of the 19th century, a unique form of positivism began to emerge in Italy. The French sociologist and philosopher **Auguste Comte** (1798–1857) is generally credited with coining the term "positivism" and is recognized as the father of sociology. He used the term "positivist" to describe what he considered the final social developmental stage, occurring when people embrace a rational, scientific view of the world, as opposed to relying on metaphysical explanations (Williams & McShane, 1994, 1999).

Cesare Lombroso and His Colleagues

In criminology, the **positivist school** was first embraced by the holy three of criminology—**Cesare Lombroso** (1835–1909), **Raffaele Garofalo** (1851–1934), and **Enrico Ferri** (1856–1929). It is Lombroso (see Box 4.6), however, who is most often recognized as the father of modern criminology. As noted above, other researchers before him had applied the scientific method to identify criminals, but it was Lombroso who focused exclusively on criminals.

Lombroso's ideas of criminality were influenced by Charles Darwin's evolutionary theory, Rudolf Virchow's ideas on organic regression, and Paul Broca's methods of describing and classifying anatomical features. To make sense of these ideas, Lombroso grounded his thinking in Comptian positivism, which emphasized the need for observable and measurable facts. Lombroso developed his biological deterministic theory of criminality based on the concept of **atavism**. He used the term to characterize those individuals who, based on some morphological (that is, bodily) characteristics, were considered not fully evolved. They were throwbacks to a more primitive time. Lombroso believed that the cause was hereditary. Among the physical malformations (he called them "criminal stigmata"), he catalogued the asymmetric face, excessive jaw, eye defects, large nose, large ears, receding forehead, long arms, and swollen lips. These physical anomalies could be inherited or indirectly manifested because of insanity, syphilis, epilepsy, or alcoholism (Martin et al., 1990) and could render the person incapable of living within the social norms of society. The fact that some physical anomalies can indirectly contribute to criminal behaviour reflects Lombroso's recognition that environment can also play a role in an individual's development. In many respects, Lombroso was the first true interdisciplinary criminological thinker, as he acknowledged the role of the environment and the physical person.

Lombroso's criminal typology involved four main categories:

1. The *born criminal*. This term, which was coined by Ferri, was used to describe criminals who were born moral imbeciles and epileptics. Born criminals supposedly accounted for one-third of all criminals.

CESARE LOMBROSO—"THE FATHER OF MODERN CRIMINOLOGY"

In his account of Lombroso, Marvin Wolfgang (1973:232) notes that "in the history of criminology probably no name has been eulogized or attacked so much.... More has been written by and about Lombroso than any other criminologist."

In 1859, at the age of 24, Lombroso obtained a medical degree with a specialty in surgery from the University of Genoa. Upon graduating, he volunteered as an army physician. With time on his hands, he decided to take anatomical measurements of soldiers as a possible way of determining from which region of Italy they came. During the course of observing over 3000 soldiers, he found a positive correlation between soldiers who had tattoos and those who were involved in some type of military or civilian rule infractions. He later obtained permission to study mental patients and began to solidify his theory of criminality. Many of his ideas and observations were first published in *L'uomo delinquente* (*The Criminal Man*) in 1876. By its fifth and final edition in 1896, the book had been expanded from 256 to 1903 pages and had received international acclaim (Schafer, 1976).

It was at the University of Turin, with the assistance of two students, Garofalo and Ferri, that Lombroso refined his general theory that criminals are distinguishable from non-criminals by different physical anomalies, which he considered to be atavistic or degenerative in origin. He would also later collaborate with William Ferrero, his daughter Gina's husband, to write the first book on female offenders. It was simply called *The Female Offender* (Wolfgang, 1973).

By all accounts, Lombroso was a celebrated, much sought after man. In fact 1908, he was asked to join the faculty of the Northwestern University in Chicago but was not able to accept the position due to ill health. On October 19, 1909, he passed away. As requested, his brain was placed in the Institute of Anatomy at the University of Turin.

2. The *criminal by passion*. This term was used mainly to describe female offenders. Criminals by passion commit crimes based on their "pure spirit of altruism"—for example, the brother who kills the man who raped his sister, or the wife who kills her unfaithful husband. Lombroso also noted that, because of their nature, these criminals suffer more from remorse than from the penalty of the law. Criminals by passion are more likely to commit suicide after the crime.

3. The *insane criminal*. Insane criminals commit crimes because they lack the mental capacity to understand or appreciate their acts. Kleptomaniacs, nymphomaniacs, imbeciles, and habitual drunkards are in this category. They tend to commit cruel, impulsive, and obscene acts.

4. The *occasional criminal*. This type has four sub-types. *Pseudocriminals* break the law by accident; *criminaloids* have weak dispositions; *habitual criminals'* constitution predisposes them to crime, and factors such as poor education, poor family upbringing, and other environmental circumstances can bring on criminal tendencies; and *epileptoids* are those who suffer from epilepsy, which becomes "the morbid condition" that serves to explain the pathological non-atavistic phenomena (Wolfgang, 1973:253) (see Box 4.7).

It is interesting to note that while Lombroso's findings have been largely discredited, the impact of the scientific method and possible deterministic or "soft" deterministic links to criminality have spawned numerous theories. Most notable among these are theories based on biological and psychological principles (see Chapters 5 and 6).

Ferri and Garofalo, both lawyers by training, not only contributed to Lombroso's ideas but also introduced some significant elements into the conception of criminal causality. For example, aside from coining the term "born criminal," which Lombroso was happy to embrace, Ferri argued that crime was caused by factors that were physical (e.g., race, geography, temperature, and climate), anthropological (e.g., age, gender, organic, and psychological factors), and social (e.g., customs, economic conditions, population density, and religion) (Williams & McShane, 2004:34).

Evaluation of the Positivist School

Which came first, the chicken or the egg? Or, in the case of traditional criminology, what is more important when trying to prevent crime: (1) changing social conditions, such as lack of opportunity, peer pressure, and early childhood socialization, through the classical model that relies on social reform via the law; or (2) changing individual factors, such as diet, drugs, alcohol, or genetic or constitutional conditions, through treatment strategies? Is there such a thing as a "criminal type" or a "constitutional crime marker"?

Both the classical and positivist schools have supporters and both continue to have an impact on the operations of the criminal justice system and research venues of criminologists today. And although Hackler (1994:109) suggests that "neither of these schools serve us well in terms of reducing crime," positivist ideas continue to have an impact on the trial process. In recent years, judges have become more willing to consider genetic conditions, dietary influences, and biochemical imbalances. Correction programs continue to experiment with "better" treatment programs such as those for particular types of offenders. In addition, young offenders continue to receive "special" treatment under the *parens patriae* doctrine (from the Latin meaning "parent of his country"), where the state acts as the guardian of minors and incompetent people—a concept derived directly from the positivist school of thought. Under English common law, the doctrine held the monarch responsible for those individuals who were deemed unable to abide by the law. This doctrine was later entrenched in the *Juvenile Delinquents Act* of 1908, which granted juvenile courts procedural rights to deal informally with young offenders in the same way as their parents would have. In addition, crime-fighting strategies such as social engineering (e.g., increased street lighting and the provision of health services and subsidized housing for the poor) are based on deterministic principles. Finally, with the emergence and growing acceptance of an interdisciplinary perspective, recent positivist-based research in the biosocial, bioenvironmental, and biopsychological areas, as well as in urban planning, has resulted in some promising findings (see Chapter 5). Some of the recent lines of inquiry that are positivist in character include sociobiology (Mednick & Christiansen, 1977) and evolutive theory (Ellis, 1982, 1988).

Nevertheless, biological, psychological, and sociological **determinism** continues to be challenged on four key issues:

- Weakness of methodology;
- Limited application to the understanding of white-collar crime, organized crime, and political crime;
- A general fear that positivist-based policies will be intrusive and possibly lead to totalitarianism; and
- The failure to distinguish clearly between the role of environment and heredity (Schafer, 1976).

In summary, the battle between law and science (free will and determinism) may not have lived up to all the expectations of either side, but the struggle has nonetheless had a major impact on criminology, criminological thought, and criminal justice.

Law vs. Science

By the turn of the 20th century the two primary schools of criminological thought had forged their identities and made their mark on how we view criminology and criminal justice. Table 4–1 illustrates how their principles have become integral characteristics of the criminal justice system.

Classicism is based on reforming criminal law and maintaining social order through criminal responsibility. It assumes that individuals are capable of intent (free will) and that punishment is therefore justified on the grounds of moral guilt and a criminal mind. Retribution and revenge are the traditional objectives of criminal law under the classical school of thought.

Positivism is an outgrowth of the scientific revolution. It embraces determinism. Someone who may not be fully capable of controlling his or her criminal actions may require special consideration and conditioning. Positivists subscribe to the doctrines of reform and rehabilitation. Scientific criminology (i.e., positivists) has given us juvenile court, parole and probation, indeterminate sentences, and special "correctional" programs for different types of offenders (e.g., sex offenders, compulsive gamblers, and shoplifters).

TABLE 4–1

LAW AND SCIENCE IN CONFLICT

Classical ideology as the basis of the criminal justice system (law)	Positivist ideology as the basis of criminology (science)
• enforce the law	• rehabilitation—mitigating circumstances
• maintain order	• best interest
• minimal discretion	• individual/public
• "follow the book"	
• apprehension	
• guilt or innocence	
• due process	
• legal rights	

Although Table 4–1 may suggest that there are two schools of thought present, operationally the criminal justice system is based on the classical legal doctrine. For example, even today, police and lawyers make decisions based on the law first, and they seldom acknowledge human nature or information from other behavioural sciences (Brantingham & Brantingham, 1984). While mandated to offer special rehabilitation and reform programs, corrections systems are usually underfunded, have insufficiently trained staff, and are overcrowded to adequately execute individualized and group treatment programs (Ekstedt & Jackson, 1997). In contrast, criminological ideas and research, are based on the scientific and positivist models and are interested in the etiology of crime and criminals.

This dualism has created conflict between the criminal justice system (i.e., law) and criminology (i.e., science). As Jeffery (1973), along with others, has noted, historically there has been a lack of theoretical integration between law and science. From Table 4–1 it can also be seen that there is no common integrated model of criminal justice by which the primary agencies operate toward a common goal through common strategies. It is essential for students studying criminology to recognize these inherent conflicts, as they play a significant role in how we study crime and criminal behaviour.

A Move Toward an Integrated School of Thought

Criminology must find a way to integrate these theoretical differences. Even though crime has been a major concern since the late 1970s, there are few positive outcomes of the expensive programs instituted to deal with crime and criminals. Crime rates, for the most part, have been steadily escalating since the early 1960s, and the per capita cost of maintaining the Canadian criminal justice system increases each year.

As has been already suggested, what is needed is an interdisciplinary approach that can study crime and criminality scientifically. Sociologists and psychologists need to know and work with the law and lawyers, while lawyers need to know the behavioural sciences. Most criminology programs across the country are staffed by people from a variety of disciplinary backgrounds. These have the foundation to offer interdisciplinary training to students. The common interdisciplinary approach that should be adopted by all programs is one that addresses the problem of crime and criminals through prevention.

Pioneers of Criminology and Criminal Justice

Before we delve further into this new, emerging criminological perspective, let us take a look at some of the pioneers who have helped shape the discipline and influenced our thinking about crime, criminality, and criminal justice.

Following the reasoning of Jeffery (1973), the pioneers are presented in chronological order, rather than in sections dealing with particular schools of thought. For practical reasons, this list of important figures has been abbreviated, but every attempt has been made to acknowledge most of the major sub-areas within criminology. However, it is these pioneers' contributions to criminological reform that are of primary interest. Box 4.8 provides an overview of a brief sample of some of the "Canadian" pioneers in criminology.

PROFILE BOX 4.8

"CANADIAN" PIONEERS OF CRIMINOLOGY

The word "Canadian" appears in quotation marks because most of the pioneers featured here are first-generation Canadians. Their varied international experience has had a noticeable impact on Canadian criminology and criminal justice.

Denis Szabo (1929–)—*The father of Canadian criminology.* Born and raised in Budapest, Hungary, Szabo received his education and training in Hungary and Belgium. Upon graduating, he taught sociology in France until 1958, when he joined the sociology department at the University of Montreal. In 1960, Szabo established the first criminology program in Canada. Since then, the program has flourished and, along with its research centre that Szabo founded in 1969, has become internationally recognized. In 1969, Szabo also founded the journal *Criminologie*. He has received numerous international awards, including the distinguished Sutherland award from the American Society of Criminology. He believes that criminology is inseparable from criminal policy.

Ezzat A. Fattah (1929–)—*Pioneer of victimology and champion of restorative justice*. Originally from Egypt, Fattah left his legal practice in the late 1950s to study under Professor Roland Grassberger, then director of the Institute of Criminology at the University of Vienna. Under Grassberger, he became interested in victimology. In 1964, he accepted a position at the University of Montreal to further his studies under Henri Ellenberger in the school of criminology and continued his work in the area of victimology. In 1974, Fattah was invited to set up a criminology program at Simon Fraser University—the first in Western Canada. Today, it is the largest English-language program in Canada, with over 25 full-time faculty. In addition to his contribution to victimology, Fattah has been a champion of human rights. He has been actively involved in Amnesty International and was instrumental in having the death penalty repealed. More recently, he has been involved in various restorative justice initiatives. Although he retired in 1997, he continues to be a prolific writer and travels extensively, sharing his ideas and views on human justice.

Tadeusz Grygier (1915–). *Champion of the social protection code*. Born and raised in Poland, Grygier became a Soviet prisoner and was sent to a gulag during World War II. The experience played a significant role in his life. After his release, he studied at the London School of Economics under the likes of Herman Mannheim (law and criminology), Sir Karl Popper (philosophy and statistics), and Sir Raymond Firth (anthropology). His doctoral thesis received considerable acclaim and helped him obtain a position in the criminology program at the University of Toronto. In 1967, Grygier moved to the University of Ottawa, where he set up a research centre in criminology and started a master's program in criminology and a professional degree program in correctional administration. In 1980, he was instrumental in establishing the school's undergraduate program in criminology. His academic interests have been diverse but almost always have focused on social justice, fair sentencing, and correctional practices. As he noted, "a criminal law oriented to the past cannot help us to build a just, peaceful and safe society."

Paul (1943–) and **Patricia** (1943–) **Brantingham**—*Environmental criminologists*. These two contemporary pioneers hail from the United States. Patricia studied mathematics and urban planning, while Paul obtained a Juris Doctor degree and a criminology diploma from Cambridge. After their paths crossed, they combined their knowledge of planning, criminology, and math and applied it to the study of the environment and of how it structures and shapes crime. Together, they developed the field of environmental criminology and the pattern theory of crime. When they moved to Canada in 1977, they joined the school of criminology at Simon Fraser University and

Prison Reform

Earlier it was noted that corrections and incarceration have not always been as we know them today. One pioneer who had a very measurable impact on penal reform is Scottish-born Captain **Alexander Maconochie** (1787–1860). In Australia, he is probably best remembered for his services at the prison colony at Van Dieman's Land on Tasmania and Norfolk Island in the Southwest Pacific. It was while serving in Tasmania as the private secretary to Van Dieman's Land lieutenant-governor, Sir John Franklin, that Maconochie formulated many of his penal reform policies, many of which were adopted and put into practice.

The treatment and transportation of English convicts to Van Dieman, which Maconochie witnessed first-hand, prompted him to point out "that cruel and harsh punishment debase not only the victim, but also the society which employs them... rather the objective be to reform the offender so that he should leave prison capable of useful citizenship, and a better man than when he entered the prison gates" (Barry, 1973:86–87). In his various writings, Maconochie put forth five ideas of prison reform, which were considered novel at the time. They were as follows:

1. Sentences should not be measured by time, but by the ability of a prisoner to complete a specified quantity of labour.
2. The quantity of labour should be determined by the gravity of the offence and the degree to which the prisoner improves himself.
3. While in prison, a prisoner should earn everything he receives.
4. When working in groups, all prisoners should be answerable for each other's conduct.
5. As a prisoner nears his release date, attention should be given to preparing him for release into society.

During his service, Maconochie introduced various novel practices, such as allowing prisoners to use proper utensils, providing educational and spiritual services, and granting other privileges. In essence, Maconochie recognized that prison was not a place to punish but a place where one served one's punishment. Barry (1973) summarizes Maconochie's major contribution in four points: (1) reward—prisoners must earn their release through industrious labour and good conduct; (2) individual influence— if they are to offer constructive support, prisons should not exceed 300 persons, or 100 for more serious offenders; (3) prisons should provide opportunities for gradual approximation of release (e.g., half-way houses); and (4) there should be strict supervision after discharge (see Box 4.9).

FYI BOX 4.9

CONFINEMENT IN CANADA

The building of Kingston Penitentiary, in 1835, marked the beginning of the prison industry in Canada. Before it was built, there was considerable debate over whether confinement should be viewed as punishment or an opportunity for reformation. The Brown Commission, of 1848–1849, produced the first major report calling for more humane treatment of prisoners.

Many of Maconochie's ideas of penal reform have found their way into Canada's penal history at one time or another, and his contributions are of utmost importance. However, other reformers have also made their mark in the history of penal reform. For example, John Haviland (1792–1852) gave us the radical model, which was used in building a number of the earlier prisons in Canada, and **John Howard** (1726–1790) (see Box 4.10) was instrumental in the establishment of prisoner advocacy groups. The writings of the French lawyer Charles Lucas (1803–1889) set the foundation for a system of maximum and minimum sentences and a system for the classification of prisoners. Lucas also emphasized the need to separate adults from young offenders (Normandeau, 1973). Many of his ideas can be seen today in Canada's correctional system (see Griffiths, 2004).

PROFILE BOX 4.10

JOHN HOWARD

Although the exact date of his birth is uncertain, John Howard was born into a life of financial independence and became a generous philanthropist. However, his life was not an easy one, as he experienced a number of personal hardships and had to deal with a frail and sickly constitution (Schafer, 1976). His poor health and unfortunate life experiences seemed to strengthen his determination to improve the well-being of others less fortunate.

Howard's experiences with prisons began in 1755 while he was en route to Lisbon, Portugal, to help earthquake victims. Captured by the French, who were at war with

---

England, Howard spent time in the dungeons at Brest castle and then in the prison in Morlaix. Upon his release, he returned to England and was elected high sheriff of Bedfordshire. He used the opportunity afforded by his position to study English prisons as well as those in Belgium, France, the Netherlands, Germany, and Switzerland. The experience left him distraught. On his return to England in 1777, he wrote and self-published his now famous book, *The State of the Prisons*. In it, he called for the classification of prisoners according to their risk of reoffending, the introduction of vocational training, the provision of opportunities for constructive work experiences for prisoners, and the general humane treatment of inmates.

Howard's interest in prison reform led to his second trip to Europe. While in Russia he contracted and subsequently died of cholera. His death did not go unnoticed. A statue of Howard was erected in St. Paul's Cathedral in London, and the organization most commonly associated with prisoner advocacy groups, the John Howard Society, is a living testament to the significance of his pioneering ideas.

Modern Law Enforcement

Policing in the Western world can be traced back to around 1035, when the Danish King Canute set up a system in which all males over the age of 12 were bound by law to keep the peace. This was referred to as the *frankpledge*, and participants were members of a *tithing*, a small administrative division. Until the 18th century, law enforcement came under the rule of the sovereign and was somewhat informal in structure (see Box 4.11). With the advent of the Industrial Revolution, the problems society faced began to change. They could no longer be dealt with on an informal basis. The solution that emerged was the creation of a bureaucracy—the foundation of modern policing (see Stansfield, 1996).

FYI BOX 4.11

THE ROOTS OF POLICING

Some of the terms and phrases we use today had very practical origins. For example, remember those old Western movies where the sheriff rounded up his *posse comitatus*? This phrase, derived from Latin, means "power of the county," and the word "sheriff" is derived from the old English practice of the king appointing a representative, called a reeve, from each shire (county) to enforce the laws. This representative became known as the shire-reeve or sheriff. As for constables, they came into being in 1285 through the Statute of Winchester. A constable (derived from Latin and meaning "officer of the stable") assisted the king in suppressing riots and other violence.

Sir Robert Peel (1788–1850) is most often recognized for his ideas on policing, at least in the arenas of criminology and law enforcement; however, he had a distinguished career in other areas. Like so many great English thinkers, he was educated at Oxford University. After graduating, he became a successful politician. In fact, Peel was the British prime minister (for only four months) in 1834–1835. He is credited as the founder of the modern Conservative Party in England, and his political efforts in 1829 succeeded in granting Roman Catholics political equality (Stansfield, 1996).

From a criminological standpoint, Peel's most significant contribution came in 1829, when he reorganized the London metropolitan police force after a somewhat frustrating and less than successful attempt by Henry Fielding (1707–1754), the author of *Tom Jones*, to establish uniformed and armed officers (see also Box 4.12).

FYI BOX 4.12

EARLY POLICING IN CANADA

The first Canadian police force was established in Toronto in 1835. In addition to the responsibilities they have today, early Canadian police officers were also required to collect taxes, serve as bailiffs, fight fires, and serve as jailers (Dantzker & Mitchell, 1998).

In re-establishing the London constabulary, Peel instituted uniforms and strict discipline, banned the bearing of firearms, and set up the fundamental principles still used in policing today. Some of the most important ones include (Normandeau & Leighton, 1990:140):

- The power of the police is dependent on public approval of the police's existence, actions, and behaviour.
- The police maintaining the respect of the public means securing the public's willing cooperation to observe and respect societal laws.
- The police must demonstrate absolute impartial service of law and readily offer individual service and friendship by exercising courtesy and friendly good humour.
- The police must use minimal force when trying to restore the law.
- The test of police efficiency is the absence of crime and disorder, and not the visible evidence of police action in dealing with them.

Peel's efforts met with considerable success. His officers became known as little *Roberts* or *bobbies*, and his system was adopted throughout England. Whether the expansion of police forces was necessary or whether it was simply an attempt by government and other power brokers to control and suppress the poor has been a subject of considerable debate.

By the 20th century, policing was well-established. Many principles from Anglo-Saxon times and Peel's criteria are entrenched in Canadian professional policing today.

Legal Aspects of Crime

Since the Hammurabi Code, law has been the cornerstone of the criminal justice system. Law is the formal means of maintaining social control, for without law there is no crime (*nulle crimen sine lege*), and without law there cannot be any punishment (*nulle poena sine lege*), two legal principles that can be traced back to the influential writings of Beccaria.

There have been many great legal reformers. Bentham introduced the principles of utilitarianism, while the American legal scholar Charles Doe's (1830–1896) writings helped clarify the meaning of criminal responsibility. Doe also called for medicine and law to work more closely together. Meanwhile, the writings of the Spanish legal scholar Pedro Montero (1861–1919) had a significant impact on North American law. Montero argued that the judiciary should be preventive in nature and that judges and lawyers should be trained in the social sciences—especially sociology and psychology—in order to better prevent crime and cure criminals.

Perhaps one of the more enduring pioneers was the American **Isaac Ray** (1807–1881), who has been described as "the most influential American writer on forensic psychiatry during the whole nineteenth century" (Overholser, 1973:177). Prior to his work, law was interpreted strictly; there were few legal provisions under which the courts would entertain mitigating circumstances, as law was essentially based on classical doctrine. In one of his early articles, Ray charged the legal profession with failing to recognize the importance of medical evidence. He wrote that the legal definition of insanity was too limited in its scope and that lawyers were ill-equipped to assess such a mental disorder. Expert testimony in cases involving insanity pleas was needed.

Being a staunch supporter of phrenology, Ray developed a line of reasoning based on a medical diagnosis that came to have a major impact on jurisprudence. In an 1835 article, he argued that criminals could experience periods during which their ability to reason was temporarily interrupted. However, this state—to which he referred to as the state of **moral insanity**—could be treated as a form of medical illness (see Box 4.13). He thought that such states could be related to the study of phrenology, and he posited that perhaps the brain was compartmentalized. While a person might act rationally in one situation, the same person might behave quite differently in others.

FYI BOX 4.13

REDEFINING INSANITY IN CANADA

Since 1992, claiming "insanity" is no longer a true defence in Canada. Under section 672 of the *Criminal Code*, an accused can be found "not criminally responsible on account of mental disorder."

Although not without his critics (see Overholser, 1973), Ray drew the attention of many legal scholars. In addition to being one of the founders of the American Psychiatric Association (APA) in 1844, Ray contributed to the bridging of the gap between law and medicine. In recognition of his contribution, the APA annually gives out an award to a lawyer or psychiatrist who promotes a closer working relationship between law and medicine—a truly integrated and interdisciplinary approach.

One scholar who was influenced by Ray, Judge Charles Doe, later wrote the decision that is now referred to as the New Hampshire Rule (see Box 4.14). This rule is still followed by a number of states when insanity is at issue in criminal cases, though since 1954, the Durham rule offers a more simplified means to the adjudication of mentally ill offenders. Both these rules can trace their roots to Isaac Ray and his enduring efforts to improve jurisprudence, not only through medicine but also through science in general.

A CLOSER LOOK BOX 4.14

THE NEW HAMPSHIRE RULE AND THE M'NAUGHTEN RULE

The New Hampshire rule, written by New Hampshire Supreme Court judge Charles Doe (1830–1896), was seen as an improvement on the M'Naughten Rule of 1843. The M'Naughten Rule allowed a plea of insanity but failed to provide any clear legal definition or universally applicable test of irrational reasoning. Daniel M'Naughten, a British citizen during Sir Robert Peel's premiership, was distraught over the prime minister's efforts to curtail human liberty. On January 20, 1843, M'Naughten attempted to kill Peel. The person he shot was not Peel but Peel's private secretary. The case drew wide attention, and M'Naughten was eventually acquitted by reason of insanity. The decision was based on the grounds that he had lost all self-control and had submitted to an "irresistible impulse."

Doe's New Hampshire rule refined the cognitive test for insanity and an irresistible impulse test as initially defined under the M'Naughten rule. Doe was the first American judge "to insist that the law should collaborate with science and particularly in the field of criminal responsibility" (Kenison, 1973:204). The New Hampshire rule was applied in 1954 in the case of *Durham v. the United States* and subsequently referred to as the Durham rule. The Canadian legal system uses the M'Naughten rule when mental disorder is at issue in criminal cases. One of the major criticisms is that regardless of the extent of one's mental disturbance, virtually everyone has some appreciation for the quality and rightness or wrongness of their act (see s. 16 and s. 672 of the Canadian *Criminal Code* for further legal clarification).

Criminalistics

Until recently, criminologists in North America gave little attention to what happens between the time of an offence and the sentencing or corrective processes. A review of several Canadian introductory criminology textbooks reveals no specific mention of this "relatively static phase...where only the administrators of social control...are in action" (Schafer, 1976:4). This aspect of the process has generally been seen as peripheral to criminology and the sub-field of criminal justice. Only when the process overlaps with criminal etiology and correctional theory have criminologists become involved. This negligence has resulted from the fact that for a long time sociology and psychology were deemed to be the only acceptable approaches to studying crime and criminality. However, to achieve an interdisciplinary perspective, criminology must embrace all aspects of social control.

Criminalistics refers to the use of scientific techniques in the detection and evaluation of criminal investigation. **Alphonse Bertillon** (1853–1914) is generally acknowledged as the first modern-day criminalist to develop the practice of *anthropometry*—that is, criminal identification. While working for the Paris police department, Bertillon refined and standardized the process of photo identification. The procedure involved positioning measuring guides beside suspects so that their physical characteristics (such as skeletal size and shape, ear form, etc.) could be determined. Photographs were then taken of both front views and profiles. Meanwhile, Sir Francis Galton (1822–1911), a cousin of Charles Darwin, popularized the use of fingerprints, which was officially adopted by Scotland Yard in 1901 (Saferstein, 1998). Although both techniques of identification have become modernized, they are still used today.

While North American criminologists focused on psychology and sociology, European criminology, has been dominated by the legal profession. Lawyer **Hans Gross** (1847–1915), born in Graz, Austria, observed that while the police were good at maintaining order, they were often less adept at solving crimes, often relying on evidence from informers who were also often engaged in criminal activity. Gross saw first-hand how poorly prepared many court cases were—there was often a serious lack of evidence. How could a case be fairly tried under such circumstances? Gross made the best of his position of "examining justice" (that is, a justice involved in criminal investigation) to gather information and formulate ideas in order to improve crime investigation techniques.

In 1883, after 13 years of careful research, Gross published his *Manual for the Examining Justice*, which eventually went to seven editions. Roland Grassberger (1973) described it as the pièce de résistance of its time. In the book, Gross says that every criminal case should be treated as a scientific problem, and every effort should be made to use and apply scientific investigation techniques in solving and resolving criminal cases. The manual provides detailed, articulate descriptions and illustrations for investigative strategies based on medicine, ballistics, chemistry, microscopy, physics, anthropometry, fingerprinting, serology, and several other relevant disciplines. Gross also argued that experts in these fields should testify in court. In addition, he developed several new methods of examining material evidence that technology has since refined (Grassberger, 1973).

The work of Hans Gross and Franz von Litz, among several other Austrian scholars, has been referred to as the Austrian school. Today, crime investigation techniques such as DNA matching, fingerprinting, photo identification, voiceprint identification, hair and fibre analysis, and crime scene analysis illustrate that Gross's pioneering work and ideas have become the heart of virtually all crime investigation practices.

Virtually every crime investigation today follows Gross's and his co-worker Ernst Seelig's seven golden rules of crime solving: who, what, where, when, why, how, and with what. These elements are more commonly referred to as the *modus operandi* of crime solving. As Grassberger (1973:316) concludes in his biographical account of Gross, scientific evidence "is the hope of any wrongfully-suspected person and it is feared by any offender conscious of guilt."

Beyond Social Defence

In 1973, Mannheim, referring to the work of French judge **Marc Ancel**, speculated that a third school of criminological thought might be emerging. It was called the school of social defence (see Box 4.15). The era of social defence emerged as a reaction against the prevailing retributive systems throughout Europe in the 1700s, through the writings of Rousseau, Voltaire, Beccaria, Bentham, and others (Schafer, 1976). Its principles were later adapted by the United Nations when it was formed in 1948 for "the prevention of crime and the treatment of offenders." C.R. Jeffery suggests that the concepts and principles of social defence might more accurately be described as the **neopositivist school**.

A CLOSER LOOK BOX 4.15

PRINCIPLES OF SOCIAL DEFENCE

1. Social defence is not deterministic.
2. It disapproves of a rigid classification of offenders into types, and stresses the uniqueness of human personality.
3. It believes in the importance of moral values.
4. It appreciates the duty of society toward the criminal and tries to establish an equilibrium.
5. While fully using the resources of modern science, it refuses to be dominated by science.
6. Its aim is not to punish a fault but to protect society from criminal acts.
7. Penal policy should promote individual resocialization rather than the collective approach to the prevention of crime currently used.
8. The process of resocialization requires a *humanization* of new criminal law, so that individual self-confidence and sense of personal responsibility can grow and human values can be respected.
9. The humanization process should be based on scientific understanding of the phenomenon of crime and the offender's personality (Ancel, 1994).

The ideas of social defence speak to the need to protect the rights of citizens against the arbitrariness of the courts, but the theory also recognizes that the state has a right to protect itself and society should an individual choose to break the law. Today, the social defence model is more widely supported in Europe and the United Nations than in North America. It is characterized by its focus on crime prevention, a theme expressed by many criminologists and criminal justice practitioners.

Prevention as a School of Thought

C.R. Jeffrey has called for a perspective that would transcend the classical and positivist schools of criminology. This new perspective would focus on prevention and would be interdisciplinary in nature. Jeffrey explained, "The Classical School said 'reform the law.' The Positive School said 'reform the man.' The environmental school would say 'reform the environment'" (Mannheim, 1973:498).

Most North American criminology textbooks have been written by sociologists and, understandably, reflect their disciplinary bias toward the concept of crime prevention. This domination has hampered the development of an integrated and interdisciplinary approach in Canada. Any notion of prevention has tended to focus attention on modifying elements within a social context.

Wolfgang and Ferracuti (1967:40) perhaps summed it up best when they wrote, "It is possible to trace the development of criminology along traditional lines of biology, psychology, and sociology without much overlapping or integration of these approaches." However, with the emergence of a new school of thought, the need to embrace an interdisciplinary approach is even more necessary.

Crime Prevention

The traditional etiologies of crime have not been able to fully explain, understand, predict, or suppress crime. It is a dismal fact that various law enforcement practices, correctional protocols, and legal reforms have failed. Combined with the general level of public distrust toward all elements of the criminal justice system, criminology needs to move away from the reactive and antiquated notion that punishment will prevent crime and protect society. Crime prevention can be achieved only through understanding what law is, why laws make some human behaviour a crime, and what guides human behaviour.

The notion of crime prevention is nothing new. Anyone who has visited European, African, or Asian countries will have seen buildings, centuries-old, that incorporate elementary yet highly effective crime prevention strategies, such as moats around a castles or absence of windows in houses facing onto a street. Many older quarters, especially in southern Europe and parts of Africa, share a common open inside courtyard for natural surveillance.

Despite the emergence of more "sophisticated" prevention methods in modern architecture and the development of crime prevention technology, crime has remained a major social problem. Crime prevention is more than advanced door locks and expensive house and car alarm systems. It is more than relying on "visibility" gimmicks such as leaving your radio or television on, using a light timer, or having someone cut your lawn and pick up your mail while you are away. And it is more than using police escorts to the parking lots on college and university campuses for night classes.

Although these strategies work reasonably well for most property-related crimes, they are less effective for crimes against a person (Jeffery, 1990). At this point you might want to take a few minutes to write down or discuss how many things you do directly and indirectly on a daily basis to minimize your risk of becoming a victim of a crime. How does it make you feel to take such precautionary steps? How does your concern about your safety make you feel about people in general, about our country, about the state of humanity? Would you rather not have to think about your risk of being victimized?

Sociology has not helped crime prevention efforts. Sociologists, along with scholars in most other social sciences and the policy sciences, have made little or no effort to acknowledge what, or how, other disciplines might contribute to the study of crime and criminals (Lejins, 1983). This lack of integration and sharing also can be seen when comparing criminology and criminal justice programs. Criminal justice students (for example, in law enforcement and corrections programs) tend to take practical courses and express minimal interest in behavioural science courses. Criminology students, meanwhile, tend to take theoretical and behavioural science–based courses.

Key Ideas

In order to embrace the crime prevention model for crime control, we must alter the goals of criminology and the criminal justice system. One of the pioneers of this model is **Clarence Ray Jeffery** (see Box 4.16). The following points are an integration of Jeffery's (1990), Schafer's (1976), and Wilson's (1975) ideas.

Crime prevention:

1. Must involve proactive measures.
2. Must accept short-term gains over immediate change.
3. Must replace punishment (i.e., revenge and retribution) as the basis for crime control.
4. Must embrace an integrative and interdisciplinary approach in which:
   a) We strive for a better understanding of the limits of law and crime; and
   b) "We do not believe that the criminal justice system should have the 'sole' responsibility for dealing with crime" (DeKeseredy & Schwartz, 1996:464).

In order for a crime to occur, three elements must be present: *skill*, *motivation*, and *opportunity*. Attempts to address skill and/or motivation, to date, have been minimally successful. Therefore, crime prevention should focus on opportunities that entail an interaction between the environment and the brain.

CLARENCE RAY JEFFERY

Jeffery was one of Edwin Sutherland's last students. His academic career has been marked with controversy, as he has challenged many conventional viewpoints on crime and criminality in North America. While at the department of psychology at Arizona State University, Jeffery developed a version of *social learning theory* based on B.F. Skinner's principles of behaviour modification, as opposed to the social control theory of Hirschi that focused on social variables. In the 1960s, Jeffery proposed replacing all of Sutherland's theory with a single statement of operant conditioning—focusing on the claim that a response is contingent on a stimulus—essentially rejecting the theory! Although his efforts were not successful, his ideas evolved into an interdisciplinary explanatory model of crime. In various writings starting around 1977, Jeffery proposed that criminal behaviour was the result of interactions among biology, human behaviour, and the environment. In his 1977 book *Crime Prevention Through Environmental Design*, he argued that all behaviour lies in the brain. This became the basis for his sociobiological theory of crime. He is currently serving on the advisory board of *Crime Times*, a publication that emphasizes research linking brain dysfunction to various behavioural problems, including criminality.

In 1963, Jeffery started the newsletter *Criminologica*, and in 1970, he became the founding editor of the journal *Criminology*, which is now the official journal of the American Society of Criminology (ASC). In 1978, he was elected president of the ASC. Many of his ideas on crime prevention and the sociobiological perspective can be found in his textbook *Criminology: An Interdisciplinary Approach* (1990). His crime prevention model is not yet widely embraced, but as criminology students develop these ideas further, this is likely to change.

Summary

- Although criminology is an evolving discipline, *classical* and *positivist* principles still dominate criminal justice practices and policies, and many criminological theories have been highly influenced by these principles.

- Criminology has moved from being reactive to proactive in its approach to the crime problem. It has also become more of an integrated and *interdisciplinary* science concerned with criminal behaviour as a result of various social, economic, individual, environmental, and biological factors (versus a focus on only one particular orientation).

- Criminological ideas, as illustrated by the work of the pioneers of criminology, are relative and therefore subject to change. This should serve as a caution—what may be "right" today may not hold true in the future.

Discussion Questions

1. How important is having a sense of criminological history when attempting to predict future criminological issues and future policy?

2. How does the classical and positivist approach to the study of crime complicate our ideas about crime prevention and criminal justice policy?

3. Which of the pioneers covered in this chapter do you feel has made the most significant contribution to current criminology? Why?

4. Discuss the ideas and work of the Canadian pioneers. How do their ideas reflect Canadian issues? What other scholars might qualify as major players in Canadian criminology? Why?

5. In this chapter, we examined four major schools of thought—classical, neoclassical, positivist, and the "school" of crime prevention. Which of these schools appears to offer the best approach for the study of crime and crime control?

Key Concepts

atavism	classical school	criminalistics
determinism	deterrence	discretion
just deserts	moral insanity	neoclassical school
neopositivist school	positivist school	utilitarianism

Key Names

Marc Ancel	Cesare Beccaria	Jeremy Bentham
Alphonse Bertillon	Auguste Comte	Enrico Ferri
Michel Foucault	Raffaele Garofalo	Hans Gross
John Howard	Clarence Ray Jeffery	Cesare Lombroso
Alexander Maconochie	Sir Robert Peel	Isaac Ray
Jan Weir		

Canadian Pioneers

Paul and Pat Brantingham	Ezzat Fattah	Tadeusz Grygier
Denis Szabo		

Weblinks

www.gov.on.ca/opp/cpdc/english/ The Ontario Provincial Police's Community Policing Section provides extensive information on community policing.

www.communitypolicing.org The website of the American-based Community Policing Consortium is a rich source for information on community policing.

www.prenticehall.ca/winterdyk This website contains a specially prepared chapter on law and crime designed to complement this textbook.

www.crimelibrary.com Crime TV's Crime Library offers a wide range of stories and accounts of various notorious criminals and criminal events.

Endnotes

1. The selection process for determining who should be highlighted is, as Mannheim noted in his preface to *Pioneers in Criminology*, "open to criticisms from many quarters" (1973:xiii). I have attempted to focus on those important pioneers who receive attention in other books covering similar topics, but I had to exercise discretion because of the limited space available. Students who would like to read more about the pioneers of criminology should consult Mannheim (1973) and Martin, Mutchnick, and Austin (1990). In fact, much of the biographical detail presented in this text has been drawn from these two sources.

2. Locke challenged the divine right of kings and argued that sovereignty should rest with the people and not the state. Many of his ideas regarding natural rights, property rights, the duty of the government to protect rights, and the democratic principle of majority rule have been embodied in the Canadian Constitution.

3. For a modern-day discussion on this controversial subject, see Peters (1995), whose article focuses on methodological issues, and Montagu (1997), whose critique is based on anthropological factors. Both suggest that in spite of the work of Canadian researchers Rushton and Ankney (1995), this line of inquiry holds little scientific merit today.

CHAPTER 5

Biology and Crime

"I have called this principle, by which each slight variation, if useful, is preserved, by the term Natural Selection."

Charles R. Darwin, On the Origin of Species, *Chapter 3*

Learning Outcomes

After you have completed this chapter, you should be able to:

- Appreciate the importance of a biological orientation and recognize the mitigating impact of the environment.

- Have an awareness of and appreciation for the research dedicated to the study of biological variables and their possible correlations to crime.

- Have an awareness of and appreciation for the research dedicated to environmental correlates of crime.

- Recognize the essential facts regarding biological explanations of crime causation.

- Appreciate and strive for an integrated and interdisciplinary theory that includes biological, social, and psychological dimensions.

Introduction to the Study of Crime in Terms of Biology

Biological explanations of crime have received limited attention among North American criminologists. When they have been addressed, they are usually grouped with psychological explanations. The rationale commonly used is that they can both be characterized as subscribing to a positivist-deterministic framework. What is ironic about this view is that criminology emerged out of the disciplines of anthropology, biology, and medicine, as can be seen in the works of Charles Darwin, Cesare

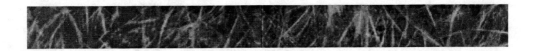

Lombroso and his colleagues, Sigmund Freud, and early geneticists such as **Gregor Mendel** (1822–1884) and Francis Joseph Galton (1822–1911). Mendel, in his famous studies involving the ordinary garden pea, discovered and proved the concept of inheritance and what would later become known as the gene.

The early positivists (circa 1920s) recognized that behaviour could be influenced by internal and external factors. The internal factors are those arising from nature, that is, biology; the external factors are those arising from nurture, that is, psychology, as well as the environment. Similar views were expressed in the frequently cited work by James Q. Wilson and Richard J. Herrnstein, *Crime and Human Nature* (1985), as well as by Shah and Roth (1974), who also argued that not adopting an interdisciplinary perspective would leave the dominant sociological explanations incomplete and inadequate as explanatory models.

Supporters of the biological perspective argue that we must identify the role of heredity and the importance of biophysical, as well as biosocial factors, in the environment. As Hippchen (1978:12) observed, "we must strive to understand what is optimum—optimum chemistry, optimum physiology, optimum psychology," as well as what is optimal socio-culturally.

In this chapter, we will examine different biological factors that have been linked to criminal behaviour. These factors fall into one of two camps: those assuming a direct inheritable link or those associated with some internal or external mediating factor. After presenting an overview of some of the most important biology-based explanations of crime, we will look at the recent theoretical developments and briefly speculate on the future of explanations rooted in biology.

Before we begin, consider the following observations, which illustrate the importance of environmental (external) and natural (internal) factors in understanding aggression, violence, and suicide in society. Throughout the chapter, we will elaborate on many of the findings.

- Children of families on welfare demonstrate twice the rate of psychiatric disorders as children from better-off families and have serious difficulties, such as alcoholism and criminality, in adulthood (Canadian Criminal Justice Association, 1989).

- A study on the prevalence of mental health problems among male federal inmates revealed that a significant number of the offenders surveyed met the criteria for anti-social personality disorders (Motiuk & Porporino, 1992).

- Comparing 41 murderers to 41 matched control participants, Raine, Buschshaum, and LaCasse (1997) found that murderers had significantly lower levels of glucose uptake in the prefrontal cortex of the brain.

- In summarizing the observations of several keynote speakers at the June 1995 conference called Violence as a Public Health Issue, held in Midland, Ontario, Carter noted that "young people are more violent than ever before" and that there appeared to be some organic (biological) linkages (Carter, 1995:28–29).

The Foundations
of Biological Determinism

According to Schafer (1976:50), the late 1800s and early 1900s were the "golden age of criminal biology." Some of the pioneering research on criminals involved the study of physical features and attributes. In scientific circles, this is known as **somatotyping** (i.e., body-typing). While scientists were busy trying to empirically verify that there is an association between body appearance and criminal behaviour, storytellers have long reflected these notions in classic good guy vs. bad guy stories. For example, in Robert Louis Stevenson's novel *Dr. Jekyll and Mr. Hyde*, the character of Hyde is portrayed as grotesque-looking and evil at the same time. In her novel *Frankenstein*, Mary Shelley describes the creation of a monster who also acts destructively. Darwin described these physical traits as *atavism*, a word that comes from the Latin *atavas*, meaning ancestors. In other words, such criminals look like a throwback to a lower level of human development. It would appear that the concept of "character" has and continues to conjure stereotypical images of physical features, stature, and accompanying psychological dispositions. (For a challenge to such views, see Box 5.1.) Let us now look at some of the early biology-based theories that tried to prove that criminal behaviour is inherited.

WHAT DO YOU THINK? BOX 5.1

CAN YOU JUDGE PEOPLE BY THEIR APPEARANCE?

William Shakespeare in his play *Julius Caesar* describes Cassius as having "a lean and hungry look...such men are dangerous." Have you ever judged someone based only on physical appearance? Do Paul Bernardo, Karla Homolka, Robert Pickton, or Kevin Vermette (believed to have killed three 20-year olds in Kitimat, British Columbia, in 2001) look like criminal types? Why might we put so much stock in judging people based on their appearance?

Early Theories of Physical Appearance

Many of our stereotypes regarding the physical appearance of "bad guys" can be traced back over two thousand years to the time of Socrates, who noted that unsavoury characters were recognizable by their physical features (Ellis, cited in Vold & Bernard, 1981:52). One of the earliest "scientific" attempts to validate such assertions was the study of *physiognomy*—that is, the judging of facial features. One of the more prolific researchers in this area was the Swiss theologian Johann Kaspar Lavater (1741–1801), who produced four volumes of work on physiognomy. He identified such classic relationships such as "shifty" eyes, a "weak" chin, and an "arrogant" nose.

Franz Joseph Gall (1758–1825) was among the first to develop a systematic method of the doctrine of *phrenology*—the study of the exterior of the skull. However, the rationale for the skull's measurements being an indicator of human behaviour can be traced back to Aristotle's notion of the brain representing the organ of the mind. While Gall identified 26 faculties of the mind on the skull, his collaborator Johann Gaspar Spurzheim (1776–1832) not only expanded the list but also brought the concept to North America (Vold, Bernard, & Snipes, 1998). Although Spurzheim's ideas reflected a biological determinist perspective, he recognized that criminal tendencies could be held in check through intellectual and moral development.

In the late 1800s and early 1900s, phrenology was widely used in penitentiaries in the eastern United States. As scientists developed better research skills, however, the concept was discredited and abandoned. Because of a lack of scientific evidence, phrenology and physiognomy have all but disappeared—or have they? (See Boxes 5.2 and 5.3.)

FYI BOX 5.2

CRIMINALITY—IS IT ALL ON YOUR HEAD?

Although it was crude, phrenology represented an early quasi-scientific method of attempting to understand the relationship between physical characteristics of the brain and criminal behaviour.

Today, other practices, such as iridology and palm reading, still rely on observable physical features or markings. It appears that, as much as we do not want to believe in fate, many people still have a fascination with (or at least a curiosity about) deterministic theories and practices such as astrology, biorhythms, the I Ching, Tarot cards, runes, and so on.

REALITY CHECK BOX 5.3

PHYSIOGNOMY AND FETAL ALCOHOL SYNDROME (FAS)

It is commonly believed that there is a strong relationship between illegal drug use and crime. We are constantly bombarded with such accounts from public officials and news media. In 2002, a special Senate committee on illegal drugs was established to assess Canada's anti-drug legislation and policy.

The problem group is those between the ages of 15–24. They consume more illicit drugs and tobacco than any other age group. Young men are more likely to use and abuse illicit and legal drugs than are young women.

Every year, the federal and provincial governments spend millions of dollars on various health expenditures. In 2000–2001, total health expenditures were $97.6 million, or $3174 per capita—up 7.2 percent from 1999–2000 (see Health Canada, 2004). Yet the "drug problem" remains a poorly understood phenomenon—culturally, politically, and from a public health perspective. According to the Canadian Institute for Health, drug expenditures rose from $537 per capita in 2001 to $578 in 2002 and exceeded $620 in 2003. In 2003, the per capita spending on drugs ranged from $192 in Nunavut to $688 in Prince Edward Island (Drug spending..., 2004). Drug sales represents one of the fastest-growing components of total spending on health in Canada. In 2003, spending on drugs reached $19.6 billion, an increase of 8.1 percent over 2002.

Even though the debate as to the relative harm of illegal versus legal drugs has been the subject of numerous publications and debates, there is little dispute over whether drugs in general take a toll on society. In recent years, the effects of fetal alcohol syndrome (FAS) and its relationship to crime and learning disabilities have received increasing attention. In 1999, a Saskatchewan psychologist reported that as many as half of the young offenders appearing in court in the province are affected by FAS. Subsequently, a growing body of research evidence has shown that FAS can be characterized by observable measures. These include intelligence scores (mean IQ score of 68), cardiac defects, central nervous system impairment, growth abnormalities, and certain physical and facial patterns (Dobbie & Bill, 1978). For example, *dysmorphic* features that appear due to prenatal alcohol abuse include the following (Schroeder, 1994):

- Eyes are widely spaced.
- Nose is often short and upturned.
- The area between the bottom of the nose and upper lip (the philtrum) is elongated and flat.
- Upper lip is thin.
- Chin is small.
- Ears are low-set and rotated to the back of the head.
- Teeth are often misplaced and misshapen.

Today, FAS has been identified as the third-ranking (behind Down Syndrome and spina bifida) cause of being mentally challenged.

Streissguth et al. (1997) found that of 415 individuals diagnosed with FAS or FAE (fetal alcohol effect), 60 percent had committed a crime, nearly 50 percent exhibited inappropriate sexual behaviour, 60 percent experienced school problems (failure and/or dropping out), and 94 percent exhibited mental problems. Streissguth and her associates have developed a Fetal Alcohol Behavior Scale that is capable of describing the behavioural essence of FAS and FAE. The scale is able to control for variable effects such as age, race, gender, and IQ and has a test-retest reliability of nearly 70 percent.

Later in this chapter, we will discuss the general biological effects of alcohol and illicit drug use on criminal behaviour.

Anthropological Measurements and Criminal Behaviour

Although Lombroso is the most famous of those who have propounded the idea that criminals can be differentiated based on their physical attributes, there have been other notable contributors to this line of inquiry. For example, although they did not focus on criminals per se, German scientist Hans Kurella and American scientist August Drahms were also strong supporters of the *somatic* approach.

Charles Buckman Goring (1870–1919), in his most noteworthy work, *The English Convict* (1913) presented data on 3000 recidivist criminals, whom he compared with a control group consisting of British soldiers, hospital patients, and university students (Vold & Bernard, 1981). Goring examined 37 mental and physical traits (such as nasal contours, colour of eyes and hair, and head circumference) that "led him to believe that a defective state of mind combined with poor physical condition *unavoidably* makes a person a criminal personality" (Schafer, 1976:51; emphasis added). Drawing on his observations from parental (father–son) and fraternal (brother) resemblance comparisons, he concluded that criminality has a hereditary link.

Goring's contribution to criminology does not lie with the specifics of his findings but with the indirect corollaries arising from his research. Unlike those before him, Goring did not restrict his explanation of crime to either the environment or heredity. Instead, he was among the first to suggest that criminal behaviour may be the result of interaction between the two:

$$\text{crime} = \text{heredity} \times \text{environment.}$$

While Goring was not able to figure out how to explain and describe that interaction, his assertion has since become the focus of and basis for numerous studies and theories. In fact, it can be found today among many criminological theories (see, for example, Williams & McShane, 1999). Few criticized his findings until **Earnest A. Hooton** (1887–1954), a Harvard anthropologist, questioned his work. Hooton's criticism focused primarily on the methodological issues and the resulting conclusions. His study (1968 [1931]) had an impressive sample size of 17 000 people, 14 000 of whom were prisoners, with the balance composed of a non-criminal control group.

Hooton did not try to imply that physical differences *caused* crime. Rather, he believed that the information could be used for predictive purposes, along with other social and environmental factors. Among his findings, Hooton reported that (Vold & Bernard, 1981:62):

- Criminals were inferior to civilians in nearly all their bodily measurements.
- Low foreheads, high-pinched nasal roots, nasal bridges and tips varying to both extremes of breadth and narrowness, excess of nasal deflections, compressed faces and narrow jaws, and thin lips fit well into the picture of general constitutional inferiority.
- The basic cause of the inferiority probably was probably due to heredity and not to situation or circumstances.
- Tattooing was more common among criminals than among civilian controls.

In spite of his impressive sample size, Hooton's findings were subjected to severe methodological criticisms. Edwin Sutherland, Robert Merton, and Ashley Montagu, among others, all pointed out that even if heredity did play a role, what was inherited was never made clear. Nevertheless, the supporters of the positivist-deterministic model did not disappear. Instead, they developed other classification strategies.

Body Types and Criminal Behaviour

"The widely held supposition that physique is irrelevant to behaviour and personality is downright nonsense. Your carcass is the clue to your character." E.A. Hooton

While Lombroso tried to establish a relationship between a person's temperament and physical characteristics, it was the pioneering efforts of the German scientist **Ernst Kretschmer**, in the 1920s, and **William Sheldon**, in the 1940s, that have been most often associated with this line of inquiry. Kretschmer believed that people fell into one of two fundamental personality types: *cycloids* and *schizoids*. In addition, there were two sub-divisions: *eliptoids* and *hysterics*. Cycloids were characterized as suffering from manic-depressive temperaments and made up 10–20 percent of the criminal population, while schizoids were generally hysterics and supposedly made up 50–90 percent of the criminal population. However, as Martin et al. (1990:129) point out, these subdivisions "did not fit any particular physical type." In addition to labelling personality types, Kretschmer identified three body types: (1) *leptosome* or *asthenic*: the tall, lean, and thin individual who typically displays a schizothyme temperament; (2) *pyknic*: the short, rotund, and soft figure representing the cyclothyme temperament; and (3) *athletic*: the broad, muscular, strong type.

Kretschmer's findings were challenged on their lack of empirical rigour. For example, his body types were not always mutually exclusive: a significant number of offenders could be characterized as having the athletic body type. In the face of such criticisms, the American physician William H. Sheldon (1898–1977) (see Box 5.4) set out to refine and improve on Kretschmer's work. Sheldon based his *constitutional* theory on the belief that human embryos are made up of three tissue layers. The inner layer is the *endomorph*, the middle layer is the *mesomorph*, and the outer layer is the *ectomorph*. Combining knowledge from his psychological training, Sheldon constructed corresponding temperaments.

The relationships between (a) the body types and (b) temperament were as follows:

1. (a) *Endomorphic*: These people have a well-developed digestive system and a tendency to put on weight and become heavy-set and soft in appearance. Their skin is usually smooth and soft, their bones small.
   (b) *Viscerotonic*: They tend to be extroverted, easy-going, and enjoy the "good" and easy life.

2. (a) *Mesomorphic*: These are predominantly muscular, strong-boned, and lean people.
   (b) *Somotonic*: They are assertive in their mannerisms and quite active in their behaviour.

3. (a) *Ectomorphic*: These people appear thin, pale, with delicate bodies, small and delicate bones, fine hair, and sharp noses.
   (b) *Cerebrotonic*: They are introverted complainers, troubled by insomnia and chronic fatigue. (This list has been adapted from Vold & Bernard, 1981:67).

PROFILE BOX 5.4

WILLIAM HERBERT SHELDON

In their account of Sheldon, Martin et al. (1990:119) write that he "represents the last of the trend setters who carried on the work of early twentieth century biological determinism.... [His] concepts became almost household words."

Sheldon was born and raised in Warwick, Rhode Island. After Sheldon's father died, the prominent American psychologist William James became a second father to the young man. Under James's influence, Sheldon entered college and pursued a degree in psychology. He eventually completed his doctoral degree in psychology, followed by a medical degree, at the University of Chicago.

After finishing medical school, Sheldon visited Europe, where he met Ernst Kretschmer. After returning to the States, he began to do research on somatotypes at Harvard. There he met another pioneer of constitutionalism, Earnest Hooton. In time, he came to believe that biology formed the basis not only for psychology and psychiatry but also for religion. In sum, Sheldon believed that the body, mind, and spiritual world were all based on biological determinism.

Sheldon's first major work *The Variety of Human Physique*, published in 1942, was devoted to arriving at somatotypes, while his second major publication, *The Varieties of Human Temperament*, also published in 1942, provided guidelines for assessing personality temperaments based on physiques (Martin et al., 1990:133). His final book on somatotypes, titled *Atlas of Men: A Guide for Somatotyping the Adult Male at All Ages*, published in 1954, consisted mainly of photographs, with little theoretical explanation or justification. Sheldon wanted to include women but was unable to secure enough volunteers to complete his detailed requirements.

Sheldon spent the longest part of his professional life (1951–1970) at the University of Oregon in Portland. After a long and distinguished career, he died of heart failure at the age of 78.

Recognizing Kretschmer's theoretical limitations, Sheldon did not view the types as being mutually exclusive but rather interrelated, to varying degrees. To quantify this assertion, he developed a seven-point rating scale, with each type receiving a score based on appearance and measurements. One meant a virtual absence of the mental or physical trait, while seven represented a preponderance of the trait. Hence, a person with a score 6–1–4 would be a strong endomorph with some ectomorphic attributes. Sheldon found that most delinquent youths were predominantly mesomorphic. However, Sheldon did not use the term "delinquent" in the same way as it was traditionally used in sociology and the law; instead, his notion of delinquency was more akin to psychiatric ideas. He used the term "biological delinquents" to describe those youths who possessed mesomorphic attributes.

Subsequent strong support for Sheldon's findings came from Sheldon Glueck and Eleanor Glueck's 1956 study involving 500 chronic delinquents and 500 proven non-delinquents. The Gluecks added a fourth constitutional type—*balanced*—and also used a multi-factor approach.

In the late 1980s, John Laub and Robert Sampson revisited the Gluecks' self-report data, salvaged from the basement of the Harvard Law School Library. With the aid of modern computers and more sophisticated analytical techniques, they reanalyzed the data (see Sampson & Laub, 1988, 1993; Laub & Sampson, 1993). The results were discussed in their important work *Crime in the Making* (1993), in which they used the *life course* perspective to demonstrate that delinquent behaviour can be affected by events that occur at different stages of life. They refer to these events as *turning points*. For example, two critical turning points that enable an adult offender to desist from crime are marriage and a career. Life events help people accumulate social capital and positive experiences with individuals and institutions that become life-sustaining. Similarly, negative experiences throughout adolescence and early adulthood can also influence the direction of delinquent and criminal careers.

While discussing a new integrated approach to explaining crime and delinquency, Siegel (1995) raises a number of questions that the **life course theory** has not been able to address. For example, "Why do some kids change while others resist? Why do some people enjoy strong marriages while others fail? Why are some troubled youths able to conform to the requirements of a job or career while others cannot?" (ibid.:286).

The body type theories eventually lost their credibility as an explanatory model when they were not able to provide convincing evidence regarding the influence of the biological factors. The lack of a sound methodology continued to plague those who championed this perspective. However, as noted in Box 5.5, Ayurvedic medicine, which is premised on physical constitution and temperament and on principles that emphasize understanding the body as a whole—as body, mind, and spirit—has received widespread support and interest. It would appear that some constitutionally based ideas continue to find support—even outside of the criminological arena.

In summary, if criminology is going to continue to move forward, it cannot think simply in terms of biology versus environment. Such approaches are not only simplistic but counterproductive to understanding the complexity of human behaviour. Future studies should attempt to see body physique as a potential risk factor along with social risk factors for violent and/or anti-social behaviour. It might be useful to ask here, who are typically the bullies in public school? Who usually starts trouble?

Chromosomes and Criminal Behaviour

In spite of the criticisms levelled at the positivists, the belief that physiological and behavioural tendencies have a constitutional foundation continued to evolve. The positivists' interests were spurred on by the development and discovery of new methods of measurement and by improved methodologies. One area of inquiry that was dependent on the discovery of an appropriate scientific measurement instrument involved the study of a possible link between an abnormal number of sex chromosomes and criminal behaviour.

Sex chromosomal abnormality is a biological defect in the pair of sex chromosomes that each human possesses. It may be inherited (i.e., caused by nature), or it may be the result of some genetic mutation (i.e., caused by nurture) during conception or during the development of the fetus in the uterus. One of these pairs consists of the gender chromosomes that determine gender and gender characteristics. In the genetically normal female, the chromosomes are both similar in size and shape. Under a microscope, they resemble two X's, hence their name. By contrast, the normal male has an XY pairing, with the Y chromosome being smaller in shape and size than the X chromosome.

For reasons not yet fully understood, when there is improper separation of the chromosomes during *meiotic* cell division (see Box 5.6), sex chromosomal abnormalities occur. According to Herrnstein (1989a), this occurs in less than one tenth of one percent of the male population. There are several known combinations of abnormal numbering of sex chromosomes, two of which have been reported to be associated with criminal behaviour. The possible combinations wherein a new embryo has more or less than the usual gender chromosomal constellation include:

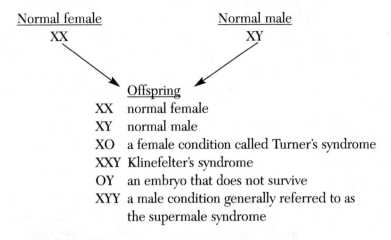

Normal female
XX

Normal male
XY

Offspring
XX   normal female
XY   normal male
XO   a female condition called Turner's syndrome
XXY Klinefelter's syndrome
OY   an embryo that does not survive
XYY a male condition generally referred to as the supermale syndrome

FYI BOX 5.6

THE ULTIMATE "JIGSAW" PUZZLE

Genes, hundreds and thousands of them, are situated along amino acid chains known as chromosomes. Once the female's egg and male's sperm have formed a union, the meiotic process of cell division, in which the number of chromosomes are reduced to half, begins. The meiotic process is different in females and males. For females a part of the meiotic division is complete at birth, while in males the entire process occurs at birth. Geneticists note that the male is the weaker of the sexes. From birth to death, males are more prone to birth defects, adolescent diseases, mental illness, heart attacks, behavioural problems, learning disabilities, and criminal behaviour. Depending on the type of crime, males are 5 to 10 times more criminalistic than females (Jeffery, 1990).

The first of the criminal sex chromosomal abnormalities to be discovered was the XXY karyotype, or Klinefelter's syndrome. While Dr. Harry Klinefelter first described the condition in 1942, at the Massachusetts General Hospital in Boston, it wasn't until the 1950s that researchers began to identify males with the extra sex (X) chromosome. The syndrome is reported to be associated with degeneration of the testes, sterility, breast enlargement, tallness and thinness, and social and/or school learning problems. Alcoholism, homosexuality, frustration-based outbursts, and overrepresentation among the mentally challenged have also been reported among those with the XXY karyotype (Vold, Bernard, & Snipes, 1998). It is probably the most common chromosomal variation in humans, occurring in approximately 1 in every 500 to 1000 live-born males.

Research by Patricia Jacobs and her associates in 1965 drew considerable criminological interest when she demonstrated the existence of males with an extra Y chromosome.

Jacobs found that a disproportionate number of the institutionalized males had the XYY constellation. These males were characterized as being exceptionally tall (mean height 6' 1" vs. 5' 7" for other patients), more introverted, and having a strong propensity toward violent and criminal behaviour. Later, Borgaonkar and Shah (1974) identified other traits that were commonly observed among males found to have the XYY makeup. These included a predisposition to facial acne, abnormal EEG patterns, extra-long extremities, and additional testosterone. Their findings were based on a limited sample size and should therefore be viewed with caution (see Sex chromosome abnormalities..., 2004). For example, none of the studies demonstrated an increased link between those who have an XYY constellation with an increased risk of developing violent or anti-social tendencies. This is due in part to the fact that the exact function of the extra Y chromosome is still poorly understood.

Perhaps the most infamous case to draw public and academic attention to the **XYY chromosome theory**, positing a link between the extra Y chromosome and violent behaviour, was that of Richard Speck. In 1968, Speck was convicted of killing eight Chicago nurses. Because of his physical size and emotional instability, he was suspected of having an extra Y chromosome; ironically, he was never tested for the condition during the trial. Years later, it was discovered that Speck did not have an extra Y chromosome (Fox, 1969). However, there were other international trials throughout the 1960s that put forward the XYY condition as the basis of a plea of insanity. These cases included that of Daniel Hugon in Paris in 1968, Ernst-Dieter Beck in Germany in 1962, Sean Farley in New York in 1969, and Raymond Tunner in Los Angeles in 1968 (Shah & Roth, 1974). Although experts testified that these men were predisposed to be criminally dangerous, the XYY syndrome was not considered a valid excuse by the courts. Given the expense, time, and socio-political environment surrounding this controversial relationship, it is unlikely that such evidence will be entertained in the near future. For example, in the 1970s, Sarnoff Mednick had his XYY research referred to as "demonism revisited" and (as a result of a major newspaper story) saw the funding for research on the subject withdrawn (see Mednick, Moffitt, & Stack, 1987).

Yet the XYY chromosome theory has prompted a call for an interdisciplinary approach to the study of criminal behaviour. One of the first non-biologists to engage in such work was Nicholas Kittrie, a law professor at the Washington School of Law at the American University. Kittrie (1971:28) observed that we must employ an eclectic framework to explain the cause of crime and that the XYY constitution "is merely one more piece of evidence that man is not his own master."

While such lines of investigation are not readily supported by mainstream criminology, Jeffery (1990:184), a supporter of the positivist frame of reference, writes, "we can put criminals in a hell-hole called prison, and we can execute them, but we cannot do research as to the causes of criminal behaviour." And even though the XYY pattern is rare enough not to represent a major factor in law-breaking (see Stoff & Cairns, 1996:6), this should not prevent criminologists from recognizing the role biological factors play in criminal behaviour.

Twin and Adoption Studies and Criminal Behaviour

With each of the biological lines of investigation described above, researchers have not been able to:

- Clearly delineate the biological influence;
- Account for possible intervening variables such as IQ, emotional instability, EEG patterns, etc.;
- Determine at what stage of development biological factors begin to exert their influence on behaviour; and
- Determine why the influence is not the same for all people who possess the biological characteristic(s).

Aside from the methodological criticisms, we are left with the following question: Just how important—if at all—is the environment in explaining human behaviour?

Twin Studies

Another biological line of inquiry that has tried to clarify the relationship between the biological basis of criminality and the environmental basis involves identical and fraternal twin studies.

Identical twins share identical genes and are the product of a single fertilized egg called a *monozygote*, while fraternal twins are the products of two eggs fertilized by two separate spermatozoa called *dizygotes*. The physical traits (such as height, weight, blood type, and general appearance) and personality traits of identical twins are more similar than those of fraternal twins. While identical twins may share common traits, careful attention reveals differences.

In spite of what the term "identical twins" (monozygotic twins) might imply, the concordance rates—that is, rates of agreement across key physical and personality traits—among these twins are not perfect. This suggests that, in addition to heredity, the environment also plays a role. However, the extent of the environment's influence and the question of whether it is possible that some of the gender trait genes are not reproduced are unclear.

One of the first twin studies to focus on criminality was conducted by the German scientist Johannes Lange in the late 1920s (cited in Schafer, 1976). Using 30 pairs of twins of which one of each pair had been incarcerated, Lange found that the concordance rate was significantly higher among identical twins than among fraternal twins. Based on these findings, he suggested that there was evidence for inherited criminal behaviour. Although Lange's work initially received much acclaim, his methodology quickly became the subject of much criticism. Nevertheless, over the years, many studies of monozygotic (MZ) and dizygotic (DZ) twins have been conducted. While the concordance rates for MZ twins were always higher than for DZ twins, none of the studies reported a concordance rate of 100 percent (for a comprehensive review, see Rowe, 2002; Wilson & Herrnstein, 1985). Given the consistent differences between MZ and DZ twins, it seems fair to conclude that the differences indicate some degree of genetic predisposition for criminal behaviour (see Box 5.7). And as Raine (1993) points out, the evidence speaks for itself; with better biometric modelling and measurement, twin studies are likely to make increasingly important contributions to genetic research on crime.

Adoption Studies

Another methodological approach to determining the effects of heredity on criminality involved the comparison of the records of adoptees with those of the biological and adoptive parents. One of the first such studies was undertaken by Fini Schulsinger in the early 1970s. It involved 57 psychopathic adoptees who were matched with 57 non-psychopathic adoptees on the basis of age, gender, social class of adoptive parent, and age of transfer to adoptive home. The concordance rate among the psychopathic patients was 14.4 percent, compared with only 6.7 percent for the biological relatives of the non-psychopathic adoptees. Again, while the concordance rates were not 100 percent, the results were statistically significant. However, they did raise the question, How do we account for the difference? Rowe (2002), among others, has attempted to unravel this puzzle through twin studies. He estimates that "38% of the individual differences in delinquency were heritable, that 28% were due to shared environment, and that 34% were due to nonshared environment" (ibid.:30).

In summarizing their findings from a longitudinal study of 344 families with two or more children, Rowe and Farrington (1997:197) further observe that "unless criminologists routinely adopt behavioural genetic research designs that estimate genetic components in environmental effects (e.g., twins or adoptive studies), no unambiguous evidence can be obtained for family environmental effects on children's criminality."

In summary, the volume of research evidence demonstrating a heredity link between MZ twins and criminality is quite impressive, though not conclusive. International studies indicate that while heredity does play a role, the environment is also a factor whose influence has not yet been clearly understood. Yet Stoff and Cairns (1996:7) note that children are more vulnerable than adults and suggest that "common environment may play a more important role than it does for adults." In his summary of the research on twin studies, **Richard Herrnstein** (1922–1994) (1989:4) concludes, "the evidence suggests a more complex chain of connections: genes affect psychological traits that in turn affect the likelihood of breaking the law. Intelligence and personality are the two traits most strongly implicated in this chain." We will examine these two next.

Before we move on, however, let us reflect on the impact of biological determinism on the study of crime. We have explored a variety of inheritable factors that have been, and in some cases continue to be, linked to criminal behaviour. While some of the earlier notions such as phrenology, somatotyping, and physiognomy have met with considerable skepticism, there still remain elements of these perspectives that cannot, or should not, be completely discarded. Just as allopathic medicine is beginning to re-evaluate some of the complementary practices (e.g., acupuncture, colour therapy, homeopathy, and naturopathy), criminologists should not be so anxious to reject ideas for which there is substantial evidence. Until a theory comes along that can solve and/or prevent all crime, criminologists should continue to entertain all new ideas and subject them to scientific scrutiny. In the next section, we examine some of the main biology-based explanations that have been advanced more recently and continue to influence criminology. Many of them point to a combination of inheritable and internal and external mediating factors instead of relying strictly on inheritance as the sole determinant or predictor of crime.

Beyond Biological Determinism: The Impact of Other Factors

Intelligence and Criminal Behaviour

"How a person behaves is determined largely by how he thinks. Criminals think differently." S.E. Samenow, 1984

There is a plethora of evidence showing that a majority of the criminal population has an average IQ of about 91–93, compared to an IQ of 100 for the general population (see Herrnstein, 1989a; Quay, 1987). The premise of criminal behaviour being related to mental abnormality was first proposed by the prominent German psychiatrist Gustav Aschaffenburg (1866–1944).

Henry Herbert Goddard (1866–1957), in his pioneering study on "feeble-mindedness," the 1912 book titled *The Kallikak Family: A Study in the Heredity of Feeble-Mindedness*, used a new intelligence test that had been developed by the French team of Alfred Binet and Theodore Simon (today known as the Stanford-Binet IQ Test). Goddard was the first to translate the French text into English, and he also established the first laboratory for the psychological study of intellectually challenged persons in 1911. Goddard suggested that intelligence, like criminal behaviour, is inherited. In his study of the Kallikak family in 1913, Goddard went so far as to conclude "that crime is the result of low-grade mentality; primarily feeblemindedness, which is an inherited quality" (cited in Schafer, 1976:60–61). He had chosen the Kallikak family because one of them, Martin Kallikak, had had an affair with a feeble-minded girl who gave birth to an illegitimate son, but later he married a girl of good reputation. Goddard traced 480 relatives of the son and 490 relatives of Martin's wife. He found that a significant number of the son's relatives had a wide variety of problems, ranging from prostitution to criminal behaviour and psychiatric problems; however, these were few such issues among the relatives on Martin's wife's side. Goddard's study also prompted him, in 1911, to play a major role in drafting the first American law mandating special education for intellectually challenged persons. During the 1870s, Richard Dugale made similar observations in his study of the Juke family (Vold & Bernard, 1981).

So powerful were these claims that they led to the sterilization of feeble-minded women in an attempt to prevent future generations of feeble-minded people. Science, as it was then understood, was used to justify this practice of eugenics. Even the Supreme Court of the United States got into the act by condoning sterilization. For example, Justice O.W. Holmes said, when referring to a case involving a feeble-minded woman, that "three generations of imbeciles are enough" (Rennie, 1978, cited in Jeffery, 1990:181).

Contrary to the findings of Goddard and Dugale, intelligence *does not* predict delinquency or crime very well (Rowe, 2002). Unfortunately, neither study examined the environment and the role it might play. For example, lower standards of living and being raised in a family with limited education are strong environmental cues that can predispose youth to deviant behaviour. Recent research cited by Kotulak (1997) and others, however, suggests that there has been sufficient evidence to indicate that we should not completely discard the relationship between intelligence and criminal behaviour. McCord and McCord (1959) were among the first to suggest that parental discipline, family cohesion, religious upbringing, and exposure to peer and social opportunities are better indicators than IQ at predicting criminal behaviour. Several years later however, Gordon (1987) demonstrated that the higher the verbal IQ score, the lower the probability of delinquent behaviour, especially when combined with high SES (i.e., social economic status) (Walsh, 2002). Herbert Quay's (1987) evidence indicates that, on the average, delinquents have IQs of about 92, which is about one-half of a standard deviation lower than the general population. In addition, Quay believes that a lower IQ places youths at social risk, and Ward and Tittle (1994) add that a lower IQ often leads to poor parenting due to compromised thinking and reasoning skills, eventually resulting in a negative spiral of disadvantages for these youths.

Finally, recent evidence from research done at the John Radcliffe Hospital in Oxford, England appears to link intelligence to pH levels in the cortex of the brain. The study found that teens with higher IQ scores tended to have higher alkaline pH readings than those with lower IQs. Graci (1997) notes that this is the first time that intelligence has been linked to a potential biochemical marker in the brain.

In an attempt to synthesize the vast volume of literature that has accumulated over the years, Akers (1994:78) concludes, "it is difficult to dismiss entirely the evidence of correlation between IQ and delinquency." Don Gibbons, a prominent sociologist, arrives at a similar conclusion but cautions that it is difficult to tell the extent to which "measured intelligence is itself a social product of sub-cultural variations in learning environments and similar factors, rather than an index of innate intelligence" (1992:148).

Notwithstanding this observation, Herrnstein (1989b) suggests that given the growing redistribution of child-bearing toward lower social strata, there will be a drop in the average intelligence of the population. One of the reasons is these parents are likely to have a lower-than-average verbal IQs, as opposed to lowered spatial/performance IQs, which makes them unable to provide the stimuli needed to nurture the intellectual growth of their children. According to Herrnstein, this trend is likely to continue through successive generations at a declining increment of one point per generation. Unfortunately, he argues, schooling alone does not guarantee success of improved IQ.

So while schools and homes can be improved to ensure that intelligence does not decline any further, it must be recognized that while environmental factors play a role, genetic factors in intelligence also contribute significantly to IQ. In addition, future researchers need to examine the mechanisms by which low IQ predisposes individuals to crime and to determine the extent to which low IQ is a product of the social and cultural environment, as opposed to early brain dysfunction.

Personality and Criminal Behaviour

Walsh (2002:112) defines personality as "the relatively enduring, distinctive, integrated and functional set of psychological characteristics that results from an individual's temperament interacting with his or her culture and personal experience." How do we acquire personality? The popular answer is that personality is the product of psychological factors, since personality refers to characteristic patterns of acting, feeling, and thinking as defined by age, gender, race, ethnicity, and geographic region. However, as with language, personality may also have a biological foundation (see, for example, Lenneberg, 1967).

Because of poor methodology and flawed measurement, early research found little or no relationship between the personalities of offenders and non-offenders. The biological component of personality is still not well understood because measurements of personality have not been standardized. As Herrnstein (1989a) notes, personality tests measure only an approximation of personality. Even though most tests nowadays have reliability and validity scores, they are all subject to an error measurement as well. In recent years, however, there has been an abundance of evidence suggesting that most offenders' personalities are distinctive, though not necessarily abnormal.

Perhaps the strongest link between personality and criminality appears in the work of Hans Eysenck (1916–1997). In the 1970s, Eysenck suggested that psychotocism, extraversion, and neuroticism—the three basic elements of personality—were able to predict criminality (Murder in the UK..., 2004).

The validity of personality and intelligence tests is premised on standardized psychological assessment procedures, which are seen to measure primarily one's experience. Herrnstein (1989a) suggests, however, that the different aspects of personality may have different heritabilities. Just as there are genes for the colour of our eyes and hair and for the growth and development of our limbs, it might well be possible that certain inherited personality traits predispose individuals to criminal behaviour. Combined with environmental cues (i.e., experience and context), these factors provide the opportunities for committing certain crimes. Hence, personality and intelligence are not likely simply determined by the environment alone but are the result of an interaction between the environment and the brain (see Box 5.8).

WHAT DO YOU THINK? BOX 5.8

TRANSCENDING CONVENTIONAL THOUGHT

"Significant problems we face cannot be solved with the same level of thinking we were at when we created them." Albert Einstein (1879–1955)

How might we begin to overcome socio-political resistance and look more closely at the possible relationship between biological influences and criminality?

Alcohol and Illicit Drugs and Criminal Behaviour

Extreme drunkenness has been used as a legal defence for various crimes; for example, see court cases such as *R. v. Esau* (1997) and *R. v. Lemky* (1996). Such a defence is premised on the assertion that the offender did not have the mental capacity to appreciate his or her actions. While the drunkenness defence is based on legal principles (i.e., Sections 1, 7, and 11(d) of the Charter of Rights and Freedoms), a biochemical malfunctioning must occur in order for the brain not to function properly.

Smart and Jansen (1991) found that most Canadian and American surveys report that use of alcohol among adolescents varies between 60 and 90 percent. Perry (1996:147) notes that, "the late 1960s and early 1970s saw adolescent substance use become more widely publicized," perhaps accounting for some of the increased usage among adolescents. Substance abuse became a legitimatized way of expressing frustration and rebellion (see Box 5.9). And although it was not the only factor identified, two of Canada's most notorious serial killers, Clifford Olson and Robert Pickton, were known to drink excessively when not in prison (see Box 5.10). The Canadian Centre on Substance Abuse (2004) reports that experimentation with illicit drugs not only is increasing but tends to begin at a younger age than in the past.

LEGAL BUT DEADLY: OXYCONTIN

OxyContin is a powerful prescription painkiller that falls under the federal government's Narcotic Control Act. It was approved for sale in 1995. In 2003, six people died in Newfoundland from overdosing on the drug. In response to the growing public concern, Newfoundland and Labrador established a task force to assess the extent of the abuse and develop strategies to deal with the issue. An interim report was released in January 2004 and can be accessed online at **www.gov.nf.ca/health/publications/oxycontininterim/**.

In May 2004, police in Thunder Bay, Ontario, declared that three pharmacy robberies were motivated by the desire to steal OxyContin. While some of the abuse of OxyContin is the result of such thefts, some doctors and pharmacists have been known to prescribe the drug indiscriminately. How might one address the abuse of prescription drugs? What about the inappropriate dispensing of prescription drugs?

ALCOHOL AND ILLICIT DRUG USE AND CRIME

The following examples are but a small sample from the growing body of literature showing a link between substance use or abuse and criminal behaviour.
From the Canadian Centre on Substance Abuse (2004):

- Impaired driving is a major cause of death in Canada.
- One in six deaths in Canada is caused by smoking.
- In 1997, 439.6 kg of cocaine and 244 949 kg of marijuana were seized.
- Indigenous Canadians have a relatively high rate of illicit drug use.
- Substance abuse costs exceeded $418.4 billion in 1992—that is, 2.7 percent of the GDP.

From Synnott (1996):

- More than half of the 5500 criminals sent to jail since 1990 had consumed either alcohol or used drugs on the day they committed the crime. More than two-thirds had related problems requiring treatment while in prison.

From the British Crime Survey (2003), which is conducted by the British Home Office annually and is based on interviews with some 40 000 people 16 years of age or older:

- During 2000–2002, nearly half of all offenders convicted of violent crime had been under the influence of alcohol. Some 45 percent of crimes committed under the influence of alcohol involved domestic violence.

Given the dominant sociological perspective in North America, these trends have been explained from a social constructionist perspective, which views society as a constructed representation of reality in which the world has no underlying objective character (see Pfuhl & Henry, 1993). However, as the evidence suggests, a perspective grounded in biology may provide greater predictive and explanatory potential as far as crime and the use of alcohol and drugs are concerned.

The effects of alcohol and drugs (both legal and illegal) on metabolic processes and the central nervous system have been extensively studied in the medical arena. For example, Cadoret's (1995) findings showed that the chance of alcohol abuse by an adoptee whose biological parent was an alcoholic was statistically high. They also showed, however, that the environment played a role. Having an alcoholic in the adoptive home increased the risk of alcohol problems in the adoptee, but not to the same extent as having a biological parent who was an alcoholic. As new and more sophisticated techniques have been developed, researchers have been attempting to localize the genes or genes responsible as well as find out how they operate (Wijsman, 1990).

Other investigators have been looking for risk factors or markers for alcoholism and drug use. Tabakoff, Whelan, and Hoffman (1990), for example, have found neurotransmitters in the brain that are related to alcoholism. Julius Axelrod (who won a Nobel Prize for his work on brain chemistry) demonstrated that when cocaine was placed on the brain of dead rats, it was absorbed into the brain and subsequently displaced the existing neurotransmitters. Axelrod found that, over time, "drugs actually drive out the brain's own chemicals" (cited in Burns, 1989:49).

In summary, while studies have shown that drugs and alcohol correlate highly with aggression and risk of suicide, homicide, motor-vehicle accidents, and domestic violence, a clear causal relationship has not been established. We know that drugs act on the neurotransmitter system of the brain, but research is less clear about the influence of environmental, cultural, gender, and individual differences. Future studies should look at the effects of alcohol and drugs from a multiple-level and interdisciplinary perspective.

Brain Chemistry and Criminal Behaviour

Endocrine Imbalances and Criminal Behaviour

Hippocrates and Galen, two of the most influential physicians of ancient Greece, believed that the human organism is a single hierarchical complex in which mind (e.g., imagination and humour), body (e.g., nerves, blood, and muscle), and soul (e.g., vital spirit) are closely linked. In fact, Hippocrates, the father of modern medicine, asked his students to divide their patients into categories according to blood, phlegm, and colour of the bile. These ideas have since evolved into the relatively new science of endocrinology (from two Greek words, *within* and *separate*).

In 1928, Max Schlapp and Edward Smith wrote the first criminological textbook to try to explain criminal behaviour as a product of hormonal imbalances. The idea of being able to explain certain criminal behaviours based on endocrine imbalances was popular in the 1930s, but at the end of that decade, a study conducted by Matthew Molitch seemed to put to rest any assertions that endocrine imbalances were related to crime (see Vold & Bernard, 1981:111). Today, however, there is a growing body of literature that relates various behavioural conditions to endocrine imbalances.

It was not until the pioneering work of the German chemist Fredrich Wohler in 1828 that it became possible to study endocrine systems (Vold & Bernard, 1981). After synthesizing the organic compound urea, Wohler speculated that humans are chemical entities. Excited by this new line of thinking, researchers began to identify some of the physiological and psychological effects of the endocrine glands—that is, the glands that produce hormones. Louis Berman (1938, cited in Vold & Bernard, 1981:109) was among the first to develop a chemical-glandular theory of personality differences. One of the areas that received considerable attention in this regard was the brain.

Our brain is responsible for managing all the hormones released from our *pituitary gland*, located near the middle of the brain (see Figure 5–1). The *hypothalamus* is the nerve centre for the autonomic nervous system and is also the control centre for sex hormones—our libido. It is also the seat of our emotional reactions: fear, aggression, hunger, and thirst. Jeffery (1990:200) refers to the functions of the hypothalamus as the "food, sex, fight or flight" syndrome. Below it is the *substantial nigra*, whose main function is to send signals throughout the body. The brain communicates with itself by

FIGURE 5—1

THE BRAIN

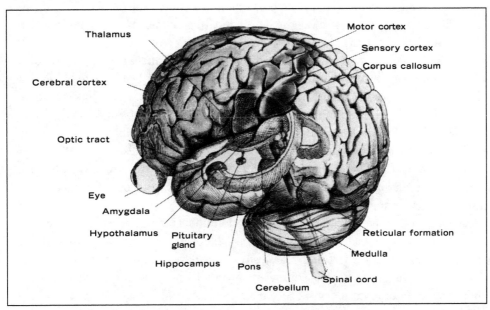

Source: C.R. Jeffery (1990:200). Criminology: An Interdisciplinary Approach. Englewood Cliffs; NI-P-H.

neural transmission. The *thalamus* is the sensory relay location that transmits neural information from the sensory organs to other parts of the brain. The chemical transporters that carry the message along the *axons* are the *neurotransmitters*. How information gets around the brain depends on the amount of each neurotransmitter present at the synapses where the neurons join. Information is transmitted through the neurons and their dendrites and axons via an electrochemical and biochemical impulse (Burns, 1989; Colgan, 1996). There are four main types of neurotransmitters.

Neurotransmitters can either increase (excite) or decrease (inhibit) the level of activity of receptor neurons. The primary excitatory neurotransmitters are *dopamine* (DA) and *acetylcholine* (ACh), while the two main inhibitory neurotransmitters are *serotonin* (5-HT) and *noradrenalin* (norepinephrine) (NE). While considerable efforts have been made to understand how hormonal imbalances lead to health problems (such as low sex drive, lack of mental alertness, prostate problems, and female reproductive problems), criminologists have not been very interested in examining the role that hormone imbalances might play in understanding criminal behaviour. For example, consider the well-documented medical finding that shows that depression among women increases dramatically after normal births (Colgan, 1996). While there are sociological (e.g., strain) and psychological (e.g., frustration) explanations for such behaviour, could the depression be related to hormonal and biological factors? There is no strong evidence that links female depression to crime—not because it may not exist, but because it does not fall within the conventional lines of criminological inquiry.

One of the first studies to examine the influence of hormonal changes on female behaviour found that 46 percent of the samples (N=156) committed their crimes four days either before or following menstruation (Dalton, 1961). However, in spite of more recent supporting evidence (e.g., Fishbein, 1992), it is still not clear whether the psychological and physical stress of aggression might trigger menstruation and not vice versa. Nevertheless, in the 1980s, there were a number of successful defences of women who had killed men while experiencing PMS (see Katz & Chambliss, 1995).

As for hormones and their effect on men, a study by James Dabbs (cited in Gibbs, 1995) found that those male prison inmates with higher testosterone concentrations are more likely to have committed violent crimes. If hormonal imbalances in the hypothalamus and striatal cortex can affect our health, is it not also possible that certain hormonal imbalances might predispose us to criminal behaviour? Walsh (2002:140) points out that adolescent males have about 20 times more "free" testosterone than females and that the activation of this hormone is thought to "partially account for the onset of antisocial behavior among most young men."

Canadian researchers Philippe Rushton and Julie Harris (1994) tested salivary testosterone levels in male and female twins (228 pairs) exhibiting pro-social and aggressive behaviour. They found that testosterone levels among those males who expressed more aggressive behaviour were higher than among those who did not exhibit violent tendencies. They suggested that male violence is largely genetic in origin, whereas female violence is often triggered by environmental factors, and posited that the differences between the genders in violence patterns are related to testosterone levels. What remains unclear, however, is the effect of the interaction among biology, gender roles, and socialization processes.

Finally, there is a growing body of research into the possible link of low serotonin (5-HT) levels to violent behaviour and impulsive and suicidal behaviour among criminals and psychiatric patients. While most of these studies have been conducted on animals, some recent human-based ones report links between adolescent and adult aggressive and anti-social behaviour and serotonin levels (Stoff & Vitiello, 1996). However, due to the limited number of studies and some questionable methodologies, the use of serotonergic drugs to treat childhood aggression does not have any scientific clear basis. In fact, the studies "do not reveal the consistent pattern of reduced 5-HT function" (ibid.:116), but the growing body of literature does offer results that should prompt continued research along these lines.

Since brain levels of serotonin may be partially determined by genes, a percentage of individuals may be genetically predisposed to violent behaviour (see Box 5.11). Issues such as this warrant further research. Increasingly, criminologists are revisiting the possible links between brain chemistry and criminal behaviour and incorporating findings from other fields of inquiry, such as biochemistry and neurology, to form an interdisciplinary theory of human behaviour.

FYI BOX 5.11

SEROTONIN AND PROZAC

Since low levels of serotonin have been linked to suicidal tendencies, the serotonin system has been the target of anti-depressant drugs such as fluoxetine—better known by its trade name, Prozac. Prozac has also been used as treatment intervention for certain types of criminals (Rowe, 2002).

EEG Abnormalities

In 1952, in a study conducted on 100 serious offenders, Dennis Hill and D.A. Pond found that approximately half of them had abnormal electroencephalograms (EEGs). However, since the authors did not use a control group, no conclusions could be drawn from these findings. Referring to some longitudinal research conducted in Scandinavia, Wilson and Herrnstein (1985) observed that the results confirmed that there was a relationship between low-level arousal and certain crimes. Low levels of brain arousal have also been linked to psychopathic behaviour and criminality. Similarly, Raine, Buschshaum, and LaCasse (1997) used a brain imaging device (a positron emission tomographer) on 41 murderers and found a network of abnormal cortical and subcortical brain processes that they suggested may lead to a pattern of violent behaviour. More recently, Pillmann and colleagues (1999) found that left hemisphere abnormalities were significantly more associated with violent offenders than non-violent offenders.

Given the results of the medical research on brain chemistry, perhaps we need to pay closer attention to the possible relationship between criminal behaviour and occurrences of endocrine imbalances and EEG abnormalities. In the next section, we will examine the relationships between crime and nutrition and environmental toxins.

Nutrition and Environmental Toxins and Criminal Behaviour

When asked what she would do about violence in Canada if she were given a blank cheque, Dr. Marnie Rice, director of research at Oak Ridge Psychiatric Hospital in Penetanguishene, Ontario, said she would "spend it feeding good food to young mothers-to-be" (Carter, 1995:34).

If, as the adage goes, you are what you eat (and drink and breathe), then perhaps there is a connection between nutrition and crime. While we may exercise free will in what we eat, we have less control over how certain foods affect our body and mind or, more specifically, our brain.

Food

Perhaps the most frequently documented example of nutrition that may be a source of crime is *hypoglycemia*, or low blood sugar. And perhaps the most famous case involving the use of diet as a defence involved Dan White, who, in 1979, was convicted of the voluntary manslaughter of San Francisco's mayor and his supervisor in a case dubbed the "Twinkie defence." White's successful defence was based on the premise that he suffered from "diminished capacities" as a result of eating too many junk foods high in sugar (e.g., Coca-Cola, chocolate, and Twinkie bars), which aggravated a chemical imbalance.

One of the functions of the pancreas is to secrete insulin into the blood system to remove sugar in order to convert it to fat for energy use. The fat is stored in the liver until the body needs it. The brain regulates and controls blood sugar levels in the body. Philpott (1978:128) found that after studying blood sugar levels "before and after exposure to addictants in known narcotic, alcohol, and food addicts I arrived at convincing evidence that hypoglycemia can consistently be observed as relating to the stress of the addictive withdrawal state" (also see Virkkunen & Linnoila, 1996).

In 1980, **Alexander Schauss** was among the first to popularize the notion that violent delinquent behaviour might be related to bioenvironmental factors—more specifically, dietary factors that produce biochemical imbalances. Along with several associates, he found that on average juvenile offenders ingested 32 percent more sugar than those in a control group, which consisted of youths with behavioural disorders but no criminal record. A recent CBC story reported that in 2003 Canadians averaged 23 teaspoons of sugar per day, while the WHO recommends no more than 12 (Sugar surprise, 2004).

And while the concept of diet being related to violent crime may have appeared out-landish to criminologists with conventional training, students of nutrition have amassed considerable data showing a link between dietary habits and anti-social behaviour.

The following summaries represent a sampling of the growing body of literature that links the effects of certain dietary practices to criminal behaviour and general behavioural disorders:

- In his review of the literature, Adams (1998a) found that there was a link between **attention deficit disorder (ADD)** and a diet high in saturated fats. ADD is char-acterized by restlessness, hyperactivity, and forgetfulness. It has been related to conduct disorders, sensation-seeking, and early adult offending among delinquents (Farrington, 1994). In a follow-up article, Adams (1998b) reports that two-thirds of ADD cases likely go unreported and undetected. It is estimated that ADD affects between 5 and 12 percent of Canadians—including 1.2 million children.

- While research has linked reduced serotonin levels to aggression in men, Bond et al. (2001) found that they may also contribute to aggressive behaviour in women during the premenstrual phase of their monthly cycle. Similarly, Smith and her col-leagues (1997) reports that women whose diets are low in the amino acid *trypto-phan* are at greater risk of depression than those who have normal diets. Tryptophan-deficient diets are more commonly found among women with eating disorders.

- Schoenthaler et al. (1995) point out that the improvement in behaviour may be not so much due to decreased sugar consumption as to an increased intake of the vit-amins and minerals contained in the fresh fruits, vegetables, and whole-grain foods. In their 15-week study, two groups received different strengths of vitamin and mineral supplements (100 percent vs. 300 percent of the United States rec-ommended daily allowances) and one group received a placebo. Those in the group receiving supplements were, on average, found to decrease their rule-violating behaviour (a mean reduction of 16 percent for the 300 percent group and of 38 percent for the 100 percent group), while the placebo group had a mean rule vio-lation increase (of 20 percent). The authors concluded that while environment should still be considered when studying violent behaviour, more research needs to be done to understand the relationship between nutritional intervention and controlling anti-social behaviour.

- After reviewing several methodologically sound studies, Challem (2001) reports that it is possible to dramatically improve offender's attitude and behaviour by reducing his or her diet and mineral imbalances.

In 1959, Dr. Frank Boudreau, of the Milbank Fund of New York, said, "If all we know about nutrition were applied to modern society, the result would be an enormous improvement in public health, at least equal to that which resulted when the germ the-ory of infectious disease was made the basis of public health and medical work" (Williams & Kalita, 1977:ix). A major study cited in Williams and Kalita reported that in 1975 one-half of the population was suffering from some degenerative disease and the number of children classified as hyperactive, retarded, or schizophrenic was steadily increasing. Why? The authors point a finger directly at the changing dietary habits of North Americans and at environmental pollutants. Along similar lines, Beasley and Swift (1989) reported that the average Scholastic Aptitude Test (SAT) scores among young people have been steadily declining over the past 25 years. Why? They also point to diet and environmental deterioration as possible markers.

Dr. Emanual Cheraskin surveyed over 1400 healthy individuals over a 20-year period and found that not only do healthy people eat better than less healthy people, but that their diets consistently exceed the government-recommended daily allowance (RDA) in terms of nutritional needs anywhere from five to nine times. His work has been replicated with young people and the results were very similar. The authors of the latter study report that only 5 percent of the American population is "clinically well" (University Medical Research Publishers, 1993). The overall implications, aside from the obvious one—that most North Americans have a substandard diet—is that it subjects them to physical and emotional problems and that dietary deficiencies may result in genetic mutations. For example, in a 1992 article that appeared in the prestigious medical journal *Lancet*, Dr. Lucas reported that pre-term children who had not been fed mother's milk but cow's milk and/or soya-based infant formula had, by the age of 8.5 years, an average IQ score 8.3 lower than those who had been fed mother's milk.

Vitamins and Minerals

Research on the possible links between nutrition and crime includes studies on an excess or undersupply of vitamins such as C, B_3, and B_6, as well as studies on the relationship between food allergies and anti-social behaviour (see Raine, 1993). Excessive exposure to or high intake of certain common minerals—such as cadmium, copper, lead, magnesium, manganese, and zinc—has been linked not only to learning disabilities and cognitive deficits but also to aggression (for reviews of this literature, see Denno, 1988; Marlowe, Bliss, & Schneider, 1994). Of these minerals, manganese has received considerable interest in recent years. The following is a brief list of some observations and findings relating to a possible link between manganese and crime:

- The notion that manganese might be a dangerous substance can be traced back to 200 BC, when the Greeks referred to it as the *voodoo metal* because of its apparent harmful effects on humans (VRF, 1994).

- In 1989, Cawte and Florence reported that, based on 50 years of data, the incidence of violence and murder was 299 percent higher on Groote Eylandt, where manganese is mined, than in any other area in Australia (see also Box 5.12).

- James Huberty, who in 1984 killed 21 innocent people after firing into a McDonald's restaurant in San Ysidro, California, and Patrick Purdy, who in 1989 went on a killing spree in a Stockton, California school, were both found to have excessively high levels of cadmium and manganese in their hair (Walker, 1994).

- While volunteering at the Stateville Prison in Illinois, Bill Walsh had an opportunity to conduct hair analysis on 24 pairs of brothers—one being a "good guy" and the other the "boy from hell." The delinquent boys consistently had high levels of copper, very low levels of zinc, sodium, and potassium, and elevated levels of lead and cadmium when compared to their brothers (Challem, 2001) (see Box 5.13).

FYI BOX 5.12

ENVIRONMENTAL TOXINS INHERITED

An in-depth study of Canada's 1991 Gulf War veterans raises "serious questions about the incidence of birth defects in the children of soldiers" (Bronskill, 1998). The study revealed that children born to veterans of the war were 20 percent more likely to have physical defects. Meanwhile, the veterans themselves expressed feelings of depression, insomnia, and irritability. The study speculates the causes of the symptoms to include exposure to chemical and biological weapons, use of anti–nerve gas pills, toxic fumes from oil fires, and war-related stress.

Roger Masters, from the United States, conducted one of the most comprehensive studies that examined the possible relationship between high rates of violent crime and geographic variations. Along with his colleagues, he found that neurotoxic metals such as lead and manganese are absorbed into the brain due to poor diet and deficiencies in vitamin and minerals, interrupting normal brain development and functions. Masters notes that environmental pollutants could interact with poverty, poor diet, alcohol and drug abuse, and social stress to put some individuals at risk for subclinical toxicity, manifested by a loss of impulse control and increased violent crime (Montague, 2004).

A CLOSER LOOK BOX 5.13

NUTRITION AND LIFESTYLE

In 1994, Dr. G. Bonham, then medical officer of health for the city of Calgary, spoke publicly about the increase in the percentage of babies who were born small. He attributed this shift to improper nutrition and a variety of lifestyle factors of the mothers. He further stated, "If you think prevention is expensive try treatment for size" (Reich, 1994:1), referring to the higher cost of treating the increased incidence of psychiatric and physical diseases that occur in these children as they grow up. A few years later, Dr. Brent Friesen, the new medical officer of health reiterated the same observations (Lowey, 1997). He further suggested that many of the social ills in Canadian society (such as alcohol and drug abuse, depression, suicide, and crime) may be based on specific nutritional deficiencies combined with increased indoor work and recreation lifestyles. Together, these deficiencies can compromise our states of mental and physical well-being.

In summary, there is a growing body of evidence that links nutrition to crime. However, the factors are quite divergent, with no consistent food type, mineral, or vitamin emerging as the ultimate marker. Similarly, most of the evidence suggests that there may be environmental and/or psychosocial factors playing mitigating roles. Overall, the findings point to the complexity of human behaviour and to how it may be altered through what we eat, drink, or breathe.

Contemporary Biosocial Theories

Until recently, the biosocial perspective has received minimal support among criminologists. It appears that the aftermath of earlier biological determinism studies has tainted the way that more recent variations of theories rooted in biology are received. In their success theory text, Williams and McShane (1999:41–42) allocate only about two full pages to the perspective. Barak (1997:123), however, offers a more promising assessment by stating that "much of this work is provocative and promising, and, I believe, certainly worth pursuing."

The Birth of Sociobiology—Biosociology!

In 1975, Edward O. Wilson, a professor of zoology at Harvard, wrote a comprehensive and controversial book entitled *Sociobiology: The New Synthesis*. It presented a theoretical synthesis of biology, studies of individual behaviour, and evolutionary ecology. He defined sociobiology as "the systematic study of the biological basis of all social behavior" and as "a branch of evolutionary biology and particularly of modern population biology" (1975:4).

Wilson believes that our genetic makeup predisposes us not only to protect our own kin but to eliminate those who appear as threats. However, he is careful to note that "there is no universal 'rule of conduct' in competitive and predatory behavior" (ibid.:247). So how do we control innate aggression? According to Wilson, "we should design our population's densities and social systems in such a way as to make aggression inappropriate in most conceivable daily circumstances and, hence, less adaptive" (ibid.:255).

More recently, Raine, Brennan, Farrington, and Mednick (1997) identified four major interactive biosocial theories of crime. We will address only three, as the fourth is considered too broad and too difficult to test empirically. All these perspectives emphasize the need for theory to become integrated and interdisciplinary in nature and also to evolve in terms of the complexity of its explanatory power.

Sarnoff A. Mednick's Biosocial Theory

For **Sarnoff Mednick** (1928–), all behaviour is triggered by the autonomic nervous system (ANS). He believes that we are all occasionally prone to do things that violate the norms, values, and rules of society. The reason most of us do not follow through on these impulses is that we learn to control those impulses as part of our socialization process and our desire to avoid punishment. We become law-abiding individuals as we learn to fear punishment. As we learn to avoid fear, the behaviour gets reinforced.

Mednick theorized that those who have an ANS that recovers quickly from fear easily learn socially proscribed behaviour, whereas those who have an ANS that recovers slowly have difficulty learning to inhibit anti-social behaviour. Accordingly, learning non-criminal behaviour involves both certain individual abilities (ANS response rate) and environmental factors ("consistent and adequate punishment for aggressive acts"). An absence of these factors greatly predisposes a person to anti-social behaviour.

Hans J. Eysenck's Biosocial Theory

As early as 1964, in his then controversial but frequently cited book, *Crime and Punishment*, **Hans J. Eysenck** (1916–1997) argued that certain personality features that are inherited (introversion vs. extraversion) are more prone to cause anti-social behaviour when they interact with various socialization processes.

Eysenck further theorized that, combined with our autonomic and central nervous system characteristics, these biological factors affect our responsiveness to punishment and our propensity for anti-social outcomes. More specifically, he found that extraverts experience cortical under-arousal and are less responsive to punishment. In other words, they do not condition well with the use of punitive discipline—yet most of our correctional practices include such elements!

Terrie E. Moffitt's Biosocial Theory

While her work has also been described as being part of the life course theory, **Terrie E. Moffitt** (1955–) proposed that "the biological roots of antisocial outcomes are present before or soon after birth" (Raine, Brennan, Farrington, & Mednick, 1997). Relying on longitudinal data from her New Zealand study, Moffitt theorized that congenital factors such as heredity and perinatal complications produce neuropsychological problems in the infant's nervous system. These deficits then manifest themselves in childhood complications ranging from poor motor skills development to poor memory and temperamental difficulties.

Moffitt's theory asserts that while some children may be born with neuropsychological deficits, a deficient social environment might also predispose a child to perinatal complications, poor nutrition, and abuse—which, in turn, may result in some biological deficiency in the child.

According to Raine, Brennan, Farrington, and Mednick (1997), the biosocial theories we just discussed offer solid support for a biosocial approach. They build on the strengths of existing models while providing a broader framework in which to study biosocial interactions. Furthermore, as can be seen in Figure 5–2, they do not have violence as the only outcome variable. Behaviour that results in violence is the outcome of a complex interaction of social and biological factors, both of which need to be considered when

FIGURE 5-2

HEURISTIC BIOSOCIAL MODEL OF VIOLENCE

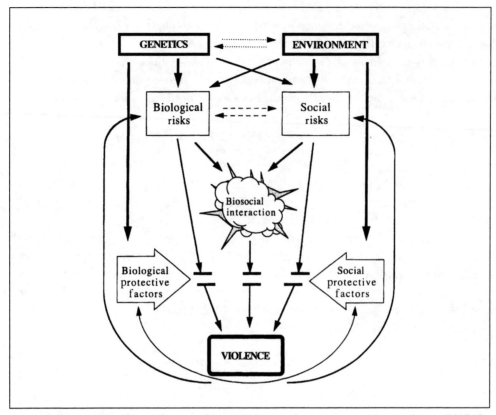

Source: Raine, Brennan, Farrington, & Mednick, *Biosocial Bases of Violence*. New York, Plenum (1997:15).

attempting to understand violence or any other form of criminal behaviour. Figure 5–2 clearly illustrates this interdisciplinary, interactive, and integrated approach to understanding deviant behaviour.

The Future of Explanations Rooted in Biology

Biology-based perspectives continue to be something of a dark horse within the criminological arena. Most of these theories focus on aberrant genes, hormones, physiological features, poor nutrition, perinatal complications, and so on, but there is limited support within society to allow overt manipulation of such conditions. Issues such as genetic engineering, for example, raise many ethical and policy concerns. And while the biosocial perspectives and related versions (such as biopsychology and bioenvironmental perspectives) appear to be transcending the more traditional criticisms, for the most part none of the theories are able to account for how much psychological or social factors interact with biology. Perhaps Terrie Moffitt summarized the biological position best when she said, "I would prefer that the basic research be conducted for the goal simply of generating new knowledge and that the individuals who are in charge of deciding how [biology-based] research can be applied would be a separate group from the scientists" (Ghosh, 2002).

While "recognition of biological factors is gaining importance among criminologists" (Beirne & Messerschmidt, 1991:487), it is clear that biological factors alone cannot explain criminal behaviour. As James Short, Jr., the president of the American Society of Criminology, put it in his presidential address in 1996, "the future development of causal theory is dependent upon our movement toward integrated theories that involve biological, social, and cultural dimensions" (Wellford, 1997:4).

Summary

- Biological explanations of criminal behaviour emerged in an era when social control took the form of retribution and just deserts. Issues of eugenics and concerns about implications of racial and class bias had not yet become social concerns.

- Most of the early explanations were plagued by methodological problems. Each perspective's efforts to explain all criminal behaviour remained incomplete.

- When analyzing criminal behaviour, environmental factors (nurture = experience and context) seem to be inseparable from questions of inheritance and biology (nature). In other words, biology might affect experience or context, but environment also influences biology. Therefore, both approaches need to be studied, and we need to recognize that criminal behaviour (and behaviour in general) is a phenomenon that has many possible causes spanning the sciences and social sciences.

- The biological perspective does not assume that social control can be exercised only through law and order. Much current research is based on an *integrated* and *interdisciplinary* approach that emphasizes individualized treatment through various biological-based and environment-based intervention strategies.

- Among the newer explanations rooted in biology, the biosocial perspective has received some support. There are currently different models, but they all subscribe to an interdisciplinary and integrated approach to studying criminal behaviour.

Discussion Questions

1. In spite of the growing body of research suggesting that criminal behaviour may have a biological basis to it, which issues pose the greatest hurdle for criminology? How might we overcome them?

2. Describe the major theories discussed in this chapter. What are the relative strengths and weaknesses of each theory? What are the primary differences between early versus more recent biology-based approaches to criminal behaviour? Which theory do you think has the most explanatory power? Why?

3. To what extent might other aberrant behaviours have a biological basis to them? To what extent might psychopathic behaviour be the result of an interaction between brain function abnormalities and social or familial factors?

4. To what degree do you think that biology-based explanations of crime have been, and are, currently grounded in scientific principles?

5. How might the various components of theories rooted in biology be incorporated into an integrated and interdisciplinary criminological perspective? Which components do you think would be the most important?

Key Concepts

attention deficit disorder (ADD)   life course theory   somatotyping
XYY chromosome theory

Key Names

Hans J. Eysenck   Franz Joseph Gall   Charles Buckman Goring
Richard Herrnstein   Earnest A. Hooton   Ernst Kretschmer
Sarnoff Mednick   Gregor Mendel   Terrie E. Moffitt
Alexander Schauss   William Sheldon

Weblinks

www.crime-times.org *Crime Times* is the most up-to-date and comprehensive source for research in the area of biology and crime.

www.ccsa.ca The Canadian Centre on Substance Abuse offers a rich array of up-to-date information on issues ranging from consumption patterns to economic impact to crime and laws related to drug use and abuse.

CHAPTER 6

Psychology-Based Perspectives of Criminal Behaviour

"...there is now much evidence to discredit the type of sociological theory so prominent and widely accepted...; criminals require socialization by properly planned conditioning treatments."

H.J. Eysenck, 1977:12–13

Learning Outcomes

After you have completed this chapter, you should be able to:

- Recognize and appreciate the impact psychology has had on the understanding of criminal behaviour.

- Appreciate the complexity of human behaviour.

- Be familiar with the major psychology-based theories of criminal behaviour.

- Recognize and be familiar with some of the important methods of treatment advocated by therapists.

- Appreciate the importance of the learning theory for understanding criminal behaviour.

Phrases like "this is what makes that person tick," "he must be really warped to be able to commit that kind of crime," or "that person really needs some serious help" can sometimes be heard when people talk about the behaviour of a criminal. As we learned in Chapter 4, this type of approach belongs to the positivist school of thought. This perspective assumes that behaviour is deterministic and is related to individual and/or environmental factors. Scientific psychology divides the causes of human behaviour along the continuum between *nature* and *nurture*.

Examining individual factors to explain behaviour is probably the oldest explanatory mode known to us. Like sociology (which will be discussed in Chapter 7), the field of psychology is both broad and diverse in its study of human behaviour. In this chapter, we will examine those explanations of criminal behaviour that focus on psychological factors.

Until recently, psychological approaches to understanding criminality were not always distinct from the somatic-biological approaches, which we discussed in the previous chapter. In fact, Schafer (1976) saw them as being on a continuum. As recently as a few years ago, introductory criminology textbooks typically grouped the biological and psychological explanatory approaches together. Today, with the growing volume of research in both the biological and psychological arenas, it is prudent to divide the two perspectives. As criminology becomes more integrated and interdisciplinary in focus and recognizes the need to separate theories of law and criminal justice from theories of human behaviour, biological and psychological theories and research are starting to receive individualized attention.

We will begin by reviewing the oldest known explanatory model of deviant behaviour—demonology. Then we will review several of the main psychological explanations of criminal behaviour. As in the other theory chapters, the objective is to provide an overview of the most important theories in this stream, as opposed to an exhaustive and detailed examination; to this end, what follows is a cross-sectional introduction to how psychology attempts to explain and predict human behaviour. It is also worth nothing that while psychological theories focus on identifying individual factors as the primary cause of criminality, most also acknowledge the influence of social and/or environmental factors.

In this chapter, we will examine five major ways of explaining criminal behaviour from the perspective of psychology: demonology, psychodynamic explanations, cognitive explanations, moral development theories, and behavioural explanations. As diverse as these psychological perspectives are, they all tend to "focus their examinations on basic components of human nature, such as appetites and aversions, motives and emotions that are viewed as characteristic of the human species" (Barak, 1997:127).

The Legacy of Demonology and "Evil"

"The devil made me do it." Flip Wilson (comedian)

Flip Wilson was a popular comedian during the 1970s and early 1980s who would use the above phrase to excuse his actions whenever he got into trouble on his show. The insinuation was that he became possessed by a "bad seed" or evil thought beyond his control. Although this excuse was usually good for a laugh, as the old saying goes, there is usually a grain of truth in every joke, and the idea of being possessed by an evil spirit forms the basis of **demonology**. In his thought-provoking and widely acclaimed book titled *The Soul's Code*, James Hillman (1996) uses the term "bad seed" to describe a psychopathic criminal. Using case studies ranging from Adolf Hitler to Jeffery Dahmer, Hillman argues that there are those who are born without a *soul* and in whose character one can see evil—in psychological terms, *psychopathic* traits. Many of his ideas are a refinement of Lombroso's earlier notions of the born criminal (see Chapter 4). Moreover, in keeping with the positivist model, Hillman describes how it is possible to exorcize the "bad seed"—"redressing the balance between the psyche's weakness and the daimon's (soul's) potential" (1996:242).

Anthropological and historical records describe how people in primitive and preliterate societies believed that all living and non-living objects held some symbol of power. Depending on the source, the powers could represent either good or evil. Out of these beliefs emerged the practice of black magic, witchcraft, and satanic worship. Today, we can still find evidence of these metaphysical belief systems. Some people believe that gemstones, pyramids, and various bioenergetic devices possess certain healing properties. Certain religious groups still practise ceremonial sacrifices or pay homage to deities to appease them in light of people's wrongdoings. There is no shortage of alternative practices that share the common theme of placing faith and trust in constructs whose influence has never been proven. Although their characteristics may vary, all these practices provide a means of balancing the good and evil in us and subscribe at some level to a belief in a "mystical" or "supernatural" power. Up to the Enlightenment period, most European authorities thought that criminal behaviour was caused by supernatural forces or "some other-world power or spirit" (Vold & Bernard, 1986:5), a view that was supported by the church. As European societies evolved from primitive tribes to agrarian cultures and then underwent urbanization, growing weaknesses in the Catholic Church led it to form an alliances with the existing ruling bodies (DeKeseredy & Schwartz, 1996). Abstract faith was being substituted by formal intervention agencies created by the state. In their zeal to convert and control the populace, these agencies engaged in a reign of terror that spanned the Middle Ages. The practices are today referred to as the Inquisition. Both the church and the state tortured and executed anyone they felt was a threat to them. The most common victims were the poor. Pfohl (1994) estimates that over a two-hundred-year period, approximately a million people, mostly women, were burned alive. Were these people possessed by evil thoughts or were they simply the victims of a narrow-minded social, cultural, and political mindset?

A historical overview of demonology serves to highlight several of the points about the *relative* and *evolutive* nature of people's views on crime (see Chapter 1). Throughout the ages, the associations between evil and criminal behaviour have been well-documented, but we can also see that the meaning of evil took on different connotations over time. We can also see how the *consensus* and *conflict* perspectives of justice emerged from these views. In ancient times, there appeared to be a greater level of consensus as to what constituted evil. However, as societies evolved and became more heterogeneous, so did the meaning of evil. Chambliss (1988), for example, suggests the Inquisition was a time when those in power used their influence to attack and use as scapegoats those less able to defend themselves. The poor, and often innocent, were punished in order to mask the shortcomings of the state and the church.

Another way of interpreting the behaviour of those thought to be engaging in evil acts is to view it as "*subjectively adaptable* to a response pattern that a person has found to be effective, or thinks to be effective, in certain circumstances" (Bartol, 1995:92). In other words, people simply act in accordance with what they feel enables them to cope and deal with life. In other words, evil behaviour can be seen as a form of maladaptive behaviour rather than as a psychopathology. When some people are exposed to a sudden shocking or violent scene, they simply faint. Humans and animals alike regularly engage in subjectively adaptable behaviour in order to suit their needs and environment. As Shakespeare once wrote, "All the world's a stage, and all the men and women merely players."

The notion that people must possess, or be possessed, by an "evil mind" to be guilty of crime has been refined over the years (see Box 6.1). Today, our criminal law doctrine of responsibility and punishment is based on the principles of *mens rea* (the ability to form intent) and *actus reus* (the physical element of crime). We do not punish people unless they have committed a wrong with foreknowledge of the act. While we may not talk openly about the intent being a product of a possessed mind, our criminal justice system still advocates the use of punishment to condemn the criminal act. Or the system might attempt to rehabilitate, treat, or simply prevent the offender from "infecting" others with his or her evil ways. In the sentencing process, we cloak such notions by framing them in a legalistic context.

REALITY CHECK BOX 6.1

MODERN-DAY DEMONOLOGY: "TAMING THE DEMONS"

The notion that individuals can be possessed by evil spirits can still be found today. "Taming the Demons" was the title for a 1998 *Calgary Herald* article that discussed the challenges researchers face in trying to help people who suffer from attention deficit disorder.

During the Roman Empire, the notion of demonic possession was used to justify persecuting Christians. Later, the Christian church used it to persecute witches. More recent examples include the Nazis' persecution of Jews and it the ethnic cleansing in Yugoslavia during the late 1990s.

Various religious and spiritual groups still subscribe to the notion of demonic possession as a means of expressing their beliefs and controlling their followers. Among the extremist groups, some continue to engage in ritual abuse exercises to rid the victim of demonic possession. The practices have included cult-related abuse, satanic ritual abuse, ritualized abuse, and sadistic abuse (Ritual abuse, 1996).

Many of our ritual behaviours are harmless—for example, getting up every morning and brushing our teeth before we have breakfast. Virtually every society has rituals related to important life situations, such as those of baptism, marriage, graduation, and death. By contrast, ritual abuse has been defined as psychological, physical, and/or sexual assault on an unwilling victim. It can be committed by one or more individuals whose primary motive is to act out a sequence of events in order to satisfy the perceived needs of their deity. The Aztecs used to sacrifice young virgin girls to appease their gods. Christians and Mormons, among others, give financial donations and perform other rituals (such as regular church attendance, prayer, abstaining from certain foods and drink, etc.) as an expression of their devotion to their deity. Where do we draw the line between acceptable and non-acceptable rituals?

Six different forms of ritual abuse can be identified in the literature. They all share the common theme of religion. In recent years, there have been reports (although difficult to substantiate) of an infant dying of exorcism in Ontario and a young child dying in Alberta as a result of satanic exercises. Another Canadian example was the ill-fated Order of the Solar Temple and its leader Luc Jouret in 1994 in Quebec. Portraying himself as the "New Christ," the Swiss-born Canadian preached of an impending catastrophe. Then, after a series of macabre events, 19 members were found dead, dressed in their ceremonial robes and lying in a circle with their feet pointing toward a common centre. Another group that garnered media attention toward the end of the 1990s was the Doomsday religious movement Heaven's Gate, with their apocalyptic belief that the year 2000 AD would bring about peace and harmony only for those would follow their movement while everyone else would experience some kind of a devastating end.

In summary, reliance on demonic approaches and other metaphysical explanations of behaviour have been used throughout the ages by some people to excuse their behaviour, while the church, religious sects, and state used it as a means of justifying social control. And since the wrongdoing was considered something supernatural, people were subjected to horrific punishment. Yet, according to a scientific perspective, there has never been any demonstrable proof of God's existence or the existence of evil. Nevertheless, the notion of spirits and demons as possible causes of criminal behaviour prevail. With the emergence of the *classical* and *positivist* schools of thought, psychological theories emerged as one means of trying to explain and predict human behaviour through scientific methods.

The Emergence of Psychology-Based Attempts to Explain Criminality

Interest in the psychological and psychiatric aspects of crime emerged during the middle to late 1800s. Jeffery (1973) identifies three essential individuals (also see Box 6.2 and Chapter 4).

1. **Gustav Aschaffenburg** (1866–1944), a pioneer of psychiatric criminology argued that we are influenced less by heredity than by our social environment (von Hentig, 1973). Aschaffenburg's ideas were instrumental in forging the notion that, from a psychological perspective, criminal behaviour is not a mental pathology but a form of socially maladaptive behaviour.

2. **Henry Maudsley** (1835–1918), described as a brilliant medical doctor, believed that criminals are the product of "moral degeneracy"—lacking in moral development (Scott, 1973). Many of the principles that were expanded on by the famous Swiss child psychologist Jean Piaget were further developed by Lawrence Kohlberg (1969:195). Beginning in the 1970s, their ideas also formed the basis of Canadian prison education programs (see Duiguid, 1979; Ross, Fabiano, & Eweles, 1988).

3. Isaac Ray (1807–1881), the "father" of the American Psychological Association and a very influential forensic psychiatrist, wrote a great deal on the subject of "moral insanity." He considered it a "disease ... never established by a single diagnostic symptom" (Overholser, 1973:183).

FYI BOX 6.2

JAMES MARK BALDWIN: THE FATHER OF CANADIAN PSYCHOLOGY

After the untimely death of George Paxton Young, a revered professor of metaphysics at the University of Toronto, James Mark Baldwin (1861–1934) assumed the position and established the first psychology laboratory in the British Empire. He was a strong proponent of the German scholar Wilhelm Wundt, who pioneered experimental psychology. Although Baldwin left Toronto in 1893, he had left a permanent mark on Canadian psychology.

A widely cited article by two well-known psychologists, Samuel Yochelson and Stanton Samenow (1976), argued there may be a **criminal personality**, or at least a different thinking pattern among criminals. Their research was based on extensive case studies of criminally insane patients in a Washington, DC, hospital. Although they overgeneralized the evidence, their work drew considerable attention from federal government circles. The view that there might be something "wrong" with the mind of a criminal gave support to the notion that sentenced individuals should be required to undergo various sorts of treatment.

The psychological explanations of criminal behaviour can be divided into two major theoretical categories: those that emphasize family conflict or *intrapsychic* factors, and those that attribute the origins of criminal behaviour to learning factors (Johnson &

Fennell, 1983). Within the later classification, there various sub-classifications, each focusing on different elements of learning. Because the learning approaches are more widely accepted, in this chapter we will focus on three primary sub-categories of this school of thought: cognitive explanations, moral development theories, and behavioural explanations. First, however, let us review the intrapsychic or psychodynamic approach, as it was one of the first approaches to consider individual personality as an observable and measurable factor in criminal behaviour.

Intrapsychic Theories: Psychodynamic Explanations

Perhaps the best known psychodynamic theory is the Viennese Freudian-based approach of **psychoanalysis**. It is a mixture of the Kantian model (rationalism) and the Lockean model (the assertion that behaviour is the result of sensations and experiences). According to the Freudian approach, criminal behaviour is the result of internal conflict and tension among the three aspects of one's personality that emerge in early childhood because of developmental and/or interaction problems between parents and their children.

Sigmund Freud (1856–1939) (see Box 6.3) believed that the mind has three levels of *consciousness*: the unconscious, the preconscious, and the conscious. According to Freudian theory, the operations of the **id**, **ego**, and **superego**—which constitute different drives and aspects of personality that function on these levels—can result in criminal behaviour. The outcome of our behaviour is dependent on how we process our early childhood experiences—traumatic or otherwise.

The id and the superego are considered part of the *unconscious* mental processes, while the ego is considered part of the *conscious* mental processes of the personality. The id consists of basic unconscious biological urges and desires for immediate gratification and satisfaction, which include the desire for food (i.e., the will to live), sex (i.e., pleasure), and survival (i.e., aggression). The id is also referred to as the *pleasure principle* because it attempts to avoid pain and unpleasant experiences.

The power of the unconscious can be used to explain how some people are driven to steal or fight for their survival—out of necessity. The id is the amoral, immature instinctive passion within all of us. As Freud noted, the id is our life source or *eros*, our creative side, and the basis for both positive and negative aggression. However, due to the influence of the id and its self-centred focus, we start life in a state of immorality. The humanist-oriented existential psychologist Rollo May (1969) later simply referred to the id as *will* in what has been considered by many to be his best book: *Love and Will*.

SIGMUND FREUD: THE FATHER OF PSYCHOANALYSIS

Freud was born on May 6, 1856, at Freiberg, Moravia, which at that time was part of the Austro-Hungarian Empire. His family moved to Vienna in 1860. On entering the University of Vienna, he became a medical student and specialized in anatomy and physiology. Because he was a Jew, opportunities were not readily available for him (Hall & Lindzey, 1970). Out of necessity, he opened a private practice where, amongst other things, he specialized in the treatment of nervous disorders. He subsequently developed a treatment modality based on patients talking about their problems, which he later called *free association*. Freud believed that sexual factors were the key to understanding hysteria.

Freud was a prolific writer, and some of his writings today are classics in the field of psychoanalysis. His commitment to clearly explicating his psychoanalytic theories and the importance of dreams is perhaps best reflected in the observation that at the end of the day he would set aside half an hour for self-analysis (Hall & Lindzey, 1970).

When the Nazis overran Vienna in 1938, Freud fled to London, where he died of cancer 16 months later, on September 23, 1939. While many critics have tried to debunk Freud's psychoanalytic theories, his ideas gained many prominent supporters over the years—such as Alfred Adler, August Aichhorn, Eric Ericson, Erich Fromm, Karen Horney, and Alice Miller—and have withstood the test of time.

The ego and superego, by contrast, are products of our individual learning experiences. We each experience different events throughout our childhood, adolescence, and adult years. Our ego—the "I" or *reality principle*—represents an adaptive outgrowth of our id. Based on early childhood experiences, our ego learns to weigh the consequences of acting out the id within the boundaries of social convention, and it serves as our control mechanism.

The other unconscious aspect of our personality, the superego, represents outer world influences. The superego arises out of the relationship between our early life experiences and the moral values of our parents and the community at large. The superego is an indicator of our socialization process. This notion is well illustrated in August Aichhorn's classic book *Wayward Youth* (1935). In addition to defining delinquent groups according to the id and the ego, Aichhorn notes that those with criminal superegos belong to criminal groups or identify with a delinquent father—a very sociological orientation of criminality according to Jeffery (1990). The superego is our "psychic police officer" (Bischof, 1964) that polices our id through conscious thought. Redl and Wineman (1951) coined the concept *delinquent ego* to describe those youths who, because of inadequate ego and superego development, are able to rationalize their delinquent aggression and frustration. They also reported that such youth lack close personal relationships with adult figures.

The three aspects of our personality—id, ego, and superego—can be in conflict. In fact, they usually are to varying degrees. Some of the more common forms of intrapsychic conflict take the form of *neuroses* such as anxiety, phobias (fear of different things), amnesia, or sexual disorders.

The source of the conflicts can be either organic or functional in nature. Organic disorders are based in the brain or result from brain chemistry, whereas functional disorders have no known physical base but rather a mental, experiential, or psychic base.

Internal psychic conflict can lead to the *repression* of desires or unpleasant memories, which in turn can lead to personality problems. For example, victims of sexual abuse can sometimes go for years without remembering the traumatic experiences they were subjected to as children (see Box 6.4). These repressed feelings can lead to

A CLOSER LOOK BOX 6.4

FREUD AND HUMAN PSYCHOSEXUAL DEVELOPMENT

Freud argued that since the id represents the core of our personality and is the dominant force at birth, it is our early childhood experiences that most directly affect our later psychological development. In particular, Freud believed that since sex is an instinctual need, how we progress through the five stages of child development significantly influences our *psychosexual* development.

The first stage is the *oral* stage (birth–age 1), which centres on the mouth and the pleasures associated with sucking and eating. Examples of its manifestation in later life include being passive or dependent, or chewing gum or smoking.

The *anal* stage (ages 1–3), which includes the toilet training period, focuses on the control and elimination process. Examples of its manifestation in later life include being compulsive, stingy, and concerned with orderliness.

The *phallic* stage (ages 3–5) is when children discover their sexual parts and derive pleasure from masturbation and their genitals. This is also the stage when boys form an attachment to their mother and when they must compete with their father for their mother. When this happens, conflict arises between son and father. Freud labelled this the *Oedipus complex*, named after the Greek tragedy in which the son kills his father. The son normally resolves the conflict by identifying with and obeying his father. This is a superego development.

The *sexual latency* stage (ages 6–13) is one of repression of sexual feelings and interest in young people. This is when boys play with boys and girls with girls.

The final stage of development is the *genital* stage (age 13 and beyond), when the superego is well enough developed for youth to move into the phase of socially and culturally acceptable behaviours and to act in morally and socially prescribed ways.

Problems experienced during any of these phases could trigger psychological problems, and thus unacceptable or criminal behaviour. The means to determine if a person is experiencing problems is through dream analysis and through free association. Freud, along with many of his followers, believed that our dreams contain many of the repressed feelings and hostilities that our conscious mind (i.e., superego) would not let surface for fear of embarrassment or some other unpleasant experience.

fundamental personality problems in these people, such as difficulty feeling close to someone for whom they care or not feeling comfortable engaging in certain sexual acts that they were subjected to. If left unattended, the unconscious memories can cause anxieties around the repressed desires and memories. Victims are then likely to resort to one of four defence mechanisms in order to avoid confronting the reality of their hidden desires.[1] According to Freud, when the mental anguish begins to negatively affect their behaviour, they are suffering from neuroticism—which can be expressed through incomprehensible distress, psychosomatic symptoms, hallucinations and delusions, and other behaviours and symptoms.

Freudian Explanations of Criminality

In accordance with the basic assumptions underlying Freudian theory, human behaviour is inherently anti-social and delinquent, and criminal behaviour is an indication of personality conflict. For example, Freud used the term *thanatos* (meaning "death" in Greek) to describe violent instinctual urges that some people experience under various social and/or psychological conditions. He further noted how the id (the pleasure principle) and ego (the reality principle) serve to mostly moderate these urges or instincts. Hence when violent urges prevail, the ego can lead criminals to feel the need to be punished, but the id may prevent them from confessing to the crime. However, when the perceived harm diminishes (e.g., they know they are dying), the superego might lead them to confess to their wrongdoing.

Criminals on death row are given the opportunity to spend time with a minister before being executed. Halleck (1967), among others, has observed how many criminals readily tell all and feel a sense of relief after being caught. For example, serial killer Heriberto "Eddie" Seda, known as the Zodiac killer, used to leave an encircled cross with three sevens at the scene of each crime. Even after signing his confession statement to the police, in 1996, Seda sealed his statement with his trademark—a confession? Psychoanalytical interpretation suggests this type of behaviour allows criminals to shed their guilt—the classic battle, in Freudian terms, between the driving forces, *cathexes*, and the restraining forces.

As Warren and Hindelang (1986) observed, Freudian explanations of criminality hold that:

- Criminal behaviour is the product of an uncontrolled id. It is a form of neurosis—an unconscious internal conflict that is expressed through an overt act.
- Criminals have an unconscious need to alleviate their sense of guilt and anxiety.
- Criminal activity may be an alternate means to gratify those needs that were not fulfilled by the criminal's family.
- Some criminal and delinquent behaviour is the result of traumatic (non-pleasurable) experiences the memories of which have been repressed.
- Some forms of delinquent behaviour may be the result of displaced hostility and/or an unconscious desire for punishment.

Freudian theory has met with varying criticism, as has Freud's treatment modality of psychoanalysis. Nevertheless, Freud can in many ways be considered, along with Darwin, a founding father of the psychobiological concept of humankind (Sulloway, 1979), for he attempted to find both a neurological and biological link to personality. In fact, his ideas were interdisciplinary in nature, as he placed a strong emphasis on biological and social factors as well as on multiple mechanisms to explain behaviour.

Today, researchers continue to think of new ways to validate the theoretical assertions of the psychoanalytic approach. And since no one theory has yet been able to explain all aspects of criminal behaviour, perhaps any theory that has withstood so much debate deserves some serious consideration in our quest to understand criminal behaviour.

Learning Theories
Cognitive Explanations

Plato and Kant both suggested that human behaviour is the product of mentalism, which involves processing the physical and social factors in our lives (Mannheim, 1973). In psychology, the term **cognition** is used to refer to the ability of individuals to make sense of their sensory experiences. In the 1970s, the American psychologist Stanton Samenow challenged the foundation of Freudian theory when he suggested that an offender "chooses to be criminal." Jeffery (1990:213) offers the following illustration of the mentalistic/cognitive model of human behaviour:

ENVIRONMENT———> MIND————> BEHAVIOUR

How the mind processes its sensory experiences is based on the premise of free will and intentionality. This general premise of explaining behaviour is related to cognitive and learning theories in psychology. Cognitive explanations claim that criminal behaviour is the result of faulty or irrational thinking.

Frustration-Aggression Model

The notion that frustration and aggression are linked is a popular conception of anti-social behaviour. For example, a growing concern in many North American cities is the increase in road rage (see Box 6.5). This occurs when a driver's temper flares up at the slightest provocation (e.g., being cut off, someone not merging properly).

THE ISSUE OF ROAD RAGE

The issue of road rage began to draw considerable attention in the late 1990s. Various associations have attempted to understand it and implement programs to curb the growing numbers of irate drivers. In one report, Vest, Cohen, and Tharp (1997) observed that road violence has gone up 51 percent in the 1990s. In the cases studied, 37 percent of offenders used firearms, while 35 percent used their cars! Obscene gestures are also very common. The American Department of Transport estimates that two-thirds of road fatalities are partly caused by aggressive driving. One expert suggests that we are simply reacting to having our sense of space constantly violated, since cars represent an extension of our personal space (Coyle, 1998). In March 1998, the Ontario Provincial Police introduced a traffic section nicknamed the "Highway Rangers," whose members drive around and spot people expressing road rage. These people are pulled over and given a survey. Based on their responses, they are either given a warning or a ticket (Question: How do you feel ..., 1998). In 2001, a study conducted in Australia compared road rage in Australia, Canada, United Kingdom, and the United States. The UK had the highest score for road rage (57.5), while Canada had the lowest score (52.9) (Results: Analyze..., 2001).

The modern frustration-aggression conception of criminality can be traced back to the work of Dollard, Doob, Miller, Mowerer, and Sears in 1939. They identified several premises that have become widely accepted under this social learning model of behaviour. These premises "linked Freudian concepts with the methods and concepts of an emerging behavioural perspective of human behaviour" (Andrews & Bonta, 1994:93). Freud believed that we are susceptible from birth to a buildup of aggressive energy, and from time to time it must be drained—"to blow off steam." Andrews and Bonta (1994) identified five elements of Dollard et al.'s study.

1. Aggression is always a consequence of frustration. Strasburg (1978) observed that communication problems are more common among violent young offenders than non-violent offenders. He also noted that speech and language disorders are more common among young males than young females. Frustration results from a negative reaction toward a valued outcome. There are two types of aggression (Feshbach, 1964). *Hostile aggression* refers to expressive or acting-out (e.g., insults and physical assault) behaviour. *Instrumental aggression* occurs when the offender weighs his or her options in order to obtain his or her desired outcome—using just enough coercion (physical and verbal) to gain another person's compliance.

2. The risk of aggression escalates with the degree of outside interference, frequency of frustrating experiences, and intensity of the event that instigated the frustration.

3. The greater the risk and perception of punishment resulting from an aggressive act, the greater the likelihood the act will not be committed. This is one of the premises of the classical doctrine; certainty and severity of punishment can serve as an effective deterrent.
4. If the victim perceives that the cost of directing aggression toward the offending agent could result in more harm, then he or she will likely redirect his or her aggression. Rather than take your hostilities out on the police officer who ticketed you, you might go home and verbally vent your frustration on your partner.
5. Once a person has vented his or her aggression, there is a temporary reduction in the desire to act out. This is also referred to as *catharsis*. You feel better after getting it off your chest—at least for a while.

A CLOSER LOOK BOX 6.6

COPYCATS AND MODELLING

Alfred Bandura of Stanford University and his fellow student Robert Walters (who taught at the University of Toronto and the University of Waterloo before his tragic death in 1968) conducted a number of studies on aggression and violence that were based on the learning model. Bandura (1965) identified three kinds of learning:

1. Observation learning is based on *modelling* in which the observer copies behaviour with which he or she identifies. For example, children may mimic television characters from their favourite programs or they might mimic the behaviour patterns of their parents.
2. *Response stimulation* is similar to the "monkey see, monkey do." Children who grow up in an environment where their father abuses their mother might grow up to copy that behaviour. Research has shown that viewing violent movies or sexually explicit videos can stimulate a desire to copy that behaviour.
3. *Raising or lowering restraints* depends on how our view of a model affects our attitude. If we admire someone and see his or her conduct pay off, we are more likely to emulate him or her. We tend to identify with winners, not losers. Studies have shown that young offenders become more aggressive after viewing "warranted" violence in which "unwarranted" aggression is directed toward a sympathetic movie character. These stereotypes are often played out in the wrestling world where the "hero" is momentarily beaten into near defeat before rising from a choreographed devastating loss to avenge his punishment, all to the adulation of his fans.

Bandura and Walters (1959) argue that while violence and aggression may result from neurological mechanisms and/or brain damage, most types of aggression in young people are based on emotional arousal that is learned and based on certain environmental cues. They also note that the type of reinforcement present affects the likelihood of violent acts being repeated (see classical conditioning on page 165). These ideas are very similar to the those put forward in learning theories developed by sociologists.

Although the state of criminological knowledge was still in its infancy in the 1930s, this model was thought to provide a viable explanation for most criminal acts.

Subsequent research on the frustration-aggression perspective by Leonard Berkowitz (1962) both updated and refined the theory. For instance, Berkowitz divided criminal personalities into two main classifications: the *socialized* and the *individual* offenders. The socialized offender's behaviour is a result of learning, conditioning, and modelling. By contrast, the individual offender's behaviour is a product of persistent, intense episodes of frustration resulting from unmet needs (see Box 6.6).

Andrews and Bonta (1994) note that the frustration-aggression model is regularly used for treatment programs that target the control of anger. It might appear quite appealing as an explanatory tool, but among the difficulties confronting this perspective are the following questions: How does one measure concepts such as frustration, aggression, or feeling better? What is an "attitude," and how does the mind assimilate and process sensory stimuli (the triggering observation)? How intense do the stimuli need to be, and are some environmental factors more important than others? The questions highlight the fact that the mind can never be directly, empirically observed (Jeffery, 1990). However, the model does assume a mind–body dualism that is congruent with the key elements of criminal law—that is, *mens rea* and *actus reus*.

In summary, the frustration-aggression model is based on social learning theory that is part of cognitive psychology. While Dollard et al. (1939) based their social learning approach on imitation, Bandura advocated a social learning approach based on cognitive process coupled with life experiences. Other variations of the social learning model include modelling (see Box 6.6) and symbolic interaction (see Blumer, 1969).

The social learning theory does not account for individual biological states due to the brain, genetics, or learning differences. We do not all respond in the same way to similar stimuli. In Chapter 7, we will see that sociology interprets social learning differently than does psychology. For example, sociology uses social learning theory as an all-encompassing experience of learning rather than as an aspect of the cognitive process.

Moral Development Theories

"Kids have no respect for people or property." "Such a heinous act! How could anyone do a thing like that?" Such statements might well reflect elements of another learning-based theory—**moral development** theory. There are different theories of moral development, but a central theme to all of them in understanding criminality is their focus on individuals' development of a sense of *morality* and *responsibility*.

The Swiss psychologist **Jean Piaget** (1896–1980) was the founder of the mental and moral development theory. Piaget hypothesized that children experience four primary stages of mental development. The *sensorimotor* period (birth–age 2) involves children learning to respond to their immediate environment and developing their motor reflex skills. The *preoperational* period (ages 2–7) involves learning language, drawing, and other skills. The *concrete operational* period (ages 7–11) involves the development of logical thinking and problem solving skills. The final *formal operational* period (ages 11–15) involves learning to deal with abstract ideas. Piaget believed that children learn to progress from being self-focused in their mental awareness to being able to understand and integrate their outer environment. As they mature, children learn to process moral-conflict situations in an intelligent manner.

Moral Development and Criminality

Piaget did not concern himself directly with delinquency or criminality; it was the American psychologist **Lawrence Kohlberg** (1927–1987) who applied the concept of moral development to criminality. Kohlberg (1969) theorized that all individuals pass through the same stages, in which they develop their moral reasoning skills. As we progress through the stages, we learn to make decisions about right or wrong and determine the ethically/morally acceptable course of action based on the surrounding circumstances.

Kohlberg divided moral development into three levels, each with two stages of moral reasoning (see Figure 6–1). For example, adolescents typically reason at the

FIGURE 6-1

KOHLBERG'S LEVELS OF MORAL REASONING

LEVEL OF MORAL DEVELOPMENT	STAGE OF REASONING	APPROX. AGES
Preconventional "do's and don'ts"	*Stage 1:* Right is obedience to power and avoidance of punishment. *Stage 2:* Right is taking responsibility and leaving others to be responsible for themselves.	< 11
Conventional	*Stage 3:* Right is being considerate: "uphold the values of other adolescents and adults' rules of society." *Stage 4:* Right is being good, with the values and norms of family and society at large.	adolescence and adulthood
Postconventional	*Stage 5:* Right is finding inner "universal rights" balance between self-rights and societal rules—a social contract. *Stage 6:* Right is based on a higher order of applying principles to all humankind, being non-judgmental, and respecting all human life.	after 20

Source: Adapted from Kohlberg, 1986:57–58.

conventional level. At this level, they believe in and adopt the values and rules of society. Hence, they try to abide by the laws—not to steal, not to lie, etc. However, according to Kohlberg and his colleagues, most young offenders (and criminals, in general) reason at the preconventional level. They might be familiar with the dos and don'ts, but they think in terms of, "If I commit a break and enter, what are the chances of getting caught and/or being punished?" By contrast, if a youth was at the postconventional level, his or her reasoning would include respect for human rights and the dignity of human life.

Kohlberg theorized that not everyone makes it through all the stages of moral development or progresses at the same rate. Moral development depends on how we deal with the learning experience at earlier stages. Based on these ideas, he reasoned that incomplete moral development was a major reason for criminal and deviant behaviour. Studies by Kohlberg and his associates (1973), among others, found that adolescent and adult offenders were significantly lower in their moral development than non-criminals of the same social background.

Given the impression some people have of the character of many types of criminals, it is not surprising the moral development theory has been an important cognitive theory for criminology (Siegel, 1995). Steven Duiguid (1979) developed a training module to help inmates develop their moral reasoning skills. He has reported some success with his model.

In spite of its pragmatic appeal, the theory also has its critics. For example, Kohlberg's approach does not clarify whether an individual's lower level of moral reasoning predisposes him or her to offending or whether offending predisposes him or her to staying in the lower stages of moral development. Peer pressure, family conflict, or biochemical imbalances might have triggered this developmental behaviour for a variety of reasons.

At what level of moral development might the following individuals be?

- The boxer Mike Tyson, who bit the ear of his opponent Evander Hollyfield during a match in retaliation for an alleged low punch.
- Alan Eagleson, former head of the NHL Players' Association in the 1980s, who was found guilty of mail fraud and of skimming profits intended for NHL pension funds. (Earlier, however, he had been bestowed the Order of Canada—the highest civilian award in Canada.)
- Former Bre-X owner David Walsh, who allegedly defrauded thousands of Canadians of their investments in the mid-1990s.
- Albert Walker, who was charged in 1998 with the cold-blooded killing of Ronald Platt, the man whose identity he assumed during the final three years of his six years on the run from Canadian authorities; he had fled Canada after bilking many of his clients in Paris, Ontario, of their savings.[2]

Gilligan (1982) argued that Kohlberg's theory is biased in favour of males. She points out that there are variations in moral standards between men and women. Women, she suggests, tend to be more care-oriented while men are more justice-oriented when making moral decisions. This difference has never been clearly resolved.

A final criticism pertains to the ability to quantify moral development. Although the general evidence suggests that the level of moral reasoning is related to behaviour (the theory is not able to differentiate between types of criminal behaviour and stage of moral development), "the correlations reported in many studies are often quite low" (Zapf, Cox, & Roesch, 2004:267).

Behavioural Explanations

Most psychological theories of crime support the assertion that human behaviour emerges from the mutual interaction between a personality variable and situational variables. However, Bartol (1995:106) notes in his review of the literature that "much crime research and theory neglects situational variables in favour of dispositional factors." An exception to this limited frame of reference lies in the behavioural approach. Of all the psychological theories, behavioural psychology has been described as perhaps the most economical and elegant (Jeffery, 1990). Rather than focus on abstract concepts such as attitudes, interests, nature of past experiences, or personality patterns of the individual, proponents of the theory of **behavioural learning** focus on specific behaviour (see Figure 6–2).

With respect to criminal behaviour, behaviourists view crime as the result of learned responses to life situations—responses that are not necessarily abnormal or morally immature. For example, the wife who kills her abusive husband or the starving survivor of a plane crash who resorts to cannibalism in order to survive do not necessarily commit these acts because they have some personality pathology or maladaptive personality trait.

There are two basic behavioural models of associative learning: classical conditioning and operant conditioning.

Classical Conditioning

The *stimulus-response* (S–R) theory can trace its origins to the pioneering work of the renowned Russian physiologist **Ivan P. Pavlov** (1849–1936), who won the Nobel Prize in physiology and medicine in 1904. Using dogs, Pavlov was able to demonstrate that through the simultaneous presentation of an *unconditional stimulus* (UCS) (piece of meat) combined with a *conditioned stimulus* (CS) (sound from a tuning fork, a neutral stimulus), the conditioned stimulus, through repeated presentations, would eventually

F I G U R E 6–2

SIMPLIFIED MODEL OF BEHAVIOURAL LEARNING

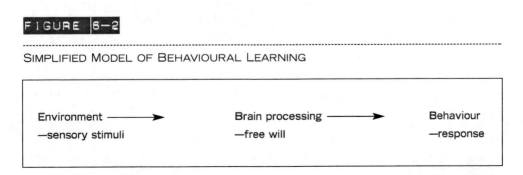

Environment ⟶   Brain processing ⟶   Behaviour
—sensory stimuli   —free will   —response

elicit a conditioned response (CR) (salivation) in the absence of the *unconditioned stimulus* (UCS). This type of learning was referred to as *conditioned response* (CR), *Pavlovian conditioning*, or **classical conditioning** (see Box 6.7). The model asserts that the dog— or person—has no control over the situation or over what happens to it (Bartol, 1995).

FYI BOX 6.7

IS DOING PSYCHOLOGY ALSO AN ART?

Although Pavlov is describe as the father of classical conditioning, he considered himself more a physiologist and had little respect for psychology. He once said, "it is still open to discussion whether psychology is a natural science...at all" (cited in Adams, 1976:91).

There are four kinds of classical conditioning that are defined by the relationship between the CS and the UCS (Adams, 1976):

- *Simultaneous conditioning* occurs when the CS and UCS come together and go off together. In treating certain pedophilias, a picture of a child (CS) is accompanied by an electric shock, noxious smell, or aversive taste (UCS) to extinguish any sexual arousal (CR).

- *Delayed conditioning* occurs when the CS precedes the onset of the UCS and may continue after the commencement of the UCS. With the pedophile, a picture may be displayed to see if it elicits a reaction before the shock is administered (see Box 6.8). The picture and shock may stay on together until the patient's sexual reaction subsides.

- *Trace conditioning* occurs when the CS is terminated before the onset of the UCS. There is delay between the two stimuli.

- *Backward conditioning* occurs when the UCS precedes the CS. Adams (1976:94) notes that "little or no conditioning is found with backward conditioning...so it is dubious as one of the main kinds of conditioning."

Applied to the treatment modality, classical conditioning is often based on a process called **avoidance learning** or aversion therapy. By associating the fear of punishment with the crime or diversion, the offender would learn to avoid and "extinguish" the behaviour. In addition to controlling the type of conditioning, the therapist can also control the duration and intensity of the punishment to the individual patient (Maletzky, 1991).

Over the years, behaviourists have compiled a considerable volume of literature demonstrating that an aversive stimulus has a strong effect on behaviour. Maletzky (1991:90), in reviewing aversion therapies for sexual offenders, concludes that "their techniques not only were highly effective but also provided a framework upon which to develop theories about the origin of maladaptive sexual approach disorders." However, Lykken (1957, cited in Bartol, 1995:80–81) was among the first to

PARAPHILIAS

Pedophilia is categorized in the *Diagnostic and Statistical Manual of Mental Disorders (DSM-IV)* as one of several paraphiliac mental disorders. Pedophilia involves sexually oriented activity by an adult with an underage person (usually a prepubescent child). Behaviour can range from undressing and looking inappropriately at a child to more direct physical sexual contact. The disorder is a type of paraphilia (from the Greek *para*, meaning "beside," and *philos*, meaning "loving") that refers to abnormal or bizarre sexual practices that involve children, animals, or others who cannot grant consent; humiliation (sadomasochism); or non-human objects (e.g., leather, shoes, and underwear) (see Holmes, 1991).

The American psychologist Seymour Halleck (1967:176) observed that the line between what is legally defined as a sex crime and what society considers sexual deviation "is almost incomprehensibly muddled by value judgements, conflicting concepts of normality and an aura of secrecy." For example, in the 1960s, it was illegal to have intercourse outside of marriage in 10 American states. Referring to patients he has treated, Halleck also points out that many sex offenders readily confess their "sins." He wonders whether their problems should be treated solely as crimes or as deep personal troubles over which they feel shame and guilt and for which they wish to be punished.

demonstrate that **psychopaths** have an unresponsive autonomic nervous system that does not respond in the classical reflex manner.

Noted researchers such as Robert Hare and Hans Eysenck have focused on social learning related factors, such as poor parenting and an impoverished learning environment. Although their models differ slightly, both argue that psychopathic and anti-social behaviour is linked to a breakdown in learning inhibition and/or the ability to process information. Other psychologists have pointed out that psychopaths suffer from a lack of *empathy*—the capacity to put oneself in another person's shoes. Yet, in spite of the growing volume of research on criminal psychopaths, Bartol (1995) concludes that while we know they do not seem to think like the rest of mainstream society, there is much we still do not understand about them; treatment programs have been only marginally effective.

Hans Eysenck (1977) coupled his personality theory of criminality with classical conditioning to suggest that the problem with criminals is that they do not condition in a socially accepted manner. The break-and-enter offender, for example, may not be deterred (UCR) by the presence of a house alarm sticker (UCS). Based on Eysenck's theory, the alarm decal is not critical enough to deter the offender because of his or her personality traits. Yet the decal might deter another potential offender.

Operant or Instrumental Learning

While **John B. Watson** (1878–1958) is often recognized as the father of experimental psychology and behaviourism (Bartol, 1995), **B.F. Skinner** (1904–1990) (see Box 6.9) has been one of the most influential behaviourists in North America. Although Skinner accepted the belief that human cognition exists, he maintained that unless one can observe and measure it, cognition cannot be scientifically studied. Only that which has a physical basis, and can be publicly observed, can be studied.

PROFILE BOX 6.9

BURRHUS FREDERICK SKINNER

Skinner was born and raised in Susquehanna, Pennsylvania. He majored in English in university, determined to become a writer, but his attempts to make a living in this way did not work out. He went back to school to study psychology at Harvard University. On graduating in 1931, he quickly became an acclaimed leader in experimental psychology and later received the distinguished President's National Medal of Science (Hall & Lindzey, 1970).

In addition to his numerous academic works, Skinner wrote the famous utopian novel *Walden II,* published in 1948, in which he "described the evolution of an experimental society based on psychological principles" (Hall & Lindzey, 1970:478). His model community was based on a planned order that eliminated punishment, along with any form of aversive control. In 1967, an actual community, Twin Oaks, based on the book, was established in Virginia. In 1971, Skinner published his scientific position in another popular book, *Beyond Freedom and Dignity.* On its release, *The New York Times* suggested that if one read only one book that year, it should be Skinner's book.

On the value of punishment, Skinner (1971:68) wrote, "the trouble is that when we punish a person for behaving badly, we leave it up to him to discover how to behave well." This view may have been influenced by his father, a lawyer, who had taken him on prison tours while young, and from his grandmother, who constantly stressed the evils of wrongdoing (Skinner, 1979). Skinner has been described as the most influential representative of behaviourism and the author of one of the major psychological theories of the 20th century.

For Skinner all behaviour is situational, deterministic, and void of independent thinking. That is, we are at the mercy of stimuli in our environment—we simply react to them. In addition, while our environment might appear complex and filled with stimuli, careful research can identify the causal factors of any behaviour.

This line of reasoning is known as *operant conditioning* and forms the basic principles of *behaviour modification* or *behavioural therapy.* Behaviourists believe that behaviour is influenced whenever someone attempts to exert some power and control over others. Thus, behaviour is not based on free will but instead is the product of chains of stimuli and responses. One of the most powerful elements of behaviourism is *reinforcement*.

We can probably all relate to examples of how our behaviour was changed as a result of being rewarded for some responses and not others. In grade school, you might have earned stars for work well done. Conversely, if you did something wrong, you might have been grounded or had a curfew levied. Psychology has extended this general knowledge to changing the anti-social behaviour of delinquent boys, as well as changing inappropriate behaviour through treating emotionally challenged patients. This is known as **behaviour modification**. The key to initiating any change is dependent on the *discriminative stimuli*, which—when present—can bring about the desired change. The discriminative stimuli can offer *positive* reinforcement (which results in increases or rewards behaviour) or *negative* reinforcement (which reduces, eliminates, or causes the avoidance of undesirable behaviour) (Bartol, 1995).

One common form of positive reinforcement used in many correctional settings is the use of **token economy**. "Tokens" such as poker chips, points, and stamps are symbolic rewards that are given whenever the desired response occurs. The tokens can be submitted in exchange for "backward reinforcement" of value to the participant (such as food or being allowed to watch a favourite television program).

Negative reinforcement focuses on trying to extinguish undesirable responses by creating a negative association between the response and the discriminative stimulus. As noted above, negative reinforcement has been used in a variety of programs designed to treat sex offenders.

Reinforcement is not always delivered in the same manner. The two basic methods involve the use of different schedules, as follows:

- *Ratio schedules*: Reinforcement occurs after a specific number of responses regardless of time frame.
- *Interval schedules*: Reinforcement is delivered on a time schedule independent of the number of responses.

These two schedules can be further classified into *fixed* and *variable* schedules, "depending whether number of responses or time between reinforcements is fixed or is variable with a statistical definition" (Adams, 1976:47).

Behaviour modification (BM) involves applying these elements in a treatment or therapeutic setting. The principles and elements of this treatment modality have been derived largely from research in experimental psychology—hence its often stark and sterile image. Some of the key aspects of BM are as follows:

- The purpose of BM is, first, to define the problematic behaviour (e.g., shoplifting).
- Unless the specific problem can be identified, behaviour cannot be properly changed. For example, it may be that when the client feels stressed, he or she turns to shoplifting to alleviate his or her tension.

Psychology-Based Perspectives of Criminal Behaviour

- Treatment usually involves designing contracts for patients that involve specific contingency elements, such as being placed under house arrest and not being permitted to leave the property between certain hours, having to report in every day at a predefined time, etc.
- The aim of the program is to shape the behaviour of the offender using either an *aversive* approach (e.g., fines, lockdown, loss of privileges) or a *positive* approach (e.g., earned remission, praise, "tokens" that can be put toward a reward of choice).

Applying Behavioural Conditioning

In their extensive review of Canadian correctional programs, Gendreau and Ross (1987) identified a number of advantages and disadvantages of treatment programs based on behavioural conditioning. The advantages include the following:

- Treatment does not dwell on past experiences. There is no need to assess the validity of such experiences.
- Because patients must focus on the current aspects of their behaviour, they cannot use explanations of prior experiences or events to excuse their behaviour.
- BM-oriented programs do not require trained therapeutic personnel to administer them.

Among those elements that are considered limitations of the behavioural treatment approach, Vito and Holmes (1994) found the following issues:

- When reinforcement is based on negative conditioning, it may be used to simply gain control of "troublemakers" instead of serving as a treatment or offering a constructive learning opportunity. Sometimes it may even be unconstitutional, as all offenders are entitled to an opportunity to reform their behaviour. Negative reinforcement involves the withdrawal of reward.
- Adequate steps may not always be taken to protect the rights of the inmates.
- BM programs tend to create artificial situations that do not resemble the natural environment in which the patient must live. As Vito and Holmes (1994:132) observe, "not all good behaviours are rewarded."

In summary, behavioural learning stands in stark contrast to most of the other learning-based theories. The model—in both its classical and operant conditioning versions—asserts that behaviours change in response to the stimuli in the individual's environment. Behaviourists do not assume that behaviour is rooted in an inherently abnormal personality.

Applications of the behavioural approach constituted popular models of treatment during the 1970s (see, for example, Gendreau & Ross, 1987). Treatment modalities varied in their description, but they all emphasized modifying behaviour through a variable system of rewards and punishments. Targeted behaviour was based on observable and quantifiable actions.

In the 1980s, in response to a variety of ethical and practical concerns, there was a waning of the behavioural approach in certain areas of the criminal justice system, in particular within corrections (see Winterdyk, 2001). Nevertheless, in keeping with theoretical trends in criminology, behaviourism has evolved, embracing a broader integrated and interdisciplinary model of learning.

The Future of Explanations Rooted in Psychology

To paraphrase one of the intellectual icons from the 1970s, Thomas Szasz (1970), psychological explanations are constantly looking to expand their domain of experimentation and treatment base. A historical review of the American Psychiatric Association's *DSM-IV* reveals that the manual continues to expand, providing a growing list of ailments that apparently require psychological intervention and/or treatment.

While there are a wide range of theories rooted in psychology, their protocols for intervention and treatment tend to have little regard for the context within which people act. As Schissel (2002) notes, treatment and intervention is dependent on being able to label a person as potentially criminal or at risk based on an assessment tool that lacks credible reliability and validity (see Cao, 2004). Furthermore, the instruments tend not to account for such factors as age, social class, culture, gender, or race (Schissel, 2002).

Although none of the psychology-based approaches to the study of crime and delinquency have been very fruitful in explaining or identifying a single criminal personality type, efforts continue to identify a cluster of traits that can account for certain types of offenders and offending behaviour. And while psychological explanations may not be able to help us understand geographic or temporal variations in crime rates, they have helped explain offending patterns in terms of age, race, gender, and social class. Psychology-based perspectives on crime causation continue to be used by the criminal justice system to determine the criminal responsibility of a defendant.

Summary

- The roots of psychological theory can be traced to the influence of demonology and its the assertion that criminal behaviour is the result of a possessed mind/body.
- Psychological explanations are premised on a deterministic model that asserts that the causes of crime originate within the individual. Psychological explanations subscribe to a medical/positivist model of treatment and intervention.
- *Intrapsychic* explanations subscribe to the notion that criminal behaviour is the result of internal conflict and tension among various aspects of one's personality. *Cognitive* explanations subscribe to the notion that criminal behaviour is the product of choice based on how an individual processes sensory experiences; frustration

is seen as a key trigger in predicting anti-social behaviour. *Moral development theories* subscribe to the notion that criminal behaviour is the product of lower-development skill sets, which may be the result of poor learning or compromised cognitive processes. *Behavioural* explanations subscribe to the notion that criminal behaviour emerges from the mutual interaction between a personality variable and situational rather than dispositional variables.

- The main criticism of psychological theories is that they pay minimal attention to the relative nature of crime (see Box 6.10).

- Treatment and intervention strategies are dependent on being able to label various behaviours as unacceptable. Aside from the questionable merit of most psychometric tools, the labels generally lack a sensitivity to various contextual factors.

A CLOSER LOOK BOX 6.10

SUMMARY: PSYCHOLOGICAL THEORIES OF CRIME

PERSPECTIVE	THEORIST	CAUSES OF CRIMINALITY AND CORE ELEMENTS
Demonology		• Demons, evil spirits, and gods cause evil behaviour
Intrapsychic theories		
Psychodynamic explanations	Sigmund Freud August Aichhorn	• Intrapsychic processes – unconscious conflicts – importance of childhood experiences – defence mechanisms – anger
Learning theories		
Cognitive explanations	John Dollard et al. Alfred Bandura	– frustration-aggression – modelling
Moral development theories	Jean Piaget Lawrence Kohlberg	– morality and responsibility
Behavioural explanations	B.F. Skinner Hans Eysenck	– classic conditioning – operant or instrumental conditioning

Discussion Questions
----

1. There has been an increase in the number of offenders who experience some degree of mental/emotional challenges. How might we explain this trend from a psychological perspective? Apply at least two different theoretical models to explain the phenomenon.

2. Describe the major psychological theories discussed in this chapter. What are the relative strengths and weaknesses of each theory? Which theory do you think has the most explanatory power? Why?

3. What challenges might exist in accepting any one type of psychological theory over another type?

4. Is there a "criminal personality"? How do the different theoretical orientations compare and contrast in terms of identifying specific personality traits that might be common in all, or a majority, of criminals?

5. How might psychological factors be used to explain differences in crime rates across Canada, over time, and according to such factors as gender, age, and social class?

Key Concepts

avoidance learning	behaviour modification	behavioural learning
classical conditioning	cognition	criminal personality
demonology	id, ego, superego	moral development
psychoanalysis	psychopath	token economy

Key Names

Gustav Aschaffenburg	Alfred Bandura	Sigmund Freud
Lawrence Kohlberg	Henry Maudsley	Ivan P. Pavlov
Jean Piaget	B.F. Skinner	John B. Watson

Weblinks

www.heavensgate.com The website of the cult group Heaven's Gate offers a glimpse into the group's agenda and propaganda.

www.schizophrenia.ca Although it doesn't strictly deal with crime, the website of the Schizophrenia Society of Canada offers lots of interesting information about an illness that many criminals seem to suffer from.

www.drivers.com/topic/31/ This site offers a variety of articles that discuss the social aspects of road rage and links to other sites that deal with this issue.

www.crimelibrary.com/criminal_mind/psychology/robert_hare/ This article from the online Crime Library offers an in-depth profile of Robert Hare, a Canadian expert on psychopathy.

Endnotes

1. According to Freud, there are four main defence mechanisms established by the ego. *Displacement* or *sublimation* is the process by which the ego handles conflict between the drives of the id and the constraints of the superego. In other words, in sublimation, the drives of the id are usually diverted to activities approved by the superego. *Repression* occurs when memories (e.g., of sexual abuse)

are forced into the unconscious mind and the individual denies that they exist. *Reaction formation* takes the form of an irrational adjustment to anxiety. For example, you might not like somebody, but you pretend to get along. *Projection* occurs when an individual rationalizes an appropriate motive for an inappropriate one (Vold, Bernard, & Snipes, 1998). One of the better known sociological applications of Freud's defence mechanisms is the *technique of neutralization* developed by Graham Sykes and David Matza in the later 1950s. The theory was used to explain how youths come to commit delinquent acts.

2.   For an intriguing account of the Walker case, you might be interested in reading Alan C. Cairns's *Nothing Sacred: The Many Lives and Betrayals of Albert Walker* (Toronto: Seal Books, 1998).

CHAPTER 7

Sociology-Based Perspectives of Crime

"The sociological imagination enables us to grasp history and biography and the relations between the two within society."

Charles Wright Mills (1916–1962)

Learning Outcomes

After you have completed this chapter, you should be able to:

- Appreciate the contribution that sociologists have made to the study of crime and the uniqueness of the perspective they bring to such study.

- Identify the factors that contributed to the emergence of the sociological school.

- Identify the different sociological perspectives.

- Appreciate the strengths and limitations of the major sociology-based perspectives of crime.

- Better understand and appreciate the need for a multidisciplinary approach.

In Chapter 1, it was noted that *crime*, in an absolute sense, refers strictly to violations of criminal laws, while the term *deviance* is used (primarily by sociologists) to mean the violations of certain norms. Together, criminal acts and acts of deviance are largely recognized as social problems. People, as social beings, are shaped by social forces in their environment. As the prominent American sociologist C. Wright Mills (1959) observed, individual problems are rooted in their **social structure** (see Box 7.1). This general perspective, in North America, has dominated the study of crime and deviance.

Even though other disciplines (such as biology, economics, political science, and psychology) are vying for acceptance in criminology, the sociological approach is still the dominant discipline used to describe, explain, and predict crime. No other discipline

offers as many theories of crime, and no other discipline has influenced criminal justice policy as has sociology.

Given the historical dominance of the sociological tradition, it is a somewhat daunting task to offer a representative overview of sociological theories. In fact, some might feel that certain sociological perspectives have been ignored in this chapter. However, given the integrated and interdisciplinary orientation of this textbook, the purpose is simply to present a cross-sectional and summative overview of some of the major sociological theories.

A CLOSER LOOK BOX 7.1

A SOCIOLOGICAL ASSESSMENT OF CRIME

Sociologists suggest there are two central questions in the study of criminology. According to Barkan (1997:3), they are:

1. Why do crime rates differ across locations and over time?
2. Why do crime rates differ according to the key dimensions of structured social inequality: race/ethnicity, class, and gender? For example, the routine activities theory (Felson, 1997) suggests that the decline in crime in the 1990s is due to a reduction in suitable targets. People are carrying less cash, and consumer goods such as televisions weigh more than they did in the late 1970s, when property crime was much higher. The explanation changes as our social environment changes over time.

Let us begin by examining the meaning of social structure and its significance for sociology and for criminologists trained in the sociological tradition. We will then proceed with a brief historical overview of sociology as a discipline before discussing several of the more established and traditional sociological theories of crime. Each of the theories, although different in approach, shares a common sociological orientation to the study of crime and deviance. Afterward, we will look at some contemporary theories of crime and deviance.

Social Structure and Crime

One of the questions many sociologists typically ask is whether as social beings we are innately "good" or "bad." While biologists and psychologists look to the individual and some personal trait or attribute for an answer, sociologists look to the social structure and social forces of society for their answers.

While recognizing the diversity of sociological perspectives addressing the issues of crime and deviance, it is possible to speak of a "sociological approach." Rooted in the classical statements of Émile Durkheim, Karl Marx, and Max Weber, sociology starts with the idea that all behaviour is social—that is, it is shaped by the social structure.

Instead of placing emphasis on the processes of personality or individual determinants for behaviour, sociology stresses behaviour through the internalization of social roles. Sociology makes a significant departure from both the classical model and positivism when it asserts that individuals are socialized into any given social structure through the parameters of their social roles and that, in this way, social structures pressure individuals toward conformist behaviour.

In relation to crime and deviance, sociology is concerned with the impact the social structure has on deviance and criminality and the pressure within the social structure on some people to engage in non-conformist behaviour.

Our social structure provides an environment for learning, or socialization. What is considered acceptable behaviour is defined through *prescriptive norms* (which outline what we may do) and *proscriptive norms* (which outline what we may not do). Some of our norms are informal, in that there are no written laws defining what we may or may not do. Rather, these rules are simply part of our social environment and have been established over time. However, as societies move from more informal structures to more formal ones, it becomes necessary for some laws to be converted into formal laws (Wright & Fox, 1978). Sociologists argue that since not all aspects of our social environment can be controlled, or all laws enforced, the result is crime and deviance.

One of the founding fathers of sociology is **Émile Durkheim** (1858–1917) (see Box 7.2), who perhaps best encapsulated these ideas when he observed that even in a society of saints there would be deviance. Durkheim believed that human groups make rules and someone within the group always breaks some of these rules. The exact reasons, according to Durkheim, are not always clear, but the individual's behaviour is perceived as being related to his or her social environment rather than intrinsic traits. For example, when you were younger and had your group of "best friends" (social environment), were you ever asked to keep a secret and never tell anyone? Did you tell the secret to someone else (intrinsic traits)? Is it possible, as the great English philosopher Thomas Hobbes, Sigmund Freud, and others have suggested, that without a hegemonic (i.e., preponderant influence or authority) social structure—that is, one that has preponderant influence or authority—crime and deviance are simply expressions of disharmony? If so, then criminal laws are necessary as a means of social control and as a reflection of the social consciousness of society at large. Furthermore, this line of reasoning lends support to a sociological interpretation and analysis of what can be viewed as a social phenomenon.

PROFILE BOX 7.2

DAVID ÉMILE DURKHEIM

Durkheim was born on April 15, 1858, in Epinal, France. His life has been described as "stoical, devoid of humor, and with near total devotion to study and scholarly pursuits" (Martin, Mutchnick, & Austin, 1990:47). His schooling was marked by strict discipline, and by the age of 16 he already held a baccalaureate degree.

Durkheim became absorbed with the moral philosophers of his time and in particular with the work of Auguste Comte (Lunden, 1972). His interest in moral philosophy and social structure were further fuelled by the impact of the French Revolution
(1788–1789) and the defeat of Napoleon Bonaparte in June of 1815 near Waterloo,
in what is now Belgium. The late 1700s and early 1800s were also marked by a dramatic move from a feudal-agricultural system to an industrial economy. As Martin et al.
(1990:48) point out, Durkheim became interested in trying to understand and explain
"societal influences upon morality, religion, deviance, and the general breakdown of
traditional social institutions."

Durkheim first introduced his famous concept of anomie, which he used to
describe how a society could change rapidly, in his doctoral dissertation, *The Division
of Labor in Society*, published in 1893. Then in 1895, he wrote another classic, *The
Rules of Sociological Method*, in which he further delineated his theory of anomie and
the function of crime in society. This was followed two years later by another seminal
work, *Suicide*. In this book, Durkheim displays his astute knowledge of the scientific
method to explain the social meaning of suicide. Drawing on his theoretical principles
and available data, Durkheim argues that Catholics commit fewer suicides than
Protestants because their doctrine is stricter, they have clearer norms, and (unlike
Protestants) they condemn the practice of suicide. Hence, he asserts, Catholics have
a strong collective conscience that is necessary for a stable society.

After Durkheim's death, his work received limited attention, primarily because it was
not translated into English. However, in the 1930s, it was rediscovered and translated. It
quickly drew the attention of sociologists and, indirectly, criminologists. And although
Durkheim is recognized as a sociologist, Lunden (1972:398) offers a quotation from
Durkheim's work that reflects a deep awareness of human behaviour that transcends a
strict sociological perspective: "man's characteristic privilege is that the bond he accepts
is not physical but moral: that is social. He is governed not by a material environment brutally imposed on him, but a conscience superior to his own."

Since the 1930s, there has been a significant volume of work developing various
aspects of the sociological approach to crime and deviance, but the link between current expressions and the traditional statements is clear. As the American sociologist
Robert Merton said, the aim of the sociological explanation is to discover how some social
structures exert pressure on certain persons in society to engage in non-conformist rather
than conformist conduct.

History of Sociological Criminology

"In the first place crime is normal because a society exempt from it is utterly
impossible." Durkheim, 1893, cited in Jacoby, 1994:65

Sociology emerged from the social and political philosophies of 19th-century Europe, in a period characterized by considerable social unrest. **Auguste Comte** (1798–1857), in addition to being recognized as the founder of sociology, was also the founder of the positivist school of philosophy. The positivist school advocated the study of social phenomena through the use of a "systematic observation and the accumulation of evidence and objective facts within a deductive framework" (i.e., moving from the general to the specific) (Williams & McShane, 1994:32).

Comte believed that the social development of humankind could be classified into what he referred to as the *law of the three stages*:

1. *Theological*: Events are largely attributable to supernatural forces that cannot be directly observed or measured. For example, the phrase "it is God's will" may be used to explain an experience, but it is a statement that cannot be proved or disproved.
2. *Metaphysical*: Natural events are seen to be the result of fundamental energies or ideas. For example, a murder might be explained as the result of an offender's soul being occupied by an evil spirit.
3. *Positive*: Phenomena are explained through observation, hypothesis, and experimentation. This is the basis of scientific inquiry.

According to Comte, the explanation of crime and criminality passed through these three stages until the 19th century, when the positivist school of thought emerged.

The final stage has two main elements. The first is the notion that our behaviour is a function of external forces beyond our immediate control. These forces can range from elements such as wealth and class to famine and war. They are examined by *macro-based* sociological theories (Williams & McShane, 2004). Macro-level theories are broader in scope and attempt to explain social events in terms of their social structure and their effect on behaviour.

The second element in Comte's final stage focuses on individual traits and characteristics, including brain structure and an individual's biological makeup. As Comte further developed his theory, however, he adopted a hierarchical view of the sciences and eventually placed sociology above all others. While he recognized the role of individual traits, he felt that the social environment was the best indicator and predictor of human behaviour.

While Comte may have been somewhat conciliatory in his approach to explaining social behaviour, his fellow compatriots **Gabriel Tarde** (1834–1904) and Émile Durkheim were not. In his effort to explain criminal acts at a social level, Durkheim rejected both biology and psychology. Gabriel Tarde's work, meanwhile, initially made significant contributions to the analysis of social and environmental influences on human behaviour. His ideas about behaviour being learned largely by association have now been replaced by more contemporary theories such as Edwin Sutherland's differential association theory, Daniel Glaser's differential identification, and C.R. Jeffery's differential reinforcement theory. Yet Tarde's book *Laws of Imitation*, published in 1890, offers "eloquent expositions of the association, or learning theory of criminality"

(Schafer, 1976:233). Focusing on the social environment, Tarde believed that everyone behaves according to customs of the cultural environment. He suggested that there are two basic social processes:

1. *Invention*: It occurs infrequently, as most "original" acts can be traced back to earlier variations. For example, during antiquity, unwanted children were simply killed at birth. Today, it is illegal to kill a newborn child, but women have abortions to rid themselves of unwanted pregnancies. Some consider abortion simply a prototype of infanticide, that is, child killing (see s. 233 of the *Criminal Code*).
2. *Imitation*: According to Tarde, this is the typical element of social life: we tend to behave in very similar ways. When someone chooses to commit a crime, he or she typically commits a crime that others have already committed.

Tarde identified three laws of imitation, as follows:

1. *Law of proportion*. We imitate events in proportion to the frequency, the closeness, and that stability that they have with those events we experience.
2. *Law of direction*. A superior act (i.e., low risk of apprehension and high return for effort) is usually imitated by those who are impressed and influenced by prestige. Tarde observed that deviant and criminal behaviour that originates in one country (e.g., the skinhead movement in Europe) may be imitated in another (e.g., North America). The superior act reflects a sense of continuance and continuity in social structures.
3. *Law of insertion*. This occurs when two mutually exclusive fashions (see Box 7.3) are in opposition (e.g., abortion vs. infanticide) and one tends to be substituted for the other. Substitution is influenced by what is fashionable or superior. Such changes in social behaviour may reflect social, economic, or political shifts occurring at the time within a community.

WHAT DO YOU THINK? BOX 7.3

FORMS OF IMITATION

According to Tarde, imitation could be expressed in one of two forms—fashion and custom. *Fashion* tends to occur where contact is close and frequent. *Custom* occurs where contact is less frequent and change occurs less often. Using these distinctions, how might we explain differences in crime in urban as opposed to rural settings?

Unlike Durkheim, Tarde treated crime as a social phenomenon and likened it to the destructive nature of cancer. Hence, he argued society should spare no effort to combat it.

Sociology in North America

Sociology emerged in 1892 as a disciplinary area of inquiry when the first sociology department was established at the University of Chicago (Williams & McShane, 2004). Since it was located in an urban centre, it is not surprising that the early sociologists focused on urban life and the influences of urban life and the urban setting. For example, the pioneering work and ideas of **Ernest W. Burgess** (1886–1966) and **Robert E. Park** (1864–1944) can still be found in Cohen and Felson's (1979) very popular routine activities theory today.

In 1921, Burgess and Park collaborated to write *Introduction to the Science of Sociology*, which was more commonly referred to as the "Green Bible" at the University of Chicago. Even today, it is considered "among the most important treatises ever written in sociology" (Martin et al., 1990:101).

While at the University of Chicago, Burgess developed his **concentric-circle theory** of crime. The theory involved the study of ecology—the distribution of phenomena and their relationship to the environment. In particular, Park and Burgess "produced a conception of the city as a series of distinctive concentric circles radiating from the central business district" (Williams & McShane, 1994:53). Burgess and his colleagues attempted to explain crime as a function of social changes that were accompanied by environmental change. This mode of sociological inquiry has been referred to as the Chicago School or **ecological school** (see page 191).

Borrowing from animal and plant ecology studies, Burgess applied the ecological concepts of dominance, invasion, and succession to explain how human beings could be physically mapped into zones. His theory divided the city into five major zones, with each zone being characterized by different social and organizational elements. For example, Zone 1, the central business district, is defined by light manufacturing, retail trade, and commercialized recreation, while Zone 5, the outermost area, is seen as the commuters' zone where wealthier residents live (see Figure 7–1). By contrast, the inner zones tend to attract the poorer and more crowded housing.

In addition, between the zones are areas in transition where the physical and social environment are less defined. These are the areas where newly arrived immigrants initially settle, where divorce rates are higher, and where housing is less well maintained—and where crime rates tend to be higher. They are areas of *social disorganization*—hence the general term **social disorganization theory**.

For a period, the concentric-circle theory enjoyed considerable success. However, as the social structure changed, the social ecological approach shifted from a focus on individual crime to the crime site and from physical characteristics of the environment to social traits (Brantingham & Brantingham, 1984). For example, during the pre-automobile era, our mobility patterns tended to be more confined than they are today. With the advent and popularity of cars, our social structure changed and our awareness of space became more fluid. The traditional social ecological approach could no

FIGURE 7–1

ZONE RATES OF MALE JUVENILE DELINQUENTS, 1927–33 SERIES

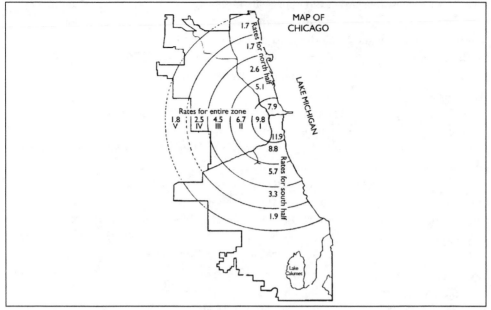

Source: Clifford R. Shaw & Henry D. McKay, *Juvenile Delinquency and Urban Areas* (Chicago: University of Chicago Press, 1972), 69. Reprinted with permission of the publisher.

longer adequately explain criminal behaviour. This set the stage for the emergence of numerous sociological theories that can trace their origins to the influence of human ecology and its evolution into social ecology.

Jane Jacobs's *The Death and Life of Great American Cities*, published in 1961, was the first influential work to suggest that by modifying the physical environment one could reduce the opportunity for crime. Jacobs's ideas were later expanded on by C.R. Jeffery and Oscar Newman in the 1970s (see pages 193–194). Their works signalled the emergence of the integrated social ecological model known as **Crime Prevention Through Environmental Design (CPTED)**. Although today the ecological orientation can be found in a number of different theoretical models, the contemporary school of social ecology generally concentrates on the environment of the potential victim rather than that of the criminal.

In spite of several methodological critiques, the intellectual heritage of the Chicago School runs deep and has had a lasting influence on North American sociological criminology. Its influence can be seen in Fredrick Thrasher's work on youth gangs in the 1920s, in Edwin Sutherland's formation of the differential association theory in the 1930–40s, in Howard Becker's labelling theory in the 1960s, and elsewhere (see Williams & McShane, 2004).

Canadian Sociology

Sociology in Canada was slower to emerge and evolve.[1] Because of colonial ties, Canadian academics have historically looked to Europe for leadership. At the outset of the Canadian sociological movement, anglophone schools followed their British counterparts in "hesitating to give recognition to sociology which was viewed as a present-oriented and shallow American discipline" (Hiller, 1983, cited in Teevan & Blute, 1986:12).

In the 1920s, McGill University was the first Canadian school to establish a sociology department, led by **Carl A. Dawson**, who was influenced by functionalist approaches of the University of Chicago and at Columbia. Throughout the 1930s and 1940s, most of the research done in the area can be viewed as historical sociology with little emphasis on crime or deviance (Teevan & Blute, 1986).

However, this changed as the baby boomers of the 1960s entered universities in record numbers. Schools sought new solutions to a growing number of social problems (e.g., problematic ethnic relations, poverty, and separatism), and universities established sociological programs to provide an academic venue for studying social conflict. With the rapid growth of sociology departments, the demand for trained faculty could not be met by Canadian sociologists. Teevan and Blute (1986) note that by 1970–1971 only 40 percent of sociology and anthropology faculty members were Canadian citizens; most of the remainder were American. As sociology emerged as an academic discipline, Canadian programs were based on the dominant American perspective of *functionalism* or a systems approach. Teevan and Blute (1986) comment on how difficult it has been for Canadian sociology to emerge—an observation reflected in the fact that most of the theoretical material presented in this chapter has American roots.

In summary, the discipline of sociology is a little more than a hundred years old. While its roots can be found in Europe, American universities were the first to embrace it as a mode of scientific inquiry into human behaviour. Canadian sociology did not come into existence until the 1920s.

As sociology gained popularity and refined its methods, many different sociological perspectives and theories have emerged. Box 7.4 provides an overview of the most important of these approaches. In this chapter, we will look at four sociological theories that have been used extensively to explain crime and criminality: anomie theory, ecological school, differential association theory, and labelling theory. Taken alone, each theory provides useful insight into crime and deviance; collectively, they serve as powerful explanatory models. While, as Schafer (1976:49) observed, sociology alone is not "able to offer satisfactory explanations of the causes of crime," it has made significant contributions to the study of crime and deviance and has drawn attention to the importance of studying social process, social structure, and the social environment. We will conclude our overview of sociology-based perspectives by summarizing several of the more contemporary theories and their efforts to explain crime and deviance.

OVERVIEW OF SOCIOLOGICAL PERSPECTIVES AND SOME RELATED THEORIES

PERSPECTIVE	KEY POINTS	RELATED THEORIES
Social/process learning	– behaviour is learned in social context – law-breaking and motives are acquired through interaction with others	Differential association Neutralization/drift
Social reaction	– focus is upon social and institutional response to an individual – focus is not on initial delinquency but on how social control agents respond – individuals are passive beings forced into delinquency/crime as a result of societal definition	Labelling Dramatization of evil
Social disorganization	– societies strive for a state of equilibrium/stability – changes in social structure and environment create instability, which can lead to crime	Concentric circle
Strain	– stress, frustration, or strain prompt deviance – norms are violated to alleviate the strain – the greatest pressure is within the lower social echelons	Anomie
Social conflict	– society is composed of competing interests – competing values and interests lead to conflict between groups vying for power – state represents the interests of those groups with the most power	Conflict
Social control	– crime and deviance result from inadequate social roles or association with deviant others – social policy focuses on changing responsibility of the offender	Differential association Social learning Social control

Anomie/Strain Theory

The idea of **anomie** was first set forth by Émile Durkheim and later modified by the eminent American sociologist Robert K. Merton. Durkheim introduced the term in his 1893 book *Division of Labor in Society* to describe a condition of "deregulation" or "normlessness" occurring in society. Two themes are central to Durkheim's thesis: (1) social organization is necessary to keep our natural (i.e., innate) tendencies in check, and (2) under conditions where social order breaks down and social norms lose their influence, a condition of anomie develops and crime significantly increases (Durkheim, 1951, cited in Wright & Fox, 1978:135–136).

Durkheim argued that all societies start in a mechanical form that is socially characterized by *homogeneity* "of the lives, work, and beliefs of their members" (Vold, Bernard, & Snipes, 1998:126). Mechanical societies are self-sufficient and autonomous, with little division of labour. However, all societies evolve (at different rates) from simple toward more complex; as they do, they are characterized by increasing labour specialization. As societies become more specialized, they need more laws to maintain social order.

Believing that every social structure is in a state of flux, Durkheim regarded crime as a natural and inevitable element of society. He recognized two types of criminals: altruistic and common. The *altruistic criminal* is one who becomes offended by the rules of society and is intent on trying to change them for the better. The *common criminal* is the more typical offender—one who rejects the laws and norms of society and intentionally violates laws with little regard for the rights of others (Vold, Bernard, & Snipes, 1998). Together the crimes of altruistic and common criminals produce the social ills of society.

Although it provided a compelling interpretation of social structure and the appearance of crime in society, Durkheim's theory lacked empirical references, and his concept of anomie was never clearly operationalized. Why and how do some criminals choose to commit altruistic crimes while others choose common crimes? Why doesn't everyone commit crime? How do criminals come to choose the type of crime they commit? Where do the criminals acquire their unconventional means? Why do some disenfranchised people choose suicide over crime?

In spite of its conceptual limitations and generality, Durkheim's thesis found wide support at a time when sociology was the dominant perspective for studying human behaviour in Europe. It was not until 60 years later that the American sociologist Robert Merton became aware of Durkheim's work and modified and applied the theory to other forms of deviance.

Robert K. Merton and Anomie/Strain

It was in his seminal article published in 1938 titled "Social Structure and Anomie" that **Robert K. Merton** (1910–2003) began to define his explanation of crime. In the opening paragraph, Merton notes that the earlier "tendency in sociological theory to attribute the malfunctioning of social structure primarily to those of man's imperious biological drives" should be discounted (Merton, 1938, cited in Jacoby, 1994:130). Instead, he argues, "certain phases of social structure generate the circumstances in which infringement of social codes constitutes a 'normal' response" (ibid.:130).

While Durkheim saw anomie as arising out of some upheaval in society, Merton believed that societies did not necessarily have to be undergoing rapid social change in order for crimes to occur. To support this orientation, Merton's (1968) version of anomie is premised on the following four major assumptions about modern societies:

- All modern societies have a core of common values.
- The majority of the members of modern societies have internalized these values (that is, they have accepted them).
- The significant values are those that channel energy toward the achievement of certain success goals.
- All members of society do not have equal opportunity to gain access to socially approved means of reaching socially approved goals.

Merton's theory, based on these assumptions, became known as **strain theory** because of his emphasis on "social structure strain." Merton developed a typology involving five modes of "structural," as opposed to individualistic, adaptations to anomie to explain crime. Unlike Durkheim, whose theory focused on rapid social change to explain crime, Merton emphasized the role of relatively stable social conditions that, because of their nature, limit the opportunity and ability of certain groups to meet or attain their needs through legitimate means. He argued that crime occurs when individuals are unable to achieve their goals through legitimate means. In such situations, the individual becomes frustrated—that is, strained—and may either attempt to resolve his or her frustration through legitimate means or turn to unconventional methods of attaining his or her goals.

For example, in Canada, we are encouraged at a very early age not only to do well in school but to strive to be the very best we can. Have you ever heard the following phrases: "winning's not everything, it's the only thing," or "no pain, no gain," or "push it to the limit"? Such phrases reflect the perception that we need to succeed and be task-driven. As impressionable young people wanting to please and fit in, most of us strive to internalize and achieve socially prescribed goals. At the same time, we are taught socially prescribed (legal) means by which to attain these goals, such as hard work, honesty, and patience. However, not everyone can become a Rhodes scholar, an outstanding athlete, or valedictorian. According to Merton, we adopt different modes of aspiring to the goals—some legitimately and others illegitimately.

Merton classifies these different responses into five categories, each describing the prevailing adaptation strategies that a certain type of person adopts in response to pressures to fit in. The five types are:

1. *Conformist*: Without conformity, there would be no social order. Most people, in spite of their social and personal circumstances, are conformists. They remain

law-abiding and do their best to finish school, get a job, and raise a family. These people subscribe to the cultural goals of society and have internalized the means by which to achieve them.

2. *Innovator*: These people accept the goals of society (e.g., getting an education) but reject the socially accepted means by which to achieve them. However, they do not necessarily select deviant or unlawful means in their efforts to attain socially approved goals. It is quite possible to be innovative without violating any significant norms. A student, for example, might participate in a field study tour rather than attend regular class as a means of learning. According to Merton, this adaptation strategy is more prevalent among the lower class, where there are more obstacles to attaining legitimate goals. Crime can be further exacerbated when criminals (e.g., drug dealers, pimps, and gangs) flaunt their wealth and their fancy clothes in a way that says "crime pays" (Cohen & Machalek, 1988).

3. *Ritualist*: Individuals who adapt a ritualistic approach to the goals of society might be described as phony. They accept the means to goals but reject the goals themselves. An example could be the student who attends school because the law requires it, does well enough to pass, and then drops out. Ritualists may not be goal-motivated, but they usually continue to give deference to the norms of hard work, honesty, etc. They go along with the program but make no real effort to aspire beyond their immediate situation. They might be described as the Archie Bunkers of society (Vito & Holmes, 1994).

4. *Retreatist*: These individuals reject both the goals and means of society. A youth who does not want to go to school or does not want to work for his or her keep could be described as a retreatist. This model of adaptation is likely to occur when the socially approved means (e.g., working to afford a downpayment on a house) are perceived as being unlikely to result in success or perhaps even unattainable. Retreatism becomes an escape mechanism for some people in this predicament. They pour what little savings they are able to accumulate into alcohol and/or drug use—giving up the means and the goal. They may even contemplate suicide.

   Not all forms of retreatism are necessarily harmful or wrong. For instance, the growing number of street people in Canada may be the result of a system that could not meet their needs. On the other hand, those who abuse drugs and alcohol and then proceed to drive their cars are not only retreatists but also criminals.

5. *Rebel*: As the term implies, rebels not only reject legitimate goals and means but also attempt to bring about a new society whose goals are more egalitarian. They are the radicals and revolutionaries. The youth movements of the 1960s and 1970s represent rebellion. For example, the Vietnam War draft dodgers not only refused to participate in the war; many of them fled to Canada to evade prosecution. More contemporary forms of rebellion include terrorist acts in which extremist groups use violence and propaganda to convey their objections to society.

Assessment of Merton's Theory

In accordance with Merton's theoretical principles, the lower classes should be disproportionately represented among the criminal population, because they have less opportunity to reach their goals legitimately. Based on a review of more than 100 studies, Braithwaite (1981) found general support for the assertion that lower-class people do commit more crimes than those in other social classes. However, the results could not account for the fact that not all lower-class people commit crimes. The failure of the 1960s US War on Poverty campaign—an idea put forth by Lloyd Ohlin and Richard Cloward and administered during the Lyndon B. Johnson presidency—serves as a clear example that trying solve social malaise through social class is insufficient. There are obviously some other factors that need to be accounted for. Thornberry and Farnsworth (1982) suggest that the model also needs to take into account other social factors such as race, the seriousness of the offence, and the education level of the family. However, when one begins to incorporate a wide variety of other factors, the model becomes too complex and overwhelming to be of much practical use. The ensuing result has been the emergence of reformulations of Merton's theory.

Robert Agnew's Strain Theory

One of the more prominent revisions of Merton's theory is that of sociologist Robert Agnew (1953–). His general strain theory implies that strain is caused by a failure to achieve certain material goals. Agnew and White (1992) identify three general forms of strain: (1) strained caused by failure to achieve positively valued goals, (2) strain caused by the removal of positively valued stimuli from the individual, and (3) strain caused by the presentation of negative stimuli. This theory offers a more comprehensive account of the cognitive, behavioural, and emotional adaptations to strain, since the authors acknowledge that individuals have differing abilities to cope with stress, based on past experience, peer influence, temperament, financial resources, etc.

While the theory is able to address some of Merton's limitations, it fails to clearly measure the type of strain needed to achieve positively valued goals. Mazerolle and Maahs (2000), using the American National Youth Survey data developed four measures of strain different from Agnew and White's, but their results were no more promising in reliability or validity of the constructs.

Cohen's Subcultural Theory of Male Delinquency

Albert K. Cohen (1918–), a former student of Robert Merton and Edwin Sutherland, developed a theory to explain male delinquent cultures in working-class neighbourhoods. Like many other theorists in the 1950s, he focused on young offenders and used a sociological positivist perspective. His theory combined elements of the Chicago School, Merton's anomie theory, and Sutherland's differential association theory.

Cohen's classic 1955 book *Delinquent Boys: The Culture of the Gang*, in which he put forward his ideas about gangs and their activities, triggered a rash of interest in both his theory and his attention to delinquent gang behaviour. It also spawned the transition from anomie theory to strain theory. In the book, Cohen introduces the notion that "status frustration" can be the result of an entire subculture's life experiences and life opportunities. He suggests that delinquency among lower-class males is the product of the status frustration that lower-class boys experience when confronted with the dominant middle-class values within the public school system (see Figure 7–2).

Based on his observation of delinquent males in the United States, Cohen found:

- As members of a society, we all share similar goals. Most of these goals are dictated by the middle-class members to those in the lower social classes.
- Among males of the lower social echelons, gang delinquency is common.
- Gang behaviour becomes an accepted way of attaining status within the social subculture because conventional avenues of attaining social status are less readily available to youth from the lower socio-economic classes than those from the middle class.
- "Over time the 'delinquent solution' is passed on through the transmission of values from youth to youth and generation to generation" (Williams & McShane, 1994:111).

In summary, the subcultural approach emphasizes the importance of the social values of informal lower social class groups, especially among delinquent boys. Subcultural explanations were very popular in the 1950s and 1960s, but they were not able to explain all delinquency (particularly female criminality) or account for social class differences in the crime rates. Nevertheless, the general concept of a campaign for the underprivileged spawned a number of multi-million–dollar projects during this era. The "War on Poverty" saw the birth of the Peace Corps, the Job Corps, and Project Head Start, among others, all designed to provide the lower classes with employment opportunities and easier access to some middle-class values

FIGURE 7–2

COHEN'S MODEL OF SUBCULTURAL THEORY

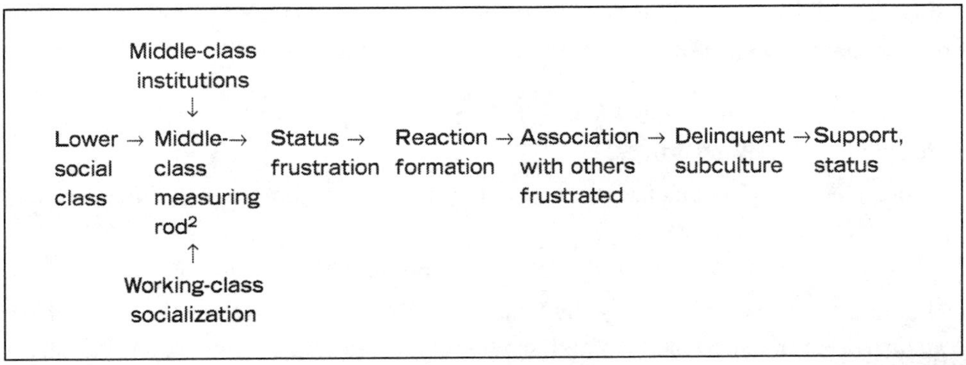

```
              Middle-class
              institutions
                   ↓
  Lower → Middle-→ Status →   Reaction → Association → Delinquent →Support,
  social   class    frustration formation  with others   subculture   status
  class    measuring                       frustrated
           rod²
             ↑
          Working-class
          socialization
```

and status. The programs met with varying degrees of success. But perhaps the biggest blow to the subcultural orientation was the emergence of self-report studies (see Chapter 3). These studies revealed that delinquency and subcultural activities are not the exclusive domain of the lower classes, nor is gang behaviour the exclusive domain of males.

Today, subcultural theory has found a new ally in sociological theories that have attempted to integrate its elements with the study of other informal groups. Instead of focusing only on social class subcultures, sociologists have expanded their definition of subculture to include such groups as anarchists, computer hackers, drug cultures, extreme religious groups, and organized crime groups. Among these newer theories is Cloward and Ohlin's differential opportunity theory (Williams & McShane, 2004).

Summary and Evaluation

It is clear that Durkheim's and Merton's ideas about anomie have had a major impact on sociological criminology. In general, the anomie theory has "drawn attention to the interplay between social structure, cultural context, and individual action" (Cao, 2004:79).

While the anomie theory tries to explain the relationship between social conditions and deviance, it fails to explain why and how people from identical social situations can differ in their reaction to states of anomie (Williams & McShane, 2004). It has also been criticized for not addressing middle-class and white-collar crime (Hirschi & Gottfredson, 1987); for example, Merton's theory focuses almost exclusively on the poor and assumes that most crimes are committed by this segment of the population. Furthermore, the adaptation modes of the anomie theory do not effectively explain violent crimes of assault, homicide, and rape (Barkan, 1997). Finally, MacLean and Milovanovic (1991) note that the theory is not able to recognize the social process by which criminal statistics are constructed and why the working class is overrepresented in these statistics.

With recent revisions and extensions of the theory, such as Robert Agnew's *general strain theory*; Albert Cohen's *delinquency and frustration theory*, and the popular *differential opportunity theory* of Richard Cloward and Lloyd Ohlin, the anomie/strain perspective will likely continue to draw a strong following (see Box 7.5 for an example of recent research). However, future research will need to:

- Discern to what extent social factors either precipitate and/or predispose some people to committing crimes;
- More clearly operationalize the level of strain that differentiates criminal from non-criminal behaviour;
- Focus on how strain works at the aggregate and individual levels; and
- Be able to explain the process by which neighbourhoods progress from a stable state to a "disorganized state" and then potentially return to a stable/organized state.

STRAIN THEORY AND HATE CRIME

Hate crime, which we will examine in more detail in Chapter 8, is a growing global concern. While the *Criminal Code* prohibits dissemination of hate literature within Canada, computerized material transmitted across phone lines is considered to be originating outside sovereign borders. Hence, the internet has been used to fuel hate crime activity. According to Canadian researcher Jeffery Ross (1995:166), "hard economic times and consequential loss of jobs and inflation" also contribute to the spread of hate crime. These factors represent blocked opportunity and create strain and frustration. However, in another publication, Ross (1995) notes that all the different sub-types of violence by and against Canadians have their own causes.

Ecological School

We have already glimpsed at the pioneering work of Ernest Burgess and Robert Park in the 1920s when we discussed the history of sociology in North America. As we saw, drawing on the relationship between animals in natural settings, Burgess and Park reasoned that humans must also display behavioural patterns in their natural setting—urban environments. Using Chicago as their study area, they developed the concentric-circle theory (see pages 181–182), which is based on the relationship between particular environmental characteristics and human relationships. Crime is but one aspect of urban ecology. In general, the ecological school asserts that crime can be understood through the study of the physical and social structure of an environment. The theory focuses on the *socio-spatial* environment in which people live (Brantingham & Brantingham, 1984). Instead of seeing crime as a product of heredity, it views it as one of *social disorganization* and of *conflict* within existing American culture.

Before Burgess and Park, others have also used ecological principles to explain crime. The earliest studies based on these premises were those done in the 1830s by André-Michel Guerry and Adolphe Quetelet, who examined the physical and seasonal spatial patterning of crime. Their work is referred to as the *cartography school*. It eventually led to the school of social and human ecology, which focused on the interrelationship between people and their environment and on how different social conditions might result in social disorganization.

Shaw and McKay's Work

Although Burgess and Park's work received considerable attention, it was the work of two fellow scholars from the University of Chicago, **Clifford R. Shaw** and **Henry D. McKay**, that is perhaps more widely known. Focusing most of their research on young offenders, Shaw and McKay (1969) applied the principles of the concentric-circle theory to rates of delinquency, tuberculosis, and infant mortality. They found that the rates follow the same "decreasing pattern as one moves away from the central business district" (Williams & McShane, 1994:54). Based on ecological data they developed their theory of *social disorganization*, which was buttressed "on a conception of primary relationships similar to those found in a village" (ibid.:54). In essence, the more stable or homogeneous the family and neighbourhood, the greater the likelihood of a stable community. As primary relationships break down, so does social control. Subsequently crime increases. Williams and McShane (ibid.:54–55) cite research by Robert Sampson and Byron Groves, who list four elements that contribute to social disorganization:

- Low economic status;
- A mixture of different ethnic groups;
- Highly mobile residents moving in and out of the area; and
- Disrupted families and broken homes.

Fernandez and Neiman (1997) presented data to suggest that the perception of increased crime risk (fear of crime) is related to general variations in assessments of the quality of life and satisfaction with social and public institutions. They further argued that overall satisfaction with life varies along with a geographic gradient to quality of life. In other words, fear of crime was found to be related to how people perceive their physical conditions. However, what is not clear is the cultural relativity of such perceptions. Shaw and McKay report that the zones of transition are more socially disorganized than other areas due to the "high degree of mobility, the decaying neighborhoods, and the encroachment of the business and factory districts" (ibid.:55).

Another variation of the ecological perspective that emerged out of the Chicago School to explain crime was Shaw and McKay's **cultural transmission theory** or cultural deviance theory. This theory tried to explain the *process* by which social disorganization leads to unavoidable conflict, which in turn can de-motivate youth's conformity to cultural values and norms and predispose them to acting in a delinquent manner. As the institutional control mechanisms break down within an area or neighbourhood, some youths choose delinquency. Over time, they develop norms and values that reinforce delinquency and criminal behaviour and eventually create a subculture of delinquency. Delinquency is transmitted to future members of the neighbourhood, from one generation to the next, through the process of *cultural transmission*.

More Recent Applications of Ecological Principles

In the decades that followed, researchers have modified the ideas of Shaw and McKay to more accurately account for discrepancies in their explanatory model. Georges-Abeyie and Harries (1980) posited that in order to more fully understand the social/ecological elements of crime, research needs to include the site of the crime, the offender's residence, and the location where the offender was arrested. Others, such as the Canadian team of Paul and Patricia Brantingham (1984:18), have observed that even more recently there has been a "shift from the sociological to the geographical imagination" (see Box 7.6). The term "geographic imagination" refers to understanding how an individual perceives his or her physical environment. In the early 1970s, American architect Oscar Newman was among the first to note how our physical environment can influence our sense of territoriality and personal space. In an updated edition of his acclaimed textbook *Defensible Space* (1996), Newman presents the latest information on how to physically build or refurbish urban communities to reduce crime. The intent is to promote a sense of community through the physical design and layout of homes, office buildings, and other structures that make up the community.

A CLOSER LOOK BOX 7.6

ZEROING IN ON CRIME SPOTS

Kim Rossmo, a former Simon Fraser University criminology graduate student currently teaching in the United States, has applied the principles of geographic mapping to the study of violent serial and sexual crimes. This approach is the latest variation of the ecological perspective.

As we already discussed in Box 3.3, Rossmo developed a sophisticated computer software system called Rigel. The program relies on the latest technology in digital mapping and powerful visual three-dimensional presentation (referred to as "jeopardies") to study violent serial crimes. Combined with investigative police work, this method of geographic profiling has been used to indicate whether "a series of crimes may have been committed by the same offender and victims are being hunted in a particular manner" (Orion, 1996:2).

A unique attribute of the software is its ability to analyze data on an ongoing basis. As new information is obtained, the program recalibrates to construct a new geoprofile, thereby eliminating information not considered essential to the modelling procedure. Recognizing that it is not possible to determine which crimes are linked, the software is capable of constructing different scenarios. Then, as the profile database evolves, the number of scenarios can be narrowed to pinpoint likely crime and victim sites.

As we saw in Box 3.3, Rossmo's software has already been used by a number of Canadian police departments across the country to help them solve violent serial crimes, and his research and expertise are being made available to international police organizations (Thompson, 1996). Rossmo's work shows the importance of combining academic research with concrete criminal justice issues. Like the developments in DNA analysis, geographic profiling is a new and vital strategy for combating crime.

Perhaps one of the more powerful theories to emerge from the ecological school of thought has been the routine activities theory, which is premised on the notion that crime is determined by a motivated offender, the absence of capable guardians, and the presence of a suitable target (see the discussion on pages 204–207). In recent years, it has been extensively used to explain social and socio-ecological elements to criminal activity. For example, Hakim and Buck (1989) found that after casinos were legalized in Atlantic City, the greatest crime increase was in violent crime and auto theft and the lowest was for burglary. They also observed that there was a spillover effect in the surrounding areas—that is, as people moved away from the city to outlying communities, their crime rates also went up. Several years earlier, Reppetto (1974) wrote that when a criminal's awareness of space expanded or efforts were made to deter the criminal, a phenomenon referred to as *crime displacement* took place. Crime displacement could take the form of a temporal displacement (a different time) and/or a physical displacement (a different area).

The ecological school and its various theoretical derivatives have played a major role in crime prevention strategies. Oscar Newman (1972, 1996), Paul and Patricia Brantingham (1991), John Baldwin and Anthony Bottoms (1976), Henry Cisneros (1995), and Ralph Taylor and Adele Harrell (1996), among others, have all produced practical works in which they have employed ecological principles to suggest ways of deterring crime and building community.

In their review of the ecological school, Williams and McShane (1994) point out how social disorganization theory and cultural transmission theory are similar to the theories of social control, differential association, situational choice, routine activities, and human ecology, among others (for a complete list, see Einstadter & Henry, 1995:121). Hence, it can be argued that the ecological school, and in particular the work of Shaw and McKay, played a significant role in the sociological criminological theories that came after them. For example, Paul and Patricia Brantingham (1991) have taken the ecological concepts to new levels in their work on environmental criminology. Today, their research and theory, along with the research of Rossmo, have drawn international respect and attention.

Summary and Evaluation

In its development, the ecological approach has been influenced by human geography and biology. It assumes that particular characteristics of the physical and social environment can precipitate crime—that is, that human behaviour is a product of the social environment and that the environment defines the boundaries of our cultural values and behaviour.

As we have seen in this section, the ecological school has evolved to provide some powerful explanatory models for crime. However, as any theory, it has also had its critics. Some unanswered questions (Cohen, 1959) include: What does "social disorganization" (SD) mean? How does one measure it? What is the demarcation line between SD and deviant behaviour? As well, as Cao (2004) argues, economic status, ethnic heterogeneity, and residential mobility have not been very reliably and accurately measured. Cao points out, however, that many of the new tests of SD continue to not only model Shaw and McKay's original study but also refine the concepts and the measuring methods. It is likely that this reorientation of SD will continue and is worth further exploration.

One important theoretical perspective that can trace its origins to the ecological school but is considered to have moved beyond them is the theory of differential association.

Differential Association

Sociological theorists such as the French sociologist Gabriel Tarde and the American sociologists Edwin Sutherland and Howard Becker, among others, view the "relationship between the individual and society as integral to the formation of not only the deviant but also the adjusted personality" (Vito & Holmes, 1994:177). Although each developed his own theory, they all examined crime as a social process involving the interplay between the individual and society. In other words, the social situations that people encounter play a major role in determining their behaviour. This orientation can be described as focusing on a social-psychological process that is derived from operant conditioning in psychology (see Chapter 6) (Einstadter & Henry, 1995). As a result, this general theoretical stream is referred to as *social process theories*. Notable contributions to the social process stream have included Gabriel Tarde's work in the 1890s on the *law of imitatio*, Graham Sykes and David Matza's *neutralization theory* in the 1950s, and Albert Reiss's pioneering work on the social control theory in the early 1950s (for a comprehensive review, see Einstadter & Henry, 1995).

Sutherland's Theory of Differential Association

Edwin H. Sutherland (1883–1950) (see Box 7.7) first outlined his theory of **differential association** in his 1939 *Principles of Criminology*—one year after Merton put forward his anomie theory. Conceptually, it is a refinement of Tarde's 19th-century concept of imitation, even though Sutherland made only three references to Tarde and none of them were to Tarde's laws of imitation (Martin et al., 1990). Sutherland explained crime as a function of a learning process that could affect any individual in any culture.

In his works, Sutherland expressed the belief that people learn how to commit crimes primarily through social interactions. The more intimate the contact, the more likely it is that the behaviours will be imitated. Through interactions with others, people learn not only the technique of committing crime, but also the attitudes, motives, and rationalizations that support crime. Sutherland further believed that while criminal behaviour is a politically defined construct, learning criminal behaviour is a social, not a political or legal process (Martin et al., 1990).

EDWIN HARDIN SUTHERLAND

Martin et al. (1990:139) begin their biographical sketch of Sutherland by noting that his reputation spanned the full spectrum from ardent critic to messiah, "but most would certainly agree that he was the leading criminologist of his generation" in North America. In fact, some have described him as the "Dean of American criminology" (Reid, 1982:153).

After receiving his bachelor's degree, Sutherland taught at a Baptist College from 1904 to 1906. There he enrolled in a home study course in sociology through the University of Chicago. The following year he moved to Chicago, where he took three courses in the Divinity School. One of them was his first criminology course, titled Social Treatment of Crime. The course appeared to have a major impact on him, and he began to take more sociology courses.

Between 1909 and 1911, Sutherland taught at Grand Island College before returning to Chicago to complete his degree. He quickly became disenchanted with sociology (or at least the department), which he felt "led to nothing more than empty moralizing" (Martin et al., 1990:141). He switched to political economy, and in 1913 was granted his doctorate with a double major in sociology and political economy.

It was not until 1919, while teaching in the sociology department at the University of Illinois and through the encouragement of the chair, Edward Carey Hayes, that Sutherland wrote his now classic introductory criminology textbook entitled *Principles of Criminology*. It was published for the first time in 1924, and Sutherland went on to complete three revisions—in 1934, 1939, and 1947. After his death, Donald Cressey, one of his last doctoral students, published six more editions before his own death in 1987. Among Sutherland's other noteworthy publications were his *Twenty Thousand Homeless Men* (1936), *The Professional Thief* (1937), and *White Collar Crime* (1949). This last book has been described as "a pioneer work and one that has remained controversial and provocative" (Martin et al., 1990:160).

Regardless of how one views his work, there is little doubt about the enduring influence that Sutherland has had on criminology.

The Nine Fundamental Principles of Differential Association

Sutherland outlined nine fundamental principles of differential association:

1. Criminal behaviour is learned. Unlike previous theoretical assertions, Sutherland's theory asserts that criminal behaviour is largely a process of cultural transmission and not an inherited characteristic.
2. Criminal behaviour is learned in interaction with other persons in a process of communication. However, just because we may be living in a criminogenic environment does not mean we will become criminals. Criminality cannot occur without direct interactions with others.

3. The principal part of the learning of criminal behaviour occurs within intimate personal groups. Vicarious exposure (e.g., watching crime-rated TV shows) may provide the "script," but intimate personal relationships provide the motivation (Vito & Holmes, 1994).

4. Learning criminal behaviour includes: (a) learning the techniques of committing the crime, which are sometimes very complicated, and (b) learning the specific direction of motives, drives, rationalizations, and attitudes. It is through the strength of the association with other criminal types that the individual learns how to commit crime.

5. The specific direction of motives and drives is learned from definitions of the legal codes as favourable or unfavourable. A person receives different messages as to how to respond to the prevailing laws of society depending on which group he or she belongs to.

6. A person becomes delinquent because of an excess of definitions favourable to violations of law over definitions favourable of the law. Every day we make value-neutral decisions that have nothing to do with crime. However, when youths talk about engaging in some deviant act, their attitudes about the legitimacy of the act begin to shift. These views then become part of their collective consciousness. In operant conditioning terms, the delinquent attitudes get reinforced.

7. Differential association may vary in frequency, duration, priority, and intensity. The extent to which criminal behaviour is learned is dependent on the frequency with which the message is reinforced, as well as the length of time that the individual is exposed to the criminal messages.

8. The process of learning criminal behaviour by association with criminal and anti-criminal patterns involves all the mechanisms that are involved in any other learning. Vito and Holmes (1994:182) observe that the processes for learning criminal behaviour are no different from those processes involved in learning non-criminal behaviour and that it "is more than simple imitation by associating with others."

9. While criminal behaviour is an expression of general needs and values, it is not explained by those general needs and values, since non-criminal behaviour is an expression of the same needs and values. Instead, since the motives for criminal behaviour are not the same as those for conventional behaviour, they can be explained only by understanding the nature and extent of association with criminality and deviant norms.

In summary, differential association theory is a positivist, macro-level theory that focuses on criminals and their behaviour and attempts to connect psychological and sociological principles. According to the DA theory, criminal behaviour represents an interaction between operant conditioning principles (i.e., association) and social group relations and environmental factors.

While Sutherland's textbook is considered a classic in its field, his theory of DA has met with varying degrees of support. Matsueda (1992) attempted to measure Sutherland's three key concepts—definition favourable to criminality, attitude toward peers, and attachment to deviant friends—but found a relatively low reliability coefficient, rendering the concepts less than satisfactory.

More Recent Social Process and Learning Theories

Since the development of the differential association theory, there have been three general trends in the way the DA has been treated (see Matsueda, 1988). Since the late 1980s, attention has focused on testing "various theoretical concepts, particularly the notion of association" (Williams & McShane, 2004:88). The different trends aside, most of the social process and learning theories are premised on the assertion that people commit crimes as a result of learning and socialization experiences with significant others—a view that can be contrasted with Skinner's theory, discussed in Chapter 6. For example, this idea is reflected in Jeffery's (1965) theory of differential reinforcement (DR). Einstadter and Henry (1995:176) observe that Jeffery's theory "recognized the differences in people's reinforcement history and the different meaning stimuli have to them." Borrowing heavily from Skinner's theory of operant conditioning, the differential reinforcement theory views crime as a learned behaviour based on the variability and intensity of the exposure to experience. However, in spite of its logical soundness, it has not received much attention.

Building on Jeffery's work are other social process–oriented approaches, such as Ronald Akers and Robert Burgess's (1966) differential association-reinforcement (DAR) theory (see Box 7.8). Akers and Burgess combined Albert Bandura's psychology-based behaviour modelling (i.e., observation learning; see Chapter 6) with Sutherland's sociology-based differential association theory.

What neither theory is able to account for is:

- How personality and/or biochemical makeup might predispose some to learn criminal behaviour and not others.
- Why some people who learn behaviour patterns never engage in criminal acts. For instance, I know how to break into a house but I have never done it.
- How the techniques and crimes originate.
- How the definition of the crime came into existence.
- Why children are more apt to model behaviour than adults.

Despite these and other criticisms, social process theories continue to attract a strong following. Supporters are likely to continue to revise this approach in an effort to counter its critics. Cullen and Agnew (1999) observe that the main arguments of social differential association and social learning theory are largely supported and will likely continue to play a vital role in directing attention of criminological inquiry to the process of learning criminal behaviour.

DIFFERENTIAL ASSOCIATION-REINFORCEMENT THEORY

Akers and Burgess tried to provide a comprehensive and scientific revision of Sutherland's learning process. They integrated some of Skinner's and Bandura's behavioural principles into Sutherland's theory, hoping that this would make the revised theory more testable while at the same time clarifying the learning processes involved. According to Akers (1977), people learn social skills by operant conditioning that is controlled by stimuli that follow the behaviour. As described in Chapter 6, behaviour is reinforced when positive rewards are associated with an act and weakened when a negative reinforcement accompanies a behaviour.

Akers argues that people learn to evaluate their own behaviour according to their interactions with significant others. The evaluative process involves making use of such social concepts as attitudes, norms, and orientations (Siegel, 1995). The interpretation of such concepts is important in reinforcing and serves as a cue for behaviour. Once a criminal is initiated, his or her behaviour can be reinforced by exposure to deviant models. The likelihood that a criminal act will be committed depends on the frequency, intensity, and duration of the exposure.

Siegel (1995:213) observes that the theory "is an important view of the cause of criminal activity" and that it "considers how both the *effectiveness* and *content* of socialization condition crime." However, Akers and Burgess's theory has not escaped criticism. Reed Adams (1973), for example, argues that the theory has misused the principles of operant conditioning and thereby misled criminologists and sociologists in understanding criminal and delinquent behaviour. Vito and Holmes (1994:184) further note that while the theory has been generally well received, it has not been able to define the "role of patriarchy in crime and delinquency."

Specifically, Sutherland's differential association theory seems to still have appeal, as reflected in the shift toward testing the various theoretical concepts (see Cao, 2004). Researchers have been asking what constitutes "excess association," how the proportion of association can be measured, and what role tutelage plays in a criminal's planning. If you ever had a close friend who got into trouble, did you copy his or her behaviour or did he or she copy yours? Why? Several years ago, Canadian researcher Bill McCarthy (1996) attempted to pursue this topic. Using six crime-specific questions (three on drug selling and three on theft) to measure tutelage, he found substantive support for introducing tutelage to improve the models of differential association theory. There appears to be something intuitively appealing about the differential association theory that continues to prompt researchers to seek better methods by which to operationalize and measure its principles.

Perhaps the most dramatic illustration of its enduring influence has been the application of the theory's principles to intervention programs. For example, the innovative program Head Start teaches disadvantaged children and/or troubled youth to deal with their environment. Former US president Lyndon Johnson approved the program in the 1960s; in 1993, Bill Clinton acknowledged the program's success (Kantrowitz & Wingert, 1993).

More recently, programs attempting conflict resolution have rapidly spread in North America. These programs are designed to teach youths and adults to resolve their frustration in a non-violent manner. Exercises used often include role-playing situations.

The LaMarsh Centre for Research at York University in Toronto engages in research projects aimed at understanding anti-social and deviant behaviour and in developing constructive response techniques to resolve such conflicts (see the weblink at the end of the chapter). In recent years, several of its studies have focused on iden-tifying vengeful attitudes, hockey violence, and abuse.

Labelling Theory

Although the three theoretical perspectives we have discussed so far in this chapter are able to explain serious crime in general terms and locate its causes either in individu-als or in the social environment, none of them is able to answer two fundamental ques-tions: How and why do some behaviours come to be defined as normative while others are defined as deviant? What are the individual/psychological and social consequences of being called a criminal or delinquent, of being apprehended, and/or convicted? **Labelling theory** concerns itself primarily with these two questions. It adopts an interactionist perspective by integrating social process and structural explanations and shifts toward a micro level of analysis.

It was noted at the outset of this chapter that no act is inherently criminal; rather, the law defines which acts are criminal. Unlike traditional sociological theories identi-fied above, which embrace an "absolutist" definition of crime (crime is learned or inherited), the labelling theory adopts a "relativist" definition. That is, crime and deviance (i.e., behaviour that violates or deviates from the social rules and/or norms) is not a property of a behaviour but rather the result of how others regard that behaviour (Barkan, 1997).

Origins of Labelling Theory

Williams and McShane (2004) point out that during the 1950s, when the labelling the-ory emerged, it focused on the individual. Social scientists observed that the ideals that North Americans fought to preserve abroad—liberty and equality for all—had not been reached on the home front. Blacks and Aboriginal peoples were still treated as second-class citizens, and unemployment and social stigmatization were still evident. Then in the 1960s, the orientation shifted toward examining and explaining the way people react to deviance. Subsequently, this new position "became known as the *societal reaction school*" (ibid:140). These researchers began to ask some probing questions, such as:

- How and why do certain behaviours become defined as deviant or criminal?
- Why do society and the criminal justice system seem to discriminate and apply official labelling and sanctions?
- What are the effects of labelling on continued criminality?

The labelling theory belongs to the conflict-based theoretical tradition and is rooted in the symbolic interaction theory of Charles Horton Cooley and George Herman Mead from the 1930s. However, it was not until the 1960s that the labelling theory became more popular. The era was marked by social unrest, the Vietnam anti-war movement, the beginning of the contemporary women's movement, the Quiet Revolution in Quebec, the emergence of the FLQ and the New Democratic Party, and such socially significant events as the introduction of our maple leaf flag. The theory became very popular among sociologists and criminologists in large part due to the work of **Howard S. Becker** (1928–) who, like so many other prominent sociologists of his time, came from the Chicago School. In his classic 1963 book *The Outsider*, Becker presented the theory's definition of deviance. However, it was Frank Tannenbaum, also from the Chicago School, who back in 1938 coined the phrase "dramatization of evil" to describe the process of how youths adjust to a delinquent group. Given how similar Tannenbaum's ideas were to the labelling theory in the 1960s, many criminologists view his work as representing the roots of the labelling theory.

Labelling theory does not view criminals as inherently evil but as individuals who have a criminal label conferred upon them because of some legal and/or social process (see Box 7.9). Hence, this theory focuses not the offender but on society's reaction to the offender. Becker (1963) felt that once an individual is "tagged" or labelled (e.g., liar, thief, junkie, stripper), it is often difficult for him or her to live down or live up to the tag. The degree to which a person can shed his or her stigmatization is dependent on the sanction that is levied against that person.

The negative impact that labelling can have on individuals has been used as a rationale for recommending that the young offender system employ alternative sanctions when dealing with youth in conflict with the law. Similarly, it has been suggested that penalties vary according to the characteristics of the offender, not the severity of the crime. It is well documented that Canada's Aboriginal people are overrepresented in the criminal justice system and that they get more severe sentences than non-Aboriginal people for similar offences (see generally Bonta, LaPrairie, & Wallace-Capretta, 1997). Such examples support the notion that the law is selectively enforced, since different groups are labelled as being more crime-prone than others.

Primary and Secondary Deviance

Labels can stigmatize an individual in a negative way. Until Canadian Rick Hansen rolled his wheelchair around in the mid-1980s, people confined to wheelchairs were thought to be incapable of achieving much. Similarly, an "ex-con" usually has a more difficult time finding employment because of a past criminal record (Bracken & Leowen, 1992). Labelling theorists suggest that labels create a self-fulfilling prophecy.

Primary deviance is deviance that results from such labels but is not socially labelled as deviant. In other words, primary deviants are those who engage in deviant acts but are not considered deviant or "bad" people. Others do not label them as "bad," nor do they themselves apply such labels. For example, the carpenter who takes home a few nails after work without being detected is not recognized as deviant and may not recognize that he or she has committed theft. Later, he or she might recognize the implications of that act and chastise him- or herself, but if the theft remains undetected, it does not affect the individual's self-concept. The social consequences of primary deviance are minimal.

Edwin M. Lemert (1912–1996) modified Becker's labelling theory to include **secondary deviance**, to further explain how the legal system can amplify the offender's

---

A CLOSER LOOK BOX 7.9

THE DEVIANCE PROCESS FROM THE PERSPECTIVE OF LABELLING THEORY

1. A person commits a deviant or criminal act. (If undetected, the act remains primary deviance.)
2. Society reacts in a retributive or punitive way.
3. The individual responds by committing more infractions (secondary deviance), which in turn draw additional attention. The deviant cycle begins to escalate (in frequency and/or intensity).
4. The labelled individual develops more hostility and resentment toward criminal justice agents.
5. Society and the legal system respond by further labelling and stigmatizing the offender.
6. As the individual's options become increasingly restricted, the criminal justice system sees the offender as a problem and the offender sees him- or herself as deviant.
7. The probability for future acts of deviance increases (deviance amplification). Therefore, once labelled and stigmatized, the offender's identity and self-concept evolve around deviance.

General Outlines of the Labelling Process: Primary deviance, informal reaction, continuance of deviance, escalation of response (e.g., stereotyping, rejection, alienation of tagged actor), more delinquency (secondary deviance), formal intervention, individual begins to see self as delinquent.

criminal behaviour through intervention (Cao, 2004). He pointed out that self-labelling combined with the social stigmatization of being labelled can result in "deviance amplification." The transition from primary to secondary deviance is summarized in Box 7.9.

As Lemert noted, secondary deviance sets in after the community, or society, has become aware of a primary deviance—real or socially created. Once an individual is tagged, the stigma can bring about dramatic behavioural changes. Secondary deviance involves the process of resocializing into a deviant role. For example, imagine a big-time media tycoon who might have been accused of embezzling funds from his company. He is subsequently forced to retire and asked to pay a considerable fine if he cannot prove his innocence. With his future prospects dashed, he turns to trying to bribe and lie his way out of being at fault. He eventually gets caught and is incarcerated. The label has served to amplify his criminal behaviour.

The labelling theory stresses the importance of societal reactions whose focus lies on the criminal, not the act. Therefore, what is important for criminologists using the labelling perspective is the label. Those responsible for making the rules are referred to as **moral entrepreneurs** (Becker, 1963). The rule-makers are interested in criminalizing certain behaviours so as to elevate their own social status, while the rule enforcers are concerned with enforcing the law. Based on his analysis, Becker feels that laws are not made unintentionally. Consequently, he urges criminologists to shift their focus from the offender to the process of criminalization.

Summary and Evaluation

How likely would you be to date or marry someone if you knew he or she had done time? Would you like your children to associate with a junkie, a stripper, or a known gang member? For most of us, the answer would probably be no. The stigma we associate with certain labels can colour our perceptions.

The labelling theory has found many supporters, but—like phenomenological approaches in general[3]—it has also had its critics. The following questions are among those that the labelling theory has not been able to answer:

- Why do people become involved in deviance even though they know they may get labelled?
- Labelling theory seems to imply that people are passive, but are they?
- Why do some people return to a life of deviance and/or crime after they have been subjected to treatment/intervention?

Various researchers have shown that the stigma of crime does not necessarily result in an escalation of crime (see Murray, 1990). In addition, Schur (1972) points out that the theory does not explain the onset of primary deviance, while Manning (1973) draws attention to the fact that not all labels are bestowed with discrimination. Nettler (1984) suggests that labelling does not always affect everyone in the same way. Finally, Gibbons (1994) goes so far as to argue that the labelling theory isn't a theory. Rather, he suggests, it is only "a collection of 'sensitizing' notions" (ibid.:83).

However, as we have already seen in previous chapters, no one theory is able to address all issues. In reference to the labelling theory, Cao (2004:140) notes that "societal reaction is a complex and its effect has yet to be understood fully." The theory has done much to enrich the study of crime and deviance, but by itself it cannot explain all issues related to crime and criminality.

The labelling theory—like the anomie theory, the ecological school, and the theory of differential association—has sparked various attempts at revision. In recent years, researchers have examined the existing operational, methodological, and/or conceptual limitations of these theories and attempted to offer new approaches to the study of crime and criminality. We will now look at some of these contemporary theories rooted in sociology.

Contemporary Theories Based on Sociology

Routine Activities Theory

Lawrence Cohen and **Marcus Felson** (1979) are credited with developing the **routine activities theory** (RAT). The theory marked a notable shift in sociological inquiry, as no previous theory "contained an assumption of a rational, thinking individual" (Williams & McShane, 1994:221). Cohen and Felson's "rational choice" perspective argues that motivation alone is insufficient to explain the cause of crime. Crime risk is largely dependent on the situational determinants for criminals and victims (Kennedy & Forde, 1995). The theory is premised on a deterministic model in that it links changes in routine activities to changes in crime rates.

The RAT quickly gained popularity, as it offers a very practical approach to the study of crime and victimology, since it attempts to integrate theoretical principles into social policy—something that has been largely lacking among criminological theories (Barkan, 1997). The theory also recognizes humans as rational beings. It considers both individual processing and the social environment, especially as each leads to social disorganization. Even though Cohen and Felson maintain that predatory crime is a matter of rational choice, they also hold that criminal opportunity is affected by the victim's behaviour and lifestyle. Hence, the RAT can be described as an integrated type of theory among the rational theories (see Box 7.10).

MAJOR RATIONAL THEORIES

- *Lifestyle theory* M. Hindelang, M. Gottfredson, and J. Garafalo

  Lifestyle is influenced by three elements: (1) social roles played by people; (2) position in social structure—the higher one's status, the lower one's risk of victimization; and (3) rational component—how one chooses to process options based on life experiences.

- *Opportunity theory* P. Mayhew, R. Clarke, A. Sturman, and J. Hough

  Crime is related to four key factors that are necessary and interrelated: (1) the abundance of goods; (2) the physical security of goods; (3) the level of surveillance; and (4) the occasion and temptation for crime.

- *Rational choice theory* D. Cornish and R. Clarke

  Crime is both offence- and offender-specific. Offenders rationally evaluate and assess the level of skill required, the personal gain to be obtained from the act, and the risk of detection/apprehension. The offence becomes the act that fits the individual's rational decision process.

- *Cognitive theory* G. Walter and T. White

  This psychology-based theory stresses the importance of the role of cognition in the individual. It argues that social and environmental factors tend to limit individual options rather than determine behaviour. Hence, crime is viewed as a product of irrational thinking.

- *Life-course theory* D. Nagin, D. Farrington, and T. Moffitt

  This theory was initially introduced by Sheldon and Eleanor Glueck in the 1930s. Moffitt and several of her colleagues have been conducting a longitudinal study along these lines since the 1970s in the province of Dunedin in New Zealand. Their life-course–style analysis has revealed that a number of elements interact to predispose youth to criminal behaviour; among these are poor neuropsychological scores, impaired communication skills, and poor nutrition. They note that the various elements manifest themselves at different developmental stages. They relate their concepts to a biosocial perspective (see Chapter 5) and suggest a variety of prevention programs.

- *Routine conflict theory* L. Kennedy and D. Forde

  This theory focuses on the lifestyle of the victim and low self-esteem as predisposing factors to crime and/or victimization. The theoretical model is based on Kennedy and Forde's (1995) survey of over 2000 respondents from Alberta and Manitoba. The victim's behaviour is a product of rational choice based on learned repertoires for responding to conflict. As evidenced by the Canadian Urban Victimization Survey and General Social Surveys, this repertoire is influenced by the person's relative circumstances in society, such as age, gender, income, race, and social class. The theory combines sociological and psychological factors.

FIGURE 7-3

ELEMENTS OF RAT

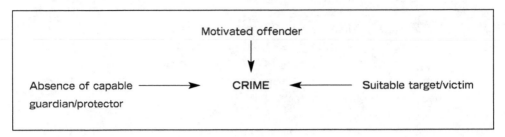

Instead of focusing on the factors that influence an offender's decision-making process to commit a crime, Cohen and Felson's theory focuses on the "routine" (daily activities) of people. Their theory includes three major elements (see also Figure 7–3):

1. A motivated offender (e.g., an unemployed person, substance abuser, unsupervised youth);
2. A suitable target (e.g., an unguarded home, unlocked vehicle, unprotected commercial residence, unmarked items); and
3. The absence of a capable guardian (e.g., homeowners, police, or neighbourhood watch groups).

Since its conceptualization, the routine activities theory has been the subject of numerous studies. It has become a popular theory that seems to complement criminal justice philosophy as well as the public's concern over victims' rights.

Evaluation of the Routine Activities Theory

The concepts of the routine activities theory are intuitively strong, and policy based on it can be readily adopted. Many of the crime prevention programs today involve practices such as target hardening (e.g., using deadbolts in doors or using security bars) and providing education programs for those who are at risk or feel they are at risk. In addition, the RAT has drawn attention to the important role of the victim in a criminal event.

The routine activities theory has undergone a number of refinements as other micro- and macro-level elements have been variably incorporated into different variations of the RAT. These elements include:

- *Opportunities of a target*. What is the visibility and physical accessibility of the target? For instance, how visible and accessible is a university parking lot filled with cars during the day?
- *Risk factors*. For example, is the target located at some distance from heavily populated areas? The parking may be located away from student activities and there may be no surveillance.

- *Exposure*. Can the target (in this example, car) be readily accessed?
- *Proximity*. How familiar is the offender with his or her target area? While the parking lot may represent a suitable target, the chance of a crime being committed there also depends on whether potential offenders are familiar with the area.
- *Structural/cultural proneness*. Are the targets considered suitable?
- *Defensive/avoidance behaviour*. To what extent do potential victims take steps to protect/secure the targets (in this example, secure their cars from being stolen)?
- *High-risk activities*. To what extent is the area under natural or technologically aided surveillance?

In spite of its practical appeal, not all criminologists support the RAT. Birckbeck and LaFree (1993) argue that the empirical tests of routine activity are generally based on false and ambiguous assumptions. For instance, the RAT asserts that those from a lower socio-economic position are more prone to victimization than the more affluent because the latter have the means to purchase security. Yet those with the means are also more likely to be seen as suitable targets. The theory does not provide an adequate explanation as to why the more affluent are not more frequently victimized.

Although the RAT acknowledges the role of choice, Canadian researchers Leslie Kennedy and Stephen Baron (1993) found that criminal choices among young offenders are also influenced by peer group pressures and cultural norms. These elements orient the potential offenders' choice of action. They argue that the RAT does not account for how these factors shape individual choice.

Nevertheless, numerous researchers continue to use the theory to help explain rates of victimization for specific crimes and crime "hot spots," among other criminal activity. RAT's future appears secure for the time being.

Social Conflict Theories

The modern variations of criminological conflict theories "emerged on the heels of labelling theory" in the 1960s (Williams and McShane, 1994:155). They are premised on certain social conditions, ranging from social and political unrest to situations involving gender, race, and social class discrimination to exploitation of the working class.

There are several primary derivations of the social conflict perspective. In this section, we will briefly examine three of the most popular social conflict orientations. They are: conflict theory, peacemaking theory, and feminist perspectives.

Conflict Theory

According to **conflict theory**, crime is caused by the inter-group conflict and rivalry that naturally exists in every society at every level, from individuals to groups. Its origins are both instrumental (actual enforcement or control function) and symbolic (product of the social environment). The perspective has also been referred to as **critical criminology** because it challenges the social context of conditions such as poverty, racism, and sexism (Schwendinger & Schwendinger, 1970).

The first wave of critical theorizing in Canada emerged in the early 1980s and was followed by a second wave in the mid-1980s. Some of the key Canadian scholars have included Tullio Caputo, Thomas O'Reilly-Fleming, Brian MacLean, and Robert Ratner. However, Austin Turk was among the first to introduce the conflict perspective in his 1969 publication *Criminality and the Legal Order*. His University of Toronto colleague John Hagan (1977) was the first Canadian to conceptually define the difference between a conflict and a consensus interpretation of social order.

Even though the second wave did not emerge until the mid-1980s, O'Reilly-Fleming (1996) points out that by the early 1990s the critical conflict perspective had begun to wane. It was replaced with new theoretical forms such as postmodernism, feminism, left-realism, and (more recently) peacemaking (see below).

For policy-makers, the conflict theory presents some practical challenges. Rather than attempting to explain crime, it tries to identify the sources of social conflict and social processes through which definitions of deviance and crime are created and enforced. Its proponents point to discriminatory practices within the criminal justice system, the discrimination against the lower classes, and the ways in which the law is used to support the status of those who make it. Yet in spite of their confrontational charges against the system, conflict theorists generally call for a peaceful evolution, rather than a revolution, to eliminate social conflict and improve the existing criminal justice system.

Austin Turk (1995) is among the few conflict theorists who identify concrete measures to reduce crime. These range from stopping the building of more prisons to decriminalizing public order offences such as consensual sexual activities and recreational gambling. Unfortunately, virtually none of his policies has received any attention from policy-makers.

Aside from practical problems, conflict theorists have been criticized for their inability to clearly define the structural causes of conflict. These and other dilemmas have spawned various modifications to the conflict perspective. Among these is the peacemaking theory.

Peacemaking Theory

Former conflict theorists such as Harold E. Pepinsky and Richard Quinney have been strong advocates of this relatively new school of thought in North America (Friedrichs, 1991). Quinney initially gained prominence in criminology with his powerful and influential work on the conflict theory titled *The Social Reality of Crime*, published in 1970. One of his propositions included the assertion that the social reality of crime is "constructed by the formulation and applications of criminal definitions, the development of behavior patterns related to criminal definitions, and the construction of criminal conceptions" (Williams & McShane, 1994:161).

Pepinsky's ideas on conflict theory, meanwhile, were first expressed in his 1976 book titled *Crime and Conflict*. Pepinsky argued that rather than rely on punishment and prisons, society should make better use of policies involving mediation and conflict resolution. While such ideas were not readily embraced in the 1970s, they have come into vogue in recent years.

Dissatisfied with the traditional conflict perspective, both Quinney and Pepinsky searched for a "radical humanistic understanding of social existence and human experience" (Friedrichs, 1991:102). They recognized that even though most people see peace as being superior to and more powerful than violence, sometimes the use of violence seems unavoidable. But is it necessary? Or natural?

Quinney and Pepinsky argue that the traditional way of perpetuating the "we–they" dualism and the criminal versus non-criminal orientation has done little to alleviate the crime problem. No matter how we express crime and punishment, we cannot punish acts, only the actors (see Pepinsky, 1991). As the esteemed Norwegian criminologist Nils Christie observes, "you're more likely to see that that person's soul is not embodied in any single act, and that you can not punish an act without contaminating a complex actor" (cited in Pepinsky, 1991:107). Therefore, there can be no justification for using punishment as a means of resolving disputes. Thus, **peacemaking theory**, like all conflict-based theories, posits that fundamental changes in the structure of society must take place if crime is to be reduced.

Pepinsky and Quinney, among other peacemaking theory advocates, point out that the criminal justice system is based on a "warlike" principles in which punishment is used to avenge wrongdoing (see Braswell, Fuller, & Lozoff, 2001). They see punishing or controlling someone as just as violent an act as committing the crime. As Tifft (1980:6) writes, "in such instance these acts reflect an attempt to monopolize human interaction." Hence, non-retaliation, according to Graeme Newman and Michael Lynch (cited in Pepinsky, 1991:109) is the "only way to break cycles of violence." Pepinsky adds that non-retaliation alone is not enough. He adds, as noted above, that people need to participate in the democratic process, which requires empathy, which in turn requires letting go of obedience.

Judging from the main anthologies on the subject, the peacemaking model has not been embraced in any noticeable way (see Pavlich and Ratner in O'Reilly-Fleming, 1996; MacLean & Milovanovic, 1991). But perhaps peacemaking criminology is making itself felt in more practical ways. For example, starting in the mid-1990s and gaining increasing support since 1997, the concept of restorative justice has been drawing considerable attention (see Chapter 14).

Feminist Perspectives

Even though Lombroso, more than a century ago, was among the first to write a book on female criminality, the subject remained largely ignored in criminology until the late 1960s. Typically, criminologists have focused only on crimes such as prostitution and shoplifting when studying female crime. In fact, Leonard (1982) points out that theoretical criminology had been unable to address female crime because it was dominated by men trying to explain male patterns of crime and delinquency. However, all this changed in the 1970s, when the women's movement provided the opportunity for female issues to be taken seriously. Freda Adler's *Sisters in Crime* and Rita Simon's *Women and Crime* were the two main works on the subject. While Adler and Simon reached different conclusions, they both attributed the growth in female crime to the emancipation of women. This interpretation did not sit well with other feminists (Daly & Chesney-Lind, 1988). But Adler and Simon's ideas, along with those of other feminists, did challenge the assumptions underlying traditional research on gender and criminal justice.

Daly (1989) comments on the relationship between feminism and criminology by identifying several issues: (1) with the exception of rape and intimate violence, criminology has not felt the impact of feminist thought; (2) some continue to believe that gender is simply another variable for the "regression equation," which asserts that the personalities of women (and men) who commit crimes are somehow flawed; (3) most often, one hears that women are simply so underrepresented they are not interesting subject matter; and (4) criminology cannot evolve unless it recognizes all components and aspects of the system—women being only one element.

According to Herman and Julia Schwendinger (1991), since the pioneering efforts of Freda Adler and Rita Simon, proponents of the **feminist perspective** have introduced a number of significant innovations in legal discourse, such as:

1. Universalizing rape laws. In January of 1983, the existing rape law was repealed and replaced with the general offence of assault. The new law consisted of three new categories: sexual assault (s. 246.1); sexual assault with a weapon, threats to a third party, and bodily harm (s. 246.2); and aggravated sexual assault (s. 246.3) (see Chapter 8).
2. Redefining gender crimes. Recognition of changes in women's gender roles in our evolving society leads to these changes being reflected in women's rates of criminal involvement.
3. Redefining gender relations in criminology. Through their writings and research, feminists have helped criminological theory move beyond the male-dominated perspectives. Some of the leading Canadian female scholars include Ellen Adelberg, Dorothy Chan, Dawn Currie, Karlene Faith, Shelley Gavigan, and Rita Gunn.
4. Widening the level of awareness of how women are handled differently from men throughout the criminal justice system, from the point of arrest to judicial processing to incarceration. For example, LaPrairie (1990) points out that even though Aboriginal people in Canada are disproportionately represented in crime statistics, there are even more Aboriginal women held in institutions than Aboriginal males.
5. Calling for new methodological strategies that focus on women's experiences of oppression and discrimination.

Depending on one's source, there are three to four primary strands or variations of feminism and feminist theory. Sally Simpson (1989) identifies three versions, while Williams and McShane (2004) add a fourth. All of these versions "share a concern with identifying and representing women's interests, interests judged to be insufficiently represented and accommodated within the mainstream" (ibid.:606) and have made significant contributions to criminological theory and criminal justice practices.

1. *Liberal feminism*: These feminists advocate for women's equality and freedom of choice. They see gender inequality being expressed in most spheres of influence, such as education, politics, and the workplace. They believe it is neither necessary nor natural. They do not accept the notion that private or public division of power and labour should exist within society. Instead, they call for a more "androgynous" approach (i.e., blending of male and female traits and characteristics). The adoption of this approach, they argue, would eliminate inequality and promote greater social harmony both within society and in the criminal justice system.

   In spite of its appeal, the liberal feminist perspective has been unable to "provide an adequate assessment of the origins of gender roles" (Hinch, 1994:4).

2. *Socialist feminism*: Proponents of this perspective see gender oppression as an inherent feature of capitalist societies. They attempt to unite radical and Marxist principles. The perspective sees criminality as a by-product of the class-based system. For socialist feminists, the only solution is a society free of gender and class stratification. They feel that in the existing social structure men are more likely to commit violent street crime, while women are more likely to commit property and vice crimes (Williams & McShane, 2004).

   In his summation, Hinch (1994:9) notes that the socialist perspective, like the radical approach, is unable to "account for variations in patriarchy over time."

3. *Radical feminism*: The supporters of this version of feminism believe that the origins of patriarchy are rooted in male aggression and control of women. They view male aggression as existing not only within the labour force but also in men's exploitation of women for their sexuality. They feel that "sex not gender is the crucial analytical category" (Williams & McShane, 2004:261) and that male domination is the origin of female subordination. They see patriarchy as a system that defines women as subjects, with men exercising their right of control through the law. Radical feminists believe that eliminating male domination will not only reduce crime rates for women, but also "precipitate a decrease in male violence against women" (Williams & McShane, 2004:261).

   The basic assertion of the radical feminists that "female subjugation is universal and originates in the biological differences between men and women" has not been supported in the literature (Hinch, 1994:6). In addition, their notion that rape somehow can exist separately from other forms of violent offences is an overstatement and a simplification of the crime.

4. *Marxist feminism*: Marxist feminists "see the capitalist system as exploiting subordinate groups (often based on race and gender) for capital production (profit)" (Williams & McShane, 1994:238). Hence, they see women as being relegated to lower occupational status and lower pay for equal work. That oppression and exploitation influences female crime directly, since it relates to labour and gender; that is, women are more likely to commit property offences

and sex offences such as prostitution. A natural continuation of the Marxist orientation is the socialist-feminist model described above.

While we have been referring to this perspective as being part of the feminist theories it has also been classified as part of the "new" gender-based theories (see Einstadter and Henry, 1995). In fact, in his review, Barak (1997:163) notes that there has been a tendency for the different feminist perspectives to become more inclusive and shift toward "the commonalties of gender, power, and conflict." This more general classification can perhaps be best illustrated by the following two points that describe the basic function of the gender-based theories. First, the various theoretical forms all criticize traditional male *androcentric* approaches to studying crime, and second, they all attempt to develop gender-sensitive interpretations of deviance (also see the weblinks at the end of this chapter).

The jury is still out as to how significant the feminist perspective is, and will be, in helping to understand and explain crime and delinquency. However, Barkan (1997:248) suggests that "without full consideration of gender and its intersection with race and class, the study of crime and criminal justice will remain incomplete." Given the changing social experiences of women and their increasing access to a wider range of opportunities (including in areas such as crime), criminology must recognize and seriously consider women's role in society in its study of crime.

Evaluation of Social Conflict Theories

Collectively, the social conflict theories view crime as the product of social inequality. Accordingly, the only way to achieve real change in crime patterns is through major social reforms, in some cases bordering on revolution. Only through aggressive social reforms is it possible to correct social and/or economic inequalities that are seen as the primary causes of crime.

Can such changes be achieved? To expect a sudden and dramatic reversal of existing social and political conditions is highly unrealistic. However, we have been witness to the emergence of what Lynch and Groves (1989:128) refer to as "middle-range policy alternatives" such as the abolition of mandatory sentences, prosecution of corporate crime, increased employment opportunities, and an increasing shift toward community-based alternatives to incarceration.

While social conflict theories appear promising, they are still unable to answer the following question: Why do some do it and others do not? Hence, while the social conflict–based approaches are important, they need to be linked with other disciplinary perspectives such as biology and psychology. In this way, as Barak (1997) and other integrationists argue, the different perspectives can be combined to analyze the elements of the individual, the group, and the society in an integrated and interdisciplinary explanatory model.

This is an interesting time for criminologists. After several decades of minimal progress, criminology appears to be going through a growth spurt. In the next section, we will examine one of the more popular contemporary criminology theories rooted in sociology—the general theory of crime.

General Theory of Crime

The History of the Theory

How should the **general theory of crime** (GTC) be classified? Does it represent a "new" theory, or is it simply a variation of existing perspectives? As you may have gathered by now, there are no hard and fast rules for classifying theories. For example, Williams and McShane (1994) place the general theory of crime in a chapter that includes several other "newer and emerging theories of criminology," while Barkan (1997) places it along with the group of theories that emphasize social process. Schmalleger and Volk (2001) make no mention of the GTC in their Canadian text, even though their book emphasizes theories. Their 2005 edition includes but a few sentencing in the opening chapter under the general heading of "theoretical criminology." In the 1991 edition of their textbook, Siegel and McCormick place their description of the GTC in their discussion of social structure theories, but in 2003 it has been moved to the section on integrated theories. The point is, there doesn't appear to be any consistent means of classifying some of the contemporary theories.

Intellectually, the GTC can trace its roots back to Travis Hirschi's (1969) popular social control theory, a theory representative of the conservative social movement of the 1970s and 1980s. It was also influenced by the resurgence of the basic principles found in the classical school. Along with rational theories and gender-class-based theories, the GTC has been called a neoclassical theory, as it represents the new generation of class theories (see Williams & McShane, 1999:ch. 10).

The general theory of crime represents a modified and somewhat refined articulation of Hirschi's social control theory. In his original version of social control, Hirschi emphasized the importance of our identification with conventional social control mechanisms in society; in the new theory, Hirschi and Gottfredson focus on how we use *self-control* as a mitigating force. Although social control and self-control represent two different concepts of control, Hirschi and Gottfredson (1989) assert that they are both acquired through early experiences of effective parenting. In response to the limitations of social control theory, the GTC has also integrated the concepts of control with those of the biosocial, psychological, routine activities, and rational choice theories.

In formulating their new theory, Hirschi and Gottfredson (1989) were interested in being able to explain a wider range of criminality and to shed conventional social concepts, such as class and gender, that they felt contribute to our understanding of crime. Instead, they focused on the problem of low self-control. So essential is the principle of self-control to the GTC that Williams and McShane (1994:227) suggest the theory will soon become known as the low self-control theory.

Gottfredson and Hirschi (1990) argue that we all have personality traits (ranging from impulsivity to insensitivity to basic intelligence) that affect our self-control. They argue that these traits are learned early in life through child-rearing practices and tend to persist throughout life. Poor parenting, deviant parents, and/or parents who are unable (or unwilling) to meet basic needs (e.g., development, security, and survival) are likely to negatively affect the child's self-control. When poor child-rearing practices are present, social bonds weaken and criminal opportunities become attractive options. The GTC model is not strictly deterministic; rather, it is based on soft determinism. That is, while the presence of poor child-rearing practices does not guarantee that children will turn to crime, these children will indeed be more predisposed to crime than those who have experienced positive child-rearing practices.

Gottfredson and Hirschi (1990) also point out that the concepts of the *criminal offender* and the *criminal act* are separate and should not be confused. The acts simply reflect rational choices and criminal opportunity, while criminal offenders are those individuals predisposed to criminal activity because of low self-control and faulty personality traits. It is here that we see the role of a biosocial element being a factor in self-control. Based on an individual's biological traits and the quality of family (social) upbringing over the individual's life course, the propensity to commit a crime may be present, but there is still opportunity to change it.

Gottfredson and Hirschi (1990) list six elements of low self-control (see Box 7.11). They claim that the principles can be used to explain a variety of criminal behaviours, ranging from break and enter to fraud, murder, and rape, and that they can even be used to explain white-collar crime, such as the infamous Bre-X gold mine hoax (see Box 7.12).

A CLOSER LOOK BOX 7.11

SIX CHARACTERISTICS OF LOW SELF-CONTROL

1. Human beings have innate impulsive tendencies to self-gratification.
2. Conventional socialization process is necessary to establish self-control mechanisms.
3. Improper or inadequate child-rearing practices predispose a child to trait developments that can precipitate low levels of self-control.
4. Low self-control weakens social bonds and promotes a digression to short-term, pleasure-seeking behaviours.
5. Crime and deviance become suitable self-fulfilling opportunities and behaviour.
6. Taking steps to improve self-control results in lower levels of crime as well as in other positive behaviours.

Source: Adapted from Williams & McShane, 2004:277.

DAVID WALSH, FOUNDER OF BRE-X MINERALS LTD.

- David Walsh was born in 1945 and grew up in the affluent Westmount area of Montreal.
- He had a string of mediocre successes in the investment industry, first with Midland Walwyn in Montreal and then with a number of junior mining companies based in Alberta.
- In 1988, he founded the Bre-X mining company, which was headquartered in his basement.
- In 1992, while on the verge of another bankruptcy, he hooked up with another Canadian, John Felderhof, who allegedly told him that there was gold in the head-waters of the Busang River in Borneo.
- After the founders claimed to have struck the "motherlode of all motherlodes" in late 1996, the shares of Bre-X went from penny stocks to nearly $280 per share almost overnight. Walsh was claiming the existence of about a 200 million–ounce resource. The going rate for gold in 1996 was about $350 (US) per ounce!
- In 1997, shortly after the American firm Freeport-McMoRan Copper and Gold (led by a friend of Indonesian president, General Suharto) began to test the area for gold prior to signing a deal with Bre-X, the mysterious death of one of Bre-X's lead geologists, Michael de Guzman, raised suspicion around the company and its purported gold find. Within days, Freeport reported there was an insignificant amount of gold in the area, and within a few short weeks the largest gold hoax of the century was revealed. Walsh unloaded about $8.7 million in Bre-X stock before the hoax became public.
- Walsh retreated to his residence in the Bahamas and claimed no knowledge of the hoax.
- In 1997, the legal firm Deloitte and Touche became Bre-X's bankruptcy trustee and filed a class action suit against Bre-X, the Toronto Stock Exchange, securities regulators, and firms that promoted the stock.
- In 2004, the RCMP were trying to bring Felderhof, the last living major player in the Bre-X saga, to court on four counts of issuing misleading press releases. But, since he still lives in the Cayman Islands, with which Canada has no extradition agreement, it is not certain whether the case will be able to move forward.
- Even after Walsh's death in 1998, close friends continued to defend his innocence, claiming he was not involved in the scam. What do you think?

Sources: Duffy, 1997; Rubin, 1998.

How might the GTC be applied to the case of David Wash, the head of Bre-X? It could be argued that after years of only mediocre success in the mining industry, Walsh became preoccupied with self-gratification as a result of weakened social bonds. On the verge of bankruptcy and unable to control his downward slide, he may have become directly or indirectly involved in shady business transactions. This could have been done with the intent of reclaiming some of his family's former image.

Evaluation of the General Theory of Crime

Williams and McShane (1994:229) suggest that the "combination of propensity and event within one theory shows promise." In addition, the theory is both integrated and interdisciplinary, and it combines biological and psychological concepts with social structural processes.

Unlike the social conflict theories discussed earlier, the GTC is a positivistic theory that focuses on the *process* of committing a crime. An important underlying assumption is that social order is *consensus-oriented* as opposed to conflict-based. Furthermore, Williams and McShane (1994:229) note that the GTC, while tending toward a microtheoretical approach (e.g., different degrees of socialization process), shares characteristics of the macrotheoretical approach. They point out that Gottfredson and Hirschi acknowledge that social institutions such as schools can "uniformly regulate child-rearing," implying that low self-control "has origins in, or is critically influenced by, the social structure."

Of course, the GTC has also drawn criticism. Williams and McShane (1994:229) argue that the theory's greatest problem is the fact that "the prediction of crime requires the identification and prediction of other outcome events as well, such as drug use, aggression, and truancy." Polk (1991) feels that its definition of crime is too restrictive, and Bartol (2002) suggests that the theory is based on tautological reasoning, since crime and other behaviours that are seen as "weaknesses" in character (e.g., drinking alcohol, smoking, doing drugs, and gambling.)—or low-self-control—are being used to explain these same exact behaviours. Akers (1991, cited in Williams & McShane, 2004:277) suggests that the GTC is really no different from his own social learning theory. Finally, Schulz (2003) offers one of the most insightful analysis of the GTC. He notes that while the theory offers theoretical explanations of crime, the explanations (such as the notion of self-control) have not been overly well operationalized or reliably measured. Schulz also suggests that the theory overestimates the contribution of low self-control to the crime problem.

Relying on secondary analysis of data from the Ontario Ministry of Transport, Keane, Maxim, and Teevan (1993) tested the GTC by examining the relationship between self-control and driving under the influence of alcohol. Overall, their findings revealed a positive relationship between risk taking and the effects of alcohol. They conclude that while their model was incomplete with regard to a number of exogenous factors, the findings lend support to the GTC.

In spite of some of the possible theoretical limitations, Gottfredson and Hirschi have not been shy to discuss the policy implications of their theory. They see no value in short-term strategies or in addressing the supposed traditional causes of truancy and delinquency, since they believe they are symptoms of low self-control. They also feel that any efforts to reduce poverty or other social ills will not directly affect crime because such conditions alone do not cause crime.

Instead, Gottfredson and Hirschi (1990:272–273) emphatically declare that "policies directed toward enhancement of the ability of familial institutions to socialize children are the only realistic long-term state policies with potential for substantial crime reduction." Familial institutions may involve traditional family settings composed of a natural father and mother or programs that focus on parenting skills and improving self-control in children. As for other forms of crime, the GTC is less specific, but Williams and McShane (2004) suggest that perhaps the use of environmental design concepts might make crime more difficult to commit.

Overall, the theory has meet with mixed levels of support. It does not appear to adequately explain all forms of crime (see Polk, 1991), but only continued testing and practical application of the theory's concepts will provide evidence as to its ultimate merit.

We have reviewed a wide range of theories based on sociology, each offering its own unique explanation of crime and deviance as well as its own approach to crime control. While most of these theories meet the general criteria for assessing a "good theory" (see Williams & McShane, 2004), none of them has been able to provide convincing evidence in a manner that is readily understandable and that works when applied to policy. As Jack Gibbs (1972:4) observed, "sociologists probably agree that testable theories are desirable, but...the proliferation of untestable theories surly signifies that testability is not taken seriously." In 1970, Thomas Kuhn (cited in Cao, 2004:184) noted that "the game of science is, in principle, without end." Our challenge as students and professionals is to critically evaluate and assess what we know and strive to refine our understanding in order to create a better and safer world.

Summary

- Sociological inquiry emerged in Europe and was popularized at the University of Chicago at the beginning of the 20th century. Sociology did not really find a home in Canada until the early 1960s.
- Sociological theories focus on some aspect of social structure and social process. Concepts range from the effects of social disorganization to people's abilities to adapt to their societal goals through legitimate means.
- The *anomie theory* focuses on the breakdown of social norms and the conditions under which the conventional norms are no longer able to maintain social order. The *ecological school* examines the role that our socio-spatial environment plays in crime trends and criminal behaviour. *Differential association theory* emphasizes the importance of social learning and subcultures and focuses on how those with whom we interact can influence our behaviour. The *labelling theory* emphasizes societal reactions to what people do or don't do.

- Contemporary sociology-based approaches to crime and deviance include routine activities theory, social conflict theories (including conflict theory, peacemaking theory, and feminist perspectives), and the general theory of crime.
- There appears to be a concerted move toward theory integration and an interdisciplinary understanding of crime. While the future of criminological theories remains unclear, we must remain optimistic and strive to refine our understanding of crime and deviance.

Discussion Questions

1. To what extent do you think crime rates differ according to the important dimensions of structured social inequality, such as urban social life, race/ethnicity, social class, and gender? Which of these factors do you feel are the most important for understanding crime? Why?

2. Describe the major theories discussed in this chapter. What are the relative strengths and weaknesses of each theory? Which theory do you think has the most explanatory power? Why?

3. What challenges might exist in accepting any one type of sociology-based theory over another type?

4. How have social structures affected criminological theory, crime research, and crime policy?

5. How might sociological components be incorporated into an integrated and interdisciplinary criminological perspective? Which components do you think would be the most important?

Key Concepts

anomie
Crime Prevention Through Environmental Design (CPTED)
feminist perspective
moral entrepreneurs
routine activities theory
social structure

concentric-circle theory
critical criminology
differential association
general theory of crime
peacemaking theory
secondary deviance
strain theory

conflict theory
cultural transmission theory
ecological school
labelling theory
primary deviance
social disorganization theory

Key Names

Howard S. Becker
Lawrence Cohen
Émile Durkheim
Robert K. Merton
Edwin H. Sutherland

Ernest W. Burgess
Auguste Comte
Marcus Felson
Robert E. Park
Gabriel Tarde

Albert K. Cohen
Carl A. Dawson
Henry D. McKay
Clifford R. Shaw

Weblinks

www.arts.yorku.ca/lamarsh/ The website of the LaMarsh Centre for Research at York University, the mandate of which is "to support, conduct, and disseminate the results of research on violence and conflict resolution in the broad sense," offers the full text of various reports.

www.westga.edu/~jfuller/peace.html This site, managed by John Fuller, one of the leading proponents of peacemaking theory, offers related links.

critcrim.org/peacemaking.htm Hosted by the Critical Division of the American Society of Criminology, the site addresses peacemaking, restorative justice, and related social conflict theories. It also provides links to other sources and individuals who specialize in one or more of the related theoretical areas.

faculty.ncwc.edu/toconnor/301/301lect14.htm This page contains an overview of the feminist perspective.

www.crimetheory.com The Crime Theory site is an excellent resource, as it contains information about most of the criminological theories covered in Chapters 5–7.

Endnotes

1. Hiller (1982) provides one of the first and most comprehensive reviews of the history of Canadian sociology, as well as a review of Clark, one of the pioneers of Canadian sociology.

2. During the 1950s, Walter Miller developed a variation of Cohen's theory and coined the term "middle-class measuring rod." The term refers to the set of standards that the lower classes try to attain. They include such social behaviours as sharing, delaying gratification, setting long-term goals, and respecting others' property (Williams & McShane, 2004). If these goals are unattainable, the result can be frustration and a subcultural reaction, such as deviance. The subcultural behaviour becomes a learned collective solution to the problem of not being able to attain certain goals.

3. A phenomenological approach holds that criminal behaviour is knowable only to those who participate in it. For example, a criminal event means one thing to the offender, another thing to the victim, and something different again to the various practitioners within the criminal justice system.

CHAPTER 8

Violent Crimes

"Murder! Rape! Robbery! Assault! Wounding! Theft! Burglary! Arson! Vandalism! These form the substance of the annual official criminal statistics on indictable offences.... they constitute the major part of 'our' crime problem. Or at least, we are told so daily by politicians, police, judges, and journalists who speak to us through the media of newspapers and television. And most of us listen."

Steven Box, 1983:1

Learning Outcomes

After you have completed this chapter, you should be able to:

- Recognize and be familiar with the major forms of violent crimes and the general trends of major violent crime types.

- Understand that an "absolute" explanation of violent crime causation is currently unavailable.

- Appreciate the importance of using crime data to understand violent crime trends and patterns, explain crime, and recommend social policy.

- Appreciate the importance of applying an integrated and interdisciplinary approach when using crime data.

- Appreciate the benefit of using comparative criminology to lend further insight into the study and control of violent crimes.

Introduction to Violent Crime

According to the media, crime has been on the increase, although actual crime rates have been declining since 1991 at an average of 3 percent per year. Various media may be quick to point out, however, that statistics still indicate that the 2002 crime rate

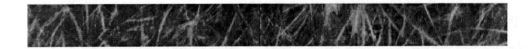

remains 9 percent higher than the rate 25 years ago.[1] So is Canada becoming a safer place to live? Are our perceptions of crime distorted and incorrect? What might account for the declining crime rate trend? Is the trend uniformly experienced across all criminal offences?

In the next two chapters, we will focus first on violent crimes and then on property crimes. As noted in Chapter 1, these types of crimes are generally referred to as *conventional crimes*. This chapter will examine three major violent crime offences—homicide, sexual assault, and robbery—and several "new" forms of violent crime—abduction, hate crime, stalking, and terrorism). However, it should be noted that official Canadian crime statistics also divide these crimes into various sub-classifications. For example, **assault** is further classified into 11 categories, ranging from "aggravated sexual assault" to "unlawfully causing bodily harm."

In addition, the police also record incidents involving prostitution, gaming and betting, offensive weapons, and a host of other *Criminal Code* offences. They also record offences that violate federal statutes, provincial statutes, and municipal bylaws. Together, these crimes make up all the police-reported incidents. Some of these crimes will be covered in Chapters 10–13.

The purpose of this chapter is not to provide an exhaustive review of all reported crimes but rather to introduce some of the trends and patterns of various forms of these violent crimes in Canada. Throughout this chapter, keep in mind that the general observations and conclusions are more important than the numbers themselves. Although violent crime represents only approximately 10 percent of the total *Criminal Code* incidents, it commands considerable media and public attention. In 2003, there were 304 515 reported incidents of violent crime, as compared with over more than 1.3 million property-related infractions (CCJS, 2004, 24(6)). But given most people's fascination with violent crime and the fact it can potentially result in the most serious harm (emotionally and/or physically) that can be inflicted on anyone, we will examine it first (see Box 8.1).

FYI BOX 8.1

YOUTH VIOLENT CRIME RATE

Between 1962 and 1995, instances of violent crime quadrupled. The youth violent crime rate rose even faster after the introduction of the *Young Offenders Act* in 1984 (CCJS, 1998, 18(12)). Between 1999 and 2003, however, there was only a slight but gradual increase in the youth violent crime rate, and after the introduction of new the *Youth Criminal Justice Act* in 2003, the number of youth charged with violent crime dropped—an occurrence largely attributed to changing police practices in response to the new legislation (CCJS, 2004, 24(6)).

In Chapter 1, we noted that the meaning of crime is dependent on one's perspective. Rather than focus on the various meanings, we will base our observations on factual data that has been collected. We will also focus on those forms of **violent crime**—that is, crime involving bodily harm, such as assault, murder, rape, and robbery—that are officially recorded by Statistics Canada. However, as the boxes scattered throughout this chapter will demonstrate, violent crime does exist in a variety of other forms as well—for example, hate-motivated crime (see Box 8.2), corporate violence, and family violence. Given that we will be relying mostly on official data, it bears reminding that these statistics have limitations and that they do not necessarily represent the "real" picture (see Chapter 3). As well, it is not possible to discern from official violent crime data exactly who is committing these crimes and why; this area deserves immediate and closer attention from policy-makers.

REALITY CHECK BOX 8.2

HATE-MOTIVATED VIOLENCE

Typically, when we think of violence caused by racial or ethnic factors, we think of the United States (e.g., the Rodney King case in March 1991) or some other foreign country. Yet Canada has a long history of hate-motivated violence toward Aboriginal and racial and ethnic minorities. As early as 1907 in Vancouver, a mob of whites attacked the local Chinese and Japanese communities, causing extensive damage to property and, reportedly, several casualties (Data on hate..., 1995). A 1994 report by the Department of Justice offers a list of references to sources on hate-motivated violence against racial and ethnic minorities in Canada during the 20th century. At times, these occurrences were thought to be related to "alleged fears of economic competition, especially at a time of recession," but Patel (1980, cited in Data on hate..., 1995:1) suggests that latent racism has been behind a number of such incidents.

In his 1977 report, Pitman (cited in Data on hate..., 1995) observed that in the "majority of incidents reported and investigated, the victim did not know his assailant and had done nothing that could be reasonably construed as a provocation." Focusing on Toronto and the surrounding area, Pitman found that most of the victims were males of South Asian origin. Few of the assailants were over the age of 22 and all were male. Alcohol had been consumed just before each attack.

While Canada is not as progressive at addressing hate-motivated violence as Canadians might think, we have set up a reporting mechanism to enable "a more comprehensive national picture of the scale of hate-motivated behaviour" (Data on hate..., 1995). Hate-motivated crime and violence have nevertheless become a serious issue in Canada, especially in light of the growing proportion of racial and ethnic minorities (see Hate and bias..., 1998; CCJS, 2004, 24(4)).

Violent Crime Rates and the Cost of Crime

As Table 8–1 shows, the violent crime rate at the national level has been fairly stable throughout the 1990s, with a slight decrease each year since 2000. The extent of violent crime varies by type, geography, and other important characteristics.

TABLE 8–1

VIOLENT CRIME IN CANADA, 1993–2003

YEAR	RATE PER 100 000	NUMBER
1993	1072	310 201
1994	1038	303 745
1995	995	294 603
1996	990	269 746
1997	980	296 737
1998	979	296 166
1999	958	291 327
2000	984	302 098
2001	984	305 186
2002	969	303 946
2003	963	304 515

Source: CCJS, *Crime Statistics in Canada* annual reports.

The financial cost of crime to Canadians has been increasing over the years (see Table 8–2). According to Statistics Canada, between 1988–1989 and 1994–1995, total criminal justice expenditures have increased 13 percent, as calculated on an inflation-adjusted basis (CCJS, 1997, 17(3)). In the 1970s, the per capita cost was approximately $170 (Griffiths & Verdun-Jones, 1994), while in 1994–1995, every person in Canada paid $324, for a total of nearly $9.4 billion on police, courts, corrections, legal aid, and criminal prosecution (CCJS, 2002, 22(11):14). However, given the recent decrease in violent crime rates, are the formal measures working, or do criminologists need to explore alternative measures to maintain social control? In 2000–2001, the per capita cost was $362, with a total budget of $11.1 billion.

As in Canada, violent crime rates in the United States increased gradually following the Great Depression until the 1960s, when they began to increase sharply. Interestingly, the homicide rate declined between the 1930s to the 1970s, at which point it began a period of sharp increase (Siegel, 1995). Between 1983 and 1993, the violent crime rate increased about 40 percent, and it appears to be experiencing a fluctuating increase still.

TABLE 8-2

THE COST OF ADMINISTERING JUSTICE BY SECTOR,
IN MILLIONS OF DOLLARS

	1990–1991	1994–1995	1997–1998	2000–2001
All sectors:	8520	9750	9470	11 100
Police	5240	5780	5900	6800
Courts*	766	838	907	1000
Legal aid	412	646	455	512
Youth corrections	434	526	499	n/a
Adult corrections	1790	1890	2070	2100

* Figures for courts are collected every second year.

Sources: CCJS, 1997, 17(3); 2002, 22(11).

When we take a moment to compare our violent crime trends with those of other countries (see Box 8.3), the picture may seem less alarming. Since a majority of the Canadian population lives within 200 kilometres of the American border, most of us have probably spent some time reading (or hearing) about the crime problem in the United States. By all counts, violent crime is a much more serious problem there than it is in Canada.

BY THE NUMBERS BOX 8.3

INTERNATIONAL (VIOLENT) CRIME RATES— UP AND DOWN

- Western Australia: Crime rates increased 5 percent during 2000. Property crime increased 6 percent, while violent crime declined 1.4 percent (Western Australian..., 2001).
- England and Wales: The 2003 British Crime Survey reveals that crime declined from 1993 through 2000, at which point overall crime rates began to increase slightly. The rise is attributed to a slight increase in property-related rather than violence-based offences (British Crime Survey, 2003). Since 2002, under the new Labour government, Home Office data reveal that crime rates have risen significantly and are among the highest in the Western world today. Violent crime had increased 11 percent between 1995 and 1996. Homicide, rape, and robbery rates went from 41 per 100 000 people in 1986 to 101 in 2002 (Welsh & Farrington, 2002).
- In general, the Home Office study reports that "nearly all countries covered by Western Europe, North America, and Japan have shown a sharp increase in recorded crime between 1987 and 1995" (Welsh & Farrington, 2002).

Changing demographics, economic recession and economic restructuring, and increasing drug use might account for some of the similarities in international trends, but they do not explain variable rates. Different police recording and administrative practices may account for some of these, but in general, more sophisticated, integrated models are required to explain these differences. In the meantime, there is considerable merit in criminologists doing comparative research and applying their theories to comparative data (see Barbaret, 2004).

The "Causes" of Violence

How do we account for all this violence? Researchers have been preoccupied with trying to explain, understand, and control one form of violent behaviour or another since criminology first became a disciplinary study in the 1800s. Yet, aside from providing descriptive information and advancing a variety of theoretical interpretations, criminologists have not been able to explain what causes violent crime.

We do know, however, that sources of violent tendencies have been said to stem from: (1) abusive families, (2) competing cultural values, (3) firearm availability, (4) gang motivation, (5) human instinct, (6) personality traits, (7) regional values, and (8) substance abuse. Numerous articles can be found describing how these various factors contribute to violence in society, and many of them have been incorporated into theoretical explanations.

One of these explanations is the deterministic model (focusing on human instinct and personality traits), such as that of Sigmund Freud, who argued that we possess a basic instinct for violence, or that of Konrad Lorenz (1966), who suggested that since violence is instinctive within the animal kingdom, it is only natural that it is part of human nature too. Other explanations have focused on social structures (for example, abusive families) and/or social forces (for example, gangs and regional values) to measures of anomie (for example, substance abuse). However, no one theory has been able to completely explain the etiology—that is, causes—of violence. Recently, a number of criminologists have begun to suggest that an interdisciplinary perspective may prove more promising. To date, insufficient research has been conducted in this area to bear out whether this line of inquiry will prove fruitful. Nevertheless, it is incumbent on criminologists to explore new theoretical directions if violence, in its diverse forms, is to be curbed.

Let us now examine some of the trends and patterns of violent crime in Canada. We will begin with the most serious of these—homicide.

Homicide

Under s. 222 of the 2004 Canadian *Criminal Code*, "a person commits homicide when, directly or indirectly, by any means he causes the death of a human being." The law goes on to define specific elements of culpable and non-culpable homicide. In Canada, some homicides are legally justified—for example, in self-defence. Culpable homicide refers to first-degree and second-degree murder, manslaughter, and infanticide.[2]

Students reading about homicide for the first time might ask, "What is the difference between homicide and murder—are they synonymous?" While both terms pertain to the death of a human being caused by another, "murder" refers more narrowly to the unlawful, often planned, and deliberate taking of another's life, whereas "homicide" is a more general term that, in addition to murder (both first- and second-degree), encompasses other ways of causing death, such as infanticide and manslaughter.

The *Criminal Code* divides homicide into four sub-categories: (1) first-degree murder, (2) second-degree murder, (3) manslaughter, and (4) infanticide. Aside from infanticide, the basis for placing murder in a sub-category is the offender's intent and the nature of the act that causes someone to die.

Homicide Rates

Up to 2000, homicide rates were on the decline. In 2002, the homicide rate in Canada was 1.85 per 100 000 people, an increase of 4 percent from 2001 (see Table 8–3). Internationally, Canada's homicide rate is well below that of such countries such as Russia and the United States but generally greater than that of most European countries (see Table 8–4).

Why Do People Kill?

What might account for the increase in the murder rate since 1999? Aside from incidents such as the mass murders uncovered at a farm outside of Vancouver in 2003, which artificially inflate the murder rate, the increase has been rather modest, and the

---

TABLE 8–3

CANADIAN HOMICIDE RATES, 1992–2002

YEAR	RATE (HOMICIDES PER 100 000)	TOTAL
1992	2.58	732
1993	2.18	627
1994	2.05	596
1995	2.00	588
1996	2.14	635
1997	1.95	586
1998	1.84	558
1999	1.76	538
2000	1.77	546
2001	1.78	553
2002	1.85	582

Sources: CCJS, 1996, 16(11); 1997, 17(9); 1998, 18(2); 2003, 23(8); 2004, 24(8).

Section III: Contemporary Issues in Canadian Criminology

TABLE 8-4

HOMICIDE RATES FOR SELECTED COUNTRIES, 2002

	RATE (HOMICIDES PER 100 000)
Russia	20.54
United States	5.52
England and Wales	2.01
Hungary	1.99
Canada	1.85
Australia	1.85
Switzerland	1.18
Austria	0.80

Source: CCJS, 2003, 23(8):3.

murder rate is now lower than throughout most of the 1990s. Nevertheless, this is a question that taxes even the most learned of scholars. Silverman and Kennedy (1993:5) observe that while the media want simple answers to explain homicide rates to their viewers, listeners, and readers, the reality is that "these crimes need to be understood in all their complexity, especially when it comes to planning ways of preventing their occurrence."

As noted above, in spite of all the research, the question remains: Does the etiology of violence (including homicide) rest within the social structure of society, within the biological makeup, or within the personality of the perpetrator? In their book on murder, Silverman and Kennedy suggest that there are two classes of theories that deal with homicide.

The first involves "individual social interaction and conflict." Among the theories under this classification are Hirschi's social control theory (see Chapter 7) and its newer derivations (for example, the general theory of crime and the power control theory). Also included is the routine activities theory.

Theories in the second class focus on the level of society. Silverman and Kennedy start their review of the theories in this class by pointing out that human behaviour does not operate in a vacuum but is subject to the effects of the economy, inequality, and the social disorganization in the environment. They cite a variety of studies that lend support to the relationship between the presence of such factors and homicide rates. Certain questions, however, remain unanswered by these explanations. For example, with regard to economic inequality, how extensive does this inequality have to be before murder rates increase? Also, what are some of the mediating preventive elements, and to what extent can economic inequality be used to explain the different types of homicide? Similar criticisms can be made of the social disorganization condition. For example, Blau and Blau (1982, cited in Silverman & Kennedy, 1993:60) found a high correlation between divorce and crime rates. But what is not clear is the level at which crime rates "suddenly" increase. To what extent do support groups for divorcees mitigate crime rates? Do the circumstances surrounding the divorce affect the likelihood of crime? These and other factors related to social disorganization have not been clearly operationalized (see Box 8.4).

FYI BOX 8.4

THE FEMALE SERIAL KILLER

Relatively little is known about the female serial killer. While researchers have developed typologies for male serial killers, there is insufficient data to offer similar explanations for female killers. Hickey (1991), among others, suggests that female serial killers represent only about 8 percent of American killers (the US has about 85 of all known serial killers in the world). Consequently, he refers to them as the *quiet killers* but says they are as lethal as their male counterparts. Kelleher and Kelleher (1998) argue that female serial killers are more successful, careful, precise, methodological, and quiet in committing their crimes.

The first officially apprehended female serial killer in North America was Aileen Wuornos, a Florida woman who killed at least seven men starting back in 1989. She was executed through lethal injection in October 2002. Her life was rather sympathetically yet realistically portrayed in the 2003 Oscar-winning film *Monster*.

Aside from these two classes of theories, Silverman and Kennedy (1992:53–58) offer a brief overview of "alternative approaches" to explaining homicide. Here they discuss some of the micro-level approaches, such as the sociobiological perspective, biology-based explanations, psychological approaches that emphasize the role of moral frustration, and psychological theories that emphasize particular psychiatric disorders.

As with the two main classifications mentioned above, this last group of theories may be able to explain some types of murder, but each of these theories, given its narrow theoretical perspective, is limited in its coverage. Until criminologists begin to recognize the complexity of human behaviour and the importance of applying an interdisciplinary approach to the study of murder, or any crime, we will have to settle for interesting but limited theoretical explanations. Consequently, our ability to control and prevent such incidents will continue to fall short of our objectives.

Patterns, Trends, and Characteristics of Homicides

In 2002, 77 percent of all reported homicide incidents were solved by the police. Between 1992 and 2002, the percentage fluctuated between 75 and 83 percent. However, since the process of solving homicides can take some time, some incidents are not solved until years after they were initially recorded. For example, in Nova Scotia, Donald Marshall spent nearly a dozen years imprisoned for a murder he didn't commit. In other cases of wrongful convictions—such as those of Thomas Sophonow, Norman Fox, David Milgaard, Guy Paul Morin, Gregory Parsons, and Romeo Phillion—it has taken years to discover that the sentenced people were innocent (see Box 8.5). Therefore, these data underestimate final police **clearance rates**.[3]

It would be interesting to know what role new police investigation strategies (such as DNA analysis and surveillance technology) are playing in solving homicides, but no official statistics available. What is available, however, is data on the manner in which homicide incidents were cleared. In 2002,

- 90 percent were cleared by a charge being laid or recommended;
- 9 percent were cleared by the accused having committed suicide immediately following the offence; and
- The remaining 1 percent (4 cases) were cleared either because the Crown chose not to proceed or because of the death of the accused (by means other than suicide).

Other interesting data available through Statistics Canada provide useful information by which to profile homicide victims and the accused. Findings include the following:

- Homicides continue to be committed by someone known to the victim (84 percent of all homicides solved in 2002). The risk of being killed by a stranger has remained relatively stable over the past decade, ranging between 12 to 17 percent of all homicides.
- Almost all of the 2003 homicide incidents were single-victim incidents (96 percent or 529 of the total 548 reported homicides); the remaining 19 multiple-victim homicides represent a decrease from the average of 31 over the past decade (CCJS, 2004, 24(8)).
- The number of victims of gang-related homicide nearly doubled from 46 in 2002 to 84 in 2003. In contrast, there were only 13 gang-related homicides in 1993 (CCJS, 2004, 24(8)).
- Just over 70 percent of those charged with homicide in 2003 had consumed, at the time of the offence, alcohol and/or drugs, while 61 percent of all homicide victims had consumed alcohol and/or drugs.

- Contrary to some media images, police work in Canada is still relatively safe. In 2002, only one police officer was killed in the line of duty. Since 1961, the average number of officers killed in the line of duty per year has been three (CCJS, 1998, 18(12); 2004, 24(8)).

In recent years, domestic violence has received considerable press, but victimization surveys still show that people are more fearful of being victimized by strangers. Yet, between 1993 and 2003, 47.3 percent of homicide victims were killed by acquaintances and 37.2 percent were killed by a spouse or other family member; strangers made up only around 15 percent of perpetrators (CCJS, 2004, 24(8)). The data also show that in 2003, nearly two-thirds of the victims (63 percent) were killed in a private residence. Areas outside of the victims' residence where homicides occurred included open public areas (26 percent of homicide incidents), commercial areas (6 percent), private vehicles (2 percent), and institutions (3 percent). Overall, the patterns reflect the social characteristics of the incident.

Homicide by Method

"The attitude here is that guns are, for the most part, just useful implements... (while) in the United States, they are an end in themselves." Donald Webster, curator of Canadiana at the Royal Ontario Museum in Toronto, cited in Simonds 1996:45

If you relied on the media to deduce which method of killing was the most common, you would likely conclude it was shooting. (Consider, for example, Michael Moore's 2002 movie *Bowling for Columbine*, which offers a strong message on guns in the United States.) This is true, though official data reveal that stabbing and beating victims to death is also fairly common (see Table 8–5).

Data such as these are of interest to criminologists because they help answer such questions as whether gun control legislation is an effective deterrent, how many deaths involve firearms as opposed to rifles, how many homicides involve stolen versus owned weapons, etc.

In recent years, there has been considerable concern and debate about the availability of firearms and their relationship to homicide. Bill C-17, passed in 1992, allows ownership of semi-automatic weapons (similar to those used by Marc Lepine in 1989) but places a strong emphasis on their control.[4] Similarly, the controversial Bill C-68, passed on January 1, 1996, required firearm owners to both register and license, under the *Firearms Act,* all their firearms and to reregister every five years. Although the Supreme Court has made it clear that Canadians have no legal right to own a firearm without registering it, during the 2004 federal election Conservative leader Stephen Harper talked about the right to own and use guns responsibly and spoke of scrapping the registry (Myths and facts..., 2004). Yet the Coalition for Gun Control in Canada reports that the number of homicides resulting from the use of a firearm is considerably lower than it was before the legislation was introduced in 2003. Some 85 percent of all firearm owners (over 5.9 million) are now registered, and most owners (approximately 77 percent) support the legislation, even though it costs them money.

Section III: Contemporary Issues in Canadian Criminology

TABLE 8-5

HOMICIDE BY METHOD, 1993–2003

	1993	1994	1995	1996	1997	1998	1999	2000	2001	2002	2003
All methods	627	596	588	635	586	558	538	546	553	582	548
Shooting	195	196	176	212	193	151	165	184	171	149	161
Stabbing	191	154	183	195	168	186	143	149	171	182	142
Beating	116	106	121	132	115	125	125	128	122	124	120
Strangulation	77	84	70	59	53	61	55	39	47	64	63
Fire	17	17	20	8	30	12	11	4	8	8	12
Poisoning	6	11	6	6	8	6	5	4	8	3	6
Injuries caused by a vehicle	–	–	–	–	6	3	13	14	5	6	6
Shaken Baby Syndrome	–	–	–	–	6	6	7	13	8	8	8
Others	21	22	6	12	2	2	6	4	5	9	7
Not known	4	6	6	11	5	6	8	7	8	29	23

Sources: CCJS, 1998, 18(12); 1996, 16(11); 2004, 24(8).

HOMICIDE AND CAPITAL PUNISHMENT

Capital punishment was officially abolished in Canada in 1976. In 1999, Conservative MP John Reynolds introduced a private member's bill to reinstitute the use of capital punishment for certain capital offences. Around the same time, a national survey revealed that 65–75 percent of Canadians supported the provisional use of capital punishment (Honeyman & Ogloff, 1996). The last Canadian hanging (see Box 8.7)—a double one—took place at Toronto's Don Jail on December 11, 1962. Ronald Trupin was hanged for shooting and killing a Toronto police officer and Arthur Lucas of Detroit was hanged for killing an undercover narcotics agent.

In the 1990s, there were a number of cases involving Canadians who were charged with murder in the United States and placed on death row. One of these involved Charles Ng, who escaped from prison prior to his trial and fled to Calgary. Shortly after arriving, he was arrested for shooting a security guard while shoplifting in a Hudson's Bay store. It took six years before he was extradited back to California to stand trial for the killing of 12 people. In November 2004, *San Francisco Chronicle* reported that Ng's trial was still ongoing.

The last Canadian executed in the United States was Joseph Faulder of Jasper, AB. He was executed on June 19, 1999 in Texas for the killing of a Texas woman. However, as of December 2004, a number of Canadians were on death row in the United States—for example, Thomas McCray, Tony Dameron, and Ronald Smith.

Has all this legislation helped reduce homicide rates? Has it helped reduce homicides involving the use of firearms? Since 1979, firearms have been involved in about one-third of all homicides, and handguns were involved in about 40 percent of these homicides. In 2002, the percentage of homicides involving firearms dropped to 26 percent—the lowest since 1961! In 2003, it climbed to 29.4 percent (CCJS, 2004, 24(8)), and the use of firearms was the most common method of committing homicide. In the same year, stabbing, occurring in 25 percent of incidents (down from 31.3 in 2002), was the second most common method used for committing homicide (CCJS, 2004, 24(8)). While the number of firearm homicides is down from prior to 1999, Statistics Canada notes that this does not imply a causal relationship. Based on the data, it is difficult to conclusively assert that the various legislative measures have produced the impact they were designed to have (see also Box 8.6). What do you think?

FYI BOX 8.7

CAPITAL PUNISHMENT IN CANADA

"In 1833, Ontario reduced its catalogue of capital crimes from over 100 to 12— murder, treason, rape, child molestation, homosexuality, bestiality, robbery, robbery of the mail, burglary, arson, and accessory to murder" (Boyd, 1988:22). The common method of capital punishment was hanging. After 1867, hangings were conducted out of sight. Do you agree with the use of capital punishment? Why or why not?

Kids Who Kill

Young offenders (ages 12–17) have been receiving considerable attention in recent years from the public and politicians. In 2003, 57 youths were charged with homicide (up from 42 in 2002), constituting 8 percent of all of those charged with homicide in that year, a figure close to the previous decade's average of 9 percent. Although the 2003 figure represents the second consecutive increase and is the highest in over 10 years, it is only slightly higher than the 10-year average of 49 youths charged with homicide per year (CCJS, 2004, 24(8)).

Fifty-four percent of the victims in homicides committed by youths were between the ages of 12 and 24 years, as compared with 20 percent of victims of homicides committed by adults (CCJS, 2004, 24(8)). And, as might be expected, the victims of young offenders tended to be family members (about 45 percent) and friends or acquaintances (31 percent).

While researchers are able to provide detailed descriptive information on kids who kill, they have been less successful at explaining why they do it. The factors on which their explanations are based run the gamut from interpersonal conflicts (e.g., gang-related killings) to risky lifestyles (e.g., drug and alcohol abuse) to greed.

Ecology and Homicide

One fact frequently overlooked by the public is that homicides, like all crimes, are characterized by certain environmental, ecological, and social factors. For example, homicide rates have tended to be higher in Western provinces than in Eastern ones, though in 2002 Eastern provinces led the way. Ontario had the highest number of homicides (178 cases), followed by British Columbia (126 cases, including the 15 homicides in Port Coquitlam related to the Robert Pickton case) and then Quebec (118 cases). Newfoundland (2 cases) and PEI (1 case) had the least number of murders. Part of the shift from the West to the East could be due to the fact that more people now live in Ontario and Quebec than do in British Columbia or any of the other Western province. Various other key social, cultural, and economic factors are also likely contributors (see Box 8.8).

A CLOSER LOOK BOX 8.8

WHY IS CANADA LESS VIOLENT THAN THE UNITED STATES?

Being the United States' next-door neighbours, we are often drawn to making comparisons between Canada and the US. The two countries have many things in common—the predominance of the English language, the ability to trace the inhabitants' heritage to European and Aboriginal peoples, the consumer-oriented cultural outlook, and the general outlines of the criminal justice system, among other things. Yet they differ on a number of economic, social, and political counts (see Box 1.1). As well, the crime rates in the two countries are dramatically different. As indicated below, violent crime rates in the United States over the past decade were significantly higher than Canada's, despite a notable overall decline in violent crime.

In 1984, the Canadian environmental criminologists Paul and Patricia Brantingham observed that homicide rates vary not only with geographic region but also between nations, in regions within a country, in communities, and even within urban neighbourhoods. For example, homicide rates vary between cities, in a way that is not necessarily related to population. Looking briefly at 2003 numbers, Winnipeg, with a population of 688 746, reported a homicide rate of 2.61 per 100 000, while Montreal, with a population of 3.5 million, reported a rate of 1.59. Smaller cities (of 100 000–499 000 people) generally tend to have lower homicide rates; for example, Sherbrooke, with a population of 146 501, had a rate of 0.00—no murders. However, cities such as Regina have historically had comparatively high homicide rates; in

2003, the rate was 5.06, while the population was 97 734. A significant number of the murders in Regina involve Aboriginal people. However, caution needs to be used when looking at the rates among smaller cities because a "small increase in the number of homicides will have a large impact on the rates" (CCJS, 2004, 24(8):4).

While a variety of social factors, including economic deprivation and inequality, have been used in an effort to explain the variations, less is known about the distribution of criminal opportunities that may affect the distribution of homicide rates. Furthermore, as Canadian researchers Bursick and Grasmick (1993) point out, little is understood about how and why offenders target certain neighbourhoods over others.

CANADIAN AND AMERICAN VIOLENT CRIME RATES, 1993 VS. 2002

	Violent crimes per 100 000			
CRIME	CANADA		UNITED STATES	
	1993	2002	1993	2002
Homicide	2.1	2.0	9.5	5.6
Aggravated assault	11	9	440	310
Robbery	104	85	256	146

Source: Canada—CCJS, 2003, 23(5); United States—Federal Bureau of Investigation, 2003.

A variety of reasons have been offered to account for these differences.

- Canada has less inequality than does the United States.
- Canada has stricter gun control legislation than does the United States.
- Handgun ownership is considerably lower in Canada than in the United States.
- Canada was settled in a more peaceful fashion than the United States. The Canadian Northwest Mounted Police helped ensure an orderly and peaceful settlement in the West.
- As a nation, Canada evolved peacefully. Our Constitution and independence were obtained without civil war or revolution. As a Canadian columnist observed a few years ago, "the Canadian cowboy's most beloved possessions were his horse and saddle, not his gun" (Simonds, 1996:51).

In summary, contrary to media portrayal and coverage, homicide is still a comparatively infrequent phenomenon in Canada, though homicide rates have increased marginally since 1999. There is also a notable geographic variation, the majority of victims know their killer, and youths are more likely to kill other youths and young adults than adults (CCJS, 2004, 24(8)).

Explanations as to why people kill cover the spectrum from sociological and psychological to biological and sociobiological perspectives. In light of our current limited ability to understand and develop social policies that can reduce homicide rates, however, what is needed is an integrated and interdisciplinary approach that deals with ecological factors, lifestyle factors, motivations, personalities, and social settings. But developing a model based on these principles to profile offenders is a major challenge to criminologists. For example, Holmes and DeBeurger (1989) identified four types of serial murderers, but as Ainsworth (2001) points out, typologies or classifications have less than a 20 percent success rate.

Only when criminologists gain a better understanding of the characteristics of people who kill can they recommend, and subsequently implement, sound policies to apprehend, detect, punish, or treat offenders and to protect citizens. In the meantime, the criminal justice system should not put too much stock in profiling or relying on criminal typologies.

Sexual Assault

As the examples in Box 8.9 show, sexual assault cuts across all social classes and ages in North America. It is an issue that the courts may not be taking seriously, despite the legal measures that have been introduced.

REALITY CHECK BOX 8.9

WHOM CAN YOU TRUST?

- Former hockey coach Graham James was sentenced to three years for sexually assaulting two young hockey players more than 10 years earlier. In 1997, Sheldon Kennedy of the NHL's Detroit Red Wings became the first professional hockey player to publicly disclose that he had been sexual abused by his former junior hockey coach. In 2004, a former Calgary minor hockey coach received six years for sexually assaulting a five-year-old youth.
- In June 2004, former British Columbia provincial court judge David Ramsay was sentenced to seven years for sexually assaulting several young Aboriginal women.
- Based on a study of more than 1000 cases, Edward Renner, a psychology professor at Carleton University in Ottawa, found the courts do not appear to take sexual assault cases seriously when meting out punishment (Sexual assaults not..., 1997).
- In 1999, Regina doctor John Schneeberger received six years for sexually assaulting two female patients and trying to fool DNA experts by inserting a tube of another man's blood into his arm.

In 1983, under Bill C-127, a new section (ss. 271 and 272) was added to the Canadian *Criminal Code*, replacing the offences of rape and indecent assault with the current offences of sexual assault, aggravated sexual assault, and sexual assault with a weapon. This section allows police to arrest a suspect when they have "reasonable and probable grounds" to believe that an assault was committed.

The *Criminal Code* recognizes three levels of sexual assault:

1. Level 1 assault: There is no serious bodily harm or physical injury to the victim. This type of assault is also known as common assault.
2. Level 2 assault: A greater degree of force or threatened force (e.g., with weapon) than in Level 1 assault is used, and a degree of bodily harm, such as broken bones, bruises, or cuts, is involved. A slap across the face does not constitute a Level 2 assault.
3. Level 3 assault: The victim is disfigured, maimed, wounded, or has his or her life endangered. This type of assault is also known as aggravated assault.

Sexual Assault Rates

In 2003, there were 23 376 sexual assaults reported to police, representing 8 percent of all violent crime in Canada. Level 1 offences constituted 97 percent of the reported assaults, while Level 2 and 3 offences accounted for 2 percent; other sexual offences constituted the remaining 11 percent. (Since offenders can be charged with more than one sexual offence, the percentages add up to over 100 percent.) These numbers break down to a rate of 92 per 100 000 people for Level 1 offences, 2 per 100 000 for Level 2 offences, and 1 per 100 000 for Level 3 offences (CCJS, 2004, 24(6)). The rate of sexual assault has remained relatively unchanged since 1998, after steadily increasing throughout the 1980s and into the 1990s.

Before 1983, approximately 30 percent of all Level 1 charges laid were cleared. In 1983, the clearance rate rose to 40 percent. In 1995, it climbed to a high of 74 percent, but in 2002, it was down to 62 percent. By comparison, clearance rates for other violent offences were over 75 percent from 1991 to 2002 (CCJS, 2003, 23(6)). Why the decline in clearance rates? According to police information presented by Statistics Canada, "it seems plausible that the charging policies police have adopted with respect to spousal violence, and the special training given to police to handle these cases, have encouraged greater numbers to come forward, which, in turn, has increased the rate of assault recorded by police" (CCJS, 2004, 24(6):8) (see Box 8.10).

FYI BOX 8.10

SEXUAL ASSAULT IN URBAN SETTINGS

In 2003, Saskatoon had the highest sexual assault rate among all 25 census metropolitan areas (CMAs) in Canada, which averaged 118 per 100 000 people. In comparison, Saskatoon's rate was 155, while the lowest rates were recorded in Ottawa and London—both 41 per 100 000. How might we explain these figures?

Between 1983 and 1993, there was a steady increase in Level 1 sexual assault rates (Johnson, 1996). Then, in a pattern similar to that for other forms of violent crime, the rates for all three types of sexual assault declined (see Table 8–6). For example, between 1993 and 2003, reported sexual offences declined 36 percent (CCJS, 2003, 24(6)). Can this recent decline be attributed to law reform?

Referring to several studies, a Statistics Canada report suggests that while the law has made it easier to report sexual attacks, it has both broadened the sentencing options and increased the severity of punishments, thereby adding to the deterrent effect. However, the research does not support the premise that the law alone can account for a 17 percent increase in Level 3 sexual assaults in 2003—the first in nearly a decade, but still down 54 percent from 1993. The data provide no evidence to indicate that the increase in child victims, prostitutes, or increased reporting of spousal abuse cases are sufficient to account for the increase the Level 3 rate for 2003. Instead, recent studies suggest a number of alternative explanations for the increase in reported sexual assaults. They include the following (Johnson, 1996:146–147):

- The 1970s and 1980s saw significant changes in the social, economic, and political status of women (although many feminists still contend that police statistics significantly underreport the true extent of sexual assaults).

- The media gave increasing attention to the rights of victims—in particular women.

- The women's movement grew.

TABLE 8-6

TOTAL SEXUAL ASSAULT OFFENCES AND RATES, 1992–2003

YEAR	NUMBER	RATE (ASSAULTS PER 100 000)
1992	38 395	135
1993	38 925	136
1994	35 524	122
1995	31 728	108
1996	30 369	102
1997	30 663	102
1998	28 998	96
1999	23 859	78
2000	24 001	78
2001	24 044	78
2002	24 499	78
2003	23 425	74

Sources: CCJS, 2003, 23(6):14; 2004, 24(6):17.

- Sexual assault support centres became more accessible.
- An increasing number of hospitals had specialized teams trained to deal positively with victims of sexual assault.
- Sexual assaults that occurred in the victim's distant past were disclosed more often.
- Women's groups lobbied intensively for the passage of the rape reform legislation.

Starting in 1993, the rates of Level 1 sexual assaults declined, and they have remained constant since 1999, at about 76 per 100 000. The rates for Level 2 and 3 assaults have also remained relatively constant, varying between 1 and 4 per 100 000. However, when one takes into account the fact that almost 4 in 10 women have experienced at least one form of sexual assault in adulthood, it turns out that four million Canadian women have been affected by this crime (CCJS, 2003, 23(6))! In addition, of those women who have been sexually assaulted, almost 60 percent have been assaulted more than once. Of that number, 26 percent were assaulted four or more times (Johnson, 1996a:139). These are alarming figures.

In spite of the 1983 *Criminal Code* amendments and all the public awareness programs and support services, the gap between official counts and Statistics Canada's Violence Against Women (VAW) survey findings reflects the fact that "very few cases of sexual assault are reported to the police" (Johnson, 1996a:143). This is also in spite of the federal government's designation of December 6th as the National Day of Remembrance and Action on Violence Against Women, in memory of the 1989 shooting of 14 women by a lone male shooter at l'École Polytechnique in Montreal.

According to various studies (e.g., Roberts & Geboyts, 1992; Roberts & Grossman, 1994), the official data underestimate the number of sexual assaults. In one recent study, 44 percent of respondents informed Statistics Canada that they considered the assault (in the legal sense) to be "too minor" to report, while 12 percent wanted to keep the incident private and 9 percent were ashamed or embarrassed to report it (CCJS, 1994, 4(7)). The 1999 General Social Survey (GSS) indicates that "victims 15 years of age and older did not report 78% of sexual assaults to the police that year." According to the surveys, sexual assault victims in Canada chose not to report assaults for one or more of the following reasons: (1) they preferred to deal with the problem in another way (61 percent), (2) they felt that it was a personal matter (50 percent), (3) they considered the incident too minor to report (50 percent), (4) they did not want police involvement (47 percent), (5) they did not think the police could do much to help them (33 percent), or (6) they did not think the police would provide them with assistance (18 percent). Others choose not to report for fear of retribution from the offender (19 percent) or fear of publicity (14 percent) (CCJS, 2003, 23(6):17).

Nevertheless, a comparison of the official statistics with the 1999 GSS results reveals that, while victimization rates have not increased, there has been an increase in official reporting. In addition to demonstrating that the two surveys are measuring the same phenomenon in different ways, the differences reveal that changing social attitudes and policies are having a positive impact on the reporting rate.

According to a 1998 federal report on family violence involving 154 reporting agencies, women continue to outnumber men nine to one as victims of assault by a spouse/partner, and girls are at greater risk of sexual assault by a family member while they are between 12 and 15 years of age (Violence against women, 2002). The 1999 GSS found that only 37 percent of women who had been victims of sexual violence reported the incident to police (CCJS, 2003, 23(6)). This figure, however, represents a noticeable increase over the 1993 GSS findings of 10 percent (Violent crime in Canada, 1996).

Clearance rates for sexual offences have been decreasing since 1995. Between 1991 to 1995, they fluctuated between 70 and 74 percent; in 2002, they dropped to 63 percent. Sexual offences are cleared at a lower rate than other violent offences.

Characteristics of Perpetrators and Victims of Sexual Assault

The characteristics of the sexual attacker accord with the generally held notions about such people. In 2002, over 40 percent of sexual offenders were drinking at the time of the incident. Women under the age of 18 were the most common victims of sexual offences (61 percent), and most sexual assaults (64 percent) occurred in a private residence. Most victims were assaulted by someone they knew—an acquaintance (41 percent of cases), a friend (10 percent), or a family member (28 percent). Only 20 percent were assaulted by strangers. Meanwhile, males made up only 15 percent of victims of sexual assault overall. The proportion was higher for younger victims, such as boys under the age of 12, who made up 29 percent of the male victims, compared to 8 percent among adults (CCJS, 2003, 23(6)).

In recent years, there has been increased interest in and awareness of **date rape** (see Box 8.11). Bunge and Levett (1998) found that some 28 percent of female victims were assaulted by a former or estranged partner. Although Statistics Canada has been conducting an annual family violence survey since 1995, there have been no recent national data on assaults by a date or boyfriend, but the 1993 GSS survey reported that 12 percent of women had been assaulted by a date or boyfriend. Various American studies report the incident rate ranging from 14.3 percent to 60 percent (see Flanagan, 2003). Given the nature of relationships these days, this is an area that merits closer examination.

A CLOSER LOOK BOX 8.11

DATE RAPE AND DATE-RAPE DRUGS

- In North America, the issue of date rape gained front-page attention when Katie Koestner went public with her story in 1991. She had been sexually assaulted by a fellow student at a US college.
- In 1996, a story on a new date-rape drug attracted considerable media attention. The drug had originated in Europe during the 1970s and spread illegally to North

America in the early 1990s. Flunitrazepam pills, marketed under the trade name of Rohypnol and known as "roofies," look like aspirin but are tasteless and odourless and cost $2–5 per 2 milligram pill. They decrease blood pressure and have the ability to send the victim into a deeply relaxed state. The effects of the drug usually start within 20–30 minutes of taking the pill and can last up to eight hours. When used for the purpose of committing a sexual offence, a pill is slipped into a person's drink without the person's knowledge. The offender waits until the pill takes effect before following through with their intention. What is particularly alarming is that Rohypnol causes amnesia—the victims don't remember what happened during the time they were on the drug (Date rape drug, 1997). In 1999, police began to respond to the growing concern about date-rape drugs. One house raid in Vancouver resulted in the seizure of 3500 doses of Rohypnol, and similar raids in other major Canadian cities resulted in seizures of Rohypnol and similar drugs (Williams, 1999). In 2003, a nationwide campaign was initiated by James Moore of the Canadian Alliance party to create legislation to address the problem. Subsequently, a number of schools established programs to inform students of the risk of date-rape drugs. In 2004, a product called Spikeys appeared on the market; it is a bottle stopper with a hole just big enough for a straw to prevent tampering. The product was designed by a man whose daughter had her drink spiked.

- Other recent date-rape drugs that are appearing include GHB (gammahydroxybutyrate), also known as "liquid ecstasy" and "easy lay." Unlike Rohypnol, GHB is a homemade drug and has been promoted as a steroid alternative for bodybuilders. Like Rohypnol, GHB has a short lifespan in the bloodstream—between 12 and 36 hours (Date rape: Drug..., 1998). However, unlike Rohypnol, GHB has prosexual properties, as it causes a loss of muscle control and reduces inhibitions. These attributes make it difficult for police to investigate rape incidents if the victims do not come forward quickly and if defendants can claim that the sexual encounter was consensual. Prosecution is further complicated by the fact that GHB is difficult to detect in the urine. Variations of GHB include GBL and 1,4 Butanediol.

- Ketamine hydrochloride, or "Special K," became something of a teen rave drug in the late 1990s. Originally, the drug was intended as an anaesthetic for pediatric patients and was used in veterinary clinics. Among its reported effects are memory impairment and deep sleep, heightened sexual elation, and "the capability of the victim to respond to verbal commands while asleep" (Brenzinger, 1998:29).

- Burundanga is an extract from the Datura arborea tree in Columbia. The extract takes effect immediately, and the victim usually has no recall while under its influence (Brenzinger, 1998:29).

These and probably yet-to-be discovered drugs are being used to commit sexual assaults. Is it possible to try to control the making of such clandestine drugs? What kinds of proactive steps might law enforcement agencies initiate? Should legislators introduce new and stricter penalties for the abuse of such drugs?

The various legal developments and amendments to the laws surrounding sexual offences since 1983 do not seem to have had a significant effect on the way police respond to suspects (see CCJS, 2003, 23(6):11–12 for a detailed summary). For example, according to the VAW survey, the perpetrator was charged in only 34 percent of all reported sexual assault cases—54 percent if the offender was known to the woman and 24 percent if he was a stranger (Johnson, 1996a). (The difference between these two rates is accounted for by the fact that positive identification of a stranger may be more problematic.)

Unfortunately, data on conviction rates and sentencing of perpetrators are limited. However, a 2002 Canadian Centre for Justice Statistics report does provide a breakdown for sentencing practices for 2001–2002 (see Table 8–7).

TABLE 8–7

SENTENCES IN ADULT CRIMINAL COURT FOR CASES INVOLVING SEXUAL OFFENCES, 2001–2002

DISPOSITION	SEXUAL ASSAULT			OTHER SEXUAL OFFENCES
	LEVEL 1	LEVEL 2	LEVEL 3	
Prison	46	74	69	52
Conditional sentence	16	15	5	19
Probation	30	4	10	25
Fine	2	0	3	0
Other	2	2	0	2
Unknown	4	5	13	2

Source: CCJS, 2003, 23(6):22.

Explaining Sexual Assault

Efforts to explain sexual violence have been varied, but among the more common theoretical orientations are those that relate sexual assaults to the offenders' personal pathologies. Using a psychology-based approach, Groth (1979) asserts that sexual perpetrators are driven by pathologies, such as anger, sadism, or desire for power.

Sociological studies, meanwhile, point to such factors as the social learning processes within lower-class subcultures, where violence may be seen as a way of life, and the mass media, which often depict the sexual exploitation of women in ways that reinforce such actions (Ellis, 1989). One of the issues Gwynn Nettler examines in his 1982 book titled *Killing One Another* is whether violence breeds violence. If we watch sporting events or watch kids in the playground during recess, the answer seems obvious—yes, violence does breed violence! Drawing on the social learning model and by careful examination of the literature, Nettler came to the same conclusion.

Feminist theorists consider sexual violence to be the product of deep-rooted patriarchal traditions in which men are encouraged to dominate all aspects of life, including women. In this view, women are seen as little more than property to be used and sexually exploited.

Even biology and sociobiology have offered their interpretation of sexual violence. Drawing on the notion of evolution, sociobiologists assert that men have an innate drive to create offspring. The lower the degree of certainty of so doing (e.g., as a result of impotence, personal unattractiveness, or social conditioning), the greater the man's tendency to turn to inappropriate sexual behaviours such as rape, child molesting, voyeurism, or collecting of pornographic material (see Holmes, 1991). Maccoby and Jacklin (1974) reported that men tend to be more visual than women are and more aggressive, curious, and dominant. Hence, they may be more biologically predisposed to respond inappropriately to women under certain circumstances. For example, when a 29-year-old known pedophile was charged with violating probation, possessing pornographic material, and being within a block of an area where young children were often present, the court demanded he "take any treatments provided, including chemical castration," not possess any pornographic material, not consume alcohol, and not go near children. Claiming that he wanted to control his urges, the pedophile agreed to all the conditions (Slade, 1999).

Unfortunately, these varied explanations make it difficult to identify which line social policy needs to, or can, take to curb the problem. Furthermore, some of the "newer" forms of assault—such as elder abuse, child abuse, and date rape—present additional ethical and moral concerns and challenges. Therefore, criminologists should perhaps look more closely at adopting an integrated and interdisciplinary approach that might provide better prospects of insight into this and other violent crimes.

Robbery

On September 10, 1904, CPR train No. 1 was robbed just after it left Mission, BC. This was Canada's first train robbery, and the ring leader, Billy Miner, was credited with using the phrase "hands up" (Mission Museum, nd).

In his book on robbery in Canada, Desroches (1995:1) describes robbery as "one of the most feared crimes common to large urban centres" because of "its sudden nature and the threat of death or serious injury." Robbery entails a double element of fear: fear of losing one's property and fear of suffering physical harm. Next to murder, robbery easily attracts our attention, perhaps because of its lack of predictability, but robberies are not that common. In 2002, they accounted for only about 10 percent of all violent crimes in Canada (CCJS, 2003, 23(6)).

Clermont (1996) observes that popular literature and the media often romanticize robbery. The fictional story of Robin Hood, a 12th-century romantic hero who took from the rich and gave to the poor, is among the most famous of such accounts. The story has been portrayed in television shows, cartoons, books, and movies, such as Kevin Costner's 1992 version.

Robbery, as defined in s. 343 of the *Criminal Code*, has certain broad characteristics. Section 343 states that "every one commits robbery" who in stealing uses violence or threats of violence against a person or property; steals from any person and, at the time of the offence wounds, beats, strikes, or assaults the victim; and, one who steals from another person while armed with an offensive weapon or imitation thereof. This definition clearly reflects the notion that robbery is an act of violence. Normandeau (1968) points out that in the United States, in contrast, robbery is more commonly associated with property-related crimes or "burglary" rather than violence. There robbery is defined as "the unlawful taking or attempted taking of property that is in the immediate possession of another by force or threat of force or violence and/or by putting the victim in fear" (Normandeau, 1968:64). Desroches (1995:9) further notes that in some states "penal codes define robbery as a property offence while other states define it as an offence against the person."

The various types of robbery include highway robbery, street robbery (e.g., using force to steal a woman's purse or mugging), armed robbery (e.g., bank robbery), drug-related robbery, and (more recently) home invasions (see Box 8.12). Research shows that the various types of robbery differ not only in terms of practicalities, such as the exact method used, but also in terms of offender traits, motivation for the crime, and modus operandi (i.e., method of operation).

FYI BOX 8.12

TWO-SIDED VERSIONS OF HOME INVASIONS

Unfortunately, home invasions are happening with increasing frequency these days. In June 2002, Anne McLellan, then minister of justice and attorney general of Canada, responded by introducing amendments to the *Criminal Code* that toughened sentencing provisions for home invasions and enhanced the efficiency and effectiveness of the criminal justice system. Although these changes were well intended, the legislation does not include provisions for police officers who break into the wrong house looking for drug suspects or high-risk offenders.

In this section, in addition to examining recent trends with regard to robbery in Canada, we will look at some of the different types of robbery and of robbers. We will see that certain types of robberies are more prevalent than others and that not all robbers are "cut from the same cloth."

Characteristics of Robbery and Robbers

In 2003, there were 28 332 robberies in Canada, which meant a rate of 90 per 100 000 people. Nearly half of the robbery incidents in 2003 were committed without a weapon; in robberies involving a weapon, handguns were used in 80 percent of cases. Although this number represents an 14.2 percent decline from 1993, there was a 5.4

TABLE 8–8

ROBBERY RATES ACCORDING TO WEAPON USE, 1978–2003

	ROBBERIES PER 100 000	
YEAR	INVOLVING A FIREARM	NOT INVOLVING A WEAPON
1978	30	38
1980	35	46
1982	36	48
1984	27	41
1986	26	40
1988	23	42
1990	27	46
1991	32	53
1992	31	48
1993	28	42
1994	25	42
1995	23	45
1996	22	48
1997	18	47
1998	18	44
1999	17	43
2000	14	42
2001	12	43
2002	11	42
2003	12	44

Sources: Adapted from Clermont, 1996:90; for years 1978–1993, see CCJS, 1995, 15(12); for other years, see CCJS, 1998, 18(11) and 2004, 24(6).

percent increase in robberies in 2003. But, as reflected in Table 8–8, robbery rates involving firearms have fluctuated over the years. The lowest rate recorded was 11 per 100 000, in 2002, and the highest rate was 36 per 100 000, in 1982—a notable fluctuation over the years. In 2002, the most popular targets for robbers were commercial establishments—such as banks (accounting for 9 percent), gas stations (6 percent), and convenience stores (11 percent) (CCJS, 2003, 23(5)). What might account for the fluctuations in robbery rates?

"Causes" of Robbery

Clermont (1996) suggests that a high unemployment rate among males in the age 15–24 age group might explain the robbery trends. Tracking the robbery rates and the unemployment rates between 1978 and 1993, Clermont shows that in the early 1980s, when unemployment increased for young males, so did the robbery rates. Similarly, as the unemployment rates dropped in the late 1990s, so did the robbery rates.

What Clermont does not take into account are the different types of robberies; as well, he does not demonstrate whether males between the ages of 15 and 24 are actually accountable for the changes. For example, is there a decline in opportunistic robberies—those robberies committed on impulse—or a decline in "professional" robberies versus those committed by "addict" robbers? In an earlier study, Dunn (1976) provides data to support the notion that variations in robberies correspond to one or more area attributes. Robberies are more likely to occur in areas with certain "geosocial attributes." Dunn's explanatory approach is somewhat interdisciplinary, as it acknowledges both environmental factors and social attributes within an area (see Box 8.13). For example, in 2003, Winnipeg had the highest rate of robberies, at 235 per 100 000, while Saugueny's rate was only 18 per 100 000 (CCJS, 2004, 24(6)).

BY THE NUMBERS BOX 8.13

BANK ROBBERIES IN CANADA

- In 1982, the *Canadian Banker* published the results of a bank robbery study comparing five major Canadian cities: Montreal, Toronto, Calgary, Edmonton, and Vancouver. Between 1967 and 1972, Montreal and Toronto bank robbery rates were fairly similar, but then suddenly Montreal's bank robbery rate jumped. The city became the bank robbery capital of the country. In 1980, Montreal's bank robbery rate was 83.9 per 1000 branches, compared with Vancouver's rate of 37.4 and Toronto's rate of 11.4. The authors of the article conclude by refuting possible explanations, such as economic differences and cultural characteristics of Quebecers, and suggest that, instead, the problem in Montreal can best be explained in terms of an *amplification process*. This process includes a variety of factors: low rate of solution, changes within the criminal element of the population, the number of targets, and possibly the targets' architectural aspects.

- In 1999, there were 1326 bank robberies in Canada, and approximately $5.6 million was stolen. Up to that year, there was a steady increase in the number of bank robberies across Canada for nearly two decades. Desroches (1995:35), among others, suggests that this increase "reflects the emergence of the so-called 'beggar-bandit'—the robber who works alone, enters the bank, and passes a note to the teller demanding ('begging for') money." The baby boom could also account for the increase, since young offenders commit most robberies. This line of reasoning is consistent with social control theory. Desroches's observations are supported by Jacobs and Wright (1999), who note that the values and beliefs of robbers reflect their street subculture and prevailing situation—that is, their being in constant need of "fast cash" to support their lifestyle.

Finally, Desroches (1995:208) offers a comprehensive overview of other possible explanations for robbery but ends by concluding, "little is presently known about offender decision-making in their selection of target victims" or about what motivates someone to become a robber. Using the rational choice theory, Desroches reasons that the robbers' rationality is "limited to what seems reasonable at the time, given their financial needs and the limited alternatives and opportunities open to them" (ibid.:106). But why then do some people turn to certain forms of criminal activity while others in the same predicament do not? How does one measure "rationality" and "what seems reasonable," and what constitutes the robbers' "financial needs"?

Robbery offenders are more likely to use weapons than are other types of offenders. However, data show that in 2003 only 12 percent of robberies involved the use of firearms (see Table 8–8), while another 34 percent involved the use of an offensive weapon (such as a club or a knife). Yet between 1993 and 2003 there was a 56.3 percent decline in the rate of robberies involving firearms (CCJS, 2004, 24(6):17).

The perceived seriousness of robbery is reflected in the fact that more than 80 percent of those convicted of robbery are incarcerated. Of those, over 75 percent are placed in federal institutions (Desroches, 1995). However, in their study of federal inmates, Motiuk and Belcourt (1995) found that those convicted of robbery made up only one-third of the federal inmate population. In 2001–2002, their representation in federal institutions dropped to 20 percent in terms of sentenced admissions, whereas 54 percent of cases of sentenced offenders involved violent crimes (CCJS, 2003, 23(11)).

One Canadian report indicated that "the age of onset of criminality for armed robbery offenders was, on average, 12, while occasional armed robbery offenders didn't tend to begin their criminal career until 15" (A profile of robbery..., 1995:3). The study further pointed out that association with robbers and/or thieves, "both during adolescence and adulthood," seemed to be more strongly correlated to the likelihood of a person becoming involved in armed robbery than corresponding association for other types of offenders. These findings seem to agree with the assumptions of the differential association theory. However, this interpretation may be too simplistic, as the report fails to operationalize or clearly define what is meant by "association." Furthermore, the study neglects to clarify how "association" was empirically measured.

The same report indicated that regular alcohol and/or drug use was common to about half of the robbery offenders (A profile of robbery..., 1995). Perhaps not surprisingly, these offenders were likely to have become involved in stealing when they were young in order to support their recreational habits. Between 1993 and 2003, the rate of youths charged with robbery increased 4 percent, compared to a 25 percent decrease in the rate among adults. But between 2002 and 2003, the rate among youths dropped 2.6 percent (CCJS, 2004, 24(6)).

In summary, robbery tends to capture the public's interest because of the double-edged fears of injury and loss of property. There is much that can be said about the nature, extent, characteristics, and various motivational components of robbery, based mostly on correlations between robbery and various aspects of different social, individual, and cultural variables.

However, we have also seen that no criminological theory can clearly link a causal explanation to any specific set of variables. For example, why is it that female robbers' chief motivation is financial gain? Why do female robbers tend to act in response to external circumstances such as intoxication, financial need, or peer pressure (see Fortune, Vega, & Silverman, 1980)? None of the criminological theories appears able to provide a clear answer. When it comes to social policy and robbery prevention, criminologists can offer little—and what they do offer should be used with considerable care (see Box 8.14).

REALITY CHECK BOX 8.14

THE VANCOUVER ROBBERY PREVENTION PROGRAM FOR CONVENIENCE STORES

While the monetary loss involved in convenience store robberies is not as significant as that in other types of theft, such as shoplifting, employee theft, fraudulent cheques, or break and enter, robberies of convenience stores are nevertheless an important and unique form of crime (Kingsbury, 1973). In the early 1970s, convenience store robbery was becoming a serious concern. The convenience store chain 7-Eleven became one of the first companies to conduct studies to learn why convenience stores are prevalent targets and what can be done to diminish their risk of being targeted. Based on the findings, employees were taught how to deter robberies, reduce the amount of cash in their register, and remove signage from store windows. These measures were based on a modified environmental crime prevention model.

The chain observed a 30 percent decrease in robberies in their study area of southern California. The Robbery Information Program (RIP) for convenience stores quickly spread, and Vancouver became one of the first cities in Canada to introduce it. The RIP was designed to proactively deter store robberies and to make it easier for employees to identify robbers.

The pilot study done in Vancouver showed that the program had a positive impact on those stores that participated. These stores averaged lower financial losses per incident. As well, there was a marked decline in the number of injuries to staff, and staff were generally better informed about the procedures that should be followed in case of a robbery. One of the limitations of the RIP was obtaining store compliance: the compliance rate was less than 20 percent (Roesch & Winterdyk, 1985).

The concept of robbery prevention has expanded and has led to the use of home security systems and closed-circuit TV surveillance camera systems. Although there are no comparable data in Canada, the robbery rate at 7-Eleven stores in the United States has declined some 70 percent since the first program was introduced in 1976! Yet, as successful as such measures might be, a study in England found that muggers in London have simply taken to moving just out of view of the cameras to commit their crimes. In 1997, muggings went up 20 percent in England. The police have taken to soliciting more community support (Hyder, 1998).

"New" Forms of Violence

So far, we have examined the more traditional forms of violent behaviour. In recent years, however, there has been an increase in other forms of violence. In this section, we will focus on a few of these emerging crimes: abduction, hate crime (see Box 8.2), stalking, and terrorism. As in the previous sections, we will examine the trends and patterns of these forms of violence and explore some attempts at explaining them.

Abduction

As can be seen from the recent examples in Box 8.15, **abduction** can be committed for different reasons and usually carries the risk of harm for those being abducted. When abduction takes the form of hostage taking and involves risk of harm or violence, the act may then be defined as an act of terrorism (see the discussion later on in this chapter). Since 1988, when the RCMP established the National Missing Children Services (NMCS), the organization has been involved in over 7000 cases of abducted and/or runaway children. The NMCS provides investigative services to all law enforcement agencies in the search, recovery, and return of missing children. Given the growing concern with the problem of abduction and the often international context of such crimes, NMCS now also networks with law enforcement agencies in the United States and other countries, especially those belonging to the Hague Convention on the Civil Aspects of International Child Abduction (Dalley, 2003).

In the index of the *Criminal Code*, the entry "Abduction" refers the researcher to "Kidnapping and Hostage Taking." These crimes are defined in ss. 280–283, 279, and 179.1 respectively. We will address only abductions here, as the official statistics do not provide a breakdown for kidnappings or hostage takings. Legally, an abduction involves the unauthorized taking of a person under the age of 16 and holding him or her more than 20 feet from his or her residence for more than one hour (Dalley, 2003). Abduction can be perpetrated either by a stranger or by an estranged or former guardian. Motivations vary by type of abduction. Abductions by strangers usually involve sexual exploitation, while the more common form of abduction revolves around conflict over custody arrangements. A child is removed because the abductor is unable to gain the type of access he or she prefers, is perhaps worried about how the legal guardian is caring for the child, etc.

RECENT ABDUCTIONS

- In 2002, a two-year-old toddler went missing and was murdered in Ontario. The father was later charged with the crime (National Missing Children Services, 2004).
- In 2002, a 14-year-old female was found murdered in Quebec. Investigations revealed multiple stab wounds and sufficient evidence to suggest that the offender may have known the victim (National Missing Children Services, 2004).
- On May 12, 2003, Holly Jones was abducted from near her home by Michael Briere. Jones was sexually assaulted, murdered, and then further degraded. It took police almost three months to catch Briere. At his trial, Briere confessed to his crime and apologized for his actions (Walsh, 2004).
- In 2003, Robert Pickton was charged with the abduction and killing of 28 prostitutes. The case received international attention after the bodies were uncovered on Pickton's pig farm in Port Coquitlam (just east of Vancouver). It is believed that the abductions began as early as 1986, during Expo '86.
- The National Missing Children Services, under the auspices of the RCMP, recorded 66 532 cases of missing children in 2002. The number includes kidnappings, parental abductions, runaways, unknown disappearances, accident-related disappearances, and cases of children wandering off. There were 429 parental abductions in 2002, compared to 387 in 2001 and 407 in 1993.

Between 1993 and 2002, the number of cases of missing children has fluctuated from a low of 55 749 in 1995 to a high of 66 994 in 2001 (National Missing Children Services, 2004). The number of abductions has fluctuated from a low of 354 in 1995 to a high of 429 in 2001. The majority of abduction cases involve contravening custody orders. In these cases, children are often helpless pawns caught in the bitter struggle between divorced or separated parents.

As Kiedrowski and Jayewardene (1994) report, research has not yet produced helpful psychological or sociological profiles of abducting types. However, legal abductors are usually employed fathers and unemployed mothers who don't have legal access to their child. The majority of children being abducted are between the ages of 3 and 7. There is no gender bias in who gets abducted, and children are usually taken during weekends or summer or winter holidays. Seldom is physical force used. Lord, Bourdreaux, and Lanning (2001) have recently called for increased use of computer-aided case management systems and geographic profiling services to assist in tracking missing youth.

A recent concern related to abductions is the use of the internet to lure children. While the internet is a wonderful educational and communication tool for many Canadian youth, American data suggest that as many as one in five children receive some form of solicitation over the internet (National Missing Children Services, 2004).

Abduction is a social problem that requires the attention of criminologists, social workers, psychologists, and sociologists if this type of violent crime and the motivations behind it are to be better understood.

Hate Crime

In the 2001 census, Canadians collectively identified themselves with more than 200 ethnic origins, with 58 percent of these being Asian and Middle Eastern. Only 13.4 percent described themselves as visible minorities. Since 1991, however, the visible minorities population has grown nearly six times faster than the total population (CCJS, 2004, 24(4)).

While **hate crime** is generally classified as a crime of violence, it can be a property-related offence. The current definition of hate crime in the *Criminal Code* (ss. 318 and 319) pertains to such acts as advocating genocide, public incitement of hatred, and/or the willful promoting of hatred against any other group within society (CCJS, 2004, 24(4)). In 1996, in response to the growing concern about hate crime, section 718.2 of the *Criminal Code* was amended to allow courts to "take into consideration whether the offence was "motivated by bias, prejudice, or hate based on race" (CCJS, 2004, 24(4). The amendment now allows to courts to regard hate motivation as an aggravating circumstance.

In the 1999 GSS, potential victims were asked whether they had been a victim of a range of violent and property-related crime within the context of what could be described as hate-motivated crime because of their gender, ethnicity, race, religion, sexual orientation, age, disability, culture, or language (CCJS, 2004, 24(4)). A 2002 report found that more than 273 000 Canadians believe they have been victims of hate crime.

Jacobs and Henry (1996) suggest that hate crime in North America started from the moment European settlers arrived and made Aboriginal people a target. Since then, recent immigrants, along with other minority groups, have also been targeted. According to Jack McDevitt and Jack Levin (1993), hate crimes usually involve some planning.

Hate crimes can be divided into three types based on the motives for the crime, as follows:

- *Thrill-seeking hate crimes*: Occasionally, a group of hate-mongers decides to "raise a little hell" by terrorizing ethnic or other minorities and/or violating their property. Gerstenfeld (2004) notes that this is the most common type of hate-motivated crime and accounts for about two-thirds of all reported incidents of hate crime. The perpetrators derive a sadistic sense of satisfaction from threatening and/or terrorizing these groups. In June 1997, the family dog of a Filipino sailor seeking refugee status in Canada was killed and the family threatened. Why? On arriving in Halifax, the sailor's fellow Filipino crew members had reported to authorities that they had witnessed six Taiwanese officers throwing three stowaways overboard in May 1996 (Purdy, 1997). The attack on the family dog was an attempt to scare the family out of the community because they were a visible minority and silence the sailors so that they would not testify in court against the officers. In addition to acting out their ethnic hatred and trying to impress their friends, the offenders found it exciting to instill fear into the family.

- *Reactive hate crimes*: When an "outsider" is seen as a threat, he or she may become the victim of a reactive hate crime because of the perpetrator's sense of righteousness and community. For example, in June, 1997 a man from Missoulian, Montana, stabbed his roommate three times with an ice pick after failing to convince him to become a heterosexual. The two men had been drinking, and the offender had been trying for some time to "convert" his roommate (Moore, 1997).

- *Mission hate crimes*: White supremacy groups, such as the Ku Klux Klan, Identity Church, Aryan Nations, and various skinhead groups, think it is their duty to rid the world of "evil"—from their point of view, people of other races. They see it as their mission, and their right, to seek out and eliminate people who they believe threaten their religious beliefs, racial purity, and power. Skinheads, for example, have been associated with such acts as "gay bashing," "Jew bashing," and attacking certain East Indian groups. In 1989, Marc Lepine, whose Muslim father taught him to hate women, killed 14 women in Montreal. As many other mission hate offenders, Lepine was a deeply troubled individual and committed suicide.

In 1999, the Canadian Centre for Justice Statistics received financial support to conduct the first comprehensive national study on hate crime with the intention of enhancing our understanding of hate crime and investigating the feasibility of collecting reliable police information on the crime. Preliminary findings for 2001–2002 from 12 major Canadian police forces indicated a total of 928 hate crime incidents. Jewish people were the most frequently targeted (in 25 percent of all reported incidents), followed by black people (15 percent) and Muslims (11 percent) (Pilot survey..., 2004). In Canada, hate crimes tend to be more concentrated in large metropolitan areas (CCJS, 2004, 24(4)). As for the United States, data from the FBI indicate that there were in excess of 7400 hate crime incidents in 2002 (Hate crime statistics, 2003). The incident rate in the United States has remained relatively stable since new legislation was introduced in 1990 that included tracking the incident rate. However, because of fears of reprisal, hate crime is probably vastly underreported. It is also possible that the trends have changed in the aftermath of the events of September 11, 2001.

Although the concept of hate crime in Canada arrived with European colonization, hate crimes have probably always been a part of societies where there is social, cultural, and/or ethnic diversity. In terms of the current legal definition used in Canada, hate crime incidents can be traced back to French settlers' dealings with Aboriginal peoples after Samuel de Champlain established the first permanent settlement at Quebec in 1608 (Carrigan, 1991).

Can the roots of hate crime be found in social, individual, political, or biological traits? The research provides no clear answers. As a result, policy-makers face major dilemmas when attempting to address the problem. For example, amendments to the *Criminal Code* are not likely to affect individuals who are driven by some warped sense of reality. Educational programs may sensitize some of us to certain issues, but the history of prejudice and hostility is a long one.

Whatever its cause, hate-motivated violence offers a sad commentary on humanity. Hate crime deserves our concerted attention so that constructive social policy measures can be introduced to combat the problem.

Stalking

As Canadians, we value our freedom and independence. In fact, we have not only entrenched these rights into the Canadian Charter of Rights and Freedoms but in recent years have also passed specific legislation that more clearly defines these rights. Today, **criminal harassment** under s. 246 of the *Criminal Code* refers to being followed, being repeatedly contacted, being watched at home and/or at the office, etc., to the point that it gives the victim good reason to fear for their personal safety, as the pursuant has no legitimate purpose for engaging in such behaviour. The common non-legal term for this type of offence is **stalking**. Although the practice of stalking has been around a long time, only recently has stalking been classified as an offence and studied by criminologists. Prior to 1993, stalking was not against the law.

It is difficult today not to hear stories about all kinds of harassment. In 1997, a highly respected Simon Fraser University swim coach was charged with sexual harassment by a female former swim team member. The story, while not an isolated incident, received considerable media coverage. Then it was found that the female swimmer had been stalking the coach for some time before filing the complaint! The issues raise interesting questions about the difficulty in differentiating between harassment and flirting. In the 1980s, the Canadian singer Anne Murray had to get a special court order to stop an ardent Saskatchewan fan, Robert Kieling, from constantly harassing her. In 1998, Erwin Sillipp from Edmonton became the first person to be prosecuted under the new stalking law. He was convicted, essentially on hearsay evidence, of stalking his ex-wife; a CBC movie was later based on his case. In 2002, a Department of Justice survey showed that 9080 incidents of criminal harassment were reported to 123 police departments—constituting around 4 percent of the violent crimes recorded among the departments (Criminal harassment, 2004).

The increase in stalking may be a response to laws against domestic violence. Restraining orders provide minimal protection for the victim and, according to the Department of Justice, may in some cases incite stalking. However, it is hoped that the recent legislation provides police with the power to prevent more serious crimes. A 2001 amendment increased the maximum penalty for criminal harassment from 5 to 10 years.

While all stalkers share a common behaviour, their motivations differ. The RCMP and Ontario provincial police use a theoretical threat model that classifies stalkers into one of three types: simple obsessional, love obsessional, and erotomanic (Criminal harassment, 2004). There are several different typologies of stalkers in the literature. Holmes and Homes (1993), for example, list six different types of stalkers: *domestic* (e.g., estranged husband following his ex-wife), *hit* (e.g., hired killers), *lust/celebrity* (e.g., stalkers of David Letterman, Leonardo di Caprio, or Madonna, who believe that the victim loves them as much as they love the victim), *scorned* (e.g., the rejected lover), and *political* (e.g., Kenneth Starr's obsession with the Clinton and Lewinsky case).

It has been estimated that in 2002 there were 16.8 million internet users in Canada (McCall, 2004). This mode of communication has spawned the most recent variation of stalking—cyberstalking. This type of stalking usually involves the use of email, cell phones, and/or other electronic means of communication to harass, threaten, and possibly even intimidate the victim (McCall, 2004). For example, one British business company found that 41 percent of their female users had been sent unsolicited pornographic material or had been harassed or stalked (Driscoll, 1999).

Aside from some preliminary studies, there is no concrete data on stalking in Canada, but due to certain social changes, such as increased sensitivity to people's rights and high divorce rates, stalking has become a social concern. A 2002 survey of 123 police forces and court data relating to criminal harassment across the country revealed that female victims tended to be younger than male victims; 8 out of 10 accused were male; nearly one-third of the female victims were harassed by a former intimate partner, while 4 in 10 males were criminally harassed by a casual acquaintance; and two-thirds of all harassment incidents occurred at the victim's home. From 1995 to 2001, the police forces reported a 40 percent increase in criminal harassment incidents (Criminal harassment, 2004). An earlier American survey offered similar results (see Stalking and domestic violence..., 1999).

In late 1997, the federal justice minister doubled the maximum sentence for stalking, from 5 to 10 years, in response to various pleas. The concern was perhaps also prompted by the sexual harassment policies implemented at virtually every work setting. Introducing special legislation is a first step in addressing this new form of violence, but more needs to be done to understand this crime before it happens.

Terrorism

Canadian criminologist Gywnn Nettler (1982:227) describes **terrorism** as involving "the calculated instilling of fear through cruelty, killing, or the threat of both as a means to obtain or maintain power." In addition to being an act of violence, terrorism is also classified as a political crime, as terrorists usually reject the goals and objectives of their society and seek to install their own goals and objectives. Stephen Schafer (1976) uses the term "convictional criminal" as a way of characterizing the political convictions underlying their illegal behaviour.

Overall, attempts to define and describe terrorism have been somewhat broad and subject to interpretation. For example, if you were an ardent environmentalist and put spikes into trees in an effort to deter logging in an area, could you be considered a terrorist? Or, if a group commits a robbery in order to support their revolutionary cause (as have members of the Aryan Nations), should the act be treated as a political or terrorist crime, or as an armed robbery? In the aftermath of September 11, 2001, Canada, along with many other countries, introduced legislation to deal with acts of terrorism. In 2001, Bill C-36 enabled the courts to deal more effectively with terrorist threats. The bill created the *Terrorist Financing Act* and amended the *Criminal Code* and other acts. In addition to providing clearer definitions of terrorism and terrorist groups, these changes allowed the government to restrict the financing of terrorist groups and prompted new strategies for identifying and curbing money laundering. Many of these legal changes comply with the various United Nations conventions on terrorism. For example, Operation Apollo, established in 2001 by the Canadian government, involved committing some 2000 troops (air, sea, and land) to combating terrorism on foreign soil. Do you think this is right?[5]

Whatever form they take, politically motivated crimes against a sovereign state have had a long history. Some of the more recognizable people to be considered political criminals in their time include Socrates, Joan of Arc, Martin Luther King, Jr., and Canada's own Louis Riel, who led a campaign against the federal government during the late 1800s. Another major terrorist incident in Canada was the FLQ crisis of 1970. For more recent examples, see Box 8.16.

In recent years, terrorism has not only increased—it has also evolved into new and deadly forms. Today, terrorists have access to and occasionally use such deadly means as chemical and biological warfare; many can also use nuclear threats.

REALITY CHECK BOX 8.16

EXAMPLES OF TERRORISM, 1990S–2004

- February 1993: Bombing of the World Trade Center in New York City killed six people and injured more than a thousand.
- April 1993: David Koresh's followers at the Branch Davidian compound in Waco, Texas, are believed to have killed themselves after US federal agents attempted to investigate the community's weapons stockpile.
- March 1995: Shoko Asahara, leader of Japan's Aum Shinrikyo ("Supreme Truth") sect, placed several canisters of deadly sarin nerve gas in the Tokyo subway. The gas killed 10 people and injured over 5000. Both the Waco and the Asahara incidents are examples of a new type of terrorism perpetrated by what are socially characterized as extremist groups.

- April 1995: Bombing at the Federal Building in Oklahoma City killed 168 people. In June 1997, Timothy McVeigh, one of the members of a right-wing militia group, was convicted of the bombing.
- December 1997: For several decades, the Provisional Irish Republican Army had been targeting British buildings as part of their campaign for Irish independence. In December 1997, Billy Wright, the infamous King Rat and a Protestant terrorist, was murdered. His killing triggered retaliation killings and threatened to end the multi-party peace talks between the feuding factions.
- November 1998: Steve West, Alberta energy minister, lashed out against so-called ecoterrorists who have been targeting the oil and forestry industries as well as electrical utilities across the province. Since 1996, there have been approximately 160 acts of vandalism causing $2 million in damage.
- September 11, 2001: The intentional collision of two jet planes into the twin towers of the World Trade Center in New York City and the attack on Pentagon in Washington were led by Muslim extremists.
- October 2002: A Muslim extremist by the name of Iman Samudra masterminded the bombing of a nightclub in Bali that resulted in the death of 202 people from 21 countries. His motive? To avenge the injustice against Muslims worldwide.
- For a current listing of terrorist activities and safety measures taking place in Canada, see **www.safecanada.ca** under "National Safety and Security. " For information pertaining to the rest of the world, see the American-based Terrorism Research Center, which monitors terrorist activities on a daily basis at **www.terrorism.com**.

WHAT DO YOU THINK? BOX 8.17

TRYING TO DEFINE A TERRORIST

In an interview with *Time* magazine in January 1999, Osama bin Laden called upon Muslims to attack Britons and Americans in revenge for the air attacks on Iraq in 1998 (Sapstead, 1999). Is bin Laden a terrorist, a crazed idealist? How do we counter such terrorist agendas?

Saddam Hussein was accused of possessing weapons of mass destruction and being linked to various terrorist groups, but coinciding with his trial, which began in July 2004, CIA evidence revealed that there were no such weapons and no clear links. Were the accusations based on an error in intelligence gathering, or are the arguments raised in Michael Moore's controversial 2004 movie *Fahrenheit 9/11* valid?

Typologies of Terrorism

The difficulty in defining terrorism is reflected in the varied typologies used to describe it. Simple dichotomous models include Jeffery's (1991) classification according to the target of the terrorists' violence: (1) *violence against foreigners* and (2) *violence against one's countrymen*. Paul Smythe (1996) offers a three-tiered model, for describing terrorist groups, as follows: (1) *ethnic separatists* and *emigrant groups* (e.g., Armenians or Sikhs), (2) *left-wing radical groups* (e.g., the Squamish Five in British Columbia), and (3) *right-wing racist groups* (e.g., Heritage Front groups). These groups are usually a combination of Jeffery's groups 1 and 2. They are not averse to using violence, and they actively recruit new members. Finally, Jonathan White (2003) suggests five fairly broad types of terrorism: (1) *revolutionary terrorism*, whose perpetrators use violence to invoke fear in those in power (e.g., Palestinian Liberation Organization, Iranian-backed Hezbollah); (2) *political terrorism*, which is directed at specific individuals or groups who oppose the terrorists' ideology (e.g., Aryan Nations and other supremacy-oriented groups); (3) *nationalistic terrorism*, whose perpetrators are intent on promoting their own minority ethnic or religious factions (e.g., the Provisional Irish Republic Army); (4) *non-political terrorism*, which champions particular religious or social causes (e.g., anti-abortion groups, Greenpeace, Animal Liberation Front); and (5) *state-sponsored terrorism*, which tends to involve repressive political regimes who rely on force and violence to force compliance (e.g., the death squads in Nigeria, Brazil, Guatemala, and Iraq, among others).

Regardless of the typology used, attempts to control terrorism through law (e.g., the *War Measures Act* in 1970 with the FLQ crisis and Bill C-36 in 2001) or the use of force (the Oka uprising in 1990) have usually not resulted in satisfactory resolutions. In addition, as Smythe (1996:19) notes, the face of terrorism is changing; today, there is "faction sponsored terrorism; issue-motivated terrorism; and crime-related terrorism," among others (ibid.:19). Terrorism will likely be a major area of interest to criminologists in the future.

The emergence of the "new" forms of violence provides impetus for criminologists to attempt to better understand the purpose, meaning, characteristics, and theoretical causes underlying such acts. Violence seems to be evolving and spreading throughout society. We must recognize the problems that new forms of violence pose, work toward understanding their causes, and develop social policy and support programs to ameliorate the problems.

Summary

- Although violent crimes vary in their nature and form, they all share the common element of violence. While different violent crimes have fluctuated in their incidence over time, official statistics indicate that the last decade has seen a general decline. However, the rates of violent crimes still far surpass the numbers first recorded in the 1960s.

- Not all types of violent crime have declined. And, aside from traditional forms of violent crime, we are witnessing new forms of violence for which no official statistics are yet kept. Media reports often reflect the fact that violence takes many forms and can be found almost anywhere.

- Criminologists tend to view violent crime in traditional legalistic terms and use conventional disciplinary explanations to explain and describe such crime. However, as discussed throughout this book, criminologists may need to deviate from this approach. They may need to begin viewing and interpreting violent crime as a problem rooted in behaviour.

- Describing the extent and nature of violence in our society is not enough—criminologists must embrace an interdisciplinary approach toward understanding the dynamics of violence and violent behaviour and in this light examine the various forms violence can take.

Discussion Questions

1. What can the violent crime statistics tell us about the crime trends and patterns in Canada? Has the picture changed in recent years? Why?

2. Who is primarily responsible for committing violent crimes? Are there any common denominators? What are some of the major explanatory models for the different types of crimes covered?

3. Are there any common causal factors that can be used to explain violent crimes?

4. Why are the crimes covered in the chapter referred to as conventional crimes? How do they differ from non-conventional crimes?

5. Collect at least a dozen articles related to the "new" forms of violence. What do they tell us about the nature and extent of the problem? What kinds of solutions, if any, are offered? Do these forms of violence pose a more serious threat to society than traditional forms?

Key Concepts

abduction	assault	clearance rate
criminal harassment	date rape	hate crime
stalking	terrorism	violent crime

Weblinks

www.statcan.ca The Statistics Canada website offers tables containing current Canadian justice and crime statistics. By using the search engine on the site, you can access different crime data. Some of this information may involve paying a fee, though most college and university libraries have free access for academic purposes.

www.guncontrol.ca/Content/GunControlLaws.html This page from the Coalition for Gun Control provides an overview of Canada's gun control laws.

canada.justice.gc.ca/en/ps/fm/harassment.html This Department of Justice page offers information on criminal harassment.

www.ncvc.org/src/ The website of the Stalking Resource Centre in the United States offers a wide range of related information about stalking.

www.uncjin.org United Nations Crime and Justice Information Network offers numerous international links.

You can use internet search engines, such as **www.google.com** or **www.altavista.com**, to easily locate violent crime information for virtually any country, as well as specific reports on any type of violent crime.

Endnotes

1. Good statistics on crime in Canada can be found at Statistics Canada's website at **www.StatCan.ca/english/pgdb/state/justic.htm**.

2. Silverman and Kennedy (1993) point out that even though the research they discuss refers to "homicide," the precise definition varies with the jurisdiction and the context in which death occurs. For example, the law does not hold accountable manufacturers who through negligence cause the death of those who work for them or of those who purchase their products (Box, 1983). After the Westray mine disaster in May 1992 at Plymouth, NS, where 26 men died in a methane fire and coal-dust explosion, the deaths were dealt with in civil, not criminal court.

3. In June 2000, Anne McLellan then justice minister, introduced changes to s. 690 of the *Criminal Code* enabling the minister of justice to use his or her discretion to respond to persons who believe they have been wrongfully convicted.

4. Bill C-51, passed in 1978, prohibited the ownership of firearms that did not have a legitimate sporting or recreational purpose (e.g., sawed-off shotguns and fully automatic firearms) and restricted the ownership of handguns. This bill introduced the Firearm Acquisition Certification (FAC).

5. For additional information on Operation Apollo, see **www.forces.gc.ca/site/operations/apollo/index_e.htm**. Additional information on terrorism and counter-terrorism can be found at the website for the International Policy Institute for Counter-Terrorism at **www.ict.org.il** or the counter-terrorism site at **www.emergency.com/cntrterr.htm**.

CHAPTER 9

Property-Related Offences

*"Greater Vancouver is proportionally [given its size and popu-
lation] the metropolitan area in Canada for property crime...
[costing] industries, businesses, government and insurance
organizations more than $128M annually." Vancouver's
property-crime rate is second highest (after Miami)
in all of North America.*

Vancouver Board of Trade, 2003

Learning Outcomes

After you have completed this chapter, you should be able to:

- Recognize the major forms of property crime and be familiar with the general trends in property crime.

- Understand that an "absolute" explanation of property crime causation is currently unavailable.

- Appreciate the importance of using crime data to understand property crime trends and patterns, explain crime, and recommend social policy.

- Appreciate the importance of applying an integrated and interdisciplinary approach when using crime data.

- Appreciate the benefit of using comparative criminology to lend further insight into the study and control of property crimes.

As we saw in the previous chapter, while violent crime captures a lot of public attention, it occurs infrequently when compared to crimes against property. In 2002, **property crimes** accounted for 51 percent of all crimes known to the police (CCJS, 2004, 24(5):4). Although nationally "the rate of property crime has been decreasing over the past decade" (CCJS, 2003, 23(5):8), the rates in the latter half of the 1990s were still

50 percent higher than they were in the late 1970s and early 1980s. In 2002, Canada experienced its lowest property crime rate since 1973, with a slight increase in 2003 (CCJS, 2004, 24(6):17). At the regional level, however, provinces such as PEI, Newfoundland and Labrador, and Alberta have experienced increases (of 8 percent, 6 percent, and 6 percent respectively) (see Box 9.1).

FYI BOX 9.1

THE PRICE OF MATERIALISM

We live in a society that values material goods. News stories about people fighting, and even killing, to illegally obtain certain goods (for example, running shoes, sport jackets, bicycles, or motorized vehicles) are frequent. While the overall property crime rate continued to edge down until 2002, theft was the one area that showed an increase (approximately 5 percent over 2001). As well, between 1993 and 2003, there was an astounding 911.1 percent increase in the counterfeiting of currency (CCJS, 2004, 24(6):17).

Though these two crimes are quite different, they both involve theft and are reflective of our society's preoccupation with wealth and material goods. Possessing or being able to purchase something can be a source of joy, but it can also be the motivation behind a property crime. In addition, while property crimes are legally considered less serious than violent crimes, victims may still have a sense of personal violation and feel significant emotional distress after a property crime occurs.

Crimes against property take various forms, but all have an economic element to them, since they involve either the theft and/or destruction of property. In this chapter, we will focus on five major conventional forms of property crime: break and enter, fraud, theft, arson, and motor-vehicle crime. We will examine offender and victim characteristics, the impact of each type of crime, and policy implications and prevention strategies.

Break and Enter

Is there a difference between **break and enter** (B & E) and burglary? These terms are sometimes used interchangeably. The United States and England still use the common law term "burglary," while in Canada we use the modern term "break and enter" (see Box 9.2). Legally, they are comparable, except that in the United States a burglar might use force if he or she encounters someone in the course of committing the crime. Technically, in Canada, such an act would be classified as a robbery.

REDEFINING BURGLARY

Under old English common law, burglary was an offence only if it was "breaking and entering of a dwelling during the night with the intent to commit a felony." Canada used this classification and description until the law was amended in 1985. The new law no longer specified that burglary had to be in a dwelling (that is, businesses and other non-residential properties were included), and the amendment omitted the specific time frame of "night time" (Carrigan, 1991). Today, the term "burglary" is used in reference to such offences as damage to buildings, safety deposit boxes, safe boxes, etc.

In Canada, both robbery and burglary involve theft, but the critical difference between these offences is the presence or lack of a person-to-person confrontation. Unlike robbery, a burglary—or break and enter—does not involve face-to-face contact or the threat of force, because it is undertaken when the resident or owner of the property entered is not present. For this reason, break and enter is considered a property crime, whereas robbery, which involves contact between victim and offender, is considered a violent crime.

Break and enter, as discussed in ss. 348–353 of the *Criminal Code*, is usually done to steal something from a residence, business, of some other fixed setting. Compared to robbery, it is a more passive, non-violent crime. As depicted in movies, the burglar usually conducts his or her activities in a clandestine manner. However, that does not mean that victims of this crime are any less victimized than those of other crimes. After then prime minister Jean Chrétien and his wife had their official residence broken into in 1995, there was an investigation into providing property security for them. In 1998, the residence underwent a $417 629 "security boost" to ensure such incidents would not happen again (Naumetz, 1999). In 2004, vandals broke into the historic Lougheed mansion in Calgary and caused $150 000 worth of damage. The offenders gained entry through the only unlocked window (Myers, 2004).

Patterns and Characteristics in Break and Enters

In 2003, there were 284 496 break and enter incidents reported to police, the lowest number in 25 years. Between 1993 and 2003, the overall B & E rate decreased 36.5 percent (CCJS, 2004, 24(6)) (see Table 9–1).

TABLE 9—1

BREAK AND ENTERS, 1993–2002

YEAR	B & ES PER 100 000	NUMBER
1993	1416	406 421
1994	1336	387 867
1995	1331	390 784
1996	1338	397 057
1997	1245	373 316
1998	1160	350 774
1999	1042	318 054
2000	953	293 357
2001	898	279 461
2002	879	275 573
2003	899	284 573

Sources: CCJS, 2004, 24(5); 2004, 24(6).

There are three categories of B & Es—residential, business, and those involving other "non-residential private structures, such as detached garages, sheds, and storage and transportation facilities" (CCJS, 2004, 24(5):2). In 2003, the majority of B & Es were residential (58 percent), followed by business B & Es (30 percent) and other B & Es (11 percent) (CCJS, 2004, 24(6):10). Since 1991, residential B & E rates have declined, decreasing 37 percent between 1996 to 2002 (CCJS, 2004, 24(5):3). Between 1993 and 2003, business-related B & E rates declined 32.3 percent, and other types of B & E rates declined 36.5 percent (CCJS, 2004, 24(6)).

B & Es represent approximately 25 percent of all reported property crimes (CCJS, 2004, 24(6):9) and account for about $2.6 billion in stolen household goods each year.

Data from the 1999 General Social Survey (GSS) indicate that urban dwellings were more likely to be targeted than rural dwellings, and that semi-detached homes, row houses, and duplexes were more likely targets than single, detached dwellings. Rented dwellings were a more likely target than owner-occupied dwellings.

The GSS victimization survey also reveals that victims of B & Es were more likely to report their victimization to the police than were victims of other types of crime. Only about one-third of victims of B & Es choose not to report their victimization. People are likely to report B & E incidents in order to file an insurance claim.

The Insurance Bureau of Canada reported that in 2002, homeowner insurance claims from B & E–related thefts totalled $290 million, up from $267 million in 1994. The most frequently stolen items were audio and video equipment (32 percent of incidents) and jewellery (13 percent of incidents). Another $63 million was involved in tenant insurance claims, and $110 million in commercial claims. In 2002, the most common item stolen in residential B & Es was audio and video equipment (22 percent of incidents), while money, cheques, or bonds were the most common items stolen in business B & Es (22 percent of incidents) (CCJS, 2004, 24(5):4). In other types of B & Es—for example, those involving garages and sheds—machinery and tools were the most common targets.

In a unique study, Wright and Decker (1994) interviewed active burglars, rather than those who were incarcerated, and reported that efforts to reduce B & E rates through target hardening (for example, better locks and home security devices) were not very effective. The primary reason was that most homeowners become careless about maintaining their security devices. In addition, even if the home alarm was functioning, most burglars spent less than five minutes in a house—much less time than it takes an alarm company to respond.

Rengert and Wasilchick (1985) found that the more experienced burglars engage in systematic selection of a home. They take time to "case the joint." They look for subtle clues (such as closed windows, no lights, mail in the mailbox, etc.). They also take into account the location of the target, ease of escape, and general familiarity with the area. However, the general consensus in the literature is that most break-and-enter offenders are opportunistic young offenders. However, a Vancouver study reports some contradictory findings. The study found that there is perhaps only a core group of 40–50 property criminals who are responsible for a significant proportion of property crimes in the city and that the majority of the offenders are young males (i.e., ages 18–24) (Vancouver Board of Trade Information, 1997). But both reports note that the primary underlying causes for B & Es are socially based factors.

Burglars do not want to spend a lot of time planning, do not want to make noise, and prefer not to be seen. Therefore, it is not surprising that houses on the edge of an unoccupied area are at greater risk than those in the interior of a residential setting (Brantingham & Brantingham, 1991). In addition, Rhodes and Conly (1981) found that residential burglars usually live within approximately 2 kilometres of their target, compared to 3.4 kilometres for robbers and 1.9 kilometres for rapists.

In 2004, a CBC report noted a new trend that involves thieves from urban settings going out into the country to commit break-ins. This trend speaks to the notion that break-ins are crimes of opportunity and rational choice. As more people move to the country, they create new opportunities for offenders. Wright and Decker (1994) found that the summer months account for about 30 percent of annual B & Es. This is the time when school is out and people take their holidays, leaving their homes less secure. In keeping with the rational choice theory, the majority of B & Es take place between the hours of 6 p.m. and 6 a.m., when people are either out or asleep. In 2002, 63 percent of those charged with B & Es were adults, while people aged 12–17 were responsible for the remaining 37 percent.

HOME INVASION: B & E OR ROBBERY?

Home invasions or intrusions are quickly becoming one of Canada's scariest forms of property crime. This crime involves the victim being robbed and terrorized in his or her own home. The robbery can turn violent, resulting in physical injury. Media reports show that home invasions have included sexual assaults, beatings, gunfire, and even murder. The motives range from wanting material goods, such as money, valuables, or drugs, to crime-related revenge.

While there are some perceptions that people of Asian decent are prime targets, police officials note that no particular culture or ethnicity is singled out. However, certain Asian groups may be hit because many choose not to put their money in banks and are targets of Asian-based organized crime groups.

The first home invasion to be officially reported in Calgary occurred in 1991. It involved a Chinese family who was robbed during the daytime (Mofina, 1991). By 1993, Vancouver was reporting that home invasions were becoming a serious concern in their city (Hall, 1993). In 2004 in Halifax, a decorated World War II veteran and his wife were brutally assaulted by a 20- and a 14-year-old youth. In 2003, in the aftermath of several such high-profile cases, the minister of justice and attorney general of Canada introduced an amendment to the *Criminal Code* that toughened sentencing provisions for home invasions.

Do we need such an offence in the *Criminal Code*? Consider the case several years ago when six police officers in Abbotsford, BC, barged into a house where there was a birthday party going on for the family's daughter. The police shot a dog in front of a group of children. The reason for their actions was a drug search—which produced no drugs (Selick, 1999). Or think of the 1997 case involving two Peel Regional Police officers who were sentenced to 23 months for engaging in a home invasion robbery in November 1995. Both officers were in their mid-20s at the time and both have since resigned (Canada News Wire, 1997).

As regular experienced burglars, home invasion perpetrators usually know their victims and carefully plan their crimes.

Clearance Rates and Explanations

Crime clearance rates often tell us something about the nature of a crime and how effective crime prevention or intervention strategies are. In both Canada and the United Sates, B & E clearance rates are around 15 percent! Fortunately for police, when offenders are ultimately caught, they usually confess to a string of B & Es, as part of a plea bargain arrangement (Wright & Decker, 1994).

One of the major explanations employed for B & E is rational choice theory, in which the offender weighs the potential costs and rewards of the act (Cromwell, Olson,

& Avary, 1991). It could be argued that in some urban centres there is an informal symbiotic support network that serves to perpetuate B & Es. The Vancouver Board report (1997:13), for example, noted that pawnshops often serve as "primary distribution centres for stolen goods."

Along similar lines, Bursik (1995) suggests that burglars rely on environmental cues. Burglars tend to select homes that they are familiar with, that are less visible to their neighbours, that have ease of access and a general appearance of affluence, and that appear unoccupied. The police regularly provide crime prevention tips that focus on many of these issues. For example, if you are going to be away, have someone collect your mail and cut your lawn. Do not leave "gone on vacation" messages on your answering machine. Also, mark your belongings and post the decals in a visible place. These precautions cannot guarantee you will never be a victim of a B & E, but they reduce your risk. However, as Reppetto (1974) observed, these measures are likely to produce a crime displacement effect—that is, a move of the target location, setting, time, etc.—rather than prevent such crimes.

In summary, while B & Es do not involve direct confrontation, they are often traumatic for the victim. They also pose a serious problem for the criminal justice system and insurance companies. They are one of the most prevalent crimes, but their clearance rates are extremely low. In addition, research shows that in most B & Es, there is no prior relationship between the thieves and the victim. While some theories provide sound explanations for burglaries, they have done little to develop programs or strategies to abate them. As Greenberg (1996:165) observes, "fears about public safety among the general public appear to be on the rise. Clearly, restoring public faith in the justice system should be at or near the top of the Canadian agenda." How are the police going to do this? Given their general lack of success in clearing B & Es, many police departments now regard B & Es as a low priority. Is encouraging people to fortify their homes or not trust anyone the answer?

Fraud

There are 16 sections (ss. 380–396) in the *Criminal Code* dealing with various aspects of fraud. **Fraud** is the taking of another's property (i.e., possessions) through deception, falsehood, or cheating.[1] For example, imagine someone sold you a used car, claiming it had never been in an accident. You bought it in good faith, only to find out later that it had been in a serious accident. This transaction would be fraudulent.

In this section, we will deal only with property-related fraud. Many fraud cases could easily fall under the general heading of white-collar crime or organized crime (see Chapter 10), since they are committed by businesses and professionals. Typically, property-related fraud includes cheque fraud, credit-card fraud, and "other" fraud, which may involve breach of trust, false pretenses, forgery, mail fraud, identity theft, telemarketing fraud, fraudulent manipulation of the stock exchange, or counterfeiting (see Boxes 9.4, 9.5, and 9.6).

Patterns and Characteristics of Fraud

According to crime statistics, the rate of fraud has steadily declined since 1991, from a high of 487 per 100 000 people to 294 in 2003 (CCJS, 2004, 24(6)). Fraud accounts for approximately 7 percent of all property crime—a proportion relatively unchanged since 2000.

McPhie (1996) notes that in spite of media reports that the dollar value of losses through fraudulent activities rivals the dollar values normally associated with organized crime, Statistics Canada reports neglect to present a breakdown of the crimes. Total dollar loss through fraudulent activities exceeded $200 million in 2003, down from $227 million in 1999.

As for the methods used in fraudulent acts, McPhie (1996:167) observes that most frauds are still "practiced by individuals or small groups who pass bad cheques, use found, stolen, or altered credit or bank cards, or who misrepresent themselves in some manner during financial transactions." Persons charged with fraud are generally older than those accused of other property crimes.

As with all crimes, there are geographical variations in fraud across the country. Unfortunately, no regular data are collected within Canada. However, several years ago, Statistics Canada data revealed that Saskatchewan reported the highest rate (540 per 100 000), while Newfoundland and Quebec had the lowest rates (291 and 250 respectively) (CCJS, 1998, 18(11)). It is interesting to observe that "other" fraud accounts for the majority of fraud cases in the above three provinces. No studies have been conducted to examine or explain the variations. However, we can assume that the differences are the result of a mix of social, cultural, and personal circumstances.

Credit-card fraud has remained the most popular type of fraudulent activity, with 42 242 cases reported in 2002. A 2004 RCMP report noted that by the end of 2003 there were 50.3 million credit cards in circulation with sales exceeding $154 billion. The most rapidly growing problem area is counterfeiting. In 2002, counterfeit credit-card use accounted for 37 percent of all dollar losses (Counterfeiting..., 2004).

Efforts to counter credit-card fraud, which involves such things as counterfeiting holograms, photographs, fingerprints, and personal histories, have all had only limited success because criminals can easily circumvent these deterrent measures. Companies continue to explore new technological deterrents as the world becomes ever more dependent on "plastic." By the year 2000, for example, gross bank card volume is expected to total $9.9 trillion; given current trends, this would mean $14 billion in fraud! The RCMP report that organized criminals "have acquired the technology that allows them to 'skim' the data contained on magnetic stripes, manufacture phony cards, and overcome such protective features as holograms" (see Box 9.7) (Counterfeiting..., 2004). In addition to increased police resources being directed to countering credit-card fraud, new technological solutions are being used. One of the latest deterrent strategies that may make counterfeiting difficult is the use of smart-card technology (cards with built-in computer chips) (Counterfeiting..., 2004).

PROTECTING YOUR MONEY

Keep your card in a safe place and never lend it to anyone. Don't write your PIN down—memorize it. Avoid using obvious identifiers for your PIN. Always remember to remove your card and transaction record when using an ATM machine. If card is stolen or lost, notify your financial institution immediately (Counterfeiting..., 2004).

Fraud in general is one type of crime in which youth is not well represented. In 2003, the fraud rate among young persons was only 108 per 100 000, as compared to 294 for adults (CCJS, 2004, 24(6)). Given that fraud is a non-violent act and requires no physical force, it may not be too surprising to find women more likely to be involved in fraud, as compared to other types of property crime. Official data show that women are most likely to engage in cheque fraud—or at least get caught at it. Vito and Holmes (1994) report that women who had been arrested have a high rate of recidivism.

Some contemporary examples of fraud include misleading direct-mail marketing and phone fraud that involves charging callers a nominal fee per minute for a service with the promise that they will receive something of worth in return when in fact they might receive something worth considerably less, and placing scam ads in local newspapers. Starting in the 1990s, numerous scams involved postcards being sent to people announcing that a prize was being held for them. At face value, it appeared that the recipient was guaranteed a wonderful prize, such as an exotic trip or an expensive automobile. To claim the prize, the person had to call a 900 telephone number—at a cost of $9.90. Subsequent investigation revealed that the chances of anyone winning any of the main prizes were extremely slim. Typically, the exotic trip might be available, but the winner had to pay his or her own air fare at greatly inflated prices through participating hotels (Remar, 1991). Yet another example of fraud involves live "sex lines" that charge at posted "regular long-distance rates." What they fail to mention is that the calls are run through a foreign country, where the rates are considerable higher. These and other techniques—such as false advertising, bogus celebrity endorsement offers, price-fixing, telemarketing swindles, and the ever-popular knock-off rip-offs (e.g., buying a watch that is advertised under a brand name but in fact is a fake)—are all schemes that people have devised to fraudulently prompt others to give them something of value (see Rosoff et al., 2004). Fraud often capitalizes on people's greed and the ability of the perpetrator to win the victim's trust or confidence.

Explaining Fraud

In his classic study of cheque forgers, Edwin Lemert (1953) observed that most forgers are naive and tend to commit the offence out of economic need. He also found that they tend not to be involved in other forms of property crime and to be older than most property offenders.

Has forgery evolved as a crime? Trembley (1986) notes that in recent years there has been an increase in professional forgers who have developed sophisticated schemes and sometimes work in teams. "The elderly are among the preferred targets of such groups" (McPhie, 1996:173). Seniors are easily accessible; some of them are looking for a little extra income on their fixed pensions; and many are reluctant to report their victimization because of possible embarrassment (Brennan, 1999). RCMP reports reveal that seniors are particularly prone to telephone fraud scams (see Box 9.8).

FYI BOX 9.8

CANADA AS A PHONE FRAUD HAVEN

RCMP reports suggest that there are hundreds of telephone fraud businesses operating in Canada. Project COLT, established by the police in 1995 to counter phone fraud, estimates that phone fraud generates about $70 million a year in North America. The techniques used vary, but they usually involve offering a significant reward in order to qualify for which the victim must pay a registration fee. In 2003, a company operating out of Toronto swindled thousands of investors out of $40 million—perhaps the largest case of phone fraud in Canadian history (Canada a haven..., 2003).

Other explanations emphasize techniques of neutralization. In the case of business fraud, perpetrators rationalize their actions by claiming that businesses make so much money that they will not be hurt by a "little" loss. As for fraudulent transactions with people, offenders might rationalize that if certain people are naive enough to fall for the false pretence, they deserve to be taken advantage of.

In summary, fraud is a commonly occurring form of property crime that can also take the form of organized criminal activity and white-collar crime (see Chapter 10). The total value of financial losses incurred through fraud is not known because of the high rate of unreported incidents (McPhie, 1996). However, based on available data, fraud costs individuals, organizations, and the government billions of dollars every year. And while the overall official rate for fraud may have declined in recent years, new forms of fraud may simply be one step ahead of police detection.

As long as most Canadians value economic success, it will be difficult to develop social policies that significantly reduce crimes of fraud. Meanwhile, although certain target hardening programs have been devised, criminals seem to find new twists to the old "snake oil" scam.

Theft

There are 14 sections in the *Criminal Code* dealing with theft, ranging from theft of cattle (s. 338) to theft by spouse (s. 329) to theft with intent to deprive (s. 322). The large number of sections implies that theft is considered a serious form of property crime and that tremendously variety exists in methods of committing theft. Even before Confederation, theft was one of the more common crimes reported to police (Carrigan, 1991). In general terms, **theft** refers to the unlawful taking of property from the possession of another. However, unlike robbery, theft does not involve the use or the threat of force or overt deception.

Patterns and Characteristics of Theft

Theft offers an excellent illustration of how crime is *evolutive* and *relative* (see Chapter 1). When the Canadian *Criminal Code* was first enacted, theft was known as "larceny." Later, it was defined as theft and eventually sub-divided into theft under $200 and theft over $200. In 1986, the amount was raised to $1000. Most recently, in 1995, it was again altered to $5000 (see Box 9.9). These changes reflect our social economy and the relative value of goods. And while general comparisons can be made over time, these comparisons should be viewed with caution, since not all property has increased equally in value. Therefore, when the trends in theft are described here, the terms "theft over" and "theft under" will be used, without specifying an amount.

REALITY CHECK BOX 9.9

THE DIFFERENCE BETWEEN "THEFT OVER" AND "THEFT UNDER"

One of my research assistants who used to be employed by a bank shared with me an interesting story she was told recently by bank employees. During a low-key bank robbery, the teller was passed a note by the robber demanding $4999.00, which he was given. The bank employees speculated that the robber requested this amount in case he was later apprehended—which would result in a charge of "theft under" versus "theft over."

Between 1993 and 2003, there was a steady decline in the rate of "theft over" incidents reported to police, amounting to 84.5 percent. By contrast the rate of "theft under" has fluctuated modestly since 1993 (see Table 9–2). In 2003, "theft under" accounted for 54 percent of all property crime and "theft over" for only 2 percent (CCJS, 2004, 24(6)).

In 2003, the largest increase occurred in Manitoba—18 percent over 2002—with Winnipeg experiencing a 21 percent jump. The Winnipeg police attribute the dramatic increase to a new telephone reporting system.

TABLE 9-2

"THEFT OVER" AND "THEFT UNDER," 1993–2003

| | THEFTS PER 100 000 | |
YEAR	OVER	UNDER
1993	408	2680
1994	398	2486
1995*	142	2772
1996	90	2747
1997	79	2503
1998	79	2352
1999	74	2231
2000	70	2161
2001	67	2126
2002	63	2128
2003	64	2220

* Note that the definition of "theft over" and "theft under" changed in 1995; see explanation in the text.

Sources: CCJS, 1997, 17(8):15; 1998, 18(11):18; 2003, 23(5):16; 2004, 24(6):17.

In 2003, theft from a motor vehicle was the most common type of theft (38 percent of theft incidents), followed by shoplifting (12 percent), theft of bicycles (9 percent), and other theft (42 percent) (CCJS, 2004, 24(6):11). This last type includes theft of such items as personal accessories, radios, televisions, money, and identification (see Box 9.10).

FYI BOX 9.10

IDENTITY THEFT

According to RCMP reports, "Identity theft has become an increasingly popular crime in Canada as a result of advances in technology" (Identity theft, 2004). Identity theft involves stealing or hijacking the identity of another person or business for the purpose of committing other crimes. It may involve stealing passwords, PINs, and other vital personal information. In 2003, the Canadian anti-fraud call centre recorded 13 359 identity theft complaints involving losses of over $21.5 million.

Based on his survey findings, Ray (1987) reports that men and women are equally likely to shoplift. The "five finger discount," while often involving items considerably less than $5000 in value (e.g., clothes, CDs, jewellery, etc.), costs some major retailers millions of dollars every year. Shoplifting has increased in recent years, and some studies estimate that about one in every nine shoppers steals from department stores.

Buckle and Farrington (1984) suggest that shoplifting is so prevalent because of its low risk of detection: less than one percent. However, accurate counts of shoplifting are difficult to establish because many businesses blend shoplifting losses into their inventory shrinkage—a figure that includes merchandise bookkeeping errors, breakage, employee theft, and damages, as well as shoplifting losses. Although shoplifting occurs every day, the Christmas season is prime time for shoplifting and fraud. Given the staffing cutbacks in some retail outlets, the problem may grow even worse, although most major department stores now have hidden security cameras and have hired their own in-house security staff. (For more on shoplifting, see Box 9.11).

A CLOSER LOOK BOX 9.11

THE AMATEUR VS. PROFESSIONAL SHOPLIFTER

In a pioneering study on shoplifting, Mary Owen Cameron (1964) developed a typology of shoplifters, to which Ronald Holmes (1983) added another category. The types of shoplifters identified are as follows:

- The *snitch* is an amateur pilferer. This is the most common type of shoplifter and is usually a respectable person. Cameron believes that snitches are not driven by impulsive urges but usually respond to an opportunity that has been preceded by a stressful experience. When caught, older persons usually change their behaviour, while youths are less likely to be deterred (Klemke, 1978). Cameron estimates that snitches make up nearly 90 percent of all shoplifters.
- The *booster* or *heel* is the professional shoplifter who may steal for personal interest, like the snitch, but more often intends to resell the stolen merchandise. Boosters usually sell the stolen goods at half to one-third the original retail cost. However, some boosters will steal to order.
- The *kleptomaniac*, identified by Holmes (1983), is driven to steal not for material gain but for the thrill and arousal gained from the experience. Kleptomaniacs are usually women, though there are exceptions. Holmes notes that only a small percentage of shoplifters fit this category. More recent support for this observation can be found in Klemke's study (1992).

In 2003, property crime rates increased 4 percent over 2002 among young persons. The increase was driven up by break-ins (which increased 7 percent) and theft under $5000 (which increased 6 percent) (Crime statistics, 2004). In 2002, there was a total of 26 748 adult convictions, with some 50 percent being given probation, 38 percent receiving a custody disposition, and almost 5 percent being given a conditional or absolute discharge. The balance of cases mostly involved the use of fines (Cases in adult..., 2004).

Although male and female rates of victimization were nearly equal in 2003, younger women were more likely to be victimized than their male counterparts. Not surprisingly, living in an urban setting places a person (regardless of age) at greater risk than living in rural settings. This general trend, however, does not reflect the fact that theft rates in the Yukon, which is mostly rural, are very high (CCJS, 2004, 24(6)).

Overall, it might be speculated that given the prevalence of theft, the current sentencing dispositions are not having a deterrent effect on offenders—especially among young offenders (see Carrington & Moyer, 1998). Are the dispositions too lenient or are we simply using an ineffective approach? Criminologists need to examine such issues. However, it might also be the case that public apathy undermines crime prevention efforts. Most people view theft as a nuisance rather than a real threat (unless they are the victims); with limited resources, criminal justice agencies may simply be mimicking public apathy. For example, in 2004, there was a rash of inflatable SpongeBob thefts from roofs of various Burger King fast-food outlets in the United States. The pop icon was a hot item on eBay, selling for as much as $1000. In addition to being a financial burden, the thefts represented a nuisance to Burger King, but the company is not actively pursuing the missing inflatables: "at the moment, it is a sort of very amusing phenomenon" (Inflatable..., 2004).

Explaining Theft

In his study of college students, Klemke (1992) found that nearly 60 percent of those surveyed had been involved in at least one shoplifting offence. Katz (1988) suggests that students participate in shoplifting as a release from boredom rather than out of financial need. However, any general explanation of theft must consider both individual and cultural factors. For example, after the wall came down in Berlin and Eastern Europeans were allowed to travel freely to the West, there was a sharp rise in shoplifting (along with other forms of criminal activity). Klemke (1992) offers the anomie and strain theories as plausible explanations. One of the North American dreams is economic success. Not being able to afford certain items may cause some (especially young) people to break the law quite readily for economic gain.

Other explanations of theft (and property theft in general) include the routine activities theory and the idea of crime for thrills. According to this second explanation, people commit acts that are "sensually compelling" (see Katz, 1988). In a 1995 study involving almost 2000 respondents, Bill McCarthy found that males and adolescents were more likely than females and adults to report getting a "high" from an object they considered stealing. Could this "high" be explained using an interdisciplinary perspective?

In summary, theft is one of the oldest crimes and one of the first common-law crimes codified by English judges. Throughout our history, the criteria of theft have undergone various updates reflecting social and financial change. Other than theft from motor vehicles, shoplifting is the most common type of theft in Canada. Explanations have ranged from stealing for the thrill to neutralization—the justification that the store already makes enough profit. Those at risk tend to be the young, the single, the urbanite, the well-educated, the high-income earners, and the homeowners (Hendrick, 1996).

Attempts to control theft have focused on target hardening strategies such as using hidden cameras, hiring undercover staff, placing tags with electronic devices, and securing some items to racks. But, overall, these and other criminal justice measures appear to have had little impact.

Arson

Sections 433–436.1 in the *Criminal Code* pertain to the legal definition and parameters of arson.[2] While not classified as a property crime, **arson** is defined as the destruction of property through the use of fire or an explosion to property, either against another for fraudulent purposes, or by negligence. Arson is considered to be a form of vandalism, but its increase has caused it to be defined as its own offence. Arson is an extremely destructive act. While arson is far less common than theft or other types of property or economic crimes, the motivations for it tend to be more diverse (see Box 9.12).

A CLOSER LOOK BOX 9.12

THE MANY FACES OF ARSON

The following stories represent a cross-section of recent incidents that reflects the diversity of the reasons for committing arson.

- In February 1997, about 500 tradespeople, many unemployed, descended upon a construction site in Sydney, NS, to protest against the use of non-unionized workers. The new apartment construction site was set ablaze in protest by the tradespeople (Protest by arson, 1997).
- In 2004, a 39-year-old man was charged with torching a Quebec band chief's home over politics in the Mohawk community of Kanesatake. Shortly before the torching of his house, the chief had fired the community police chief. Reports indicated that some 40 people stood by and watched the house burn (Arrest in Kanesatake..., 2004).
- In 2004, the 21-year-old son of a Calgary couple was charged with setting fire to his family garage, which then spread to the family home. The son was annoyed for having been grounded (Son charged..., 2004).
- In 2004, Toronto police began a manhunt for an arsonist suspected of setting five fires on a Saturday night. Fires were set to garbage, porches, and a vehicle. Witnesses reported seeing two young males, 17–20 years, leaving the scene. Their motive was egging each other on for the thrill and excitement.

Patterns and Characteristics of Arson

Between 1993 and 2003, the rate of arson incidents reported to police remained stable (see Table 9–3). It is interesting to observe that while the *Juristat* reports provide numerical account of the number and rate of arson incidents, the publication does not offer any discussion or description of the crime, despite the fact that annual estimated losses reach $2.2 billion in direct property damages (see Box 9.13).

TABLE 9–3

ARSON, 1993–2003

YEAR	ARSONS PER 100 000	NUMBER
1993	43	12 470
1994	46	13 509
1995	44	13 156
1996	43	12 830
1997	42	12 799
1998	43	12 947
1999	42	12 756
2000	45	13 733
2001	47	14 484
2002	42	13 192
2003	44	13 851

Sources: CCJS, 1997, 17(8):15; 1998, 18(11):18; 2003, 23(5):16; 2004, 24(6):17.

All provinces have a fire commission that keeps fire-related statistics. For illustrative purposes, a snapshot of fire-related deaths in Alberta and in all of Canada is provided in Table 9–4.

Males are far more likely to be charged with arson than women: 86 percent versus 14 percent of offenders. In addition, while the median age of male fire-setters is 19, for women it is almost double that: 33 years (Noblett & Nelson, 2001). Why is there such an age difference? Why are targeted areas typically economically depressed? Why are companies with ongoing labour problems and vacant buildings targeted? Part of the explanation might lie in understanding the different types of arson and the motivations underlying such acts.

In his study of young arsonists, Wayne Wooden (1991) identified four categories of juvenile arsonists:

1. The *playing with matches fire-setters* are children, usually between the ages of four and nine, who start a fire accidentally while playing with matches carelessly left around.

ARSON: MISCHIEF, VANDALISM, OR AGGRAVATED VANDALISM?

Under common law, the offence of arson was broad in scope. It was defined as "the malicious and willful burning of the house or outhouse of another man" and was generally classified as a form of vandalism (*Working paper 36*, 1984:5). However, as societies evolved, so did the meaning of property and a desire arose to legally enunciate the gravity of the act (*actus reus*) and its underlying intent (*mens rea*).

In response to the increase in arson attacks, the *Law Reform Report* (*Working paper 36*, 1984) attempted to clarify why arson should be treated differently than vandalism. Five recommendations were offered in "an attempt to eradicate the complexities and redundancies of an area of law, which despite some unique problems, may be clearly and simply enunciated in our new *Code*" (*Working paper 36*, 1984:29).

The recommendations set out to treat arson as an aggravated form of vandalism that carries a higher maximum penalty. In 1985, the recommendations were incorporated in the *Criminal Code* amendments. Today, arson is treated more seriously than mischief or vandalism, reflecting the emotional and personal value we place on our property.

Do you agree with these changes? Socially, what might arson represent?

TABLE 9-4

FIRE DEATHS AND DEATH RATES, ALBERTA AND CANADA

YEAR	POPULATION (MILLIONS)	FIRE DEATHS	ALBERTA DEATHS INVOLVING FIRE	FIRE DEATH RATE	CANADA FIRE DEATH RATE
1993	2.57	29	7	1.1	1.5
1994	2.60	22	3	0.8	1.3
1995	2.61	31	5	1.2	1.4
1996	2.67	34	7	1.3	1.3
1997	2.74	24	13	0.9	1.4
1998	2.78	12	8	0.4	1.1
1999	2.87	34	17	1.2	1.3
2000	2.93	19	8	0.6	1.1
2001	2.96	27	16	0.9	n/a
2002	3.05	16	15	0.5	n/a

Source: *Alberta Fire Commissioner's Statistical Report, 2002*, Alberta Municipal Affairs 2004.

2. The *crying for help fire setters* tend to be a little older (ages 7–13) and set fires to reduce anxiety or stress. The source of such feelings is usually related to family-based issues such as divorce, abuse, death, or family strife. These youths have difficulty expressing their pain, so they act it out. Gaynor and Stern (1993) suggest that they usually feel remorse for their actions.

3. The *delinquent fire-setters* are youth aged 14–18 who set fire to property in retaliation for some criticism they might have received). Gaynor and Stern (1993) found that delinquent fire-setters are mostly males (10 for every female) characterized by anger, anti-social personalities, and a lack of regard for social rules and norms.

4. The *severely disturbed fire-setters* are youth who have some personality disturbance. These fire-setters are likely to set numerous fires. The word "pyromaniac" is sometimes used to describe them.

More recently, Swaffer and Hollin (1995) studied a group of female and male adolescent fire-setters and came up with some slightly different categories. Although their sample size was small—only 17 adolescents—the results are nevertheless interesting. Five youths said they set fires out of "revenge." Three said they set fires either to conceal a crime or because of peer pressure. What is interesting to note is that all three females reported self-injury as their motivation.

Pioneering FBI profilers such as John Douglas note that arson at a young age may be symptomatic of greater future problems. Douglas and Olshaker (2000) claim that their studies of rapists and other violent offenders yielded numerous commonalities in the offenders' past. The three "prongs" of what is known as the "homicidal triad" are arson/fire-setting, cruelty to animals, and enuresis (bedwetting) at an inappropriate age. Douglas and colleagues assert that when adolescents frequently engage in two or more of these behaviours, a red flag should be raised. These arguments have been substantiated by reviewing the history of many well-known offenders, such as David Berkowitz, better known by his nickname Son of Sam, who started over 2000 fires before evolving into a serial killer (Douglas & Olshaker, 2000).

Not unlike juveniles, adults commit arson for a variety of reasons. The most common form is *arson for profit*. For example, the owner of a failing business might torch his or her building in order to claim insurance money. In an effort to reduce the risk of being caught, the owner might hire a professional lawyer (Bennett & Hess, 1984). Today, many insurance companies require a fire inspection before insuring buildings in an effort to make it more difficult to file fraudulent claims.

Another motive is *revenge* (Somers, 1984). This is the most common motive for serial arsonists and involves retaliation for some injustice or imagined injustice. For example, a young offender may torch his school in retaliation for a real or imagined wrong, a suspension, or failing grades.

In addition, some psychologists state that adult fire-setters commonly suffer from *personality disorders*. Webb and her colleagues (1990) argue that most adult arson should be viewed as a mental health problem—not a criminal act. The *Alberta Fire Commissioner's Statistical Report, 2002* (2004) notes that some 26 percent of all fatal casualties were impaired at the time of the fire. The emotionally disturbed *pyromaniac* usually attempts to cover or destroy evidence of another crime. Vito and Holmes (1994:315) cite an example in which a husband set fire to his house after killing his wife, hoping to incinerate the evidence. However, the fire department was able to put the fire out and find his wife's remains. The Alberta report notes that 51.6 percent of fire-related deaths and 39.7 of injuries occur between 10:30 p.m. and 6:29 a.m.

Finally, organized crime groups and political terrorists are also known to use arson. Between 1976 and 1980, Cecil Kirby, a Satan's Choice motorcycle club member, carried out over 100 contracts for the Mafia in Canada. The crimes he committed included arson, assault, bombing, and attempted murder (Carrigan, 1991). The Provisional Irish Republican Army is probably the best known terrorist group to frequently resort to arson. Over the years, its activities are believed to be responsible for over 1000 deaths and many more injuries.

According to research by Pettiway (1988), arson patterns can be explained by environmental and ecological theories. Pettiway found that the rate of arson was significantly related to the age of the housing—the older the house, the greater the likelihood of arson. Stahura and Hollinger (1988) were also able to explain arson using the routine activities theory. They found that criminal motivation (e.g., poverty, lack of employment, and age), criminal opportunities (e.g., percentage of old and multiple housing, number of commercial and industrial buildings), and guardianship (e.g., police resources, female labour force participation) were directly and/or indirectly related to arson rates.

In summary, arson, although not legally defined as a property offence, involves the willful destruction of private or public property. While the rate of arson has not changed significantly in recent years, the dollar loss due to arson is extremely high. The motivations of arsonists are varied. Virtually every major fire department has specialists who try to determine the cause of a fire, but their efforts are not always successful. Because arson is so destructive and relatively easy to commit, criminologists need to better understand the motives underlying arsonist attacks so that such attacks can be prevented.

Motor-Vehicle Crime

North Americans love their automobiles. In 2003, there were over 24.6 million motor vehicles registered across Canada, of which approximately 17.7 million were passenger automobiles (Motor vehicle registrations, 2004). Canadians spend billions every year maintaining and nurturing these vehicles. It should come as no surprise that **motor-vehicle crimes**—such as carjacking, joyriding, theft, and vandalism—have fluctuated since 1993 (see Box 9.14).

MOTOR-VEHICLE CRIME: BIG BUSINESS

In September 1996, the Ontario Provincial Police (OPP), in cooperation with several regional police forces and then Canada Customs (known as Canada Border Service Agency since December 2003), successfully smashed a sophisticated ring of car thieves. The ring involved at least six members. The police had recovered 95 luxury vehicles valued at $2.5 million, destined mostly for Vietnam. The gang hired youths and adults and paid them from $300 to $500 to steal cars for a Mississauga import-export business (Mitchell, 1996).

The head of the OPP theft team pointed out that Ontario has the highest rate of stolen vehicles in Canada and observed that since 1990 auto theft had increased by 100 percent (ibid.). The *Juristat* reports that "[t]he rate of motor vehicle thefts increased in 2003 (+5%)—returning to the same level as 2001, but still stands 10% higher than a decade ago" (CCJS, 2004, 24(6):6).

In the early 1990s, the recovery rate for stolen vehicles was 95 percent but fell to 61 percent in 1999. Why? Police officials point to the proliferation of organized vehicle theft around 1995. Insurance companies indicate that stolen motor vehicle claims now exceed $600 million annually (Toronto automobile..., 2004). Meanwhile, in the United Kingdom, since 1997 vehicle crimes dropped 30 percent (Secure your motor, 2004).

The *Criminal Code* deals with the theft of a motor vehicle under the subheading "Offences Resembling Theft" in section 335. Regardless of the high value Canadians place on their vehicles, the taking a motor vehicle without consent is punishable only on a summary conviction (see Box 9.15).

IS YOUR CAR SECURE?

Car theft in North America occurs on average every 20 seconds (Shaw, 1997).

Patterns and Characteristics of MVC

In this section, we will look at some of the general patterns and characteristics of motor-vehicle crime (MVC), in particular motor-vehicle theft (MVT). We will also examine some of the strategies that have been introduced to combat the problem.

Motor vehicle theft involves the illegal use of a motorized vehicle (e.g., automobiles, buses, vans, trucks, or motorcycles) for the use of joyriding, short or long-term transportation, profit, and/or the commission of another crime. Motor vehicle crime refers to the broader range of offences involving a motor vehicle that includes theft from vehicles, theft of vehicles, criminal damage to vehicles, and vandalism.

After a relatively stable period between 1981 and 1987, the motor-vehicle theft (MVT) rate increased 62.7 percent between 1988 and 1993. Starting in 1994, the rate began to nudge up (see Table 9–5). Alberta experienced the highest increase in MVT—15 percent—while the Maritime provinces averaged around 12 percent each. Only Ontario and Quebec rates remained stable (CCJS, 2004, 24(6):10).

TABLE 9–5

MOTOR VEHICLE THEFT, 1993–2003

YEAR	THEFTS PER 100 000	NUMBER
1993	546	156 685
1994	549	159 469
1995	551	161 696
1996	607	180 123
1997	591	177 130
1998	549	165 920
1999	529	161 388
2000	521	160 315
2001	543	168 595
2002	516	161 912
2003	541	171 017

Sources: CCJS, 2003, 23(1); 2004, 24(6):10.

Like other property-related crimes, MVC varies geographically. While Quebec had the highest motor vehicle theft rates in the early to mid-1990s, the rates began to shift dramatically thereafter. Since 1999, Manitoba has had the highest MVT rates (1148 per 100 000 in 2001), while Newfoundland and Labrador had the lowest (119 per 100 000). In 2001, Quebec's MVT rate was only slightly above the national average: 567 versus 548 (CCJS, 2003, 23(1)). Roy (1988, cited in Trembley et al., 1996:264) offers an explanation as to why Quebec may have had a higher rate than other provinces in the early 1990s. He points that "junked vehicles are allowed to go back on the street in Quebec and not in Ontario ... as a result, wrecked vehicles are purchased by Quebec-based 'retag operators'... and their vehicle identification numbers subsequently used to provide a legitimate number for a locally stolen vehicle." As for urban variations, Statistics Canada suggests that the high incidence of youth offending can account for the high MVT rates in Regina and Winnipeg (1996 and 1581 per 100 000 respectively) (CCJS, 2003, 23(1)).

Interestingly, in 1996, Canada's rate of MVT exceeded that of the United States. In 2000, Canada's rate was 26 percent higher than in the United States (CCJS, 2003, 23(1):4), and it remains higher today. However, international trends show that between 1996 and 2000, 14 countries reported decreases in the number of MVTs reported to police. Canada experienced an 11 percent decrease, while Germany had a 43 percent drop. Conversely, Austria had a 49 percent increase in MVTs!

Which kind of car should you not own if you are worried about car theft? Over a decade ago, the two-door Ford Mustang Cobra GT and the two-door Volkswagen Golf were the most common targets, while the Mercury Sable and Oldsmobile Ninety-Eight were least likely to be targeted (Morrison, 1996). Of the 1999–2000 models, the most frequently stolen vehicles in 2001 were (CCJS, 2003, 23(1):5):

1. Two-door Hyundai Tiburon (FX);
2. Two-door Acura Integra; and
3. Two-door Honda Civic Si.

Vehicles with the lowest theft frequencies were:

1. Toyota Tundra 4-wheel drive V8;
2. Buick Park Avenue; and
3. Mercury Sable Wagon.

Although the rate of youths charged with motor vehicle theft in 2001 was 35 percent lower than it was a decade ago, almost half of all persons charged with MVT are still young people (CCJS, 2003, 23(1):5). When youths steal a vehicle, most of their acts (approximately 76 percent) amount to *joyriding*—taking vehicles for a short period for purposes of pleasure or transportation. Youths are more likely to steal vehicles during July and August—the summer holidays. However, research shows they rarely are suspected or apprehended. In 2001, only 13 percent of MVTs were solved by the police. The General Social Survey shows that in 1999 approximately 40 percent of all motor-vehicle vandalisms "cleared otherwise" involved youths aged 12–17. Another 16 percent involved youths under the age of 12. The data indicate that most young offenders are dealt with through avenues other than the formal criminal justice system.

Explaining Motor-Vehicle Crime

Why are motor-vehicle crimes so prevalent and why do people become involved in them? Based on his review of the literature, Morrison (1996) cites a number of common explanations for MVC in North America. For example, vehicles are stolen or vandalized, especially by youth, because of the symbolic value of having something of status. In North America, cars are a status symbol. They can be stolen for a joyride, to be sold, or simply to be vandalized, following the thinking that if the offender can't have it, then the owner shouldn't either. The action provides the offender with a sense of power. Also, initial MVC may be motivated by peer pressure or boredom, commission of another crime, or money reward. The risk of auto theft is further enhanced by the fact that potential victims leave their valuables insecure and often in plain view.

Light, Nee, and Ingham (1993) found that offenders who steal vehicles for profit develop a dependency on this type of income. However, they found that most youths simply grow out of the activity. It is not the legal sanction that deters them but simply growing up.

Borrowing from Felson's routine activities theory, Trembley et al. (1996) suggest that one approach that might be used to understand the motivation of joyriders is to undertake a cross-sectional analysis of their responsiveness to structural features or urban environments. However, they point out that the process of developing a fruitful explanatory model requires "a much more detailed investigation of the routine activities and concerns" of all the factors that could be involved.

A number of years ago, Karman (1979) raised a number of interesting questions about the motivation of motor-vehicle crimes. Karman pointed out that it is important to understand not only the relationship between motor-vehicle thieves or vandals and their victims but also the role that the automotive industry plays in the design and security of cars. For example, why are cars easy to damage but expensive to repair? Why are cars still relatively easy to steal? Does the automotive industry have a stake in car theft and vandalism? Surveys indicate that most people are willing to pay higher purchase prices for effective security features.

Recently, several automakers have taken steps to target harden their vehicles. In 1997, Ford, in its Ford Taurus model, introduced an electronic key that eliminates the ability to hot-wire a car. Several leading automakers have equipped cars with GPS and Boomerang devices that enable the vehicle to be tracked via a satellite to pinpoint its location. Both systems include a monitoring fee. A passive arming system includes immobilzers that shut off the electrical circuit when the car is shut down and prevents the car from being started without a special coded key. A novel program introduced in the United States is the national Watch Your Car Program. Owners of vehicles "voluntarily display a decal or device, such as a state-issued, customized licence plate on their vehicles to alert police that their vehicles are not normally driven between the hours of 1 a.m. and 5 a.m." (The Watch Your Car Program, 1996). The decals are tamper-resistant. Some states also use decals that indicate that the car is not normally operated near international borders or ports. For a nominal fee, all participants are registered with law enforcement officials. Perhaps the most common device, which has received endorsements from the police as well as considerable media attention, is "The Club"—a relatively inexpensive mechanical barrier system that attaches to the steering-column.

When one takes into account all the target hardening measures that have been introduced and tried over the years, perhaps it is time to consider an alternative strategy. For example, crime prevention strategies should consider both the types of vehicles being targeted and the motivation of the perpetrator.

In summary, motor-vehicle crimes have increased in recent years. The patterns vary geographically. The characteristics and motivations of offenders are also varied. The problem of motor-vehicle crime is not unique to Canada or North America. Sophisticated professional car stealing rings serve as reminders that all the security devices and safety programs that have been introduced have done little to curb the problem.

As long as we continue to value automobiles and as long as the average cost of vehicles remains high, the opportunity for motor-vehicle crime will not go away. We need to not only focus on security measures but also better understand the motivation behind motor-vehicle crime. This will require an integrated and interdisciplinary approach. In the meantime, we might want to see what countries with low rates of MVC are doing and adopt some of their methods.

Summary

- Property crimes are generally committed with the aim of providing financial reward to the offenders. Offenders are either amateurs capitalizing on an opportunity or professional criminals. Most offenders are young males.

- Most property crimes (in particular, theft) have evolved over time, reflecting social and economic changes, and may readily cross over into other crime classifications such as violent crime (theft), organized crime (fraud), or white-collar crime (arson).

- Most explanative theories relating to property crime are grounded in sociology, and the policies resulting from them have had a questionable impact in reducing property crime incidents. Most property crime prevention approaches have focused on target hardening strategies, which have been marginally, if at all, successful. An integrated and interdisciplinary approach may be more effective, focusing instead on other environmental, political, and individual factors motivating property-related criminality.

- The nature of property crime has evolved beyond the conventional categories of simple theft, arson, etc. We are experiencing new variations of property crime that are having a broader impact on society.

- Despite the fact that conventional crime rates have been declining, current rates are still alarmingly high when compared with earlier rates. Social policies should endeavour to incorporate interdisciplinary and integrated approaches in their efforts to study and remedy such crimes.

Discussion Questions

1. What can the property crime statistics tell us about crime trends and patterns in Canada? Has the picture changed in recent years? Why?

2. Who is primarily responsible for committing property crimes?

3. Are there common denominators for property crime offenders?

4. What are some of the major explanatory models for the different types of crimes covered in this chapter? Are there any common causal factors that can be used to explain both violent and property crimes?

5. Collect at least a dozen media articles related to the "new" forms of crimes against property. What do they tell us about the nature and extent of the problem? What kinds of solutions, if any, are offered? Do these forms of property crime pose a more serious threat to society than traditional forms?

Key Concepts

arson

break and enter

fraud

motor-vehicle crime

property crime

theft

Weblinks

www.statcan.ca/english/Pgdb/justic.htm This page from Statistics Canada offers links to tables containing current Canadian justice and crime statistics.

www.uncjin.org/Statistics/statistics.html This page from the United Nations offers international crime statistics.

http://www3.gov.ab.ca/hre/library/fire/index.asp Hosted by the Department of Human Resources and Employment in Alberta, this page offers lists of videos related to fire and arson prevention. Most provinces have similar sites.

www.rcmp.ca/scams/tfraud_e.htm Hosted by the RCMP, this site offers information on fraud, scams, telemarketing, identity theft, and related property and personal crimes.

www.ibc.ca/vehinfo_pub_howcarsmeasureup.asp This page, from the Insurance Bureau of Canada, includes information on motor-vehicle theft and motor-vehicle crime across Canada.

You can use internet search engines, such as **www.google.com** or **www.altavista.com**, to easily locate property crime information for virtually any country, as well as specific reports on any type of violent crime.

Endnotes

1. Fraud used to be called "false pretence." It was introduced by the English Parliament in 1757 to cover an area of law not addressed by larceny (theft) statutes. The Canadian *Criminal Code* used the term "false pretence and fraud" until it was changed to simply "fraud" (Carrigan, 1991).

2. Prior to 1985, arson came under s. 392 (now s. 436).

CHAPTER 10

Organized and Corporate Crime

"The reason why crime doesn't pay is that when it does it is called by a more respectable name."

Justice Tom Clark

Learning Outcomes

After you have completed this chapter, you should be able to:

- Describe the nature and significance of organized crime.

- Discuss the various types of organized crime groups in Canada.

- Assess the extent of corporate crime and the difficulty in regulating it.

- Discuss the causes of corporate crime.

- Evaluate the ways in which corporate crime and organized crime can be controlled.

Introduction

In the previous two chapters, we dealt with conventional crimes or "crimes of the street"—violent crimes and property crimes. Conventional crimes are typically (but not always) committed by the middle and lower socio-economic classes. For the most part, conventional crimes can be committed by individuals or small groups. Information on violent and property-related crimes is readily available through official police records. There are, however, other forms of crime whose impact can be more devastating and which can present very different challenges to criminologists.

Organized crime and corporate crime are two forms of crime typically committed by powerful and/or influential groups or individuals. As illustrated in Box 10.1, because of the status or power that these groups or individuals hold, the impact of their crimes can be very costly in both human and financial terms. These crimes can also have an international dimension, which makes them difficult to combat.

In this chapter, we will examine a variety of organized crimes and corporate crimes. We will look at the characteristics, methods, motives, and trends associated with them and review some of the major theoretical perspectives used to explain them. We will also examine the various strategies that criminologists have recommended and the steps that the state has taken to deal with these powerful groups and individuals and their illegal activities.

REALITY CHECK BOX 10.1

THE MANY FACES OF ORGANIZED CRIME

- December 1996: Two Iranian nationals living in Toronto were charged with smuggling illegal immigrants (mostly Iranians) into Canada by using false travel documents. The smuggling ring originated in the Netherlands. The smugglers charged between US $5000 and $6000 per immigrant. It is estimated that over a three-year period as many as 5000 people were smuggled into Canada (Refugee smuggling ring smashed, 1996).
- October 1997: An organized group of poachers in northern Alberta were arrested and charged with 185 counts of illegally selling fish and wild game. Several local restaurants were also charged with trafficking in illegal fish and wild game. Authorities said that understaffing prevents them from better monitoring this lucrative activity (Arnold, 1997).
- July 2002: After an 18-month investigation, Canadian, US, and Caribbean police and customs infiltrated one of Canada's largest-ever drug smuggling rings, seizing $95.7 million in drugs. The largest raid took place at the Port of Halifax. The group included members of the Hell's Angels (Aldred, 2004).
- August 2004: A series of brazen heists of cigarettes and tobacco have prompted the RCMP to conclude that what was once the work of lone street-corner thugs is now being conducted by organized gangs (Brewster, 2004)

Organized Crime

While the public's image of organized crime usually involves Colombian cartels, the Italian Mafia, the Asian Triads, and motorcycle gangs, organized crime can also involve legitimate businesses. In this section, we will examine various forms of **organized crime**.

History of Organized Crime

Probably since the dawn of time, human beings have been interested in gathering "goods and services" of one sort or another. As societies moved from hunting and gathering to mercantile and feudal systems and from rural settings into urban settings, people's methods of acquiring "profit" illegally began to flourish (Wright & Fox, 1978).

Piracy is among the earliest examples of organized crime. Some of the ancient Phoenicians (c. 1200 BC to 146 BC) roamed the Mediterranean Sea and plundered ships. From the close of the eighth century, the Vikings of Scandinavia were also known to practise acts of piracy and plunder throughout France, Scotland, England, and Ireland. However, the most famous examples of piracy, made popular today through movie images, occurred during the 1600s. Flamboyant, swashbuckling pirates, wearing eye patches and bandanas, roamed the seas to plunder and pillage ships carrying goods to and from colonies in the New World.

Historically, Canada and the United States have shared more than the world's longest border. Brodeur (cited in Koenig, 2003:47) points out that while neither the FBI or the RCMP have "found much evidence for such a conceptualization of organized crime ... it would be ... accurate to speak of associations [between the two countries] of criminals *organizing* crime." While its nature and scope have evolved, organized crime has been entrenched in virtually every culture and society.

Defining Organized Crime

Howard Abadinsky (1994), one of the leading North American authorities on organized crime, observes that organized crime has been poorly defined. He suggests that there is no ideal type of organized crime; rather, organized crime exists as a "degree" of criminal activity or as a point on the "spectrum of legitimacy."

The following represent a cross-section of definitions of organized crime:

- "Organized crime is a continuing criminal enterprise that rationally works to profit from illicit activities that are in great public demand. Its continuing existence is maintained through the use of force, threats, and/or the corruption of public officials" (Abadinsky, cited in Definitions..., 2003).

- According to Interpol, organized crime constitutes "any group having a corporate structure whose primary objective is to obtain money through illegal activities often surviving on fear and corruption" (Interpol, cited in Definitions..., 2003).

- "The illegal activities carried out by structured groups of three or more persons for a prolonged period of time and having the aim of committing serious crimes... in order to obtain, directly or indirectly, a financial or other material benefit" (Council of Europe, 2002, cited in Definitions..., 2003).

While most definitions vary in their terminology, they tend to share several themes: (1) the supplying of illegal goods and services; (2) predatory crime (e.g., fence rings, gangs, and terrorist activities); and (3) increasingly transnational dimension.

One of the challenges in offering a clear definition is the difficulty of "captur[ing] the essential aspects of the 'process' that certain criminals use in carrying out criminal activity" (Beare, 1996:266). Loree (2004:10) points out that since each nation "creates its own legal definition of organized crime, [it] complicates international collaboration, data collection and analysis."

Appreciating the difficulty of defining organized crime, Abadinsky (1994), along with several other scholars, has focused on identifying a set of attributes that are commonly found among organized crime groups. (For a Canadian definition of "criminal organization," see Box 10.2.) Among other things, organized crime groups are:

- *Non-ideological*: Most organized crime groups have no political affiliation. Their goals are not directly motivated by political concerns.
- *Hierarchical*: There is a chain of command. Three or more permanent positions of authority usually exist within the group.
- *Limited or exclusive in membership*: Organized crime groups are sometimes formed along ethnic, racial, kinship, and prior criminal records lines.
- *Perpetuous*: These groups constitute an ongoing criminal conspiracy designed to persist over time.
- *Organized through specialization or division of labour*: Members have certain areas of responsibility (e.g., enforcers, soldiers, money movers).

FYI BOX 10.2

DEFINITION OF "CRIMINAL ORGANIZATION"

In February 2002, the passing of Bill C-24 allowed for an amendment to the *Criminal Code* adding three new offences and toughening sentences that target involvement in criminal organizations; simplifying the definition of a criminal organization; and providing special measures to protect those who assist in apprehending and/or prosecuting members of a criminal organization. Section 467.1(1)(a) of the *Criminal Code* states that a "criminal organization":

- Is composed of three or more persons in or outside of Canada; and
- Has as one of its main purposes...the facilitation or commission of one or more serious offences that...would likely result in the direct or indirect receipt of a material benefit...by the group....
- Does not include a group of persons that forms randomly for the immediate commission of a single offence.

In September 2000, the RCMP estimated that between $5 and 17 million is laundered every year by organized groups in Canada (Facts about..., 2003). In September 2002, the federal, provincial, and territorial ministers responsible for justice declared combatting organized crime a national priority (ibid.).

- *Monopolistic*: Organized crime groups strive for hegemony (dominance) over a geographic area, thereby restraining competition and increasing their own profit.
- *Governed by rules and regulations*: Virtually all organized crime groups require their members to take an oath of secrecy. Members of the Japanese yakuza used to have to submit to having a joint of their little finger removed. Some gangs require new members to undergo a hazing or beatings by fellow members, while others require a criminal act as part of their initiation.

What are the main criminal activities of criminal organizations? We will discuss the specific activities of various types of criminal organizations shortly, but the following are some of the main activities as recognized by the RCMP and Interpol:

- Alien smuggling;
- Armed assault;
- Car theft;
- Drug dealing;
- Fraud;
- Trafficking in humans, radioactive material, and weapons;
- Robbery and smuggling of precious and antique goods;
- Exploitation through prostitution;
- Chemical terrorism;
- Gambling;
- Embezzling from industries and financial institutions up to infiltration and control of private and commercial banks; and
- Controlling of black market.

One can readily see from this list how criminal organization is big business and how it poses a threat to the economic stability of countries.

Organized Crime Groups in Canada

We will now turn to several of the more prominent types of organized crime groups that exist in Canada today. Although they may differ in their orientation, all of these groups share many of the characteristics defined by Abadinsky (1994).

Aboriginal Crime Groups

Once thought to be little more than low-level groups of thugs lacking formal structure, **Aboriginal crime groups**—such as Indian Posse, Redd Alert, and Warriors—have been drawing increasing attention since the early 1990s as a result of their escalating involvement in criminal activities. Beare (1996:272) describes the Aboriginal organized crime activities as "a perfect example of a 'manufactured' organized crime problem," since certain groups choose to turn to seek out illegal ventures by which to attain their goals as a result of perceived

RCMP NOT AS WELL ORGANIZED AS ORGANIZED CRIME FAMILIES

Between 1990 and 1994, an undercover RCMP operation inadvertently helped Colombian drug traffickers and their associates import and sell almost 5000 kilograms of cocaine. The drugs had an estimated street value of $2 billion. A report revealed that the sting operation failed as a result of insufficient police personnel, a reluctance of senior RCMP officials to respond to requests for assistance, and internal security breaches by at least two corrupt officers. The RCMP fiasco is even suspected of helping "the clandestine drug pipeline between Colombia's cocaine cartels and Canadian biker gangs and Italian Mafia gangs that import, distribute and sell cocaine to users and addicts in Canada" (McIntosh, 1998:A2).

Koningsfeld (1998) points out that the art of money laundering has become very sophisticated through the use of "foreign legal persons" (e.g., companies, legal entities, or foreign legal persons) and the internet. He calls for international cooperation and the establishment of data banks of all companies and their beneficial owners. As he states, "the weakest link is the problem of identification of the beneficial owner."

limited economic opportunities and of being marginalized on a number of social levels. The following are some recent examples of Aboriginal organized crime activity:

- In the early 1990s, residents of three Native reserves in Eastern Canada were involved in cigarette smuggling operations and illegal gambling operations (Beare, 1996).
- In 2003, several prairie-based Aboriginal gangs were working with more sophisticated gangs—such as Hell's Angels and Asian gangs—in selling drugs at the street level (Dolha, 2003). In 2004, there were an estimated 300 Aboriginal gang members incarcerated in the Prairie Region.
- In 2004, an Aboriginal gang was responsible for 12 arson attacks against a chief in Quebec in an effort to establish its territory and engage in drug trafficking and other smuggling with support from various bike gangs (Nickerson, 2004).

Because of their special rights, tax exemptions, and location near the US border, Aboriginal organized crime groups can make a profit of over a million dollars with a single tractor trailer loaded with 1200 cases of cigarettes (Stamler, 1996). Such opportunities, combined with the ability to make easy profits, have made intervention difficult. The problem of controlling or regulating smuggling activities and other criminal activities among First Nations people is further compounded by their efforts to seek self-government rights over their reserves, since politicians do not want to push for standard policing (Nickerson, 2004).

What can be done? Because these are crimes of opportunity, it is difficult for law enforcement agencies to counter them. In 1994, the situation became so critical that the government dramatically reduced cigarette taxes, but in 2001, in response to Ottawa calling tobacco the most serious health problem facing Canada, it raised the price of a carton by $4 and allocated $480 million for anti-smoking programs and for combatting cigarette smuggling. Other measures involved closer cooperation among law enforcement agencies, better prosecution, and cooperation with Customs and Revenue Canada.

These measures have received varying support. Would you choose not to buy smuggled products at a reduced price if you knew you would likely not be prosecuted for it? Do you think it is right to levy such high taxes on alcohol and tobacco? Are there alternative strategies that could be considered? For example, in 2000, Ovide Mercredi, former national chief of the Assembly of First Nations, prepared a report in which he calls for initiatives that promote a path of healing and positive contribution in the community for gang members, based on a restorative justice model (see Chapter 14). Similar views were expressed at the Round Table on Aboriginal Organized Crime held in March 2004 (Dickson-Gilmore, 2004).

Cartels

Cartel can be defined as a combination of independent commercial enterprises designed to limit competition. A special report in *Criminal Justice International* (Hill, 1994) described cartels as a new breed of international organized crime that transcends nations. They are seen as threats to democracy, national security, and development. The report estimates that in the early 1990s there were over 2600 organized cartels around the world. Illegal narcotic sales in North American generate an estimated US $57 billion a year, mostly in cash (Drug cartels, 2003).

The Colombian cartels, for example, specialize in importing and trafficking in cocaine (see Box 10.4). They were the most violent and sophisticated cartel operation that emerged in the early 1970s. Before Pablo Escobar, one of the Cali Cartel leaders was caught, it is estimated that he had made US $4 billion from trafficking in cocaine. It is also estimated that in Colombia alone there are 20 organized crime families, four of which have major international operations (Stamler, 1996). Collectively, they provide at least 75 percent of the cocaine that is used in Canada and the United States (ibid.).

FYI BOX 10.4

COCAINE—A MEDICINAL DRUG?

Cocaine is derived from the leaves of the coca shrub, which has grown naturally in the Andean highlands since 1500 BC and has been used for medicinal and tonic purposes. Abuse began after 1862, when a German chemist was able to extract an alkaloid that he labelled cocain. Its potent properties were soon being touted as a "magical substance" by Sigmund Freud in 1886. Today, cocaine is used in a variety of pharmaceutical products. However, in 1961, a treaty ratified by 125 nations introduced a ban on producing or processing cocaine—except for medicinal purposes. It was shortly thereafter that cocaine became the drug of choice and a marketable item for organized crime groups (White, 1989).

Although the Colombian government, helped by financial aid from the United States, has made efforts to curtail the drug cartels, the cartels' multi-billion–dollar operation is not likely to be easily eradicated. Their sophisticated infrastructure, ability to corrupt officials, and preparedness to defend their **illicit market** will not readily succumb to government raids and the odd arrest. In fact, the Colombian drug cartels recently developed a new strain of coca plant that yields up to four times more cocaine, "dealing a setback to a campaign against production ... that was beginning to show results" (McDermott, 2004:A13).

Other drug cartels operating in Canada and elsewhere in the world include Nigerian operations, Japanese yakuza or boryokudan groups, and Jamaican groups known as posses. Among the newer cartel groups in Canada and the United States are the Russian organized crime groups (see Box 10.5). These groups are also established in other countries and are known for their excessive violence and wide range of organized criminal activity.

A CLOSER LOOK BOX 10.5

THE RUSSIAN "MAFIYA"

"The law cannot keep up with crime which is no doubt the biggest industry in Russia." *Moscow Times*, cited in Goodwin, 1995:3

With the collapse of the Soviet Union in 1991, Eastern European organized crime began to flourish. However, its roots go back to the 1970s and 1980s, when it became increasingly involved in the black market. This period coincided with the weakening of the Russian economy.

In 1991, the Russian Ministry of the Interior reported that there were at least 785 organized crime groups operating throughout Russia. By 2000, their numbers had swelled to 5600—over 700 percent growth (Finckenauer & Waring, 2001). Today, their influence plagues both economic and institutional reform in Russia. Murder rates have risen 25 percent each year since 1991. The CIA estimates that more than "half of Russia's 25 largest banks have illegal ties to Russian organized crime."

Coinciding with the 1991 collapse, the Russia Mafiya began to move beyond national borders. In 2002, the number of Europeans applying for immigration status was 38 811. Unfortunately for criminological purposes, Citizenship and Immigration Canada does not provide a breakdown of how many of the new immigrants are or might be associated with the Russian Mafiya. Yet, according to CSIS, a number of those applying for immigration status in Canada are suspected to be members of Russian organized crime groups. In 2002, the newly formed Criminal Intelligence Service of Alberta declared these groups as among the most troublesome in the province.

Unlike conventional organized crime groups, Russian organized crime groups involve themselves in anything that will gain them a profit, rather than specializing in a specific market. Although recent reports note they have become principal traffickers of MDMA (ecstasy) and steroids (Alberta Solicitor General, 2002), they have also been known to be involved in several drug "rip-offs" against the Hell's Angels and various Asian gangs. Their growing sophistication and ruthlessness has caused Canadian law enforcement agencies to establish a special task force to deal with the growing problem (CACP, 1994). One recent report noted that "nowhere has the influence of the mob been more evident than Russia itself" and that its tentacles are rapidly spreading around the world (Ward & Kinney, 1999:5).

Cartels are a prime example of the changing face of organized crime. Once little more than glorified regionalized gangs, they have evolved to become international threats to national economies and political stability of states. Changes in the global economy and political instability in various parts of the world have created an environment favourable to the flourishing and spread of criminal organizations. The widespread and international nature of many cartels poses a major problem in terms of fighting this type of crime. Most attempts at a solution have called for cooperation between law enforcement agencies that crosses jurisdictions and international borders (Smyth, 2001). Laws could also be revised so that they are easier to enforce and can transcend international boundaries as far as dealing with certain organized crime groups is concerned. Criminologists should also explore proactive and interdisciplinary approaches in their efforts to understand and address the problem.

Ethnic Crime Groups

Canada is a country made up of many cultural and ethnic groups. Some of these groups come from war-torn areas where violence, corruption, and extortion have become a way of life and—due to cultural and ethnic differences—may not assimilate as readily as others. On arriving in Canada, members of these groups may occasionally bring their conflicts with them. Their activities may receive a fair bit of attention, while those of members of certain other minority groups may go largely unnoticed because of the image the group projects (see Box 10.6).

Pace (1991) observes that ethnicity may affect a group's tendency to violence, its market of specialization, and accessibility to legitimate markets. Different groups are involved in different types of activities and use different strategies when engaging in criminal behaviour.

Asian Triads, Vietnamese gangs, and Caribbean gangs can be found in every province. The greatest amount of activity, however, takes place in British Columbia, Ontario, and Quebec (Alberta Solicitor General, 2002). Influenced by social and political circumstances in their native countries, these groups are known for their violence (manifesting itself in, for example, drive-by shootings, home invasions, and extortions).

Among the more serious ethnic organized crime groups in Canada are Asian-based crime groups, whose roots can be traced back to the first wave of Chinese immigrants, predominantly goldfield or railroad workers in the mid-1800s (Emerging gangs, 1997). At the 14th Annual International Conference on Organized Crime, held in Calgary in 1995, a wide range of Asian Triad operations was identified. These groups are involved in illegal activities ranging from running prostitution rings, making counterfeit credit cards, engaging in forgery, trafficking in drugs, selling contraband goods, operating nightclubs to launder their illegally gotten monies, and organizing home invasions and break and enters.

The Alberta Solicitor General (2002) has expressed concern over the influx of Asian criminals after the Chinese takeover of Hong Kong in July 1997. The wealth of many new Hong Kong immigrants in Canada may make them prime targets for extortion, drug trafficking, and other activities of Chinese crime groups. Tong Sang Lai, the leader of the Wo On Lok, also known as the Shui Fong (Water Rats), one of the most powerful Triads operating in Hong Kong, is living a posh life in east Vancouver while his gang (reported to be 3000 strong) continues its turf war in Hong Kong (Criminal lands..., 1997).

Vietnamese gangs (for example, 14K, Sun Yee On, Wo Hop To, Wo On Lok, United Bamboo, Born to Kill, Viet-Ching, and AOC) are known for their violence and general disregard for law enforcement (Asian-based..., 1999). In Canada, they often prey on members from their own communities through extortion and robbery, taking advantage of immigrants who are unfamiliar with Canadian ways and who, because of their cultural background, are afraid to go to the police (Carrigan, 1991). Many gang members see going to jail as better than being in a refugee camp. The extent of these groups' involvement in organized crime is not known because it is suspected that a significant number of their activities go unreported. One Vietnam-born police officer estimated that as much as "75 per cent of the crime committed by the Asian community is not reported" (ibid.:194).

In her study of Vietnamese criminal organization in Canada, Prowse (1994:2) observes that "the most powerful gang is the most violent gang; with violence, you get power, and with power, you get money." Criminal activities among Vietnamese gangs first came to the attention of Canadian authorities in the early 1980s, but these groups were often mistaken for Chinese Triads. Starting in the 1990s, their level of violence escalated, and they have since "undergone a transformation from loosely-structured crime groups...to well armed and semi-structured criminal organizations" (ibid.:5). Involvement in Vietnamese gangs, according to Prowse, is grounded in the members' "conflicting demands of culturally-rooted financial obligation to family and the lack of a legitimate means of fulfilling their obligations" (ibid.:8).

Outlaw Motorcycle Gangs

Historically, Quebec has been a hotbed for motorcycle gangs in Canada, but these gangs can be found in every province. In 2002, there were over 350 000 registered motorcycles and mopeds in Canada. Most of them were owned by law-abiding citizens who may attend Harley Davidson motorbike conventions but do not engage in any form of criminal activity. Some motorcycle clubs, however, are involved in organized crime.

The Hell's Angels are one such outlaw motorcycle gang (OMG) (see Box 10.7). Its members also own Harleys and may attend some of the conventions, but the orientation of the club is criminal. In 2000, there were three Hell's Angels chapters in Alberta, with a combined membership of 48 people (Alberta Solicitor General, 2002). Approximately 500 people were members across the country (Outlaw..., 2004). Other OMGs in Canada include the Outlaws, Bandidos, Quebec's Rock Machine, and the oldest Canadian OMG—the Red Devils (located in the greater Hamilton area). These gangs compete for control of exotic dancer clubs, are involved in extortion and intimidation of many other bars, and engage in drug trafficking, prostitution, contract killing, and (more recently) the cultivation and distribution of hydroponic marijuana. In 2001, this last activity netted a street value of $2.7 million (Alberta Solicitor General, 2002). The illegal drug market is valued at between $7 and 10 billion annually (Smyth, 2001).

FYI BOX 10.7

HELL'S ANGELS

Formed in the late 1940s, in Hollister, California, the Hell's Angels was made up of mostly ordinary individuals who were looking for a little recreation and excitement after the war. They called themselves the Pissed Off Bastards of Bloomington and formed the first American Motorcycle Association. It was only after a member of the group was arrested and not released that the group became more violent and renamed itself the Hell's Angels (Stamler, 1996).

Wolf (1991) uses a sociological perspective to interpret bikers' lives and subculture. He notes that most of the members come from the lower and working classes where they experience a sense of anomie—lack of purpose and identity. Being a member of the bike gang allows them to superficially romanticize their mundane life. With the backing of other members, they are able to lead a wild and carefree existence—a form of rebellion. The colours they wear and the bikes they ride (for example, riding only Harley Davidsons, wearing the Rebels' logo on jackets) add the dimension of ritualism to their lifestyle. These practices are also used to express the members' commitment to the gang and even serve as a form of intimidation. In addition, members of bike gangs have their own jargon (see Box 10.8), reinforcing their retreatism.

FYI BOX 10.8

GLOSSARY OF TERMS USED BY OUTLAW MOTORCYCLE GANG MEMBERS

AFFL: Angels Forever, Forever Loaded.

Angels' Bible: Harley-Davidson motoring manual, frequently used for Hell's Angels' weddings and torn up for divorce proceedings.

Back pack: Full colours tattooed on member's back.

Chopper: Chopped or cut-down motorcycle with all unnecessary equipment, such as front brake and fender, stripped off.

Crash truck: A van, panel truck, or converted school bus that follows or precedes the bike gang run and picks up broken down bikes.

Hawg or HOG: Law enforcement officers; also known as "the man."

Mama: Any woman sexually available to all club members.

Patch over: A situation where a stronger major club takes over defeated or probationary clubs; this can be accomplished peacefully or through war.

Suck the bulls: Talk or act friendly toward a police officer.

Tattoos and patches worn:

13: The letter "M" is the 13th letter in the alphabet. It signifies methamphetamine and/or marijuana.

22: Signifies having been in prison.

24: Signifies having drunk 24 beers in less than 8 hours.

81: Hell's Angels. "H" is eighth letter of alphabet; "A" is first.

666: Satan's sign; replaces the "filthy few" but signifies the person has engaged in acts of violence.

*: An asterisk tattooed between the thumb and forefinger indicates how many times the wearer has been in prison.

Note: This is only a sample of the terms/vocabulary used among outlaw bikers.

Sources: Adapted from *RCMP Gazette*, 1994, (56)3 and (56)4:39, as well as courtesy of N. Tusikov, Assistant Editor of the *RCMP Gazette*.

Wolf suggests that motorcycle gangs persist partly because they represent an outgrowth of a capitalist system in which certain members of the working class feel alienated. In the gang subculture, these people are able to share a common set of social norms that are usually in contrast to those of the society at large. Adoption of such norms draws social rejection and further reinforces rebellious attitudes and behaviours.

What Wolf does not explain is why more working-class people don't join motorcycle gangs or other subcultural groups. Why don't women become involved more in subcultural groups? Are violent subcultural groups a product of social conditions, or is it possible that individual biological factors are also involved? After all, very few societies have ever been crime-free and gangs, mobs, and organized crime groups seem to have existed since the beginning of recorded history.

Motorcycle gangs have become very sophisticated in their activities and have extended their activities to the international arena (see Scaramella, Brenzinger, & Miller, 1997). In North America, the Hell's Angels have a very strong presence and are involved in many of the same activities regardless of their location (prostitution, illegal drug trade, money laundering, fraud, trafficking in weapons, and so on). It is believed that the Italian Mafia hires bikers as muscle men and hit men. The Mafia has also allegedly employed bikers to move drugs and carry out violent tactics such as bombings and arson (ibid.).

Police efforts to control outlaw motorcycle gangs have been limited, as evidenced in Montreal during the mid-1990s and the takeover of the Grim Reapers by the Hell's Angels in Alberta in the late 1990s. Other than harassing the bikers with various traffic violations as they ride into town, the police are unable to prevent the bike groups from going where they please and doing what they want. Yves Lavigna (1996), a noted Canadian expert on the Hell's Angels, describes the Angels and similar motorcycle gangs as North America's equivalent of the ethnic gangs commonly found in the underworld. Bikers have their own roots in what Lavigna calls "white trash"—the social outcasts and rebellious youths. Yet, just as most of the ethnic crime groups have evolved and become more sophisticated, so have the Hell's Angels. While groups like the Hell's Angels are spreading their power and influence into new territory, law enforcement agencies in provinces such as Alberta and Quebec are facing financial cutbacks and a dearth of investigators and tactical analysts (Slobodian, 2000). This makes it increasingly difficult for them to counter the spread of organized crime alone. The situation is further compounded by police forces having to deal with legal constraints and court rulings that are undermining some of their efforts (see Palango, 1997; Hall, 2004).

In spite of several successful law enforcement stings between 2000 and 2004, efforts to combat outlaw motorcycle gangs are hampered by the gangs' level of organization (Hall, 2004). The gangs consist of a vertical chain of command with at least three tiers. In addition, because of their organizational structure, they are able to continue operating despite a loss of key members. And, as is common among organized crime groups, they are prepared to use violence and bribery as a means of creating and maintaining their existence and monopoly over certain criminal activities (Scaramella,

Brenzinger, & Miller, 1997). Finally, organized motorcycle groups have a clearly defined set of rules and regulations that govern membership, making them both difficult to join and difficult for law enforcement to infiltrate (Abadinsky, 1994).

The only way to fight sophisticated crime is with sophisticated methods. This requires an integrated approach involving cooperation among all the elements of the criminal justice system and the input and support from society. Neither the police nor the law can on their own arrest the growth of organized criminal activities. Nevertheless, the Criminal Intelligence Service Canada (CISC) has made combating OMG a major priority, and the infusion of $584 million to the RCMP budget over three years should assist them in fighting organized crime (Smyth, 2001).

The Italian Mafia

Traditional Italian-based organized crime has been reported in every province, with particular strongholds in the major urban settings in southwestern Ontario and, to a lesser extent, in Calgary and Vancouver (Traditional..., 2004). Although the primary specialization of these groups has been drug trafficking, they have also been known to engage in illegal gambling, loan-sharking, union racketeering, counterfeiting, extortion, distribution of illicitly operated video poker machines, and money laundering (Beare, 1996). Of particular concern to law enforcement agencies is their "extensive investment in legitimate businesses. These operations are used to invest their profits, to serve in a money laundering capacity, and as a cover or front for criminal operations" (Beare, 1996:271).

It is believed that the Mafia originated during the ninth century on the island of Sicily, when Arab invaders tried to oppress the original inhabitants. To survive, the inhabitants sought refuge in the hills of the island. The word "Mafia" means "refuge" in Arabic (*Mafia history*, 1997). Subsequent attempts to force out the native inhabitants of the island led Sicilian families to form a secret society with its own infrastructure. Members were required to take an oath on initiation whose intention was to help create a sense of family based on ancestry and Sicilian heritage. To this day, the oath includes five fundamental principles:

- *Omerta*: A code of silence; that is, a vow never to reveal any Mafia secrets or expose Mafia members under the threat of torture or death.
- Total obedience to the boss, or "don."
- A promise to assist any befriended Mafia faction, no questions asked.
- A promise to avenge any attack on members of the family, because an attack on one is an attack on all.
- A vow to avoid any contact with the authorities (*Mafia history*, 1997).

The Mafia grew into a strong organization that relied on extortion and other forms of crime to gain what it needed. When Mafia members did not get their way, they resorted to violence to force compliance. Soon families began to compete for power and territory, leading to the emergence of organized crime families so often depicted in the movies. Al Capone, Charles "Lucky" Luciano, Bugsy Siegel, and Meyer Lansky have all been the subjects of various gangster movies.

Today in Italy, the Mafia poses a serious problem for the government. Its *modus operandi* has evolved over time; in recent years, for example, the Mafia has formed alliances with the Colombian cartels and outlaw motorcycle gangs as a means of facilitating international drug trafficking.

In spite of a few sensationalized cases in which "big-time" mobsters are arrested and prosecuted, efforts to weaken the influence of the Mafia in Canada have not been very successful (Traditional..., 2004) (see Box 10.9). When arrested, Mafia members usually get relatively light sentences by plea-bargaining, since they have access to the best legal talent available. While in prison, they tend to be model prisoners and are usually paroled as soon as they become legally eligible. Furthermore, because they are not placed in isolation, they are still able to continue their entrepreneurial activities. Better policing, the use of informants, and successful prosecution bring occasional success, but the impact has been minimal.

WHAT DO YOU THINK? BOX 10.9

INVESTIGATING MAFIA-RELATED INCIDENTS

In July 1997 in the Niagara Region, the powerful mob figure Carmen Barillaro was shot to death execution-style when he answered his door. Barillaro had been convicted of cocaine trafficking and had hired a woman to murder an ex-biker of the Outlaw biker gang over an outstanding drug debt. However, the woman turned informer and got Barillaro sentenced to three years.

While the killings appeared to be characteristic of a mob war, police were not able (or willing) to confirm such an association. They simply said, "our goal and intention is to solve the homicide," although there had been a series of other bombings and killings in the preceding months (Wilkes & Edwards, 1997). For interesting details on the Mafia, see Pierre de Champlain's 2004 book *Mobsters, Gangsters and Men of Honour: Cracking the Mafia Code*, published by Harper Collins Canada. Champlain is a RCMP intelligence analyst.

Explaining Organized Crime

We have examined a variety of organized crime groups in Canada and seen that organized crime is pervasive and has a dramatic impact on the social economy of the country. We have also noted that organized crime groups have become more sophisticated over the years as law enforcement and criminal justice efforts to counter organized crime have been introduced. In 1997, the Nathanson Centre for the Study of Organized Crime and Corruption was established at Osgoode Hall, the law school at York University, to study the growing problem in Canada.

Hackler (1994:308) notes that explanations of organized crime activities differ and observes that one approach is to describe and explain these activities as "cancers that invade and destroy healthy societies." Because of the economic consequences of most organized crime on governments, the cancer analogy is a popular interpretation. It enables governments to justify taking extreme measures, such as enacting the *War Measures Act*, passing special legislation to control outlaw motorcycle gangs, exercising special provisions for screening new immigrants, confiscating property, and so on. The assertion is that through aggressive crime control and intervention efforts, organized crime can be rooted out—or at least controlled.

Criminologists have also used a functionalist approach that sees organized crime as representing deficiencies in society. This approach emphasizes such factors as strain, blocked opportunity, and anomie (see Chapter 7). In this sociological tradition, organized crime is seen as a normal adaptive response to the structural organization of society. Of particular importance are: "(1) the division of labour, (2) the nature and distribution of occupational roles, and (3) the opportunities available to obtain them" (Einstadter & Henry, 1995:145).

For groups such as the Mafia, Colombia cartels, and Aboriginal crime groups—often relegated to the lower working class, without the same opportunities for upward mobility—the functionalist approach offers a plausible, albeit tenuous, explanation. However, the functionalist perspective does not explain crime groups such as the yakuza in Japan, the criminal tribes of India, and the roving pickpocket gangs of Paris (Hackler, 1994). Furthermore, social disorganization, anomie, and subcultural theories cannot readily explain gender differences within organized crime.

As a macro approach, the functionalist theories are good at focusing on the criminogenic conditions of societies, but they are less adept at explaining the more micro social processes by which individuals choose to become involved in organized crime. In addition, the functional perspective, in accordance with its principles, assumes that organized crime performs some function. However, this is a tautological argument and not necessarily true. For example, if organized crime is *dysfunctional* to the stability of society and the state, then it could be reasoned that it would eventually cease to exist rather than evolve and expand.

In terms of the criminogenic conditions, organized crime is fluid. Its existence is more dependent on public and official readiness to cooperate with its illegal activities than on legislation or lack thereof. As Potter (1994:147) observes, organized crime does not produce the desire for vice (e.g., taking drugs, viewing pornography, or prostitution); rather, "it merely fills an already existing social gap."

Should criminologists then study which vices might or should be legalized as a means of crime control? It is possible that organized crime does serve a functional symbiotic service, as governments are still able to operate with varying degrees of corruption? If we legalized drugs, pornography, prostitution, and other vices (other countries have experimented with such measures), would this serve to lessen organized crime's power and related problems? Whether such solutions would help or generate new problems is not clear, and it is the subject of considerable debate. However, criminologists could engage in comparative studies and evaluations involving countries that have legalized certain Canadian vices to see whether such measures might work. Kappler, Blumberg, and Potter (2004) point out that the very existence of laws against **consensual crimes**—that is, crimes in which otherwise law-abiding people are willing participants—simply serves to create the opportunity for organized crime, both nationally and internationally (see Box 10.10). Furthermore, it would also be prudent for researchers to engage in an integrated and interdisciplinary approach because organized crime is an evolving phenomenon that takes many forms. Criminologists need to view organized crime in terms of how society has structured its economic, political, and social resources to create an environment in which organized crime can both thrive and evolve.

A CLOSER LOOK BOX 10.10

THE EFFECTS OF GLOBALIZATION: TRANSNATIONAL CRIME

Until recently, organized crime has been largely a regional concern. However, with improvements in transportation, computers, and communications, organized criminal activity has increasingly become devoid of national borders. The more sophisticated and organized criminal syndicates have become involved **transnational crime**. The problem has become so evident that the United Nations now holds special sessions on transnational criminal activity. In 1998, members of the G8 summit labelled such activity one of the three major challenges facing the world today (Transnational criminal activity, 1998).

Organized Crime versus Governments: Is There a Difference?

As was noted above, the definition of organized crime is not clear; in many respects, it is socially and politically relative. For example, it could be argued the Crusades of the 11th–13th century were a form of organized crime. Although sanctioned by the Roman Catholic Church, they amounted to little more than groups of armed Christians invading Muslim lands to kill, steal, and rape. In recent years, the terrorist activities of various Islamic factions have been interpreted as a type of organized crime.

One person's fight for freedom may be seen by another as terrorist activities. Perhaps one of the most famous of all "terrorists" was the notorious guerrilla leader Ernesto "Che" Guevara (1928–1967), who after meeting Fidel Castro in 1954 became involved in the invasion of Cuba. The Baptista regime in Cuba described him as being involved in organized crime during his activist days. After Guevara left Cuba, he travelled the world and attempted to spread communism in Bolivia before being killed in 1967. In 1997, when his remains were returned to Cuba, he was treated as a national hero, and thousands lined up to pay their respects.

Governments have many of the same administrative, operational and organization traits as do organized crime groups. Hence, it is perhaps not surprising that some governments, or levels of government, sometimes engage in behaviour that is illegal. Like those of organized crime groups, illegal government activities are difficult to detect. Several examples that blur the line between governments and crime include the following:

- Various governments have used criminal elements for their own ends. Examples include the cooperation of the CIA and Mafia against Castro in the 1960s, Japan's use of yakuza to ensure the cooperation of construction workers, and General Chiang Kai-shek's rise to political power with assistance from the Green Gang of Shanghai (*Committee for a Safe Society*, 1997).

- The use of lotteries by governments has also been described as a legalized version of organized crime and number rackets. Although prizes are awarded, the value of the prizes or money given out is considerably less than the government makes from such ventures. Hence, the government profits considerably more than do those who participate in the lottery.

- Government officials in many parts of the world are routinely bribed or receive campaign funding from organized crime groups (e.g., in Colombia, the United States, Italy, and the Philippines).

- Governments in Nigeria, Cambodia, and Myanmar have been completely taken over by organized crime groups (*Committee for a Safe Society*, 1997).

- The RCMP paid Clifford Olson $100 000 for disclosing information about the murders he committed during the 1980s.

The activities in which certain organized crime groups are involved may not be so dissimilar from some of the activities in which governments engage. These differences may be more subjective than based on fact. The differences are *relative*, as both parties share many of the characteristics described under "Defining Organized Crime" above.

Whatever their similarity to government, organized crime groups are widespread and increasingly heedless of national boundaries. The economic impact of organized crime is far greater than that of conventional crime. Crime, and attempts to control it have done little to hamper its growth (Loree, 2004).

Corporate Crime

Although substance abuse can be classified as a crime against public order (see Chapter 11), consider the issue of alcohol marketing and availability in relation to corporate responsibility. According to the *Multinational Monitor* (2001), alcohol producers are luring young drinkers with sweet fruit-flavoured drinks that have bright, colourful labels and resemble the non-alcoholic drinks they are used to drinking. And even though some companies add warning labels related to drinking and driving, they take no responsibility for promoting the use of their product. For example, in 2002,

Transport Canada reported that almost 30 percent of those fatally injured were impaired at the time of the accident. Similarly, data on incarcerated Canadians reveal that a significant number of them have a substance abuse problem and/or were under the influence of alcohol when committing their offence.

In spite of these statistics, and depending on which province one lives in, various types of alcoholic spirits can be easily obtained at wine specialty stores. With the exception of Quebec, this was not always the case. Liquor sales used to be completely controlled by the Liquor Control Board stores across the provinces. However, in the 1970s and 1980s (depending on the province), wine specialty stores began to get licencing privileges, and then in the 1990s various provincial governments began to decentralize the operations of liquor stores. They saw an opportunity for free enterprise to take over, offering more employment opportunities and generating more revenue for provincial coffers.

Is this flagrant availability of a potentially dangerous drug an example of state corruption? Is it still possible for the government to ensure that underage youth do not gain easier access to alcoholic beverages? Should the provinces be allowed to place high taxes on a product that is the source of many social ills? Like organized crimes, corporate crimes are committed by powerful groups in society. Organized crime groups and corporate crime offenders share several of the characteristics identified by Abadinsky (1994), as discussed above, and both are interested in maximizing the profits of their organization. The difference is that corporations are legitimate and are run by high-status members of society.

Corporate crime involves illegal acts by big-business officials that benefit the corporation. As Kramer (1984:31) points out, it is "the result of deliberate decision making by persons who occupy structural positions within the organization. The organization makes decisions intentionally to benefit itself." Many of these officials hold prestigious social positions, and their individual incomes are well above the national per capita income. Yet, as Snider (1993:1) observes, "corporate crime ... actually does more harm, costs more money, and ruins more lives" than conventional crimes. Snider goes on to point out that more deaths result from corporate crimes in a month than all the deaths caused by mass murderers in a decade (see Box 10.11).

Corporate crime is a modern-day phenomenon. Only after the emergence of industrialization and the market economy was it possible for corporate crime to manifest itself. And it was not until Edwin Sutherland's ground-breaking 1949 book titled *White Collar Crime* that corporate crime became a subject of interest to criminologists (see Box 10.12). Sutherland's work was based on an analysis of the "life careers of the 70 largest U.S. manufacturing, mining, and mercantile corporations, examining the following legal violations: restraint of trade; misrepresentation in advertising; infringements of patents, trademarks, and copyrights; labour law violations; illegal rebates; financial fraud and violation of trust; violations of war regulations, and finally some miscellaneous offences" (Keane, 1996:282). The corporations studied averaged 19 judgments against them, with the maximum number being 50! The most common violation,

CANADIAN AND US EXAMPLES OF CORPORATE CRIMES

At the end of each year, the *Multinational Monitor*, founded by the renowned corporate watchdog **Ralph Nader**, publishes an annual survey on corporate crime in the United States. The following is a sample from the 2002 list.

- Between 2000 and 2004, a staggering number of significant business improprieties took place. Examples include front-loading income, improperly booking expenses, and insider trading. Among the noteworthy offenders were Enron, WorldCom, Global Crossing, Tyco, and ImClone.
- In 2002, Xerox was found guilty of using overseas bribery to gain business favours in India.
- In 2002, Merrill Lynch was found guilty of publicly touting stocks that they privately derided as "junk."
- In 2002, accounting scams and financial scams capped a US $5 trillion loss in market value. Carrigan (1991) compiled a list of Canadian companies that have committed an assortment of corporate crimes. The following is a cross-section of the cases and the penalties imposed, the first four in the 1980s and the remaining two in the 1990s.
  - Stone Consolidated Inc. was charged with spilling PCB-laced transformer oil; fined $35 000.
  - Shell Canada was charged with price fixing; fined $100 000.
  - Amway Canada was charged with tax evasion; settled lawsuit for $45 million.
  - Zellers Inc. in Nova Scotia was found guilty of listing sales prices above advertised levels; fined $35 000.
  - In 1999, Litton Systems was charged with fraud; fined $16.5 million (Mokhiber, 2003).
  - The Westray mine explosion in 1991 in Nova Scotia, which took the lives of 26 people, was found to be the result of corporate negligence, but by 1998 the courts had to drop several charges against some of the mine's managers. Since the bereaved family members of the miners received workman's compensation, the Supreme Court said they were not entitled to any further civil compensation, even if the Nova Scotia government was negligent in licensing and administering an unsafe mine (McMullan, 2004).

Yet, as one study recently found, Canada still remains relatively free of corruption. In a survey of 133 countries, Transparency International (2004) reports that Canada ranked as the ninth least corrupt country. Finland was the most honest, while Bangladesh was the most corrupt.

found in 60 companies, involved restraint of trade. Sutherland suggested that 90 percent of the corporations were habitual criminals and 97 percent were recidivists.

While corporate crime refers to criminal offences that are chargeable to a corporate entity, it involves the efforts of individual employees and officers—that is, white-collar offenders. Hence, **white-collar crime** refers to business-related crime such as embezzlement and other corporate-related offences. The offender uses his or her entrepreneurial or professional status for personal and/or corporate gain.

A CLOSER LOOK BOX 10.12

THE NATURE OF BUSINESS CRIME

In his 1939 presidential address to the American Sociological Society, Edwin Sutherland argued that criminologists needed to extend their focus beyond the study of crimes committed by the social underclass and look at those committed by the upper socioeconomic class and professions, which he referred to as *white-collar crimes*. These are crimes committed by respectable individuals who have high social status as part of their occupation for their own benefit (Rosoff et al., 2004). White-collar crime or professional crime involves the linkage of social status and prestigious occupational standing. Related to white-collar crime is corporate crime—also referred to as business crime and/or elite deviance—which involves employees in a business setting (e.g., Enron, ImClone, Xerox, etc.) intentionally engaging in "corporate illegalities on behalf of the corporation and in accordance with formally specified corporate goals" (Gomme, 1993:395). White-collar crime and corporate crime involve victims both directly and indirectly, but the legal system has had a difficult time trying to define, regulate, and prosecute such crimes.

Although Sutherland's methodology and definition of white-collar crime have been criticized (see Geis & Goff, 1982), his general findings have been replicated in more recent studies. For example, Clinard and Yeager (1980) studied 1553 federal files collected by government agencies. In addition, while virtually every kind of corporation was represented in their sample, the motor-vehicle industry accounted for half of the hazardous product violations.

Our economic history is rich with examples of corporate crime activities ranging from counterfeiting, embezzlement, forgery, and fraud to regulatory offences (see Snider, 2002). Yet until the pioneering work of Goff and Reasons (1978), Canadian criminologists virtually ignored this area of inquiry, since corporate crime was not seen as "real" crime and since conventional criminological theory was not oriented toward the study of white-collar crime.

Since Goff and Reasons' (1978) landmark study, however, there have been a number of other noteworthy studies conducted in an attempt to shed light on, and explain, Canadian corporate criminality (McMullan, 1992; Keane, 1996). Topics have included:

- Corporate violence against women (DeKeseredy & Hinch, 1991);
- The effectiveness of jurisdictional laws in protecting consumers and the labour force (Snider, 2002);
- The nature and impact of crimes against consumers and employees through such activities as price fixing, illegal mergers, industrial espionage, and environmental pollution (Goff & Reasons, 1986); and
- The origins of anti-combines legislation (Smandych, 1985) (see Box 10.13).

FYI BOX 10.13

REGULATING CORPORATE/BUSINESS CRIME

Most forms of white-collar crime are dealt with not as corporate crimes per se but simply as fraud or embezzlement, as defined under the *Criminal Code*. For the most part, regulatory agencies ranging from municipal governments to the federal government define corporate offences and monitor their violation. The primary jurisdictional body concerned with overseeing corporate transgressions is the Ministry of Consumer and Corporate Affairs.

Until 1986, the most important regulatory statute was the *Combines Investigation Act (CIA)*. Introduced in 1889, the act was intended to enable the state to protect consumers from unethical business practices such as price fixing, establishment of a market monopoly, pollution, and safety and health violations, among others. However, only two convictions were made under this act. In 1986, it was replaced with the *Competition Act.*

Cases now appear before a Competition Tribunal consisting of not more than six judicial members and not more than eight lay members. The minimum number of judges and lay people are two and one respectively. This tribunal decides whether a company has violated its monopoly powers. Cases are tried under civil law.

In 2004, the Competition Bureau responded to some 350 complaints of alleged price fixing by petroleum companies. At the time of preparing this chapter, no resolution had been reached on any of them! However, in the same year, PetNet was fined $150 000 for misleading thousands of pet owners through a deceptive mail campaign (PetNet..., 2004).

Canada is one of the 11 countries that comprise the G10: Belgium, Canada, France, Germany, Italy, Japan, the Netherlands, Sweden, Switzerland, the United Kingdom, and the United States. These countries consult and cooperate on economic, monetary, and financial matters. In 1997, the G10 attempted to establish international regulations for several international business operations (e.g., electronic banking). No consensus could be reached because of "the different approaches that various countries have taken to regulations in the field" (Pressman, 1997).

In examining the evolution of legislation aimed at preserving a competitive and free-enterprise system, researchers have observed how inept the government has been at enforcing the legislation. In a similar vein, Ralph Nader's Center for the Study of

Responsive Law points out that about 1 percent of the public owns 40 percent of the wealth, whereas the bottom 95 percent of the public owns as much as the top 1 percent!

Gordon and Coneybeer (1995:400) offer several general conclusions about corporate crime:

- The losses in materials, property damage, and physical injury are considerable. For example, Reasons, Ross, and Paterson (1981) noted that occupational deaths ranked third after heart disease and cancer. While not all occupational deaths could be directly associated with corporate wrongdoing or carelessness, the authors argue that these do account for a proportion of the deaths. An American study by Bohm (1986:195) estimated that "each year at least 10,000 lives are lost due to unnecessary surgeries, 20,000 to errors in prescribing drugs, 20,000 to doctors spreading diseases in hospital, 100,000 to industrial disease, 14,000 to industrial accidents, 200,000 to environmentally caused cancer, and an unknown number to lethal industrial products."

- Criminal law regulating corporate crime is poorly defined, and violators are usually dealt with outside the criminal justice system. Compensations and victim appeasement are common strategies. Perhaps the clearest example is the American and Canadian governments' attempt to take legal action against the tobacco industry. After considerable legal posturing, tobacco companies made a number of concessions. All cigarette packages now carry clear warnings about health hazards, and by around 2020 the industry will pay out US $360 million in North America, most of which will go to anti-smoking campaigns. In return, tobacco companies will never face class-action lawsuits (*Newsworld*, 1997, June 20). Yet tobacco is recognized as the number one cause of premature death and illness in the United States, costing US $52 billion in health care.

- Laws designed to prohibit certain forms of corporate behaviour are not only poorly enforced but are not effective deterrents.

- Because of their symbiotic relationship, governments usually work with corporations in constructing "appropriate" legislation and in determining measures to handle violators.

- The causes of corporate crime involve the complex interactions between individual, organizational, and social structural factors.

- High-quality investigations into corporate crimes by criminologists are stymied by a variety of methodological problems, such as limited access to funding and data and the complexities of corporate businesses.

Computer Crime: A New Form of Corporate Crime

As we have observed, corporate crime is both highly profitable and relatively risk-free, and it appears to be growing. One of its more recent forms is computer crime. Although many computer crimes involve some form of theft, this type of crime is addressed in this chapter because the victims and/or offenders often involve businesses. In general, **computer crime** is any crime that involves the use of computer equipment and technology as the means of committing the crime. Commonly known forms of computer crime include:

Unauthorized access to networks and their data: Knowledge is power. Gaining access to protected information—whether that of an individual or a corporation—can be used to gain an illegal advantage. When corporations engage in this type of computer crime, it is referred to as *industrial espionage*. Companies have been known to hire "cyberspies" or "cyberpirates" to illegally access information from a competitor's system without leaving any trace of intrusion. For example, in July 2004, Air Canada accused WestJet of engaging in cyberspying. Relying on powerful and sophisticated technology, cyberspies can operate from virtually anywhere, making detection extremely difficult.

Another version of unauthorized access and use is *software piracy*. Have you ever obtained a copy of software from a friend and put it onto your computer? The duplication process is relatively simple. More sophisticated piracy ventures might involve individuals or businesses copying software and then selling it as the original product—usually at a lower price. For some of the ways of preventing unauthorized access to data, see Box 10.14.

FYI BOX 10.14

PREVENTING ACCESS TO DATA

One of the techniques used to prevent access to sensitive data involves *physical security*, such as key-operated hard disks and removable storage media. Another is *screen blanking*, in which the screen at a data entry station goes blank if left unattended for a fixed period of time (Carter, 1995). Yet another method is the use of *passwords* or other forms of identification. Most of us use a secret password and can set a limit on the number of wrong entries before the system shuts down. More advanced systems use optical imaging (eyeball scanner) to recognize the owner's network of blood vessels on the retina (Dolu, 2004). *Data encryption methods* involve using either hardware or software to convert information into gibberish until it is decoded by authorized users. Did you ever learn to write backward or use pig Latin? Data encryption is the same sort of thing, just more sophisticated.

Willful destruction of data: If you use a computer, you have most likely heard of those dreaded computer viruses. Hackers may be lay people or professionals with advanced computer programming skills (see Box 10.15). Remember the Melissa virus planted by David Smith in March 1999? Smith disguised the virus as an email message marked "important message" from a friend. A more recent example is the Klez virus, which arrived as an email attachment, or the W32.Sober.I@mm in 2004, which started

HACKERS

Computer hackers can do a lot of damage. For example:

- In 1998, a 22-year-old Sudbury man was charged with hacking into NASA's computer system and in one case causing more than $70 000 in damage (Police make arrest..., 1998).
- In 1995, Kevin Mitnick was arrested and charged with breaking into the system of an internet provider and stealing more than 20 000 credit-card numbers.

Who are computer hackers? An Australian-based survey revealed some interesting findings. Based on a sample of 101 respondents from around the world, Bavinton (1998) found that:

- Less than 4 percent of hackers were women.
- Respondents were between 12 and 54 years of age. The average age was 22.
- The majority of respondents indicated that they hacked for the challenge, curiosity, fun, and thrill. They were not the demented cybernerds typically depicted in the media.
- 82 percent said stricter criminal laws would not serve as an effective deterrent.
- 78 percent said more prosecutions would also not serve as an effective deterrent.
- The majority did not see their hacking activity as criminal as long as they were not doing "any harm."

Since part of the act of hacking involves a challenge, hackers will always try to keep ahead of the technology. As a result, no matter what deterrents or preventive strategies are used, there are new viruses to be aware of all the time. Some internet providers warn their customers, if they are able to find out about the virus. In addition, there are software programs that have anti-virus detection devices. The more sophisticated programs provide free downloads for virus updates. Yet Zuckerman (2000) reports that some 70 percent of systems professionals reported being victims of computer crimes.

But not all hackers are bad—there are those who actually help ensure the security of networks. Doing business is a competitive enterprise, corporations and governments believe it is necessary to protect their interests, and many companies spend considerable sums of money trying to ensure that their networks are secure. In 1992, a company was set up in Calgary to test the security of networks. M-Tech employs professional hackers who are paid by companies to try to break their security systems. The company prefers to use the terms "penetration testing" and "ethical hacking" to describe its activities (Knapp, 1998).

in November 2004 and averaged almost 10 000 complaints per day worldwide. Today, new viruses emerge virtually on a daily basis. Viruses can be spread from one computer to another through disk swapping, using pirated or counterfeit software, or over access lines that link computers to another source. Some hackers might use their skills to access networks and plant a set of hidden instructions that cause the computer to destroy its data or alter information.

Data manipulation: Data manipulation may be one of the most serious forms of computer crime. It involves unauthorized entry into computer files and subsequent modification of data. The late 1980s movie *The Net* depicts a scenario in which a computer user accesses the internet, accidentally discovers confidential information, and uses it to create havoc. Shortly after the release of the movie, an article in *Maclean's* magazine reported on the real-life risk of international terrorism being conducted with computers. The article notes that banks already transfer several trillion dollars around the world each day—money that is potential prey for technologically sophisticated computer criminals (Crime in the computer age, 1988).

Data manipulation can range from students accessing their school grades and modifying them to criminals accessing data banks of big companies and stealing files and/or money. An area of data manipulation that has posed a major challenge for law enforcement agencies has been child pornography on the internet. Those who post such information on the internet can use sophisticated technology to strategically hide and alter images (a technique referred to as *morphing*), making detection and apprehension difficult.

Combatting Computer Crime

Legally, ss. 342.1 and 430 of the Canadian *Criminal Code* define computer crime as involving destruction, altering data, rendering data meaningless, and/or interfering with someone using legitimate data. However, as noted above, the likelihood of apprehending and prosecuting offenders is very slim. Aside from using sophisticated technology, offenders tend to be well-educated, highly skilled, and generally young.

Law enforcement resources are limited. There is a dearth of RCMP members who are trained in computer-related crime techniques, and only about one-half are assigned to commercial crime units across Canada. Members are trained to provide technical guidance and expertise on techniques known to the offenders—but, unfortunately, once an offence has been recognized, it is usually too late.

Although the intentions of computer criminals are in many cases similar to those of property offenders—namely, financial gain—their crimes tend to be far more costly and more difficult to detect. Law enforcement agencies don't have the resources to effectively combat computer-based crimes, and criminal law does not appear to be an effective deterrent—taking a "byte" out of crime, so to speak.

Computer crimes provide excellent support to the argument that traditional intervention and prevention strategies are both outmoded and ineffective. What is needed is an integrated and interdisciplinary approach that redefines our cultural structure by drawing on the ideas presented in Chapter 7. As Barak (1997) argues, we are all capable of adapting, changing, growing, and "reintegrating" in a manner that will help redefine our social contract so that we will all want to work toward eliminating crime. Currently, many businesses, for example, are reluctant to report being victims of computer crime, likely fearing bad publicity. However, by so doing, they further isolate themselves from community support and involvement.

Organized and Corporate Crime: Cut from the Same Cloth?

We have examined two different forms of crime by the powerful in society, noting that they share some common operational goals and motivations. The primary difference between the two is that most organized crime involves participants from the middle and lower classes, while corporate crime participants often come from the upper class and are esteemed members of society. However, in their efforts to explain the crimes of the powerful, criminologists have found a number of other characteristics that suggest that the participants in both of these kinds of crime share one important characteristic—they have criminal propensities. While one might wonder why someone in a position of power would engage in criminal activity, these types of criminals, like others, simply choose to capitalize on their position and power—as the opportunity theory suggests—for a range of real or perceived pragmatic reasons. Unlike those involved in organized crime, however, corporate offenders operate under a guise of public trust and legitimacy (Webb, 2004).

Although no direct comparison has been made, research shows that participants in organized crime begin their criminal careers early in life, while white-collar criminals begin their careers a little later (Weisburd, Chayet, & Waring, 1990). Weisburd et al. (1990) also found that white-collar criminals are often repeat offenders. Recidivism rates varied from 10 percent for bank embezzlers to 46 percent for credit-card offenders. Similarly, corporate offenders also tend to be repeat offenders, since enforcement, prosecution, and deterrence are difficult to carry out effectively (Goff & Reasons, 1978).

But why exactly would a big successful company risk engaging in criminal activity when it appears to have so much going for it?

Explaining Corporate Crime

In his landmark 1949 book, Edwin Sutherland used his theory of differential association (see Chapter 7) to explain white-collar crime. The theory, however, emphasizes the individual rather than the organization, which—given the general definition of corporate crime—poses a conceptual problem. Therefore, as Clinard and Quinney (1973) suggested, Sutherland's theory is more applicable for explaining *occupational crimes*—that is, crimes in which a person takes advantage of his or her occupation, such as fraud, embezzlement, and theft. Is there any real difference between occupational crime and corporate crime? Do criminologists need to make a distinction? Without an individual to initiate it, a crime cannot take place. Hirschi and Goffredson (1989) appear to recognize this point when they suggest that criminologists do not need a separate theory of crime to explain corporate or white-collar crime.

One possible solution is for criminologists to use a narrower definition of white-collar crime, by limiting the term to the realm of corporate or business crime, and to regard crimes committed by individuals as common-law property offences. Accepting this line of reasoning would require using an organizational theory that considers the factors that make up the environmental setting of the corporation, such as market competition, organizational stratification, and profit motivation. The objective of organizational theory is to understand what determines the variations within a business setting that allow it to engage in illegal activities.

In contrast, the conflict perspective focuses on "external factors of influence" (Keane, 1996:283). According to this perspective, businesses in a market economy are motivated to maximize profit, ensure perpetual growth, monopolize their market, and have free rein over their operations. Government regulations only serve to restrict natural growth. From a conflict perspective, capitalism contains the seeds of its own destruction. The price of success for corporations is to "run a tight ship" so as to maximize their profits. So, while companies may not intentionally set out to cause harm, there will always be trade-offs, since the pressure to succeed and excel can create conflict, prompting some to engage in social deviations.

In her book on corporate crime, Snider (1993) argues that the interests of corporations and the state are not always compatible and this can, and does, lead to the creation of distorted public images of "big business." For example, governments are sensitive to public pressure for job creation and keeping unemployment rates down. These are usually major issues during election campaigns. In 1997, then BC premier Glen Clark offered the lumber industry financial incentives to create more jobs. However, as the lumber industry has become more mechanized in an effort to compete on the international market, it has not needed to employ more people to support itself.

On the other hand, government regulatory bodies have served as watchdogs to minimize the risk of corporations destroying the environment in their zeal to make profits. For example, these bodies have been instrumental in drafting regulations restricting clear-cut logging, setting limits on how close to rivers and streams loggers can cut, setting catch limits for the fishing industry, requiring pollution controls to be placed on emission devices, etc. Corporations now have to engage in a balancing act between meeting social and environmental obligations and conducting business (see Box 10.16).

Another theory that has a certain level of appeal in explaining corporate crime is Sykes and Matza's (1957) theory of **neutralization**. In his chapter on corporate crime, Carl Keane (1996:228–229) offers a concise account of how the techniques of neutralization can be applied to the way corporations can justify illegal behaviour. We will use the tobacco industry as an example of how the culprit might neutralize any responsibility. The following are the main neutralization techniques:

- *Denial of responsibility*: The tobacco industry does not force people to smoke its cigarettes—smoking is an individual choice. The industry is simply satisfying a market demand. It places warnings on its packages.

THE DELICATE BALANCING ACT—THE "GOOD" CORPORATE CITIZEN

- Lake Erie was almost totally void of life because of pollution in the 1960s and 1970s. Today, because of the work of regulatory bodies, the lake has returned to life.
- Acid rain from pollutants emitted from factories in the 1970s was destroying lakes across Canada. New regulations have helped curb the trend.
- In Newfoundland, the Grand Banks and other rich fishing holes were being depleted until the fisheries ministry stepped in and placed a moratorium on the fishing industry (Carrigan, 1991).
- Many companies use sound, ethical business practices. For example, The Body Shop and many financial institutions use a percentage of their profits to support environmental causes.
- Do corporations become involved in various environmental and social causes because they are concerned corporate citizens or because they want to present an image behind which they can deflect their preoccupation with making more money? This question is often difficult to answer. One clear-cut case, however, is that of Ted Turner, vice-chairman of Time Warner Inc. and founder of CNN. In September 1997, Turner pledged to donate one billion dollars to the United Nations over the following 10 years. The money is going to United Nations humanitarian programs (*Newsworld*, 1997, September 19).

- *Denial of injury*: There has never been conclusive evidence proving that tobacco causes cancer. Millions of smokers have lived long and healthy lives and died of natural causes. Deaths may be attributed to other related factors. By placing warning ads on packages, the industry is fulfilling its legal obligation to warn people of the possible hazards.
- *Denial of victim*: Not all smokers die of lung cancer. If they are smokers and die, it is probably because they were predisposed to getting lung cancer.
- *Condemnation of the condemners*: Why does the government focus on cigarettes when alcohol, sugar, fast cars, and many other products are major potential risks? (This is the "everyone is corrupt" defence.)
- *Appeal to higher loyalties*: When the tobacco industry was under attack, a number of people pointed out that the government had been quite happy for years to collect the revenue generated from the high taxes levied on cigarettes. The tobacco industry was supporting the economy. Is it not hypocritical to sanction this industry and yet continue to profit from its profits? Who is the real offender?

Criminologist Stanley Cohen (2001) used the term "culture of denial" to describe the fact that there is virtually no information (official or unofficial) on corporate crime. Moreover, when someone is caught and charged, the penalty is nominal. For example, after the 1989 *Exxon Valdez* oil spill in Alaska, Exxon was not forced out of business. Similarly, in spite of the overwhelming evidence linking tobacco to cancer, tobacco companies are allowed to continue business. The list goes on.

The various explanations of corporate crime have focused on micro- or macro-level external, internal, or individual factors impinging on how organizations conduct their business. Each approach has its strengths but also its limitations. For example, although neutralization techniques have appeal, they do not in themselves explain crime. Therefore, as some investigators have suggested, a more prudent approach might be to synthesize these findings in an integrated format.

Keane (1996) suggests that one of the underlying themes of most explanations is the concept of *stress*. The idea of stress could be used, for example, to link the micro- and macro-level external, internal, and individual elements. Strain is an external factor as corporations strive to compete in an open market. Internal stress is expressed by the owners and employees as they try to conduct business within the confines of existing regulations. Individual stress can result from the potential risk of failure or shutdown. In other words, the causes of corporate crime are as involved and as complex as operating a successful corporation.

A more realistic way to integrate macro and micro elements is to apply an interdisciplinary approach. As much as we might want to analyze corporate crime at an organizational level that consists of external, internal, and individual factors, the white-collar offender is still a biological and psychological individual. Without *mens rea* and *actus reus*—which only an individual can possess and effect—there can be no crime. The only difference between conventional types of crime and corporate crime is that the offender commits the crime within the organizational structure of the corporation. Therefore, when studying corporate crime, criminologists must adapt an interdisciplinary approach and integrate biological, psychological, social, and legal levels of analysis.

Regulating Corporate Crime

There is little doubt that corporate crime has a major social and economic impact. What is more difficult to agree on is how the state should respond to this type of crime. With regard to corporate crime, the state follows traditional punishment rationales of retribution and just deserts—but should it prosecute the individual offender or the corporation? Or should prosecution involve the individual *and* the corporation? In addition, is the traditional approach of shaming the offender effective (see Box 10.17)?

Attempts to control corporate crime are further complicated by the interests of the state. For example, as noted above, penalizing the tobacco industry would result in considerable loss of government revenue. So would prohibiting video lottery terminals and lottery tickets, as these generate millions of dollars every year. Yet in sanctioning such activities, the state opens the way for people to become addicted to these vices, and many end up ruining their lives to support their habit.

The criminal justice system has been, and continues to be, largely reactive in its approach to economic crimes. Economic crimes happen because criminals are proactive

SHAME ON YOU!

In 1989, **John Braithwaite** introduced his theory of **reintegrative shaming** in *Crime, Shame, and Reintegration*. This approach has been described both as a general theory of crime and as an integrative explanation of crime. The theory combines elements of "labeling, subcultural, control, opportunity, and learning—the positive and negative aspects of lawbreakers" (Barak, 1997:203).

According to Braithwaite, not all forms of social disapproval are the same. Braithwaite distinguishes between *disintegrative shaming* and *reintegrative shaming*. The former is negative in orientation and does not provide the offender with any opportunity to make amends for his or her behaviour. This type of shaming usually results in driving the offender into further acts of deviance or crime. Reintegrative shaming involves efforts to bring offenders back into the community. While the offender is expected to experience some shame around his or her behaviour, it is through the efforts of community involvement that the offender is given an opportunity to reintegrate. The general concept works well in homogeneous societies such as Japanese society, Aboriginal communities, and other "communitarian" societies that are characterized by a high degree of concern for the welfare of others.

Braithwaite's ideas have been applied in many settings. One of the earliest studies related to corporate crime involved interviews with 70 offenders who had been convicted of a corporate crime. Benson (1990) found that most of the offenders experienced disintegrative shaming, usually at the hands of the media. While reintegrative shaming has been adapted into restorative justice–based programs for conventional crimes and youth, there is little evidence that it has been used in relation to white-collar offenders.

and are able to take advantage of opportunities. In order to regulate corporate crime, criminologists and criminal justice agencies must learn to be sensitive to international issues, differences in law, differences in law enforcement, changing technology, and market and social trends. For example, the ways in which different countries respond to corporate offenders vary. According to Hackler (1994), government tolerance is less common in Australia, Britain, Japan, and Sweden, while in the United States and Canada corporations have a tendency to resist regulation.

In summary, the economic, social, and political implications of corporate crimes are often far reaching, and yet the public is usually not well informed about these crimes. Unfortunately, methodological problems make the study of this type of crime particularly difficult. Criminologists and policy-makers have a tall order in front of them. At present, we are ill-equipped to address economically motivated crime (Kappler, Blumberg, & Potter, 2004). The state cannot financially afford to combat the spread of these types of crimes, and criminal justice systems, by themselves, have been slow to change their traditional—and failed—approaches. It is time to look beyond our parochial views. In order to combat these crimes, criminologists and criminal justice agencies must collaborate and share their ideas. In addition, since single explanations and strategies will never work, an integrated and interdisciplinary approach will be required.

Summary

- Organized crime and corporate crime—or simply economic crimes of the elites— are difficult to define. They are subject to change with the passage of time and are often culturally relative, which further complicates the gathering of information and enforcement.
- While organized crime and corporate crime differ in many ways, their *modus operandi* are very similar. Both share the motive of economic gain through illegal means; both strive to monopolize the economy; and both resort to varying forms of threats, intimidation, and deceptions to succeed. As well, the organizational structure of many organized crime groups mirrors the business model.
- Organized crime is becoming increasingly diverse within countries as well as more transnational in its dimensions, coinciding with improved technology and communications.
- The rapid expansion of governments and corporations has given rise to an increase in organized crime and corporate crime.
- Traditionally, sociological theories have been used to explain organized crime and corporate crime, but they have had limited success. Criminology must extend its approach to embrace an integrated and interdisciplinary perspective as well as adopt an international and comparative view of organized and corporate crimes.

Discussion Questions

1. What are the similarities and differences between organized crime and corporate crime?

2. Should organized crime and corporate crime be treated differently than conventional crimes (robbery, murder, theft, etc.)?

3. Why is it difficult to detect and prosecute organized crime and corporate crime offenders?

4. Why is it better to apply an interdisciplinary approach to the study of organized and corporate crime?

5. Do outlaw motorcycle gangs serve a useful function in society? Aside from these gangs' level of organization, why can authorities not stop the expansion of these organized groups? What should criminologists focus on when studying such groups in order to offer sound advice?

Key Concepts

Aboriginal crime groups

consensual crimes

neutralization

transnational crime

cartel

corporate crime

organized crime

white-collar crime

computer crime

illicit market

reintegrative shaming

Key Names

Howard Abadinsky

Ralph Nader

John Braithwaite

Weblinks

www.yorku.ca/nathanson/Links/links.htm The website of the Nathanson Centre for the Study of Organized Crime and Corruption at York University offers a comprehensive bibliographical database search engine, as well as many informative links.

www.rcmp-grc.gc.ca/crimint/sparkplug_e.htm The RCMP's organized crime and automobile theft page provides an excellent overview of the topic.

mafiasite.8m.com This page about the Mafia contains some offensive information but is nevertheless worth the educational visit.

multinationalmonitor.org The website of the *Multinational Monitor*, a watchdog magazine of corporate crimes contains interesting articles on the topic and every year publishes a list of the 10 worst companies around the world.

CHAPTER 11

Crimes Against Public Order

"The greatest happiness of the greatest number is the foundation of morals and legislation."

Jeremy Bentham (1742–1832)

Learning Outcomes

After you have completed this chapter, you should be able to:

- Recognize the relationship between law and morality.

- Be familiar with the various types of public order offences.

- Be familiar with the characteristics and nature of public order offences such as gambling, prostitution, pornography, and substance abuse.

- Have an awareness of the implications of public order offences on society.

- Appreciate the difficulty in regulating public order offences.

In earlier chapters, we discussed several of the important elements of crime. We also observed that the criminalization of certain behaviours is *relative* and *evolutive*. Perceptions of what constitutes "wrongful" behaviour vary widely throughout society. That is, there is little consensus as to what behaviours should be classified as criminal as opposed to being seen as *deviant* or simply as constituting *social diversions*.

Within criminology, certain acts are often referred to as public order crimes—or by a variety of other names, such as consensual crimes, victimless vices, or victimless crimes. The term "victimless crime" is somewhat confusing, in that it implies that there is no complaining victim; for this reason, some criminologists question whether or not these acts should be considered criminal. **Public order crimes** are usually characterized as

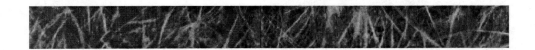

victimless crimes because they involve a degree of compliance by the victim. Public order crimes are based on moral principles and are consequently subject to controversy. They include gambling, prostitution, pornography, substance abuse, vandalism and graffiti, and some hate crimes.

Law and Morality

"Good laws lead to the making of better ones; bad ones bring about worse." J.J. Rousseau (1712–1778)

Consider the following questions:

- If it is legal to buy lottery tickets, why are other forms of gambling considered illegal?
- If it is legal to have intimate relations with partners of one's choice, why is it illegal to pay someone for such services?
- If Charter rights guarantee freedom of speech and press, why are some forms of music censored and/or sanctioned?
- It is legal to watch most forms of exotic dancing, yet in March 1997 the Supreme Court declared lap dancing to be illegal and indecent. Is there a discernable difference between suggestive behaviour as opposed to overt sexual expression?
- If women are allowed to sell their eggs for profit (to donor banks), why is the public at large not permitted to sell organs?
- The Bible implies that God destroyed the ancient cities of Sodom and Gomorrah because their residents engaged in deviant behaviour and supposed homosexual practices (see Box 11.1). Why is the practice of homosexual behaviour legal today when public support is mixed?

FYI BOX 11.1

HOMOSEXUALITY

Prior to 1968, homosexuality was a punishable crime in Canada. Because of social and cultural changes in the 1950s and 1960s, Bill C-150 was passed, legalizing the practice of homosexuality. For some years after, homosexuality was viewed as a disease rather than a crime (Duhaime, 1996). Since mid-1996, Alberta, Ontario, British Columbia, and Nova Scotia have granted restricted rights to gays and lesbians (Religious tolerance, 2003).

The primary purpose of the law is to protect society by legislating behaviours that society at large considers immoral and socially harmful. However, what is the foundation of morality? Surely, as the German philosopher Immanuel Kant (1724–1804) argued, morality cannot rely on religious doctrines. Rather, according to more recent philosophers such as Rauhut (2004), morality must be established on grounds that can withstand skeptical challenges and enrich the lives of all.

These philosophical points have been the subject of many debates. How does one determine whether an act presents a clear and immediate harm to all those who partake? For example, how should criminology respond to certain acts that take place between consenting individuals (e.g., gambling, prostitution, and euthanasia)? Answers to the above questions are complicated due to an assortment of related variables. How old are the participants? Is there a greater social and moral issue at stake? For example, does allowing prostitutes to walk the streets send an inappropriate message to young impressionable people? Does it promote the entry of the homeless and runaways into prostitution as a means of survival? Does it result in their unnecessary exploitation? These are questions of morality for which there are no clear-cut answers. As will be discussed throughout this chapter, it is uncertain whether criminal law can be effectively used to regulate these subjective behaviours.

Since antiquity, social conventions and rules of etiquette have been the guiding principles for maintaining social harmony. As societies evolved, they needed to codify their norms and values in order to maintain a sense of social harmony. This codification resulted in the creation of formal criminal law. Law can be interpreted as subscribing to one of two general theoretical orientations—the consensus model or the conflict perspective—which are not necessarily mutually exclusive.

Among criminologists who subscribe to the consensus model (see Figure 1–1, p. 11), laws are seen as representing the interests (i.e., needs and values) of a given society. Conversely, those criminologists who adopt a conflict perspective interpret laws as representing the interests of the vocal minority and those who are in a position of power.

The architects of the Canadian Constitution recognized a dilemma inherent in the law. In formulating the Constitution, they attempted to strike a balance between respecting natural law (i.e., utilitarian principles) and the relative and evolving nature of social norms and values. The balance between protecting the public from certain behaviours and not limiting the freedoms guaranteed in the Charter is the rich domain of legal scholars. In general, public order crimes are determined by legal jurisprudence. A number of criminology programs, most law schools, and some political science programs offer courses on the history of criminological thought that usually address some of public order crimes and social concerns.

From a criminological (primarily sociological perspective) standpoint, criminal prohibitions have their roots in the social forces of society. In courses on the sociology of law, for example, students explore the forces and elements that contribute to the formation of criminal law. Among the aspects studied are the moral entrepreneurs who campaign to have their values legitimized and embodied in law. Canadian examples include the prohibition movement, environmental groups such as Greenpeace and the Sierra Club, abortion activists, gay and lesbian groups, and hemp growers and users. Although these groups do not represent a majority or necessarily hold high social positions, many have gained a voice by using various laws, along with appeals to public sympathy, in an attempt to have their rights protected.

The tension between social order and individual freedoms is one that is unlikely to be resolved in our multi-ethnic, multicultural, and pluralistic society. We will now examine four different types of public order crimes: gambling, prostitution, pornography, and substance abuse.

Gambling

"Gambling is not a healthy commercial activity. It is an activity that shows a society is morally bankrupt." Marie Lucie Spoke (Citizens Against Gambling Expansion), 1998.

Have you ever bought a lottery or a raffle ticket? Have you ever been to a casino, played bingo, or participated in nambling (net gambling)? Have you ever made a bet with a friend, at the track, or with yourself? If you are like most people, you have probably participated in one or more of these activities "just for fun" (see Box 11.2). However, why are some forms of gambling considered socially acceptable and quite innocent while other forms have been prohibited by law? What is the point of the dress code in casinos? What does the law say about gambling?

Gambling and the Law

Gambling in the Canadian *Criminal Code* is covered under ss. 197–210 and is referred to as "gaming and betting." But the line between what is defined as acceptable chance-taking and what is defined as illegal has become less clear since the late 1960s, when certain types of lottery sales were legally approved. Since then, increasingly, many forms of gambling are being legalized. Why? Some of the reasons are as follows:

- Legalization undermines the exploitation of gambling by organized crime groups.
- The public has become more tolerant with regard to a variety of vice crimes, including gambling. Today, it is possible to buy lottery tickets in every province and territory, and legally operating casinos have been established in various places.
- Federal, provincial, and municipal governments can use gambling venues to generate much-needed revenue. For example, First Nations peoples have been granted the right to run casinos in most provinces. A 2001 survey by Aboriginal Tourism showed that casinos generated $4.9 billion for First Nations people.

Are the legislative bodies preying on human weakness? Moral entrepreneurial groups such as Gamblers Anonymous and the Canadian Foundation on Compulsive

IS IT JUST FOR FUN OR IS IT SOMETHING MORE SERIOUS?

AADAC Gambling Test

1. In the past 12 months, have you:
   - ☐ played bingo
   - ☐ bet on sporting events
   - ☐ purchased lottery tickets
   - ☐ played games of skill for money (e.g., cards)
   - ☐ played slot machines, video lottery machines (poker machines)
   - ☐ gambled in a casino
   - ☐ gambled at the track (include off-track betting as well)
   - ☐ participated in any other form of gambling?

2. In the past 12 months, have you spent more money than you intended on any of these activities?
   - ☐ Yes   ☐ No

3. In the past 12 months, has your involvement in the above activities created financial difficulties for you or your family?
   - ☐ Yes   ☐ No

4. In the past 12 months, has anyone expressed concern about your involvement in these activities?
   - ☐ Yes   ☐ No

5. In the past 12 months, have you been concerned about your involvement in these activities?
   - ☐ Yes   ☐ No

If you answer "yes" to any one of questions 2–5, or if you show significant gambling activity in question 1 but answer "no" to questions 2–5, further assessment is recommended. All provinces have an AADAC office and most have a Gambling Help Line.

Source: Lesieur, H.R. & Blume, S.B. (1987). South Oaks Gambling Screen (SOGS): *A new instrument for the identification of pathological gamblers*. American Journal of Psychiatry, 144(9), 1184–1188. Adaptation by Alberta Alcohol and Drug Abuse Commission (AADAC) (www.aadac.com).

Gambling, along with many religious groups, warn against the temptation and vice of gambling. While their reasoning may differ, they all agree that the harm done to families and individuals and the impact of gambling on crime are serious issues.

Characteristics and Trends

- Three-quarters of adult Canadians spent money on some form of gambling in 2002 (*The Daily*, 2003).

- In 2002, $11.3 billion was spent on lotteries (including video lottery terminals, lottery tickets, bingo, and slot machines), by approximately 18.9 million adult Canadians (*The Daily*, 2003) (see Box 11.3).
- Stinchfield and Winters (1997) found that 61 percent of adult gamblers were male, 16 percent were college graduates, 66 percent were employed full-time, and 49 percent had previously sought assistance for their gambling problem. The average age of those who gambled was 39.
- According to the 2002 Canadian Community Health Survey, 1.2 million Canadians were at risk of a gambling problem or were compulsive gamblers (*The Daily*, 2003).

WHAT DO YOU THINK? BOX 11.3

VLTs

In 1998, several Alberta MLAs suggested that one solution to the problem of numerous video lottery terminal (VLT) outlets throughout the province would be to limit their presence to casinos. In June of 1998, Ontario announced that it was opening four giant casinos that include VLTs. Three of the casinos border the United States—hoping to lure American gamblers the way Niagara Falls and Windsor already do (Welsh & Donavan, 1998). A 2003 study found that at least 25 percent of VLT users were either at-risk or problem gamblers (Smith & Wynne, 2004). What do you think about VLTs in general?

Today, every province sponsors local lotteries, and the federal government is involved in sponsoring several national lotteries. As Walker (1994, cited in Barkan, 1997:449) notes, "the old moralist objections have collapsed" as the line between legalized gambling and illegal gambling, in many respects, has been reduced to mere legal discourse.

A recent news article observed that cash-starved Atlantic provinces were looking for ways to capitalize on legalized gambling. In the article, the auditor general of the Atlantic Lottery Corporation was quoted as saying that the lottery industry was a "cash cow" for the Eastern provinces. For example, New Brunswick, with its 3588 gambling machines, generated $82 million in 1996; Nova Scotia, with its 2573 machines, generated $105 million; Newfoundland generated $74 million from its 2084 machines; and Prince Edward Island managed a profit of $14 million from 621 machines. The article went on to point out that although New Brunswick has the most machines, it does not generate the most money. Suggestions were made about how to improve this ratio.

As we saw in Chapter 10, many organized crime groups are heavily involved in gambling-related activities (sometimes referred to as the "numbers racket"). Any attempt to estimate the amount of profit organized crime groups make from illegal gambling activities is sheer speculation. Criminal justice agencies are aware of the extent of the problem and prefer instead to direct their attention to understanding and curbing it. The recent liberalization of gambling laws throughout North America has reduced organized crime's income from gambling. In response, organized crime groups have turned to other illegal pursuits, such as extortion, illicit drugs, immigration fraud, money laundering, and pornography.

What is sometimes overlooked when presenting raw data on gambling are the moral consequences of gambling. What is the social impact? What kind of spinoff consequences might result? What is the impact on organized crime?

Now that many forms of gambling have been legalized, more people have become problem gamblers, and the negative social effects have escalated accordingly. Although there are no hard data, there is sufficient research to demonstrate that gambling is a social vice that threatens public order, increases health care costs, and increases criminal activity.

Those individuals who experience serious gambling problems are sometimes referred to as compulsive gamblers. Their problem is generally seen as symptomatic of an emotional or behavioural disorder—low self-esteem, inability and/or unwillingness to accept reality, immaturity, or obsessive behavioural patterns. While the indicators of compulsive gambling behaviour are dependent on varying environmental, psychological, and social factors, it is possible to identify certain warning signs (see Box 11.2).

In 1995, it was reported that in Alberta there were an estimated 100 000 people who are "slaves" to gambling. Of those who sought help, many said that the VLTs provided them with an escape from reality that became addictive. In one reported case, an individual spent nearly five hours in his van with a gun and a ski mask trying to get up enough courage to rob a local pub to recover all the rent and food money he had gambled away on VLTs (When it's ..., 1995). Fortunately, he finally turned himself in. Such stories are not isolated examples. Yet, in spite of the fact that two-thirds of Albertans oppose VLTs, they have not been removed or declared illegal.

Gambling is seen as a social problem, and problem gamblers require attention. In January 1957, Gamblers Anonymous (GA) was formed to help people deal with their compulsion to gamble. GA operates on the premise that gambling is an illness; that it is progressive in nature; and that it cannot be cured, only arrested. Gamblers Anonymous does not believe willpower will work. Only adherence to spiritual principles can help control this moral vice.

Today, this organization has chapters all around the world. In 1997, the Calgary Addiction Centre of Alberta set up the very first residential program in Canada, intended exclusively for women who are gambling addicts. The executive director of the centre believed that the problem would get only worse as the provinces further relaxed laws on gambling. She noted that women are less likely to disclose their addiction problems to men than they are to women. She also suggested that women are turning to gambling as a way to escape boredom, marital problems, and depression (Treatment planned..., 1997). Other provinces are looking into setting up similar programs.

Explaining Gambling

Why do people gamble? Three main schools of thought provide varied explanations:

- *Psychological theories* focus on individualized factors such as "too much" or "too little" parenting, suggesting that the basic emotional needs of gamblers were not met when they were children. Another psychological perspective is that gambling is an unconscious desire to take risks and lose, in response to feelings of guilt, emotional isolation, and pain.

- *Biological theories* interpret gambling as an impulse disorder with a biochemical link. Berman and Siegel (1992) cite studies showing that compulsive gamblers have low levels of serotonin and increased responsiveness of the noradrenergic system, associated with poor control impulse.

- *Learning/perception theories* view gambling as a learned behaviour that is dependent on random reinforcement.

Attempts to explain gambling are about as diverse as the methods by which people can engage in gambling. What is evident is that gambling is a complex social, cultural, and personal phenomenon that could perhaps be best explained and addressed through an interdisciplinary perspective—one in which individual, social, biological, and personal characteristics are all considered.

Criminologists will likely have to accept the fact that, for better or worse, gambling is here to stay. As has been said in many different ways, life itself is a gamble (see Box 11.4).

WHAT DO YOU THINK? BOX 11.4

GAMBLING AND THE STOCK MARKET

One small irony of possible gambling venues is the fact that organized crime has not infiltrated the greatest gambling enterprise in North America—the stock market! Why is it that criminologists typically direct their attention to "ordinary" forms of gambling and pay minimal attention to people who play the stock market? As the Bre-X scandal of 1997 showed, the cost of playing the stock market can be more financially devastating than ordinary gambling.

In addition to defining the characteristics of gamblers and identifying those forms of gambling that pose a greater risk than others, in the future criminologists should focus on articulating the extent to which gambling is or is not a victimless crime. In terms of social policy, they should study whether offering help lines, establishing support groups or programs, and having trained staff at gambling facilities can minimize the damage gambling causes.

Prostitution

We have probably all heard that prostitution is the oldest profession in the world. As a social institution, it has run the gamut from being tolerated and even condoned to being defined as a serious moral interdiction.

In ancient Greece, prostitution was openly accepted. Also during ancient times, there existed a class of sacred prostitutes in the Middle East known as *qedesha* or *kedesha* (*Britannica*, 1997). Geishas were considered desirable for marriage in pre–20th-century Japan because "they knew how to please a man" (Vito & Holmes, 1994).[1] During the 1700s and 1800s, many European cities permitted licensed brothels and required the women to submit to regular medical examinations (Bullough & Bullough, 1987). Closer to home, during the Yukon gold rush in the late 1800s, prostitution services operated openly. Most of the prostitutes during this period were Aboriginal women, "many of whom were lured into the business through alcohol addiction, or were forced into it by fathers, husbands, and others who bought and sold Native women for prostitution" (Carrigan, 1991:263).

Although there is a considerable volume of Canadian literature on prostitutes or sex workers today, most of it did not begin to emerge until the early 1980s. Prostitution became a politically relevant issue when special interest groups such as POWER (Prostitutes and Other Women for Equal Rights), CORP (Canadian Organization for the Rights of Prostitutes), SWAV (Sex Workers Alliance of Vancouver), and Dans La Rue attracted considerable attention to the needs and rights of prostitutes.

In 1981, the Committee on Sexual Offences Against Children and Youth examined child abuse and youth prostitution. Its report—commonly referred to as the **Badgley Report**, after its primary author—revealed that young prostitutes were more likely to be sexually precocious than youth not involved in prostitution. It also showed that a significant number of young prostitutes were the victims of unwanted sexual acts committed against them as children and/or adolescents. However, as Lowman (1995) and Brannigan (1996) point out, the report did not specify the nature of abuse, examine its prevalence, or describe how often abuse occurred. Notwithstanding the methodological shortfalls, the Badgley Report, along with subsequent studies (for a general review, see Lowman, 1995) indicated that many young prostitutes come from dysfunctional family backgrounds. The growing body of evidence prompted a review of laws pertaining to youth prostitution.

Although no amount of adolescent prostitution should be tolerated, the increase in official counts needs to be placed in perspective. The new legislation against prostitution—specifically Bill C-15, known as "the child exploitation law" (section 153 of the *Criminal Code*)—resulted in significant changes in law enforcement practices. It provided the criminal justice system with additional leverage to apprehend and allow the court to administer more severe penalties for the exploitation of a child.

However, according to Statistics Canada, there has not been any significant change in the conviction rate of prostitutes (CCJS, 2004, 24(6)). In fact, between 1993 and 2003, the rate of conviction of prostitutes dropped 39.8 percent. As for those who exploit children, organizations such as the Sex Alliance Workers of Vancouver argue that legislation alone cannot curb the problem. This observation would appear to be supported by the prevalence of child pornography on the internet. The United Kingdom and Australia experienced similar trends after the introduction of new legislation to protect children from exploitation.

Adult prostitution was addressed by the Special Committee on Pornography and Prostitution (SCPP), frequently called the Fraser Committee, whose mandate was to review the status of prostitution and pornography and their related regulatory laws. The committee released its report, referred to as the **Fraser Report**, in 1983. One of its recommendations was to amend the outdated 1850 *Bawdy House Act* (see s. 212 of the *Criminal Code*). The authors of the report argued that the act represented an outmoded morality law that made criminals of people who might simply be living an alternative lifestyle. Under the law, it was not only illegal to operate a bawdy house (i.e., a place used "for the purpose of prostitution or the practice of acts of indecency"—s. 197 of the *Criminal Code*); it was also a crime to simply be found in a bawdy house. The problem of the act revolved around the concept of "acts of indecency," which are not defined in the *Criminal Code* (see Lowman, 1995).

Section 197 of the *Criminal Code* contends with the criminological (and social) dilemma of whether prostitution should be criminalized, regulated, or abolished. Davis and Shaffer (1994:3) point out that these three solutions share two common policy considerations:

1. "The protection of prostitution from exploitation by third parties; and
2. The protection of the public from adverse affects of exposure to prostitution."

Defining Prostitution

Technically speaking, prostitution is legal in Canada. What is illegal is practising and soliciting prostitution. In fact, it is almost impossible for a prostitute to work without violating laws. And while other Western countries have moved away from criminalizing prostitution, Canada appears to have moved in the opposite direction. In 1990, for example, the Standing Committee on Justice recommended that on arrest prostitutes should be fingerprinted and photographed and that those charged with communication have their driver's licences removed. Subsequent studies have placed an emphasis on better enforcement of existing laws (Davis & Shaffer, 1994).

In the 2004 *Criminal Code*, sections 210–213 pertain to "keeping common bawdy-house" (indoor prostitution), "procuring" or living off the avails of prostitution, and "offences in relation to prostitution" (e.g., any person in a "public place" who attempts to stop any person for the purpose of engaging in prostitution). These sections constitute the legal meaning of prostitution. Lowman (1995) argues that sections 210 through 212 are intended to protect prostitutes from third parties, while section 213 is designed to protect the public from the nuisance effects of prostitution. Do these laws work? Davis and Shaffer (1994) and McIntyre (1994), among others, argue that they do not. They point out that the law has only prompted prostitutes to devise better means of avoiding detection rather than focusing on health and safety issues.

Historically, prostitution was more narrowly defined. As with much of our legal heritage, Canada's first prostitution laws were based on British law. Prostitution was initially prohibited by vagrancy laws (Lowman, 1995); the first vagrancy act was the *Nova Scotia Act* of 1759. The laws were not directed at prostitution per se but at the "nuisance that was created by streetwalkers and 'bawdy-house' activities" (ibid.:333), and enforcement was superficial. In the frontier areas of Canada and the United States especially, red-light districts were openly tolerated by the police (see Brannigan, Knafla, & Levy, 1989) (see Box 11.5).

FYI BOX 11.5

RED-LIGHT DISTRICTS

The term "red-light district" became popular in North America during the railroad-building era in the 1800s. When visiting a prostitute, a railroad worker would hang his red signal light outside the woman's tent, so that if he was suddenly needed for work he could be quickly found (Bullough, 1978).

In 1957, a commissioned study on laws governing sexual behaviour in Great Britain eventually brought about new standards. The commission produced the Wolfenden Report, which argued that any legislation pertaining to sexual behaviour should focus on the sexual acts that offend public decency or disrupt order and not concern itself with trying to legislate morality. This idea was enshrined in the *Sexual Offences Act* in 1967.

While the law grapples with the definition of prostitution and public decency (see Box 11.6), the public also has varying perceptions as to the meaning of prostitution. The SCPP (1985) reported that only 62 percent of Canadians surveyed felt that exchanging sex for money was indecent and worthy of disapproval. A 1994 poll by *Maclean's* magazine showed that 49 percent of Canadians believed that prostitution should be legalized (*Maclean's*, 1994). However, after Sweden legalized prostitution in the late 1960s, the sale of drugs increased, a significant number of prostitutes became drug addicts, and various other social problems escalated, to the point where, in 1998, the law was amended to criminalize prostitution. A clear solution is not readily obvious.

PROSTITUTION IN OTHER COUNTRIES

The following examples illustrate variations that exist in attitudes toward prostitution, age of consent, and related issues in different countries.

- Australia: Prostitution is not illegal, but street prostitution is in some regions. In Victoria, for example, street prostitution is legal but prohibited near schools, churches, and hospitals. Age of consent is generally 16.
- Costa Rica: Prostitution is legal, and workers are required to be licensed and to carry ID cards. Age of consent is 18.
- Denmark: Prostitution is legal, but it is illegal to make a living off it. In other words, a prostitute must have another source of income. Age of consent is 15.
- Greece: Prostitution is legal. Recent provisions have been proposed to require prostitutes to retire at 55, with the state providing social and medical benefits. Workers are required to undergo health checks every two weeks.
- Netherlands: Prostitution has never been outlawed in the Netherlands. Since 1988, prostitutes have joined the Service Sector Union as a legal profession, and workers have been required to pay income taxes since 1996. No health checks are required. Age of consent is 16.
- New Zealand: Although prostitution is not officially legal, prostitutes advertise their services in the yellow pages, magazines, and even on the radio. Age of consent is 16.
- Vietnam: In the mid-1970s, after North and South Vietnam united, the communist-oriented government began a major campaign to rid the country of prostitution. Today, giant billboards warn against illicit sex, gambling, and other vices, but prostitution is thriving. Authorities attribute the resurgence of prostitution to the emergence of the market economy.

There is no consensus among Canadians on a definition of prostitution—other than stating in general terms that it involves providing a sexual service. Such being the case, how can we expect the law to adequately address and control prostitution? Both American and Canadian studies have found that regardless of how strict the laws are and how well enforced, they do not serve as effective deterrents (Davis & Shaffer, 1994; Cao, 1987).

Characteristics and Trends

Drawing on a variety of studies, we can identify some of the key characteristics and trends of prostitution in Canada:

- The average age of female prostitutes is 28, while the average age of male prostitutes is 35. The average age of entry into prostitution among female prostitutes is around 15 (Bittle, 1999).

- In 2003, 1 percent of those charged in relation to prostitution were between the ages of 12 and 17 (CCJS, 2004, 24(6)).
- In 2003, those charged were divided equally in terms of gender: 51 percent were males and 49 percent were females (ibid.).
- British Columbia averages the highest rate of charges per capita (1792), followed by Ontario (1653) and Alberta (851) (CCJS, 2003, 24(1)).
- One in every five charges laid for procuring the services of a prostitute involves an assault, sexual or otherwise (Bittle, 2002).
- One in 20 of the people murdered between 1991 and 1995 was a known prostitute. It is believed that 50 of the 63 murdered prostitutes between 1991 and 1995 were killed by their customers, while the rest were killed either by their pimps or partners (CCJS, 2003, 24(1)).
- The clearance rate for murders involving prostitutes is 34 percent, compared to 77–85 percent for non-prostitutes (Bittle, 2002).
- Mortality rate among female prostitutes is 40 times higher than the national average (Special Committee..., 1985).
- Prostitutes are a common target for victimization. For example, 80 percent of these women have been victims of rape (Durkan, 1997).

Most people view prostitutes in stereotypical terms, as social misfits suffering from low self-image who use prostitution to support their drug habits, work for pimps (those living off the avails of prostitutes), and do not like men or enjoy sex (SCPP, 1985). Most of these perceptions have not been empirically supported. For example, Carman and Moody (1985) found that most male and female prostitutes are heterosexual and have satisfying sex with their partners. The SCPP (1985) found that only 1 percent of male and 10 percent of female prostitutes worked for a pimp. The SCPP survey also found that approximately 60 percent of Canadians surveyed believed that prostitution is controlled by organized crime. While there is some evidence that organized crime is involved in prostitution, that influence is not as pervasive as imagined. Another common perception (Report on assessing..., 1994) is that prostitutes are drug users—they prostitute themselves to support their drug habits. However, a number of North American studies found that this is not the case (for Canada, see Committee on Sexual Offences...(1984); for the United States, see James (1977)).

The extent of prostitution is also commonly underestimated. If one can believe what one obtains through the media, prostitutes are well established in society as they can be found in virtually every urban centre across the country. For example, the Vancouver police estimate that there are some 600 women involved in the sex trade in the city on any given day. Meanwhile, Lowman (1997) estimates that the "murder rate of British Columbia women involved in street prostitution was roughly 60 to 120 times the rate of other adult women" (see Box 11.7). Solving murders involving prostitutes is very difficult given their low social status and the number of strangers with whom they come into contact (ibid.).

CANADA'S LATEST SERIAL KILLER?

"After having stabilized over a two-year period, the national homicide rate climbed 4 percent in 2002.... The increase in the number of homicides at the national level was driven by a large increase in British Columbia, up from 84 homicides in 2001 to 126 in 2002. Part of this increase is a result of 15 homicides which occurred in Port Coquitlam in previous years being reported by police in 2002." CCJS, 2003, 23(8):1

As of July 2004, Robert "Willy" Pickton, a Port Coquitlam pig farmer, was facing charges relating to the disappearance and murders of 15 missing prostitutes—although prosecutors indicate they have enough evidence to proceed with a total of 22 first-degree murder charges, though they have yet to file a formal indictment. Following an extensive search of Pickton's property, traces of other missing women began to surface, and the murder charges have continued to mount. The victims are among 60 women (many of them prostitutes from the area) who have been missing since between the late 1970s and the late 1990s. Pickton's trial is expected to commence sometime in 2005.

One of the earlier Canadian studies on prostitution found that prostitutes usually enter the profession in one of three ways. Lautt (1984) found that the younger prostitutes (ages 12–16) are often recruited through *exploitation* (see Box 11.8). Street pimps patrol bus stops, airports, train stations, and other entry points into a city looking for prospective young girls and boys who can be enticed into prostitution with the promise of food and shelter. MacLauren (2004:188) reports that "a percentage of runaway and homeless youth become involved in prostitution while living on the streets." Yet he goes on to note that these youth do not leave home "with the goal of taking up prostitution, but rather, that entering into prostitution occurs as a result of the street situation" (ibid.:188).

A second method of entry into prostitution is through the influence of a *"big sister."* In this situation, an older prostitute recruits a naive 15- to 19-year-old girl. While participation may initially be for "fun" because of the sexually active lifestyle, Lautt (1984) points out that the girls get hooked on it for financial gain.

The third way of entering the trade is through *independent pragmatic decision*, usually taken by more mature individuals aged 18–24, who choose prostitution usually out of economic necessity. These women, and occasionally men, come from all walks of life; they include students and employed women seeking extra money (SCPP, 1985).

YOUTH AT RISK

The first piece of legislation introduced to protect young children from being exploited in Canada came into effect with the *Seduction Act* of March 1837. The act enabled the "domestic servant's father to sue the daughter's employer for seduction of the daughter" (Bailey, 1991:159). It also amended the common law by making the father liable for the support of his illegitimate child. Until the *Family Law Act* was introduced in 1986, laws protecting the exploitation of children underwent a number of revisions. However, in spite of the laws intended to protect the exploitation of children, Bailey (1991) notes the number of girls exploited and abused is substantially greater than that for boys.

In 1999, Alberta became the first province to put into effect the *Protection of Children Involved in Prostitution Act* (*PCIPA*). Under revisions to the act, a police officer or any director working under the provincial *Child Welfare Act* may "apprehend and convey the child to a protective safe house" where the child can be confined for a period of up to five days to ensure the safety of the child and assess the risk (*Protection of children...*, 2004; Bittle, 2002). In response to this legislation there has been criticism that the broader social and economic conditions that lead to prostitution are ignored, as well as the protection of the legal rights of youths (Bittle, 2002). Opponents, however, argue that "the beneficial impacts of secure care clearly out weigh the negatives." This opinion appears to be reflected in the courts as well (see *Director of Child Welfare v. K.B. and M.J.* 2000 ABQB) (Bittle, 2002).

Silbert and Pines (1982, cited in McIntyre, 1994:54) found that approximately 32 percent of young persons acquire their knowledge of prostitution through movies, books, and/or magazines. Similarly, Brannigan et al. (1989) found that 39 percent of those they interviewed knew someone working in the sex business. This figure was reaffirmed by McIntyre (1994), who found that 36 percent of those involved in prostitution became involved because of someone they knew in the business. For some who are products of dysfunctional families, suffer from personal problems, or are in economic need, entering into the sex trade for "easy money" becomes compelling.

Types of Prostitutes

There are several different types of prostitutes. Furthermore, as in most professions, there is a status hierarchy among prostitutes. We will look at the seven main types of prostitutes, beginning with the "lowest" level on the hierarchy and ending with the "highest" level. However, it is important to note that, regardless of the level, most prostitutes are subject to criminal exploitation by other criminals, such as organized crime groups (see Box 11.9). The hierarchy is a social construct based on the manner in which the prostitute practises his or her trade and the level of risk involved in that mode of practice.

ORGANIZED CRIME AND SEX SLAVE MARKETS

In many parts of the world, organized crime has been involved in prostitution. In the 1990s, the fastest-growing crime groups to become involved in sexual slavery have been organized Eastern European crime groups. Stone (1998:7) reports that this has "become one of the fastest growing criminal enterprises on the international black market" and that, since the fall of the USSR, "Slavic women have become the most valuable commodities on this market." For example, Stone observes that:

- Slavic sexual slaves outnumber those of all other nationalities.
- In Milan, Italy, 80 percent of the prostitutes are foreigners.
- Gangs lure women with the promise of good jobs and better wages; in some cases, they use mail order ads and front companies such as modelling agencies to recruit innocent victims.
- Each prostitute can average about US $215 000 per month for the gang.

In 1999, Canada joined a number of other countries to combat the "dark side of globalization—transnational organized crime," which includes the illegal trafficking of human beings. Unfortunately, to date there is very limited information available on the extent of the problem, but there have been a number of studies that serve to illuminate the gravity of the crime (see Antonopoulos, 2004; Bensinger, 2000).

1. *Streetwalkers*:
   - Are the most visible and common prostitutes.
   - Generally represent the lowest rung of the prostitution hierarchy;
   - Are the most commonly researched.
   - Are offered the greatest number of intervention strategies.
   - Are at the greatest risk of arrest and injury (due their regular engagement with strangers).
   - Are at the greatest risk of rape, payment evasion, robbery, and exploitation by their pimps.
   - Have a clientele that is garnered through street solicitation.
   - Wait for the john to initiate discussion and interest so as to avoid entrapment risks.

2. *Bar prostitutes*:
   - Are also known as B-girls.
   - Operate out of public drinking establishments such as bars and taverns (ranging from seedy watering holes to luxurious hotel lounges).
   - Usually work these establishments with cooperation of the management.

- Approach prospective clients and engage in flirtatious discussion leading to an arrangement, thereby avoiding solicitation.
- Experience less police interference than streetwalkers.
- Maintain a higher social status than streetwalkers.

3. *Massage-parlour prostitutes*:
   - Work in parlours that use suggestive language to indicate type of services available (e.g., "all muscle massages"); fees charged are comparable to those charged in legitimate parlours to avoid entrapment.
   - Rely on clients to request "extra services" and negotiate fees. (Sansfacon [1985] reports that fellatio—performing oral sex—and sexual intercourse are usually not part of the fee structure but other sexual services can be negotiated.)
   - Are rarely charged by the police because of the method of operation.

4. *House prostitutes*:
   - Work in brothels. (There are no legal brothels in Canada, but American states such as Nevada have special provisions under which brothels may operate if a county so elects.)
   - Are generally considered higher on the social ladder than massage and street prostitutes (depending on the nature of the brothel).

5. *Rap session booth prostitutes*:
   - Converse with clients in adult bookstores or shops that provide such booths (for example, in Amsterdam and in London's red-light districts); such booths are illegal in Canada today.
   - Sit behind glass; money is passed through an opening in the booth.
   - Remove their clothing for a fee determined based on an informal fee structure; there is no direct sexual contact between the prostitute and the john.

6. *Call girls*:
   - Are the aristocrats of all illegal prostitutes and charge the most.
   - Keep an exclusive and comparably small and select group of clients.

7. *Escort services prostitutes*:
   - Are also known as call girls.
   - Fall outside the legal definition of prostitution, since they do not engage in solicitation; it is incumbent on the client to request "extra" services for an additional fee.
   - Take out ads in the yellow pages or in the classified ads section of newspapers.
   - Usually use (or have their own) escort agency that screens for vice squads and clients considered unsuitable. Prospective clients may be shown photos, video clips, and/or audio tapes of potential escorts (all of which costs a fee) and are guaranteed discretion and confidentiality.

- Are recognized as belonging to a legal operation; therefore, clients can pay with credit cards, cheques, or cash.
- Are seldom targeted by the police because of the privacy of the transactions and because of the relatively high social standing of many of the clients (Sansfacon, 1985).

Male Prostitution

Until recently, the subject of male prostitutes was largely overlooked. One of the first of studies on this topic was conducted by the sociologist Albert Reiss (1961). While studying young offenders, Reiss found that a number of them had been involved in homosexual contact with older men as a means of making money. Yet, when questioned, they denied they were prostitutes. Nevertheless, Reiss's work has helped to perpetuate the myth that most male prostitutes are gay.

More recent studies by Cates and Markley (1992) and the Vancouver-based Sex Workers Alliance of Vancouver (Walnet Institute) (2000) lend support to Reiss's general finding that the major reason males engage in prostitution with older males is to find a "sugar daddy" who will support them. This financial motivation is also found among many female prostitutes.

Relying on interview data, Wright (1997) found that 84 percent of the male prostitutes interviewed in Vancouver were survivors of sexual abuse. He also observed that, like female prostitutes, male prostitutes experienced a lack of belonging and intimacy and felt more like a commodity. Furthermore, most of the male prostitutes coped with their pain and sex-trade work through disassociating from it. Yet, the most important factor appears to be that males are drawn to sex work as a way of discovering and exploring their sexuality (Matthews, 1988) or "coming out" and meeting other gay males (Brannigan & Fleischman, 1989).

Like female prostitutes, male prostitutes are harassed by police and raped and/or assaulted by johns. They are often also the subject of gay bashing, even though many are not gay. In her follow-up study of male sex workers across Canada, McIntyre (2002) concludes that there is a serious service gap for men who are prostitutes—as well as an information gap, which criminologists should be addressing. In the meantime, McIntyre recommends that "prevention material be developed to create awareness that sexual exploitation trade is a form of sexual abuse" (ibid.:37).

Explaining Prostitution

Explanations as to why women and men enter prostitution are varied. Based on his review of the literature, Lowman (1995) notes there are at least six types of theoretical perspectives on prostitution, ranging from biological positivism to feminist approaches. He also suggests that no perspective is particularly Canadian, but since prostitution is a universal phenomenon, there is no reason for specifically Canadian responses to exist. Nevertheless, there are a number of perspectives that have been favoured in Canadian-based research.

The Badgley Report of 1984 offers a social-psychological perspective on prostitution, focusing on such characteristics as family stability, social background, and unwanted sexual acts and/or physical violence. While it is much acclaimed for its groundbreaking efforts, Lowman (1995) identifies a number of limitations of the study and its theoretical approach. For example, "very little is said about the effect of unemployment structures and the marginal position of youth." The study also "negates any kind of structural analysis of the family as a social unit" and pays limited attention to gender relations (ibid.:349). These are elements that are usually examined when using a social-psychological perspective.

In a follow-up to a series of studies on prostitution over the years, Van Brunschot and Brannigan (1997) adopted a social-psychological approach with an emphasis on social control theory. Consistent with other social-psychological studies, the authors found a significant relationship between involvement in prostitution and a history of physical abuse, non-traditional familial structures, expulsion from school, and a history of running away. Similarly, McIntyre (1994, 2002) found that almost 75 percent of male and female prostitutes began sex work prior to their 16th birthday. Over three-quarters of those interviewed had been sexually and/or physically abused prior to their involvement in sex work. Furthermore, and consistent with other studies, running away, school difficulties, and a low self-image were common features among those in the study group.

By contrast, the Special Committee on Pornography and Prostitution, working for a conservative think-tank, presents a **political economy perspective** on prostitution (Lowman, 1995). Influenced by the feminist approach, this perspective stresses inequalities in job opportunities, earning power, and "sexual socialization as the structural factors responsible for making prostitution appear to be a choice at all" (ibid.:349). Hence, prostitution is described as being motivated by economic necessity, with women being the victims of a patriarchal power structure. Brannigan et al. (1989) found that 77 percent of women and 84 percent of men stated that money was their primary motivation for entering the sex trade. By contrast, McIntyre (1994) found that the need for money accounted for only 30 percent of those who entered the business.

Some feminists view prostitution as one of the ways in which men exploit women, using them as expendable commodities to be bought and sold. Liberal feminists have argued that some women become involved because they do not have access to legitimate opportunities. Marxist and socialist feminists view prostitution as a product of women being subjugated into the trade. Radical feminists "believe that prostitution is the result of the role women are trained into in the serving of men" (McIntyre, 1994:144). All feminist groups, regardless of their theoretical orientation, support the decriminalization of prostitution.

Another perspective that has received some support is the functionalist approach. Drawing on the work of sociologist Kingsley Davis in the late 1930s, functionalism views prostitution as part of our social institution. And while it condemns the practice of prostitution on the one hand, functionalism also suggests that it contributes to stability in society by providing men with a sexual outlet. This view reflects a double standard and reinforces the status quo. For example, in 1982, Portugal legalized prostitution, in partial response to the number of upper-class men who saw prostitutes while their wives stayed at home (Geis, 1989). Feminist groups applauded the liberalization of laws but still opposed the exploitation of women. It can be argued that only if the needs of society are equated with the needs of men could prostitution be considered functional.

Finally, Lowman argues that Canadians need to "cut the hypocrisy and work out what we want prostitution law and social policy to accomplish" (Sterling Prize..., 1997). Accordingly, he identifies four goals in a decriminalization process: "prevent sexual procurement of children and youth; protect prostitutes from pimp coercion and customer violence; encourage prostitute self-employment; and protect bystanders from nuisance" (ibid.). While evocative, Lowman's goals neglect a fundamental aspect of criminology that has repeatedly been noted throughout this book: laws and policy cannot prevent crime. Criminology needs to examine the causes and meaning of prostitution from an interdisciplinary perspective.

In summary, prostitution is one of history's oldest professions—and one of the most dangerous ones for the worker. In spite of this long history, there are many misconceptions as to who prostitutes are and why they enter this profession. While many come from abusive backgrounds and/or are coerced into prostitution, Carman and Moody (1985) report that a small percentage come from respectable backgrounds. They enter the profession for economic gain, understand the risks, and are not emotionally upset by their work or hooked on drugs.

The issue of whether prostitution should be legalized remains controversial. There are competing groups and organizations that offer compelling arguments on both sides of the debate. One area in which there is strong consensus, however, is the exploitation of youth in prostitution. Based largely on social and cultural values, it is often argued that young prostitutes are not capable of making an informed decision about such a lifestyle. In terms of enforcement, since other crimes are considered more serious than prostitution, it is not likely that sufficient resources will be directed to addressing the issue.

Pornography

"[I]f true equality between male and female persons is to be achieved, we cannot ignore the threat to equality resulting from exposure to audiences of certain types of violent and degrading material. Materials portraying women as a class as objects for sexual exploitation and abuse have a negative impact on the individual's sense of self-worth and acceptance." *Regina v. Red Hot Video Ltd.*, 45 C.R. 3d 36, 43-44 (B.C.C.A. 1985).

Have you read *The Stone Angel* by Margaret Laurence, *Ulysses* by James Joyce, *Lady Chatterley's Lover* by D.H. Lawrence, *Fanny Hill* by John Cleland, or *Moll Flanders* by

Daniel Defoe? These books were all considered to be obscene at one time or another. Have you ever looked at a copy of *Chic*, *Forum*, *Hustler*, *Penthouse*, *Playboy*, or *Playgirl*? These are legitimate magazines for those over 18, although there are other pornographic magazines that are illegal in Canada, such as ones containing child pornography (but see Box 11.10). Have you every listened to the rap group 2 Live Crew? In 1990, they were charged in the United States for producing obscene material. Several of their songs (e.g., "Me So Horny") contain sexually explicit lyrics. Yet in the 1970s, the wife of former Beatle great John Lennon, Yoko Ono, produced an album on which it sounds very much like she is having an orgasm. Why did her album not receive the same bad press as Marilyn Manson or 2 Live Crew? When does art become obscene or pornographic?

FYI BOX 11.10

VIOLENT IMAGES IN ADULT MAGAZINES

In conducting a content analysis of 373 issues of *Playboy*, *Penthouse*, and *Hustler* from between 1953 and 1984, Reisman (1997) found 6004 child images as well as over 14 000 images of crime and violence. Reisman further observed that since 1975, *Penthouse* and *Hustler* have increased their coverage of children, crime, and violence.

Like prostitution, **pornography** has been around a very long time. Plato is sometimes credited with beginning, over 2300 years ago, the debate on the role of the arts in a good society. His simple question as to what is the proper role or function of art continues to be relevant. Pornography was common in ancient Greece and Italy and was especially popular in ancient India and Japan. For example, the Indian manual *Kama Sutra* provides readers with ways to use their bodies for love. The term "pornography" is derived from the Greek *pornē*, meaning "prostitute," and *graphō*, meaning "to write." Therefore, the term literally means writing about the activities of prostitutes. Today, pornographic material is available from a wide range of sources, including books, magazines, videos, and the internet. Most major cities have specialty stores that specialize in providing "adult" entertainment.

A term that is sometimes used interchangeably and considered by some moral entrepreneur groups to be synonymous with pornography is "obscenity," derived from the Latin *caenum*, meaning "filth." The *Concise Oxford Dictionary* defines obscenity as "indecent, especially grossly or repulsively so; lewd, ...morally repulsive." The difficulty in controlling pornography revolves around the legal definition of obscenity. Law enforcement officials can seize only material that is defined as obscene. In 1987, the US Supreme Court modified its 1973 ruling by stating that pornographic material could be judged obscene, and thus banned, if a "reasonable person" could conclude that the work lacked any social value. However, as Albanese (1996) points out, the term "reasonable person" lacks any objective standards. And despite two presidential commissions, the US Supreme Court is no closer to successfully defining the term.

Pornography and the Law

Crimes pertaining to pornography, or more precisely obscenity, are listed under "Offences Tending to Corrupt Morals" in sections 163–69 of the Canadian *Criminal Code*. Section 163.1 specifically deals with child pornography (see Box 11.11). Introduced in 1993, the law prohibits the exploitation of children (i.e., anyone under the age of 18) in any manner that involves explicit sexual activity. The maximum penalty is five years imprisonment. The law also prohibits the importation, selling, or any other distribution of child pornography.

WHAT DO YOU THINK? BOX 11.11

THE CHALLENGE OF TRYING TO LEGISLATE MORALITY

Although Canadian law criminalizes the possession, creation, and distribution of child pornography, a recent case heard by the Supreme Court—*R. v. Sharpe*—caused considerable controversy, both prior and subsequent to the highest court's final ruling. John Robin Sharpe, the accused, had in his possession self-created writings and drawings of a sexual nature involving children under 14 (the legal age of consent). The Court was asked to decide whether or not this constituted possession of child pornography (see s. 163 of the *Criminal Code*). The Court held that self-produced visual or written material created for personal use (such as writings, journals, and drawings) and other self-created visual material (such as photos and videos) that do not depict illegal sexual activity and are exclusively for personal use are permissible under the law. What do you think?

The British legal system has adopted a different approach: its definition of pornography does not refer to any inherent danger. In fact, pornography may be prescribed by a sex therapist for patients experiencing sexual difficulties. Using a functional theory approach, Ellis (1987:31) suggests that "prostitution and pornography are functional for society, because by permitting the expression of anti-social sex, they act as a safety valve and so help keep families together." The British legal definition focuses on the negative effect on public morals, especially those of children. For example, the British Home Office (1979:103) defines pornography as follows: "A *pornographic* representation combines two features: it has a certain function, or intention, to arouse its audience sexually, and also a certain content, explicit representation of sexual materials (organs, postures, activity, etc.)." Finally, Ellis (1984, cited in Scott & Schwalm,

1988:40) simply defines pornography as "anti-culture, anti-conscience, anti-God, anti-family, anti-child, and anti-women. Pornography brutalizes and insults society."

All these definitions share a common theme: they all view pornography as a violation of social values and norms. However, none of them provides a clear and concise explanation. Since we live in a heterogeneous society with diverse moral standards, it may not be possible to reach a consensus; hence, any attempt to find a universal definition or an acceptable societal response is further complicated.

Does Pornography Cause Violence?

Recently, criminologists have shifted their focus from moral issues to the question of whether pornographic material contributes in any way to violence and victimization of women and children (and possibly of men). As Chelsea Draeger (1997) notes, there is ample literature indicating that many women are being forced to participate in pornography and in some cases are being harmed while participating.

Public surveys conducted in the United States in the 1980s showed that most Americans believe there is a relationship between pornography and violence and/or crime (*The Report of the Commission...*, 1986). However, after reviewing the academic literature, the US Presidential Commission on Obscenity and Pornography (1970) concluded that exposure to erotic materials is *not* a causal factor in sex crimes or sex delinquency, though the report neglected to differentiate between the kinds and the extent of erotic materials. Many thought the issue would quickly die, but hundreds of studies were conducted on this question in the following years, spurred partly by the women's movement and by religious fundamentalists. After reviewing many of these studies in 1984, the US Attorney General's Commission concluded that while erotic material may not cause sex crimes, viewing such material can lead to a greater acceptance of sex crimes through a habituation to pornography (Adler, Mueller, & Laufer, 1991). These findings provided feminists with the evidence to argue that pornographic material should be censored and that it does undermine the status of women in general.

Today, the literature generally concurs on the point that regular exposure to erotic material can facilitate expressions of anger and violence (Conklin, 2003). Radical feminists, for example, argue that exposure to pornography often leads to violence against women by linking coercion and violence with sexual stimulation (Berger et al., 1991). However, it does not appear to be the sexual acts per se but the degree of violence depicted in pornographic materials that triggers violence. Scott and Schwalm (1988) point out that after Denmark repealed all bans of sexually oriented material in the late 1960s, sex crimes actually declined in the country. Similarly, Japan has a flourishing pornography trade, and yet its rape rate is less than one-quarter the rate in Germany or Great Britain and one-fourteenth the rate in the United States (cited in Livingston, 1992). As pointed out in Chapter 8, sexual assault in Canada has increased since new legislation was enacted in the 1980s. Although a percentage of the increase may be due to reporting patterns, greater public awareness, and changes in the legal definition of rape, surely such factors cannot entirely account for the dramatic increase.

The comparative rates lend credence to the idea that sex crimes are related to certain cultural climates. If so, criminologists need to explore what the possible critical cultural factors are that differentiate countries with high rape rates from countries with low rape rates. Knowing such factors may enable countries to better regulate pornography. We have seen dramatic changes in our society's level of tolerance in terms of acceptable norms and values as well as lifestyle choices—such as gay marriage and the presence of graphic depiction of sex and violence in movies, music videos, and on the internet. The notion of pornography is a relative concept that poses a major challenge to criminologists interested in studying any criminogenic relationship. The fact that pornography not only involves questions of morality but also is closely tied to the notion of constitutional right to freedom of speech and the press further complicates matters.

The two primary opponents of pornography, religious fundamentalists and feminists, continue to be vigilant about how society embraces pornography. The fundamentalists adopt the argument that pornography erodes public morality and respect for human life. For example, in the early 1980s, the Squamish Five, protesting against businesses that degraded women by selling pornographic videos, bombed several pornographic video stores in British Columbia (see Salomon, 1988). Feminists view pornographic material as being anti-women. They also argue that it violates women's civil rights on the grounds of equality and free speech (Scott & Schwalm, 1988). The "rape shield" law in the mid-1980s received considerable impetus from feminist groups across the country. Women's groups have also been instrumental in limiting access to child pornography, by getting magazine distributors to put shrink wrap on their materials and having businesses display the magazines above normal eye level. However, if the influx of pornographic material is any indication, these moral entrepreneurs are fighting a losing battle.

In summary, there is no conclusive evidence that either completely refutes any link between pornography and sex crimes or supports possible links. Sex surveys show that most adults engage in acts that are found in pornographic literature. Exactly when does sexual contact or sexual interaction constitute a moral wrong that deserves to be legislated?

Since many non-consenting acts are precipitated by drugs or alcohol, is there a possible biological or biochemical cause for obscene behaviour, or is the behaviour learned through association? To date, there is no conclusive empirical evidence to support one theoretical perspective over another. Pornography will likely continue to fuel the underground economy (through organized crime groups and other means). Criminologists need to adopt an interdisciplinary approach that enables them to recognize the unique elements of the environment and individual characteristics and/or traits associated with pornography and violence. It may also be time to deal with the issue as a civil matter, not a criminal one.

Substance Abuse

> "She threw into the wine which they were drinking a drug which takes away grief and passion and brings forgetfulness of all ills." Homer, *The Odyssey*

In Chapter 5, we looked at the relationship between the biochemical effects of alcohol and criminal behaviour. It was also noted that an inordinate number (as high as 65 percent according to Single et al., 1996) of violent crimes involved the use of alcohol and/or drugs. For example, between 1992 and 2002, the number of official drug-related offences increased from 55 881 to 92 591 (a rate per 100 000 increase from 207 to 295). This represents a 42 percent rate increase (CCJS, 2004, 24(1):1).

Abuse of alcohol and legal and illicit drugs can affect the sense of public order as a result of the altered behaviour expressed by the substance abuser. And if we can believe the media, there has been a drug epidemic in North America since at least since the 1960s. Millions of dollars are spent every year to curb the abuse of alcohol and drugs. The social, financial, and personal costs of abuse are staggering.

History of Substance Use and Abuse

There is virtually no society in which people cannot be found using mind- and mood-altering substances (Schlaadt, 1992). We can find numerous examples of how alcohol has been used throughout the ages in everything from religious rites to social celebrations to simply complementing a meal.

While in the ancient times alcohol was not the only psychoactive substance—that is, a substance affecting mood or behaviour—that was used, it was the most prevalent. Both the Greeks and Romans had gods of wine; for the Greeks, it was Dionysus, also the god of vegetation, while for the Romans it was Bacchus. As the Roman Empire spread throughout Europe, the Romans brought their love of wine and copious consumption with them. The French, Spanish, Germans, and even the British were quick to embrace the practice and began to cultivate their own vines. Schlaadt (1992:3) observes that some historians believe that the eventual downfall of the Roman Empire was due in part to alcoholism—along with greed, corruption, and self-indulgence. After the birth of Christianity, even the Catholic Church got into the act, using wine in such rituals as the sacrament of Communion. To this day, certain monasteries throughout Europe are known for the alcoholic beverages they produce. Not surprisingly, Europeans brought their drinking habits with them to the Americas. By the 19th century, alcohol was both plentiful and frequently used and abused throughout the Western world.

In Eastern Europe, there is also a long history of drinking spirits such as vodka. In 2004, the *Christian Science Monitor* noted that the average Russian consumes about five gallons of vodka per year (Weir, 2004)! In Japan, although beer arrived only about 100 years ago, it has become very popular among men, with an estimated several million problem drinkers. It is not considered socially acceptable for Japanese women to drink, especially in public; however, unlike in North America, public drunkenness among men is quite common, especially at night (Alcohol in Japan, 2004). As for other parts of the world, there is often limited information available, for various reasons. In Muslim countries, for example, alcohol is forbidden.

The use of drugs has an equally long, if not longer, history. Egyptian records show that as far as 1500 BC opium was already being used for medicinal purposes. The inhabitants of ancient Peru chewed coca leaves containing cocaine, and Native Americans discovered the use of mescaline as a mood-altering substance. It appears that most cultures have chosen some drug that can be readily found in their area as a socially accepted way for altering the state of consciousness.

It was not until the late 1800s and early 1900s that drug regulation became an issue in North America. Fishbein and Pease (1996) suggest there were two important factors that contributed to this awareness and the subsequent move to regulate drugs. The first was an alarming increase in the rates of addiction and the second was "the association of drug use with minority groups" (ibid.:11).

Drugs and the Law

What exactly is meant by "drug abuse"? Generally, we think of drug abuse as overuse or physical and/or psychological dependency. But, as Blackwell (1988) notes, the meaning is ambiguous. For example, how many drinks, joints, or pills does one need to take before they qualify as harmful?

The *Controlled Drugs and Substances Act* replaced the *Narcotic Control Act* in 1996. The new act covers everything from "possession of substance" to "punishment," "forfeiture of proceeds of crime," and "determination of amount." Schedules I through VIII, which are located at the end of the act, provide a list of all the controlled substances. With respect to this list, what is interesting to note is s. 60 of the act, pertaining to "amendments to schedules," which reads:

> The Governor in Council may, by order, amend any of Schedules I to VIII by adding to them or deleting from them any item or portion of an item, where the Governor in Council deems the amendments to be necessary in the public interest.

The wording of the section reflects recognition of how new drugs can be manufactured and used in harmful ways. What is less clear is what constitutes "necessary in the public interest." For example, cannabis is a banned substance and yet it has been used for medicinal purposes. In 1999, the mayor of Grand Forks in British Columbia suggested that the city obtain federal licensing to become Canada's primary supplier of medical marijuana. The mayor pointed out that the region is well suited for growing marijuana and that the crop would be a boost for the economically depressed community (Ketcham, 1999).

Alcohol the Drug

If you have ever set a match to alcohol, you know how rapidly it evaporates. When put into the body, alcohol is absorbed quickly and completely. In fact, there are few other drugs that can be as quickly absorbed into the bloodstream. However, absorption and rate of impact are also moderated by the concentration of alcohol in the drink, which can range from 5 percent in regular beer to 40 and 50 percent in distilled liquor.

The psychological and psychoactive effects of alcohol are well-documented. For example, one of the serious consequences of drinking is that over time drinkers develop a tolerance for alcohol, meaning they require more in order to get the same effect. As they drink more, there is an increased tendency to develop a dependency on the alcohol to sustain the false sense of well-being. Then, because of the biochemical changes that occur with sustained heavy drinking, drinkers develop withdrawal symptoms when they try to go without. The addiction begins to take hold, and the symptoms escalate. Another damaging consequence of alcohol addiction is the transference of biochemical changes into newborns. Babies born to mothers who are chronic drinkers are highly susceptible to fetal alcohol syndrome (King et al., 1999).

Illicit Drugs

There are three broad classes of psychoactive drugs that affect the central nervous system: *stimulants*, *depressants*, and *hallucinogens*. While these categories describe the general effects created by the drugs that fall into them, they are not always mutually exclusive. For example, marijuana is known as a crossover drug, as it initially acts as a stimulant and then a depressant as the effects wear off. Depending on the potency and amount smoked, it can also create sensory distortions similar to those created by hallucinogens.

Stimulants tend to elevate the user's sense of well-being. Sometimes referred to as "uppers," these drugs keep the user alert and able to resist fatigue. The most common examples are nicotine and caffeine—that morning pick-me-up cup of coffee. Other examples include cocaine, crack, and the synthesized drugs called amphetamines. As all drugs, stimulants vary in potency and addictive properties. According to a study cited by Fishbein and Pease (1996:85), nicotine is the most addictive (nearly 100 percent of first-time users get addicted) of the stimulants, with crack being a close second. Caffeine is the least addictive of the stimulants (approximately 85 percent among first-time users).

Depressants, as the term suggests, slow down the central nervous system. They are also referred to as "downers." They can induce sleep, alleviate pain, relax muscles, reduce anxiety, and create a false sense of euphoria—a "nothing bothers me" effect. The most common depressant is alcohol. The opiate drugs (heroin, morphine) and barbiturates, antihistamines, PCP (phencyclidine), and a variety of aerosol sprays act as depressants. Alcohol is the most addictive of the depressants (approximately 87 percent for first time users), followed closely by heroin.

Hallucinogens create an altered state of awareness—a distortion of reality. Users of hallucinogens report "out-of-body" experiences such as hearing sounds, seeing images and colours, and experiencing a distortion of time and place. The most popular hallucinogen is marijuana, although in the 1960s peyote (a type of cactus) was very popular. Peyote contains mescaline, which can also be made synthetically. Other synthetic hallucinogens include LSD (lysergic acid diethylamide) and PCP (phencyclidine). LSD is derived from a natural fungus known as ergot, which grows on such grains as rye. PCP, also known as angel dust, hog, or green, is easily made, is comparatively inexpensive, and is the most addictive of the hallucinogens. Stories of hallucinogens (e.g., LSD and PCP) causing violent and uncontrollable behaviour seemed to make them less desirable. But just as preferences for other social vices go in cycles, is it possible that hallucinogens might regain status among different social groups who are looking for something different and perhaps unpredictable. The most popular hallucinogen is cannabis. It is the most prevalent illegal drug among young users: almost 40 percent of 18–19-year-olds reported having used it in the past year (*The Daily*, 2004).

Table 11–1 offers a breakdown of the various drugs used by Canadians and the impact associated with each drug. As illustrated in the table, Canadians are more likely to use/abuse legal drugs, which posed much higher health risks. Why do so many people continue to use/abuse drugs?

TABLE 11–1

CANADA'S DRUG USERS, COSTS, AND ATTRIBUTABLE DEATHS

DRUG	ANNUAL NUMBER OF USERS	COST PER WEEK FOR THE AVERAGE USER	POSSIBILITY OF OVERDOSE DEATH	DRUG-RELATED DEATHS PER YEAR
Alcohol*	16 000 000	$10–$100	YES	3000–15 000
Amphetamines	<100 000	$100–$500	YES	<100
Cocaine	300 000–500 000	$10–$5000	YES	<100
Heroin	<100 000	$50–$5000	YES	<100
LSD	<100 000	<$20	NO	<10
Marijuana	1 500 000–2 500 000	$10–$100	NO	<10
Tobacco*	6 000 000–8 000 000	$30–$100	NO	35 000
Tranquilizers*	1 500 000–2 500 000	$0–$20	NO	<10

* Denotes drugs that are legal.

Source: Used with permission from Neil Boyd, *High Society* (Toronto: Key Porter Books, 1991).

Characteristics and Trends

Statistics Canada reports that in 2002 approximately 8.8 percent of Canadians had an alcohol dependency problem that ranged from slightly to highly probable (Statistics Canada, 2003). The Canadian Centre on Substance Abuse (CCSA, 1999) noted that 6503 alcohol-related deaths occurred and that over 80 946 hospitalizations were attributed to alcohol in 1998. At some level, Canadians are aware of the risks associated with alcohol consumption. Nearly 75 percent of Canadians supported increases in prevention programs, while 75.5 percent supported severe intervention programs. Furthermore, 66.7 percent were opposed to selling alcohol in convenience stores, and 69.5 percent were in favour of placing warning labels on bottles containing alcoholic beverages (ibid.). A question that was not asked was: Do Canadians favour the privatization of liquor store operations? In Alberta, for example, there has been an explosion of liquor outlets since the government relaxed its licensing laws.

With the exception of those countries where religion forbids its consumption, alcohol is consumed in great quantities. Knowledge about the harmful effects of alcohol and tobacco has had no significant impact on consumption. As a vice, should we view alcohol as a disease rather than a crime? How should criminologists deal with the latest scientific evidence that suggests that people who use modest amounts of alcohol are less likely to experience health problems such as arteriosclerosis, heart attacks, and strokes? John Bland from the University of Vermont College of Medicine points out that there are "cleansing and neurophysiological benefits to alcohol" (cited in Pela, 1997:74).

While there is considerable literature and research on alcohol and tobacco abuse, the effects of illicit drug abuse are not as well documented. Single et al. (1996) reported that there were an estimated 732 deaths in 1992 related to illicit drug use, versus 33 498 deaths related to tobacco and 6702 deaths related to alcohol use. The majority (88 percent) of the deaths involved males, and some 42 percent of the deaths were suicides. Opiate poisoning and cocaine poisoning were most common for suicides (14 percent and 9 percent, respectively). The authors of the study point out that compared to deaths resulting from alcohol and/or tobacco, deaths resulting from the use of illicit drugs are relatively infrequent. Yet, in 1992 there were 7095 hospitalizations and 58 571 days spent in hospital as a result of illicit drug use.

Based on more recent but not as comprehensive research conducted by Health Canada, use of cannabis among Canadians aged 15 or older had nearly doubled between 1994 and 2002; 7.4 percent reported using it in 1994 versus 12.2 percent in 2002. The same survey found that the use of other illicit drugs, such as cocaine, ecstasy, LSD and other hallucinogens, amphetamines, and heroin had increased from 1.6 percent in 1994 to 2.4 percent in 2002 (*The Daily*, 2004).

Single et al. (1996) estimated the economic cost of illicit drugs in 1992 at $1.37 billion, or $48 per capita. This amount was significantly less than the costs of the abuse of alcohol ($265 per capita) and tobacco ($336 per capita). Nevertheless, substance abuse is a serious social consequences in terms of health, family disorders, problems in the workplace, and crimes instigated under the influence of drugs.

Research evidence shows a strong link between controlled substance abuse and criminal behaviour. Several studies have found that offenders with a substance abuse problem commit a high percentage of violent crimes (Gropper, 1985; Zawitz, 1992) and that drug addicts commit more crimes while under the influence than when sober (Nurco, Cisin, & Ball, 1985). Speckart and Anglin (1986) observed that substance abuse was significantly related to high levels of property crime.

In many respects, the public seems hypocritical in its condemnation of the illicit drug problem in Canadian society, since more Canadians die every year from legal drugs than from illicit drugs. As well, the focus shifts from decade to decade. In the 1960s, the evils of marijuana were the main concern; in the 1970s, the focus shifted to hallucinogens (e.g., LSD, PCP, and MDA); and in the 1980s, cocaine and crack (a synthetic form of cocaine) became the main targets of public condemnation. All the while, little attention or concern seems to have been directed at the number one drug killers—alcohol and tobacco (see Box 11.12).

FYI BOX 11.12

ALCOHOL AND TOBACCO AS THE MOST DEADLY KILLERS

In 1995, the abuse of illicit drugs cost 804 Canadians their lives (CCSA, 1999). This number, however, does not even begin to come close the number of deaths caused by the most costly and deadly drugs—alcohol and tobacco. In 2003, 17 013 people were killed in alcohol-related crashes, which translates into an average of one every half an hour (MADD, 2004). According to Health Canada's 2003 Canadian Tobacco Use Monitoring Survey, over five million (21 percent) of Canadians over the age of 15 currently smoke, of which 17 percent smoke daily. The rates have been declining slightly since 1991, shortly after Health Canada started administering the survey. Yet the number of deaths recorded in 1996 puts the gravity of smoking into perspective: murders: 510; alcohol: 1900; car accidents: 2900; suicides: 3900; and tobacco: 45 000 (Graphic health warning labels, 2004).

It is true that the government has set limits on how alcohol and tobacco can be advertised, but out of fear of losing millions of dollars in revenue from the high taxes levied on these products, and because of the majority of society's acceptance of alcohol and general tolerance toward soft drugs, the government is not prepared (or able) to ban them. Boyd (1991) is quite critical about the hypocrisy that sees Canadians viewing legal drugs as less harmful than illegal drugs. As he states, "we are a country of drug takers" (see Box 11.13).

MAKING MONEY FROM SOCIAL VICES

Next to military arms and oil, coffee is the largest commodity-based industry in the world, with North American sales exceeding $10 billion (US) annually (Equator, 2004). Health Canada reports that some six million Canadians use tobacco every day, even though the consumption rate declined from 35 to 24 percent between 1985 and 2000 (Health Canada, 2003). Figures are somewhat skewed by the increase of illegal smuggling and selling of cigarettes due to the high taxes placed on them (Tobacco Act challenge, 2003). For 2000–2001, persons aged 15 and over purchased on average 103.8 litres of alcoholic beverages, up from 99.5 litres in 1996–1997 but down significantly from a high of 134 litres in 1976.

Perhaps one of the reasons the public is not inclined to think of cigarettes as a drug is that, other than the physiological addiction to the nicotine, there is no psychomotor or cognitive impairment involved. In other words, smoking does not alter one's ability to drive, talk, or perform delicate tasks. But smoking is a silent killer and a relatively inexpensive one. In 2004, a package of cigarettes cost approximately $8.80, while a gram of cocaine cost approximately $80–$100, a marijuana cigarette cost about $5, and a bottle of spirits cost around $20. Withdrawal from smoking has been reported to be more difficult than withdrawal from heroin. The relapse rate is nearly 70 percent (Canadian Cancer Society, 2004).

Explaining Addiction

Fishbein and Pease (1996:82) point out that while there are many theoretical explanations of drug use and addiction, "many theories do not distinguish between those factors that contribute to the reasons to first use a drug, reasons to maintain drug use, and reasons for relapse." After reviewing biological, psychological, and a variety of sociological theories of addiction, they note that none of the perspectives is able to address all the factors, suggesting that an interdisciplinary approach is necessary. Specifically, they embrace the **diathesis-stress model**, which recognizes elements of the social environment, perceived environment, personality, biological/genetic factors, and behavioural factors. Each element has risk factors as well as protective factors. An individual's risk of developing alcohol problems is dependent on the extent of the stressors within each of the major elements.

Fishbein and Pease (1996) note that while the diathesis-stress model offers a comprehensive view of the problem, the conditions necessary for predicting alcoholic tendencies are still too non-specific. However, they believe that only through this line of inquiry will we be able to predict and prevent alcohol abuse.

We have noted that throughout history some of the drugs that are illicit today were once legal and even used for medical purposes. A conflict interpretation of the relative legal status of drugs focuses on drugs being viewed as a social problem by various social classes who feel that a certain drug threatens their social stability (i.e., power). In other words, they would sanction a drug only if they could monopolize the making and selling of the drug. From this point of view, the best way to combat an "evil" drug is through thought reform and education.

Drugs present a moral dilemma for society. Whether one subscribes to the psychological position of Erich Fromm—that we learn to desire those things that go along with our economic and social system—or the sociological position put forth by Max Weber—that society rewards those who are industrious—it is cultural values that dictate what "pleasure-seeking" outlets are acceptable or unacceptable. If our desire to use drugs can be traced back to earliest recorded history, perhaps the drug controversies are a reflection of a cultural lag between existing laws and people's changing feelings and values.

Society is forever evolving, and some of these changes are accompanied by social consequences that pose challenges to criminologists. Only by adopting an interdisciplinary perspective can we try to understand the complex relationship between crime and morality.

Summary

- Although public order offences represent the "most widespread organization of lawlessness" (Sutherland & Cressey, 1955:230), attempts to legislate issues of morality in a heterogeneous society are controversial and complex. Most people engage in various forms of vices, and criminal—and often non-criminal—organizations feed society's demands.

- Gambling is an ancient pastime that continues to plague certain individuals and sectors of society. Gambling generates revenue for governments and various groups but at the same time is the bane for those who become addicted to it. Efforts to explain and control gambling have met with minimal success.

- Both prostitution and pornography have a very long history. Prostitution has run the gamut from being held in the highest esteem to being viewed in derogatory terms. And although it has endured the full criminological spectrum of theoretical explanations, no theory has been able to provide a complete understanding of why people enter into prostitution or offer sound advice on how to provide a solid basis for controlling its practice. With regard to pornography, no clear definition, boundaries, effects, or answers to the problem have been offered.

- Substance abuse parallels the trends and patterns of the other vices covered in this chapter. Whether legal or not, all drugs have potential addictive and destructive consequences and their differentiation in legal status is a social construction.

- Criminologists must bridge the gap between laws and social science when considering public order offences. They must focus on the acts as they relate to human behaviour from an integrated and interdisciplinary perspective. Only by recognizing the complexity of behaviour in this manner will criminologists begin to understand what such behaviours mean and how to more appropriately respond to them. However, it does not necessarily follow that society will be able to precisely control all of them, or that it should even endeavour to do so.

Discussion Questions

1. Should criminologists try to legislate issues of morality? What issues need to be taken into consideration when making such a decision? To what extent might trying to control public order offences contribute to the criminal population? To what extent does it promote the involvement of organized crime groups?

2. To what extent does involvement in any public order offence involve voluntary participation?

3. Where does one draw the line in defining obscenity? How do these laws affect the right to freedom of speech and expression?

4. Should people suffering from serious illnesses be allowed to use soft drugs like marijuana for medicinal purposes? What moral and/or ethical issues might be involved?

5. Why have conventional theories been relatively ineffective in explaining public order offences and in helping to formulate effective social policy? How could an interdisciplinary and integrated approach be applied to address public order crimes?

Key Concepts

Badgley Report

political economy perspective

diathesis-stress model

pornography

Fraser Report

public order crimes

Weblinks

www.ccsa.ca The Canadian Centre on Substance Abuse provides statistics and other resources on its website.

www.acjnet.org Canada's Access to Justice Network offers information on a wide variety of public order issues such as prostitution, gambling, and substance abuse.

www.marijuanaparty.com The official site of the Marijuana Party of Canada contains some interesting information on its political platform, as well as links.

walnet.org/swav/ The page of the Vancouver-based Sex Workers Alliance of Vancouver includes numerous useful links addressing prostitution and related issues.

www.gov.ns.ca/heal/gambling/ The website of the Nova Scotia government's Problem Gambling Services offers extensive information on gambling.

Endnotes

1. Japanese prostitutes do not have the same status today.

CHAPTER 12

Victims and Victimology

"I am a man; more sinn'd against than sinning."

Shakespeare, King Lear, *Act III, Scene 2*

Learning Outcomes

After you have completed this chapter,[1] you should be able to:

• Understand the role of victimology within the criminological area.

• Identify and describe the key theories of victimology.

• Identify some of the key findings regarding victims of crime.

• Understand and discuss the new challenges and direction of victimology.

• Recognize and identify the range of government services for victims.

How does one address the 2003 case of 10-year-old Holly Jones, whose brutal and sense-less murder in the west end of Toronto attracted both national and international atten-tion? Aside from her family, how many peoples' lives were negatively impacted by the crime? What of the life of the accused Michael Briere? This 35-year-old who has been described as a loner was charged approximately 40 days after the crime. His picture was posted on the internet and distributed through the media before he was proven guilty. How can the rights of people such as Briere be ensured? What direct or indirect impact does the availability of information about the accused have on the accused's family? How do special interest groups influence such cases, and what role do comments from those affected—such as Holly Jones's parents—play in the judicial proceedings?[2]

Introduction to Victimology

By definition, a crime does not occur in a vacuum. As with physics, there is a conse-quence to every action, be it financial or personal loss, or the direct or indirect suffering

of crime victims. Crime can also result in emotional distress or fear that compromises one's life, and it can cause a reciprocal effect of triggering anti-social behaviour within the victim. Several Canadian researchers (e.g., MacLaurin, 2004; MacIntyre, 2002) have shown that being the victim of abuse or neglect as a child increases the odds of becoming both a juvenile and an adult offender. As Hans von Hentig (1948:383) noted in his landmark work *The Criminal and His Victim*, "crime, for the most part, is injury inflicted on another person." Until recently, however, North Americans have given little attention to the intended or unintended target of deviant or criminal act—the victim.

In one of the first North American introductory textbooks to dedicate an entire chapter to victimology, Stephen Schafer observed (1976:143) that "the implications of early criminologists have not shed any clear light upon the nature of this correspondence [that is, the importance of the victim's relationship to the crime] and interplay, and they did not evolve the dynamic possibilities of victimology." However, since the late 1980s, Canada has been at the forefront in this area of study; in fact, some of the major victimologists have been trained and have taught at Canadian institutions.

What Is Victimology?

As already noted, for a crime to occur there must be an offender and recipient of the offence—the victim. The recipient can be a person or an inanimate setting, such as a building or an office that is vandalized. According to the World Society of Victimology (cited in van Dijk, 1997:4), **victimology** is defined as

> the scientific study of the extent, nature and causes of criminal victimization, its consequences for the persons involved and the reactions thereto by society, in particular the police and the criminal justice system as well as voluntary workers and professional helpers.

Elias (1993) offers a definition that is somewhat broader in its scope, reflecting the fact that the subject matter can be approach from different perspectives.

The Roots of Victimology

The plight of the victim began to receive attention in the mid-1940s from legal scholars, lawyers, the media, sociologists, psychologists, and politicians. And as criminology emerged in the following decades, it became, as the Dutch criminologist Hermanus Bianchi observed, a "tremendously huge and hybrid science" (cited in Fattah, 1997:167). The study of victims now lies firmly rooted within its scope of interest. For, as Dennis Chapman noted in 1968, to focus exclusively on the criminal and neglect "the causal role of the victim, is unlikely to establish a satisfactory theory, that is, one from which reliable predictions may be made" (cited in Fattah, 1997:181). However, when **Benjamin Mendelsohn** (1900–1998), one of the pioneers of victimology, advocated that victimology should "not be a part of criminology but 'a science parallel to it,' or better, the reverse of criminology" (cited in Schafer, 1976:144), his statements may have compromised its evolution into mainstream criminology.

Brief History of Victimology

The historical heritage of victimology can be traced back to the Middle Ages, to German common laws. German law included a system of "composition" (compensation) or "wergeld" in which victims were to be compensated, usually in financial terms, for the harm or injury incurred. This system replaced the prior practices of revenge and the blood feud. This historical foundation aside, victimology, as Fattah (2000) observes, did not originate with lawmakers, sociologists, psychologists, or other social scientists. It was poets, writers, and novelists such as Thomas de Quincey, Kahlil Gibran, and the Marquis de Sade, among others, who first spoke about the plight of victims.

While Mendelsohn was the first social scientist to recognize the importance of the victim, it was—as Marvin Wolfgang notes in the preface to Schafer's (1968) *The Criminal and His Victim*—**Hans von Hentig** (1887–1974), "more than anyone, [who] wrote tellingly in theory about the role of the victim in the duet of crime" (Schafer, 1968:v). Wolfgang suggests that no discourse on victimology is complete without recognizing or crediting the contribution of von Hentig (see Box 12.1).

The idea that a "crime is more indicative of a subject-object relation than of the perpetrator alone" (von Hentig, 1948:384) led early researchers to argue that the victim can shape and mould the criminal. Consider the following example. On November 14, 1997, Reena Virk, of Victoria, was brutally attacked and eventually drowned by a group of youths. Why? She was a victim partly because she was "brown" (i.e., East Indian) in a predominantly white society. She was also overweight in a society that values slimness. In other words, she was different. Within the social and cultural context, these differences served to precipitate her victimization. The subject–object relation is also evident in the case of Dr. Harold "Fred" Shipman, an English family physician who in 2000 was charged with the killing of 15 women and with forging wills. Why? Some reports suggested that he was suffering from schizophrenia and had control issues with women. He used his position to take advantage of elderly women who would seek his medical advice. To take another example, the motivation behind the case of Michael Briere that links the offender and the victim is his self-admitted fantasy to have sex with a child. Holly Jones was the first child he saw when he went outside after viewing the pornography. Other cases that were not resolved at the time of preparing this chapter but serve as useful illustrations include the Toronto case of Cecilia Zhang and the Regina case of Tamra Keepness (both young girls at the time of their death), in which the suspects were known to the victims.

Early on, victimology was concerned mostly with theoretical issues, as reflected in the works of Hans von Hentig. Inquiries evolved around the causal explanations of crime and the victim's role in those explanations. Von Hentig's theoretical work was followed by that of others who tended to focus on specific types of crime and on conducting empirical research on the topic—for example, Wolfgang (1958) on homicide, Amir (1971) on rape, Normandeau (1968) on robbery, and Helworth (1975) on blackmail.

HANS VON HENTIG

After disagreeing with Hitler's social and political ideology in the late 1930s, Hans von Hentig left Germany for the United States to pursue his academic interests. His first work of note appeared in the *Journal of Criminal Law, Criminology and Police Science* in 1940. In this article, von Hentig used violent crimes to illustrate his point about the perpetrator–victim dilemma, noting: "the victim not only contributes amply to the commitment of the crime, but his way of cooperation is often such that it prevents him from having the felon reported and prosecuted effectively in court. After rendering himself a victim he obstructs the course of justice and grants the criminal immunity" (von Hentig, 1940:308). This line of reasoning reflects an indictment of some people who claim victimhood.

Although he never used the term "victimology" in his work, von Hentig spent considerable effort identifying "general classes of victims"—such as the young, women, the elderly, the mentally challenged, immigrants, and ethnic minorities. He noted how criminals, as much as the victim, face many of the same personal challenges and are referred to with words regularly used to describe inmates. Von Hentig used a range of similar terms to describe types of victims—yokel, clown, lout, bumpkin, apple-knocker, sucker, etc. He also classified victims according to their personality (e.g., the depressive), traits (lethargic, apathetic, passive, cooperative, contributing, provocative, instigating, soliciting, and submitting), and acquisitiveness (the desire to take advantage of others through fraudulent ploys).

Von Hentig believed that understanding the role of the victim would result in a better prevention of crime. His approach was championed by several other early pioneers in victimology, including Stefan Schafer in the United States, Willem Nagel in the Netherlands, and Ezzat Fattah in Canada. The International Victimology Society has named an award after von Hentig to recognize his contributions in this area of study.

In part due to the changing political and ideological climate throughout the 1970s and 1980s, theoretical victimology fell on somewhat hard times as it was criticized in some circles as "the art of blaming the victim" (see Clark & Lewis, 1977). Fortunately, the rhetoric began to shift (but not completely) from "blaming" to "helping and assisting crime victims, alleviating their plight and affirming their rights" (Fattah, 2000:25). Slowly, the theoretical concerns moved into the political arena, where the interests of crime victims were championed. The growth of victimology and victim's rights was also fuelled by the feminist movement, which brought forth such concerns as victims of rape, sexual assault, and domestic violence (Fattah, 1997, 2000). This shift in focus helped broaden the scope of victimology from an academic curiosity to a humanistic movement, as well as providing a connection between scholarly research and political activism. For example, gays and lesbians have used the support for victim's rights to plead their case.

The first symposium on victimology was held in Jerusalem, Israel, in September 1973, with 307 delegates from around the world. Canada had five attendees. It was at these meetings that Mendelsohn reiterated his views about victimology being a separate science from criminology. Judging from the conclusions and recommendations of the symposium, his views were not widely embraced (Schafer, 1976). Some of the key conclusions included the following (Drapkin, 1976):

- Criminology is enriched by a victimological orientation.
- Focus should shift from simple person-to-person interaction to a multi-dimensional one, thus including the bystander and other relevant people.
- Research of hidden victimization is needed.
- More research into why certain individuals are prone to repeat victimization should be conducted.
- Research is needed on the extent to which victimization may lead the victims to become offenders.

The 10th International Symposium on Victimology (which is held every three years) was held in the first year of the new millennium in Montreal. The proceedings were compiled by Paul Friday and Gerd Kirchhoff (2000) in an anthology that is dedicated to the lifetime effort of the internationally acclaimed German criminologist and victimologist Hans Joachim Schneider. The book clearly illustrates how far the study of victimology has come since the 1973 symposium. As Canadian scholar Irvin Waller noted in his contribution, the field of victimology, like that of criminology, can and does benefit from investing in prevention programs that are intended to be proactive rather than reactive (Waller 2000:363). However, as Albrecht et al. (2002:22) recently observed, "is it possible to predict crime problems within a complex set of variables, and, how should crime prevention be weighted against other evenly legitimate goals." Some of these issues were further explored at the 11th International Symposium on Victimology, held in July 2003 in Stellenbosch, South Africa, where the main focus was on new horizons in victimology.

Like criminology, victimology has not followed the same path in every part of the world; it has evolved in the "more developed countries and while legislation advanced in some parts of the world, in others it is non-existent" (Fattah, 2000:21). Some criminology and criminal justice programs across Canada still do not offer courses on victimology. The University of Montreal, however, now offers a post-doctoral program in the subject.

While the nature of victimological study has changed considerably over the years, its focus on the importance of offender–victim relationships, the degree of harm or damage done to the victim, and the appropriate compensation for this harm or damage remains the same.

Victimology has emerged as an applied science and has been confronted with many of the challenges that criminology is facing in trying to bridge theory and practice. As Fattah (2000) notes, while the 1950s and 1960s can be characterized as a period of dramatic changes, the 1980s and 1990s are representative of a period of consolidation, data gathering, and theorizing. These two decades also correspond to new legislation, victim compensation, victim assistance and service-based programs, and policy changes on many levels. But perhaps most important for the field has been the formal approval and recognition by the General Assembly of the United Nations on November 11, 1985, of the UN Declaration of Basic Principles of Justice for Victims of Crime and Abuse of Power. In framing the declaration, the United Nations recognized the plight of millions of people around the world.

Victimization Surveys

As victimology began to shift from a focus on theoretical issues toward empirical testing of some of these ideas in the 1940s and even more so in the 1960s, empirical instruments were needed. The method of inquiry that emerged as dominant was the victimization survey. Victimization surveys involve asking respondents to comment on whether they had been a victim of a crime and sometimes also asking specific questions about the event and the ways in which it was handled by the various elements of the criminal justice system.

Advantages and Disadvantages of Victimization Surveys

Although it is tempting to make comparisons between Uniform Crime Reporting (UCR) data and victimization data, since they focus on the same categories of crime, these two sources of information are very different: they access different populations (either offenders or victims), and they make different assumptions. As such, they complement rather than replicate each other.

Evans and Legar (1979) identified four major objectives and advantages of victimization surveys (VS). According to them, victimization surveys:

- Measure the extent and distribution of selected crimes, generating data that provide a more complete picture of crime than may be possible based on official sources. VS shed light on the dark figure of crime—the amount of crime not known to or recorded by the police.

- Measure the impact of selected crimes, such as injury and cost to victims (i.e., financial, emotional, and physical). Such information is unavailable through the UCR.

- Help assess the risk of victimization. VS can obtain information on known factors that affect a person's risk of being victimized and can also produce information about *perceived risk* of criminal victimization.

- Help assess the victim's perception of the functioning and effectiveness of different aspects of the criminal justice system, which can be contrasted with the perceptions of non-victims.

As useful as the VS appear, do we really learn enough from them to justify the investment of time and money in advocating certain policies? And are there possible negative repercussions, such as inciting unnecessary anxiety and fear? For example, various studies have shown that the sale of house alarms closely parallels the media presentation of victimization. Yet it is usually the people who need protection the most (people with low incomes and the young) who are least able to afford high-quality systems.

Although VS have become more commonplace in recent years, their results at times pose more questions than they offer answers (see Skogan, 1981). For example, measures of crime through general population surveys are problematic because, among other barriers, crime (especially serious and/or violent crime) is relatively infrequent; crime is not evenly distributed; and most criminals try to avoid detection.

Canadian Victimization Surveys

The first victimization survey was conducted in the 1720s in Denmark (Clinard, 1978). Interest in victims was somewhat cyclical until the 1980s, when social scientists and crusading journalists focused their discussions and debates on this topic. As a result, victimization surveys and research on victims have become somewhat more mainstream.

Starting in the early 1980s, Canada began to conduct the **Canadian Urban Victimization Survey (CUVS)**, which involved the participation of seven cities and the use of telephone interviews with some 60 000 randomly sampled Canadians over the age of 17. The survey covered eight categories of crime: assault, break and enter, motor-vehicle theft, robbery, sexual assault, household theft, theft of personal property, and vandalism.

In 1988, Statistics Canada began conducting a victimization survey as part of the **General Social Survey (GSS)**. The GSS served to replace the CUVS and introduced a more standardized and consistent format for gathering victimization data. Data was collected in 1988 (on personal risk), 1993 (on personal risk), and 1999 (on victimization) (see Box 12.2). Then in 2000, Statistics Canada switched to an annual survey; however, each year, the GSS focuses on a different topic (e.g., health and well-being, work and education background, social support, or victimization) (see Box 12.3). The survey is conducted by telephone and takes approximately 30 minutes to answer.

Another significant Canadian victimization survey was the first national **Violence Against Women Survey (VAWS)**, conducted in 1993. It involved telephone interviews with over 12 000 women 18 years of age and older. The questions focused on experiences of physical and/or sexual violence after the age of 16 as well as perceptions of personal safety. About half of the respondents had experienced at least one incident of violence since the age of 16, and about the same percentage said their assailant was by a male known to them. The VAWS has been the only study of its kind, but issues related to violence against women in Canada—such as fear of crime, stalking, sexual assault, and spousal violence—were explored in the 1999 GSS.

Finally, the federal government conducts annual surveys on family violence in Canada under the Family Violence Initiative and presents findings in publications titled *Family Violence in Canada: A Statistical Profile*. According to the 2001 and 2002 reports, which focused, respectively, on child abuse and the impacts and consequences of family violence, and the 1998 report, which provided a general overview of family violence, the victimization rate for seniors is 14 times lower than that for persons 18–24 years of age (157 versus 2226 per 100 000). Youth under the age of 18 are victims in 21 percent of all victimizations reported to the police. They also account for 60 percent of those who are victims of sexual offences and 20 percent of those who are victims of physical assault. The number of women and dependant children who have had to seek shelter from abusive settings increased around 10 000 to 101 248 in 2001–2002 in the 483 shelters across the country.

International Victimization Survey Initiatives

Given the growing interest in international and comparative research, let us briefly review the results from several other international survey initiatives.

Victimization in Britain

The Home Office in England has been conducting the British Crime Survey periodically since 1982. The survey focuses on people's experiences as victims in the previous year and on their attitudes toward crime and the criminal justice system. The 2001 data show (Crime Reduction Programme, 2002):

- A 13 percent drop in the amount of crime experienced by members of the public;

- From 1999 to 2000, a 12 percent fall in crimes against people living in private households;

- Statistically significant falls in the levels of burglary (17 percent), all vehicle-related theft (11 percent), other household theft (16 percent), and violent crime (19 percent);

- Small—and statistically insignificant—increases in theft from the person (2 percent) and theft of vehicles (1 percent); and

- Reduction in the overall fear of crime, but an increase in the levels of fear amongst those living in high-crime areas and those who were recent victims.

WHAT DO YOU THINK? BOX 12.4

AFRAID OR ANGRY?

Have you ever been a victim of a crime? If so, how did you feel? What was your reaction? One of the perceived benefits of conducting a victimization survey is to obtain a sense of the fear of crime among the populace being surveyed. Yet, as often happens when a relatively new field of study emerges, the concepts used to describe and/or explain the relevant phenomena may not be adequately operationalized. Such may be the case with the concept "fear of crime."

Jason Ditton and his colleagues (1999) conducted a study in which they explored the merit of the concept. Based on interview data, they found—contrary to expectation—that measures of fear do not always correlate with measures of anger. They noted that being "angry about the prospect of criminal victimization has been shown to be reported at higher levels than being afraid of it" (ibid.:98). They speculate that anger may stem from the general perception that crime is seemingly ever-increasing and that the criminal justice is not able to effectively fulfill its mandate. They conclude that it may be worthwhile to concentrate on the nature and meaning of anger in the context of victimization and that such a focus may actually help "resolve the issue more swiftly than has been the case with research into the 'fear of crime'" (ibid.:98). Such ideas raise methodological and practical concerns about how data is collected and used.

Victimization in the United States

In the United States, periodic victimization surveys have been conducted since the first systematic effort undertaken in 1966. Since 1972, the federal Bureau of Justice (BJS) has regularly carried out victimization surveys. In 1992, the survey was revised to include wider and better coverage of crimes. It is administered annually to a representative sample of some 100 000 respondents aged over 12 in 50 000 households. The survey addresses the frequency, characteristics, and consequences of criminal victimization in the United States. The following are some highlights from the 2000–2001 and 2002 surveys (Bureau of Justice Statistics, 2003):

- In 2002, the violent crime rate declined 10 percent since 1998, reaching the lowest level in National Crime Victimization Survey history.
- Property crime declined 6 percent, continuing a more than 20-year decline.
- In 2002, US residents aged 12 or older experienced approximately 23 million crimes, down from 24.2 millions crimes in 2001. Of these:

  - 76 percent (17.5 million) were property crimes, down from 18.3 million in 2001;
  - 23 percent (5.3 million) were crimes of violence, down from 5.7 million in 2001; and
  - 1 percent were personal thefts.

- In 2002, for every 1000 people aged 12 or older, there occurred:

  - 1 rape or sexual assault;
  - 1 assault with injury; and
  - 2 robberies.

- Murders were the least frequent violent victimization, at a rate of about 6 murder victims per 100 000 people in 2001.

The International Crime Victims Survey

The International Crime Victims Surveys (ICVS) has been conducted four times—in 1989, 1992, 1996, and 2000—in numerous countries (Nieuwbeerta, 2002). With each survey, the methodology has been refined to ensure more representative samples, and the resulting data allows international comparisons of crime. Yet, as Kury (2002) notes, this does not mean that the survey is without methodological limitations (also see Aebi et al., 2002). Such shortcomings aside, van Dijk and Shaw (2002:16) argue that international comparative statistics are needed because "crime in societies across the globe is converging, not diverging." The ICVS is one of the few surveys that has established a significant foundation in the industrial world and "has made useful inroads into collecting additional data from the developing world" (ibid.:20). However, due to financial limitations and political factors, it has been difficult to retain a consistent number of participating countries from developing nations (see Del Frate and van Kesteren, 2002).

The following findings are some of the highlights from the 2000 ICVS (CCJS, 2002, 22(4)):

- For 13 of the 47 countries that participated in the survey, an average of 22 percent of people surveyed had been victims of at least one of the 11 offences listed in the survey in the previous year. For Canada, the figure was 24 percent.
- The rates of victimization for those countries who participated in the 1996 cycle were fairly stable.
- The most prevalent victimization in 2000 was car vandalism; approximately 7 percent of respondents had their vehicle vandalized during the previous year.
- On average, just over half of the incidents were reported to the police. Scotland's reporting rate was the highest, at 65 percent; Japan's was the lowest, at 39 percent; and Canada's was 49 percent. While most property crime is reported, few sexual assaults are. The breakdowns vary across jurisdictions, which might suggest, for example, different levels of victims' confidence in the criminal justice system and/or different demands from other organizations, such as insurance companies.
- Levels of punitive attitudes toward offenders in Canada increased from 32 percent in 1989 to 45 percent in 2000. According to the survey, the trend toward harsher punishment was also witnessed in seven other countries.
- Most Swedes (85 percent) and Canadians (83 percent) felt safe when walking alone at night. Australians and Poles felt least safe (64 percent each) (CCJS, 2002, 22(4)).
- Contrary to previous surveys, the 2000 cycle did not find a relationship between prior victimization and fear of crime.

The number and quality of national and regional victimization surveys is growing. For example, in 1996, the first national crime victimization survey was carried out in the British West Indies by Painter and Farrington (1996). Similarly, national surveys have also been conducted in Germany (Kury et al., 1992) and Switzerland (see Aebi et al., 2002). In 2000, Brienen and Hoegen conducted a victims of crime survey in 22 member nations of the Council of Europe. They also evaluated how well the member countries have implemented the council's Recommendation (85)11 on the position of the victim in the framework of the criminal law and procedure.

Although these and other surveys have been productive in helping to illuminate the picture of reported and unreported crime, they have not been without their critics. In particular, concerns have been raised about the methodology. For example, how effective are the surveys in actually measuring the extent of crime in a society? How accurately can respondents remember what happened over the past year or two? Are respondents truthful in their answers? Does the fact that surveys tend to question only people in urban centres affect the results? However, researchers have made concerted efforts to address such shortcomings. For example, **Jan van Dijk** (1947–) (see Box 12.5) continues to try to standardize the manner in which the data are recorded and make the surveys consistent between countries. Due to the diligence of those who engage in victimization research, victimization surveys have slowly gained acceptance and have had a modest impact on the development of policies to address crime.

PROFILE BOX 12.5

JAN VAN DIJK: FATHER OF THE ICVS

Jan van Dijk got his auspicious introduction into victimology in the early 1970s, after he was asked to assume the class of the noted Dutch criminologist Willem Nagel. Nagel had left some unfinished notes pertaining to victims of violent crime. Van Dijk followed up on the research, eventually becoming more involved in the field. In subsequent years, he worked on various victimology projects for the Dutch government, as well as a number of related studies for the United Nations. He helped develop the first comprehensive national Dutch victimization survey and was regularly consulted by the Dutch government as it explored new avenues to address to address criminal events. In 1987, he became the founding president of the Dutch National Association of Victim Support.

Jan van Dijk was also instrumental in the creation of the first ICVS, conducted in 1987. The initial survey involved the participation of 14 countries. Since then, some 80 countries have participated in the various cycles of the survey, with 47 countries participating in the 2000 cycle, and the questionnaire has become the world standard for such surveys.

In addition, van Dijk has played a major role in the formation of the World Society of Victimology. He co-organized the 1997 symposium in Amsterdam and, with significant support from the Dutch Ministry for Justice, helped establish a newsletter and a website for the society. The website, located at **www.victimology.nl**, offers the most comprehensive collection of literature and information on victimology-oriented work.

Although van Dijk has been involved in numerous other ventures over the years, he is perhaps best known for his work on the ICVS and for spearheading initiatives within the UN that address the rights of victims.

Victim Characteristics

Virtually every victimization survey gathers social and demographic details that are used to differentiate victims from non-victims and/or identify those who might be a greater risk of victimization based on various characteristics. In this section, we turn our attention to these characteristics.

Age

According to the 1999 GSS, youths aged 16–24 are officially responsible for 40 to 50 percent of victimizations. Various studies also show that because a considerable proportion of offences occur within the same age group, young persons face much greater risk of victimization (e.g., bullying and minor assaults) than do older persons. *Juristat* data from 1999 indicate that the rate of victimization among those between the ages of 15 and 24 is 405 per 1000, as compared to 64 per 1000 for the 55–64 age group (CCJS, 2000, 20(10)). There also appears to be a strong relationship between one's lifestyle, age, and victimization. Adolescents and young adults tend to stay out late at night, frequent bars, restaurants, and other public places, and just hang out. Research indicates that while some 50 percent of victimizations occur in or around a private dwelling, nearly 30 percent occur at a public institution, and some 29 percent in public places such as pubs and parking lots (see, for example, Gomes et al., 1999).

In one of the first Canadian studies to examine victimization and fear of victimization among the elderly, Brillon (1987) reported that rates for fear of crime seem to increase among successively older age groups. However, as reflected in the 1999 CCJS report and the annual *Family Violence in Canada* (1998) report, those 65 years of age or older) are at considerably less risk (12 per 1000). However, given their physical, emotional, and often financial limitations, they tend to *feel* more vulnerable.

One of the more alarming findings from victimization research is the fact that homes are not as safe for children as one might expect. In 1984, the Badgely Report reported that young persons were more commonly victims of sexual abuse in the home than had been previously thought to be the case. Various subsequent studies pointed out how difficult it is to provide reliable estimates of abuse and neglect, but a comprehensive study in 1998 reported that approximately 45 percent of all cases investigated by welfare staff involved confirmed abuse (Trocme et al., 2001). Although researchers were somewhat aware of such facts, little had been done until recently to protect the rights and safety of children. Victimization research in this area has contributed significantly to programs and legislation to address this problem. For example, Irvin Waller, from the University of Ottawa, was instrumental in forging the UN Declaration on Children (see Winterdyk & Cao, 2004).

Gender

Gender is a major factor in certain crimes and social responses to them by society. According to the 1999 GSS, men are more likely to be victims of such crimes as robbery and assault, while women are more likely to be victims of sexual assault and theft. Overall, women are more likely to be victimized than men, although only by a slight margin (189 versus 183 per 1000).

Karlene Faith (2002) notes that, despite the 1990 report of a task force on women's imprisonment in Canada, the plight of incarcerated women has changed little. In 2002, more women were being detained for relatively minor crimes than for other forms of crime. They were arguably victims of a system that is unable, or unwilling, to bring about necessary reform. The discriminatory treatment of women has also been evidenced across college and university campuses across the country. For example, in 2003, the University of Calgary had to apologize to its female students for not notifying them earlier that three women had been assaulted in a university parking lot. In 2003, women were the victims of about 77 percent of reported criminal harassment such as stalking.

While the discriminatory treatment of women has garnered much needed attention, there has also been a growing body of research focusing on men being victims of domestic violence (DV). In his study of family violence in Canada, Hoff (2001) reports that over a five-year period of study, the prevalence of DV was 8 percent among women and 5 percent among men. Hoff further notes that the incident rate for men has been increasing over the study period. The results were comparable to available data from the UK and the United States. The author notes that men tend to report DV far less than do women. This lower rate is likely reflective of social norms, yet the underlying cause has to do with power and control (e.g., "she isn't sensitive to my needs").

Social Status

The most recent GSS data confirm that those Canadians in the lower social economic strata are more likely to live in areas that are crime-prone: in the inner city, in urban neighbourhoods, and on reserves. Official data show that households with incomes below $15 000 had victimization rates of 254 per 1000, while the national average was 186 per 1000. More specifically, violent crime among the lower social status groups was 192 per 1000, while the national average was 111 per 1000. Yet those with incomes over $60 000 represent the second highest victimized group. For example, those in higher income brackets are among the typical targets of home invasions (Kowalski, 2002).

Whether rich or poor, the targets of home invasions reflect the principles of the routine activities theory, which asserts that a perceived opportunity with low risk of apprehension and/or detection are conducive to resulting in a crime target. Other factors found to contribute to home invasions include a sense of impunity, perceived opportunity, and attractiveness of the target because of the target's lifestyle.

Marital Status

It is perhaps ironic that the CUVS failed to provide much information on spousal abuse since questions on this topic were simply not asked of the respondents. Furthermore, the survey neglected to include information about non-physical violence. The 1988 and 1993 GSS did gather information on attacks by family members but not specifically in relation to domestic violence. Consequently, the early GSS findings are conservative estimates, at 15 per 1000 women. In 27 percent of the cases, the accused was a family member; in 36 percent, an acquaintance or friend; and in 26 percent, a stranger. The data support the relationship between risk of victimization and lifestyle. A 1998 report by the Women's Bureau of Health Canada reported that three times as many female spouses are killed as male spouses. These issues are explored in greater detail in Chapter 13.

In response to these statistics and to the 2002 federal report on assessing violence against women, the federal government has taken steps to initiate special programs to protect and educate women about potential risks. Among the initiatives is the National Day of Remembrance and Action on Violence Against Women, the establishment of which was prompted by the 1989 massacre of 14 women at l'École Polytechnique in Montreal. Also, the *Criminal Code* has been amended to protect women and children in many contexts.

Race and Ethnicity

Because the issues of race and ethnicity are politically sensitive, it is difficult to obtain statistical data that addresses victimization based on these characteristics. However, there is plenty of anecdotal information to suggest that the relationship between victimization and race and ethnicity deserves closer attention.

In the aftermath of September 11, 2001, numerous Canadians of Arab origin became victims of racial profiling and discrimination. For example, the former head of the Canadian Arab Foundation and a once-esteemed member of the immigration review board of Citizenship and Immigration Canada was jailed for six days in 2001. She fell prey to a scam perpetrated by two men who came to her for immigration advice and convinced her that charging an illegal fee to expedite the applications of prospective immigrants from Arabic countries was worth the risk. To take another example, a Toronto man of Kuwaiti origin who had lived and taught for 32 years in Canada had his insurance on a building he owned cancelled by his insurance company without any explanation. As well, in 2003, a man of Sudanese origin was shot to death by a Calgary police officer; witnesses claimed that the man had only a knife. Similar incidents of victimization of people of different racial and ethnic origins abound. Every year, Immigration Canada deals with dozens, if not hundreds, of cases in which innocent refugees are denied access to the country. They are victims of a political system that is simply incapable of always knowing if it made the right decision.

As well, Canada's Aboriginal people are often the victims of racial discrimination. For example, an article in the *Toronto Sun* in February 2000 accused the Saskatoon police of "ethnic cleansing" (Mandel, 2000) or, in less controversial terms, prejudicial treatment of Aboriginal offenders. In one incident, they allegedly took an intoxicated Aboriginal man to the outskirts of the city and dumped him at the roadside in the dead of winter. The individual died from exposure. Similar stories have surfaced across the country over the years.

The connection between victimization and race and ethnicity remains a controversial and politically charged issue.

Repeat Victimization

In the late 1800s, Cesare Lombroso coined the term "born criminal." Today, the notion that there may be such a person as a "born victim" seems at times a possibility. Many of us know someone who just seems to always be getting into trouble, be the target of bad jokes, or simply have "bad karma." Aromaa (1974) found that about 25 percent of victims of violence are repeat victims. However, the fatalistic notion of the born victim has been replaced in contemporary victimology by such relativistic concepts as "predisposition," "propensity," "proneness," and "vulnerability." These factors refer to the victim's role and to how the victim might contribute to his or her own victimization.

While some victims become so by mere chance (i.e., being in the wrong place at the wrong time, as in the Taber High School shooting in 1996 or the Red Deer school shooting in 2004), the evidence increasingly reveals that risk of repeat victimization involves an interaction among such factors as one's age, personality, occupation, and lifestyle. The risk for young people can be further complicated by the fact that, according to a Toronto-based youth crime and victimization survey (Tanner & Wortley, 2002), more than half of those surveyed do not report their victimization to adult authority figures.

Theoretical Models and Victim Typologies

The victimological field has essentially come full circle. Initially, the focus was on trying to explain the process of victimization, and these theoretical ideas were applied to practice without much data. Today, the field is rich with data that are being used to reforge some of the theories of victimization.

Victim Precipitation Theory

The first attempts to develop victim typologies can be found the works of Mendelsohn and von Hentig. Unfortunately, these models were not based on any empirical evidence. For this reason, they receive little attention today. However, a brief summary is in order, to shed light on how the offender–victim relationship was viewed in the past. In essence, both Mendelsohn and von Hentig used what can be referred to as **victim precipitation theory**, which states that a victim, through his or her actions (or a lack thereof) presents him- or herself as a potential target for being victimized. In other words, the victim is a direct, positive precipitator in the crime; he or she shapes and moulds the crime. For example, the prevailing stereotype was that the more provocatively a woman was dressed, the greater was her risk of being victimized.

Mendelsohn's typology—the "correlation of culpability (imputability)"—focused on the degree of the victim's contribution to the crime. Mendelsohn identified six types of victims, ranging from the "completely innocent victim," such as a child or a person who is victimized while being unconscious, to the "simulating/imaginary" victim, such as a person who is paranoid, senile, or otherwise detached from reality—or, to use a modern-day variation, one who subscribes to conspiracy theories. For example, one sardonic website suggests that the American government intentionally put Céline Dion's music in the *Titanic* movie to stir negative emotions against Canadians. The site reflects a detached sense of reality about how a high-profile musician through her anti-patriotic lyrics can supposedly stir American patriotism by directing American anger toward Canadians for not respecting them.

Von Hentig's typology, according to Schafer (1976), was more sophisticated. He included psychological, sociological, and biological factors in developing his categories. He emphasized that there is no such thing as a "born criminal" or a "born victim"; rather, there are society-made victims. Von Hentig proposed 13 categories of victims. They included:

- *Young victim*: Because of his or her youth, this type of victim tends to be weak and inexperienced both intellectually and physically and can therefore easily become a target of sexual assault or kidnapping (legally defined as abduction). According to the RCMP's Our Missing Children organization (Our Missing Children, 2003), there were 387 reports of parental abductions in Canada in 2001.

- *Female victim*: Like the young, this type of victim demonstrates (overtly or passively) certain physical weaknesses. Since most offenders are male, they tend to have a physical advantage over this victim.

- *Minority victim*: This type of victim is a target because of racial prejudices. Hate crimes are among the offences against this victim.

- *Tormentor victim*: This type of victim tortures others to the extent that ultimately he or she becomes the victim.[3]

In the 1950s, the Swiss-Canadian psychiatrist Henri Ellenberger took several of von Hentig's concepts and conducted one of the few theoretical studies of the psychological relationship between the offender and the victim (cited in Fattah, 1991:179). Ellenberger identified three different types of psychological relationships: neurotic, psychobiological, and genetic-biological. Unfortunately, this vein of inquiry remains relatively untapped.

Lifestyle Model

According to Fattah (2000), one of the first important models that are more empirically oriented is the lifestyle model developed by Hindeland, Gottferedson, and Garofalo in 1978. In essence, these researchers suggested that one's risk of victimization correlates significantly with one's lifestyle. In other words, the more active and social you are, the greater your risk. For example, young college students, because of their generally active lifestyle, may take to such risky behaviours as excess drinking or use of illicit drugs. It is not only their grades that might suffer as a result of such lifestyle—these individuals are at considerably greater risk for becoming victims of a non-fatal crime (see, for example, Indicators of school crime and safety, 2002).

The lifestyle model shares many similarities with the opportunity model, which attributes the risk of victimization to demographic, social, and economic conditions or situations. A young person who goes out to the bars of Halifax or Winnipeg is at greater risk than a young person who goes camping on his parents' property in northern British Columbia.

There are three related hypotheses that are derived from the lifestyle model:

1. *The equivalent group hypothesis* suggests that the offender and victim share similar characteristics. This hypothesis seems most valid in relation to personal victimization. The GSS reports and various *Juristat* reports indicate that child victims, for example, are more likely to be victimized by someone they know than by a stranger.

2. *The proximity hypothesis* suggests some people knowingly place themselves at risk by choosing a high-risk lifestyle (e.g., frequenting certain bars or hanging out with gangs). It is generally acknowledged that such individuals do not actively encourage their own victimization; they just happen to make bad choices.

3. *The deviant place hypothesis* asserts that some areas are more conducive to criminal activity regardless of the precautions one takes. A bouncer at a bar, for example, deals nightly with individuals who sometimes have had too much to drink and is then required to remove them from the premises. The bouncer is obliged to fulfill these responsibilities as part of the job. Unfortunately, from time to time, a reluctant patron might take issue with the bouncer's actions.

Routine Activities Theory

Another model that has endured the test of time is the routine activities theory (RAT) (also discussed in Chapter 7), developed by Cohen and Felson in 1979. Its basic premise is that there are always individuals who are motivated to commit crimes. This theory focuses on the opportunity or suitability of targets; the lack of capable guardians or protectors of property, and motivated offenders. This approach encourages potential victims to consciously choose to reduce their potential risk of victimization by using various crime prevention strategies that make them less suitable victims (Davis, Lurigio, & Skogan, 1997).

There are several contemporary variations of the RAT that have met with varying degrees of success in explaining victimization (Cao, 2004). They are all part of the rational choice perspective and include the lifestyle theory, the rational choice theory, and situational theory. The lifestyle theory asserts that people can decrease or increase their potential risk of being victimized based on their lifestyle. For example, some people have lifestyles that involve very high risk (e.g., homeless or street people, prostitutes, bouncers, etc.). The basic premise is that the more one places oneself in harm's way, the more likely it is that one will be harmed. However, potential victims can take constructive steps to reduce their risk of victimization. According to the lifestyle theory, risk of victimization is related to the similarities in the lifestyles of potential victims and offenders; the proximity of potential victims to offenders in terms of living arrangements, and the type of areas in which potential victims live.

Collectively, these classical choice-oriented theories can be characterized as integrated theories, as they consider both individual and social and/or physical settings. These theories view victims as products of their situation within the social and economic context in which they life and/or work. Hence, one's living arrangements play a role in one's risk of being victimized. General support for this orientation can be found in the work of Miethe and Meier (1994), who also argue that there is considerable congruence between the RAT and life course perspective. However, Cao (2004:35) points out that "rational choice is not a measurement-oriented perspective...as it only assumes a limited rationality." Furthermore, Cao argues that the key concepts (such as guardianship, proximity, etc.) lack clear operational characteristics, which makes them difficult to measure in an objective manner. Nevertheless, the RAT and other rational choice perspectives have been widely used to provide policy-makers with a framework in which to think about crime prevention and its control.

Integrated Theory of Victimization

Since the 1970s, there have been a number of attempts to offer an integrated theoretical approach that might enrich our understanding of victim issues as well as reconcile differences found in previous theories (see Thornberry, 1989). For example, in 1991, Fattah attempted to integrate the various models described above in a comprehensive system. The main factors considered were:

- Opportunities;
- Risk factors;
- Motivated offenders;
- Exposure and associations;
- Dangerous times and dangerous places;
- Dangerous behaviours;
- High-risk activities;
- Defensive/avoidance behaviours; and
- Structural/cultural proneness.

While Fattah's attempt was a commendable effort with intuitive appeal, it has not been widely embraced, the reasons being perhaps that there are too many factors to be considered and that there is no clear direction as to how to weigh the various factors.

While it is not the purpose of this chapter to espouse the virtues of one theoretical model over another, it can be said that the field of victimology has established itself, like criminology, through the use of a variety of different theories. These theories have been used to explain victimization, forge research, and direct effective policy.

While theories of victimology have made significant advances since the 1940s, we should avoid the risk of placing victims in the new role of scapegoats in crime explanations. To this end, sound theory must guide sound policy. As with criminological theories, no one theory can provide a clear answer to all forms of victimization. Yet the different theoretical perspectives serve as objective models by which to better understand and possibly prevent, or at least reduce, the risk of victimization.

From Theory to Practice:
The Emergence of Victims' Rights

"Tears shed for the accused are traditional and 'trendy' but has the law none for the victim of crime, the unknown martyr?" Justice Krishna Iyer of the Supreme Court of India (cited in Rao, 1988:213).

As noted earlier, perhaps the most significant international document relating to victims' rights has been the 1985 UN Declaration of Basic Principles of Justice for Victims of Crime and Abuse of Power, which catapulted the study of victimology into the political realm. Irvin Waller, from the University of Ottawa, was instrumental in bringing this declaration into existence. The full text of the declaration can be accessed at **www.unhchr.ch/html/menu3/b/h_comp49.htm**.

Although countries such as the United States have been slowly trying to amend their Constitution to ensure the protection of crime victims' rights, at the time of preparing this chapter, the Constitution Subcommittee of the Senate Judiciary Committee had not yet passed the requested amendment. By contrast, legislation pertaining to crime victims' rights has been passed in England, several European countries, Australia, and Canada. In Europe, victims' rights have been recognized since the 1980s by the Council of Europe. In 2001, the council updated the rights to ensure the following main principles (New rights for victims..., 2003):

- Victims of crime are entitled to a high level of protection.
- The laws and regulations of member states should be approximated to achieve the main rights set out in the framework decision.
- The needs of crime victims should be addressed in a comprehensive and coordinated manner to avoid secondary victimization; thus provisions are not confined to criminal proceedings.
- Cooperation between member states should be strengthened through networks of victims' organizations.
- Suitable and adequate training should be given to people who come into contact with victims of crime.

In 2003, federal, provincial, and territorial ministers responsible for justice endorsed a new Canadian Statement of Basic Principles of Justice for Victims of Crime (2003). These principles reflect those found in the UN Declaration of Basic Principles of Justice for Victims of Crime. The Canadian principles are intended to promote fair treatment of victims and are supposed to be reflected in federal, provincial, and territorial laws, policies, and procedures. These principles are as follows:

1. Victims of crime should be treated with courtesy, compassion, and respect.
2. The privacy of victims should be considered and respected to the greatest extent possible.
3. All reasonable measures should be taken to minimize inconvenience to victims.
4. The safety and security of victims should be considered at all stages of the criminal justice process and appropriate measures should be taken when necessary to protect victims from intimidation and retaliation.
5. Information should be provided to victims about the criminal justice system and the victim's role and opportunities to participate in criminal justice processes.
6. Victims should be given information, in accordance with prevailing law, policies, and procedures, about the status of the investigation; the scheduling, progress and final outcome of the proceedings; and the status of the offender in the correctional system.
7. Information should be provided to victims about available victim assistance services, other programs and assistance available to them, and means of obtaining financial reparation.
8. The views, concerns and representations of victims are an important consideration in criminal justice processes and should be considered in accordance with prevailing law, policies and procedures.
9. The needs, concerns and diversity of victims should be considered in the development and delivery of programs and services, and in related education and training.
10. Information should be provided to victims about available options to raise their concerns when they believe that these principles have not been followed.

These principles are intended to ensure the fair and equitable treatment of all victims throughout the criminal justice process.

Victim Impact Statements

Victims have a right not only to be assured that the offender is justly punished for the transgression committed against them, but also to be permitted the opportunity to offer their impressions to the court during its decision-making process. These contributions are formally known as **victim impact statements (VIS)**. In these written statements, victims can describe the effect that crime has had on them. VIS represents one attempt to meet the needs and interests of crime victims. Yet, it is not clear whether the victims should have a right to influence the sentencing of an offender, especially in an adversarial criminal justice system, where a crime is an offence against the state and a person in punished by the state.

The VIS was first introduced in the United States in the mid-1970s, and today it is used in all but a few states. Canadian legislation did not come into effect until 1988, when an amendment to the *Criminal Code* (see Box 12.6) allowed victims of crime to present in writing a victim impact statement. In the statement, they can describe the harm done to them or the loss suffered as a result of the crime. With the passing of this amendment, courts are now obliged to consider a VIS in their decision-making process. The rights of a victim were further extended in 1995, when Bill C-37 was proclaimed, allowing VIS to be presented in youth courts.

A CLOSER LOOK BOX 12.6

SECTION 722 OF THE *CRIMINAL CODE*: VICTIM IMPACT STATEMENT

(1) For the purpose of determining the sentence to be imposed on an offender or whether the offender should be discharged pursuant to section 730 in respect of any offence, the court shall consider any statement that may have been prepared in accordance with subsection (2) of a victim of the offence describing the harm done to, or loss suffered by, the victim arising from the commission of the offence....

(2) For the purpose of this section and section 722.2, "victim," in relation to an offence,

  (a) means a person to whom harm was done or who suffered physical or emotional loss as a result of the commission of the offence; and,

  (b) where the person ... is dead, ill or otherwise incapable of making a statement referred to in subsection (1), includes the spouse or common-law partner or any relative of that person, anyone who has in law or fact the custody of that person or is responsible for the care or support of that person or any dependant of that person.

Although the *Criminal Code* is a federal law, the lieutenant-governor in council of each province directs how a VIS is to be prepared. For example, in Alberta, the VIS program is provided by police services and victim assistance programs such as the John Howard Society. In New Brunswick, victims are given the opportunity to prepare a VIS form that is provided by the New Brunswick Department of Public Safety. The department's victim service staff can assist the victim in preparing the statement.

Preparing a VIS is voluntary, and the victim has the option of reading the statement in court, but such a reading should not be seen an opportunity for the victim to seek private retribution for any harm done or to be emotive toward the offender and/or the court. However, Dugger's (1996) study found that it is somewhat conducive to the retribution goal. Alternatively, the victim may choose to not appear in court but have the statement read by the police or representative from a victim's assistance program (Victims of crime research series, 2004). The Crown, prosecution, and offender are privy to the content before the reading of the statement. A third scenario is that the presiding judge may elect to read the statement out loud to the court, in which case the name of the victim is disclosed. As Canadian experience has shown that the nature of the statement and the demeanour of the victim can play a significant role in how the court receives a VIS.

An American study of VIS in New York found that VIS resulted in a number of negative outcomes ranging from undue public pressure on judges, additional court costs and court delays, and impact on the uniformity in sentencing (Davis & Smith 1994). Conversely, a study of VIS in South Australia revealed that "any concerns about negative effects of VIS on the criminal justice system were unwarranted" (Erez et al., 1994:70). Judges and prosecutors rarely reported cases of a VIS that was inflammatory or otherwise unacceptable. The VIS did not appear to artificially increase the sentences delivered or result in increased restitution or compensation. The majority of the victims' were satisfied with the outcome of the case.

In their survey on the perception of Canadian judges of VIS, Roberts and Edgar found that the judges "appear to find material in the victim impact statements that is relevant to the task of determining the sanction to be imposed" (2003:8). However, there was a lack on continuity in how the information from VIS was presented. Since then, this problem has been effectively addressed through recent changes in legislation to assist in ensuring a standardized approach to presenting such testimony. For example, the 1995 *Witness Protection Program Act* allows the RCMP to place witnesses and informants under protection while they testify. Nevertheless, victims are still reluctant to submit statements, and there have been few cases in which victims were permitted to present their statements orally (see Roberts & Edgar, 2003). For example, in the late 1990s, only about 14 percent of victims of crime filed statements in Alberta.

Victim Assistance Programs

Victim Compensation

In 1976, Stephen Schafer observed that regardless of which country's legal system one examines, "one seeks in vain a country where a victim of crime enjoys the expectation of full compensation or restitution for the injury, harm, or loss he suffered" (1976:162). As Schafer and others have noted, while the state has concerned itself with the punishment of the crime, how the statement impacts the outcome of the trial has been regarded almost as a private matter.

In the past 25 years, considerable progress has been made in the area of compensation. A growing number of different compensation systems can now be found around the world. However, it can be argued that there is still room for improvement. One of the challenges of most government indemnification programs is that most face budgetary restraints. These restraints tend to limit the scope of compensation, not to mention the number of victims who can be assisted. Miethe and Meier (1990) argued that state compensation is essentially a symbolic gesture to appease the victim, as the remuneration is token in nature. In fact, Fattah (2000:35), citing his own research, notes that "in some countries there is a deliberate attempt not to publish these state compensation schemes."

On an optimistic note, in 1988, the Canadian federal government amended the *Criminal Code* under subsection 655.9(1) so that the minimum amount of a victim fine surcharge applied to the offender is $35. In accordance with section 737 of the *Criminal Code*, the offender must make the payment within two months or two years, depending on the nature of his or her sentence. The minimum fine has been subsequently increased to a minimum of $50 for offences punishable by summary conviction and to a minimum of $100 for offences punishable by indictment. The surcharge can be imposed even when the sentence is for a victimless crime (Fattah, 2000). For example, in 2003, NOCO Canada Inc., based out of Perth, Ontario, was fined $2000 for failing to comply with provincial environmental waste laws and was also required to pay a victim fine surcharge, collected by the courts (NOCO Canada..., 2003). Most provinces have regulations that allow them to apply a victim fine surcharge of up to 25 percent. For example, in addition to the $80 000 fine for violating the Ontario *Occupational Heath and Safety Act*, the Great Atlantic & Pacific Company of Canada Limited was required to pay a 25 percent victim fine surcharge as required under the *Provincial Protection Act* (The Great Atlantic..., 2003).

Court Services

The Canadian Statement of Basic Principles of Justice for Victims of Crime, quoted earlier (see page 371), directly and indirectly recognizes and endorses principles that ensure the provision of court program services designed to assist victims and address their needs when attending court and in dealing with the criminal justice system process. Services can range from providing transportation to and from court to providing a counsellor who may accompany the victim in court to answer relevant questions.

Victim Service Programs

As of 2003, every province and territory offered some form of victim/witness assistance program. These programs are fairly diverse in their nature and organization, often in accordance with local needs, conditions, and resources. For example, the Calgary Police

Service's Victim Assistance Unit, operating since 1977, provides (on a free and confidential basis) (Victim Assistance Unit, 2004):

- *Support* through its 35+ volunteers, seven days a week, 24 hours a day. Programs include hospital and home visits, court accompaniment, restitution request, victim impact statement (VIS), court preparation, and robbery trauma support.
- *Information* and answers to such key questions as: Has an arrest been made? When is my court date? How does one file a VIS? How does one report any additional stolen property? Who is the officer in charge of the case?
- *Referral services* for victims who might be in need of additional services. In Calgary, the organizations referred to include counselling agencies, distress/crisis lines, public trustee, and medical examiner's office.

Public Education

The federal Department of Justice supports various provincial and territorial public legal education and information initiatives that serve to inform the public about the law and how it affects people. In addition, specific victim assistance projects offer information and assistance to certain types of victims to help them deal with their victimization. One example is CAVEAT (Canadians Against Violence), founded in 1982. The organization relied on donations to operate, but in May 2001 it had to close it doors due to a lack of resources and legal complications. During its 10-year existence, it offered public educational programs that increased people's awareness of their level of risk and taught prevention skills, among other constructive initiatives.

Crisis Intervention

Given that victims are often negatively impacted emotionally, psychologically, and/or financially, many victim service programs make referrals to organizations and programs from which victims can obtain specialized help. The list of these organizations and initiatives is extensive, covering areas such as domestic violence, physical child abuse, sexual assault (e.g., see sections 161, 810.1, 264, and 718 of the *Criminal Code*), and terrorism. Although most provinces have legislation specific to victims of crime, the range of services and crisis intervention varies among the provinces. For example, the Ontario Victim Crisis Assistance & Referral Services (VCARS) program is a community response program that works in conjunction with the local police services. In 2004, there were 38 sites throughout the province offering crisis intervention and related services (Victim Crisis Assistance..., 2004). In addition, victims who are in need of special support or help can use services provided by the RCMP, through the Canadian Resource Centre for Victim Assistance of Crime; the federal government, through its Policy Centre for Victim Issues; and the Department of Justice, though its Victims of

Crime Initiative (see Victims of Crime Initiative, 2004). As virtually every organization notes, crisis intervention is an important element of the healing process for victims and should be an important element of each agency or organization that deals with victims of crime. In addition, such services need to be delivered in a humanistic, orderly, and structured manner. This involves the use of such basic strategies as providing empathy, understanding, and validation of the fact that the victim is entitled to feel anger and hurt.

As extensive as some programs have become, there are areas where improvements are still needed. Groups of victims that specifically need to be addressed are teens, children, men, family members of offenders and the victim, the homeless and others who make their living off the streets, and various ethnic groups. For example, while federal government has funded various initiatives to support female victims of domestic violence and while there are 508 shelters for women, there are less than a handful of privately funded organizations and shelters for men (More men..., 2003).

Victim–Offender Reconciliation Programs

Victim–offender reconciliation programs (VORP) have been established as a result of the restorative justice movement. Although restorative justice has been widely practised for centuries in agrarian and less formalized cultural settings of the world (for example, among Aboriginal people of Australia, in Canada's First Nations and Inuit communities, and in the Mennonite Church in North America), it has just recently entered mainstream criminology.

Beginning in the early 1970s, the Mennonite Church began to set up victim–offender reconciliation programs in Canada and the United States. By 1996, there were well over 300 of them in the US, about 20 in Canada, and over 500 in Europe and the UK, while more were scattered in about 20 other countries (Price, 1996). Today, the concept has evolved and has adopted different nomenclatures, ranging from victim–offender reconciliation programs and victim–offender mediation programs to peacemaking conferences. Many of these programs are run by volunteers, and it is not possible to obtain reliable numbers as to the extent to which victim–offender reconciliation has grown. However, the spread and growth of the programs does speak volumes about the efforts of many communities to respond to the needs of both the victim and the offender.

Evaluation of Victim Assistance Programs

As extensive and expansive as victim assistance programs have become, it is unclear whether they are reaching all those in need. International data suggest these programs are not as accessible as they should and perhaps could be. For example, Maguire (1991) estimated that about only 1 percent of the crime victims in Britain come into contact with victim services programs. An American study conducted in New York found that "between only 2% and 10% of the victims who filed criminal complaints used the services of the program" (Davis et al., 1999:102).

Also, are the programs meeting victims' needs? Although there has been some research into this issue, considerably more work needs to be done. Based on their British study, Davis and his colleagues suggest that such services need to improve "in terms of outreach, speed of intervention and service priorities...as well as their responses to the most vulnerable groups of crime victims" (1999:114). But various studies reveal that the level of satisfaction among the victims and offenders who participate in initiatives founded on the restorative justice model tends to be fairly high, lending support to the idea that it is better to restore social harmony than punish transgressions (see Wemmers, 2002). Victims who participate in restorative justice programs often get support and recognition. They also feel a higher level of procedural justice. These factors contrast with the experiences of victims in the traditional criminal justice system—hence the push for victims' rights to information, consultation, and participation.

Finally, as much as respect and support for the victim is important, the manner in which society responds might require a degree of caution. Canadian criminologist Brian MacLean (1992) argues that the study of victims simply represents an excuse for the state to exert social control by enhancing fear within society. The total amount spent on of house alarms, for example, far exceeds the financial losses incurred as a result of theft from houses. While views such as MacLean's may be in the minority, they highlight the dangers in seeing victimological research as a total solution to the criminal justice system.

New Directions in Victimology

Fattah (2000:39) observes that victimology, like criminology, appears to have gone through its idealistic state of focusing on the "poor suffering victim" to a more realistic, sophisticated, "defensible view of two human being caught in a web of intricate social relationships and human emotions." Striving for more rights for the victim is not necessarily better per se; it may be just as counterproductive as it is to overcriminalize!

The concept of being a victim typically conjures up images of pity, empathy, and a need to provide support. As the interest in victims became more mainstream, an enterprising host of "victim therapy" programs spring up. A perusal of the internet will reveal a lot of such programs and services, ranging from special services for children who have been victimized to more generic "victim treatment and therapy services." In his keynote address to the 9th International Symposium on Victimology in Amsterdam in 1997, Fattah argued that just as rehabilitation and treatment initiatives for offenders have met with questionable success, the same will hold true for programs for the victim. In the future, he suggests, current victim therapies will be replaced with alternative healing practices, "reinforcing the natural healing powers of the human psyche, [and] strengthening the family and social networks of potential and actual victims" (Fattah, 2000:42).

Today, both criminology and victimology (perhaps somewhat ironically, given the history of past tension between them) are being equally influenced by the restorative justice model, which offers new ideas about offender–victim relationships and our responses to them. Restorative justice initiatives are having a profound influence on justice paradigms For example, Fattah (1999) feels that the arbitrary distinction between crimes and civil torts will disappear and that we will likely be witness to a breakdown in the current barriers between criminal and civil courts.

One thing is certain: the victim no longer is—nor will likely ever again be—the forgotten factor in a criminal event. While victimization methodology and its data have improved significantly over the years, they still do not provide sufficient information on offenders. For those who are interested in studying the causes of criminal behaviour, this lack of thoroughness is a notable shortcoming. Ultimately, to obtain a more comprehensive picture of the offender–victim relationship, we will need to continue to improve official Uniform Crime Reporting data, self-report data from offenders, and victimization data.

Based on current trends, in the coming years and decades we will likely see the much-needed research into the effectiveness of victim assistance programs and the effects of victimization. For just as we learned in criminology that policy not supported by research tends to become bad policy, we can see that victimology, across all its venues, needs to be grounded in solid theory and backed by sound research. As the area gains additional momentum and government support, these objectives are likely to be fulfilled, and victimology will become a major area of study within criminology. While there were but a handful of presentations related to victimology a few years ago at such major North American conferences such as that of the American Society of Criminology, there were several dozen sessions on the topic in 2004.

Summary

- The study of victims has become a major focus in recent years and is referred to as victimology.
- Those at greatest risk of being victimized are young females, persons living in lower socio-economic settings, married people, and those leading risky lifestyles.
- Among the dominant theories of victimization are victim precipitation theory, lifestyle model, and routine activities theory.
- Practical applications of theories include victim impact statements, public education, and victim–offender reconciliation programs. Despite the growth in victim services, gaps in coverage and service availability remain.
- In recent years victims' rights and interests are being entrenched in restorative justice initiatives as well as various compensation schemes.

Discussion Questions

1. How are a victim's needs to be assessed?

2. Should all victims receive compensation, or should victim compensation be contingent upon the victim's actions not contributing to the crime?

3. Which of the theories covered in this chapter seems the most plausible to you? Explain why and offer an example to illustrate your point.

4. Explain the basic assumptions of routine activities theory and the lifestyle model. Discuss how these theories may or may not be supported by examining victimization data.

5. How might one design a policy to reduce victimization among those groups most likely to experience victimization? Incorporate a discussion of at least three situational crime prevention techniques into your answer.

Key Concepts

Canadian Urban Victimization Survey (CUVS)

victim impact statement (VIS)

victimology

General Social Survey (GSS)

victim precipitation theory

Violence Against Women Survey (VAWS)

Key Names

Benjamin Mendelsohn   Jan van Dijk   Hans von Hentig

Weblinks

canada.justice.gc.ca/en/ps/voc/ The website of the Policy Centre for Victim Issues at the federal Department of Justice offers government publications on the topic of victims of crime, as well as news updates, details of related legislation, and links to resources at the provincial level.

crcvc.ca/en/ The Canadian Resource Centre for Victims of Crime is an advocacy organization whose aim is to "ensure the equitable treatment of crime victims in Canada." The site offers information about CRCVC as well as online publications and links.

www.vaonline.org/prov.html This page offers a comprehensive directory of victim services across Canada.

Endnotes

1. This chapter was prepared largely on a Visiting Fellowship at the Max Planck Institute in Freiburg, Germany. I am indebted to the Institute for its kind support and wonderful resources and am particularly thankful for the assistance and support of Professor Hans-Jörg Albrecht.

2. On June 14, 2004, Briere pleaded guilty to first-degree murder. DNA evidence from a soda pop can he discarded was used to link him to the crime. He claimed to have acted upon an urge after viewing child pornography on the internet.

3. For a complete listing and description of both Mendelsohn's and von Hentig's typologies, see Schafer, 1976:154–156.

CHAPTER 13

Women and Crime

"There can be no doubt about women's violent potential."

Heidensohn, 1992

"Women commit the majority of child homicides."

Pearson, 1998

Learning Outcomes

After you have completed this chapter, you should be able to:

- Appreciate the history of the study of women and crime.
- Identify the most important gender issues in criminology.
- Appreciate the need to see female crime not only as a social construct but also as a biosocial disorder.
- Identify the characteristics of female offenders.
- Understand the main explanations of female crime.

Crime is ever-present in our world, and it cuts across all demographic categories such as age, gender, and class. Hardly a day goes by when we do not hear or read about a criminal incident in the news. If you have paid attention, you have probably noticed that while women are typically portrayed as victims (e.g., of rape or assault), they also commit crimes. Boritch (1997) has observed that, until recently, criminologists have tended to focus on female victimization instead of studying women and crime.

Two rationales for this lack of attention are that "women represent a minority of all offenders, across time and culture" (Boritch, 1997:4–5) and that most crimes committed by women tend to be petty property-related offences. In addition, the patriarchal aspects of society (including the criminal justice system) have typically viewed female offending as "sick" or "pathological" and therefore not a serious social problem.

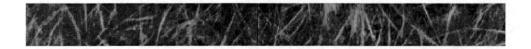

Swigert and Farrell (1976) observed that being a female seemed to serve as a mitigating factor when women's criminality was assessed. They used the term **pedestal effect** to describe a social and definitional orientation that they feel contributes "to the less severe treatment accorded women accused of homicide" (ibid.:80). The view of women as needing protection means that they have traditionally been less likely to be arrested and incarcerated and more likely to receive lighter sentences. This benevolent attitude toward women has also been referred to as the **chivalry hypothesis**.

In spite of an apparent lack of interest in female offenders, the number of women being charged with criminal offences in North America has nudged upward over the years. This has been especially true among adolescent females (Reitsma-Street, Artz, & Nicholson, 2004) (see Box 13.1). Today, earlier attitudes have been mostly discredited (see DeKeseredy, 2000). It is important for criminology to pay attention to criminal behaviour trends and patterns among women.

BY THE NUMBERS BOX 13.1

FEMALE OFFENDERS IN THE CRIMINAL JUSTICE SYSTEM

- In 1997–1998, 12 percent of all Canadians charged with violent crime were women. By 2003, the figure climbed to 16 percent (CCJS, 2004, 24(6)). However, the majority of the offences committed by women involved minor assaults.
- In 2003, Aboriginal women made up 3 percent of the population of women in Canada, but represented 29 percent of all federally sentenced women. Between 1997 and 2002, their representation in federal prisons increased by 36.7 percent. Yet it is estimated that 87 percent will experience physical violence at some time in their lives (CAEFS, 2004).
- Worldwide, women constitute the fastest growing prison population. Many of those who are increasingly incarcerated are "racialized, young, poor women and women with mental health disabilities" (ibid.).
- "Young women represent a greater proportion of youth sentenced to custodial care than do young males" (ibid.).

This chapter will begin with a brief historical overview of the role of women and the female offender. As Boritch (1997:5) points out, being familiar with "the legacy of the past [is important] in understanding the contemporary context of women's criminality and the criminal justice system response to women." Boritch claims many of the issues surrounding our misconceptions about female offenders and their treatment are the product of stereotypical images perpetuated throughout the ages.

We will proceed to discuss the extent and nature of female offending and focus on how female offenders differ from male offenders on such variables as motivation, age, race, and social class. We will also examine a number of specific crimes that are perpetrated by women. Where possible, Canadian information will be used, but as many researchers have observed, most "sources available for literature searches in Canada are primarily American or North American" (Shaw & Dubois, 1995:2).

This empirical discussion will be followed by an overview of some of the early and more recent theoretical explanations of the reasons women commit crimes. We will begin by looking at the early biological explanations that stigmatized the female offender and progress to the feminist perspectives that attempt to provide an integrated and interdisciplinary approach to understanding the female offender. But before we get into these issues, let us look at the history of women and crime.

The History of Female Offenders

One of the first works on female offenders was written by one of the pioneers of criminology, Cesare Lombroso (see Chapter 4). Lombroso, in collaboration with his son-in-law, Guglielmo Ferrero, wrote *La donna delinquente, la prostituta e la donna normale*. First published in 1893, it appeared in English (and several other languages) in 1895 and was titled *The Female Offender*.

Many of the stereotypes that preceded Lombroso's work can be found in this book. For example, Lombroso described women as being very child-like in their emotions and level of sensibility. Relying on historical and some ethnological material, Lombroso suggested that "prostitutes and prostitution represent reversionary or atavistic phenomena"[1] (Wolfgang, 1973:254). Relying on the examination of women's physical traits, he argued that genuine female offenders "are endowed with the same fundamental peculiarities found in male criminals, and that prostitutes and other genuine criminal feminine types are characterized by a lack of 'mother-sense'" (ibid.:255). While popular in the 19th century, such views have since been largely discredited. However, consistent with today's crime statistics, Lombroso did point out that while females commit fewer crimes than males, they commit far more crimes than official statistics show.

Between 1893 and the 1960s, very little was written on female offenders. Among the more noteworthy studies was a 1930s research project undertaken by Sheldon and Eleanor Glueck in which the authors attempted to discover the biological and environmental causes of crime. The Gluecks included women in their study project, and although their findings were decidedly sociological, their work inspired others to examine the causes of female crime. In the 1950s, **Otto Pollak** was among the first to attempt to break the stereotype that women offenders are biological aberrations. Instead, he emphasized the importance of family structure in determining women's activities. He suggested that women tend to commit crimes that are deceitful in nature, such as fraud and shoplifting, supposedly using deceit to compensate for their physical weaknesses. Pollak described crimes committed by women as "masked crimes." Since he did not use empirical data to support any of his assertions, the feminist movement that subsequently emerged was quick to condemn him for perpetuating stereotypes and for being unable to provide supporting evidence (see Gavigan, 1987:52).

Many early studies not only lacked empirical support—they were also at times demeaning. For example, in the 1938 *Report of the Royal Commission to Investigate the Penal System of Canada* (known as the Archambault Report), when referring to the 32 women at Kingston Penitentiary for Women, the authors concluded, "The number of trainable women is very small, and the women prisoners apart from young prisoners who are capable of deriving benefit from continued education would constitute a small class" (cited in Gavigan, 1987:79).

While the early research was sporadic, the emergence of the feminist movement led to a more concerted effort to understand both the female offender and the female victim. Specifically, the feminist writings of **Freda Adler** (1975) and **Rita Simon** (1975) caused renewed interest in the relationship between gender and crime. Both Adler and Simon argued that the **women's liberation movement** (see Box 13.2) helped women access legitimate and illegitimate opportunities. While their claims about future trends in female criminality have been overstated (see Barak, 1997), their efforts were instrumental in compelling criminology to study female offenders.

A CLOSER LOOK BOX 13.2

WOMEN'S LIBERATION MOVEMENT

The term "women's liberation" was first used by the French feminist writer Simone de Beauvoir in her 1953 book *The Second Sex*. The term was used to refer to women as deserving equal status as men in every way, whether educational, political, social, and/or economic. As Canadian author and feminist Donna Laframboise (1996:1) phrased it, "when little girls grow up they should be able to be anything they want to be—doctors, lawyers, political leaders or fighter pilots."

Canadian women have only been able to vote in federal elections since May 24, 1918, but they did not acquire legal status as "persons" until 1929. Since then, many have reached prestigious positions. Jeanne Sauvé became the first female governor general, first female Speaker of the House of Commons, and the first female MP from Quebec to be a cabinet minister. Kim Campbell was the first female prime minister, and Audrey McLaughlin was the first woman to serve as head of a federal political party in Canada and North America (*Then and now*, 1997).

The women's movement began to truly gather momentum at a societal level in the 1960s, spurring many changes at all levels of society. The following are some interesting examples of the difference it has made:

- It was illegal to distribute information about birth control as late as 1969.
- As recently as the early 1970s, many females weren't permitted to wear trousers to school or work because they were considered "unfeminine" (Laframboise, 1996).
- Canada did not get its first female Supreme Court judge until 1982.

Additional impetus for the feminist perspective on criminology came from the first anti-rape group in the early 1970s in San Francisco. Known as the Bay Area Women Against Crime, the group included criminology students expressing feminist ideas in action, ideas that were instrumental in bringing about criminal justice reforms (Schwendinger & Schwendinger, 1991). These and other efforts helped make women a central subject in criminology.

One of the first Canadian studies on women offenders appeared in the *Canadian Journal of Corrections* (now the *Canadian Journal of Criminology and Criminal Justice*) in 1969. Then, in 1976, **Phyllis Haslem**, executive director of the Elizabeth Fry Society (Toronto Branch) wrote a chapter on female offenders for McGrath's (1976) criminal justice textbook. Haslem expressed the belief that, contrary to popular opinion, female offenders are not any more difficult to work with than are men. Nevertheless, she stated that women need to be treated differently than men in order for each of them to "gain or regain a sense of her own worth" (ibid.:475). Haslem offered eight general recommendations for change. They ranged from eliminating the mandatory physical search on entry into prisons to providing "suitable, colourful, well-fitted clothing."

Throughout most of the 20th century, the **Elizabeth Fry Society** (see Box 13.3) championed the cause of female offenders and female victims. However, one of the most significant reports that helped bring the issue of female crime into the limelight in Canada was the 1986 report commissioned by the government entitled *A Feminist Review of Criminal Law*. It was the first report to approach Canadian criminal law from women's perspective. In the following year, Ellen Adelberg and Claudia Currie (1987) were among the first Canadians to write about the Canadian female offender. They said they felt "compelled to break the historical silence surrounding women offenders" (ibid.:11).

As already mentioned, the influence of feminism has been felt in criminology since the 1970s. In addition to feminist-oriented research, there has been a smattering of other studies, primarily from the critical criminology perspective, that have also focused on women's crime and on criminal justice issues related to women. Notable Canadian scholars include Walter DeKeseredy and Ronald Hinch (1991), who have written extensively on the abuse of women; Holly Johnson (1996b), who has focused on violence against women; and Sacco and Kennedy (1998), who have researched the general victimization of women.

While there is a growing body of information on female victims, there is still a dearth of literature on the female offender. Yet, based on the titles of some recent books—for example, *Too Few to Count* by Adelberg and Currie (1987, 1991), *The Invisible Woman* by Belknap (1996), *When She Was Bad* by Pearson (1997), *Casualties of Community Disorder* by Baskin and Sommers (1998), *Women, Crime and the Canadian Criminal Justice System* by DeKeseredy (2000), *Women Who Kill* by Davis (2001), and *Mothering from Inside: Parenting in a Woman's Prison* by Enos

(2001)—the interest in female offenders is increasing. However, comparing the number of studies on this topic to the extent of material available on the male offender, there is much room for research here. It is hoped that this chapter might inspire others to study female offenders, not just in terms of gender issues but as part of an integrated and interdisciplinary approach to the study of crime and criminality.

A CLOSER LOOK BOX 13.3

ELIZABETH FRY SOCIETY

Elizabeth Fry (née Gurney) (1780–1845) was born into a family of Quakers in England. Quakers were among the first denominations to believe in the equality of women. Having been brought up in such an environment had a profound impact on Fry and her work at London's Newgate Prison. She became a strong proponent of the humane treatment of female prisoners and was instrumental in promoting prison reform (CAEFS, 2004).

The first Canadian Elizabeth Fry Society was established in Vancouver in 1939. The Canadian Association of Elizabeth Fry Societies was incorporated as voluntary non-profit organizations in 1978. In 2004, there were 26 member societies across Canada. CAEFS is a federation that works with, and on behalf of, women involved with the justice system. The member societies emphasize community-based services and programs for "marginalized women, advocating for legislation and administrative reform" (CAEFS, 2004).

On May 5, 1995, Herb Gray, then solicitor general of Canada, and Marie Cadieux, director of the National Film Board productions *A Double Tour* and *Twice Condemned*, helped launch National Elizabeth Fry Society Week, held in the week before Mother's Day. Member societies organize public information events to promote awareness and support. Volunteerism is an essential part of the society (CAEFS, 2004).

Despite the gaps that exist in the research on this topic, let us now turn our attention to the female offender.

The Female Offender

"Part of reclaiming women's history is documenting our oppression in all facets of life." Adelberg and Currie, 1987:21

Gender Differences

Before we focus specifically on women, perhaps we should ask whether there are differences between the genders. How do women differ from men? Observable and measurable differences between males and females have been the subject of much controversy. In their classic study, Maccoby and Jacklin (1974) reviewed over 1600 gender difference studies, from which identified four major differences between the genders:

- Females are more verbal (left hemisphere);
- Females are less visual, aural, and spatial (right hemisphere);
- Females are less adept in science and mathematics; and
- Females are less physically aggressive, dominant, and curious.

While these traits are not universally embraced by other academics who study gender difference, Maccoby and Jacklin stressed the biological influence of gender differences. However, others have argued that biology cannot account for all the differences. For example, in subsequent work in the area, Maccoby, Snow, and Jacklin (1984) agree that social learning and the socialization process likely play a mediating role in accounting for gender differences. Yet, others contend that the differences are the product of social learning influences but that these processes also correlate with both biological and environmental contributions, reflecting a more integrated approach. The point is that we should not assume that an either/or relationship exists when making female–male comparisons. For example, both "males and females vary between being highly aggressive and very unaggressive" (McKie, 1989:19).

For these reasons, it is important to adopt an interdisciplinary perspective when trying to understand gender differences. One example that illustrates this point is the famous study done by Kalat in the late 1980s (cited in Blum, 1997). Kalat studied the impact of socialization on sexual behaviour among young males in the Dominican Republic. Because of a genetic defect, most of the boys studied did not have a fully developed penis until adolescence. Until that point, they were raised as females, but once their gender identity became clear, they were treated as males (which they were all along). Although they were raised as girls, the boys readily adapted to their "new" identity. Similar studies have been done of males who lost their penises shortly after birth due to an accident or during circumcision. Most of the documented cases indicated that the male preferred to behave in a "male way." All these studies show that both social reinforcement *and* the effects of biology (e.g., testosterone and hypothalamus differences) can play a determining role in behaviour.

The Role of the Media

As the American sociologist and criminologist Richard Quinney noted, "social reality begins in the imagination" (cited in Finley & Finley, 2003:570). Because of our cultural fascination with the media and crime, the media plays a powerful role in forging the way in which we see and think about things. Karlene Faith (1987), from Simon Fraser

University, argues that the media tend to portray female offenders as violent individuals and/or predator lesbians. She, among others, claims that female offenders "are mocked by B-grade movies about women's prisons which feature male-oriented sex-and-violence plots complete with predatory characters who prey on young, innocent types" (ibid.:183). These movies also stereotypically portray female wardens and/or female staff as cold, "masculine" females. Faith describes these movies as insulting to both female staff and those who are in prison and contends that they represent a sub-genre in which women are exploited. Such negative depictions of women in the movies also run the risk of possibly desensitizing viewers to the way women are treated in real-life penal institutions (Finley & Finley, 2003).

While Faith makes a number of excellent points, much of what she describes—sexual violence, "masculinity" among female offenders, the degradation of women in general, etc.—can also be regularly found in male-centred B-grade prison theme movies (see also the more recent work of Wilson & O'Sullivan, 2004). Since Faith does not draw gender comparisons on how women might be treated differently from men in the media (or in any other social context), it is difficult to gauge the extent to which such problems are unique to female offenders and female prisons, let alone other social settings. Katz (2004), for example, reports the results from a telephone survey on sexual harassment on over 700 workers. The authors of the study found that 31 percent of the women and 7 percent of the men claimed to have been sexually harassed on the job. In the case of the women, 100 percent of these incidents were committed by men, while women were responsible for harassing men in only 59 percent of reported incidents.

In one incident, Faith notes that a male inmate told her how he felt humiliated after being "treated like a woman," while a female prisoner told her how degrading it was to be treated like a child (ibid.:199). Unfortunately, anecdotal incidents do not a case make, but both individuals speak to the degrading treatment that offenders can receive while incarcerated. There is, however, considerable evidence showing that female victimization and fear of victimization is often associated with women being portrayed as stereotyped objects who can be controlled by men (Belknap, 1996).

At another point, Faith points out that since there was no concrete data until 1994, there was "no basis for believing that the violence that does occur in P4W" (Kingston's Prison for Women) was comparable to the amount of violence portrayed in such Canadian movies as the 1986 *Turning to Stone*. She considers the movie to be a realistic depiction of female offenders and life in women's prisons. Yet, in April 1994, P4W was the subject of one of the worst scandals in Canadian prison history. Female inmates were brutally assaulted by male prison staff, while the female warden allegedly turned a blind eye to the whole incident, though she may not have been fully aware of what had happened during the "shakedown." The incident shows how women can be, and are, the subject of male exploitation.

Notwithstanding some methodological shortfalls in her article, Faith makes a poignant observation in suggesting that the media could be used to educate the public about the realities of social and cultural issues surrounding female offenders and female prisons.

THE STORY OF MARLENE MOORE

"Marlene Moore was a woman who kept her soul, despite the brutality she experienced. She was a miracle." June Callwood (cited in Kershaw & Lasovich, 1991)

Marlene Moore (1957–1988) was the first Canadian woman to be classified as a dangerous offender after the provision was introduced in 1977, primarily to deal with violent sex offenders. Moore was the third youngest of 12 children. Her father repeatedly beat with the buckle end of his belt for her bed-wetting, which continued until she was almost 16. Her brothers allegedly abused her sexually; in addition, she was raped when she was 16.

Moore began her run-ins with the law as a young child, with repeated incidents during her elementary school years. Her first official contact with the law occurred when she was just 13, in the early 1980s. She was committed to a maximum-security institute of a training school where three-quarters of the girls had mutilated their bodies. She herself is thought to have slashed herself over a thousand times. From then on, she spent a considerable period of her time being detained in various types of facilities, which resulted from her violent acting out behaviour. In 1983, in a Toronto court, a friend requested that Moore be released into her custody, fearing that should she stay in an institution, she would act out her frustrations. In his remarks, the presiding judge ruled, "I have never heard any application that has less merit than this one. The record speaks for itself." Moore's criminal history was rife with a pattern of repetitive violence, and she was described by the Crown as a "time-bomb that was totally out of control."

Overall, after her first contact with the justice system, Moore spent almost 80 percent of her time in detention. Because of her involvement in a dramatic hostage taking incident at an Ontario jail, she was transferred while still a teenager to P4W in Kingston. In spite of various efforts by friends, institutional staff, and the Elizabeth Fry Society, Moore continued a life of crime and trouble and was in and out of various detention centres in southern Ontario until 1988, when she was sent back to P4W and was declared a dangerous offender after numerous efforts made by her various lawyers to avoid the classification.

On December 3, 1988, after getting involved in another violation, Moore requested a visit to the hospital ward because of her ill health. When left unattended, she hung herself. The following year, several of her family's members took her ashes and spread them on Lake Wilcox, where she had spent her early childhood. Mary Lasovich and Anne Kershaw wrote a book about Moore's life titled *Rock-a-Bye Baby*, and in 1997, CBC produced an award-winning documentary on Moore's troubled life entitled *Dangerous Offender*.

I would like to acknowledge the assistance of Charlene Diamond at the Calgary Elizabeth Fry Society for helping to track down the relevant information for this box in the Society's library.

WOMEN OFFENDERS: MAD, BAD, OR EXPLOITED?

In November 1994, a 21-year-old Aboriginal prostitute, Lisa Neve, told *The Edmonton Journal* that she was "public enemy number one." Her problems with the law began in the late 1980s, when she was sentenced to four months in jail for uttering threats, carrying a concealed weapon, and failing to comply with a court order. Over the ensuing years, she continued to have altercations with the law, until 1994, when she was charged with robbing and stabbing another woman. Later the same year, the court declared her a dangerous offender—only the second woman in Canada to receive this label. At 21, Neve also became the youngest person ever to be designated a dangerous offender and was incarcerated in maximum security units in different men's prisons.

Is Neve only a criminal or also a victim? At the age of 12, she had been recruited by a pimp and forced into prostitution. In an effort to escape her torturous life, she attempted suicide and engaged in self-mutilation on numerous occasions. Were her criminal acts a cry for help? Perhaps one of her statements best expresses her plight and the attitude of the criminal justice system, "I wish they'd spend half the time they did on my case sending the men who hurt me to jail" (cited in Boritch, 1997:12).

In 1998, after 15 months of deliberation, the Alberta Court of Appeal overturned Neve's dangerous offender status. Today, Neve tries to lead a normal life and gives talks on her life experience.

In Canada, life sentences and indeterminate sentences can both result in imprisonment for life. However, an indeterminate sentence is a result of a designation made by the court resulting from an application by the Crown. For an offender to be classified as dangerous, application must be made to the court, and the consequence is imprisonment for an indeterminate period (Corrections and conditional release..., 2003). As of March 2004, there were 331 individuals classified as dangerous offenders (DOs) in Canada, of which around 70 were declared long-term offenders. The number of DOs has grown steadily since 1997, when the government added the category of long-term offender to the *Criminal Code* (Moore, 2004). The rate peaked in 2001, with 29 new dangerous offenders designated by the courts. Ontario has the most of such offenders, while in 2004 Prince Edward Island had none.

Although no specific public information is available on the exact number of DOs by gender, a correction report reveals that in 2002–2003 women represented 4 percent of the indeterminate admissions (Corrections and conditional release..., 2003:54). It is perhaps because of their comparatively low numbers that women serving life or indeterminate sentences are not having their needs adequately met.

Until 1993, if asked about female crime, most Canadians would have probably pointed to such offences as prostitution, shoplifting, and fraud. Then the gruesome case of Paul Bernardo and his now ex-wife, Karla Homolka, captured media attention as few other criminal cases ever have in Canadian history. Homolka assisted her husband in the sexual slaying of two teenage girls: Leslie Mahaffy, from Burlington, and Kristin French, from St. Catharines. She also contributed to the death of her own sister, Tammy, a murder she was never convicted of. Pearson (1998) suggests that this may have been the result of Homolka's defence lawyer trying to use the "battered wife syndrome" to deflect direct responsibility to Paul Bernardo. Needless to say, the public was repelled (Boritch, 1997).[2]

Is Homolka an anomaly among women (see Boxes 13.4 and 13.5)? Do women commit crimes for the same reasons men do? What kinds of crimes do they commit? Because of the Homolka case, suddenly people wanted to know more. Female offenders finally gained a public platform.

A Growing Concern

According to official UCR data, there has been a significant increase in the absolute number of women being officially charged with criminal offences (Corrections and conditional release..., 2003). Between 1962 and 1992, the number of women charged for all offences rose from 27 530 to 115 770; it then declined until 2000, when it began to increase again. In 2002, 95 380 women were charged with criminal offences, with violent offences climbing from 14 853 in 1996 to 18 853 in 2002 (Statistics Canada, 2004). Among the adult offender population, women only represent 17 percent of the total population dealt with by the criminal justice system, of which 3 percent are sentenced to federal institutions (Elizabeth Fry Society, 2004). The number of women admitted under sentence to provincial/territorial facilities has increased by 13 percent between 1986–1987 and 2003 (ibid.). Of course, this figure does not account for those crimes that go undetected and/or unreported. It can be assumed that the actual growth in female crime is even greater than reported.

Boritch (1997:19) notes that since these absolute numbers over an extended period, "it is not immediately clear whether the growth in female criminality has kept pace with the growth in Canada's female population." However, in referring to Campbell's 1990 special CCJS report, she observes that when the numbers are converted into charges per 100 000, it is clear that female crime rates increased—from 476 per 100 000 in 1962 to 1092 per 100 000 in 1989.

Allen and Simenson (1997:302) report that "the female prisoners' population growth outpaced that of males." Between 1989 and 1998, the number of adult women incarcerated climbed from 203 to 360 (Elizabeth Fry Week, 1999) while general admission was dropping (CCJS, 2003, 23(11)). Although the number of incidents committed by female offenders has been increasing since the 1960s, *Juristat* has not released a report on female offenders since 1990 (although it did report, in 2001, on Canada's shelters for abused women). Is this scarcity of data and analysis a reflection of the criminal justice system's continuing lack of interest in the female offender? Does it reflect the ideological bias that still dominates Canadian criminology and criminological thought?

Violent Female Offenders

Kelly Blanchette (1997:14) recently pointed out that "violent crime has traditionally been viewed as a uniquely male phenomenon." In fact, as Shaw and Dubois (1995) observe, men outnumber women by a large margin, and this difference holds true "across countries, over time, at all ages, and in relation to different types of violence." Most people have been conditioned to believe that women are only the victims of crime and that when they do commit crimes, it is a result of mitigating circumstances—"acts of necessity." However, since 1986, there has been a slow but steady increase in the rates of female violent crime. Nevertheless, female offenders are less likely to be incarcerated for violent crimes than are males and they are considered to have a lower risk of reoffending than violent male inmates (CCJS, 1999, 19(5)).

Relying on slightly dated information from the Offender Intake Assessment process used in Canadian Corrections, Blanchette (1997) examined available demographic data on 182 federal female offenders since 1994. She reports that:

- 106 (58 percent) were designated as violent.
- 76 (42 percent) were designated as non-violent.
- The average age of the entire population was 33.8 years. Violent offenders' average age was 32.4, while non-violent offenders' average age was 34.5.

A 2001 federal corrections report reveals that there were 866 women with federal sentences. Of these, 40.9 percent were incarcerated, and 51 percent were placed in remand, with the balance receiving community service sentences (*Profile of women...*, 2001). And although most of the women who are sentenced to a federal institution have committed serious violent offences, in 2002 only eight mothers were accused of killing their children—the lowest number since 1965 (CCJS, 2002, 23(8)). While it costs approximately $68 000 to incarcerate a male offender in a federal penitentiary per year, it costs around $115 000 to detain a female offender in a federal institution (ibid.).

The majority of violent offences committed by women in Canada still involve minor assaults (Dell & Boe, 1998) (see Box 13.6). However, women convicted of violent offences are more than twice as likely as violent men (36 percent versus 16 percent) to commit violence against someone close to them. For example, in 1997, the victims of women in prison for homicide included relatives (in 5 percent of these women), intimates (such as husbands, friends/possible lovers, common-law partners, or boyfriends; in 33 percent), relatives of the offender (in 5 percent), acquaintances (in 18 percent), strangers (in 7 percent), own and non-biological children (in 13 percent), and prostitute clients (in 5 percent) (Lavinge, Hoffman, & Dickie, 1997). As the authors of this study note, contrary to public perception, the offender's victims were mostly not intimate partners. Yet, as Allen and Simenson (1997:304) point out, the profile of the average imprisoned (American) female inmate "hardly reflects a dangerous offender for whom incarceration in prison is required." Based on recent data produced by Corrections Canada, the same observation appears true of Canadian female offenders (Corrections and conditional release..., 2003).

WOMEN AND VIOLENT CRIME

- In 2003, 58 percent of the violent crimes committed by women were for charges classified as minor assault (The patterns..., 2003).
- Women are significantly more likely to be victimized by a spouse than are men. In 1999–2000, over 96 000 women and dependant children were admitted to 448 shelters for women across Canada (CCJS, 2001, 21(1)). The Transition Home Survey reported that 73 percent of the women and 84 percent of the children were in shelters to escape abuse (ibid.).

Female offenders in general are less likely than male offenders to have a previous criminal history, but they are more likely to have a partner with a criminal history. In addition, various reports have noted that nearly one-third of female inmates reported they were under the influence of a drug at the time of committing the offence (The patterns..., 2003). Shaw (1994) found that 53 percent of sentenced women reported having been sexually abused at some point in their lives, while another, more recent study cited nearly 40 percent (The patterns..., 2003). Whatever the exact figure, abuse clearly plays a part in many offenders' lives.

Blanchette (1997) found that violent female offenders more often lack family ties during childhood. As illustrated in Table 13–1, female offenders were also more likely to have poor employment records, to use drugs, to have weak interpersonal skills, and to have a poor attitude toward the different elements of the criminal justice system. In addition, adult female offenders with a history of family, emotional substance abuse and/or employment problems were statistically more likely to become violent adult offenders than those women who did not experience major difficulties (Blanchette, 1997).

Blanchette (1997) also found that 55 percent of those in the violent offenders group have attempted suicide in the past; in contrast, the percentage of those in the non-violent group was less than half of that. Some have used this type of data to lend support to the notion that violent female offenders are somehow psychologically (if not biologically) unstable or different than non-violent female offenders. Yet Farrell (1993), among others, argues that violent women do not experience any more psychological disorders than non-violent females or males; they simply report them more. For example, Asher (1996) reports that male suicide rates in Canada are 376 percent higher than

Section III: Contemporary Issues in Canadian Criminology

TABLE 13-1

AREAS OF EXPRESSED NEEDS OF VIOLENT AND NON-VIOLENT FEMALE
OFFENDERS AT ADMISSION

TYPE OF NEED	VIOLENT (N = 106) %	NON-VIOLENT (N = 127) %
Employment	80.2	70.1
Marital/Family	87.8	68.5
Substance abuse	73.6	45.7
Personal/Emotional	97.2	82.7
Attitude	35.8	20.5

Source: Adapted from Blanchette, 1997:15.

those among females. But male suicide rates are currently double the rates they were during the 1930s—the Depression years— which likely points to an increase in reporting rather than an actual increase. On the other hand, female federal inmates are more likely to have a history of suicide attempts (48 percent) than men (13 percent).

These and other related issues pose interesting and challenging questions for gender-based violence. Much more research needs to be conducted in relation to the female offender. For example, in recent years, just as an increasing number priests are being charged with pedophilia, an increasing number of female teachers are being charged with sexual assault for having sex with their students. The increasing number of incidents involving women and violent crime appears to further support the assertion that there is an interaction between social and biological factors. As Blum (1997), among others, notes, a growing body of knowledge suggests that genetics might also play a role.

Homicide

Women kill far less frequently than men do. In 2002, 67 women were killed by their male partner or ex-partner, as compared with 16 men killed by their female partner or ex-partner (CCJS, 2003, 23(8)). Historically, the sex ratio of partner homicide has remained fairly stable. There is a growing body of research that shows that when women do kill, their methods and reasons for killing are usually different from those of their male counterparts (see Box 13.7). A majority of women who kill their partners have been victims of abuse. Given the widespread presence of domestic abuse of women, however, it is not clear why so few women, comparatively speaking, commit murder.

FEMALE VIOLENCE

- In November 1997, Reena Virk, a 14-year-old girl from Saanich, BC, was found dead near a riverbank. Seven of her assailants were female. Only one boy was involved (Bailey, 1998). The accused claimed (though this was never proven) that Virk stole one of the girl's phone books and called her male friends to spread rumors about them. Based on evidence presented, two of the accused, Kelly Ellard and Warren Glowatski, were motivated by hatred toward Virk because of her visible minority status and physical appearance.
- A month earlier, a 32-year-old Danish nurse was charged with killing 22 patients at a home for the elderly. She said she had become emotionally distraught after her father had refused to see her in 1994 (Nurse charged..., 1997).

Lavigne et al. (1997) found many of the same demographic factors that related to violent female offenders, as reported in Blanchette's (1997) study, also related to women convicted of homicide. Women who killed usually killed only one person. Most offenders did not live with their victim, although in 18 percent of the cases the victim was an acquaintance, and in 14 percent the victim was the husband. Strangers accounted for only 7 percent of the victims, while 15 percent of the homicides involved the death of a child cared for by the offender.

Dougherty (1993:94) asserts that not only have female perpetrators of child abuse and infanticide been virtually ignored in the literature, but researchers have relied on "gender neutral psychiatric factors and defects in character structure" to explain their behaviour. Sodhi (2000) notes, however, that the penalties for women who kill children are less severe than that those for men who kill children, especially when a newborn child is involved. This is in part due to the fact that section 233 of the *Criminal Code* includes a provision for diminished responsibility for women who kill their newborns. Official data indicate that the number of mothers accused of killing their children has increased in recent years. Between 1974 and 2000, 400 (step)mothers versus 460 (step)fathers were accused of killing at least one of their children (CCJS, 2003, 23(8)). It is not clear why a woman might kill her child. One of the explanations suggested in recent years is postpartum depression.

Female Serial Killers

One aspect of female violence that has received minimal attention has been the topic of female serial killers (see Davis, 2001). Part of the problems lies in the fact that there is no universal definition of a serial killer. According to Hickey (1991:6), a serial killer is "any offender who killed three or more victims over time." While there are slight variations on the definition, it is generally agreed in the literature that serial killing among women is a relatively rare event.

Several years ago, Keeney and Heide (1994) estimated that 10 to 15 percent of serial killers are women. They found that females use different *modi operandi* than do males. For example, while males are more likely to use violence and torture and have direct physical contact with their victims, females are more likely to poison or smother their victims. Women are more likely to lure and seduce their victims, while men typically track and stalk them. Female serial killers tend to murder for "comfort" purposes, which according to Holmes and Holmes (1993) include money, insurance benefits, or business interests. However, as with any crime, there are exceptions.

One infamous female serial killer was Aileen Wuornos, the "Spiderwoman," of Florida, who in 1992 was found guilty of killing seven men. She would pose as a hitchhiker and wait for men to pick her up. She would then rob and kill them by shooting each one multiple times and leave their naked bodies at the roadside. Her motive, according to Holmes and Holmes, was "mission-oriented." Having been abused and neglected by male figures in her life, she sought to gain revenge by seducing and then killing her victims. Her life was recently depicted in the movie *Monster*.

Mann (1996) notes that female serial killers average 9.2 years of killing and 8 to 14 victims before being caught. In comparison, men average 8 to 11 victims before being caught (Hickey, 1997). In addition, Mann reports that female serial killers tend to be slightly older (32 years of age) than male serial killers (28.5 years of age) (Hickey, 1997). Nearly one-third are housewives. Davis (2001) identifies several different types of female serial killers, including power-motivated killers (e.g., Charlene Gallego and Karla Homolka) rejection-filled killers (e.g., Catherine Birnie), and revengeful killers (e.g., Aileen Wuornos).

Hickey (1997) points out how the media stereotypically portray female serial killers as having more psychopathic tendencies than their male counterparts. Gender bias is also reflected in the criminal justice system, in that female serial killers are less likely to end up on death row (in the United States), are more likely to be placed in a psychiatric facility, and generally receive shorter sentences.

Additional research needs to be conducted in order to better understand why some women kill—and why some women become serial killers. The question of why women continue to account for fewer violent crimes than do men also remains unanswered.

Aboriginal Women and Violent Crime

In terms of homicide, UCR data indicate that Aboriginal women are overrepresented in the female offender population (Corrections and conditional release..., 2003) (see Box 13.8). Although they represent only 3 percent of the adult population, in 2001–2002 Aboriginal women accounted for 20 percent of the provincial and territorial prison admissions and for 16 percent of federal institution admissions (CCJS, 2003, 23(11)). In addition, they make up some 50 percent of women who are classified as maximum-security prisoners, yet about 58 percent of them are charged with minor assaults and only 13 percent are charged with serious assaults. Lavigne et al. (1997)

found that Aboriginal women are more likely to be convicted of second-degree murder (approximately 50 percent of those convicted) as opposed to manslaughter (34 percent) or first-degree murder (11 percent). The majority of the Aboriginal female offenders are under the age of 35, and a significant number are survivors of physical and sexual abuse, are single mothers with one or two children, and often have a substance abuse problem (Elizabeth Fry Society, 2004). The Elizabeth Fry Society further points out that Aboriginal women are regularly denied services for women and access to specific programs designed for Aboriginal offenders. Regardless of the type of crimes they commit, Aboriginal female offenders continue to be marginalized.

FYI BOX 13.8

ARE ABORIGINAL WOMEN MORE LIKELY TO KILL OUT OF PROTECTION?

Although Aboriginal women commit more violent crimes than non-Aboriginal women, Silverman and Kennedy (1988) found that they are more likely than Caucasian women to defend themselves against violent men and are better at protecting themselves than Caucasian women.

A CLOSER LOOK BOX 13.9

VIOLENCE AGAINST INUIT WOMEN

As part of her doctoral thesis, Evelyn Zellerer (1996) examined violence against Inuit women in the Canadian Eastern Arctic. She noted that while there is a growing body of literature on violence against women, very little is written about violence against Aboriginal women or about abuse of women living in rural areas. Adopting an interdisciplinary perspective, Zellerer examined a variety of information and, in addition to official statistics, relied on in-depth interviews and personal observations.

Overall, Zellerer found that Inuit women were the subject of a startling amount of violence. She further noted that there were few resources available to such victims and raised concerns about community-based justice initiatives. In support of these observations, Morris (2002) reports there is a virtual absence of alternative housing arrangements for such women.

LaPrairie (1993) reports that Aboriginal women are more likely to commit violent crimes than non-Aboriginal women. She, among others, attributes the increase in Aboriginal women's violent crime to increasing marginalization and a breakdown of traditional cultural norms and values (see Box 13.9). However, as important as these social factors are, it is crucial to understand the extent to which long-term substance abuse, dietary history, and genetic predisposition exacerbate the plight of Aboriginal people. This is a politically sensitive issue that has not yet been explored. However, the Elizabeth Fry Society (2004) notes that between 1988 and 1992, six out of the seven women who committed suicide while at P4W were Aboriginal women. In 1996, another suicide occurred after an inmate was told that her children could no longer visit her.

In their review of the literature, Shaw and Dubois (1995) note that in the United States, violent crime is higher among black women and that they are more likely to be charged with violent offences than other women. Both American black women and Aboriginal women have been described as being products of historical and socio-economic factors that marginalize their opportunities. Hence, both groups must struggle against racial and cultural bias and gender prejudices.

Women and Property-Related Crime

"In Canada the first person to be officially condemned to death in 1640, was a French girl, sixteen years old. She was convicted of theft." Carrigan, 1991

Based on their practical experience gained while working in the criminal justice system, Adelberg and Currie (1987) note that most of the women charged with property-related offences they encountered were young and poor (see Box 13.10). Few had finished high school, and still fewer had any training for the job market. In addition, the institutions that housed them offered very limited opportunities for upgrading social, educational, and practical skills. Overall, Adelberg and Currie (1987:13) observed that "women offenders' lives did not seem to improve after coming into contact with the criminal justice system." Furthermore, they noted that the vast majority of Canadians are quite naive about the actual workings of the justice and corrections systems.

FYI BOX 13.10

PROPERTY CRIMES AMONG WOMEN

In 1975, the proportion of Canadian women who were charged with property offences accounted for 55.5 percent of all female offences, an increase from 45.1 percent in 1965 (Johnson, 1987). In 2001, the proportion of property-related offences committed by women was down slightly, to 43.9 percent, reflecting a steady decline for almost a decade (Profile of women..., 2001). The most common property-related offence among women is theft under $5000, accounting for approximately 30 percent of all property-related offences in 2003 (CCJS, 2004, 24(6)).

The general increase in female criminality and the absolute increase in property-related crime in particular (that is, an increase in the frequency, not the rate), can be explained partly by the changing patterns of criminal opportunity for women. Freda Adler (1975) argued that the women's liberation movement would not only help break down barriers to equality between men and women but also result in increased aggressive criminal behaviour in women. Although a number of subsequent studies supported this view, other studies pointed out that while the overall rate has declined in recent years, the number of property crimes still represents the largest increase in women's offending (see Shaw & Dubois, 1995).

The increase in the number of property-related offences has been explained in terms of increased poverty among women. Even though the percentage of women in the labour force has increased steadily since the late 1960s (from 38 percent in 1969 to 58 percent in 1989), women are still disproportionately employed in lower-paid service industry jobs (O'Neill et al., 1994). Chunn and Gavigan (1991) suggest that changing social attitudes toward prosecuting women may be a viable explanation, while Thomas (1993) argues that the changes in the roles of women (for example, women working in order to support the family) have added extra stress and subsequently predisposed both men and women to lead more aggressive lives. However, the overall impression in the literature is that no single conventional explanation can satisfactorily account for the absolute increase in property-related crime as well as violent crime.

Women and White-Collar, Corporate, and Organized Crime

The political, economic, and technological changes since the 1970s have had a major impact on the role of women at home. As noted above, since the early 1970s, an increasing number of women have entered the professional work force. Therefore, it should come as no surprise that women have also been charged with white-collar, corporate, and organized (WCO) crimes. Data on women who commit these crimes are very limited. Although there are no specific data on women in the professional workforce, several years ago an American study found that between 1990 and 1996 there was a 55 percent increase in women convicted of fraud. Consumer complaints filed during 2001 with the Internet Complaint Center show that females comprised almost 18 percent of the "individual perpetrators identified and reported by victims of fraud" (Haantz, 2002). Citing data from the UCR, Haantz (2002) notes that the most common charges against women in this area were embezzlement, followed by forgery. Kathleen Daly (cited in Haantz, 2002:2) suggests that "women's economic marginality, not liberation or occupational mobility better describes the form of female white collar crime."

Although women are still underrepresented relative to men in this area, the relationship between WCO crimes and women deserves further investigation(see Pollock, 1999). Ogle, Maier-Katin, and Bernard (1995) suggest that violence and crime committed by women may be motivated and influenced by different factors than violence and crime committed by men. Their observations include the following:

1. Women experience higher stress than men.
2. Women have more blockages on anger-coping mechanisms than men.
3. Women are more likely than men to develop overcontrolling personalities.
4. Women are more likely than men to explode in an episode of extreme uncontrolled violence when experiencing high stress.

Although Southland, Collins, and Scarborough (1997) argue that these propositions do not appear to apply directly to the workplace, they did find that women are more likely to leave the workplace and are more effective in their attempts to commit suicide. They also observed that female offenders in general are younger than their male counterparts (median age of 30 versus 36 years), and they are also more likely to receive shorter prison sentences than men for similar crimes. Overall, however, Kelta Advance Learning (2003) reports that in spite of entering into professional positions in increasing numbers, women do not appear to be responding to opportunities in the same way as men do. Women are still principally committing shoplifting and theft, although Martha Stewart's involvement in a stock scandal highlights the fact that some women do commit white-collar offences.

In summary, as criminology pays increasing attention to female offenders, research indicates that more and more women are coming into conflict with the law, although crime rates for women are consistently lower than those for men. Over time, women have become more involved in a variety of crimes, including those traditionally thought of as "male crimes," such as crimes of violence and white-collar crimes. Rather than simply focusing on gender-related issues, criminology needs to embrace an integrated and interdisciplinary perspective when trying to understand how and why women become more involved in non-conventional crimes—and why are they are generally less criminal than men.

Competing Explanations

Thanks in large part to the feminist movement, researchers have begun to study female crime separately from male crime. It has become politically and socially correct to recognize these differences. Nevertheless, the stereotype has been that women are not supposed to be criminals; if they are, they must be either "bad" or "mad." Fortunately, over the years, a number of perspectives have evolved to explain female crime. We will look at five divergent explanatory models, summarized in Figure 13–1.

Biological Positivism

The biological perspective is perhaps the oldest and most controversial approach explaining female crime. As discussed earlier in this chapter, Lombroso was among the first to offer some scientific verification of the biological determinism of female offenders.

FIGURE 13-1

PERSPECTIVES ON FEMALE CRIME

THEORIST	BIOLOGICAL/ PHYSICAL CHARACTERISTICS	PSYCHOLOGICAL/ PERSONALITY FLAWS	GENDER ROLE SOCIALIZATION	WOMEN'S LIBERATION	FEMINIST THEORY
Adler 1975			X		
Chesney-Lind 1973				X	
Cowie et al. 1968	X	X			
Hagen et al. 1979			X		
Heidensohn 1985					X
Hoffman-Bustamonte 1973			X		
Konopka 1966		X			
Lombroso 1889	X				
Pollak et al. 1961		X			
Schafer 1946	X				
Simon 1975				X	
Smart 1976					X
Steffensmeier 1978				X	
Thomas 1923		X			

Source: Adapted from Brown, Esbensen, & Geis, 1991:525.

While his ideas of being able to differentiate criminals from non-criminals based on their physical traits have since been debunked, some researchers focused on other observable traits. For example, Susan Edwards (cited in Gavigan, 1987) refers to literature that supposedly linked female crime to menstruation, menopause, and even pregnancy and childbirth. Even the Canadian media got mileage out of publishing articles in the 1980s linking pregnancy to crime (ibid.).

Such ideas reinforced the stereotype that female offenders are not "true" criminals but women who are "sick" at a given point in their life, a condition that predisposes them to commit a crime. As has been the case with much of the biological research until recently, the these studies were often methodologically weak. It is interesting to note that most discussions of any biological link are often limited to Lombroso and many of the earlier studies.

Another commonly cited work is that of **William Thomas** (1923). Although a sociologist, Thomas was influenced by the works of Lombroso and Ferrero. Examining case studies of delinquent girls, he reasoned that human behaviour was dominated by four key wishes: new experiences, security, response, and recognition. He further contended that the four wishes had a biological basis and were expressed in the form of anger, fear, love, and the desire to gain power or status. Then, based on these assertions, he inferred that women need to give and receive love and that failure to do so often leads to immoral acts such as prostitution. Although it can be seen as containing a double standard, Thomas's work had an enduring impact—especially on the male-dominated discipline of criminology. In many respects, his efforts to use social and biological factors to explain female delinquency reflect an integrated and interdisciplinary perspective.

Even the 1968 research of John and Valerie Cowie and Eliot Slater does little to give credibility to the biological perspective. For example, in the classic tradition of Lombroso and Ferrero, the authors claimed that "delinquent girls more often than boys have other forms of impaired health; they are noticed to be oversize, lumpish, uncouth and graceless, with a raised incidence of minor physical defects" (Cowie, Cowie, & Slater, 1968:166–167). But as Rosenbaum (1991) notes, the author studied only female delinquents who were more than likely to come from troubled homes. They also failed to distinguish between biological variables and cultural variables such as gender, neglecting to acknowledge any environmental influences.

While such chauvinistic attitudes might still prevail in some circles today, it is obvious that female offenders do not all come from the lower socio-economic class, are not all prostitutes, and do not look like men.

Until researchers begin to pay full attention to the possible interactions between biological characteristics and environmental factors in triggering criminal and deviant behaviour, biological factors will remain a politically sensitive area of inquiry when it comes to gender-based issues. Fortunately, however, research conducted in different disciplines is slowly finding its way into criminological literature and opening the doors for an integrated and interdisciplinary approach. For example, Kolata (1995) reports that there are measurable brain differences between women and men, which affect behavioural, cognitive, and emotional functioning. Although this area of study is still in its infancy, a number of researchers have finally begun to explore the possible interaction of biological and environmental factors and gender differences (see, for example, Raine, Brennan, Farrington, & Mednick, 1997).

Psychological "Flaws"

In 1966, Gisela Konopka interviewed several hundred delinquent girls who had been sentenced to a Minnesota institution. Relying on the traditional psychological perspective, she sought to identify some pathological traits in the girls. In adopting this approach, Konopka focused on stereotypical traits that might distinguish deviant behaviour from non-deviant behaviour among young girls.

Like Thomas (1923), she believed that women have a greater need for love and affection than men do. She noted that women who failed to make themselves lovable to men tended to come from poor and/or broken homes and that they were more likely to experience distrust, fear, loneliness, and poor self-image. She further observed that while these traits were less expressive in males, men do appreciate and value feeling wanted, loved, and trusted. Konopka concluded that female delinquency was the result of gender instability and an inability to adjust to basic female needs.

Again, although Konopka's research was methodologically flawed and her model lacked clear operationalization of fundamental constructs, such as what loneliness is and what constitutes poor homes, her work still attracted considerable attention. Rosenbaum (1991) observed that the double standard of morality and the perpetuation of delinquency among females supposedly being related to individual maladjustment justified social workers' and clinicians' treatment of female delinquents as promiscuous and unloved.

One of the more frequently cited studies from the 1960s that uses a psychological approach is Otto Pollak's (1961). Pollak believed that female criminality was more prevalent than was officially recognized because women were better able to deceive men through sexual play-acting and by manipulating situations. This assertion is not dissimilar from Farrell's (1993) discussion of why women get treatment for their psychological problems while men commit suicide. For example, Farrell notes that nearly two-thirds of female offenders seek psychological help, as opposed to one-third of male offenders, but women do not experience more psychological or emotional disorders, since various self-report studies have shown that an "equal number of men and women experience depression." The difference is that men just don't seek help for it. It may be that it is simply more socially acceptable for women to appear to suffer more from psychological disorders (Gray, 1994).

Pollak also asserted that the nature of women's social roles (in the 1960s, primarily the roles of housekeeper and caretaker of children) provided them with ample opportunities both to commit crimes and to readily disguise them. As Carol Smart (cited in Rosenbaum, 1991:511) observes, this is hardly an original notion as "it has its origins in the biblical story of Adam and Eve." Pollak also suggested that women do occasionally abuse and neglect their children but that these actions go largely unreported—they get "masked."

Both Konopka and Pollak's work focused on trying to identify female delinquent traits based in individual factors. In spite of their questionable methodologies and weak theoretical foundation, their findings were embraced by practitioners eager to address the growing concern with female criminality. The merits of their ideas appeared to be reflected in crime data. Female delinquency and female criminality *appeared* to be increasing throughout the 20th century. And even though some of the increase can be explained as a result of increased awareness, the fact remains that such perceptions contributed little to the understanding or control of female crime. The shortcomings of this approach eventually set the stage for the next wave of theoretical inquiry and explanation—gender role socialization and women's liberation.

Socialization and Women's Liberation

As noted earlier, the 1970s marked a significant change within criminology and the study of female crime. It was a period in which more women entered the field and in which women's liberation became a tour de force.

In 1973, Hoffman-Bustamonte, for example, asserted that women and men were socialized differently. Boys were socialized to be tough, to not cry, and to fight back when confronted, while girls were socialized to be caring, non-violent, and passive. Hoffman-Bustamonte suggested that since socialization processes are different, girls have less illegitimate opportunities than males, hence the lower female crime rate. But does this mean women have any less propensity for committing crimes? Hoffman-Bustamonte's work was instrumental in shifting the focus away from individual traits and *role theory* (i.e., the idea people define roles for themselves and others based on social learning and reading). It has been described as a starting point for feminist criminology (Rosenbaum, 1991).

A less controversial perspective rooted in sociology that has been frequently used is the **middle-class value approach**, which is a variation of the individual strain theory. The individual strain perspective asserts that deviance is a by-product of the conflict and frustration experienced by the individual as they look for ways to meet their needs. The middle-class value approach is premised on the observation that girls have traditionally been brought up to be quiet and well-behaved. They are expected to stay home until old enough to look after themselves. Haslem (1976) points out that such images and expectations are full of double standards. Boys who date numerous girls, engage in sex, and go out a lot with their friends are considered to be normal, while girls engaging in similar behaviour are considered to have "morally fallen." Hence, criminal behaviour among women is seen as a form of rebellion against traditional standards. Or is it that as values and norms change, society has been reluctant to accept role convergence?

In her influential book, Adler (1975) argued that the old stereotypical image of being "pregnant and barefoot in the kitchen" was no longer the dominant way in the 1970s. She suggested that the rise in female crime was related to the emancipation of women: there were more opportunities to commit crimes available to women. Adler speculated that with the convergence of gender role expectations, female crime would increasingly resemble male crime. Her argument became known as the *liberation hypothesis*.

Official crime statistics seemed to lend support to Adler's assertions, as property crime among women increased significantly in the 1970s. But how much of the increase could be accounted for as a result of increased attention to female crime and how much as a result of the manner in which the criminal justice system was responding to female offenders? And has women's liberation created a catch-22? Not surprisingly, the work of Adler and others during this period came under fire. Using data from before 1970 and into the 1970s, Steffensmeier (1978) argues that the empirical links between women's liberation and female crime were weak at best.

By this time, momentum was gathering, and the volume of research directed at women and crime was growing. The interest in researching female crime and related issues blossomed into feminist criminology in the 1980s.

Feminist Criminology

In Chapter 7, we noted that the feminist perspective is not a single perspective but can be divided into several fundamentally different orientations.

The **power-control theory**, developed by Hagan, Simpson, and Gillis (1979) and elaborated on in subsequent studies, suggests that female delinquency is linked to the patriarchal family. The authors assert that both mothers and fathers control girls more than boys—as a way of both repressing and sheltering them. This perspective exposes the society's double standard. As the control is dissipated, opportunity in which greater female delinquency can occur is created.

Although it is gender-based, power-control theory was also one of the first integrated theories of female crime. It combined Marxist, conflict, and control theories with classicist assumptions about human behaviour. While it represents a commendable effort to combine structural (macro) constructs with individual level (micro) constructs, research evidence has not been favourable.

For example, Caspi and his colleagues (1994, 1995, 2000), in their longitudinal study of more than 1000 children born in New Zealand in 1972 and 1973, found no significant difference in the personality and structural indicators suggested by Hagan and his associates. Instead, they found that delinquency among male and female youth corresponded to neuropsychological problems. Such problems could be traced to poor nutrition during pregnancy, birth complications, exposure to lead and other toxic substances—all of which, they suggest, result from preventable problems in the social and family environment of the youths. As promising as their research might appear, Caspi and his associates have not addressed the critical issue of causal order, nor have they been able to account for possible spurious relationships. However, they do draw attention to possible interactions among biological, social, psychological, and environmental elements. Their research, in many respects, can be described as interdisciplinary.

In recent years, feminist criminology has gained considerable influence. The *British realists* and *post-critical criminologists*, among others, have begun to embrace ideas put forth by feminist criminology. The volume of literature has been prodigious. Overall, the feminist perspective has played a significant role not only in bringing the issue of female crime to the forefront in criminology but also advancing the study of women, gender, crime, and criminal justice policy in general. And while the perspective is championed mostly by women, its influence has been felt in other patriarchal perspectives.

In summary, female offenders are not all that dissimilar from male offenders. For example, as noted earlier, they both tend to come from minority groups, have been brought up in lower socio-economic conditions, are often undereducated and underemployed, have a history of substance abuse themselves and/or in the family, and predominately commit property-related crimes. However, based on reported incidents, female offenders tend more often to be the victims of physical and/or sexual abuse and neglect. Rosenbaum (1991:523) suggests that, for women, the picture of the female offender is one "with survival as her goal."

Criminology needs not only to remain sensitive to female crime (and the female victim) but to explore the differences between male and female crime in the context of an integrated and interdisciplinary perspective. If we are going to truly understand the differences between female offenders and male offenders, there must be a convergence not only of feminist ideas and criminology but also of different disciplinary perspectives. After all, men are still more likely to be victims of violent crime (see Box 13.11), and they are still more likely to commit violent crimes. A balanced approach that addresses such issues must be adopted.

A CLOSER LOOK BOX 13.11

FOSTERING A BETTER UNDERSTANDING OF GENDER (IN)EQUALITY

In our politically charged climate, we sometimes neglect to see things in balance. The following points are not intended to undermine the gravity of violence directed at women today. Rather, they constitute a plea for a movement that will foster a better— and objective—understanding of both women and men. For as Farrell (1993) and others have observed, "when one gender loses, they both lose."

- Women live longer then men.
- Women tend to get shorter sentences than men when committing similar crimes and sharing comparable backgrounds (Cose, 1995).
- Women have used PMS as a legal defence, while no male offender has ever been able to use elevated testosterone as a defence (Pearson, 1998). Recent discoveries show that women suffering from premenstrual syndrome have neurotransmitters similar to men's (Moir & Jessel, 1997).
- Men are victims of violent crime far more often than women, except in the case of rape (Brott, 1995).
- In 1993–1994, over $11 million was allocated to the Canadian Panel on Violence Against Women commission. No mention was made of violence perpetrated against men (Asher, 1996).
- In some countries, such as England and Canada (under the *Infants Act*), a mother cannot be found guilty of murdering her child within the first 12 months of its life. She can be charged only with manslaughter. The rationale underlying the *Infants Act* is that it allows the court to consider a biological basis for possible postpartum depression (Moir & Jessel, 1997).
- The cost of maintaining a male prisoner in 1999–2000 was about $67 686 a year, as compared with $115 465 a year for a female prisoner (CAEFS, 2004).
- In March 2004, the MP for Yorkton-Melville in Saskatchewan introduced a private member's motion calling for a new *Criminal Code* offence for the murder of a woman carrying an unborn child. Referring to an American study, the MP said that the "leading cause of death among pregnant or recently pregnant women was homicide" (House motion..., 2004).

Summary

- Early research on women and crime yielded a view of female offenders as "sick" or morally "bad." Sweeping statements and questionable methodologies began to be replaced when the women's liberation movement took hold in the 1960s and 1970s. A number of important changes since the 1970s affected the rate at which women commit crimes, and major shifts in criminology concerned with the female offender have also occurred. Feminist criminology has garnered more widespread attention.

- Women still make up a comparatively small percentage of the offending population. The most common type of offence committed by women is property-related crime. In terms of violent crime, women tend to commit minor offences. Yet, more recently, women are also being convicted of various white-collar and corporate offences, as well as organized crime activity. Aboriginal women are disproportionately represented in the female offending population.

- Explanations of women and crime span the spectrum of perspectives, from biological and biosocial to ones based on psychology and those emphasizing socialization. Since the 1970s, the feminist perspective has also played a significant role in explaining female offending. Collectively, the theories have served to create a better awareness and understanding of female offending.

- Differences between female and male criminality have important implications for criminology and criminologists. Traditional explanations are unable to adequately account for gender crime rate differences. Future research needs to pay more attention to the plight of the female offender and not only the female victim. In general, theoretical approaches to this issue should be integrated and interdisciplinary in nature.

Discussion Questions

1. Why is it important to understand how female offenders have been viewed and understood in the past?

2. Are female offenders different from male offenders? What are the important differences that need to be considered? How can an interdisciplinary and integrated approach facilitate the understanding of female crime?

3. Is female crime increasing? Is it becoming more serious? How can we explain the trends?

4. What areas of female crime deserve further research?

5. Is there a social, political, and cultural bias between the genders? If so, to what extent does it mask our understanding of how criminology and the criminal justice system view female criminality?

Key Concepts

chivalry hypothesis	Elizabeth Fry Society	middle-class value approach
pedestal effect	power-control theory	women's liberation movement

Key Names

Freda Adler	Elizabeth Fry	Phyllis Haslem
Otto Pollak	Rita Simon	William Thomas

Weblinks

www.elizabethfry.ca/caefs_e.htm The Canadian Association of Elizabeth Fry Societies website is a rich source of information on the female offender.

www.criaw-icref.ca The site of the Canadian Research Institute for the Advancement of Women offers fact sheets and other publications.

www.usask.ca/nativelaw/awomen.html This page from the University of Saskatchewan focusing on Aboriginal women and law provides links and an extensive bibliography.

www.csc-scc.gc.ca The site of the Correctional Service of Canada offers a wealth of information, including links to pages related to female offenders.

Endnotes

1. The term "atavistic" refers to certain individuals resembling earlier, less evolved ancestors.

2. For an interesting historical overview of other Canadian women who have killed in ways that could rival Karla Homolka's, see Frank Anderson's 1997 book *A Dance with Death: Canadian Women on the Gallows, 1754–1954*. In addition to covering 49 different cases, he discusses the various reactions of society and the criminal justice system to these women.

CHAPTER 14

Future Directions in Criminology

"It was only gradually...that I realized that what is interesting is not necessarily useful."

J.Q. Wilson, 1985:56

Learning Outcomes

After you have completed this chapter, you should be able to:

- Discuss the importance of developing an interdisciplinary and integrated approach to the study of criminology.

- Be cognizant of the dynamic nature of crime and criminality.

- Recognize some of the likely future trends in crime and criminological research.

- Appreciate the need to merge criminology and criminal justice issues.

- Discuss the importance of comparative criminology in bridging criminological issues.

Criminologists have a personal stake in the issues they study, publish, and bring to the public's attention. Whether their studies focus on criminological theory, sociology of law, victimology, or any of the other elements that make up the criminological enterprise, they evolve with the ebb and flow of cultural, political, and social trends and with the growing body of scientific evidence. No matter how advanced our research and knowledge seem, however, we must always be careful about what we believe and about what we predict (see Box 14.1).

WRONG PREDICTIONS

The following list includes some hilariously inaccurate predictions and judgments:

- "Computers in the future may weigh no more than 1.5 tons." *Popular Mechanics*, 1949
- "We don't like their sound, and guitar music is on the way out." Decca Recording Company rejecting the Beatles, 1962
- "I'm glad it'll be Clark Gable who's falling on his face and not Gary Cooper." Gary Cooper on his decision not to take the leading role in *Gone with the Wind*
- "Stocks have reached what looks like a permanently high plateau." Irving Fisher, Professor of Economics, Yale University, 1929
- "Louis Pasteur's theory of germs is ridiculous fiction." Pierre Pachet, Professor of Physiology at Toulouse, 1872

In the quotation opening this chapter, James Q. Wilson is referring to the gap between what criminologists do and what criminal justice practitioners do. Although both are interested in the subject of crime control, they have not always worked in concert. Criminology lacks the stability of the natural sciences, and its research often follows fads that have short lifespans. For example, under the 1990s wave of post-positivism and **postmodernism**, many of the conventional concepts of the discipline have been challenged. Milovanovic (1997:5) recently suggested that the modernist conventional views of criminology (such as determinism, Newtonian ideas, and adherence to a structural functionalist approach to knowledge) lead him to conclude that the "search for overencompassing theories of society and social development" is fundamentally flawed. He claims the new postmodern paradigm "is neither fatalistic or nihilistic" but is an approach that views knowledge differently and in a way that may hold more promise than the ways in which we have traditionally studied crime (ibid.:23).

Throughout this textbook, we have examined the subject of criminology and its major elements. We have seen that this field of inquiry is evolving into an interdisciplinary and integrated science. As John Short noted in his 1997 presidential address to the American Society of Criminology, criminology "cuts across professions as well as disciplines." Similarly, in his 1998 presidential address to the Academy of Criminal Justice Science, Gennaro Vito called for a merging of the disciplines and said that criminal justice and criminology scholars must work toward bridging and integrating their differences.

Throughout this book, it has been suggested that criminology must move beyond its traditional disciplinary biases and that it must cross boundaries and build new bridges in order to overcome the challenges that face criminologists. Although the concept of crime has always been dynamic, the challenges that lie ahead are perhaps more exciting than ever. As crime continues to draw wide public attention, and as issues of accountability escalate, so will competing philosophies of crime control. Policy-makers will need to work more closely with criminologists. Criminologists, in turn, will have to move beyond their cherished ideologies or favourite policies that have no scientific foundation.

In this final chapter, we will examine some of the issues with which criminologists will have to contend. Crime, being *relative* and *evolutive*, constantly presents new and changing challenges. If criminology is to help improve our sense of social justice, reduce crime, and rectify inequalities, it must find a balance between responding to complex human behaviour issues and dealing with the more pragmatic policy-based criminal justice decisions.

Criminology: A Frame of Reference
Four Approaches to Crime Control

Repeatedly throughout this textbook, we have seen that the ultimate objective of criminology is crime control or the science of controlology—a term coined by Ditton (1979). The objective and rationale is to maximize the quality of life for the greatest number in society, following the utilitarian principle. However, those who espouse an integrated and interdisciplinary approach—which has been advocated throughout this text—struggle with how to best address the issue of crime control and social order.

Until recently, there have been three basic approaches to crime control: conservative, liberal, and radical (Conklin, 1998). More recently, the integrated and interdisciplinary approach has been drawing attention (Cao, 2004).

The **conservative approach**, as discussed in more general terms in Chapter 4, emphasizes:

- Preserving the status quo from criminals;
- Focusing on conventional crimes;
- Attributing crime to the lower and middle classes;
- Focusing on improving family values;
- Asserting the legitimacy of the legal order;
- Using incarceration and just deserts;
- Expanding the police force and removing restraints from it; and
- Compromising individual freedoms in the name of social control.

One of the critical issues that the conservatives grapple with is laws that are not "humanistic" in their intent but are political and power-based. The rise of such laws means that the law in general is "becoming an instrument of utility, removed from its proximity to the cultural institutions" (Christie, 1996:182). For example, Christie (1996), among others, argues that as an instrument of social control, the law is becoming more political than scientific. In the process, it is losing its roots in the "core area of human experience" (ibid.:182). However, as evidenced throughout this textbook, reliance on the law to control the crime problem has not yielded particularly good results.

The **liberal approach**, as discussed in more general terms in Chapter 7, emphasizes:

- Controlling crime by addressing the underlying causes;
- Viewing criminal activity as the result of social and economic circumstances;
- Adopting a labelling and/or interactionist approach;
- Understanding that lack of opportunity for certain groups increases the probability of crime;
- Focusing on social reform through vocational training, social assistance, job creation, and community involvement; and
- Using treatment and rehabilitation as the means to crime control (see Cullen & Gendreau, 2001).

Although the liberal approach has received considerable attention and support since the early 1970s, it struggles to explain how and why anti-crime policies have been only marginally successful and its search for crime causation has been wanting.

The **radical approach**, also generally discussed in Chapter 7, emphasizes:

- Examining crime committed by both the lower classes and the upper-class and white-collar groups;
- Relying on unofficial sources (e.g., self-report and victimization surveys) to indicate that crime can be found across all social classes;
- Adopting an anti-establishment view of social order;
- Understanding that crime problems are ultimately a reflection of media hype, competing interest groups, and recording patterns;
- Viewing competition (i.e., capitalism) as an underlying motivator of crime, and focusing on non-conventional crime (e.g., political crime, white-collar crime, and corruption);
- Shifting the focus from the offender to the system; and
- Calling for the construction of a new and fundamentally different social system.

Conklin (1998:530) notes that radicals offer few specific solutions to the crime problem. Other critics have been much harsher in their assessment. For example, Klockar (1980 cited in Fattah, 1997:296) described radical criminology as lacking in empirical evidence, representing poor scholarship, and containing embarrassing empirical failures. Klockar further criticized it for its "strident moral and political imperialism," adding that it is nothing more than "intellectual shoddiness."

Finally, the integrated and interdisciplinary approach:

- Views crime as a product of human behaviour;
- Stresses an interaction between the individual and the environment (i.e., nature versus nurture);

- Holds that an individual is characterized by his or her genetic and biological traits and attributes, and influenced by environmental factors; and

- Adapts a soft deterministic approach to the study of human behaviour (i.e., objective or quantitative analysis versus subjective or qualitative analysis).

The integrated and interdisciplinary attempt to reconcile differences between the previous three approaches is a tall order—to say the least! However, as stated in previous chapters, we can overcome the fragmentation in criminology only by embracing this relatively new approach. Doing so will require the bridging of the varieties of the criminological enterprises (see Chapter 1) and being interdisciplinary in the ways we view crime.

Although the division of crime control perspectives into four approaches described above is somewhat simplistic, what is important to understand is that each general view emphasizes a different way to interpret crime and offers different strategies of crime control. It is no small challenge for criminologists to choose which camp to align themselves with. It is perhaps an even bigger challenge for those who administer justice and legislate criminal policy.

Inevitably, choosing one perspective over another carries a price. While social control is an inherent element of criminology and a facet of political life, criminology must build a model of social control that respects people's sense of freedom and dignity. The interdisciplinary approach represents one such model. However, as Cao (2004) suggests, it still requires refinement. It remains to be seen whether criminology becomes interdisciplinary and whether the agents of the criminal justice system will be able to move from a legalistic, classical approach to a more scientific and humanistic discipline.

There are signs, however, that criminology has started to evolve in this direction. For example, at the 1998 and 1999 Annual American Society of Criminology (ASC) meetings, Margaret Zahn and David Farrington, in their presidential addresses, called for a stronger move toward embracing an interdisciplinary approach in criminological research. In 2004, the outgoing president of the ASC, Francis Cullen, offered similar support for more criminological research that embraces integrated and interdisciplinary approaches. The point is that the perspective is gaining momentum, but it remains to be seen if it becomes mainstream.

Criminology and Social Responsibility

It is easy to be critical of existing theory and social policy; however, it is an unenviable task to try to offer constructive insights. Over the years, many criminologists have espoused policy recommendations only to find that the policies met with limited success when implemented. Perhaps the most infamous of these ideas came from the work of Robert Martinson (1974) and his colleagues, who in the 1970s suggested that "nothing works" in the correctional arena. Martinson's conclusion had an enduring impact on how criminologists viewed crime and crime control. In many respects, it marked the end of an era of conservatism and a return to a model of retribution and to theories that focused on social structures as representing the underlying causes of criminality. The time following the "nothing works" observation also was marked by the growth of critical criminology, radical criminology, feminist criminology, and structural criminology. Criminologists became agents for social change—a mantle that some may be carrying with reservations. Other notable policy examples influenced by criminological research that have failed to produce the outcome postulated include the War on Poverty in the 1960s, the War on Drugs in the 1970s, and the more recent zero-tolerance policies around such things are speeding, drinking and driving, etc. Collectively, these examples serve to show that bridging criminological findings with social policy is at best a risky venture.

Human behaviour is perhaps the most complex of the phenomena that criminology must understand. However, if Charles H. Cooley (the father of sociology in the United States) was on the mark when he said that all human beings have a common ground (in that we all share the same basic human experiences), why then has it been so difficult to explain, control, and regulate criminal behaviour? As elusive at it appears to be, crime control will likely continue to occupy a prominent place in academia and in society at large. Universally, we value freedom and life. As long as we continue to do so, deviance and crime will remain focal concerns. The challenge for criminologists is to find fruitful methods of approaching these issues, which are enveloped in so many cultural, political, and social concerns.

Comparative Criminology

"It is our duty to recognize that the 'misery of men in different countries' is still with us." Sir Leon Radzinowicz, 1999:404

In the future, as in the past, the theoretical and practical direction criminology takes will follow the prevailing intellectual climate. However, as already mentioned, with increasing public and political awareness, criminology will need to undergo fundamental paradigm and theoretical shifts. In addition to adopting an interdisciplinary perspective, it will need to embrace an integrated approach that pays increasing attention to comparative criminological research within a national and international context.

Until fairly recently, the idea of engaging in comparative criminological research was met with varying support at best. Language barriers, definition barriers, different reporting and recording practices, and administrative variations were seen as interfering with the ability to do comparative research (see Winterdyk, 2001). It was thought that these and other barriers helped produce only fragmented knowledge and did little to advance the discipline. However, with advances in technology and methodology, international and **comparative research** of criminological issues has become a major area of study (see Box 14.2). For example, the Division of International Criminology at the 2004 ASC meetings had the largest membership (400 people) of the nine divisions with the ASC. Only a few years ago there were but a few dozen members! Nevertheless, Reichel (2003) cautions that even though comparative criminal justice and criminology is a "synthetic scheme," it serves an essential role in classifying and presenting information in a way that allows for constructive comparisons. A growing number of textbooks and academic journals are adopting such an approach (see Beirne & Hill, 1991; Reichel, 2003; Fairchild & Dammer, 2001; and the *International Journal of Comparative Criminology*).

A CLOSER LOOK BOX 14.2

MAKING A POSITIVE CHANGE

The Canadian Foundation for the Americas (FOCAL) is an independent and non-governmental organization dedicated to deepening and strengthening Canada's relations with countries in Latin America and the Caribbean through policy discussion and analysis. In response to the problems of civil war and social and political unrest in Latin America and the Caribbean, the foundation has provided assistance by offering expertise in crime prevention and criminal justice programs. The foundation promotes cooperation between governments. For example, through agencies such as the Canadian International Development Agency (CIDA), funds have been directed to building bridges that encourage international participation in decision-making. As Dandurand and Paris-Steffens (1997:27) have noted, FOCAL's support has been described as "tepid," yet at least it represents a constructive effort. In addition, the foundation's 2002 annual report noted that support and initiatives emanating from and through FOCAL had improved significantly.

In addition to various federally based initiatives, academic institutes such as the criminology program at the University of Montreal have also been involved in international (especially Europe-related) and comparative research projects for many years. However, because most of this work is produced in French, it is not generally known to English-speaking Canadian scholars. Another example involves the joint initiatives by the Human Justice program at the University of Regina and the School of Criminology at Simon Fraser University on international restorative justice projects.

In spite of historical antecedents, North American criminologists have been slow to embrace a comparative approach. Fattah (1997:303), for example, notes that the words "comparative research" and "comparative criminology" "hardly appear in any of the subject indexes of American textbooks in criminology." The vacuum in criminology is largely due to the "provincial attitudes" among North American criminologists and criminal justice officials. A review of criminology and criminal justice programs across Canada in 2004 reveals that very few include comparative courses as a requirements; in the few schools that do offer such courses at all, the courses are electives. Hackler (1996:258) asserts that "many anglophones still complacently assume that their legal systems are superior to others," when in fact they are "now inferior to those in most of the developed world."

For example, in examining the juvenile justice systems in Australia, France, and Fiji, Hackler (1996) suggests that some of the practices used there deserve to be examined by such countries as Canada. He notes that our juvenile offender system is fraught with political inefficiency that is not in the best interests of young offenders. In France, youths cannot be detained for more than one night, judges must undergo special training to work with young offenders, and a greater emphasis is placed on re-education than on punishment. French judges prefer a less scientific approach to assess the guilt or innocence of a youth. In many respects, the French juvenile justice system is based on the principles of restorative justice, rather than those of retributive justice, which characterize the Canadian system.

Aside from the anecdotal studies, a review of international criminology journals reveals that while there may be a plea among some criminologists for an integrated, interdisciplinary, and comparative approach, a survey of citations in major international criminology journals suggests that the practice is quite different (Cohn & Farrington, 1998). Indeed, each country tends to reflect a bias for "homegrown" criminologists. Provincialism can also be readily observed when reviewing the tables of contents of various journals. For example, the *Canadian Journal of Criminology and Criminal Justice* contains research primarily in the area of young offenders and various national criminal justice concerns (e.g., policing and punishment). In the United States, the focus is more on social control theory and the general theory of crime. In England (for example, in the *British Journal of Criminology*), there is a split between crime prevention and British realism theory. The focus in Australia (for example, in the *Australian and New Zealand Journal of Criminology*) is on restorative justice issues and reintegrative practices. Students of criminology should be sensitive to these trends and should review criminological journals published elsewhere in the world to obtain an international perspective and be able to draw comparative analyses.

The nature of crime in Canada is changing with the country's demographic composition. As Canada becomes more multicultural and multi-ethnic, it is increasingly important to understand how these cultural differences influence crime and criminal trends. For example, home invasions, drive-by shootings, and foreign-based email letter scams were virtually unknown to Canadians until the 1980s. Along with the influx of new immigrants, new forms of transnational crime are emerging. The price of globalization has brought many benefits to Canada, but it has also introduced many new forms of crime that are best dealt with from an international and comparative perspective (see Reichel, 2005).

Canadians are not the only ones who can benefit from a comparative approach. The United States has the highest incarceration rate in the world, with 701 per 100 000 of the national population (Walmsley, 2003), whereas the rates of incarceration in some European countries (e.g., Austria, Finland, and Germany) have decreased since the mid-1970s (see Winterdyk, 2004). This decrease has been accomplished largely through the use of alternative programs. Such findings should excite criminologists and criminal justice officials and encourage them to examine how these countries are able to create such trends. Only through cross-national and cross-cultural research that attempts to marry theory and practice will it be possible to learn about such programs.

Fairchild (1993:3) identifies three main reasons for criminology to engage in cross-national and cross-cultural studies. They are as follows:

- To benefit from the experience of others;
- To broaden our understanding of different cultures and approaches to problems; and
- To help us deal with international crime problems such as terrorism and drug smuggling.

Collectively, as Reichel (2003:27) notes, these points show that all provincial perspectives can benefit from a better understanding of historical, political, and descriptive context, as well as a greater appreciation of other countries' criminal justice systems, since such knowledge is based on "understanding points of contrast between the different systems."

In his informative account of the mysterious international police association Interpol, Fooner (1989) points out that criminal justice and public safety policy needs to focus on an international approach, suggesting that to date the professional community and institutions of higher learning have ignored international issues. Global crime is a reality, but criminologists and criminal justice agencies have been slow to respond (Loree, 2004).

In 2004, 181 countries and 11 territories belonged to Interpol. Canada joined in 1949. The RCMP serves as a link to the collection of documents and information pertaining to international law enforcement and forwards the information to Interpol (McKeena, 1998). Interpol Canada played a key role in the 1996 capture of Albert Walker, who had defrauded his Canadian clients of millions of dollars while posing as a financial advisor in Paris, Ontario, before fleeing to England. Until criminologists begin to work toward an international or global perspective in explaining, describing, and predicting crime and criminality, transnational and international crime "will be defining issues of the 21st century for policymakers...because these groups are major beneficiaries of globalization" (Shelley, 2004).

As noted earlier in this chapter, in recent years, there has been a groundswell of researchers who are venturing into the arena of comparative criminology. But scholars such as Nowak (1989, cited in Oyen, 1992:8) emphasize that in addition to providing descriptive comparisons of criminological concepts and criminal justice issues, studies need to ground themselves in some type of theoretical framework and sound methodology. Until criminology can bridge this gap, comparative and cross-cultural studies will likely be limited to being interesting but shallow in their findings.

At the Commonwealth finance ministers' annual meeting in 1996, a number of legal strategies were proposed to counter the expanding international problem of money laundering. It was noted that current estimates place money laundering practices at $500 billion. In an effort to curb such trends, Switzerland has proposed reporting suspicious transactions to authorities. Australia, Canada, and the United States already have such practices in place. Germany has extended police powers, including phone tapping, while Great Britain has set up a separate police unit for money laundering (Malinowski, 1996).

Although such meetings and discussions are helpful in forging international co-operation, it is unlikely that the strategies mentioned above will deter organized crime groups, which employ highly sophisticated strategies. Laws alone cannot ensure compliance with social values and norms. Criminology needs to understand the root causes of these behaviours, rather than focusing on the acts per se. An interdisciplinary and comparative approach can provide the venue for such inquiries.

In the mid-1980s, the United Nations tried to develop guidelines for the administration of juvenile justice. The UN Standard Minimum Rules for the Administration of Juvenile Justice, more commonly referred to as the **Beijing Rules** (see Box 14.3) reflect the welfare model advocated by the United Nations. However, as several researchers have noted, few countries have tried to incorporate the model or the guidelines. In fact, in 1998, then Justice Minister Anne McLellan reported that the government was planning to toughen the *Young Offenders Act* by introducing new legislation that would be called the *Youth Criminal Justice Act* (*YCJA*). The theory behind the *YCJA* (implemented April 2003) was that it was to focus more on the aspects of restorative justice—keeping youth in the community, taking into consideration victims' needs, etc. Some have noted, however, that the idea of restorative justice in the *YCJA* is questionable, given the penal nature of the act. Antonopoulos and Winterdyk (2003) offer an in-depth analysis and comparison of the restorative initiatives in the Canada and British juvenile justice system. They conclude that the legislation in both countries is liberal in orientation, but that neither system "would appear to have effectively considered the magnitude of institutional reconstruction and redesign" (ibid.:397). This represents a break from the United Nations Convention on the Rights of the Child, of which Canada was a signatory member (Bronskill & Bryden, 1998).

A CLOSER LOOK BOX 14.3

HIGHLIGHTS OF "THE BEIJING RULES" (1984)

- *Fundamental perspectives*: 1.1 To further the well-being of the juvenile and her or his family; 1.2 To develop conditions that will ensure a meaningful life in the community for the juvenile; 1.4 Administration of juvenile justice should represent an integral part of the natural development process of each country.
- *Age of responsibility*: 4.1 The beginning age shall not be fixed at too low an age level, bearing in mind the facts of emotional, mental, and intellectual maturity.
- *Aim of juvenile justice*: 5.1 Emphasize the well-being of the juvenile and ensure that any reaction to juvenile offenders shall always be in proportion to the circumstances of both the offender and the offence.
- *Scope of discretion*: 6.2 Efforts shall be made to ensure sufficient accountability at all stages and levels in the exercise of any such discretion.
- *Protection of privacy*: 8.1 Right to privacy shall be protected at all stages in order to avoid harm being caused by undue publicity or by the process of labeling. 8.2 No information that may lead to the identification of a juvenile offender shall be published.

Source: Adapted from Winterdyk, 2001:xv.

Comparative criminology is driven by substantive problems of crime, social control, and crime control. Borrowing from Robert K. Merton's notion that we should abandon the quest for an all-encompassing theory, comparative criminology may force criminology to deal with "theories of the middle range"(see Cao, 2004). As Merton notes, "our task today is to develop *special* theories, applicable to limited ranges of data—theories, for example of deviant behavior, or the flow of power from generation to generation, or the unseen ways in which personal influence is exercised" (cited in Wallace & Wolf, 1995:56). At the 1995 United Nations Crime Prevention and Criminal Justice meetings, Coldren (1995:10) emphasized the need "to rely on the best thinkers in the world and to share our ideas and experience with our colleagues because we can all benefit from such efforts." Recently, Winterdyk and Cao (2004) edited a reader in which they present 14 of the world's leading scholars in international and comparative criminology and criminal justice. Each of the contributors offers insight into his or her personal life and the lessons he or she has learned along the way. Comparative criminology has the potential to play a primary role in leading criminology out of the ideological approaches that have dominated in the past and into the interdisciplinary model.

The Knowledge Explosion in Criminology

"This is the bitterest pain among men, to have much knowledge but no power."
Herodotus (c. 485–425 BC)

As many areas of study today, criminology is an expansive discipline. Its growth can be seen, for example, in the number of journals devoted to criminology nationally and internationally. The number of criminology textbooks on the market, and even the number of true crime novels, lend credence to the perception that crime is a serious topic. At the 2004 conference of the American Society of Criminology, over 500 different sessions were offered over the four days (American Society of Criminology Conference, 2004). However, as we have already discussed throughout this book, criminology has not always been this expansive.

In the early part of the 20th century, criminology was dominated largely by sociologists—in particular, a small group based out of the University of Chicago known as the Chicago School (see Chapter 7). After World War II, the study of criminology expanded into the disciplines of psychology, geography, and biology, and even economics and political science. Slowly, criminology became a growth industry with many competing perspectives. Today, it is nearly impossible to master criminological knowledge. Although there is no shortage of criminological theories, and although these theories have been dominated by sociological and psychological perspectives, no one theoretical orientation has prevailed. Instead, the theories seem to compete in explaining criminological phenomena.

In recent years, a growing number of criminologists have commented on the pro-liferation of criminological thought but noted its general lack of soundness. For exam-ple, Henry (1990, cited in Einstadter & Henry, 1995:297) evaluated the postmodernist movement within criminology as "merely a provisional metaphor, insufficiently devel-oped to merit the grand description 'theory.'" Martin Schwartz (cited in Einstadter & Henry, 1995:298), commenting on reading postmodernism, was even more forceful in saying, "I really do not know what the hell they are talking about."

The debate as to the soundness of criminological theory appears to have reached new heights since the mid-1990s. A number of criminologists have suggested that some "scientific" theories in criminology are based on untested assumptions and that, as a result, these "theories" are in fact myths (Cao, 2004). Similarly, Matthews and Young (1986:1) noted that criminological theory is in a state of "theoretical bankrupt-cy." These charges pose a major problem, since evaluation and policy-making are sup-posed to rely on informed opinion. The vast resources available and the new high-technology information dissemination methods seem to have complicated the process of criminological study rather than expedited it. There always seems to be something else to consider.

Charles Tittle (1997:101) has cautioned that while theoretical integration is the most useful approach for criminologists interested in improving their theories, there are a number of limitations that still need to be resolved: "(1) the necessity for compatible dependent variables, (2) agreement on the purpose and nature of theo-ry, (3) difficulty in articulating interconnections of parts, and (4) inadequacy of data for checking out problematic elements." Even though his points have considerable merit, the overriding benefit of adopting an integrated and interdisciplinary approach is that it is more likely to enable a more realistic examination of crime. And, as Cao (2004) suggests, it is hoped that explanatory models will become more robust as theoretical and methodological strategies that bridge the current gaps are developed.

While the general concept of crime remains constant, its precise meaning contin-ues to shift. Criminologists must grapple with these issues when deciding what topics need to be researched, how they should be studied, from what perspective they should be examined, and what objectives should be attained. As discussed in Chapter 1, doing criminology can involve aggregate data research, experimental research, lon-gitudinal research, and/or survey research. Each technique has its strengths and weaknesses, not to mention its associated methodological and ethical issues. One of the challenges for criminology is to uniformly recognize that the causes of crime and criminality are linked to a number of interrelated variables—in other words, to rec-ognize the existence of multi-causality. Multi-causality, in addition to benefiting from an integrated and interdisciplinary approach, also requires the use of sophisticated statistical and various research techniques in order to manage the potential complex-ity of comparative issues.

The knowledge explosion in criminology has been both a blessing and a curse for criminologists. While it has helped create an identity and bolstered the discipline's image, it also proved the truth of the adage that states that the more we know, the more we realize how little we know. Criminologists must realize and accept the limits of their knowledge. They must learn to accept slow and perhaps painful growth in their understanding of criminal behaviour. To advance this understanding, they must also explore, with great care, the interdisciplinary nature of people's behaviour—a simple challenge, but one that they have not yet come close to mastering. As Einstadter and Henry (1995:318), among many others, have noted, "there are no simple explanations; there are no simple solutions. Complexity is the nature of social science." Yet Akers (1994:194) reminds us that "opinion in criminology favours the search for parsimonious, empirically valid integrated explanations of crime and criminal justice." Even so, what direction an integrated approach will take—or should take—has not been resolved. Furthermore, the way in which all the criminological information may be consolidated also remains a puzzle.

Crime in the Future

While crimes can be classified as either property-related or personal-type offences, they have taken many different forms. Humans are truly a creative, innovative, and adapting species. As the saying goes, where there is a will, there is a way. Many traditional crimes (e.g., break and enter, fraud, murder, and theft) that persist today will likely continue to do so for centuries to come, but the new, emerging forms will pose additional challenges to criminology.

Fattah (1997:286) expresses the belief that the invention of the automobile is "the most important single factor responsible for the fundamental changes in the nature of crime in the 20th century." Yet he points out that very few criminologists study the role that the "car has played in transforming many types of crime and in producing new forms of criminality" (ibid.). For example, in 2004, the Alberta RCMP reported that there was an noticeable increase in rural break and enters that were executed in ways similar to the methods used in such offences in major urban centres. Upon further investigation, it was discovered that a good number of rural break and enters were committed by individuals travelling via a motor vehicle from an urban setting. Environmental criminologists have also shown how the use of automobiles has altered the choice of targets and people's willingness to drive some distance to commit their crime, with one of the objectives being a reduced risk of being recognized.

While Fattah's observation deserves consideration, similar arguments could be made for the introduction or invention of the monetary system, airplanes, computers, credit cards, radios, telephones, the internet, and a wide variety of other technologies. People have found ways to capitalize on each new technological advance. According to the Criminal Intelligence Service Canada, high-tech ID theft and counterfeiting are among the fastest-growing crimes in North America. The cost to Canadians rose to $21 million in 2003, almost double the losses in 2002 (CISC, 2004). New technologies have changed the nature of criminal enterprises, affected the methods used to deliver criminal justice services, and influenced how we respond to crime.

Few would dispute the suggestion that crime and criminality will continue to evolve. Among the areas that *may* pose increasing challenges for criminology and crime control are (also see Box 14.4):

- Computer and other high-tech crimes;
- International sex trade;
- Smuggling of migrants;
- International criminal law (because of potential differences in legal orientations and traditions);
- International trade in human organs;
- Transnational organized crime groups;
- Transnational corporate crime;
- Transnational environmental crime;
- Drug trafficking within a transnational context;
- Biosocial factors and crime;
- International terrorism and new forms of terrorist violence, used by groups ranging from businesses and governments to religious leaders and cyberterrorists; and
- International money laundering, gemstone scams, land sale scams, etc.

FYI BOX 14.4

THE EVOLVING NATURE OF CRIME

The following examples illustrate some of the emerging forms of crime.

- In Bulgaria, one of Europe's least scientifically advanced countries, criminal gangs were writing computer software and selling it abroad with the specific aim of helping hackers break into computers from wherever they are (Moseley, 1995).
- In the Balkans, organized crime is flourishing as it capitalizes on the unstable political climate and the social unrest is filtering down into the general populace, who offer at least passive support (Roth, 2000).
- In 2003, the violence of Hmong gangs in the United States began to present a new problem for law enforcement. Gang rapes and prostitution are among the gangs' chosen activities, and these gangs are considered to be very mobile, traveling literally across the country to engage in criminal activities (Straka, 2003).
- Once thought to be regionally based, outlaw motorcycle gangs are going global, creating a greater demand for international cooperation and intelligence sharing among law enforcement agencies (Moran, 2002).

- Militant groups are spreading internationally. For example, unofficial counts of neo-Nazi skinheads range from 5000 in Germany to 4000 each in Hungary and Czechoslovakia, 3500 in the United States, 2500 in Poland, 1500 each in United Kingdom and Brazil, 1000 in Sweden, and 500 each in France, Switzerland, and Canada (Malinowski, 1996).

The question of what forms these crimes will take, assuming they emerge as major concerns, poses a great challenge for criminologists. As these crimes become more common, it will become even more important for criminologists to develop theoretical understandings that transcend cultural, gender, and political boundaries. Of course, criminologists will continue to have to pay attention to the traditional forms of crime. It will be interesting to see whether the new forms of crime will cease to exist if criminologists can identify the underlying causes of the traditional forms.

The conventional trend of theory development seems little more than an attempt on the part of criminologists to develop a "better mousetrap" as each successive paradigm is found wanting or is little more than a variation on an old theme. However, the rest of this century will be an exciting time for criminology as the discipline continues to determine whether prevention or punishment or some combination thereof will be the most effective means of crime and social control.

Social Control: Prevention or Punishment?

Consider the following facts from the Canadian-based International Centre for the Prevention of Crime (ICPC reports/papers, 2003) in Montreal:

- In Canada, Australia, the Netherlands, and the United States, the cost of crime accounts for more than 5 percent of the Gross Domestic Product.
- An international survey of seven countries, including Canada, shows that the average citizen pays annually $200 for police, courts, and prisons; $400 for the shattered lives of victims; $100 for private security; and $25 for lost property.
- The number of persons incarcerated has risen by approximately 10 percent since 1970.

These and other statistics point to the need for governments to find cost-effective ways to control crime.

In the mid- to late 1990s, the American government spent $3 billion on state and local crime **prevention** programs. A team of distinguished criminologists, led by Lawrence W. Sherman, was commissioned to evaluate the effectiveness of these programs in terms of the prevention of crime and the increased protection of society (Chin, 1997).

The authors of the report suggest that effectiveness depends on whether money and resources are being directed at urban areas with concentrated poverty. Sherman and his associates examined five different institutions involved in crime prevention efforts: community programs, family-based programs, school-based programs, policing, and criminal justice system programs. Within each major area, they looked at programs that fell within the domain of these areas (Chin, 1997).

Unfortunately, no comparable study has been undertaken in Canada. However, since Canada shares many of the same concerns as the United States, a summary of Sherman's findings are presented in Figure 14–1.

FIGURE 14–1

CRIME PREVENTION: WHAT WORKS AND WHAT DOESN'T

COMMUNITY PROGRAMS

Most programs suffer weak evaluations.

What's promising:

- Gang violence prevention.
- Community-based mentoring.
- After-school recreation.

What doesn't work:

- Gun buy-back programs.
- Community mobilization (e.g., lobbying against renewal of tavern liquor licences).

FAMILY-BASED PROGRAMS

What works:

- Early infancy and preschool visitations.
- Parent training or family therapy for high-risk adolescents and children.

What's promising:

- Battered women's shelters.
- Orders of protection for battered women.

What doesn't work:

- Home visits by police after domestic violence incidents fail to reduce repeat violence.

SCHOOL-BASED PROGRAMS

What works:

- For youth, programs aimed at building capacity to initiate and sustain innovation.
- Clarifying norms of behaviour and ensuring they are consistently enforced in schools.
- For substance abusers, using behaviour modification programs and programs on "thinking skills."

What's promising:

- Use of small groups within a school setting that provide the opportunity for supportive interaction and greater flexibility to students' needs.
- Behaviour modification programs.

What doesn't work:

- Counselling and peer counselling.
- Alternative activities such as recreation and community services for substance abusers.
- Instructional programs focusing on information dissemination, fear arousal, and moral appeal.

POLICING

What works:

- Increased police presence at "hot spots" of crime.
- Proactive arrest, drug testing, drunk driving programs.

What's promising:

- Community policing with community participation.
- Zero tolerance of disorder, if circumstances are justified.
- Problem-oriented policing generally.

What doesn't work:

- Neighbourhood Block Watch.
- Arrest of unemployed suspects for domestic assault.
- Community policing with no clear crime-risk factor focus.

CRIMINAL JUSTICE SYSTEM PROGRAMS

What works:

- Rehabilitation programs with particular characteristics.
- Incapacitation of repeat offenders (e.g. detention or capital punishment).

What's promising:

- Day fines.
- Juvenile aftercare.
- Drug courts combining both rehabilitation and criminal justice control.

What doesn't work:

- Rehabilitation programs that use vague, non-directive, unstructured counselling and programs that rely on shock intervention strategies.
- Programs with vague behavioural targets directed at low-risk offenders.
- Rehabilitation programs are effective only to the extent to which the funding agent is willing and prepared to provide target areas with high-quality assistance and information as to what works and how the initiatives are best implemented. Furthermore, the success of such programs depends on whether funding is directed to the urban neighborhoods where youth violence is highly concentrated.

    For further details, see www.ncjrs.org/works/. For specific techniques of situational crime prevention, see Clarke and Eck (2003).

A comprehensive study conducted for the American Office of Juvenile Justice and Delinquency and Prevention reported that the "only way to substantially reduce serious and violent offending is through prevention and early intervention with youth who are on paths toward becoming serious violent chronic offenders" (Howell, 1995:6). The report points out that in order to control the growth of violent youth crime, it is necessary to recognize that such behaviours are characterized by *multiple risk factors*, such as background indicators such as family, school, peers, and neighborhood characteristics. The report also notes that these factors interact and are not necessarily linear in their relation to one another. However, the authors of the report further point out that it is possible to have *protective factors*. While they may have a minimal impact on a singular basis, collectively they can serve as deterrents to prevent high-risk youth from becoming chronic offenders. Protective elements can include family, school, and peer groups, among other factors.

The study identified three *developmental pathways* that young offenders "take to problem behavior and serious, violent, and chronic offending" (Howell, 1995:5). The first is the *authority conflict pathway*, where delinquency amplifies when stubborn behaviour eventually gives way to authority avoidance (e.g., staying out late, running away from home). The *covert pathway* begins with youths engaging in secretive behaviour and then progressing to overt behaviour such as property damage, which may in turn escalate to more serious acts (e.g., break and enter, fraud, and theft). The third model is the *overt pathway*, where behaviour begins with minor aggression and progresses to more serious violence (e.g., assault and sexual assault).

Howell (1995) notes that approximately 75 percent of high-risk offenders fit into one or more of these pathways. The findings also lend support to the evidence that only a small proportion—between 6 and 14 percent (depending on the source cited)—of young offenders commit the majority—70 percent—of serious and violent crimes.

One of the prevention strategies suggested by this study involves the **social development approach**. This strategy is designed to address "target risks in a way that enhances protection" and lead to healthy beliefs and healthy behaviours. An example is the 1980s campaign to teach children to "just say no" to drugs. A similar initiative in the 1990s is the Stop the Violence campaign. Critical to the success of any such program is the ability of youths to "bond" with the message (Howell, 1995). This involves youths being able to experience a sense of involvement, being able to contribute to and/or participate in the campaign, and receiving recognition for their involvement.

Despite its impressiveness, the study reflects the traditional limitations found in explanatory models: concern with only sociological and/or psychological factors. For example, the report neglects to examine the role of victims in the implementation of crime prevention initiatives (see Tonry & Farrington, 1995).

Two crime prevention approaches that are capturing the attention of some Canadian scholars are the opportunity reduction (see Box 14.5) and social development approaches.

OPPORTUNITY REDUCTION AS A MEANS OF CRIME CONTROL

The following points reflect the varied findings about the effectiveness of crime control through opportunity reduction:

- Research from both sides of the Atlantic suggests that conventional attempts to control and/or reduce crime, such as more policing, more laws, and longer sentences, are not very fruitful (Pease & Litton, 1984).
- When the Dutch introduced a law requiring drivers of motorized bicycles to wear helmets, theft of such cycles dropped by one-third (ibid.).
- After the French introduced closed-circuit television cameras in their supermarkets, they observed a 33 percent drop in losses (ibid.).
- The Australian Institute of Criminology's Research and Public Policy Service provides a list of crime prevention initiatives that are based on opportunity reduction. For example, the Julalikari Night Patrol was set up to break the cycle of violence associated with excessive alcohol consumption. Night patrols were introduced to mediate disputes and admonish perpetrators in a culturally appropriate context (Grabosky & James, 1995).
- The Home Office in England is also involved in promoting and publishing the results of a wide range of primary crime prevention initiatives. The office hosts a website that provides practical crime prevention information on such varied topics as domestic violence, convenience store robberies, and anti-social behaviour in local housing developments. Visit the Home Office's crime reduction site at **www.crimereduction.gov.uk/cpindex.htm** for more information.

Opportunity reduction is a type of crime prevention that emerged in response to escalating difficulties in the administration of justice and the cry among criminologists for proactive intervention. Opportunity reduction can take three forms. **Primary prevention** involves addressing the conditions in the environment and includes such things as maintaining streets, fixing broken windows, and generally cleaning up disorganized communities. Primary prevention attempts to address those physical factors that are thought to be directly related to crime risk. However, community/neighborhood crime prevention initiatives, where communities take on the responsibility of monitoring their own crime problem (for example, Neighbourhood Watch), are also forms of primary prevention. The risk of embracing a primary prevention approach is that it may lead to increased fear of crime and isolation, with people sitting behind barred doors, fearful of all but their immediate friends and family members. In this way, as Fattah (1997:294) observes, such an approach may serve to "undermine the social democracy it wishes to protect."

Secondary prevention involves identifying targets (in terms of people, places, situations, time, etc.) and trying to prevent the target from being victimized. For example, because of the relationship between the use of drugs and crime, programs have been developed to educate youth about the hazards of drugs. Well-established law enforcement procedures such as patrolling crime "hot spots" and using deadbolts and house alarms are referred to as target hardening practices; other variations include natural surveillance and formal surveillance. While these ideas are appealing, Lab (1997) observes that in the future criminologists will need to focus more clearly on which strategies are the most promising and also come to terms with crime displacement, which occurs when target hardening, instead of eliminating problems, causes them to shift to another area. As well, secondary prevention poses some unanswered questions. Can such programs work for individuals who demonstrate a propensity for criminal activity? What is the risk of overpredicting?

The final form of opportunity reduction is **tertiary prevention**. This strategy is reserved for individuals who have already violated the law or situations where crimes have already occurred. The focus is on reducing the recidivism rate. In countries such as the United States, the primary method of tertiary prevention is incarceration. In Canada, efforts range from incarceration to restorative justice initiatives. While tertiary prevention does not prevent crime from occurring, it does make areas safer and reduces the risk of victimization by those removed from the setting.

Opportunity reduction means using devices to limit the likelihood of potential victimization. While such strategies may reduce the risk of criminal victimization, they provide minimal insight into why someone chooses to commit a crime in the first place. For example, why are some individuals more prone to commit crimes than others, given the same situation, and why are they more prone than others to place themselves in situations that favour criminal activity?

The social development approach is a type of primary prevention in which social or community-based programs are created to mobilize people to become more aware of and take steps to reduce their risk of being victimized. This approach assumes a social system based on linear progression rather than being "composed of interlocking, intersecting, and interpenetrating relational sets which are in dynamic change" (Milovanic, 1997:196).

Sacco and Kennedy (1994:317) note that "crime prevention through social development is focused on the serious repeat offender." The literature concurs in observing that approximately six percent of offenders account for a disproportionately large number of crimes. Yet, in spite of attempts to predict and correct the criminogenic social conditions, traditional approaches have had limited success. Sacco and Kennedy (1994:317) suggest future success may lie in such strategies as police "shifting their attention from crime fighting...to compliance policing, which is more directly integrated into the community." They assert that if the community participates in defining and solving problems, the social development concept can work (see Box 14.6).

COMMUNITY POLICING

In a two-part series on youth crime in the *Calgary Herald*, Christine Silverberg, chief of the Calgary Police Service from 1995 to 2000, publicly offered her assessment of how to solve the youth crime problem in Canadian society. Among the points she made were:

- There is no panacea for the maintenance of order or the problems of crime and disorder.
- There must be an integrated and comprehensive approach to crime control.
- The police must work in concert with governments, institutions, and the community to counter crime.
- Responding to crime necessitates both traditional and advanced investigative techniques (Silverberg, 1997).

The prevention efforts that have been put in place as part of a social development strategy have had modest success. A major survey of 589 prison inmates serving sentences for property-related crime rated crime prevention policies as poor to no good (Crime prevention..., 1988). In the future, any social development programs will have to be subject to more rigorous evaluation, larger sample sizes, and clearer operationalization of key terms (Tonry & Farrington, 1995). In addition, as former federal justice minister Allan Rock argued, the government needs to free up more money to support efforts by the Department of Justice's National Crime Prevention Council, since 1998 known as the National Crime Prevention Strategy (NCPS). Yet Rock allocated less than one percent of his department's budget to crime prevention (Alden, 1996). More recently, the government has directed significant amounts of money toward a wide range of crime prevention initiatives. For example, in 2002, the NCPS awarded some $3.4 million to 133 crime prevention projects in the Atlantic provinces alone (Communities across Atlantic..., 2002).

In 1994, the then newly elected government of the Netherlands decided to take a proactive stance on the country's growing crime problem by directing $100 million into crime prevention. As part of the initiative, the Dutch Ministry of Justice tested four hypothetical models of crime control: (1) doing nothing; (2) increasing the number of police officers; (3) increasing situational prevention measures; and (4) increasing social prevention. While situational prevention had some success, the most effective model involved social prevention. The program was introduced in four major cities and involves four levels of intervention: providing employment, particularly in the socially disadvantaged groups; improving education and reducing school dropout rates; improving target hardening for property-related offences; and facilitating the quality of life through promoting interracial harmony (Preventing crime within…, 1997). In her 2003 report on the project, Moene indicates that, overall, the initiatives have created mostly positive changes.

The Department of Public Safety and Emergency Preparedness of Canada lists a wide range of national crime prevention initiatives, reflecting a concerted effort to introduce crime prevention strategies across the country. For example, in 2004, the government allocated $2.98 million to increasing community safety in Newfoundland and Labrador and another $2 million for 42 similar projects in Saskatchewan. Crime prevention programs also include business action programs and crime prevention partnership programs.

Regardless of whether they prefer the punishment model or the crime prevention model, criminologists always have to contend with politics. While they might not want to recommend policy changes, criminologists can provide informed opinions that could then be used by decision-makers. Either way, criminologists also need to come to terms with the "true" extent of the crime problem. Although a variety of techniques can be used to gauge the level of crime, political agendas are often driven by public attitudes (Roberts et al., 2003). Research has clearly shown that fear of crime levels among the public are disproportionate to the true magnitude of crime. Hence, future techniques must be cognizant of both the real and perceived levels of crime and must be prepared to attack crime in all aspects. Ekstedt (1995:307) suggests that "policy-making is concerned with competing values and the achievement of social purpose." Criminal policy seeks to effect compromises between basic social values that are in tension—liberty and security. In other words, crime policy seeks to balance utilitarian principles with those that aim to protect society at large. This is no small task—one that, until recently, has been given only token attention by criminologists (Tombs & Whyte, 2003).

Finally, as a result of globalization, societies are becoming increasingly multicultural. Canada's rate of growth is due primarily to immigration. These cultural changes, combined with growing urbanization, ease of travel, and ease of communication affect all aspects of society, including crime and crime control. In the future, criminologists will have to think globally, and criminal policy will have to evolve with these trends. These changes will require criminologists to redefine their approach. Currently, criminologists and criminal justice officials continue to be treated, and to treat each other, as separate entities. For example, each group holds its separate conferences. Theory and practice are often also divided, and the gap widens between them. Finding the right balance in the use of the principles of restorative justice, reintegrative shaming, and other moral and value-laden programs will require diligent theoretical and methodological attention by criminologists.

A 1997 article on "innovative" incarceration practices in the state of Wisconsin and Maryland noted that inmates will be required to "wear stun belts which fire 50,000 volts through their bodies if they try to escape" (Gordon, 1997:A3). As of 2003, these states are continuing with the program in spite of continued urging from Amnesty International and the Human Rights Watch group that such practices represent "cruel and unusual punishment." Gordon (1997) concludes by observing that "shame, hard work and harsh conditions are increasingly seen as part of crime and punishment." Yet, there is no criminological theory to support the contention that such notions work.

The bulk of criminological and criminal justice efforts have been directed at punishment, rehabilitation, or some other intervention strategy, but these efforts have had a dismal track record. It will be interesting to see whether criminology can change its focus to one that is interdisciplinary in its theoretical perspective and proactive in its objective to reduce crime and fear of crime. Such changes will also require some changes to our criminal law.

Criminology and Criminal Law

Criminal law plays an important role in helping maintain social order and is therefore a crucial element in the study of crime. Yet, while the meaning of a criminal act is dependent on its legal definition, such definitions do not address any of the causal factors of crime and, historically, the study of crime and the role of criminal law have been treated as interdependent. In essence, criminal law has been in conflict with criminology and the social sciences in general, since criminal law is concerned with punishment and accountability while criminology is concerned with crime prevention and the medical model of treatment and rehabilitation (Jeffery, 1990). What is less clear is how criminal law will evolve in the future.

Norval Morris suggested that the criminal law of the future would be predominantly administrative in nature, responding to the increasing obsession with the right of property (Morris, 1982). If this were to be the case, there would be a shift in social control and social regulation, from the law focusing on imprisonment to one focusing on compensation and restitution. Should criminal law make such a shift, then the radical view of criminal law being an instrument of the elite would no longer hold true. Instead, criminal law would protect values and norms of a more universal nature.

Wollan (1980, cited in Fattah, 1997:289) observed that criminology will "become somewhat more concerned with values and, hence, to shift slightly from the empirical, scientific end of the spectrum toward the normative, philosophical end." Given that a quarter century has passed since Wollan's observations, it may be optimistic to think that criminology can make such a dramatic shift. At best, such elements may become a part of the criminal justice network.

It has been noted that criminal law has had a minimal effect in curbing crime trends. In Canada, we now have more than 90 000 laws covering substantive offences, while the United States has more than 250 000 such laws. Yet neither system has been able to demonstrate a positive relationship between criminal behaviour and crime control. If anything, it could be argued that criminal law serves only to artificially inflate crime statistics (generally, see Goff, 1998).

Criminologists need to recognize this inherent contradiction. Furthermore, current parochial attitudes are no match for the changing forms of crime. Today, crime knows no boundaries—but our legal system does. In the future, we are likely to see criminal law shift increasingly from a model of reactive response to law violation to a model wherein criminal law enforcement officials and criminologists focus on promoting observation of the law and crime prevention not only on local and national levels but also on an international level. Such a shift will require many criminologists to rethink how they view crime and how they respond to it.

Expanding the Scope of Criminology

The assertion that criminal law will move toward the normative and philosophical end suggested by Wollan is likely to be further complicated by the growth of science and technology as they become a major part of criminology. Criminalistics or forensic science, in particular, is a rapidly growing area.

In a general sense, forensic science is "the application of science to law" (Saferstein, 1998:1). Forensic science offers "the knowledge and technology of science for the definition and enforcement of such laws" (ibid.:1). For many, the term conjures up images of *CSI Miami*, *CSI Las Vegas*, *CSI New York*, *Cold Case*, *Da Vinci's Inquest*, or perhaps Sherlock Holmes. In all cases, the key figure works either in crime laboratories or specializes in trying to get into the minds of heinous criminals and is a master at finding clues that link the criminal to the crime scene.

In the real world, ViCLAS (Violent Crime Linkage Analysis System) represents an attempt by the RCMP to update its computer system for tracking the nation's most serious crimes. The system currently holds information on over 20 000 major crimes committed across Canada (ViCLAS, 2004). ViCLAS allows police to cross-reference details of crimes committed across the country. The total number of staff is about 100. This represents a lot of resources allocated to a category of crime that accounts for a small percentage of all conventional crimes—let alone non-conventional crimes. ViCLAS is a classic example of how criminology and the criminal justice system remain more preoccupied with apprehending high-profile criminals than focusing on petty crime offenders and white-collar, political, and other forms of criminality.

As with many other aspects of our life, science and technology will continue to play a bigger role in forging the identity of criminology and its growing number of sub-fields.

Crime: The Elusive Enigma

In earlier chapters, we saw that crime is very much present in society. Official statistics show us that crime rates have increased since the UCR system was introduced in the early 1960s. Self-report studies and victimization surveys generally reinforce these observations. However, we also saw that public interest is as predictable as the weather. The focus shifts as the media grapple to find news stories to pique our interest. How often now do we hear anything more about high-profile violent offenders who used to be in the spotlight, such as Clifford Olson, Paul Bernardo, Karla Homolka, or notable white-collar offenders, such as Alan Eagleson and several members of Parliament under the final term of Jean Chrétien—or, for that matter, any other individual who captured considerable media coverage at one point or another?

The point is that new social issues appear regularly, though many of them focus on similar problems—for example, young offenders, corporate crime, biker gangs, or drug abuse. Media coverage of these issues reinforces our awareness of the strong presence of crime in society. As Kappler, Blumberg, and Potter (1993:331) observe, crime waves "become mental filters through which social issues are filtered," and crime problems as portrayed in the media are in fact crime myths, since they carry no concrete (or at least a very limited) significance in and of themselves. Rather, they simply feed misconceptions of crime and criminal justice.

For example, most people continue to believe that if crime is so serious, then more police officers with high-tech equipment are needed to combat crime. Yet classic studies such as the Kansas City Patrol Study in the 1970s dispelled these myths. All the same, the police continue to argue that they need more officers and better technology to fight criminals. Similarly, the evidence strongly indicates that imprisonment of violent offenders is not an effective deterrent; all it does is temporarily remove individuals from society. Recidivism data hardly argues for continued use of imprisonment—yet new institutions are continually being built. Similarly, in the aftermath of the 1974 "nothing works" perspective, most criminologists were reluctant to revisit the rehabilitation model. Yet, judging from the recent efforts of Francis Cullen and his colleagues (2001), this approach merits more consideration. As for the judicial system, one need only look at the plight of young people to know that the punishments meted out by the courts are laughable. Furthermore, the most likely losers are minority groups and the lower and middle classes. The winners are white-collar offenders who seldom receive criminal sentences but whose crimes are often more costly to society.

Public misconceptions not only help create and perpetuate myths about crime and criminals but also serve to stymie the introduction of new ideas. While criminologists struggle to try and determine which philosophical orientations best explain and predict criminal behaviour, the criminal justice system continues to rely on antiquated ideas of punishment and treatment.

Perhaps one of the more innovative alternatives to gain momentum in the 1990s is the concept of restorative justice or communitarianism, as it is sometimes referred to in Sweden (Lindstrom, 1997).

Restorative Justice: A Glowing Light in the Dark

Throughout the textbook, we have seen that criminology and the criminal justice system in general are in a state of crisis. Despite a decline in the late 1990s, crime rates are still alarmingly high when contrasted with the rates in the 1960s, when the current recording procedures were introduced. The criminal justice system is struggling to maintain some sense of social control, public support is waning, and criminological theory is in a state of disrepair.

Throughout most of history, most societies have adopted a negative approach to crime and applied principles of retribution and revenge to crime control. The preoccupation with the Hammurabi Code's principle of retaliation—"an eye for an eye and a tooth for a tooth"—has accomplished little in our society's efforts to control crime. Perhaps it is time to break from the traditional modes of criminological thinking.

One area of criminological inquiry that began drawing considerable attention in the 1990s and is continuing to do so now is **restorative justice**. Ezzat Fattah (1995), one of the champions of this alternative form of justice, presents a list of reasons as to why punishment does not and never will work (see Box 14.7).

WHAT DO YOU THINK? BOX 14.7

PUNISHMENT: IS THERE EVER A TIME FOR IT?

- *Punishment is ineffective*: The United States sends more people per capita to prison than any other Western country, yet their crime problem shows no serious signs of reversing. China has been executing offenders liberally in an attempt to stem the tide of crime. Singapore's zero tolerance for many crimes is beginning to show signs of faltering. Do we want to embrace such concepts?

- *Punishment is costly*: The financial costs of administering criminal justice have been escalating as a result of inflation, increased number of legal cases to process, and growing prison populations. What social and financial good has ever come of placing an offender in prison?

- *Punishment treats human beings as a means to an end*: While punishing someone can have a cathartic effect on the victim and the public, it does little or nothing for the individual being punished. Those who repent and reform are few compared to those who feel degraded, humiliated, and stigmatized in ways that can never be corrected. Is there no better solution?

- *Punitive penal sanctions amount to punishing the victim*: Regardless of the etiology one uses to explain criminality, there is no logical justification for punishment. The outcome is that the offender loses and the victim has no real recourse to heal. Is this true justice?

The major principles and philosophy of restorative justice include the following:

- When a wrong (crime) is committed, the offender is obliged to make some form of restitution—for example, apologize or provide financial restitution—to the victim, and by extension to the community. Instead of moral responsibility, social responsibility is emphasized.

- The restoration process has strong psychological and sociological underpinnings for the offender. Research has shown that publicly shaming an offender can serve as a powerful tool to reintegrate the individual.
- Retribution focuses on the crime as being a violation of the state, while restoration focuses on the crime as being a violation of people. This means that instead of a guilt orientation, a consequence orientation is used in restorative justice.
- Crime is not an abstraction but an injury and violation to a person and a community that should be repaired. Instead of revenge and retribution, emotional, physical, social, and spiritual restitution is needed.
- The restorative process should respect all parties—victim, offender, and justice colleagues.

The Mennonites were among the first in North America to formally put restorative principles into practice. However, University of Calgary law professor Chris Levy (1997) has observed that evidence of these principles can also be found in the late 1800s and early 1900s in England, when the government practised a minimalist approach to justice. The community was encouraged to resolve its own disputes before bringing them to court.

Informally, the Aboriginal people of Canada had practised elements of restorative justice for hundreds of years. However, as the Europeans settled and conquered the "new world," they forced the Aboriginal people to give up the ways of their culture, subjecting them to cultural genocide. Today, our criminal justice system bears the scars of various ill-conceived notions. It is now well documented that Aboriginal people are overrepresented in the Canadian criminal justice system, as well as the child welfare, juvenile justice, unemployment, and drug and alcohol treatment systems (Carriere, 2003).

Before Aboriginal people were subjected to colonialism, they embraced principles that relied on the community to resolve disputes and emphasized informal social process, reintegrating the offender into the family and community through a gradual restoration of trust and forgiveness. The process is commonly referred to as a *circle sentencing conference*. As Hazelhurst (1996:1–2) noted, "many of these fundamental mechanisms, institutions, social processes and inter-personal skills need to be relearned or regenerated" within the Aboriginal community.

Because of the strong First Nations influence, Canada is a world leader in restorative justice. The Tsuu T'ina Peacemaker Court in Alberta is one example of how healing and restoration can be brought back into a community. Another is the Saskatchewan Cree Court, established in 2001, where offenders are diverted from jail though restorative justice programs (Parker, 2004). Restorative justice is also being implemented around the world and can be seen in such countries as Northern Ireland (a program called RECOVERY) and New Zealand (victim reconciliation programs) (Restorative Justice, 2004). In general, existing restorative justice programs include VORP (victim–offender reconciliation program), VOM (victim–offender mediation), CJJ (community justice circles), RPP (reparative probation program), reintegrative shaming, and transformative justice. Numerous books, papers, and lectures on restorative justice point to its growing importance within criminology. Whether or not restorative justice becomes the prevailing paradigm in the new millennium will likely depend on the nature of social order and the political and economic developments.

If we can continue to embrace the evolving character of crime and criminality, then we may be in for a pleasant surprise, as peacemaking and other interdisciplinary paradigms begin to emerge. However, from a pragmatic perspective, Nicholl (1997) points out that a balance needs to be struck in bridging the gap between the criminal justice system's focus on crime control and the terms of reconciling through conferencing. The Canadian Criminal Justice Association, along with various provincial associations, is trying to bridge this gap between theory and practice, but it remains to be seen whether there is enough community support to effectively engage in meaningful restorative processes. In many respects, restorative justice initiatives offer an opportunity to integrate theoretical ideas with practice, breaking from the history of discontinuities between public policy and criminological theory.

In North America, criminology has evolved from constituting a sub-field of sociology to being accepted as its own scientific discipline. However, nowadays, virtually all sub-disciplines within the social sciences and several within the sciences have become part of the family of perspectives that help explain, describe, and predict crime and its control. As a result, criminology has become both more multidisciplinary and interdisciplinary in its approach. These changes promise challenging and exciting times for students and researchers of criminology.

Furthermore, the developments in criminology taking place in non-Western countries are certain to generate ongoing challenges to the dominant Western European and North American perspectives. If approached with an open mind, these views will prompt Western researchers to re-examine, re-evaluate, and revise the current understanding of crime, criminals, and social reaction to crime (Fattah, 1997).

Another challenge students and researchers are likely to face is how to merge criminological and criminal justice issues—and to what extent to focus on basic research as opposed to applied research. There is still a considerable gap between criminology and criminal policy and between punishment and alternative approaches to controlling crime. These are issues that criminologists must be prepared to embrace as the discipline moves forward. With rapid advances in techniques, theories, and methods, students will likely have to specialize in areas of study within criminology, be it victimology, theory, penology, sociology of law, environmental criminology, criminal behaviour systems, or another subject area. However, no matter what their specialization, they will need to keep the larger issues in mind and pay attention to the context.

We must have the courage to look beyond the status quo and continue to push our boundaries of understanding. If one thing is certain, it is the fact that criminology is constantly evolving. And as the eminent criminologist Sir Leon Radzinowicz (1999:469) concluded, we must strive "to dispel the heavy clouds of opportunism, prejudice and oversimplification."

Summary

- In the future, criminology must embrace an integrated, interdisciplinary approach to the study of human behaviour and criminological issues if it is to move forward as a discipline and to help create sound policy that effectively addresses crime in our society.

- In an increasingly globalized environment, criminologists need to embrace comparative cross-cultural and cross-national approaches to the study of crime and criminality, which includes acknowledging the efforts of non-Western researchers.

- As Beccaria noted over 300 years ago, it is better to prevent crime than to punish it through means that have consistently been proven not to work. Restorative justice may represent one method of accomplishing this task.

- Criminologists should feel morally and ethically bound to develop a new approach to understand and control human behaviour while building models that universally respect human freedom and dignity.

Discussion Questions

1. Which of the four approaches to crime control do you think is best suited to address criminological concerns? How does each of these approaches reflect the relative and evolutive nature of crime?

2. What are the barriers to conducting comparative research? What are the advantages for criminology in trying to overcome them?

3. Why has the knowledge explosion been a blessing and a curse in the pursuit of finding solutions to crime and in formulating policy? How can we begin to synthesize all this knowledge?

4. Based on your readings, and regardless of what may be in vogue, what do *you* think is the most effective strategy for crime control? With which perspective does it align?

5. Using the concept of restorative justice, what could we do at a local and national level to implement new policies for social control?

Key Concepts

Beijing rules	comparative research	conservative approach
liberal approach	postmodernism	prevention
primary prevention	radical approach	restorative justice
secondary prevention	social development approach	tertiary prevention

Weblinks

----

www.realjustice.org This website from the International Institute for Restorative Practices offers information on restorative justice and provides an extensive online library of articles on the topic.

www.csc-scc.gc.ca/text/prgrm/rjust_e.shtml The Correctional Service of Canada's website for restorative justice provides information and links to numerous other related sites.

www.crime-prevention-intl.org The Canadian International Centre for the Prevention of Crime, based in Montreal, offers extensive online resources on crime prevention.

crimeprevention.jibc.bc.ca/bkgd.htm British Columbia's Community Safety and Crime Prevention Practitioners Training Program includes online training modules for crime prevention volunteers and professionals.

www.aic.gov.au The website of the Australian Institute of Criminology includes links to sites addressing various criminological issues as well as crime prevention initiatives.

References

Abadinsky, H. (1994). *Organized crime* (4th ed.). Chicago: Nelson Hall.

Adams, J. (1976). *Learning and memory: An introduction.* New York: Dorsey Press.

Adams, R. (1973). Differential association and learning principles revisited. *Social Problems,* 20:458–470.

Adams, S. (1998a, January 28). Diet found to play role in attention deficit disorder. *Calgary Herald,* B4.

——. (1998b, June 17). Taming the demons. *Calgary Herald,* B6.

Adelberg, E., & Currie, C. (1987). *Too few to count.* Vancouver: The Press Gang.

Adler, F. (1975). *Sisters in crime: The rise of the new female criminal.* New York: McGraw-Hill.

Adler, F., Mueller, G.O.W., & Laufer, W.S. (1991). *Criminology.* New York: McGraw-Hill.

Aebi, M.F., Killias, M., & Tavares, C. (2002). Comparing crime rates: The international crime (victim) survey, the statistics, and Interpol statistics. *International Journal of Comparative Criminology,* 2(1):22–37.

Agnew, R., & White, H.R. (1992). An empirical test of general strain theory. *Criminology,* 30:475–499.

Aichorn, A. *Wayward youth.* (1935). New York: Viking Press.

Ainsworth, P. (2001). *Offender profiling and crime analysis.* London: Willan Publishing.

Akers, R. (1977). *Deviant behavior: A social learning approach* (2nd ed.). Belmont, CA: Wadsworth.

——. (1994). *Criminological theories: Introduction and evaluation.* Los Angeles: Roxbury.

——. (1998). *Social learning and social structure: A general theory of crime and deviance.* Boston: Northeastern University Press.

Akers, R.L, & Brugess, R. (1966). A differential association-reinforcement theory of criminal behavior. *Social Problems,* 14:128–147.

Akman, D.D., & Normandeau, A. (1967). The measurement of crime and delinquency in Canada. *Criminal Law Quarterly,* 9:323–238.

Albanese, J. (1996). Looking for a new approach to an old problem: The future of obscenity and pornography. In R. Muraskin & A.R. Roberts (Eds.), *Visions for change: Crime and justice in the twenty-first century.* Upper Saddle River, NJ: Prentice-Hall, 60–72.

Alberta fire commissioner's statistical report, 2002. (2004, March). Edmonton: Alberta Municipal Affairs.

Alberta Solicitor General and Criminal Intelligence Service Alberta. (2002, June). Organized serious crime initiatives: Business plan 2002–2005. Edmonton: Criminal Intelligence Service Alberta.

Albrecht, H-J., Kilchling, M., & Braun, E. (Eds.). (2002). *Criminal preventive risk assessment in the law-making procedure.* Freiburg, Germany: Max Planck Institute.

Alcohol in Japan. (2004). Online: www.a1b2c3.com/drugs/alc04.htm.

Alden, E. (1996, August 26). Rock wants more money to battle crime. *Calgary Herald,* A3.

Aldred, K. (2004). Street-gang savvy. *Gazette,* 66(2):17–19.

Allen, H.E., & Simenson, C.E. (1997). *Corrections in America: An introduction* (8th ed.). Upper Saddle River, NJ: Prentice-Hall.

Alter, S. (1997). *Violence on television: Canada.* Ottawa: Law and Government Division, for the Library of Parliament.

American Friends Service Committee. (1971). *Struggle for justice.* New York: Hill and Wane.

American Society of Criminology Conference. (2004). The 2004 American Society of Criminology Conference. Online: www.asc41.com/www/2004/cmsindx.htm. Retrieved August 26, 2004.

Amir, M. (1971). *Patterns in forcible rape.* Chicago: University of Chicago Press.

Ancel, M. (1994). Social defence. In J.E. Jacoby (Ed.), *Classics of criminology.* Prospect Height, IL: Waveland, ch. 41.

Anderson, C.A., & Bushman, B.J. (2001). Meta-analysis of 35 different studies of violent video games. *Psychological Science*, 12:353–358.

Anderson, C.A., & Dill, K.E. (2002). Video games and aggressive thoughts, feelings, and behavior in the laboratory and in life. *Journal of Personality and Social Psychology*, 78(4): 772–790.

Anderson, F.W. (1997). *A dance with death: Canadian women on the gallows, 1754–1954.* Calgary: Fifth House Publishing.

Andrews, D.A., & Bonta, J. (1994). *The psychology of criminal conduct.* Cincinnati, OH: Anderson.

——. (1998). *The psychology of criminal conduct* (2nd ed.). Cincinnati, OH: Anderson.

Antonopoulos, G.A. (2004). The financial exploitation of the sexuality of migrant children in Greece. *Crime & Justice International*, 20(83):19–22.

Antonopoulos, G.A., & Winterdyk, J.A. (2003). The British 1998 *Crime and Disorder Act*: A "restorative" response to youth offending? *European Journal of Crime, Criminal Law and Criminal Justice*, 11(4):386–397.

Arnold, S. (1997, October 17). 36 arrests as major poaching ring busted. *Edmonton Journal.* (Online).

Aromaa, K. (1974). Our violence. *Scandinavian Studies in Criminology*, 5:35–46.

Arrest in Kanesatake arson case. (2004, June 10). CBC News. Online: www.cbc.ca/stories/2004/06/10/canada/kanesatake_arrest040610.

Asher, J. (1996). Deadly hazards of being male in Canada. Online: www.lvm.vom/mine/asher3.htm.

Asian-based Organized Crime. (1999). Online: www.cisc.gc.ca/AnnualReport1999/Cisc99e/Asian.htm.

Bailey, I. (1998, February 9). Doomed teen's last moments to unfold in court. Canadian Press: Vancouver.

Bailey, M. (1991). Servant girls and masters: The tort seduction and the support of bastards. *Canadian Journal of Family Law*, 10(1):153–166.

Baldwin, J., & Bottoms, A.E. (1976). *The urban criminal.* London: Tavistock.

Ballard, J.D. (1998). *The Oklahoma City bombing case, the media and public policy on domestic terrorism.* Paper presented at the Academy of Criminal Justice Science 35th Annual Meeting. Albuquerque, NM, March 10–14.

Bandura, A. (1965). Vicarious processes: A case of no-trial learning. In L. Berkowitz (Ed.), *Advances in experimental social psychology*, vol. 2. New York: Academic Press, ch. 1.

——. (1979). The social learning perspective mechanisms of aggression. In H. Toch (Ed.), *Psychology of crime and criminal justice.* New York: Holt, Rinehart, & Winston.

Bandura, A., & Walters, R.H. (1959). *Adolescent aggression.* New York: Ronald Press.

Barak, G. (1997). *Integrating criminologies.* Boston, MA: Allyn & Bacon.

Barbara, J.S. (1995). *Media violence and real life aggression and militarism.* Online: www.pgs.ca/pages/jsbmedv1.html.

Barbaret, R. (2004). Mainstreaming comparative methodology in criminal justice/criminology research methods courses. *International Journal of Comparative Criminology*, 4(2).

Barkan, S.E. (1997). *Criminology: A sociological understanding.* Englewood Cliffs, NJ: Prentice-Hall.

Barkan, S.E., & Cohn, S.F. (1994). "Racial prejudice and support for the death penalty by whites." *Journal of Research in Crime and Delinquency*, 31:202–209.

Barry, J.V. (1973). Alexander Maconochie. In H. Mannheim (Ed.), *Pioneers in criminology* (2nd ed.). Montclair, NJ: Patterson Smith.

Bartol, C.R. (1995). *Criminal behaviour: A psychological approach* (4th ed.). Englewood Cliffs, NJ: Prentice-Hall.

Bartol, C.R. (2002). *Criminal behaviour* (6th ed.). Upper Saddle River, NJ: Prentice-Hall.

Baskin, D.R., & Sommers, I.B. (1998). *Casualties of community disorder: Women's careers in violent crime.* Boulder, CO: Westview.

Bavinton, F. (1998). *Hacking: A questionnaire.* Online: www.arts.unimelb.edu.au/dept/crim/hack/quest.htm.

BC Crime Stoppers. (2003). British Columbia Crime Stoppers. Online: www.bccrimestoppers.com/statistics/index.asp.

Beare, M. (1996). Organized crime and money laundering. In R.D. Silverman, J.T. Teevan., & V.F. Sacco (Eds.), *Crime in Canadian society* (5th ed.). Toronto: Harcourt Brace.

Beasely, J.D., & Swift, J.J. (1989). *The Kellogg report.* Annandale-on-Hudson, NY: The Institute of Health Policy and Practice, The Bard College Center.

Beccaria, C. (1963 [1764]). *On crimes and punishments.* Trans. Henry Paolucci. Indianapolis, IN: Bobbs-Merrill.

Becker, H.S. (1963). *Outsiders.* New York: The Free Press.

Bedau, H.A. (1996). Capital punishment. *Microsoft Encarta 96 Encyclopedia.* Microsoft Encarta Corp.

Beirne, P. (1991). Inventing criminology: The "science of man" in Cesare Beccaria's Dei delitti e delle pene (1764). *Criminology,* 29(4):777–820.

Beirne, P., & Hill, J. (1991). *Comparative criminology: An annotated bibliography.* New York: Greenwood Press.

Beirne, P., & Messerschmidt, J. (1991). *Criminology.* San Diego: Harcourt Brace Jovanovich.

Belknap, J. (1996). *The invisible woman: Gender, crime, and justice.* Belmont, CA: Wadsworth.

Bennett, W.W., & Hess, K.M. (1984). *Investigating arson.* Springfield, IL: Charles C. Thomas.

Bensinger, G. (2000). Prostitution and trafficking in women. *Crime & Justice International,* 16(46):5–8.

Benson, M.L. (1990). Emotions and adjudication: Status degradation ceremonies among white collar criminals. *Justice Quarterly,* 7:515–528.

Berger, R., Searles, P., & Cottle, C.E. (1991). *Feminism and pornography.* Westport: Praeger Publications.

Berkowitz, L. (1962). *Aggression: A social-psychological analysis.* New York: McGraw-Hill.

Berman, J., & Siegel, M-H. (1992). *Behind the 8-ball: A guide for families of gamblers.* New York: Simon and Schuster.

Birckbeck, E., & LaFree, G. (1993). The theoretical analysis of crime and deviance. *American Review of Sociology,* 19:113–137.

Bischof, L. (1964). *Interpreting personality theories.* New York: Harper & Row.

Bittle, S. (1999). *Youth involvement in prostitution: A focus on intrafamilial violence: A literature review.* Ottawa: Department of Justice. Online: canada.justice.gc.ca/en/ps/rs/rep/tr99-3a-e.html.

——. (2002). *Youth involvement in prostitution: A literature review and annotated bibliography.* Department of Justice Canada. Online: www.justice.gc.ca/en/ps/rs/rep/rr01-13a.html.

Blackwell, J.E. (1988). Sin, sickness, or social problem?: The concept of drug dependence. In J. Blackwell & P. Erickson (Eds.), *Illicit drugs in Canada.* Scarborough, ON: Nelson.

Blakey, R. (2002). Study links TV viewing among kids to later violence. Online: archives.cnn.com/2002/HEALTH/parenting/03/28/kids.tv.violence/.

Blanchette, K. (1997, May). Comparing violent and non-violent female offenders on risk and need. *Forum on Corrections Research,* 14–18.

Blum, D. (1997). *Sex on the brain: The biological differences between men and women.* New York: Viking.

Blumer, H. (1969). *Symbolic interactionism: Perspective and method.* Englewood Cliffs, NJ: Prentice-Hall.

Boers, K., & Sessar, K. (1991). Do people really want punishment? In H.J. Kerner & K. Sessar (Eds.), *Developments in crime and crime control on victims, offenders, and the public.* New York, Heidelberg: Springer, 126–149.

Boggs, S. (1966). Urban crime patterns. *American Sociological Review,* 30:899–908.

Bohm, R.M. (1986). Crime, criminal, and crime control policy myth. *Justice Quarterly,* 3:193–214.

Bond, A.J., Wingrove, J., & Critchlow, D.G. (2001). Tryptophan depletion increases aggression in women during the premenstrual phase. *Psychopharmacology,* 156:477–480.

Bonta, J., LaPrairie, C., & Wallace-Capretta, S. (1997). Risk prediction and re-offending: Aboriginal and non-aboriginal offenders. *Canadian Journal of Criminology,* 32(2): 127–144.

Borgaonkar, D.S., & Shah, S.A. (1974). The XYY chromosome: male—or syndrome? *Progress in Medical Genetics*, 10:135–142.

Boritch, H. (1997). *Fallen women: Female crime and criminal justice in Canada*. Scarborough, ON: Nelson.

Box, S. (1983). *Power, crime, and mystification*. London: Tavistock.

Boyd, N. (1988). *The last dance: Murder in Canada*. Scarborough, ON: Prentice-Hall.

——. (1991). *High society: Legal and illegal drugs in Canada*. Toronto: Key Porter Books.

——. (1993). *High society*. Toronto: Seal Books.

Bracken, D.C., & Leowen, R.J.L. (1992). Confronting individual and structural barriers to employment: The employment and skill enhancement (EASE) program for prisons. In L. McCormick & L. Visano (Eds.), *Canadian penology: Advanced perspectives and research*. Toronto: Canadian Scholars' Press, 157–166.

Brady, T.V. (1996, December) *Measuring what matters*. National Institute of Justice. Washington, DC: U.S. Department of Justice.

Braithwaite, J. (1981). The myth of social class and criminality reconsidered. *American Sociological Review*, 46:41.

——. (1989). *Crime, shame and reintegration*. Cambridge: Cambridge University Press.

Brannigan, A. (1996). The adolescent prostitute: Policing delinquency or treating pathology? In J. Winterdyk (Ed.), *Issues and perspectives on young offenders in Canada*. Toronto: Harcourt Brace, ch. 9.

Brannigan, A., & Fleischman, J. (1989). Juvenile prostitution and mental health: Policing delinquency or treating pathology. *Canadian Journal of Law and Society*, 4:77–98.

Brannigan, A., Knafla, L., & Levy, C. (1989). *Street prostitution: Assessing the impact of the law, Calgary, Regina, and Winnipeg*. Ottawa: Department of Justice.

Brantingham, P.J., & Brantingham, P.L. (1984). *Patterns in crime*. New York: Macmillan.

——. (Eds.). (1991). *Environmental criminology*. Beverly Hills, CA: Sage.

Brantingham, P.J., Mu, S., & Verma, A. (1995). Patterns in Canadian criminology. In M.A. Jackson & C.T. Griffiths (Eds.), *Canadian criminology* (2nd ed.). Toronto: Harcourt-Brace.

Braswell, M., Fuller, J., & Lozoff, B. (2001). *Corrections, peacemaking, and restorative justice: Transforming individuals and institutions*. Cincinnati, OH: Anderson.

Brennan, B. (1999, March 22). Fraud squad: Calgary seniors tell their peers how to protect themselves against scams, cons. *Calgary Herald*, B6.

Brenzinger, M.A. (1998, May). Serial rapists and their use of clandestine chemicals. *Crime and Justice International*, 6, 28–29.

Brewster, M. (2004, August 19). Spectacular tobacco heist catch the attention of organized crime: RCMP. Online: www.canada.com.

Brienen, M.E.I., & Hoegen, E.H. (2000). Victims of crime in 22 European criminal justice systems: The implementation of recommendation (85) 11 of the Council of Europe on the position of the victim in the framework of criminal law and procedure. PhD dissertation, University of Tilburg, Nijmegan, Netherlands.

Brillon, Y. (1987). *Victimization and fear of crime among the elderly*. Toronto: Butterworths.

Britannica. (1997). Wolfenden report. Online: www.britannica.com.

British Crime Survey. (2003). What is the British Crime Survey? Online: www.homeoffice.gov.uk/rds/bcs1.html.

Brodeur, J. (2002). Campaign to counter TV violence. Online: www.acmecoalition.org/countertvviolence.html.

Bronskill, J. (1998, January 28). Vehicle thefts hit record level in '97. *Calgary Herald*, A2.

Bronskill, J., & Bryden, J. (1998, April 21). Grits fear tough laws could break UN Treaty. *Calgary Herald*, A9.

Brott, A.A. (1995, January 5). Male victims of domestic violence: A substantive and methodological research review. *Violence Against Women*, part 1, 8(11).

Brown, S., Esbensen, F-A., & Geis, G. (1991). *Criminology: Explaining crime and its context*. Cincinnati, OH: Anderson.

Buckle, A., & Farrington, D.P. (1984). An observational study of shoplifting. *British Journal of Criminology*, 24:63–73.

Bullough, V. (1978). *The history of prostitution.* New Hyde Park, NY: University Books.

Bullough, V.L., & Bullough, B. (1987). *Women and prostitution: A social history.* Buffalo, NY: Prometheus.

Bunge, V.P., & Levett, A. (1998). *Family violence in Canada: A statistical profile.* Ottawa: Statistics Canada.

Bureau of Justice Statistics. (2003). Criminal victimization: Summary findings. Online: www.ojp.usdoj.gov/bjs/cvictgen.htm. Retrieved July 4, 2003.

Burns, E.T. (1989). *Anatomy of a crisis.* Needham Heights, MA: Ginn Press.

Bursick, R.J. (1995). The distribution and dynamics of property crime. In J.F. Sheley (Ed.), *Criminology: A contemporary handbook.* Philadelphia: Temple University Press, 211–257.

Bursick, R.J., & Grasmick, H.G. (1993). *Neighbourhoods and crime.* Toronto: Maxwell Macmillan.

Business Week. (1993, December 13). Car security and anti-theft devices, 72–75, 78–80, 85.

CACP (Canadian Association of Chiefs of Police). (1994). Strategic Planning Committee, Canadian Association of Chiefs of Police, Ottawa.

Cadoret, R.J. (1995). Adoption studies. *Alcohol Health & Research World,* 19(3):195–201.

CAEFS (Canadian Association of Elizabeth Fry Societies). (2004). Fact sheets. Online: www.dawn.thot.net/election2004/issues32.htm. Retrieved September 2, 2004.

Cameron, M.O. (1964). *The booster and the snitch.* New York: Free Press.

Campbell, D.T., & Fiske, D.W. (1959). Convergent and discriminant validity by the multitrait-multimethod matrix. *Psychological Bulletin,* 56:81–105.

Canada a haven for phone fraud. (2003, December 30). Online: www.ctv.ca/servlet/articlenews/story/ctvnews/1027035705299_10?s=name.

Canada and the death penalty. (2004). Online: www.ccadp.org/can-con.htm.

Canadian Cancer Society. (2004). *Canadian Cancer Statistics 2004.* Online: www.cancer.ca/vgn/images/portal/cit_86751114/14/33/195986411niw_stats2004_en.pdf.

Canadian Centre on Substance Abuse. (2004). Canadian profile 1999. Online: www.ccsa.ca/index.asp?menu=&ID=43.

Canadian Criminal Justice Association. (1989). Cited in *Tough on crime: What you should know about youth crime.* Calgary: John Howard Society, 3.

Canadian Foundation on Compulsive Gambling (Ontario). (1993). Online: www.responsiblegambling.org/articles/Prevalence_of_problem_and_pathological_gambling_in_Ontario.pdf.

Canadian Statement of Basic Principles of Justice for Victims of Crime. (2003). Online: canada.justice.gc.ca/en/ps/voc/csbp.html. Retrieved July 7, 2003.

Cao, L. (1987). Illegal traffic in women: A civil RICO proposal. *The Yale Law Journal,* 96:1297–1306.

——. (2004). *Major criminological theories.* Belmont, CA: Wadsworth.

Carman, A., & Moody, H. (1985). *Working women: The subterranean world of street prostitutes.* New York: Harper & Row.

Carrigan, D.O. (1991). *Crime and punishment in Canada: A history.* Toronto: McClelland and Stewart.

Carrington, P.J., & Moyer, S. (1998). A statistical profile of female young offenders. Technical Report No. TR-1998-4e. Ottawa: Department of Justice Canada.

Carter, P. (1995, September). Violence: From the grave to the cradle. *Financial Post Magazine,* 23–48.

Cases in adult criminal court by type of sentence; fine, restitution, absolute or conditional discharge, other sentence. (2004). Online: www.statcan.ca/english/pgdb/legal38a.htm.

Caspi, A. (2000). The child is the father of the man: Personality continuities from childhood to adulthood. *Journal of Personality and Social Psychology,* 78:158–172.

Caspi, A., Henry, B., McGee, R., Moffitt, T., & Silva, P. (1995). Temperamental origins of child and adolescent behavior problems: From age three to age fifteen. *Child Development,* 66:55–68.

Caspi, A., Moffitt, T., Silva, P., Stouthamer-Loeber, M., Krueger, R., & Schmutte. P. (1994). Are some people crime-prone? Replications of the personality-crime relationship across countries, genders, race, and methods. *Criminology*, 32:163–194.

Cates, J.A., & Markley, J. (1992). Demographic, clinical, and personality variables associated with male prostitution by choice. *Adolescence*, 27:695–714.

Cawte, J., & Florence, M.T.A. (1989). A manganic milieu in North Australia: Ecological manganism: Ecology, diagnosis, individual susceptibility, synergism, therapy prevention, advice for the community. *International Journal of Biosocial Medicine and Research*, 11:43–56.

CCJS (Canadian Centre for Justice Statistics). (1994, 14(7)). Criminal justice processing of sexual assault cases.

——. (1995, 15(12)). Criminal justice processing.

——. (1996, 16(11)). Homicide in Canada—1995.

——. (1997, 17(3)). Justice spending in Canada.

——. (1997, 17(8)). Canadian crime statistics, 1996.

——. (1997, 17(9)). Homicide in Canada—1996.

——. (1997, 17(13)). Justice fact finder.

——. (1998, 18(2)). Homicide in Canada.

——. (1998, 18(11)). Canadian crime statistics, 1997.

——. (1998, 18(12)). Homicide in Canada, 1997.

——. (1999, 19(5)). Female inmates, Aboriginal inmates, and inmates serving life sentences: A one day snapshot.

——. (2000, 20(10)). Adult correctional services in Canada, 2000/01.

——. (2000, 20(10)). Criminal victimization in Canada, 1999.

——. (2001, 21(1)). Canada's shelters for abused women.

——. (2002, 22(4)). Criminal victimization: An international perspective.

——. (2002, 22(11)). Justice spending in Canada, 2000/01.

——. (2003, 23(1)). Motor vehicle theft in Canada, 2001.

——. (2003, 23(2)). Adult criminal court statistics, 2001/2002.

——. (2003, 23(3)). Youth court statistics, 2001/02.

——. (2003, 23(5)). Crime statistics in Canada, 2002.

——. (2003, 23(6)). Sexual offences in Canada.

——. (2003, 23(8)). Homicide in Canada, 2002.

——. (2003, 23(11)). Adult correctional service in Canada, 2001/02.

——. (2004, 24(1)). Trends in drug offences and the role of alcohol and drugs in crime.

——. (2004, 24(4)). Hate crime in Canada.

——. (2004, 24(5)). Breaking and entering in Canada, 2002.

——. (2004, 24(6)). Crime statistics in Canada, 2003.

——. (2004, 24(8)). Homicide in Canada, 2003.

CCSA (Canadian Centre on Substance Abuse). (1999). *Canadian profile: Alcohol, tobacco, and other drugs.* Online: www.ccsa.ca/index.asp?menu=Statistics&ID=43.

Challem, J. (2001). Mean streets or mean minerals? Online: www.thenutrtionreports.com/nutrition_and_crime.html.

Chambliss, W. (1975). *The box man: A professional thief's journal, by Harry King.* New York: Harper & Row.

——. (1988). *On the take* (2nd ed.). Bloomington, IN: Indiana University Press.

Chermak, S.M. (1995). *Victims in the news: Crime and the American news media.* Boulder, CO: Westview Press.

Chin, E. (1997, October). Crime prevention: Is it working? *Crime and Justice International*, 21–22.

Christianity Today. (2000, September 28). Film forum: Taking aim at media violence. Online: www.christianitytoday.com/ct/2000/139/.

Christie, N. (1996). *Crime control as industry* (2nd ed.). London: Routledge.

Chunn, D., & Menzies, R. (1997). The getting of wisdom: The ideology and experience of graduate education among students enrolled in anglophone Canadian criminology programs. *Canadian Journal of Criminology*, 39(1):1–26.

Chunn, D.E., & Gavigan, S.A.N. (1991). Women and crime in Canada. In M. Jackson & C.T. Griffiths (Eds.), *Canadian criminology.* Toronto: Harcourt Brace, Jovanovich.

CISC (Criminal Intelligence Service Canada). (2004). Annual report on organized crime in Canada. Online: www.cisc.gc.ca/Annuale port2004/Cisc2004/frontpage2004.html. Retrieved August 25, 2004.

Cisneros, H.G. (1995). *Defensible space: Deterring crime and building community*. Washington, DC: Secretary of Housing and Urban Development.

Clairmont, D. (1999). In defence of liberal models of research and policy. *Canadian Journal of Criminology and Criminal Justice*, 41(2): 151–160.

Clark, L., & Tifft, L. (1966). Polygraph and interview validation of self-reported deviant behaviour. *American Sociological Review*, 31:516–523.

Clark, L.M., & Lewis, D.J. (1997). *Rape: The price of coercive sexuality*. Toronto: Women's Press.

Clarke, R.V., & Eck, J. (2003). *Become a problem solving crime analyst*. London: University College.

Clarke, R.V., & Felson, M. (1993). Introduction: Criminology, routine activity, and rational choice. In R.V. Clarke & M. Felson (Eds.), *Routine activity and rational choice*. New Brunswick, NJ: Transaction, 1–14.

Clermont, Y. (1996). Robbery. In L.W. Kennedy & V.F. Sacco (Eds.), *Crime counts: A criminal event analysis*. Scarborough, ON: Nelson.

Clinard, M.B. (1978). *Cities and little crime: The case of Switzerland*. Cambridge, UK: Cambridge University Press.

Clinard, M.B., & Yeager, P.C. (1980). *Corporate crime*. New York: Free Press.

Clinard, R., & Quinney, R. (1973). *Criminal behavior systems: A typology*. New York: Holt, Rinehart, & Winston.

CNN interactive. (1998, April 16). Study finds more violence in prime-time TV shows. Online: www.cnn.com.

Cohen, A. (1955). *Delinquent boys: The culture of the gang*. New York: Free Press.

——. (1959). The study of social disorganization and deviant behavior. In R.K. Merton, L. Broom, & L.S. Cottrell (Eds.), *Sociology today*. New York: Harper & Row, 461–484.

Cohen, L.E., & Felson, M. (1979). Social change and crime rate trends: A routine activities approach. *American Sociological Review*, 44:588–607.

Cohen, L.E., & Machalek, R. (1988). A general theory of expropriate crime: An evolutionary ecological approach. *American Journal of Sociology*, 94:465–501.

Cohen, S. (2001). *State of denial: Knowing about atrocities and suffering*. London: Polity Press.

Cohn, E.G., & Farrington, D.P. (1998). Changes in the most cited scholars in major international journals between 1986–90 and 1991–95. *British Journal of Criminology*, 38(1):156–170.

Coldren, J.D. (1995, July/August). Change at the speed of light: Doing justice in the information age. *CJ International*, 8–12.

Colgan, M. (1996). *Hormonal health*. Vancouver: Apple Pub.

Committee for a Safe Society. (1997). The Office of International Criminal Justice. Online: www.oicj.org.

Committee on Sexual Offences Against Children and Youth. (1984). *Sexual offences against children*. Ottawa: Department of Supply and Services.

Communities across Atlantic Canada awarded support for crime prevention efforts. (2002, June 14). Public Safety and Emergency Preparedness in Canada. Online: www. prevention.gc.ca/en/whatsnew/news/index. asp?a=v&di=JNNKRKMG4.

Conklin, J. (1975). *The impact of crime*. New York: Macmillan.

——. (1998). *Criminology* (6th ed.). Boston: Allyn & Bacon.

——. (2003). *Criminology* (8th ed.). Boston: Allyn & Bacon.

Cornish, D.B., & Clarke, R.V. (Eds.). (1986). *The reasoning criminal: Rational choice perspectives on offending*. New York: Springer-Verlag.

Corrections and conditional release statistics: Overview. (2003, December). Ottawa: Solicitor General Canada.

Cose, E. (1995). *A man's world: How real is male privilege—And how high is its price*. New York: HarperCollins.

Counterfeiting helped drive crime rate higher in '03. (2004, July 28). Online: www.mytelus.com/news.

Cousineau, F.D., & Verdun-Jones, S. (1979). Evaluating research into plea bargaining in Canada and the United States: Pitfalls facing the policy makers. *Canadian Journal of Criminology*, 21:293–309.

Cowie, J., Cowie, V., & Slater, E. (1968). *Delinquency in girls*. London: Heinemann.

Cowles, E.L., & Castellano, T.C. (1995). "Boot camps," drug treatment and aftercare intervention: An evaluation review. Rockville, MD: National Institute of Justice.

Cox, D.N., Roesch, R., & Zapf, P.A. (1996). *Psychological perspectives on criminality*. In R. Linden (Ed.), *Criminology: A Canadian perspective* (3rd ed.). Toronto: Harcourt Brace, ch. 8.

Coyle, J. (1998, May 9). Road rage is driving us around the bend. *Toronto Star*. Online: www.thestar.com.

Crime and punishment: The facts. (1996). Online: www.newint.org/issue282/facts.html.

Crime in the computer age. (1988, January 25). *Maclean's*, 28–30.

Crime prevention efforts get poor rating by criminals. (1988, December). *Law and Order*, 66–67.

Crime rate drops: We're just too old? (1995, October 23). *Calgary Herald*, A3.

Crime Reduction Programme. (2002). Online: www.number-10.gov.uk/output/Page1432.asp. Retrieved July 4, 2003.

Crime statistics. (2004, July 28). *The Daily*. Ottawa: Statistics Canada.

Crime Stoppers International. (2004). Crime Stoppers International. Online: www.c-s-i.org.

Criminal harassment. (2004, June). Ottawa: Department of Justice.

Criminal harassment: A handbook for police and Crown prosecutors. (2004). Online: canada.justice.gc.ca/en/ps/fm/pub/harassment/part1.html. Retrieved September 9, 2004.

Criminal lands in Canada. (1997, July 13). *Calgary Herald*. Online: www.calgaryherald.com.

Cromwell, P.F., Olson, J.N., & Avary, D.W. (1991). *Breaking and entering: An ethnographic analysis of burglary*. Newbury Park, CA: Sage.

——. (1993). Who buys stolen property? A new look at criminal receiving. *Journal of Crime and Justice*, 56:75–95.

CSI Statistics. (1997). *Crime Stoppers International*. Online: www.c-s-i.org.

Cullen, F., & Gendreau, P. (2001). From nothing works to what works: Changing professional ideology in the 21st century. *The Prison Journal*, 81(3):313–338.

Cullen, F.T., & Agnew, R. (Eds.). (1999). *Criminological theory past to present: Essential readings*. Los Angeles, CA: Roxbury.

The Daily. (2003, December 12). Problem gambling. Statistics Canada. Online: www.statcan.ca/Daily/English/031212/d031212c.htm.

——. (2004, July 21). Health reports: Use of cannabis and other illicit drugs. Online: www.statcan.ca/Daily/English/040721/d040721a.htm.

Dalley, M.L. (2003, December). The abduction by stranger in Canada: Nature and scope. Ottawa: National Missing Children Services, Royal Canadian Mounted Police.

Dalton, K. (1961). Menstruation and crime. *British Medical Journal*, 2:1752–1753.

Daly, K. (1989). Neither conflict nor labeling nor paternalism will suffice. *Crime and Delinquency*, 35:136–168.

Daly, K., & Chesney-Lind, M. (1988). Feminism and criminology. *Justice Quarterly*, 5:497–533.

Dandurand, Y., & Paris-Steffens, R. (1997). *Beyond wishful thinking*. Vancouver: Canadian–Latin American Cooperation in Criminal Law Reform and Criminal Justice.

Dantzker, M.L., & Mitchell, M.P. (1998). *Understanding today's police* (Canadian ed.). Scarborough, ON: Prentice-Hall.

Data on hate-motivated violence. (August, 1995). Online: canada.justice.gc.ca/orientations/reforme/ naine/hate_en_7.html.

Date rape drug. (1997, July). Online: www.siamweb.org/content/News-Culture/144/index_eng.php.

Date rape: Drug smuggled from Mexico. (1998, February 5). *Calgary Herald*, B1–B2.

Daubney report (Taking responsibility). (1988, August). Ottawa.

Davis, C.A. (2001). *Women who kill: Profiles of female serial killers*. London: Allison and Busby.

Davis, R.C., Lurigio, A.J., & Skogan, W.G. (1999). Services for victims: A market research study. *International Review of Victimology*, 6:101–115.

Davis, R.C., Lurigio, A.J., & Skogan, W.G. (Eds.). (1997). *Victims of crime* (2nd ed.). Thousand Oaks, CA: Sage.

Davis, R.C., & Smith, B.E. (1994). The effect of victim impact statements on sentencing decisions: A test in an urban setting. *Justice Quarterly*, 11(3):453–470.

Davis, S., & Shaffer, M. (1994). *Prostitution in Canada: The invisible menace or the menace of invisibility?* Online: www.walnet.org/csis/papers/sdavis.html.

Definitions of organized crime. (2003). Online: familyrightsassociation.com/AMOS/cali/definitions_of_organized_crime.htm.

DeKeseredy, W.S. (2000). *Women, crime and the Canadian criminal justice system*. Cincinnati, OH: Anderson.

DeKeseredy, W., & Hinch, R. (1991). *Woman abuse: Sociological perspectives*. Toronto: Thompson.

DeKeseredy, W., & Schwartz, M.D. (1996). *Contemporary criminology*. Belmont, CA: Wadsworth.

Del Frate, A.A., & van Kesteren, J. (2002). The ICVS in the developing world. *International Journal of Comparative Criminology*, 2(1): 57–71.

Dell, C.A., & Boe, R. (1998). *Adult female offenders in Canada: Recent trends*. Ottawa: Correctional Service Canada.

DeMause, L. (Ed.). (1988). *The history of childhood*. New York: Peter Bedrick Books.

Denno, D. (1988). Human biology and criminal responsibility: Free will or free ride? *University of Pennsylvania Law Review*, 137:615–671.

Dentler, R.A., & Monroe, L.J. (1961). Social correlates of early adolescent theft. *American Sociological Review*, 26:733–743.

Desroches, F. (1991). Tearoom trade: A law enforcement problem. *Canadian Journal of Criminology*, 33(1):1–21.

——. (1995). *Forces and fear: Robbery in Canada*. Scarborough, ON: Nelson.

——. (1996). *Behind the bars*. Toronto: Canadian Scholars' Press.

Dickson-Gilmore, E.J. (2004). Aboriginal participation in organized criminal activities. *Gazette*, 66(2):27–28.

Ditton, J. (1979). *Controlology: Beyond criminology*. London: Macmillan.

Ditton, J., Bannister, J., Gilchrist, E., & Farrell, S. (1999). Afraid or angry? Recalibrating the "fear of crime." *International Review of Victimology*, 6:83–99.

Dobbie, J., & Bill, P. (1978). *Fetal alcohol syndrome*. Toronto: Alcohol and Drug Addiction Research Foundation.

Dollard, J., Doob, L.W., Miller, N.E., Mowrer, O.H., & Sears, R.R. (1939). *Frustration and aggression*. New Haven, CT: Yale University Press.

Dolu, O. (2004, November 17). Credit card fraud: The nature of the crime, how credit card fraud occurs, prevention methods—Experiences of Turkish National police. Paper presented at the American Society of Criminology, Nashville, Tennessee.

Doob, A.N., & Roberts, J.V. (1982). *Crime and the official response to crime: The views of the public*. Ottawa: Department of Justice.

Dougherty, J. (1993). Women's violence against their children: A feminist perspective. *Women and Criminal Justice*, 4(2):91–114.

Douglas, J.E., & Olshaker, M. (2000) *Anatomy of motive*. New York: Pocket Books.

Draeger, C. (1997). Law and the feminist debate about pornography and censorship on the internet. Online: www.ucalgary.ca/~dabrent/380/webproj/ChelseaD.html.

Drapkin, I. (1976). *Premier symposium international de victimologie: First international symposium on victimology*. Hebrew University of Jerusalem, Israel.

Driscoll, M. (1999, February 19). Internet breeds new kind of criminal: Cyberstalkers. *Calgary Herald*, A20.

Drug cartels. (2003). Online: www.drugstory.org/feature/drug_cartels_QR.asp.

Drug spending in Canada still on the rise. (2004, June). Online: secure.cihi.ca/cihiweb/dispPage.jsp?cw_page=media_22jun2004_e.

Duffy, A. (1997, May 18). Bre-X an epic hoax. *Calgary Herald*, A8–9.

Dugger, A. (1996). Victim impact evidence in capital sentencing: A history of incompatibility. *American Journal of Criminal Law*, 23:375–404.

Duhaime, L. (1996). Canadian law: A history. Online: www.duhaime.org/canadian_history/default.aspx.

Duiguid, S. (1979). History and moral education in correctional education. *Canadian Journal of Education*, 4:81–92.

Dunn, C.S. (1976). *Patterns of robbery characteristics and their occurrence among social areas*. Washington, DC: U.S. Dept. of Justice.

Durkan, S. (1997, February 14). Most hooker killers go free. *Toronto Star*. Online: www.thestar.com.

Durkheim, É. (1895). *Rules of sociological method*. Trans. S.A. Soloway & J.H. Mueller. New York: Free Press.

——. (1951). *Suicide*. Trans. J.A. Spaulding & G. Simpson. New York: Free Press.

Easton, S.T., & Brantingham, P. (1998). *The cost of crime and how much?* Vancouver: Fraser Institute.

Einstadter, W., & Henry, S. (1995). *Criminological theory: An analysis of its underlying assumptions*. New York: Harcourt Brace.

Ekstedt, J. (1995). Canadian justice policy. In M.A. Jackson & C.T. Griffiths (Eds.), *Canadian criminology: Perspectives on crime and criminality* (2nd ed.). Toronto: Harcourt Brace.

Ekstedt, J., & Jackson, M. (1997). *Keepers and the kept*. Scarborough, ON: Nelson.

Elias, R. (1993). *Victims still: The political manipulation of crime victims*. Newbury Park, CA: Sage.

Elizabeth Fry Society. (2004). Canadian Association of Elizabeth Fry Societies. Online: www.elizabethfry.ca.

Elizabeth Fry Week. (1999, September 20). Online: www.elizabethfry.ca/eweek99.html.

Ellis, D. (1989). *The wrong stuff*. Toronto: Collier Macmillan.

Ellis, L. (1982). Genetics and criminal behavior. *Criminology*, 20(1):43–66.

——. (1987). *Theories of rape: Inquiries into the causes of sexual aggression*. New York: Hemisphere.

——. (1988). Genetic influences and crime. In F.H. Marsh & J. Katz (Eds.), *Biology, crime and ethics: A study of biological explanations for criminal behavior*. Cincinnati, OH: Anderson, 65–92.

Ellis, R. (1986). *The politics of victimization: Victims, victimology and crime victims*. New York: Oxford University Press.

Elmer, M.C. (1982). Century-old ecological studies in France. In G.A. Theodorson (Ed.), *Urban patterns: Studies in human ecology*. Philadelphia, PA: Pennsylvania State University Press.

Emerging gangs: An international trend? (1997, October). *Crime and Justice International*, 4–5.

Ennis, B.J., & Litwack, T.R. (1974). Psychiatry and the presumption of expertise: Flipping coins in the courtroom. *California Law Review*, 62:693–752.

Enos, S. (2001). *Mothering from inside: Parenting in a woman's prison*. New York: State University of New York Press.

Equator. (2004). About coffee: Industry overview. Online: www.equator.ca/about-coffee/industry.asp.

Erez, E., Roeger, L., & Morgan, F. (1994). *Victim impact statements in South Australia: An evaluation*. Adelaide, SA: Office of Crime Statistics.

Ericson, R.V., Baranek, P.M., & Chan, J.B.L. (1987). *Visualizing deviance: A study of new organizations*. Toronto: University of Toronto Press.

——. (1991). *Representing order: Crime, law, and justice in the news media*. Toronto: University of Toronto Press.

Evans, J., & Himelfarb, A. (1992). Counting crime. In R. Linden (Ed.), *Criminology: A Canadian perspective* (2nd ed.). Toronto: Harcourt Brace.

Evans, J., & Legar, P. (1979). Canadian victimization surveys. *Canadian Journal of Criminology*, 21(2):166–183.

Eysenck, H.J. (1977). *Crime and personality*. Frogmore, England: Paladin.

Facts about organized crime in Canada. (2003, September). Ottawa: Public Safety and Emergency Preparedness Canada.

Fairchild, E. (1993). *Comparative criminal justice*. Belmont, CA: Wadsworth.

Fairchild, E., & Dammer, H.R. (2001). *Comparative and criminal justice systems* (2nd ed.). Belmont, CA: Wadsworth.

Faith, K. (1987). Media, myths and masculinization: Images of women in prison. In E. Adelberg & C. Currie (Eds.), *Too few to count*. Vancouver: Press Gang.

——. (2002). La résistance à la pénalité: un impératif féministe. *Criminologie*, 35(2): 113–134.

Family violence in Canada: A statistical profile. (1998). Statistics Canada, cat. no. 85-224-XIE.

——. (2001). Statistics Canada, cat. no. 85-224-XIE.

——. (2002). Statistics Canada, cat. no. 85-224-XIE.

Family Violence Initiative. (2003). Department of Justice. Online: www.canada.justice.gc.ca/en/ps/pb/familyv.html.

Farrell, W. (1993). *The myth of male power*. New York: Simon and Schuster.

Farrington, D.P. (Ed.). (1994). *Psychological explanations of crime*. Aldershot, UK: Dartmouth.

Fattah, E.A. (1991). *Understanding criminal victimization*. Scarborough, ON: Prentice-Hall.

——. (1995). Restorative and retributive justice models: A comparison. In H-H. Kuhne (Ed.), *Festschrift für Koichi Miyazawa*. Baden-Baden, Germany: Nomos Verlagsgesllschaft.

——. (1997). *Criminology: Past, present and future*. New York: St. Martin.

——. (1999). From a handful of dollars to tea and sympathy: The sad history of victim assistance. In J.J.M. van Dijk, R.G.H. van Kaam, & J. Wemmers (Eds.), *Caring for crime victims: Selected proceedings of the IXth International Symposium on Victimology*. Monsey, NY: Criminal Justice Press, 187–207.

——. (2000). Victimology: Past, present and future. *Criminologie*, 30(1):17–46.

Fattah, E.A., & Sacco, V.F. (1989). *Crime and victimization of the elderly*. New York: Springer-Verlag.

FBI Uniform Crime Reports. (2002). Online: www.fbi.gov/ucr/cius_02/html/web/offreported/02-table02.html.

Federal Bureau of Investigation (2003). Uniform Crime Reports. Online: www.fbi.gov/ucr/ucr.htm.

Felson, M. (1997). A "routine activity" analysis of recent crime reductions. *The Criminologists*, 22(6):1, 3.

Fernandez, K., & Neiman, M. (1997). The geography of fear of crime. Paper presented at the 49th American Society of Criminology Annual Meetings, San Diego, November 19–22.

Feshbach, S. (1964). The function of aggression and the regulation of aggressive drive. *Psychological Review*, 71:257–272.

Fetherston, D. (2004). The law and young offenders. In J. Winterdyk (Ed.), *Issues and perspectives on young offenders in Canada* (3rd ed.). Toronto: Nelson.

Feyerabend, P.K. (1986). *Against method*. London: New Left Books.

Finckenauer, J.O., & Waring, E. (2001, April). Challenging the Russian Mafia mystique. *National Institute Journal*, 2–7.

Finley, L.L., & Finley, P.S. (2003). Film portrayals of female delinquents. In R. Muraskin (Ed.), *It's a crime: Women and crime*. Upper Saddle River, NJ: Prentice-Hall.

Fishbein, D.H. (1992). Biological perspectives in criminology. *Criminology*, 28(1):27–72.

Fishbein, D.H., & Pease, S.E. (1996). *The dynamics of drug abuse*. Needham Heights, MA: Allyn & Bacon.

Flanagan, A.Y. (2003). Teen dating violence. Online: www.nursingceu.com/NCEU/courses/dating/. Retrieved September 9, 2004.

Fooner, M. (1989). *Interpol: Issues in world crime and international criminal justice.* New York: Plenum.

Fortune, E.P., Vega, M., & Silverman, I. (1980). A study of female robbers in southern correctional institutions. *Journal of Criminal Justice,* 8:317–325.

Foucault, M. (1977). *Discipline and punish: The birth of prison.* New York: Vintage.

Fox, R.G. (1969). XYY chromosome and crime. *Australian and New Zealand Journal of Criminology,* 2(1):5–19.

Fraser Forum. (1996, September). Critical Issues Bulletins. The crime bill: Who pays and how much? Online: oldfraser.lexi.net/publications/forum/1996/september/.

Friday, P., & Krichhoff, G.F. (Eds.). (2000). *Victimology at the transition from the 20th to the 21st century.* Aachen, Germany: Shaker Verlag.

Friedrichs, D.O. (1991). Introduction: Peacemaking criminology in a world filled with conflict. In B.D. MacLean & D. Milovanovic (Eds.), *New directions in critical criminology.* Vancouver: Collective Press.

G8 hems and haws on cybercrime. (2000). Online: www.wired.com/news/politics/0,1283,36398,00.html.

Gallup Polls. (2004, February 24). Wanted in Great Britain: Law and order. Online: www.gallup.com/content/default.asp?ci=10768&pg=1.

Garfinkel, H. (Ed.). (1967). *Studies in ethnomethodology.* Englewood Cliffs, NJ: Prentice-Hall.

Gavigan, S. (1987). Women's crime: New perspectives and old theories. In E. Adelberg & C. Currie (Eds.), *Too few to count.* Vancouver: Press Gang.

Gaynor, J., & Stern, D. (1993). Child and juvenile firesetters: Examining their psychological profiles. *Firehouse,* 18:24–26.

Gebotys, R.J., Roberts, J.V., & DasGupta, B. (1988). News media use and public perceptions of crime seriousness. *Canadian Journal of Criminology,* 30(1):3–16.

Geis, G. (1973). Jeremy Bentham. In H. Mannheim (Ed.), *Pioneers in criminology* (2nd ed.). Montclair, NJ: Patterson Smith.

——. (1989). Prostitution in Portugal. In N. Davis (Ed.), *International handbook of prostitution.* Westport, CT: Greenwood.

Geis, G., & Goff, C. (1982). Edwin H. Sutherland: A biological and analytical commentary. In P. Wickman & T. Daily (Eds.), *White-collar crime and economic crime.* Lexington, MA: Lexington Books.

Gendreau, P., & Ross, R.R. (1987). Revivification of rehabilitation: Evidence from the 1980s. *Justice Quarterly,* 4:349–407.

Georges-Abeyie, D.E., & Harries, K. (Eds.). (1980). *Crime: A spatial perspective.* New York: Columbia University Press.

Gerstenfeld, P.B. (2004). *Hate crime.* Thousand Oaks, CA: Sage.

Ghosh, P. (2002, February 18). Behaviour research is "overstated." BBC News. Online: news.bbc.co.uk/1/hi/in_depth/sci_tech/2002/boston_2002/182387.stm.

Gibbons, D. (1979). *The criminological enterprise: Theories and perspectives.* Englewood Cliffs, CA: Prentice-Hall.

——. (1992). *Society, crime, and criminal behavior* (6th ed.). Englewood Cliffs, NJ: Prentice-Hall.

——. (1994). *Talking about crime and criminals: Problems and issues in theory development in criminology.* Englewood Cliffs, NJ: Prentice-Hall.

Gibbs, J. (1972). *Sociological theory construction.* Hinsdale, IL: Dryden.

——. (1987). The state of criminological theory. *Criminology,* 25:821–840.

Gibbs, W.W. (1995, March). Seeking the criminal element. *Scientific American,* 100–107.

Gilligan, C. (1982). *In a different voice: Psychological theory and women's development.* Cambridge, MA: Harvard University Press.

Gilmour, G.A. (1994, March). Hate motivated crime. Ottawa: Department of Justice.

Glaser, B.G., & Strauss, A.L. (1973). *The discovery of grounded theory: Strategies for qualitative research.* Chicago: Aldine.

Goff, C. (1998). *Criminal justice in Canada.* Toronto: Nelson.

Goff, C., & Reasons, C.E. (1978). *Corporate crime in Canada: A critical analysis of anti-combines legislation.* Scarborough, ON: Prentice-Hall.

Goff, C., & Reasons, D. (1986). Organizational crimes against employees, consumers and the public. In B. McLean (Ed.), *The political economy of crime.* Scarborough, ON: Prentice-Hall.

Gollin, A.E. (1988). The media's influence is limited. In B.L. Bender & B. Leone (Eds.), *The mass media.* San Diego, CA: Greenhaven Press, 116–120.

Gomes, J.T., Bertrand, L.D., Paetsch, J.J., & Hornick, J.P. (1999). The extent of youth victimization, crime and delinquency in Alberta. University of Calgary, Canadian Research Institute for Law and the Family.

Gomme, I.M. (1993). *The shadow line: Deviance and crime in Canada.* Toronto: Harcourt Brace Jovanovich.

Goodwin, T. (1995, Winter Solstice). Crime in Russia: Bitter fruit of capitalism and democracy. *Synapse.* Online: www.nrec.org/synapse34/Goodwin.html.

Gordon, H. (1997, March 12). State has stunning plan for jailbreakers. *Calgary Herald*, A3.

Gordon, R., & Coneybeer, I. (1995). Corporate crime. In M.A. Jackson & C.T. Griffiths (Eds.), *Canadian criminology: Perspectives on crime and criminality* (2nd ed.). Toronto: Harcourt Brace.

Gordon, R.A. (1987). SES versus IQ in the race-IQ delinquency model. *International Journal of Sociology and Social Policy*, 7:29–56.

Goring, C.B. (1913). *The English convict: A statistical study.* London, HMSO.

Gottfredson, M.R., & Hirschi, T. (1990). *A general theory of crime.* Stanford, CA: Stanford University Press.

GPI Atlantic. (1999, April 14). Crime costs Nova Scotians $1.2 billion a year. Online: www.gpiatlantic.org/releases/pr_crime.shtml.

Grabosky, P., & James, N. (Eds.). (1995). Julalikari Night Patrol. Online: www.aic.gov.au/publications/rpp/01/rpp01-03.html.

Graci, S. (1997). *The power of superfoods.* Scarborough, ON: Prentice-Hall.

Graphic health warning labels. (2004). Ottawa: Health Canada.

Grassberger, R. (1973). Hans Gross. In H. Mannheim (Ed.), *Pioneers in criminology* (2nd ed.). Montclair, NJ: Patterson Smith.

Gray, J. (1994). Three fundamental emotional systems. In P. Ekman & R. Davidson (Eds.), *The nature of emotion: Fundamental questions.* New York: Oxford, 243–247.

The Great Atlantic & Pacific Company of Canada Limited fined $80,000 for health and safety violation. (2003, January 16). Online: www.newswire.ca/government/ontario/english/releases/January2003/14/c9708.html. Retrieved July 9, 2003.

Greenberg, P. (1996). Break and enter. In L.W. Kennedy & V.F. Sacco (Eds.), *Crime counts: A criminal event analysis.* Scarborough, ON: Nelson, ch. 9.

Greenfeld, L.A. (1994, March). Criminal victimization in the United States, 1992. Bureau of Justice Statistics. U.S. Department of Justice.

Grescoe, T. (1996, September). Murder he mapped. *Canadian Geographic*, 49–52.

Griffin, J.H. (1961). *Black like me.* Boston: Hougton Miffin.

Griffiths, C.T. (2004). *Canadian corrections* (2nd ed.). Toronto: Nelson.

Griffiths, C.T., & Verdun-Jones, S.N. (1989). *Canadian criminal justice.* Toronto: Butterworths.

———. (1994). *Canadian criminal justice* (2nd ed.). Toronto: Harcourt Brace.

Gropper, B.A. (1985). Probing the link between drugs and crime. Washington, DC: National Institute of Justice.

Grossman, D. (2002). Killology. Online: www.killology.com.

Groth, N. (1979). *Men who rape: The psychology of the offender.* New York: Plenum.

Guilford, J.P. (1954). *A factor-analytic study across domains of reasoning, creativity, and evaluation.* Los Angeles: University of Southern California.

Haantz, S. (2002). Women and white collar crime. Online: www.nw3c.org/downloads/women_wcc1.pdf.

Hackler, J. (1994). *Crime and Canadian public policy.* Scarborough, ON: Prentice-Hall.

——. (1996). Anglophone juvenile justice. In J. Winterdyk (Ed.). *Issues and perspectives on young offenders in Canada.* Toronto: Harcourt Brace.

Hagan, F.E. (1997). *Research methods in criminal justice and criminology* (4th ed.). New York: Macmillan.

Hagan, J. (1977). *Disreputable pleasures.* Toronto: Butterworths.

——. (1985). *Modern criminology: Crime, criminal behaviour and its control.* New York: McGraw-Hill.

——. (1987). *The disreputable pleasures: Crime and deviance in Canada* (2nd ed.). Toronto: McGraw-Hill.

——. (1989). *Structural criminology.* New Brunswick, NJ: Rutgers University Press.

Hagan, J., Simpson, J.H., & Gillis, A.R. (1979). The sexual stratification of social control: A gender-based perspective on crime and delinquency. *British Journal of Sociology,* 30(1):25–38.

Hakim, S., & Buck, A.J. (1989). Do casinos enhance crime? *Journal of Criminal Justice,* 17:409–416.

Hall, C.S., & Lindzey, G. (1970). *Theories in personality* (2nd ed.). New York: John Wiley & Sons.

Hall, N. (1993, April). Big-city crime wave hits the "burbs": Home invasion, prostitution on the rise. *Vancouver Sun,* B4.

Hall, N., & Richards, G. (2004, August 21). Criminal gangs still endanger Canadians. *National Post,* A5.

Halleck, S.L. (1967). *Psychiatry and the dilemmas of crime.* New York: Harper & Row.

Hamm, M.S. (1998). Ethnography at the edge: Crime, deviance, and field research. Paper presented at the Academy of Criminal Justice 35th Annual Meeting, Albuquerque, NM, March 10–14.

Harris, J.R. (1998). *The nature assumption.* New York: Free Press.

Hartnagel, J. (1995). Correlates of criminal behaviour. In R. Linden (Ed.), *Criminology:*
A Canadian perspective (3rd ed.). Toronto: Harcourt Brace.

Haslem, P.G. (1976). The women offender. In W.T. McGrath (Ed.), *Crime and its treatment in Canada* (2nd ed.). Toronto: Macmillan.

Hatch, A. (1995). Historical legacies of crime and criminal justice in Canada. In M.A. Jackson & C.T. Griffiths (Eds.), *Canadian criminology* (3rd ed.). Toronto: Harcourt Brace, ch. 7.

Hate crime statistics. (2003). Washington, DC: Federal Bureau of Investigation. Online: www.fbi.gov/ucr/hatecrime2002.pdf.

Hazelhurst, K. (1996). Community healing and restorative justice: Two models of recovery in aboriginal Australia. CBA Commonwealth Law Conference, Canberra, August.

Health Canada. (2003). Canadian tobacco use monitoring survey (CTUMS) 2003. Online: www.hc-sc.gc.ca/hecs-sesc/tobacco/research/ctums/.

——. (2004). National health expenditure trends. Online: secure.cihi.ca/cihiweb/disp Page.jsp?cw page=AR 31 E&cw topic=31.

Heidensohn, F. (1992). Sociological perspectives on violence in women. Paper given at the University of Montreal, February.

Helworth, M. (1975). *Blackmail: Publicity and secrecy in everyday life.* London: Routledge and Kegan.

Hendrick, D. (1996). Theft. In L.W. Kennedy & V.F. Sacco (Eds.), *Crime counts: A criminal event analysis.* Scarborough, ON: Nelson, ch. 11.

Hentig, H. von. (1948). *The criminal and his victim: Studies in the sociobiology of crime.* New Haven, CT: Yale University Press.

Herrnstein, R.J. (1989a). *Biology and crime.* National Institute of Justice. Rockville, MD: U.S. Department of Justice.

——. (1989b). IQ and falling birthrates. *The Atlantic,* 263(5):72–84.

Hickey, E.W. (1991). *Serial murderers and their victims.* Pacific Grove, CA: Brooks/Cole.

——. (1997). *Serial murderers and their victims* (2nd ed.). Belmont, CA: Wadsworth.

Hill, G. (1994). Crime prevention and criminal justice branch. *Criminal Justice International,* 10(1):5–6, 8.

Hiller, H.H. (1982). *Society and change: S.D. Clark and the development of Canadian sociology.* Toronto: University of Toronto Press.

Hillman, J. (1996). *The soul's code.* New York: Random House.

Hinch, R. (1994). Introduction: Theoretical diversity. In R. Hinch (Ed.), *Readings in critical criminology.* Scarborough, ON: Prentice-Hall.

Hindelang, M., Hirschi, T., & Weis, J. (1981). *Measuring delinquency.* Beverly Hills, CA: Sage.

Hippchen, L.J. (Ed.). (1978). *Ecological-biochemical approaches to the treatment of delinquents and criminals.* New York: Van Nostrand Reinhold.

Hirschi, T. (1969). *Causes of delinquency.* Berkeley: University of California.

Hirschi, T., & Gottfredson, M. (1987). Causes of white-collar crime. *Criminology*, 25(4): 949–974.

——. (1989). The significance of white-collar crime and a general theory of crime. *Criminology*, 27(2):359–372.

Hoff, B.H. (2001). *Family violence in Canada: A statistical profile, 2000.* Online: www.batteredmen.com/batrcan.htm. Retrieved July 15, 2004.

Hoffman-Bustamonte, D. (1973). The nature of female delinquency. *Issues in Criminology*, 8:117–136.

Holmes, R., & DeBeurger, J. (1989). *Serial murder.* Newbury Park, CA: Sage.

Holmes, R.M. (1983). *The sex offender and the criminal justice system.* Springfield, IL: Charles C. Thomas.

——. (1991). *Sex crimes.* Newbury Park, CA: Sage.

Holmes, R.M., & Holmes, S.T. (1993). *Murder in America.* Thousand Oaks, CA: Sage.

Home Office (1979). *Report of the Committee on Obscenity and Film Censorship.* London, UK: Her Majesty's Stationery Office.

Honeyman, J.C., & Ogloff, J.R.P. (1996). Capital punishment: Arguments for life and death. *Canadian Journal of Behavioural Science*, 28(1).

Hooton, E.A. (1968 [1931]). *Crime and the man.* Westport, CT: Greenwood Press.

Horowitz, I.L., & Rainwater, L. (1970). Journalistic moralizer. *TransAction*, 7(7):5–7.

House motion proposes new criminal offence for murdering an unborn child. (2004). Online: www.lifesite.net/ldn/2004/mar/0403/04031204.html. Retrieved September 1, 2004.

Howell, J.C. (Ed.). (1995). *Guide to implementing the comprehensive strategy for serious, violent, and chronic juvenile offenders.* Washington: U.S. Department of Justice, Office of Juvenile Justice and Delinquency Prevention.

Huff, D. (1954). *How to lie with statistics.* New York: W.W. Norton.

Humphrey, L. (1970). *Tearoom trade: Impersonal sex in public places.* Chicago: Aldine.

Hyder, K. (1998, May 27). Muggers defy hi-tech spies to send crime rate soaring. *Evening Standard*, 5.

ICPC reports/papers. (2003). Online: www.crime-prevention-intl.org/publications.php?type=REPORT.

Identity theft. (2004). RCMP frauds and scams: Identity theft. Online: www.rcmp.gc.ca/scams/identity_e.htm.

Indicators of school crime and safety. (2002). National Centre for Education Statistics, Washington, DC.

Inflatable SpongeBobs disappear from Burger King. (2004, December 4). Online: www.mytelus.com. Retrieved December 4, 2004.

Is chemical castration an acceptable punishment for male sex offenders? (1996). Online: www.csun.edu/~psy453/crimes_n.htm.

Jackson, W. (1995). *Doing social research methods.* Scarborough, ON: Prentice-Hall.

——. (1999). *Doing social research methods* (2nd ed.). Scarborough, ON: Prentice-Hall.

Jacobs, B., & Wright, R. (1999). Stick-up, street culture, and offender motivation. *Criminology*, 37(1):149–173.

Jacobs, J.B., & Henry, J.S. (1996). The social construction of a hate crime epidemic. *Journal of Criminal Law and Criminology*, 86:366–391.

Jacoby, J.E. (1994). *Classics of criminology* (2nd ed.). Prospect Heights, IL: Waveland.

Jahrig, G. (1996, June 22). IQ exam isn't smart testing, says Harvard researcher. *Missoulian*, B1.

James, J. (1977). Prostitute and prostitution. In E. Sagarin & F. Montanino (Eds.), *Deviants: Voluntary action in a hostile world*. Glenview, IL: Scott, Freeman.

Jeffery, C.R. (1965, September). Criminal behavior and learning theory. *Journal of Criminal Law, Criminology, and Police Science*, 56: 294–300.

———. (1973). The historical development of criminology. In H. Mannheim (Ed.), *Pioneers in criminology* (2nd ed.). Montclair, NJ: Patterson Smith, ch. 25.

———. (1978). Criminology as an interdisciplinary science. *Criminology*, 16(2):149–170.

———. (1990). *Criminology: An interdisciplinary approach*. Englewood Cliffs, NJ: Prentice-Hall.

Johnson, H. (1987). Getting the facts straight. In E. Adelberg & C. Currie (Eds.), *Too few to count: Canadian women in conflict with the law*. Vancouver: Press Gang, 23–46.

———. (1996a). Sexual assault. In L. Kennedy & V. F. Sacco (Eds.), *Crime counts*. Scarborough, ON: Nelson, ch. 8.

———. (1996b). Violence against women: A special topic survey. In R.A. Silverman, J.J. Teevan, & V.F. Sacco (Eds.), *Crime in Canadian society* (5th ed.). Toronto: Harcourt Brace, 210–221.

Johnson, H.A. (1988). *History of criminal justice*. Cincinnati, OH: Anderson.

Johnson, J.A., & Fennell, E.B. (1983). Aggressive and delinquent behaviour in childhood and adolescence. In C.E. Walker & M.C. Roberts (Eds.), *Handbook of clinical child psychology*. New York: John Wiley.

Junger-Tas, J., Terlouw, G-T., & Klein, M.W. (Eds.). (1996). *Delinquent behaviour among young people in the Western world*. New York: Kugler.

Kantrowitz, B., & Wingert, P. (1993, April 12). No longer a sacred cow: Head Start has become a free-fire zone. *Newsweek*, 51.

Kappler, V.E., Blumberg, M., & Potter, G.W. (1993). *The mythology of crime and justice*. Prospect Heights, IL: Waveland Press.

———. (2004). *The mythology of crime and justice* (4th ed.). Prospect Heights, IL: Waveland Press.

Karman, A. (1979). Victim facilitation: The case of automobile theft. *Victimology*, 4(4):361–370.

———. (1990). *Crime victim* (2nd ed.). Pacific Grove, CA: Brooks/Cole.

———. (1996). *Crime victim* (3rd ed.). Pacific Grove, CA: Brooks/Cole.

Katz, J. (1988). *Seduction of crime: Moral and sensual attraction of doing evil*. New York: Basic Books.

Katz, J., & Chambliss, W.J. (1995). Biology and crime. In J.F. Shelly (Ed.), *Criminology: A contemporary handbook*. Belmont, CA: Wadsworth.

Katz, N. (2004). Sexual harassment statistics. Online: womensissues.about.com/od/genderdiscrimination/.

Keane, C. (1996). Corporate crime. In R.A. Silverman, J.J. Teevan, & V.F. Sacco (Eds.), *Crime in Canadian society* (5th ed.). Toronto: Harcourt Brace.

Keane, C., Maxim, P., & Teevan, J. (1993). Drinking and driving, self control, and gender: Testing a general theory of crime. *Journal of Research in Crime and Delinquency*, 29:30–49.

Keeney, B., & K. Heide. (1994). Gender differences in serial murderers. *Journal of Interpersonal Violence*, 9(3):383–398.

Kelleher, M.D., & Kelleher, C.L. (1998). *Murder most rare: The female serial killer*. New York: Dell.

Kelta Advance Learning. (2004). Online: www.keltawebconcepts.com.au/efemcrime1.htm. Retrieved September 1, 2004.

Kenison, F.R. (1973). Charles Doe. In H. Mannheim (Ed.), *Pioneers in criminology* (2nd ed.). Montclair, NJ: Patterson Smith, ch. 11.

Kennedy, L., & Baron, S. (1993). Routine activities and a subculture of violence: A study of violence on the street. *Journal of Research in Crime and Delinquency*, 30:88–112.

Kennedy, L.W., & Forde, D.R., (1990). Routine activities and crime: An analysis of victimization in Canada. *Criminology*, 28:137–152.

———. (1995). *Self-control, risky lifestyles, routine conflict and crime: A respecification of the* general theory of crime. Edmonton: University of Alberta, Centre for Criminological Research.

Kerlinger, F.N. (1979). *Foundation of behavioral research* (2nd ed.). New York: Holt, Rinehart, & Winston.

Kershaw, A., & Lasovich, M. (1991). *Rock-a-bye baby: A death behind bars.* Toronto: Oxford University Press.

Ketcham, B. (1999, January 10). Mayor wants Grand Forks to go to pot. *Calgary Herald*, A6.

Kidder, L.H., & Judd, C.M. (1986). *Research methods in social relations* (5th ed.). New York: Holt, Rinehart, & Winston.

Kiedrowski, J., & Jayewardene, C.H.S. (1994). *Parental abduction of children: An overview and profile of the abductor.* Report prepared for the Missing Children's Registry, RCMP. Online: www.childcybersearch.org/rcmp/recmp6.htm.

Kinberg, O. (1960). *Basic problems of criminology.* Copenhagen.

King, A.J., Boyce, W.F., & King, M.A. (1999). *Trends in the health of Canadian youth.* Health Canada. Online: www.hc-sc.gc.ca/dca-dea/publications/hbsc_10_e.html.

Kingsbury, A.A. (1973). *Introduction to security and crime prevention surveys.* Charles C. Thomas.

Kittrie, N. (1971). *The right to be different.* Baltimore, MD: John Hopkins University Press.

Klemke, L.W. (1978). Does apprehension for shoplifting amplify or terminate shoplifting activity. *Law and Society Review*, 12:390–403.

——. (1992). *The sociology of shoplifting: Boosters & snitches today.* New York: Praeger.

Knapp, S. (1998, June 28). Hackers find the cracks in systems. *Calgary Herald*, TL16.

Koenig, D.J. (1992). Conventional crime. In R. Linden (Ed.), *Criminology: A Canadian perspective* (2nd ed.). Toronto: Harcourt Brace, ch. 13.

——. (2003). Organized crime: A Canadian perspective. In J.S. Albanese, D.K. Das, & A. Verma (Eds.), *Organized crime: International perspectives.* Upper Saddle River, NJ: Prentice-Hall, 46–77.

Kohlberg, L. (1969). Stage and sequence: The cognitive developmental approach of socialization. In D.A. Goslin (Ed.), *Handbook of socialization theory and research.* Chicago: Rand McNally.

——. (1986). The just community approach to corrections. *Journal of Correctional Education*, 37(2):54–58.

Kohlberg, L., Kauffman, K., Scharf, P., & Hickey, J. (1973). *The just community approach in corrections: A manual.* Niantic, CT: Department of Corrections.

Koningsveld, J. (1998, December 3). Money laundering and FIOD. Summary of paper presented at the FATF meeting in London, UK, November 1998.

Kotulak, R. (1997). *Inside the brain: Revolutionary discoveries of how the mind works.* Kansas City: Andrews McMeel.

Kowalski, M. (2002). Online: www.statcan.ca/english/freepub/85F0027XIE/85F0027XIE02002.pdf.

Kramer, R.C. (1984). Corporate criminality: The development of an idea. In E. Hochstedler (Ed.), *Corporations as criminals.* Beverly Hills, CA: Sage.

Krisberg, B., & Austin, J. (1978). *Children of Ishmael.* Palo Alto, CA: Mayfield.

Kuhn, T. (1970). *The structure of scientific revolutions* (2nd ed.). Chicago: University of Chicago Press.

Kury, H. (2002). International comparison of crime and victimization: The ICVS. *International Journal of Comparative Criminology*, 2(1):1–9.

Kury, H., Doermann, U., Richter, H., & Wueger, M. (1992). *Opfererfahrungen und Meinungen zur Inneren Sicherheit in Deutschland. Ein Empirischer Vergleich von Viktimisierungen, Anzeigerververhalten und Sicherheitseinschatzung in Ost und West vor der Vereinigung.* Wiesbaden: Bundeskriminalamt.

Lab, S.P. (1997). *Crime prevention: Approaches, practices and evaluations* (3rd ed.). Cincinnati, OH: Anderson.

Lad, V. (1985). *Ayurveda: The science of self-healing.* Wilmot, WI: Lotus Press.

Laframboise, D. (1996). *Am I a feminist?* Online: www.razberry.com/raz/laframboise/feminist.htm.

LaHaye, T. (1988). The media's influence undermines America's morality. In D.L. Bender & B. Leone (Eds.), *The mass media*. San Diego, CA: Greenhaven Press, 111–115.

LaPrairie, C. (1990). The role of sentencing in the over-representation of Aboriginal offenders in correctional institutions. *Canadian Journal of Criminology*, 32:429–440.

———. (1993). Aboriginal women and crime in Canada: Identifying the issues. In E. Adelberg & C. Currie (Eds.), *In conflict with the law: Women and the Canadian justice system*. Vancouver: Press Gang.

Laub, J.H., & Sampson, R.J. (1993). Turning points in the life cycle course: Why change matters to the study of crime. *Criminology*, 31:301–326.

Lautt, M. (1984). *A report on prostitution in the prairie provinces*. Working Papers on Pornography and Prostitution, report no. 9. Ottawa: Department of Justice.

Lavigna, Y. (1996). *Into the abyss*. Toronto: Harper Collins.

Lavigne, B., Hoffman, L., & Dickie, I. (1997). Women who have committed homicide. *FORUM: On Correctional Research*, 9(2):25–28.

Lazerfeld, P.F. (1959). Problems in methodology. In R.K. Merton, L. Brown, & L.S. Cottrell, Jr. (Eds.), *Sociology today: Problems and prospects*. New York: Basic Books.

Leard, F. (1980, March). Case management and the juvenile offender. *Corrections Newsletter*. Victoria, BC: Attorney General.

LeBlanc, M., & Frechette, M. (1989). *Male criminal activity from childhood through youth: Multilevel and developmental perspectives*. New York: Springer-Verlag.

Lejins, P. (1983). Educational programs in criminal justice. In S.H. Kadiosh (Ed.), *Encyclopedia of crime and justice*. New York: Free Press.

Lemert, E. (1953). An isolation and closure theory of naive check forgery. *Journal of Criminal Law and Police Science*, 44:297–298.

Lenneberg, E.H. (1967). *Biological foundations of language*. New York: John Wiley.

Leonard, E.B. (1982). *Women, crime and society: A critique of criminological theory*. New York: Longman.

Letkemann, P. (1973). *Crime as work*. Englewood Cliffs, NJ: Prentice-Hall.

Levy, C. (1997, May 22–24). Presentation given at the annual Alberta Criminal Justice Association meetings, Red Deer, Alberta.

Liberator, M. (2003). Legalized prostitution. Online: www.liberator.net/articles/prostitution.html.

Light, R.C., Nee, C., & Ingham, H. (1993). *Car theft: The offender's perspective*. Home Office Research Study No. 130. London, Home Office.

Linden, R. (2004). *Criminology: A Canadian perspective* (4th ed.). Toronto: Harcourt Brace.

Lindstrom, P. (1997). Communitarianism and restorative justice in Sweden: Potentials and pitfalls. Paper presented at the American Society of Criminology 49th annual meetings, San Diego, CA, November 19–22.

Lippert, R. (1990). The construction of Satanism as a social problem in Canada. *The Canadian Journal of Sociology*, 15(4):417–440.

Livingston, J. (1992). *Crime and criminology*. Englewood Cliffs, NJ: Prentice-Hall.

Locke, D. (1993). Court services in Canada. *Juristat*, 13(2).

Lofland, J. (1984). *Analyzing social settings*. Belmont, CA: Wadsworth.

Longmire, D.R. (1983). Ethical dilemmas in the research setting. *Criminology*, 21:333–348.

Lord, W.D., Bourdeaux, M., & Lanning, K.V. (2001). Investigating potential child abduction cases: A developmental perspective. *FBI Law Enforcement Bulletin*, 70(4).

Loree, D. (2004). What is organized crime? *Gazette*, 66(2):10–11.

Lorenz, K. (1966). *On aggression*. New York: Harcourt Brace Jovanovich.

Lowey, M. (1997, March 22). Diagnosis: We're healthy, but there's room for improvement. *Calgary Herald*, A14–15.

Lowman, J. (1995). Prostitution in Canada. In M.A. Jackson & C.T. Griffiths (Eds.), *Canadian criminology* (3rd ed.). Toronto: Harcourt Brace, ch. 10.

———. (1997, Fall). Sterling Prize winner challenges prostitution law. *SFU Alumni Journal*, 8.

Lowmann, J., & MacLean, B. (Eds.). (1992). *Realist criminology: Crime control and policing in the 1990s.* Toronto: University of Toronto Press.

Lunden, W.A. (1972). Emile Durkheim. In H. Mannheim (Ed.), *Pioneers in criminology.* Montclair, NJ: Patterson Smith.

Lundman, R.J. (2001). *Prevention and control of juvenile delinquency* (3rd ed.). New York: Oxford University Press.

Lynch, M.J., & Groves, W.B. (1989). *A primer in radical criminology* (2nd ed.). Albany, NY: Harrow & Heston.

Maccoby, E.E., & Jacklin, C.N. (1974). *The psychology of sex differences.* Stanford, CA: Stanford University Press.

Maccoby, E.E., Snow, M.E., & Jacklin, C.N. (1984). Children's disposition and mother-child interaction at 12 and 18 months: A short-term longitudinal study. *Development Psychology*, 20(3):459–472.

MacIntyre, S. (2002). *Strolling away.* Ottawa: Department of Justice Canada.

MacLaurin, B. (2004). Street youth in Canada. In J. Winterdyk (Ed.), *Issues and perspectives on young offenders in Canada* (3rd ed.). Toronto: Harcourt.

Maclean, B.D. (1986). *The political economy of crime.* Scarborough, ON: Prentice-Hall, ch. 7.

MacLean, B.D. (1992). A program of local crime survey research for Canada. In J. Lowman & B.D. MacLean (Eds.), *Realist criminology: Crime control and policing in the 1990s.* Toronto: University of Toronto Press.

Maclean, B.D., & Milovanovic, D. (Eds.). (1991). *New directions in critical criminology.* Vancouver: Collective Press.

Maclean's. (1994, January 1).

Maconochesi, E. (1973). Cesare Beccaria. In H. Mannheim (Ed.), *Pioneers in criminology* (2nd ed.). Monctlair, NJ: Patterson Smith, ch. 2.

MADD. (2004). Fast facts in on MADD Canada. Online: www.madd.org/english/about/fast fact.html.

Mafia history. (1997). Online: www.planetpapers. com/Assets/1120.php.

Maguire, M. (1991). The need and rights of victims of crime. In M. Tonry (Ed.), *Crime and justice: A review of research.* Chicago: University of Chicago, 363–433.

Maletzky, B.M. (1991). *Treating the sexual offender.* Newbury, CA: Sage.

Malinowski, S. (1996, November/December). Eastern Europe battles transnational auto theft problems. *CJ Europe*, 6(6):1, 4–5.

Man sentenced for tax fraud. (2004, November 25). *The Chronicle Herald Nova Scotia.* Online: www.herald.ns.ca/stories/2004/11/25/ fnovascotia.html.

Mandel, M. (2000, February 20). Growing allegations of racism against natives rock Saskatoon. *Toronto Sun.* Online: www.canoe. com/NewsStand/TorontoSun/home.html.

Mann, C.R. (1996). *Women who kill.* New York: State University of New York Press.

Mannheim, H. (Ed.). (1973). *Pioneers in criminology* (2nd ed.). Montclair, NJ: Patterson Smith.

Manning, P. (1973). On deviance. *Contemporary Sociology*, 2:697–699.

Marlowe, M., Bliss, L., & Schneider, H.G. (1994). Hair trace element content of violence prone male children. *Journal of Advancement in Medicine*, 7(1):5–18.

Marron, K. (1983, November 7). TV dubbed a "violent teacher." *The Globe and Mail*, 1.

Martin, R., Mutchnick, R.J., & Austin, W.T. (1990). *Criminological thought: Pioneers past and present.* New York: Macmillan.

Martinson, R. (1974). What works? Questions and answers about prison reform. *Public Interest*, 35:22–54.

Matsueda, R.L. (1988). The current state of differential association theory. *Crime and Delinquency*, 34:277–306.

——. (1992). Reflected appraisals: Parental labelling, and delinquency: Specifying a symbolic interactionist theory. *American Sociological Review*, 97:1577–1611.

Matthews, F. (1988). Familiar strangers: A critical study of adolescent involvement in prostitution. Toronto: Central Toronto Youth Service.

Matthews, R., & Young, J. (1986). *Confronting crime.* London: Sage.

——. (1992). *Issues in realist criminology.* London: Sage.

Maxfield, M.G., & Babbie, E. (1995). *Research methods for criminal justice and criminology*. Belmont, CA: Wadsworth.

May, R. (1969). *Love and will*. New York: Norton.

Mazerolle, P., & Maahs, J. (2000). General Strain and delinquency: An alternative examination of conditioning influences. *Justice Quarterly*, 17:753–778.

McCall, R. (2004). Online harassment and cyber-stalking: Victim access to crisis, referral and support services in Canada, concepts and recommendations. Online: www.vaonline.org.

McCarthy, B. (1995). Getting into street crime: The structure and process of criminal embeddedness. *Social Science Research*, 24:63–95.

——. (1996). The attitudes and actions of others: Tutelage and Sutherland's theory of differential association. *British Journal of Criminology*, 36:135–147.

McCord, W., & McCord, J. (1959). *Origins of crime*. New York: Columbia University.

McDermott, J. (2004, August 27). Drug cartels develop super-cocaine plant. *Calgary Herald*, A13.

McDevitt, J., & Levin, J. (1993). *Hate crimes: The rising tide of bigotry and bloodshed*. New York: Plenum.

McGrath, W.T. (Ed.). (1976). *Crime and its treatment in Canada* (2nd ed.). Toronto: Macmillan.

McIntosh, A. (1998, June 11). RCMP's sting aided drug lords. *Calgary Herald*, A1–2.

McIntyre, S. (1994). The youngest profession: The oldest oppression. Unpublished PhD thesis. Department of Law, University of Sheffield, Sheffield, England.

McIntyre, S. (2002, August). Strolling away. Ottawa: Department of Justice. RR2002-4e.

McKeena, P.F. (1998). *Foundations of policing in Canada*. Toronto: Pearson.

McKie, C. (1989). Life style risks: Smoking and drinking. In C. McKie & K. Thompson (Eds.), *Canadian social trends*. Toronto: Thompson, 86–92.

——. (2004). *Canadian social trends*, vol. 3. Toronto: Thompson.

McLean, G. (2000). The new age of bank security. *The Canadian Banker*. Online: www.cba.ca/en/magazine/getArticle.asp?at_id=204.

McMullan, J.L. (1992). *Beyond the limits of the law: Corporate crime and law and order*. Halifax: Fernwood.

——. (2004, November 17). Representing corporate crime: The media, the politics of truth and the denial of crime. Paper presented at the American Society of Criminology, Nashville, Tenn.

McPhie, P. (1996). Fraud. In L.W. Kennedy & V.F. Sacco (Eds.), *Crime counts: A criminal event analysis*. Scarborough, ON: Nelson.

Media Awareness Network. (2002). Special issues for young children. Online: www.media-awareness.ca/english/parents/television/issues_children_tv.cfm.

Mednick, S., & Christiansen, K.O. (1977). *Biosocial bases of criminal behavior*. New York: Gardner Press.

Mednick, S., Moffitt, T., & Stack, S.A. (1987). *The causes of crime: New biological approaches*. Cambridge, UK: Cambridge University Press.

Mennonite drug pipeline expanding. (1997). *Toronto Star*. Online: www.thestar.com.

Merton, R. (1968). *Social theory and social structure*. New York: The Free Press.

Miethe, T.D., & Meier, R.F. (1990). Opportunity, choice, and criminal victimization: A test of theoretical model. *Journal of Research in Crime and Delinquency*, 27(3):243–266.

——. (1994). *Crime and its social context: Toward an integrated theory of offenders, victims, and situations*. Albany, NY: SUNY Press.

Miller, L.S., & Whitehead., J.T. (1996). *Introduction to criminal justice research and statistics*. Cincinnati, OH: Anderson.

Miller, R.W. (1973). John Henry Wigmore. In H. Mannheim (Ed.), *Pioneers in criminology* (2nd ed.). Montclair, NJ: Patterson Smith.

Mills, C.W. (1959). *The sociological imagination*. London: Oxford University Press.

Milovanovic, D. (Ed.). (1997). *Chaos, criminology, and social justice: The new orderly (dis)order*. Westport, CT: Praeger.

Mission Museum. (nd). Online: www.missionmuseum.bc.ca/mm/localhist/milestones/milestones/billy_miner.html.

Mitchell, B. (1996, September 26). Police smash ring sending stolen cars to Vietnam. *Toronto Star*. Online: www.thestar.com.

Moene, M. (2003). *Crime prevention by community control in the Netherlands*. Den Haag, The Netherlands: Ministry of Justice.

Mofina, R. (1991, August 6). City Asians prey to home invasions. *Calgary Herald*, B1.

Moir, A., & Jessel, D. (1997). *A mind to crime*. Toronto: Signet.

Mokhiber, R. (2003). Corporate crime reporter: Top 100 corporate criminals of the decade. Online: www.corporatecrimereporter.com/top100.html.

Monachesi, E. (1973). Cesare Beccaria. In H. Mannheim (Ed.), *Pioneers in criminology* (2nd ed.). Montclair, NJ: Patterson Smith.

Monahan, J. (1981). *Predicting violent behaviour*. Beverly Hills, CA: Sage.

Montagu, A. (1997). *Man's most dangerous myth: The fallacy of race* (6th ed.). Walnut Creek, CA: Altamira Press.

Montague, P. (2004). Toxic pollutants cause violent crime. Online: www.life.ca/nl/57/crime.html.

Montreal businessman pleads guilty in immigration fraud case. (2004, Aug. 12). National News. Online: www.news1130.com/news/national/article.jsp?content=n081223A.

Moore, D. (2004, May 16). Stats show increasing number of dangerous offenders. Online: cnews.canoe.ca/cnews/Canada/2004/05/16/462257-cp.html. Retrieved August 30, 2004.

Moore, M. (1997, June 18). Argument over man's sexuality turns violent. *Missoulian*, B1.

Moran, N.R. (2002). Motorcycle outlaw clubs going global. *Crime & Justice International*, 18(64):9–10, 30.

More men victims of domestic violence. (2003, July 13). Online: www.CTV.ca. Retrieved July 15, 2004.

Morris, M. (2002). Violence against women and girls. Ottawa: CRIAW.

Morris, N. (1982). *Madness and the criminal law*. Chicago: University of Chicago Press.

Morrison, P. (1996). Motor-vehicle crimes. In L.W. Kennedy & V.F. Sacco (Eds.), *Crime counts*. Toronto: Nelson.

Moseley, R. (1995, July/August). Conference: High-tech crime looms as major global concern. *CJ Europe*, 1, 4.

Motiuk, L.L., & Belcourt, R. (1995). *Statistical profiles of homicide, sex, robbery and drug offenders in federal corrections*. Correctional Service of Canada, Research Brief B-11.

Motiuk, L.L., & Porporino, F. (1992). *The prevalence, nature and severity of mental health problems among federal male inmates in Canadian penitentiaries*. Correctional Service of Canada, Research Report R-24.

Motor vehicle registrations. (2004). Online: www.statcan.ca/english/pgdb/trade14a.htm.

Multinational Monitor. (2001, June). Online: www.multinationalmonitor.org/mm2001/01june/june01lines.html.

Murphy, C. (1995). Traditional sociological approaches. In M.A. Jackson & C.T. Griffiths (Eds.), *Canadian criminology* (3rd ed.). Toronto: Harcourt Brace., ch. 6.

Murphy, C., & Stenning, P. (1999). Introduction. *Canadian Journal of Criminology and Criminal Justice*, 41(2):127–130.

Murray, J.P. (1990). Status offenders: Roles, rules, and reactions. In R.A. Weisheit & R.G. Culbertson (Eds.), *Juvenile delinquency: A justice perspective*. Prospect Heights, IL: Waveland, 17–26.

Myers, S. (2004, July 30). Vandals deface Lougheed mansion. *Calgary Herald*, B1.

Myths and facts about gun control. (2004, February). Online: www.guncontrol.ca.

National Missing Children Services. (2004). Online: www.rcmp.ca/crimrec/misskids e.htm.

Naumetz, T. (1999, January 14). Control of death penalty could shift to regions. *Calgary Herald*, A6.

Nettler, G. (1982). *Killing one another*. Cincinnati, OH: Anderson.

——. (1984). *Explaining crime*. New York: McGraw-Hill.

——. (1987). *Explaining crime* (2nd ed.). Toronto: McGraw-Hill.

New rights for victims of crime in Europe. (2003). Online: www.victimsupport.org.uk/about/publications/new_rights/nr_new_rights.html. Retrieved December 18, 2004.

Newman, G., & Marongiu, P. (1990). Penological reform and the myth of Beccaria. *Criminology*, 28:325–346.

Newman, O. (1972). *Defensible space*. New York: Macmillan.

——. (1996). *Creating defensible space*. Washington, DC: U.S. Department of Housing and Urban Development.

Newsworld. (1997, June 20). Tobacco. Online: www.cbc.ca/newsworld/.

——. (1997, September 19). Turner donates $1 billion to UN. Online: www.cbc.ca/newsworld/.

Nicholl, C. (1997). Implementation issues in restorative conferencing. Paper presented at the American Society of Criminology 49th annual meeting, San Diego, CA, November 19–22.

Nickerson, C. (2004, Jan. 1). Crime gangs get free roam on Canada Indian reserves. Online: mytwobeadsworth.com/CAgangs2104.html.

Nieuwbeerta, P. (Ed.). (2002). *Crime perspective: Results from the International Crime Victims Survey, 1989–2000*. The Hague, NL: Boom.

Noblett, S., & Nelson, B. (2001). A psychosocial approach to arson: A case controlled study of female offenders. *Medical Science Law*, 41(4):325–330.

NOCO Canada Inc. fined $2,000 for waste-related offence. (2003, April 15). Online: www.ene.gov.on.ca/envision/news/2003/0415 03.htm. Retrieved July 9, 2003.

Normandeau, A. (1968). Trends and patterns in crimes of robbery. PhD dissertation. Philadelphia: University of Pennsylvania.

——. (1973). Charles Lucas. In H. Mannheim (Ed.), *Pioneers in criminology* (2nd ed.). Montclair, NJ: Patterson Smith.

Normandeau, A., & Hasenpush, B. (1980, July). Prevention programs and their evaluation. *Canadian Journal of Criminology*, 307–319.

Normandeau, A., & Leighton, B. (1990). *A vision of the future of policing in Canada— Challenge 2000*. Ottawa: Police Security Branch: Solicitor General Canada.

Nurco, D.N., Cisin, I.H., & Ball, J.C. (1985). Crime as a source of income for narcotic addicts. *Journal of Substance Abuse Treatment*, 2, 113–115.

Nurse charged in death of 22 seniors at Danish centre. (1997, October 22). *The Toronto Star*. Online: www.thestar.com.

Ogle, R.S., Maier-Katin, D., & Bernard, T.J. (1995). A theory of homicidal behavior among women. *Criminology*, 33(2):173–193.

O'Neil, J.A., Wish, E., & Visher, C. (1990). *Drugs and crime-1989*. Washington, DC: National Institute of Justice.

O'Reilly-Fleming, T. (Ed.). (1996). *Serial and mass murder: Theory, research and policy*. Toronto: Canadian Scholars' Press.

Orion: Geographic profiling software. (1996). Vancouver: Environmental Criminology Research Inc.

Ottawa Crime Stoppers. (2004). Upper Ottawa Valley Crime Stoppers. Online: www.renc.igs. net/~crimestop.

Our Missing Children. (2003). Online: www. rcmp-grc.gc.ca/crimrec/misskids e. htm.

Outlaw motorcycle gangs (OMGs). (2004). Online: www.cisc.gc.ca/annualreport2004/ cisc2004/outlaw2004.html.

Overholser, W. (1973). Issac Ray. In H. Mannheim (Ed.), *Pioneers in criminology* (2nd ed.). Montclair, NJ: Patterson Smith, ch. 11.

Oyen, E. (1992). *Comparative methodology: Theory and practice in international social research*. London: Sage.

Pace, D.F. (1991). *Concepts of vice, narcotics, and organized crime* (3rd ed.). Engelwood Cliffs, NJ: Prentice-Hall.

Painter, K.A., & Farrington, D.P. (1996). Criminal victimization on a Caribbean Island. *International Review of Victimology*, 6:1–16.

Palango, P. (1997). *Above the law*. Toronto: McClelland and Stewart.

Palys, T. (1997). *Research decisions: Quantitative and qualitative perspectives* (2nd ed.). Toronto: Harcourt Brace Jovanovich.

Parker, L. (2004). Peacemaking justice in Canada. Online: www.restorativejustice.org/ rj3/Feature/2004/August/peacemaking.htm. Retrieved August 26, 2004.

Paternoster, R., Saltzman, L.E., Waldo, G.P., & Chiricos, T.G. (1983). Perceived risk and social control: Do sanctions really deter? *Law and Society Review*, 17:457–480.

The patterns of violent crime by women. (2003). Online: www.csc-scc.gc.ca/crd/fsw/fsw23/fsw23e02.htm.

Pearson, P. (1998). *When she was bad: Violent women and the myth of innocence*. Toronto: Random House.

Pease, K., & Litton, R. (1984). Crime prevention: Practice and motivation. In D.J. Muller, D.E. Blackman, & A.J. Chapman (Eds.), *Psychology and law*. New York: John Wiley & Sons.

Pela, R.L. (1997, Winter). High hopes: A spirited guide to aging and alcohol. *Prime Health and Fitness*, 72–76.

Pepinsky, H. (1991). *The geometry of violence and democracy*. Bloomington: Indiana University Press.

Pepinsky, H., & Jesilow, P. (1984). *Myths that cause crime* (2nd ed.). Cabin John, MD: Seven Locks.

Perry, P. (1996). Adolescent substance abuse and delinquency. In J.A. Winterdyk (Ed.), *Issues and perspectives on young offenders in Canada*. Toronto: Harcourt Brace, ch. 7.

Peters, M. (1995). Does brain size matter? A reply to Rushton and Ankney. *Canadian Journal of Experimental Psychology*, 49(4). Online: ww.cpa.ca.

PetNet pleads guilty and pays $150,000 fine for misleading mailings. (2004, July 28). Ottawa: Government of Canada, Competition Bureau.

Pettiway, L.E. (1988). Urban spatial structure and arson incidence: Differences between ghetto and nonghetto environments. *Justice Quarterly*, 5:113–130.

Pfohl, S. (1994). *Images of deviance and social control: A sociological history*. New York: McGraw-Hill.

Pfuhl, E.H., & Henry, S. (1993). *The deviance process* (3rd ed.). New York: Aldine.

Philpott, W.H. (1978). Ecological aspects of antisocial behavior. In L.J. Hippchen (Ed.), *Ecological-biochemical approaches to treatment of delinquents and criminals*. New York: Van Nostrand Reinhold.

Pillmann, F., Rohde, A., Ullrich, S., Draba, S., Sannemuller, U., & Marneros, A. (1999). Violence, criminal behavior, and the EEG: Significance of left hemispheric focal abnormalities. *Journal of Neuropsychiatry and Clinical Neurosciences*, 11:454–457.

Pilot survey of hate crime 2001 and 2002. (2004, June 1). *The Daily*. Ottawa: Statistics Canada.

Platt, A.M. (1969). *The child savers*. Chicago: University of Chicago.

Police make arrest in NASA computer hacking case. (1998, April 6). *Sudbury Star*. Online: www.thesudburystar.com/webapp/sitepages/.

Polk, K. (1991). Book review of Michael R. Gottfredson and Travis Hirschi, *A general theory of crime* (Stanford, CA: Stanford University Press). *Crime and Delinquency*, 37:575–581.

Pollak, O. (1961). *The criminality of women*. New York: Barnes.

Pollock, J.M. (1999). *Criminal women*. Cincinnati, OH: Anderson.

Poterfield, A.L. (1943). Delinquency and its outcome in court and college. *American Journal of Sociology*, 49:199–208.

Potter, G. (1994). *Criminal organizations: Vice, racketeering, and politics in an American city*. Prospect Heights, IL: Waveland.

Pressman, A. (1997, May 8). USA: Big countries differ on regulating electronic money. Online: www.bizinfo.reuters.com.

Preventing crime within a framework of urban social development (the Netherlands). (1997). Online: www.crime-prevention-intl.org/english/how to/city action/048.htm.

Price, M. (1996). Victim-offender mediation: The state of the art. *VOMA Quarterly*, 7(3). Online: voma.org/connect.shtml.

A profile of robbery in Canada. (1995). Ottawa: Correctional Service Canada. Research Brief B-10.

Profile of women offenders: Incarcerated and community population, March 2001. (2001). Ottawa: Correctional Service Canada. Online: www.csc-scc.gov.ca/text/prgrm/fsw/profiles/nomax_e.shtml. Retrieved September 1, 2004.

Protection of children involved in prostitution. (2004). Alberta Children's Services. Online: www.child.gov.ab.ca/whatwedo/pchip/page.cfm?pg=index.

The protection of victims of crime in penal procedures. (2004). Online: www. activecitizenship.net/justice/protection_victim.htm.

Protest by arson? (1997, February 24). *Calgary Herald*. Online: www.calgaryherald.com.

Prowse, C. (1994). Vietnamese criminal organizations: Reconceptualizing Vietnam "gangs." *RCMP Gazette*, 56(7):2–8.

Public opinion polling. (2004). Canadian Coalition Against Insurance Fraud. Online: www.ibc.ca/ccaif_polling.asp.

Public perception of crime. (1996, May 24). *Calgary Herald*. Online: www.calgaryherald.com.

Purdy, A. (1997, June 17). Four charged in hate crime. *Calgary Herald*, B4.

Quay, H.C. (Ed.). (1987). *Handbook of juvenile delinquency*. New York: John Wiley.

Question: How do you feel about stupid quizzes? (1998, March 25). *Edmonton Journal*. Online: www.southam.com/edmontonjournal.

Quick facts—Media violence. (1998). Online: www.screen.com/eng/iss...olence/quikfct/vioquik.htm#canprev.

Quinney, R. (1970). *The social reality of crime*. Boston: Little, Brown.

——. (1977). *Class state and crime*. New York: David McKay.

Quiros, C.B. de (1969 [1911]). *Modern theories of criminality*. Trans. A. deSalvio. Boston: Little, Brown.

Radzinowicz, L. (1965). *The need for criminology*. London: Heinemann.

——. (1999). *Adventures in criminology*. London: Routledge.

Raine, A. (Ed.). (1993). *The psychopathology of crime: Criminal behavior as a clinical disorder*. New York: Academic Press.

Raine, A., Brennan, P., & Farrington, D., & Mednick, S. (1997). Biosocial bases of violence: Conceptual and theoretical issues. In A. Raine, P. Brennan, & D. Farrington (Eds.), *Biosocial bases of violence*. New York: Plenum.

Raine, A., Buchsbaum, M., & LaCasse, L. (1997). Brain abnormalities in murderers indicated by positron emission tomography. *Biological Psychiatry*, 42:495–508.

Random drug testing to be introduced for officers. (1996, November/December). *CJ International*, 8.

Rao, S.V. (Ed.). (1988). *Perspectives in criminology*. Sahibabad, India: New Printindia.

Rauhut, N.C. (2004). *Ultimate questions: Thinking about philosophy*. (Penguin Academic Series). Upper Saddle River, NJ: Pearson Education.

Ray, J.-A. (1987). Every twelfth shopper: Who shoplifts and why? *Social Casework*, 68:234–239.

RCMP Gazette. (1994, November). Hells Angels forever!

Reasons, C.E., Ross, L., & Paterson, C. (1981). *Assault on the worker: Occupational health and safety in Canada*. Toronto: Butterworths.

Reckless, W.C. (1970). American criminology. *Criminology*, 8(1):4–20.

Redl, F., & Wineman, D. (1951). *Children who hate*. Glencoe, IL: Free Press.

Refugee smuggling ring smashed. (1996, December 6). *Calgary Herald*. Online: www.calgaryherald.com.

Regina v. Red Hot Video Ltd., 45 C.R.3d 36, 43–44 (B.C.C.A. 1985).

Reich, C.J. (1994, March). Personal communication.

Reichel, P.L. (2002). *Comparative criminal justice systems: A topical approach* (3rd ed.). Englewood Cliffs, NJ: Prentice-Hall.

Reichel, R. (Ed.). (2005). *Handbook of transnational crime and justice*. Thousand Oaks, CA: Sage.

Reid, S.T. (1982). *Crime and criminology* (3rd ed.). New York: Holt, Rinehart, & Winston.

Reisman, J.A. (1997). *Images of children crime and violence in* Playboy, Penthouse, *and* Hustler. Washington, DC: Department of Justice.

Reiss, A.J. (1961). The social integration of peers and queers. *Social Problems*, 9:102–120.

Reitsma-Street, M., Artz, S., & Nicholson, D. (2004). Canadian girls and crime in the twenty-first century. In J. Winterdyk (Ed.), *Issues and perspectives on young offenders in Canada* (3rd ed.). Toronto: Thompson, ch. 3.

Religious tolerance. (2003, October). Same sex marriage. Online: www.pais.org/hottopics/2003/October/index.stm.

Remar, S. (1991, August). Dial "900" for trouble. *Reader's Digest*, 139:39–43.

Rengert, G., & Wasilchick, J. (1985). *Suburban burglary: A time and place for everything.* Springfield, IL: Thomas.

Rengert, G.F. (1989). Spatial justice and criminal victimization. *Justice Quarterly*, 6:543–564.

Reoffence risk high—study. (1998, June 5). *Calgary Herald*, B13.

The report of the Commission on Obscenity and Pornography. (1970). Washington, DC: U.S. Government Printing Office.

Report on assessing corporal punishment. (1994, August 13). *Missoulian*, A2.

Reppetto, T. (1974). *Residential crime.* Cambridge, MA: Ballinger.

Restorative Justice. (2004). Restorative justice. Online: www.restorativejustice.org. Retrieved Aug. 25, 2004.

Results: Analyze your driving style. (2001). Online: www.roadragers.com. Retrieved August 13, 2004.

Rhodes, W.M., & Conly, C. (1981). Crime and mobility: An empirical study. In P.J. Brantingham & P. Brantingham (Eds.), *Environmental criminology.* Beverly Hills, CA: Sage, 161–178.

Ritual abuse. (1966, January 21). Online: limestone.kosone.com/people/ocrt/ra.htm.

Ritzer, G. (1992). *Sociological theory* (3rd ed.). New York: McGraw-Hill.

Roberts, J., & Edgar, A. (2003). Victim impact statements at sentencing: Perceptions of the judiciary in Canada. *The International Journal of Victimology*, 1(4). Online: www.jidv.com. Retrieved July 18, 2003.

Roberts, J., & Geboyts, R. (1992). Reforming rape laws. *Law and Human Behavior*, 16(5):555–573.

Roberts, J., & Grossman, M. (1994). Changing definitions of sexual assault: An analysis of police statistics. In J. Roberts & R. Mohr (Eds.), *Confronting sexual assault: A decade of legal and social change.* Toronto: University of Toronto Press.

Roberts, J., & Sanders, T. (2004). Researching public attitudes towards sentencing in Canada. In J. Winterdyk, L. Coates, & S. Broddie (Eds.), *Research methods reader.* Toronto: Pearson Education.

Roberts, J., Stalans, L.J., Indermaur, D., & Hough, M. (2003). *Penal populism and public opinion: Lessons from five countries.* New York: Oxford University Press.

Roesch, R., & Winterdyk, J.A. (1985). *The Vancouver convenience store robbery prevention program: Final report.* Ottawa: Ministry of the Solicitor General of Canada, no. 1985–42.

Rosenbaum, J.J.L. (1991). Female crime and delinquency. In S.E. Brown, F-A. Esbensen, & G. Geis (Eds.), *Criminology: Explaining crime and its context.* Cincinnati, OH: Anderson.

Ross, J.I. (Ed.). (1995). *Violence in Canada: Sociological perspectives.* Don Mills, ON: Oxford.

Ross, R. (1993). Evaluating the Canadian Centre for Justice Statistics. In J. Hudson & J. Roberts (Eds.), *Evaluating justice.* Toronto: Thompson.

Ross, R.R., Fabiano, E.A., & Eweles, C.D. (1988). Reasoning and rehabilitation. *International Journal of Offender Therapy and Comparative Criminology*, 32:29–35.

Rosoff, S.M., Pontell, H.N., & Tillman, R.H. (2004). *Profit without honor: White-collar crime and the looting of America.* Upper Saddle River, NJ: Pearson.

Roth, M. (2000). Organized crime in the Balkans. *Crime and Justice International* 16(38):7–8.

Rowe, D. (2002). *Biology and crime.* Los Angeles, CA: Roxbury.

Rowe, D.C., & Farrington, D.P. (1997). The familial transmission of criminal convictions. *Criminology*, 35(1):177–201.

Rubin, S. (1998, June 3). Bre-X's Walsh suffers stroke. *Federal Post.* Online: www.sunmeadia.ca.

Rushton, J.P., & Ankney, D. (1995). Brain size matters: A reply to Peters. *Canadian Journal of Experimental Psychology*, 49(4). Online: www.cpa.ca.

Rushton, J.P., & Harris, J.A. (1994). Genetic and environmental components to self-report violence in male and female twins. Paper presented at the American Society of Criminology annual meeting, Miami, November.

Sacco, V.F. (1982). The effects of mass media on perceptions of crime. *Pacific Sociological Review*, 25(4):475–493.

Sacco, V.F., & Kennedy, L. (1994). *The criminal event*. Scarborough, ON: Nelson.

———. (1998). *The criminal event* (2nd ed.). Scarborough, ON: Nelson.

Saferstein, R. (1998). *Criminalistics: An introduction to forensic science* (6th ed.). Upper Saddle River, NJ: Prentice-Hall.

Salomon, E.D. (1988). Homosexuality: Sexual stigma. In V.F. Sacco (Ed.), *Deviance: Conformity and control in Canadian society*. Scarborough, ON: Prentice-Hall.

Samenow, S.E. (1984). *Inside the criminal mind*. New York: Random House.

Sampson, R.J., & Laub, J. (1988). Unraveling families and delinquency: A reanalysis of the Glueck's data. *Criminology*, 26:355–380.

———. (1990). Crime and deviance over the life-course: The salience of adult social bonds. *American Sociological Review*, 55:609–627.

———. (1993). *Crime in the making: Pathways and turning points through life*. Cambridge, MA: Harvard University Press.

Sansfacon, D. (1985). *Prostitution in Canada: A research review report*. Ottawa: Department of Justice.

Sapstead, D. (1999, January 4). Terrorist chief renews call for holy war. *Calgary Herald*, A1.

Scaramella, G., Breninger, M., & Miller, P. (1997, October). Outlaw motorcycle gangs: Tattoo-laden misfits or sophisticated criminals? *Crime and Justice International*, 10–13.

Schafer, S. (1968). *The criminal and his victim*. New York: Random House.

———. (1976). *Introduction to criminology*. Reston, VA: Reston.

Schissel, B. (2002). Orthodox criminology: The limits of consensus theories in crime. In B. Schissel & C. Brooks (Eds.), *Marginality and condemnation: An introduction to critical criminology*. Halifax: Fernwoood.

Schlaadt, R.G. (1992). *Alcohol use and abuse*. Guilford, CT: Duskin.

Schmalleger, F., MacAllister, D., & McKeena, P. (2004). *Canadian criminal justice today* (2nd ed.). Toronto: Prentice-Hall.

Schmalleger, F., & Volk, R. (2005). *Canadian criminology today* (2nd ed.). Toronto: Pearson Education.

Schoenthaler, S., Amos, S., Eysenck, H., Hudes, M., & Korda, D. (1995). *A controlled trial of the effect of vitamin-mineral supplementation on the incidence of serious institutional rule violations*. Unpublished manuscript (courtesy of H. Eysenck).

Schroeder, D.P. (1994). Brief overview of fetal alcohol syndrome and effects. Online: members.aol.com/creaconinc/fas.html.

Schulz, S. (2004). Beyond self-control: Analysis and critique of Gottfredson and Hirschi's general theory of crime (1990). PhD thesis, Max Plank Institute, Freiburg, Germany.

Schur, E. (1972). *Labelling deviant behavior*. New York: Harper & Row.

Schwendinger, H., & Schwendinger, J. (1970). Defenders of order or guardians of human rights. *Issues in Criminology*, 5:123–157.

———. (1991). Feminism, criminology and complex variations. In B.D. MacLean & D. Milovanovic (Eds.), *New directions in critical criminology*. Vancouver: The Collective Press, ch. 7.

Scott, J.E., & Schwalm, L.A. (1988). Pornography and rape: An examination of adult theater rates and rape rates by state. In J.E. Scott & T. Hirschi (Eds.), *Controversial issues in crime and justice*. Newbury Park, CA: Sage.

Scott, P. (1973). Henry Maudsley. In H. Mannheim (Ed.), *Pioneers in criminology* (2nd ed.). Montclair, NJ: Patterson Smith, ch. 12.

SCPP (Special Committee on Pornography and Prostitution). (1985). *Pornography and prostitution in Canada*. Ottawa: Department of Supply and Services.

Secure your motor. (2004). Online: www. secureyourmotor.gov.uk.

Selick, K. (1999, May). Home invasions by criminals or cops. *Canadian Lawyer*, np.

Sellin, T. (1931). The basis of a crime index. *Journal of Criminal Law and Criminology*, 22:335–336.

Seskus, T., & Mofina, R. (2004). Young offenders and the press. In J. Winterdyk (Ed.),

Issues and perspectives on young offenders in Canada (3rd ed.). Toronto: Nelson.

Sex chromosome abnormalities. (2004). Online: www.dor.kaiser.org/genetics/OurServices/XXY-XYY-XXXMain.html.

Sex offender recidivism predictor. (2004). Online: www.csc-scc.gc.ca/text/home_e.shtml.

Sex Workers Alliance of Vancouver. (2000). Online: www.walnet.org.

Sexual assaults not seen as serious: Professor. (1997, June 8). *Calgary Herald*. Online: www.calgaryherald.com.

Shah, S., & Roth, L.H. (1974). Biological and psychophysiological factors in criminality. In D. Glaser (Ed.), *Handbook of criminology*. Chicago, IL: Rand McNally, 101–73.

Shaw, C., & McKay, H. (1969). *Juvenile delinquency and urban areas: A study of rates of delinquency in relation to differential characteristics of local communities in American cities*. Chicago: University of Chicago Press.

Shaw, G. (1997, September 5). Car theft in North America, it occurs on average every 20 seconds. *Calgary Herald*, G12.

Shaw, M. (1994). *Ontario women in conflict with the law: A survey of women in women institutions and under community supervision in Ontario*. Toronto: Ministry of the Solicitor General and Correctional Service.

Shaw, M., & Dubois, S. (1995). *Understanding violence by women: A review of the literature*. Ottawa: Corrections Service Canada. Online: 198.103.98.138/crd/fsw/fsw23/fsw23e02.htm.

Shearing, C. (1989). Decriminalizing criminology: Reflections on the liberal and topological meaning of the term. *Canadian Journal of Criminology*, 31(2):169–178.

Shelley, L.I. (2004). Transnational crime and corruption centre. Online: www.american.edu/traccc/. Retrieved August 28, 2004.

Sherman, L.W., Smith, D.A., Schmidt, J.D., & Rogan, D.P. (1992). Crime, punishment, and stake in conformity: Legal and informal control of domestic violence. *American Sociological Review*, 49:261–272.

Short, J. (1997, September/October). President's message: On communicating, cross boundaries and building bridges. *The Criminologist*, 1.

Siegel, L.J. (1995). *Criminology: Theories, patterns, and typologies* (5th ed.). Minneapolis/St. Paul, MN: West.

Siegel, L.J., & McCormick, C. (1993). *Criminology in Canada*. Toronto: Nelson.

——. (2003). *Criminology in Canada* (2nd ed.). Toronto: Nelson.

Silverberg, C. (1997, October 19). Problem solving: The new face of community policing. *Calgary Herald*, A19.

Silverman, R.A. (1988). Interpersonal criminal violence. In V.F. Sacco (Ed.). *Deviance: Conformity and control in Canadian society*. Scarborough, ON: Prentice-Hall.

Silverman, R.A., & Kennedy, L. (1988). Women who kill their children. *Violence and Victims*, 3(2):121–135.

——. (1993). *Deadly deeds: Murder in Canada*. Scarborough, ON: Nelson.

Silverman, R.A., Teevan, J.J., Jr., & Sacco, V.F. (1991). *Crime in Canadian society* (4th ed.). Toronto: Butterworths.

Simon, R. (1975). *Women and crime*. Lexington, MA: D.C. Health.

Simonds, M. (1996, March/April). Code of arms. *Canadian Geographic*, 45–56.

Simpson, S. (1989). Feminist theory, crime and justice. *Criminology*, 27:497–538.

Single, E., Robson, L., Relm, J., & Xie, X. (1996). *The cost of substance abuse in Canada*. Toronto: Canadian Centre for Substance Abuse.

Skinner, B.F. (1971). *Beyond freedom and dignity*. New York: Knopf.

——. (1979). *The shaping of a behaviourist*. New York: Knopf.

Skogan, W.G. (1981). *Issues in the measurement of victimization*. NCJ-74682, Bureau of Justice Statistics, US Department of Justice.

Skolnick, J.H. (1994). *Justice without trial*. New York: Macmillan.

Slade, D. (1999, January 16). Unusual circumstances cited in lenient sentence. *Calgary Herald*, B1.

Slobodian, L. (2000, July 23). Biker "crackdown" has little to show. *Calgary Herald*, A10.

Smandych, R. (1985). Re-examining the origins of Canadian anticombines legislation, 1890–1910.

In T. Fleming (Ed.), *The new criminologies in Canada*. Toronto: Oxford University Press.

Smart, R.G., & Jansen, V.A. (1991). Youth substance abuse. In H.M. Annis & C.S. Davis (Eds.), *Drug use by adolescents: Identification, assessment and intervention*. Toronto: Addiction Research Foundation.

Smith, G.J., & Wynne, H.J. (2004). *VLT gambling in Alberta: A preliminary analysis*. Edmonton: Alberta Gambling Research Institute.

Smith, K.A., Fairburn, C.G., & Cowen, P.J. (1997). Relapse of depression after rapid depletion of tryptophan. *Lancet*, 349:915–919.

Smith, M. (1983). *Violence and sports*. Toronto: Butterworths.

Smyth, S. (2001, July 15). Organized crime: Some facts, issues, and concerns. *Bulletin* (Canadian Criminal Justice Association):1–9.

Smythe, P. (1996). Terrorism in Canada: Recent trends and future prospects. *RCMP Gazette*, 58(10):18–22.

Snider, L. (1993). *Bad business: Corporate crime in Canada*. Scarborough, ON: Nelson.

———. (2002). Corporate crime: Business as usual? In B. Schissel & C. Brooks (Eds.), *Critical criminology in Canada: Breaking the links between marginality and condemnation*. Toronto: Fernwood Press.

Snodgrass, J. (1982). *The jack-roller at seventy: A fifty year follow-up*. Lexington, MA: D.C. Health.

Social implications of child prostitution. (1998). Online: www.taasa.org/childprostit.htm.

Sodhi, E. (2000). The truth about family violence in Canada. Online: www.fathersforlifeorg/Sodhi/fvcan1.htm.

Solicitor General of Canada. (1998, June 02). Launch of the national strategy on community safety and crime prevention. Online: www.psepc-sppcc.gc.ca/publications/Speeches/19980602 e.asp.

Somers, L.E. (1984). *Economic crimes*. New York: Clark Boardman.

Son charged with 4 weapons charges for unloaded .177 cal pellet gun. (2004, May 21). Target Shooting Canada. Online: www.targetshooting.ca/wwwboard/message/4519.html.

Southland, M.D., Collins, P.A., & Scarborough, K.E. (1997). *Workplace violence*. Cincinnati, OH: Anderson.

Speckart, G.R., & Anglin, M.D. (1986). Narcotics and crime: A causal modeling approach. *Journal of Quantitative Criminology*, 2(1): 3–28.

Spoke, M.L. (1998, June 27). Quoted in M. Welsh & K. Donovan, Four giant casinos on the way. *Toronto Star*. Online: www.thestar.com.

Stahura, J.N., & Hollinger, R.C. (1988). A routine activities approach to suburban arson rates. *Sociological Spectrum*, 8:349–369.

Stalking and domestic violence in America. (1999). Online: www.ojd.usdoj.gov/vawgo/stalk98/chapter1.htm. Retrieved January 15, 1999.

Stamler, R.T. (1996). Organized crime. In R. Linden (Ed.), *Criminology: A Canadian perspective* (3rd ed.). Toronto: Harcourt Brace.

Stansfield, R.T. (1996). *Issues in policing: A Canadian perspective*. Toronto: Thompson.

Straka, R. (2003). The violence of Hmong gangs and the crime of rape. *Crime & Justice International*, 19(76):19–22.

Statistics Canada. (2003). *Alcohol dependence, by sex, household population aged 15 and over, Canada and provinces, 2002*. Online: www.statcan.ca/english/freepub/82-617-XIE/htm/5110096.htm.

———. (2004). *Adults and youths charged, by offence category and sex, Canada, provinces and territories, 1996–2002*. Online: www.statcan.ca/english/freepub/82-221-XIE/00604/tables/html/22142.htm. Retrieved September 3, 2004.

Steffensmeier, D.J. (1978). Crime and the contemporary women. *Social Forces*, 57:566–584.

Stein, K. (2001). *Public perception of crime and justice in Canada: A review of opinion polls*. Ottawa: Department of Justice.

Sterling prize winner challenges prostitution law. (1997, Fall). *Simon Fraser University Alumni Journal*, 8.

Stinchfield, R., & Winters, K. (1997). Gambling treatment outcome study. Online: www.cbc.med.umn.edu/~randy/gambling/gamtx.htm.

Stitt, B.G., & Giacopassi, D.J. (1992). Trends in the connectivity of theory and research in criminology. *The Criminologist*, 17(1):3–6.

Stoff, D.M., & Cairns, R.B. (Eds.). (1996). *Aggression and violence: Genetic, neurobiological, and biosocial perspectives.* Mahwah, NJ: Lawrence Erlbaum Association.

Stoff, D.M., & Vitiello, D. (1996). Role of serotonin in aggression of children and adolescents: Biochemical and pharmacological studies. In D.M. Stoff & R.B. Cairns (Eds.), *Aggression and violence: Genetic, neurobiological, and biosocial perspectives.* Mahwah, NJ: Lawrence Erlbaum Association.

Stone, M. (1999, August 28). Hackers a growing threat to security. *Computing Canada.* Online: www.findarticles.com/p/articles/mi_m0CGC/is_32_25/ai_55621896.

Stone, T. (1998, May). Slavic women in demand in sex slave markets throughout world. *Crime and Justice International*, 7–8.

Strasburg, P.A. (1978). *Violent delinquents.* New York: Monarch Books.

Straten, M. van. (1994). *Gurana.* Saffron Walden, UK: C.W. Daniel Co.

Streissguth, A.P., Barr, H.M., Kogan, J., & Bockstein, F.L. (1997). Alcohol's legacy: High crime rate seen in FAS/FAE. Cited in *Crime Times*, 3(1):5.

Stutman, S. (1995, May 1). An opportunity to prevent violence: The role of the media. Paper Presented to the Ninth UN Congress of the Prevention of Crime and the Treatment of Offenders at the Mass Media and Crime Prevention Workshop, Cairo, Egypt.

Sugar surprise. (2004, March 9). CBC News. Online: www.cbc.ca/consumers/market/files/food/sugar/.

Sulloway, F.J. (1979). *Freud: Biologist of the mind.* New York: Basic Books.

Support for capital punishment plummets. (2001, February 21). Ipsos News Center. Online: www.ipsos-na.com/news/pressrelease.cfm.

Sutherland, E. (1937). *The professional thief.* Chicago: University of Chicago Press.

——. (1947). *Principles of criminology* (4th ed.). Philadelphia, PA: J.B. Lippincott.

——. (1949). *White collar crime.* New York: Holt, Rinehart, & Winston.

Sutherland, E., & Cressey, D. (1955). *Principles of criminology* (5th ed.). Philadelphia, PA: Lippincott.

——. (1960). *Principles of criminology* (6th ed.). Philadelphia, PA: J.B. Lippincott.

Sutherland, E., & Locke, H.J. (1936). *Twenty thousand homeless men: A study of unemployed men in the Chicago shelters.* Philadelphia: J.B. Lippincott.

Swaffer, T., & Hollin, C.R. (1995). Adolescent firesetting: Why do they say they do it? *Journal of Adolescence*, 18:619–623.

Swigert, V.L., & Farrell, R.A. (1976). *Murder, inequality, and the law.* Lexington, MA: Lexington Books.

Sykes, G., & Matza, D. (1957). Techniques of neutralization: A theory of delinquency. *American Sociological Review*, 22:664–670.

Synnott, A. (1996). *Shadows: Issues and social patterns in Canada.* Scarborough, ON: Prentice-Hall.

Szasz, T. (1970). *The manufacture of madness: A comparative study of the inquisition and the mental health movement.* New York: Harper & Row.

Tabakoff, B., Whelan, J.P., & Hoffman, P.L. (1990). Two biological markers of alcoholism. In C.R. Cloninger & H. Begleiter (Eds.), *Genetics and biology of alcoholism.* Cold Spring Harbor, NY: Cold Spring Harbor Laboratory Press.

Taming the demons. (1998, June 17). *Calgary Herald*, B6.

Tanner, J., & Wortley, S. (2002). *Toronto youth crime and victimization survey: Overview report.* University of Toronto.

Taylor, A., & Anielski, M. (2001). Genuine progress indicators for Alberta. Online: www.pembina.org/publications_item.asp?ID=56.

Taylor, R.B., & Harrell, A.V. (1996). *Physical environment and crime.* Washington, DC: National Institute of Justice.

Teevan, J.J., & Blute, M. (1986). What is sociology? In J.J. Teevan (Ed.), *Introduction to sociology: A Canadian perspective.* Scarborough, ON: Prentice-Hall, ch. 1.

Then and now: Women in Canadian legislatures. (1997). Ottawa: National Library of Canada.

Theodorson, G.A. (Ed.). (1982). *Urban patterns: Studies in human ecology.* Philadelphia: The Pennsylvania State University Press.

Thomas, S.P. (Ed.). (1993). *Women and anger.* New York: Aldine de Gruyter.

Thomas, W.I. (1923). *The unadjusted girl: With cases and standpoint for behavior analysis.* New York: Harper & Row.

Thompson, M. (1996). Zeroing in on the serial killer. *RCMP Gazette*, 58(3):14–15.

Thornberry, T.P. (1989). Reflections on the advantages and disadvantages of theoretical integration. In S.F. Messner, M.D. Krohn, & A.E. Liska (Eds.), *Theoretical integration in the study of deviance and crime.* Albany, NY: SUNY Press, 51–60.

Thornberry, T.P., & Farnsworth, M. (1982). Social correlates of criminal involvement: Further evidence on the relationship between social status and criminal behavior. *American Sociological Review*, 47:505–518.

Tifft, L. (1980). Foreword to D. Sullivan, *The mask of love.* Port Washington, NY: Kennikat Press.

Tittle, C.R. (1998). *Control balance: Toward a general theory of deviance.* Boulder, CO, Westview.

Tobacco Act challenge. (2003). Health Canada. Online: www.hc-sc.gc.ca/hecs-sesc/tobacco/legislation/challenge/contents.html.

Tombs, S., & Whyte, D. (2003). *Unmasking the crimes of the powerful.* London: Peter Lang.

Tonry, M., & Farrington, D.P. (Eds.). (1995). *Building a safer society: Strategic approaches to crime prevention.* Chicago: University of Chicago.

Tories decimated by fraud scandal. (1997, August 24). *Calgary Herald*, A6.

Toronto automobile. (2004). Online: auto-insurance.easycfm.com/automobile-insurance-toronto.html.

Traditional (Italian-based) organized crime (TOC). (2004). www.cisc.gc.ca/annualreport-2004/cisc2004/traditional2004.html.

Transnational criminal activity.(1998). Online: www.globalpolicy.org/globaliz/law/law/orcrime.htm.

Transparency International. (2004). Corruption perceptions index, 2003. Online: www.transparency.org/pressreleases_archive/2003/2003.10.07.cpi.en.html.

Treatment planned for women gambling addicts. (1997, August 11). *Calgary Herald.* Online: www.calgaryherald.com.

Trembley, P. (1986). Designing crime: The short life expectancy and the workings of a recent wave of credit card bank frauds. *British Journal of Criminology*, 26:673–690.

Trembley, P., Clermont, Y., & Cusson, M. (1996). Jockeys and joyriders. In R.A. Silverman, J.J. Teevan, & V.F. Sacco (Eds.), *Crime in Canadian society* (5th ed.). Toronto: Harcourt Brace, ch. 20.

Trocme, N., MacLaurin, B., Fallon, B., Daciuk, J., Billingsley, D., & Tourigny, M. (2001). Canadian incidence study of reported child abuse and neglect: Methodology. *Canadian Journal of Public Health*, 92(4):259–263.

Turk, A. (1995). Transformation versus revolutionism and reformism: Policy implications of conflict theory. In H.D. Barlow (Ed.), *Crime and public policy: Putting theory to work.* Boulder, CO: Westview Press, 15–28.

Two provincial employees charged with fraud. (2004, August 12). Online: www.canada.com.

Underwood, N. (1991, January 7). High anxiety. *Maclean's*, 30–36.

University Medical Research Publishers. (1993). *Amazing medicines the drug companies don't want you to discover.* Tempe, AZ.

Up in smoke? Canada's marijuana law and the debate over decriminalization. (2004, November 1). CBC News. Online: www.cbc.ca.

Van Brunschot, E.G., & Brannigan, A. (1997). Youthful prostitution and child sexual trauma. *International Journal of Law and Psychiatry*, 20(3):337–354.

Vancouver Board of Trade. (2003). *Report on property crime in Vancouver.* Online: www.vancouver.boardoftrade.com/crime_report.html.

Vancouver Board of Trade Information. (1997, June). *Report on property crime in Vancouver, June 1997.* Online: www.vancouver.boardof-trade.com/crime_report.html.

van Dijk, J.J.M. (1997). Towards a research-based crime reduction policy: Crime prevention as a cost-effective policy option. *European Journal on Criminal Policy and Research*, 5(3):13–27.

van Dijk, J.J.M., & Shaw, M. (2002). The International Crime Victims Survey: Impact and future policy. In Helmut Kury (Ed.), *International comparison of crime and victimization: The ICVS*. Toronto: de Sitter.

Vest, J., Cohen, W., & Tharp, M. (1997, June). Road rage. *U.S. News and World Report*. Online: www.findarticles.com/p/articles/mi_kmusn/is_199706.

ViCLAS. (2004). Violent Crime Linkage Analysis System (ViCLAS). Online: www.rcmp.ca/vicals/viclas_e.htm. Retrieved August 30, 2004.

Victim Assistance Unit (Calgary). (2004). Online: www.calgarypolice.ca/inside/victim.html.

Victim Crisis Assistance & Referral Services (VCARS). (2004). Ontario Ministry of the Attorney General. Online: www.attorneygeneral.jus.gov.on.ca/english/about/vw/vcars.asp.

Victims of Crime Initiative. (2004). Department of Justice. Online: canada.justice.gc.ca/en/ps/pb/fsvictims.html.

Victims of crime research series. (2004). Online: canada.justice.gc.ca/en/ps/rs/rep/victims_sum-b-e.html.

Vikkunen, M., & Linnoila, M. (1996). Serotonin and glucose metabolism in impulsively violent alcoholic offenders. In D.M. Staff & R.B. Cairns (Eds.), *Aggression and violence*. Mahwah, NJ: Lawrence Erlbaum Association.

Violence against women. (2002). Online: www.hc-sc.gc.ca/english/women/facts_issues/facts_violence.htm. Retrieved September 9, 2004.

Violent crime in Canada. (1996). *Juristat*, 16(6).

Vito, G.F. (1998, March). Presidential Address. American Criminal Justice Society meetings. San Francisco, CA.

Vito, G.F., & Holmes, R.M. (1994). *Criminology: Theory, research, and policy*. Belmont, CA: Wadsworth.

Vold, G.F., & Bernard, T.J. (1979). *Theoretical criminology*. New York: Oxford.

——. (1981). *Theoretical criminology* (2nd ed.). New York: Oxford.

——. (1986). *Theoretical criminology* (3rd ed.). New York: Oxford University.

Vold, G.F., Bernard, T.J., & Snipes, J.B. (1998). *Theoretical criminology* (4th ed.). New York: Oxford University Press.

von Hentig, H. (1940). Remarks on the interaction of perpetrator and victims. *Journal of Criminal Law, Criminology and Police Science*, 31(3):303–309.

——. (1948). *The criminal and his victim: Studies in the sociobiology of crime*. New Haven, CT: Yale University Press.

VRF (Violence Research Foundation). (1994). Material forwarded by R. Hodges, President of Violence Research Foundation, Tustin, CA.

Walker, M. (1994, December). Excessive tissue manganese as a cause of antisocial behaviour. *Townsend Letter for Doctors*, 1328–1334.

Walker, N. (1987). *Crime and criminality: A critical introduction*. New York: Oxford University Press.

Wallace, R.A., & Wolf, A. (1995). *Contemporary sociological theory: Continuing the classical tradition* (4th ed). Englewood Cliffs, NJ: Prentice-Hall.

Waller, I. (2000). Towards responsible public safety. In P. Friday & G.F. Krichhoff (Eds.), *Victimology at the transition from the 20th to the 21st century*. Aachen, Germany: Shaker Verlag, 347–368.

Walmsely, R. (2003). World prison population list. Online: www.homeoffice.gov.uk/rds/pdfs2/r234.pdf. Retrieved August 25, 2004.

Walsh, A. (2002). *Biosocial criminology*. Cincinnati, OH: Anderson.

Walsh, C. (2004, June 18). Holly Jones' murderer behind bars. Online: www.canadiancontent.net/commtr/article_690.html.

Ward, D.A., & Tittle, C.R. (1994). Interpreting the IQ-delinquency relationship. *Journal of Quantitative Criminology*, 10:189–212.

Warren, M.Q., & Hindelang, M.J. (1986). Current explanations of offender behaviour. In H. Toch (Ed.), *Psychology of crime and criminal justice*. Prospect Heights, IL: Waveland Press, 166–182.

The Watch Your Car Program. (1996, November). Washington, DC: Bureau of Justice Assistance Fact Sheet.

Webb, G.R. (2004, November 17). Rollovers, recalls, and rhetoric: Corporate framing of the Ford/Firestone controversy. Paper presented at the American Society of Criminology, Nashville, Tennessee.

Webb, N., Sakheim, G., Towns-Miranda, L., & Wagner, C. (1990). Collaborative treatment of juvenile firestarters: Assessment and outreach. *American Journal of Orthopsychiatry*, 60:305–310.

Weichman, D. (1994). Caning and corporal punishment: Viewpoint. *CJ International*, 10(5):13–20.

Weir, F. (2004, September 23). Russia cracks down on beer ads. *Christian Science Monitor*. Online: www.csmonitor.com/2004/0923/p06s01-woeu.html.

Weisburd, D., Chayet, E.F., & Waring, E.J. (1990). White-collar crime and criminal careers: Some preliminary findings. *Crime and Delinquency*, 36:342–355.

Wellford, C.C. (1997, December). Two goals of criminal justice. *Crime and Justice International*, 4.

Welsh, B.C., & Farrington, D.P. (2002). Crime prevention effects of closed circuit television: A systematic review. *Home Office Research Study*, 252. London: Home Office.

Welsh, M., & Donovan, K. (1998, June 27). Four giant casinos on the way. *Toronto Star*. Online: www2.thestar.com.

Wemmers, J.-A. (2002). Declaration of basic principles of restorative justice. *The Victimologist*, 1(1):5, 7.

West, G.W. (1984). *Young offenders and the state*. Toronto: Butterworths.

West, G., & Farrington, D. (1977). *The delinquent way of life*. London: Heinemann.

Western Australian Statistical Indicators. (March 2001). Australian Bureau of Statistics. Online: www.abs.gov.au/ausstats/.

When it's no longer a game. (1995, February 27). *Calgary Herald*, B3.

White, J.R. (2003). *Terrorism: An introduction* (4th ed.). Belmont, CA: Wadsworth.

White, P.T. (1989, January). An ancient Indian herb turns deadly: Coca. *National Geographic*, 2–47.

Wijsman, M. (1990). Linkage analysis of alcoholism: Problems and solutions. In C.R. Cloninger & H. Begleiter (Eds.), *Genetics and biology of alcoholism*. Cold Spring Harbor, NY: Cold Spring Harbor Laboratory Press, 317–326.

Wilkes, J., & Edwards, P. (1997, July 25). Mobster murdered answering his door. *Toronto Star*. Online: www.thestar.com.

Williams, F.P. III., & McShane, M.D. (1994). *Criminological theory* (2nd ed.). Englewood Cliffs, NJ: Prentice-Hall.

—— (1999). *Criminological theory* (3rd ed.). Englewood Clirffs, NJ: Prentice-Hall.

——. (2002). *Criminological theory* (4th ed.). Englewood Cliffs, NJ: Prentice-Hall.

——. (2004). *Criminological theory* (4th ed.). Englewood Cliffs, NJ: Prentice-Hall.

Williams, J. (1999, February 8). Police target date-rape drug. *Calgary Herald*, B5.

Williams, R.J., & Kalita, D.K. (1977). *A physician's handbook on orthomolecular medicine*. New York: Pergamon Press.

Wilson, D., & O'Sullivan, S. (2004). *Images of incarceration: Representations of prison in film and television drama*. Winchester: Waterside Press.

Wilson, E.O. (1975). *Sociobiology: The new synthesis*. Cambridge, MA: The Belknap Press of Harvard University Press.

Wilson, J.Q. (1975). *Thinking about crime*. New York: Random House.

——. (1994, September). What to do about crime? *Commentary*, 25–34.

——. (1995). Crime and public policy. In J. Wilson & J. Petersilia (Eds.), *Crime*. San Francisco, CA: ICS Press, 489–507.

Wilson, J.Q., & Herrnstein, R. (1985). *Crime and human nature*. New York: Simon & Schuster.

Winterdyk, J. (1996). The looking glass: Canadian Centre for Justice Statistics. *Law Now*, 20(5):14–17.

Winterdyk, J. (Ed.). (2000). *Corrections in Canada: Social reactions to crime*. Scarborough, ON: Prentice-Hall.

——. (2001). *Issues and perspectives on young offenders in Canada* (2nd ed.). Toronto: Harcourt Brace.

——. (2002). *Juvenile justice systems: International perspectives* (2nd ed.). Toronto: Canadian Scholars' Press.

——. (2004). *Adult corrections: International systems and perspectives*. Monsey, NY: Criminal Justice Press.

Winterdyk, J., & Cao, L. (Eds.). (2004). *Lessons from international/comparative criminology/criminal justice*. Toronto: de Sitter.

Winterdyk, J., & Roesch, R. (1982). A wilderness experiential program as an alternative to probation: An evaluation. *Canadian Journal of Criminology*, 24(1):39–50.

Wolf, D. (1991). *The Rebels: A brotherhood of outlaw bikers*. Toronto: University of Toronto Press.

Wolff, R.P. (1971). *Philosophy: A modern encounter*. Englewood Cliffs, NJ: Prentice-Hall.

Wolfgang, M.E. (1958). *Patterns in criminal homicide*. Philadelphia: University of Pennsylvania Press.

——. (1973). Cesare Lombroso. In H. Mannheim (Ed.), *Pioneers in criminology* (2nd ed.). Montclair, NJ: Patterson Smith.

——. (1996, May). *Delinquents in China: Study of birth cohort*. National Institute of Justice. Rockville, MD: U.S. Department of Justice.

Wolfgang, M.E., & Ferracuti, F. (1967). *The subculture of violence*. London: Tavistock.

Woman complains over RCMP inaction. (1997, August 19). *Calgary Herald*. Online: www.calgaryherald.com.

Wooden, W. (1991). Juvenile firesetters in cross-cultural perspective: How should society respond? In J. Hackler (Ed), *Official responses to juvenile problems: Some international reflections*. Onita, Spain: Onita International Institute for the Sociology of Law.

Working paper 36: Damage to property—Arson. (1984). Ottawa: Law Reform Commission of Canada.

Wright, B., & Fox, V. (1978). *Criminal justice and the social sciences*. Philadelphia, PA: W.B. Saunders.

Wright, D. (1997). Acknowledging the continuum from childhood abuse to male prostitution. Online: www.netizen.org/narc/bcifv/backiss2/spring95/nf_continuum.html.

Wright, R., & Decker, S. (1994). *Burglars on the job: Streetlife and residential break-ins*. Boston, MA: Northeastern University Press.

Yochelson, S., & Samenow, S.E. (1976). *The criminal personality*, vol. 1. New York: Jason Aronson.

Young, J. (1986). The failure of criminology: The need for a radical realism. In R. Matthews & J. Young (Eds.), *Confronting crime*. London: Sage.

Zapf, P.A., Cox, D.N., & Roesch, R. (2004). Psychological perspectives on criminality. In R. Linden (Ed.), *Criminology: A Canadian perspective* (5th ed.). Toronto: Nelson Thomson Learning.

Zawitz, M.W. (Ed.). (1992). *Drugs, crime, and the justice system: A national report from the Bureau of Justice Statistics*. Washington, DC: Department of Justice, Bureau of Justice Statistics.

Zellerer, E. (1996). Violence against Inuit women in the Canadian Eastern Arctic. PhD dissertation, School of Criminology, Simon Fraser University, Burnaby, BC.

Zimring, F.E., & Hawkins, G. (1975). *Deterrence: The legal threat to crime control*. Chicago: University of Chicago Press.

Zuckerman, M.J. (2000, March 22). Criminals hot on money trail to cyberspace. *USA Today*, 8A.

Glossary

Note: The number of chapter in which the term is discussed appears in parentheses following each term.

Abduction, also referred to as kidnapping, is the illegal apprehension of another person for the purpose of financial gain, retribution, or personal or political gain. Legally, an abduction involves the unauthorized taking of a person under the age of 16 and holding him or her more than 20 feet from his or her residence for more than one hour. (8)

Aboriginal crime groups are those organized crime groups in Canada that involve Aboriginal people. These groups have been involved in crimes ranging from smuggling of cigarettes to running illegal gambling establishments. (10)

Anomie is a sociological term that refers to a state of normlessness in society. Anomie is usually attributed to decreased homogeneity, which provides a social environment conducive to crimes and criminality. (7)

Arson involves the destruction of property through the use of fire or an explosion, either for fraudulent purposes or by negligence. Legally, is considered to be a form of vandalism, but its increase has caused it to be defined as its own offence. (9)

Assault is a type of violent crime that has several sub-classifications under the *Criminal Code*. In general, it refers to the unlawful, intentional attempt to inflict injury on another person. (1)

Atavism refers to a biological condition that allegedly renders the recipient incapable of living within the social norms of a society, a notion first advanced by Cesare Lombroso. (4)

Attention deficit disorder (ADD) is a psychological and/or biology-rooted disorder that is characterized by the individual being unable to concentrate for periods of time. Many inmates are thought to suffer from some degree of ADD. (5)

Avoidance learning is a form of behavioural learning in which the individual learns to avoid an undesirable behaviour as a result of associating the fear of punishment with that behaviour. (6)

Badgley Report, released in 1984, was the first major Canadian study on the abuse of children and young people. (11)

Behaviour modification is a psychological theory and treatment that emphasizes changing behaviour rather than personality. The process relies on a series of either rewards or undesirable punishments. (6)

Behavioural learning is the psychological theory that asserts that all behaviour is learned through some type of stimulus (negative or positive). It assumes that behaviour consists of determinable relationships. (6)

Beijing Rules were created in 1984 at a United Nations meeting in Beijing. The rules established a set of guidelines that all member countries should use when dealing with young offenders. The primary emphasis is a welfare approach that asserts that young people should be given special consideration and support. (14)

Break and enter is a form of property crime that involves the illegal entry into a building or dwelling without permission and with the intent of committing a theft or an act of violence. (9)

Canadian Centre for Justice Statistics (CCJS) is the agency responsible for collecting and compiling crime data on a wide range of criminological and criminal justice topics. Its findings are published in the *Juristat* bulletins. (3)

Canadian Urban Victimization Survey (CUVS) was conducted during the 1980s and was the first major attempt to survey Canadians who had been victims of crime. The data generally show that certain crimes are far less reported than others. (12)

Cartel is a group of illegal producers whose goal it is to fix prices, to limit supply, and to limit competition through various means, some of which may be illegal and may involve violence. Although cartels are prohibited by anti-trust laws in most countries, they continue to exist nationally and internationally. (10)

Cause implies that the outcome of one event is due to the influence of another. Criminologists strive to identify causal relationships. The assumption is that if causal relationships can be found, prevention measures can be more accurately defined. (3)

Chivalry hypothesis refers to the benevolent attitude the criminal justice system is sometimes accused of using when processing female offenders. The hypothesis asserts that women need special protection. (13)

Classical conditioning, sometimes referred to as Pavlovian conditioning, is a process of behavior modification by which a subject comes to respond in a desired manner to a previously neutral stimulus that has been repeatedly presented along with an unconditioned stimulus that elicits the desired response. (6)

Classical school of criminology can trace its origins to the work of Cesare Beccaria in 1764. Its main assumptions were that criminals are rational, being capable of free will, and that the severity, swiftness, and certainty of punishment should serve as an effective deterrent to crime. (4)

Clearance rate is the percentage of reported crimes that are solved over a fixed period of time. The rate varies considerably depending on the type of offence and is generally considered a reasonable indicator of the effectiveness of crime prevention strategies. (8)

Cognition is a term used in social psychology that refers to the processes we use to organize our thoughts and make sense out of our environment. (6)

Comparative research in criminology is the cross-cultural and cross-national study of crime and its control. Researchers attempt to develop theories and strategies that cut across social, economic, and political boundaries. (14)

Computer crime is a form of high-technology crime that involves the use of computer equipment and technology as the means of committing crime. It includes illegal damage and destruction of data, theft of software via unlawful copying, and use of computers to gain illegal access to information or to steal money. (10)

Concentric-circle theory is one of the early forms of ecological theory. It is based on the premise that crime radiates out in a predictable fashion from inner cities to the suburbs. The circles relate to observable social and environmental characteristics. (7)

Conflict crimes are actions for which there is mixed support as to whether they should be considered crimes, although they are legally defined as such. Examples include using marijuana for medicinal purposes, procuring the services of a prostitute, and appearing topless in public (in some provinces). (1)

Conflict theory asserts that crime is the product of social and/or economic disparity in society. People are seen as social creatures who, when subjected to division and competition, may resort to criminal activity. (7)

Consensual crimes are crimes in which otherwise law-abiding people are willing participants. (10)

Consensus crimes are those behaviours that are generally considered to be very harmful; there is strong support to sanction and control them. (1)

Conservative approach to crime control is an ideology that relies on the criminal justice system to deter and incapacitate criminals as a means of controlling crime. (14)

Conventional crimes are those crimes that most commonly come to mind when we think of crime. They typically include violent crimes such as murder, robbery, and assault, as well as property crimes such as break and enter, motor-vehicle theft, and arson. (1)

Corporate crime is crime committed by a corporate entity that is instigated by the activities of its employees and/or officers. (10)

Correctional statistics are an official source of crime data. The data are based on federal and provincial offenders and include an array of information ranging from offenders' age, gender, and offence to prior convictions. (3)

Correlation is a statistical term used to refer to the observed association between two or more variables. The relationship can be either positive or negative. The higher a correlation between the variables, the greater the likelihood that they are associated in some way (e.g., many prostitutes have a history of sexual abuse). A correlation does not imply a causal relationship. (3)

CPTED (Crime Prevention Through Environmental Design) is an integrated social ecological model that focuses on proactive means of preventing crime. The model emphasizes and targets the physical environment to minimize target suitability. (7)

Crime is a socially constructed concept used to categorize certain behaviours as requiring formal control and warranting some form of social intervention. (1)

Crime data is the information that people and/or criminal justice agencies collect on criminal events. (3)

Crime funnel refers to the idea that crime data can be seen in terms of a funnel. The wide top represents all the crime that has occurred, and, as one moves down the funnel, the narrowing reflects the fact that the number of cases that are officially processed through law enforcement, the courts, and corrections gets increasingly smaller. The difference between the absolute number of crimes and those that are officially processed is referred to as the dark figure of crime. (2)

Crime rate refers to the number of offences in a category recorded in a fixed ratio, such as per 1000, per 10 000, or per 100 000 people. The Uniform Crime Reports provide crime rates for most crimes. (3)

Criminal harassment, also known as stalking, is a criminal offence that involves unlawful following and/or willful harassing of another person. (8)

Criminal justice system consists of the three formal elements involved in the detection, apprehension, processing, and handling of offenders: the police, the courts, corrections, plus all their supporting agencies. (1)

Criminal personality is a type of personality thought to be found in criminals, as opposed to non-criminals. Those who subscribe to its existence also often assume that in most cases the criminal personality can be corrected. (6)

Criminalistics is the science of crime detection and investigation that relies on scientific methodology. Today, there are many sub-areas, ranging from a specialization in weapons to DNA analysis. (4)

Criminological enterprise refers to what criminologists do. The broader context of criminology is made up of a number of sub-areas (such as criminal statistics, sociology of law, victimology, etc.). Together, these sub-areas make up the criminological enterprise. (1)

Criminologist is a behavioural scientist who is interested in the identification, classification, and description of types of criminal behaviour. (1)

Criminology is the integrated, interdisciplinary, scientific study of human behaviour, crime causation, crime prevention, and the punishment and rehabilitation of offenders. (1)

Critical criminology calls for a "self-critical" approach to understanding crime and criminality. It emphasizes the importance of critically examining the social, economic, political, and ideological traditions within criminology. (7)

Cultural transmission theory is a sociological theory that views crime as a socially learned behaviour that is transmitted through successive generations. It is more likely to occur in disorganized urban settings. (7)

Dark figure of crime is a term coined in the 1970s that refers to that element, or portion, of crime that goes undetected or unreported by official sources. (3)

Date rape is a form of sexual assault involving unlawfully coercing sexual interactions with someone (usually a female) against his or her will within the context of a dating relationship. (8)

Demonology is a view of crime that attributes deviant or criminal behaviour to supernatural spirit or power. (6)

Determinism is a doctrine that maintains that our decisions are decided by predictable and/or inherited causes that act on our character. It denies the existence of free will. (4)

Deterrence is one of the forms of social response to a potential offender. It is based on the premise that the risk or fear of punishment may be enough to prevent someone from committing further crime. (4)

Deviance is a sociological term that refers to a behaviour that violates a social norm but that is not necessarily prohibited by law. For example, it is impolite to stick one's tongue out at someone, but it is not a crime to do so. (1)

Diathesis-stress model is an approach for treating substance abusers that focuses on both risk and protective factors. (11)

Differential association is a sociological construct that suggests that criminal acts are the result of exposure to negative influences. Crime is seen as a form of socially learned behaviour. (7)

Discretion is a criminal justice system term denoting the process by which an authority exercises his or her judgment rather than following specific rules and facts. (4)

Ecological school of criminology involves the study of how elements of the physical environment (from buildings to climate and social settings) interact to create a criminal environment. (7)

Ego. See Id, ego, and superego.

Elizabeth Fry Society was created by Elizabeth Fry (née Gurney) in the mid-1800s in response to the perceived need to promote prison reform for women prisoners. Elizabeth Fry Societies can be found across Canada. (13)

Empiricist is an adjective used to describe those researchers who rely on an experimental approach to the study of crime and criminality. (2)

Etiology of crime refers to the study of the origins or causes of crime. (1)

Evolutive is a term coined by Maurice Parmalee in 1918 to describe the process by which the nature and characteristics of crime can change over time. For example, computer crime is a modern-day version of theft. (1)

False positive is a research methodology concept that refers to the risk of making a prediction about an event/individual that may not be true. (3)

Feminist perspective draws attention to the female offender and female victim. While there are several different strands of feminism, they all emphasize the patriarchal bias in society and call for greater equality between the genders within the criminal justice system and theory construction. (7)

Fraser Report is the 1983 report of the Special Committee on Pornography and Prostitution (SCPP), frequently called the Fraser Committee, whose mandate was to review the status of prostitution and pornography and their related regulatory laws. (11)

Fraud is the unlawful taking of another's possession through cheating or deception. (9)

General Social Survey (GSS) was a survey initiated in the 1980s by Statistics Canada to regularly gather data on social trends and to provide information on specific policy issues of current or emerging interest. Between 1985 and 2001, there have been 12 survey cycles. (12)

General theory of crime is a sociological perspective that asserts that criminal behaviour is a product of defective socialization processes that make it difficult for a potential offender to exercise self-control. The theory is a modification of the social control theory. (7)

Hate crime is a crime in which the perpetrator's conduct is motivated by bias, hatred, or prejudice regarding the actual or perceived race, color, religion, national origin, gender, disability, or sexual orientation of another group or individual. (8)

Id, **ego**, and **superego** are three principles from Freud's psychoanalytic approach that denote different aspects of personality. The id refers to the primitive, instinctual urges that address the primal need for gratification; the ego is the rational aspect that mediates between the id and superego and is the conscious aspect of personality; the superego represents the moral and ethical dimension of personality. (6)

Illicit market refers to the services provided through organized crime to meet the demands of law-abiding citizenry for illegal goods and services, such as prostitution, illicit drugs, contraband computer software and cigarettes, etc. (10)

Indictable offences are offences that are considered more serious than summary offences and usually carry a more serious penalty. They include such crimes as murder, robbery, and assault. Sentences for indictable offences are usually served in federal institutions. (1)

Integrated approach to criminology involves the general and specific attempt to combine two or more theories that are thought to complement each other (e.g., strain and differential association theory) into a more powerful explanatory model. (1)

Interdisciplinary approach to criminology involves the attempt to integrate the various sub-areas of knowledge—such as biology, economics, law, psychology, and sociology—to formulate an interdisciplinary theory of behaviour and form the basis for intervention and prevention strategies. (1)

Juristat. The regular publication of the Canadian Centre for Justice Statistics. *Juristat* bulletins address a broad range of criminal justice topics using statistical data and are considered the most authoritative source of criminal justice statistics in Canada. (2)

Just deserts is a punishment model that asserts that an individual who commits an offence deserves to suffer for it. It is also referred to as retribution. (4)

Labelling theory is a sociological theory used to explain why someone might commit a crime that asserts that a direct or indirect negative characterization can predispose the individual to be "tagged" and feel like an outcast. (7)

Liberal approach to crime control proposes to control crime by focusing on alleviating social inequalities and by providing legitimate opportunities for everyone. (14)

Life course theory is an integrated theory that involves the study of changes in the offending pattern of an individual over the course of his or her life. Researchers attempt to identify differentiating factors that predispose individuals to criminal activity. (5)

Middle-class value approach, also referred to as the "middle-class measuring rod," is a sociological theory that asserts that people from the lower classes strive to attain middle-class standards. When they fail to do so, anger and frustration with the conventional values result. These feelings may then trigger criminal behaviour. (13)

Moral development is a psychological theory that asserts that morality is a development process that is dependent on how we are able to meet certain needs at different developmental stages of life. Criminals are thought to exhibit a lower level of moral development. (6)

Moral entrepreneurs is a term used to describe those individuals who use their power and/or influence to shape the legal process to their advantage. (7)

Moral insanity is a concept devised by the American pioneer in psychology Isaac Ray in 1835 that provided physicians with an opportunity to offer a medical diagnosis in court cases and treat the condition as a form of mental illness in which the offender's ability to reason is temporarily interrupted. Today, the concept has been entrenched into the Durham Rule. (4)

Moral panic is a sociological term that refers to people's concern over crimes of morality (e.g., prostitution, pornography, gambling, etc.). (2)

Motor-vehicle crime refers to the broader range of offences involving a motor vehicle, which includes theft of a vehicle, theft from a vehicle, and criminal damage to a vehicle. (9)

Neoclassical school thinkers subscribe to the assertion that different situations or circumstances can make it impossible to exercise free will. If these circumstances can be identified, they can be used to exempt the accused from conviction. (4)

Neopositivist school is the school of thought that evolved after the positivist school and has been characterized as part of the school of social defence. It focuses on establishing rational penal policy that emphasizes the systematic resocialization of the offender through treatment and rehabilitation efforts. (4)

Net widening refers to the process by which social control mechanisms (e.g., laws, administrative decisions) are used to expand the state's control over behaviour. (2)

Neutralization is the idea that asserts that young offenders follow conventional values while "drifting" into periods of illegal behaviour. In order to drift into such behaviour, the youth must first neutralize the legal and moral values of the act. (10)

Non-conventional crimes are those illegal acts that most people tend not to associate with crime and that are often not pursued by the criminal justice system, such as organized crime, political crime, computer crime, etc. (1)

Operationalization involves defining criminological concepts or events so that they can be observed and measured in a scientific manner. (2)

Organized crime is illegal activity conducted by a group of individuals and/or organizations who act in consort. Crimes commonly committed by organized crime groups include extortion, fraud, theft, smuggling, and the sale of illicit products. (10)

Paradigm shift is a sociological term that refers to the process that takes place when a prevailing model or theoretical orientation undergoes a conceptual shift. (2)

Peacemaking theory is a sociological perspective based on a humanistic approach to crime control. Advocates of the peacemaking perspective emphasize reconciliation through mediation and dispute settlement, rather than the use of punishment and retribution as a means of social control. (7)

Pedestal effect is a term occasionally used to describe the differential treatment and processing of female offenders. It is also sometimes interchangeably used with the term "chivalry hypothesis." These terms are often used when asserting that women offenders have been treated more kindly than male offenders. (13)

Political economy perspective has its roots in feminist theory. Used to explain prostitution, the perspective emphasizes social inequalities that force some women to turn to prostitution out of economic necessity. (11)

Pornography is the portrayal of sexually offensive material prohibited by law (e.g., child pornography). It is a type of public order offence. (11)

Positivist school in criminology proclaims that the study of crime should emphasize the individual. Its adherents focus on the treatment over punishment as a means of correcting behaviour. They rely on the scientific method to quantify and measure behaviour. (4)

Postmodernism is a theoretical framework derived from critical criminology that essentially rejects the self-evident reality of distinctions made by conventional scientific knowledge and/or common sense. (14)

Power-control theory is a sociology-based perspective that emphasizes the importance of class structure within the family setting in explaining delinquency and crime. Key concepts involve the nature of power and control within a family setting and the ways in which power and control relate to patriarchy and gender role socialization. (13)

Prevention of crime focuses on proactive strategies to forestall crimes before they occur. There are three major types of prevention. **Primary prevention** involves addressing the conditions in the environment and includes such things as maintaining streets, fixing broken windows, and generally cleaning up disorganized communities. **Secondary prevention** involves identifying targets (in terms of people, places, situations, time, etc.) and trying to prevent the target from being victimized. **Tertiary prevention** is a type of prevention used for individuals who have already violated the law or situations where crimes have already occurred; the focus is on reducing the recidivism rate. (14)

Primary deviance is a sociological concept that refers to a criminal act that not been socially labelled as deviant. (7)

Primary prevention. See Prevention.

Property crime refers to the broad range of offences involving property, such as breaking and entering, fraud, theft, and motor-vehicle theft. (9)

Psychoanalysis was developed by Sigmund Freud and views crime as the expression of conflict and tension within the individual. The source of conflict is believed to stem from unresolved and often unconscious experiences during one's childhood. Treatment involves trying to resolve these conflicts. (6)

Psychopath is considered by some to be an individual suffering from a psychological and/or biological condition in which his or her behaviour is characterized by a lack of empathy, low arousal levels, and an inability to learn from experience. There is a growing body of literature suggesting that many chronic offenders suffer from some degree of psychopathy. (6)

Public order crimes are based on moral principles and are usually characterized as victimless crimes, since they involve a degree of compliance on the victim's part. They include gambling, prostitution, pornography, substance abuse, and vandalism. (11)

Radical approach to crime control addresses both conventional and non-conventional crimes by attempting to eliminate structural inequalities brought on through capitalism. (14)

Random error pertains to observations that are not predictable because of some unforeseen intervening variable. (2)

Rationalism refers to the "common-sense" process by which individuals attempt to determine the reality of a situation. (2)

Reintegrative shaming is a correctional philosophy introduced by John Braithwaite that advocates the use of public shaming and/or public acceptance of wrongdoing as a way of having offenders re-enter general society. (10)

Relative is a term that refers to the notion that the meaning and nature of crime can vary across time and location. (1)

Reliability in research methodology refers to the likelihood that an observed relationship between two or more variables can or will be observed in a consistent manner. (2)

Restorative justice is a sentencing model that emphasizes restitution and community participation with the intent of restoring a sense of community and reintegrating individuals back into their communities. (14)

Routine activities theory is a sociological explanation that views crime as a predictable function of normal activities of daily living. The risk of victimization depends on one's lifestyle, opportunity, or proximity to the crime scene; through changes in one's lifestyle (rational choice), it is possible to increase or decrease one's risk of victimization. (7)

Secondary deviance is a sociological term that refers to deviant behaviour as the result of being labelled. See Primary deviance. (7)

Secondary prevention. See Prevention.

Self-report studies involve asking individuals to disclose whether they have ever committed an offence and constitute an unofficial source of crime data. Given that a great deal of youth crime goes undetected, self-report studies are popular among this group. (3)

Social development approach is a type of primary prevention in which social or community-based programs are created to mobilize people to become more aware of and take steps to reduce their risk of being victimized. (14)

Social disorganization theory is a sociological theory that defines deviance and crime in terms of a breakdown of social control bonds, areas characterized by social decay, and/or associations involving other deviant groups. (7)

Social structure is a sociological concept used to describe consistent and stable patterns of social interactions. (7)

Somatotyping is a technique used for categorizing the behaviours or temperaments of individuals based on specific body types or physique. (5)

Stalking is a form of harassment in which the offender intentionally and repeatedly pursues another person with the intention of causing emotional and/or physical discomfort. See also Criminal harassment. (8)

Strain theory is a sociological theory that interprets emotional turmoil and conflict as the result of being unable to achieve desired goals through legitimate means. (7)

Summary offences are considered less serious than indictable offences. Penalties are restricted to six months imprisonment and/or a $5000 fine. Sentences are usually served in provincial institutions. (1)

Superego. See Id, ego, and superego.

Systematic error is the predictable error in observation. When collecting data, the observer is aware of the approximate error in the reliability of the observation. (2)

Terrorism involves the use of propaganda, violence, or dangerous acts against some organization or agency for the purpose of obtaining concessions or rewards for a cause for personal and/or political reasons. (8)

Tertiary prevention. See Prevention.

Theft is a type of property crime that pertains to the unlawful taking of another person's, business's, or organization's property or service, usually without the intent of returning it. (9)

Token economy is a term used by behavioural therapists to describe a reinforcement strategy in which a participant gets certain rewards (tokens) for desired behaviour. (6)

Transnational crime involves a criminal act or transaction that violates the laws of more than one country. Examples include international drug trafficking, terrorism, money laundering, and various organized crime activities that cross national boundaries. (10)

Triangulation is a research methods technique that involves using more than one source of criminological data to assess the validity of what is being observed. (3)

Uniform Crime Reporting (UCR) system yields the official crime data collected by Statistics Canada and offers a continuous historical record of crime statistics reported by every police agency in Canada since 1962. UCR data reflect reported crime that has been substantiated through police investigation. Information collected includes the number of criminal incidents, the clearance status of those incidents, and persons-charged information. (3)

Unofficial data pertains to crime data that is not collected by official criminal justice agencies, including self-report data, victimization data, and field observation. The research is usually conducted by academics and/or research organizations with no specific regularity and essentially serves interests of the host rather than the general public. This type of data is usually used to elucidate existing official data and verify the validity of official sources. (3)

Utilitarianism is an ethical and classical school concept that states that any laws should respect the greatest good for the greatest number. (4)

Validity in research methodology pertains to the likelihood that relationships being observed and measured are in fact real. (2)

Verstehen was a term used by German sociologist Max Weber (1864–1920) to refer to the social scientists' attempt to understand both the intent and the context of human action. (3)

Victim impact statement (VIS) is a statement from the victim that is allowed in court during the sentencing phase of the trial. It enables the victim (or another person on behalf of the victim) to inform the court of the personal impact of the offender's behaviour. (12)

Victim precipitation theory states that a victim, through his or her actions (or a lack thereof) presents him- or herself as a potential target for being victimized. In other words, the victim is a direct, positive precipitator in the crime; he or she shapes and moulds the crime. (12)

Victimization surveys involve collecting data from individuals who have been victims of crimes, or in some cases know of someone who has been a victim, and asking a range of questions regarding the incidents. (3)

Victimology is a sub-field of criminology that focuses on examining the role of the victim in a crime. (12)

Violence Against Women Survey (VAWS) was a 1993 survey of women over the age of 18 that examined the safety of women both inside and outside the home, focusing on issues such as sexual harassment, sexual violence, physical violence, and perceptions of fear. (12)

Violent crime is a general category of crime classification that includes such crimes as homicide, attempted murder, robbery, and assault. Violent crimes involve the physical violation of a person, and most are indictable offences. (8)

White-collar crime refers to business-related crime committed by employees and officers of a company who capitalize on their legitimate occupations or pursuits. The offender uses his or her entrepreneurial or professional status for personal and/or corporate gain. White-collar crimes include theft, fraud, and embezzlement. (10)

Women's liberation movement emerged in the late 1950s and drew attention to the rights of women and their unequal status to men in all economic, political, and social settings. (13)

XYY chromosome theory is a theory that asserts there is a relationship between the extra Y chromosome, found in some males, and a propensity toward criminal or anti-social behaviour. (5)

Index

Note: "f" after a page number indicates a figure; "t" after a page number indicates a table.